Conflict of Laws and Laws of Conflict in Europe and Beyond

Editor:
Rainer Nickel

Conflict of Laws and Laws of Conflict in Europe and Beyond

Patterns of Supranational and Transnational Juridification

intersentia

METRO

Ius Commune Europaeum

Editor:
Rainer Nickel

Conflict of Laws and Laws of Conflict in Europe and Beyond

ISBN 978-94-000-0123-7
D/2010/7849/116
NUR 828

Antwerp – Cambridge – Portland
www.intersentia.com

Cover picture: "The Rape of Europa" by Walentin Alexandrowitsch Serow (1865–1911)

ACKNOWLEDGEMENTS

The present volume contains the proceedings from the RECON project (www.reconproject.eu) workshop on 'Conflict of Laws and Laws of Conflict in Europe and Beyond – Patterns of Supranational and Transnational Juridification', which I organised and convened in September 2007 at the European University Institute in Florence. The event was held within the framework of RECON Work Package 9 – 'Global Transnationalisation and Democratisation Compared'.

I would like to thank John Erik Fossum and Christian Joerges as leaders of WP 9, Erik O. Eriksen as the overall scientific co-ordinator of RECON, and Geir Kvaerk and Marit Eldholm for their generous help and support, and all the contributors to this report and the participants in the discussions in Florence for their efforts. I also wish to express my gratitude to Marlies Becker (EUI) for her wonderful help and assistance with the organisation of the event, and to Ernst-Ulrich Petersmann, the Head of Law Department of the EUI, who supported this project from the beginning and gave us the opportunity to hold the workshop at the EUI.

As always, Chris Engert has done an excellent job as our language editor, and I wish to thank him for his patience and sensitive language editing.

Rainer Nickel
Johann Wolfgang Goethe University

CONTENTS

LIST OF CONTRIBUTORS

Nina Boeger is a lecturer in law at the University of Bristol, UK. She is also a fully-qualified UK solicitor and German lawyer and holds an LL.M. from the European University Institute in Florence.
Nina.Boeger@bristol.ac.uk

Alicia Cebada Romero is Professor of Public International Law at the Universidad Carlos III in Madrid (Spain) and Director of the Crisis Management and Peacebuilding Programme at Toledo International Centre for Peace (CITpax). She teaches and writes on Public International Law and European Union Law, with a focus on the external action of the European Union as well as on peace studies and conflicts resolution.
aliciacebada@der-pu.uc3m.es

Michelle Everson, LLB (Exeter), Ph.D (EUI, Florence) is Professor of European Law. She has previously held posts as the Managing Editor of the *European Law Journal* at the European University Institute in Florence, as a lecturer in Law and Political Science at the University of Bremen and as a fellow at the Centre of European Law and Politics Bremen. Michelle Everson is also Director of the Birkbeck College Research School, co-ordinating the research environment for post-graduate students across all Schools at Birkbeck College. Currently, Michelle Everson also sits on the editorial boards of *Law and Critique* and the *Journal for Socio-Legal Studies.* She is also Vice-Chair of the Academic Board for Social Sciences of the Austrian Academy of Sciences.
m.everson@bbk.ac.uk

John Erik Fossum holds a Ph.D from the University of British Columbia, Canada and is Professor in Political Science at the ARENA Centre for European Studies at the University of Oslo, Norway. He is substitute co-ordinator for RECON and co-editor of the Routledge Series on Democratising Europe (with Erik Eriksen). He has published widely on democracy, federalism, constitutionalism, citizenship and identity in the European Union and Canada.
j.e.fossum@arena.uio.no

Christian Joerges held the Chair for European Economic Law at the European University Institute in Florence from 1997–2007. Since 2003 he directs together with Josef Falke the project "Trade Liberalisation and Social Regulation" at the Collaborative Research Centre Transformations of the State in Bremen, and since 2007 the project "Transnational Governance, Deliberative Supranationalism and Constitutionalism" within the Integrated Project Reconstituting Democracy in Europe (RECON), co-ordinated by ARENA-Centre for European Studies, Oslo. After his return to the University of Bremen in 2008 he became a Research Professor there, and Co-Director of the Bremen Centre of European Law and Politics.
cjoerges@Sfb597.uni-bremen.de

Poul F. Kjaer is Alexander Von Humboldt fellow at the Cluster of Excellence "The Formation of Normative Orders" at the Goethe-University, Frankfurt am Main. He holds a Ph.D in Law from the European University Institute, Florence, and a BA and MS in Political Science from University of Aarhus. He has also studied and researched at the Humboldt University, Berlin, the University of Bielefeld, the London School of Economics and Political Science, and the Centre for Law and Politics at the University of Bremen.
Poul.Kjaer@normativeorders.net

Karl-Heinz Ladeur is Professor (em) of Public Law, University of Hamburg. He is Distinguished Professor at the Bremen International Graduate School of Social Sciences (BIGSSS). From 1994–1996 and 1998–2002 he was also a professor of public law, including environmental law and telecommunications law, at the European University Institute, Florence.
karl-heinz.ladeur@uni-hamburg.de

Miguel Poiares Maduro has been Advocate General at the European Court of Justice and is currently Professor at the European University Institute in Florence/Italy. He is an external Professor at the Law School of the Universidade Nova de Lisboa, at the London School of Economics, and at the College of Europe. His book, *We the Court – The European Court of Justice and the European Economic Constitution*, (Oxford: Hart Publishing, 1997) has won the Rowe and Maw Prize and the Prize *Obiettivo Europa.* He belongs to the editorial or advisory board of several law journals, including the *European Law Journal* and the *Common Market Law Review.*
Miguel.Maduro@eui.eu

John P. McCormick, professor of political science at the University of Chicago, is the author of *Carl Schmitt's Critique of Liberalism: Against Politics as Technology*, (Cambridge University Press, 1997); *Weber, Habermas and Transformations of the European State: Constitutional, Social and Supranational Democracy*, (Cambridge UP, 2006); and *Machiavellian Democracy* (Cambridge UP, 2011).
jpmccorm@uchicago.edu

Jürgen Neyer is Professor of European Politics at the European University Viadrina. He teaches and writes on aspects of the institutional order of the European Union, with a special focus on the legitimacy of the EU.
Neyer@euv-frankfurt-o.de

Rainer Nickel teaches European Law and Public Law at the Goethe Universität in Frankfurt am Main, where he obtained his Ph.D in Law. From 1998–2001, he served as a legal advisor at the German Federal Constitutional Court. He has been visiting professor and Schlesinger Scholar at Cornell Law School and visiting professor at the University of Florida Levin College of Law. From 2004–2006, he was a Marie Curie Fellow at the European University Institute in Florence.
nickel@jur.uni-frankfurt.de

Ernst-Ulrich Petersmann is Professor for international and European law at the European University Institute, Florence. He was previously professor at the University of Geneva (Switzerland) and its Graduate Institute for International Studies (1993–2001).
Ulrich.Petersmann@EUI.eu

Florian Rödl holds degrees in law and philosophy and received his Ph.D from the European University Institute in Florence. He was then a Research Assistant at the Centre of European Law and Politics in Bremen and is now the Head of an Independent Research Group at the Cluster of Excellence on "The Formation of Normative Orders", Goethe-Universität, Frankfurt am Main. The group's focus is on "The change in Transnational Economic and Labour Law".
roedl@normativeorders.net

Wolf Sauter is currently professor of healthcare regulation at the University of Tilburg and a senior member of TILEC (Tilburg Law and Economics Centre) as well as a competition expert at the Dutch Healthcare Authority. He obtained his Ph.D in law (with distinction) from the EUI under co-supervision by Christian Joerges in 1996, and, before moving to Tilburg, held academic posts at the Universities of Bremen and Groningen.
w.sauter@uvt.nl

Christoph U. Schmid has, since 2005, been Professor of European Private, Economic and Constitutional Economic Law, and successor to Christian Joerges and Gert Brueggemeier as Director of the Centre of European Law and Politics (ZERP) at Bremen University. He was post-doctoral research fellow and co-ordinator of the European Private Law Forum at the European University Institute (EUI) in Florence from 1995 to 2005. He holds a doctoral and a habilitation degree from Munich University and a Ph.D. from the EUI.
schmid@zerp.uni-bremen.de

Gunther Teubner is Professor (em.) of Private Law and Legal Sociology at the Goethe University Frankfurt/Main and Centennial Professor at the London School of Economics.
g.teubner@jur.uni-frankfurt.de

Ellen Vos is Professor of European Union Law at the Law Faculty of Maastricht University. She is a member of the Editorial Board of the Maastricht Journal of European and Comparative Law and of the Editorial Board of the Maastricht Working Papers on Law and the Ius Commune Book Series. She has published extensively in the field of EU Law, institutional law (comitology and agencies), market integration and risk regulation (precautionary principle). She holds a Ph.D degree in Law from the European University Institute in Florence.
e.vos@maastrichtuniversity.nl

Neil Walker has been the Regius Professor of Public Law and the Law of Nature and Nations at Edinburgh University since 2008. Before that, he was Professor of European Law at the European University Institute between 2000–8. His main area of research is the changing role of law in the post-national constellation.
neil.walker@ed.ac.uk

ABBREVIATIONS

AB	Appellate Body
AC	Andean Community
BFN	Between Facts and Norms: Contributions to a Discourse Theory of Law and Democracy by J. Habermas
BGB	*Bürgerliches Gesetzbuch* (German Civil Code)
BSE	Bovine Spongiform Encephalopathy – "Mad cow" disease/Creutzfeld-Jakob's disease
CAC	Codex Alimentarius Commission
CCB	Comparative Constitutional Borrowing
CERN	European Nuclear Research Centre
CFI	Court of First Instance
CFSP	Common Foreign and Security Policy
CM	Community Method
CoE	Council of Europe
COST	Co-operation in the field of Scientific and Technical Research
CREST	Committee on Science and Technical Research
CSD	UN Commission for Social Development
CT	Constitutional Treaty
DEU	Democracy in the European Union: Integration through Deliberation? by E.O. Eriksen & J.E. Fossum
DG SANCO	Directorate Health and Consumer Protection
DSB	Dispute Settlement Body
EC	European Community
ECHR	European Convention of Human Rights
ECJ	European Court of Justice
ECLAC	Economic Commission for Latin America and Caribbean
ECSC	European Coal and Steel Community
ECT	European Community Treaty
ECtHR	European Court of Human Rights

EEA	European Economic Area
EEC	European Economic Community
EFSA	European Food Safety Authority
EFTA	European Free Trade Area
ELDO	European Launch Development Organisation
EMBL	European Molecular Biology Laboratory
EMBO	European Molecular Biology Organisation
EP	European Parliament
ERA	European Research Area
ERC	European Research Council
ESA	European Space Agency
ESO	European Southern Observatory
ESPRIT	European Strategic Programme for Research and Development
ESRF	European Synchrotron Radiation Facility
ESRO	European Space Research Organisation
ETUC	European Trade Union Federation
EU	European Union
EUI	European University Institute
EURATOM	European Atomic Energy Community
EUREKA	Europe-wide Network for Industrial R&D
EUROSTAT	Statistical Office of the European Communities
FAO	Food and Agriculture Organisation of the United Nations
FCC	German Federal Constitutional Court
FOCEM	Convention for the Protection of the Marine Environment of the North-East Atlantic
FP	Framework Programmes
FSU	Finnish Seamen's Union
FTAs	Free Trade Agreements
GATS	General Agreement of Trade in Services
GATT	General Agreement on Trade and Tariffs
GM	Genetically-Modified
GMOs	Genetically-Modified Organisms
GSP	Generalised System of Preferences Scheme
ICANN	Internet Corporation of Assigned Names and Numbers
ICJ	International Court of Justice
IDB	Inter-American Development Bank
ILL	Institut Laue-Langevin
ILO	International Labour Organisation
IMF	International Monetary Fund
IO	The Inclusion of the Other: Studies in Political Theory by J. Habermas, edited by C. Cronin & P. de Greiff

ITER	Treaty establishing the International Thermonuclear Experimental Reactor
ITF	International Transport Workers' Federation
ITLOS	International Tribunal for the Law of the Sea
LAC	Latin-American Social (Regional) Cohesion
LC	Legitimation crisis by J. Habermas
MERCOSUR	*Mercado Común del Sur* – Southern Common Market
MS	Member States of EU
NAFTA	North American Free Trade Agreement
NATO	North Atlantic Treaty Organisation
NGO	Non-Governmental Organisation
NLR	New Left Review
ODIHR	OSCE Office for Democratic Institutions and Human Rights
OMC	Open Method of Co-ordination
OSCE	Organisation for Security and Co-operation in Europe
OSPAR	Convention for the Protection of the Marine Environment of the North-East Atlantic
PC	The Postnational Constellation: Political Essays by J. Habermas, edited by M. Pensky
Ph.D	Doctor in Philosophy
PSE	European Socialist Party
QMV	Qualified-majority voting
R&D	Research and Development
RACE	R&D in advanced communications technologies in Europe
REACH	Regulation on Registration, Evaluation, Authorisation and Restriction of Chemicals
RSC	Robert Schuman Centre for Advanced Studies
SCA	Surveillance Authority and a Court of Justice
SCF	Scientific Committee for Food
SEA	Single European Act
SGEI	Services of General Economic Interest
STPS	The Structural Transformation of the Public Sphere: An Inquiry into a Category of Bourgeois Society by J. Habermas
TCA	Theory of Communicative Action by J. Habermas
TEU	Treaty of European Union
TKG	*Telekommunikationsgesetz* (German Telecommunications Law)
TRIPS	Trade-Related Aspects of Intellectual Property Rights
U.S.	United States of America
UDHR	Universal Declaration of Human Rights
UN	United Nations
UNCLOS	UN Convention on the Law of the Sea

UNESCO	United Nations Educational, Scientific and Cultural Organisation
USO	Universal Service Obligations
VCLT	Vienna Convention on the Law of Treaties
VDI	*Verein Deutscher Ingenieure* (Asssociation of German Engineers)
VG	*Verwaltungsgericht* (Court of Administrative Affairs – 1st instance)
VIP	Very Important Person
VwVfG	*Verwaltungsverfahrensgesetz* (German Code of Administrative Procedure)
WHO	World Health Organisation
WIPO	World Intellectual Property Organisation
WTO	World Trade Organisation

Rainer Nickel

INTRODUCTION

CONFLICT OF LAWS AND LAWS OF CONFLICT – AN INTRODUCTION TO THE RESEARCH AGENDA

1. The Need for a New Approach to Supranational and International Law-Making

This volume strives to develop and formulate a new perspective on supranational and transnational law formations, and to begin a new discussion about their methods, forms and functions. It is based upon the proceedings of the 2007 RECON conference of Work Package 9 at the European University Institute in Florence, and it deals with new approaches to supranational and transnational law-generating structures. These new approaches, namely, Christian Joerges' theoretical concept based upon the conflict of laws methodology,[1] and additional ideas of constitutional pluralism and of participatory transnational governance, are discussed from private, public and international law perspectives. They strive to conceptualise the efforts to re-constitute democratic post-national constellations in legal categories. The volume seeks to find new ways for a democratisation of European and transnational governance outside traditional models, and more convincing ways of a European and transnational "juridification" that reconciles democracy, diversity, and social rights.

It appears particularly timely to talk about such a conceptual re-orientation if we take the recent developments of the EU legal structure and of the constitutionalisation process into account, a process which has dominated the European debate during this

1 Christian Joerges' conflict of laws approach is the underlying intellectual theme of the contributions to this volume. It provides us with a new, normative perspective on transnational juridification. See, most recently, Ch. Joerges, "Deliberative Political Processes Revisited: What Have we Learnt About the Legitimacy of Supranational Decision-Making", (2006) 44 *Journal of Common Market Studies*, p. 779; Ch. Joerges, "Reconceptualising the Supremacy of European Law: A Plea for a Supranational Conflict of Laws", in: B. Kohler-Koch and B. Rittberger, (eds), *Debating the Democratic Legitimacy of the European Union*, (Lanham MD: Rowman & Littlefield Publishers, 2007), p. 311, and his contribution to this volume in Chapter 18.

first decade of the new millennium. After the failure of a "formal", or denominational, constitutionalisation in 2005, the EU has nonetheless been successful in transforming itself again: This new era started on 01 December 2009 with the Treaty of Lisbon,[2] which came into effect after the second Irish referendum ended up with a "Yes", a vote that completed a long and winding ratification process.

The conflicts surrounding the new treaty and the "messy" ratification procedure mirror a growing unease about the *finalité* of the EU, and a growing concern about the primacy of its law over the laws of the member states. A couple of months before the Irish referendum the German Federal Constitutional Court (FCC) had approved the Treaty as "constitutional, but...".[3] Ironically, the Court did not join the choir of critics who stress the democratic deficit of the EU, but instead told the German parliament that it has to secure its democratic rights *vis-à-vis* the executive branch, i.e., the Federal government, while firmly stating that the EU does not need to fulfil the same criteria of fully developed democratic institutions that we take for granted within the nation state. The Court held that the Treaty of Lisbon does not lay the foundations for a new political entity in the strong sense of a constitutionalisation: the status of EU citizenship does not automatically generate such a move, nor does the introduction of a *Passerelle* procedure for simplified treaty revisions[4] represent a kind of *kompetenz-kompetenz* which is typical for sovereign entities. The FCC decision confirms that the character of the EU and its legal framework remain, even after the Treaty of Lisbon, as much in limbo as the character of the WTO, for example, which is also oscillating between a mere international organisation and a "constitutional" entity.[5] In general terms, thus, it leaves us with a cardinal question: How to conceive the emerging law of the 'postnational

2 The Treaty of Lisbon establishes a reformed EU Treaty and converts the EC Treaty into the "Treaty on the Functioning of the European Union". A consolidated version of these new treaties can be found at http://europa.eu/lisbon_treaty/full_text/index_en.htm. The Charter of Fundamental Rights is not an integral part of the Treaty package, but it will have "the same legal value" as the two Treaties, see Art. 6.1 of the new TEU.

3 *Bundesverfassungsgericht*, judgment of 30 June 2009 (2 BvE 2/08 and others). The Court formulated a number of caveats that amount to a kind of constitutional barricade against further integration. In the case at hand, however, it only nullified some provisions of the "Act Extending and Strengthening the Rights of the Bundestag and the Bundesrat in European Union Matters" (Bundestag document 16/8489). A "preliminary" English translation of the FCC decision can be found at www.bverfg.de/entscheidungen/es20090630_2bve000208en.html, on the Federal Constitutional Court's website.

4 The *Passerelle* ("bridge") procedure in Article 48 ch. 7 of the new TEU and the simplified procedure in Article 48 ch. 6 of the new TEU allow for simplified treaty amendments (similar to the previous provision in Article 42 TEU). If the European Council decided to invoke the *Passerelle* according to Article 48 ch. 7, it could only do so unanimously and would first have to seek the consent of the European Parliament and notify national parliaments. In addition, any proposal for such a decision could be blocked "if a national parliament makes known its opposition within six months of the date of such notification".

5 See the detailed discussion about different legal concepts of a WTO constitution by D.Z. Cass, *The Constitutionalization of the World Trade Organization* (Oxford: Oxford University Press, 2005) and the critique of E.-U. Petersmann, Book Review, (2006) 43 *CMLR*, pp. 890–91.

constellation' (J. Habermas) without falling back into the simple dichotomy of national and international law?

The contributions to this volume tie in with this question. They represent, in one way or another, the ambition to find third ways between, on the one hand, a constitutionalisation of the EU (or the WTO, or the UN) in the classical hierarchical sense, with a fully-fledged harmonisation of its legal order, irrespective of the legal orders of its Member States, and, on the other, a loose international co-ordination of national policy spheres and the accompanying legal instruments. As the emergence of a single World Legal Order appears as much illusionary as frightening, it is well-justified to take the continuing diversity of legal orders as a starting-point. While concepts of legal pluralism[6] have aptly described and embraced the existence of such a variety, their cognitive and explanatory force is rather limited as they cannot explain how conflicts between different legal orders can be properly defined, contextualised, and finally solved (or avoided).

Supranational and transnational courts are the first ones to be confronted with this diversity, and they have been challenged by the complexity of colliding legal orders and concepts. Most recent examples of conflictual and conflict-laden encounters can be found in the jurisprudence of the European Court of Justice (ECJ) and the European Court of Human Rights (ECHR). The ECJ, in the *Kadi and Al Barakaat* decision[7] on the application of the Security Council terror list resolution within the EU, had to strike a balance between the obligations stemming from Article 103 of the UN Charter[8] and the *Rechtsstaat* or rule of law principle which guides the EC/EU legal order. In contrast to the Court of First Instance, which rejected the request of Kadi and Al Barakaat to be deleted from the list, the ECJ held that the pleas of Kadi and Al Barakaat "in support of their actions for the annulment of the contested regulation and alleging breach of their rights of defence, especially the right to be heard, and of the principle of effective judicial protection, are well founded".[9] As a consequence, Article 103 of the UN Charter, which can be interpreted as a rule expressing the unconditional preference of the UN legal order, did not prevail within the EU legal order.

The ECHR, for its part, is constantly in a situation in which it needs to define the "European Public Order" embodied in the European Convention on Human Rights, while, at the same time, it has to pay its tribute to the national constitutional orders of the Member States. This constellation is tempting for a court with a tendency for judicial

6 For an overview, see N. Walker, "The Idea of Constitutional Pluralism", in: (2002) 65 *Modern Law Review*, pp. 317–359.

7 ECJ, joined cases C-402/05 and C-415/05, *Kadi and Al Barakaat* v *Council*, judgment of 03 September 2008.

8 Article 103 UN Charter reads: "In the event of a conflict between the obligations of the Members of the United Nations under the present Charter and their obligations under any other international agreement, their obligations under the present Charter shall prevail."

9 ECJ, joined cases C-402/05 and C-415/05, *Kadi and Al Barakaat* v *Council*, judgment of 03 September 2008, para. 353.

activism, and the court has, more than once in recent times, been accused of overstepping its territory. In its *Bosphorus*[10] decision, however, the ECHR went down a different path: It had to define its role *vis-à-vis* the EC/EU legal order, and it came up with a distinctive and creative solution. It stated that the EC/EU legal order provides for a sufficient degree of legal protection, and that a complainant has to show that, in his or her case, this general level of protection has not been met. This hurdle, although not as steep as the *Solange II* admissibility hurdle set up by the German FCC in relation to constitutional oversight over EC/EU law,[11] represents another possible path for a settlement of conflicting legal orders: mutual recognition as the rule, stricter scrutiny as the exception.

2. The Development of a Notion of Supranational Conflicts Law

Both the ECJ and the ECHR have been heavily criticised in recent times for their "intrusive"[12] and "too detailed"[13] judgments. For example, the decision of the ECJ in the *Mangold* case and the decision of the ECHR in the *von Hanover* case have been greeted, almost unanimously, with severe criticism, and they caused even alarmist and angry

10 ECHR, *Bosphorus Hava Yolları* v. *Ireland*, Application no. 45036/98, judgment of 30 June 2005, www.echr.coe.int/echr/en/hudoc.

11 See BVerfGE 73, 339 (1986), *Solange II*: Constitutional complaints that are based upon a claim for the unconstitutionality of EC/EU law are inadmissible unless the complainant shows in a detailed analysis that the *general* level of human rights protection within the EU has sunk below the *general* level of protection guaranteed by the German constitution. This is a Herculean task that has not been met in the last 23 years since the judgment was handed down in 1986. – The latest judgment in EU matters, the *Treaty of Lisbon* decision (see, *supra*, note 3) expressly allows for complaints directed at EU legal acts which are *ultra vires*, but it has again confirmed the *Solange II* rationale with regard to constitutional rights protection.

12 Roman Herzog, the former German President, and former President of the Federal Constitutional Court as well as President of the Convention which drew up the EU Charter of Fundamental Rights, demanded "Stop the ECJ" in an article written for the *Frankfurter Allgemeine Zeitung*. Herzog and his co-author Lüder Gerken found "adventurous legal constructs" in the judgments of the ECJ, and asked the FCC to take up again its watchdog function against "intrusions" of the ECJ: "Stoppt den EuGH", *FAZ*, 08 September 2008, available at www.cep.eu/fileadmin/user_upload/Pressemappe/CEP_in_den_Medien/Herzog-EuGH-Webseite.pdf. An English translation of this article is available at: www.cep.eu/fileadmin/user_upload/Pressemappe/CEP_in_den_Medien/Herzog-EuGH-Webseite_eng.pdf. A counter-critique by Carl Otto Lenz lists all cases mentioned by Herzog and claims that Herzog does not accurately restate the facts and the reasoning of the ECJ: C.O. Lenz, "Anmerkungen zu den Fällen aus dem Aufsatz von Prof. Herzog 'Stoppt den Europäischen Gerichtshof' in der FAZ vom 8.9.2008", Walter Hallstein Institut, *WHI – Paper* 1/09, www.whi-berlin.de/documents/whi-paper0109.pdf.

13 Lord Hoffmann, one of the most prominent UK law lords, has publicly criticised the ECHR and its jurisprudence as "inconsistent", that the court has "assumed power to legislate", and that its decisions are too intrusive: "It has been unable to resist the temptation to aggrandise its jurisdiction and to impose uniform rules on Member States. It considers itself the equivalent of the Supreme Court of the United States, laying down a federal law of Europe". Lord Hoffmann, "The Universality of Human Rights", Judicial Studies Board Annual Lecture, London, 19 March 2009, available at: www.jsboard.co.uk/downloads/Hoffmann_2009_JSB_Annual_Lecture_Universality_of_Human_Rights.doc, p. 14 and 21. See, also, the (critical) comment by Afua Hirsch: "Judges: can't live with 'em…", *The Guardian*, 06 April 2009, available at: www.guardian.co.uk/commentisfree/libertycentral/2009/apr/06/law-eu.

comments in Germany.[14] The *Taxquet* decision of the ECHR on jury trials not only stirred emotions in Belgium, from where the case originated, but also in Norway, where the criminal court system shows similar features and where the fear is rising that the country will have to adopt a completely new system of criminal procedure prescribed by the ECHR.[15]

However, the debate is not confined to an academic ivory tower. Some of the critics are established and internationally well-known judges who served or still serve at the House of Lords or the German FCC, and their harsh interventions were not just distributed among the expert circles of lawyers and academics. They were held at public events and were published in widely-distributed newspapers, thus reaching the general public at large. Thus, the legitimacy of the courts and of their respective jurisprudence, and even the supranational legal systems in which they operate, is also at stake. The central question is whether their judgments "deserve recognition", not only in a technical sense, but also with regard to the legal orders that they establish and develop further, and, more and more often, the answer given is "no".

EC/EU law represents one of the most challenging riddles for lawyers and political scientists alike. For many years, the discussion about the basis of its legitimacy had reached a stalemate: it was trapped between two alternatives, a conventional criticism of the "democratic deficit" of the EU (the "input legitimacy"), on the one hand, and those approaches which underlined the problem-solving capacity of the EU (the "output legitimacy"), on the other. Christian Joerges, in a joint article with Jürgen Neyer, was the first to offer us a new and fresh perspective on the discussion about supranational law-making and its legitimacy problems.[16] Together with Jürgen Neyer he developed the idea of deliberative supranationalism as a third way of thinking about European law: as a means to reconcile national political preferences and their external effects on others. In contrast to functional and output-oriented approaches, Joerges favours a normative perspective based upon Jürgen Habermas' insight that law "deserves recognition" only if the law-making procedures themselves are designed in an inclusive manner. Joerges and Neyer found elements of such a procedure that deserve recognition in the "Comitology" committees of the EU. Their peculiar features offer a starting-point for the idea that supranational deliberative structures, even if these are not democratic in the traditional sense (because, for example, they are dominated by bureaucrats, and not

14 See Herzog (note 12 *supra*). For an overview, see J. Wieland, "Der EuGH im Spannungsverhältnis zwischen Rechtsanwendung und Rechtsgestaltung", in: (2009) 62 *NJW*, pp. 1841–1845.

15 I.L. Backer, "Definition and Development of Human Rights in the International Context and Popular Sovereignty – A Comment", presented at the UNIDEM Seminar Frankfurt am Main, 15–16 May 2009, p. 8, on file with author.

16 This is, of course, their famous article on deliberative supranationalism: Ch. Joerges and J. Neyer, "From Intergovernmental Bargaining to Deliberative Political Processes: The Constitutionalisation of Comitology", in: (1997) 3 *European Law Journal*, pp. 273–299.

by democratically-elected representatives), can at least help to "compensate the shortcomings of constitutional nation-states".[17]

The concept of deliberative supranationalism found wide support among lawyers and political scientists, but also invited misunderstandings and criticism.[18] Supranational Conflict of Laws[19] is a response to these criticisms, and also a response to a new challenge to EU law: If it was once the "bureaucratic nightmare" of the Brussels regulatory complex that inspired deliberative supranationalism, it is now the, so-called, European social dimension that calls for a remodelling of its legitimation basis: "The problem of the welfare state is the practical-political *bête-noire* of the European project" (Ch. Joerges).[20] Inspired by a conflict of laws methodology (which also points to his academic roots as a private international lawyer[21]), Joerges argues for a new form of conflict of laws which may be characterised as an attempt to formulate a "conflicts law", a *Kollisionsrecht* of a new type.

We are, indeed, in need of such a new conflicts law: the de-coupling of the social from the economic constitution, which characterises the structure of the EU, is nowadays even further complicated by a clash of these different rationalities with Europe's internal diversity: the exemplary cases *Viking*, *Laval* and *Ruffert* clearly reveal these differences among the Member States' labour constitutions, and the decisions of the ECJ "solved" theses conflicts in a questionable way: The court interpreted the four freedoms of the EC treaty in all three cases as an overriding quartet, a strict doctrine which is hardly reconcilable with a conflicts law approach.

"Conflict born of diversity will continue to characterise the process of European integration",[22] and, one may add, also the processes of international and transnational juridification. The emergence of a World Society,[23] accompanied by a rapid construction of its legal patterns in the last decades, has only fuelled the need for additional conflict-solution or conflict-avoidance strategies (and concepts) that are not fixated on a constitutionalisation of a hierarchical World Order. This volume strives to prepare the ground for further inquiries into this field.

17 Ch. Joerges, "European Law as Conflicts of Law", in: Ch. Joerges and J. Neyer, *Deliberative supranationalism revisited*. 20/2006 *EUI Working Paper Law*, p. 21.

18 For an account of these criticisms, see Ch. Joerges and J. Neyer, note 17 *supra*.

19 For an early version of Joerges' approach and a first debate on its features, see Ch. Joerges, "Rethinking European Law's Supremacy" with comments by D. Chalmers, R. Nickel, F. Rödl and R. Wai, 2005/12 *EUI Working Paper LAW*, available at: http://hdl.handle.net/1814/3332.

20 Ch. Joerges, "Integration Through Conflicts Law: On the Defence of the European Project By Means of Alternative Conceptualisation of Legal Constitutionalisation", in this volume, Chapter 19, sub Part 5.

21 Ch. Joerges, Zum Funktionswandel des Kollisionsrechts. Die "Governmental Interest Analysis" und die "Krise des Internationalen Privatrechts", (Berlin-Tübingen: deGruyter/Mohr-Siebeck, 1971).

22 Ch. Joerges, note 20 *supra*, in this volume, Chapter 19, sub Part IV.1.

23 See the contributions to the collected volume by H. Brunkhorst (ed), *Demokratie in der Weltgesellschaft*, Sonderband Soziale Welt Nr. 18, (Baden-Baden: Nomos, 2009).

3. Mapping the Field: Conflict of Laws and Laws of Conflict

Part I of the volume (*Deliberative Supranationalism: Law and Democracy in the Post-National Constellation*) lays the groundwork for a normative concept of supranational and transnational juridification. It starts with a self-assurance about the philosophical, political and legal foundations that may serve as compass for the new complexity arising from the post-national constellation: Will the concept of constitutional and social democracy survive this transformation (J. McCormick)? Should we apply justice and the "right to justification" – instead of democracy – as the adequate normative yardstick (J. Neyer)? And how do we have to re-conceptualise a new international law if it was to supply "international public goods" beyond intergovernmental structures (E.-U. Petersmann)?

The EU is clearly the most advanced entity in the international sphere, both in the institutional sense, and with regard to its ever-denser internal legal order. Can the EU really compensate the shortcomings of the constitutional nation-state, as the concept of deliberative supranationalism suggests, or are they just "re-routed to the supranational level" (A. Cebada Romero)? Should the U.S. serve as a blueprint for the European Union, for a creation of the "United States of Europe", or is Canada as "another American state" more fitting a model (J.E. Fossum)? And did the EU produce a new, post-modern European citizen, or is the European project built upon "the false promise of the *homo economicus*" that tends to exclude "the common European man", and a European judiciary that effects "the *bourgeois* colonisation of the normative framework of European law" (M. Everson)?

The legitimacy of the EU rests to a considerable degree upon its ability to integrate a very diverse family, with historically very diverse rule-making traditions and techniques. The most active part of the integration machinery – and, at the same time, the least visible – has been labelled European Governance, meant here in the sense of an umbrella term for "soft law" techniques such as the Open Method of Co-ordination (OMC), as well as for the well-established "Comitology" committee system. The latter has become the role-model for legitimate law-making in the earlier works of Christian Joerges. Does Christian Joerges' new, revised concept of deliberative supranationalism, based upon the conflict of laws idea, avoid the/all the possible flaws of the original concept, and does it provide for an even better normative basis for legitimacy claims (E. Vos)? Can his conflict of laws approach also serve as a model for the development of ordering principles for a general European administrative law, as "a new species of 'conflicts law'" (K.-H. Ladeur)? And finally, will the tendency towards soft law techniques in the EU, such as the OMC, threaten not only legally-mediated political decision-making, but also the whole concept of modern law as such because it will lead to a "de-formalisation through governance" (P. F. Kjaer)?

Part II of this volume enters the debate from a different perspective (*Transnational Regulation and Societal Constitutionalism: Conflict of Laws or Law of Conflicts?*). The contributions to this part examine the supranational and transnational debate on constitutionalism. Their goal is to de-construct the traditional discourse on transnational constitutionalisation and leave the worn-out path of a hierarchical, exclusively public-law driven constitutionalisation of international law behind. Instead, they focus upon the diversity and the fine-print of the Post-Westphalian age: Do the corporate codes of multinationals, in the form of company constitutions, represent "law" and a "civic constitutionalisation" beyond the state-centred law, and can they "guarantee the preservation of high labour standards" in a situation in which the traditional preservation concepts such as the German company co-determination "is one of the casualties of globalisation" (G. Teubner)? Can constitutionalism be taken as a "route to a new state-decentred framework of legal authority", what are the frames of this "constitutionalising trend", and what are the antinomies (N. Walker)? Do academics and international judges – as the major actors behind this constitutionalising trend beyond the state – silently work on, and create, "a common core of global constitutional law", and do they represent "an emerging transnational juristocracy" which shows no signs of deference towards local knowledge and the embeddedness of all the systems of rights (R. Nickel)? Is Christian Joerges' concept of a "proceduralised conflict of laws" the right choice for "entities which are not states, but are condensed contractual regimes" with a trend to constitutionalisation, and what does this mean for the concept of the unity of law, especially with regard to private international law (F. Roedl)?

Market and state are often seen as separate spheres, equipped with different rationalities as well as with different legal structures. State action is measured on formalized procedures, individual rights, and the rule of law principle, whereas market activities are bound by a completely different set of rules. If modern state intervention in markets takes the form of a *Flucht in das Privatrecht* as well as the opposite masquerade – giving "a 'public form' to private behaviour in order to exempt itself from certain community rules" – how can European law deal with this type of "chameleon state" and its "blurring of the private/public distinction in the market" (M. Poiares Maduro)?

Part III deals with a central aspect of today's debates on the EU, namely, *Social Rights and Social Justice: Can "the Social" survive European integration?* A preference for market-driven integration and a neglect of the social sphere is often held responsible for the present stalling of the EU's integration project. The rift is mainly caused by the fact that the (Member) States remain without a market and the (European) market remains without a state, and this situation creates much irritation. If, indeed, European integration is in crisis, can this crisis also be traced back to a "new methodological expansionism of the ECJ", especially in private and labour law, that has lead to a situation in which a concept of an *effet neolibéral* replaces the traditional EU law orthodoxy of an *effet utile* (Ch. Schmid)? As the regulation of the Services of General Interest (SGEI) is situated at the interface between national social policy and EU competition and service law, "can community law resolve the conflict between the Member States' individual concern to control their public services, and their common concern to integrate Europe's service markets and keep them competitive" (N. Boeger)?

And finally, "what is the scope for using the legal concept of Services of General Interest to guarantee the provision of universal service in curative health care" (W. Sauter)?

Part IV leaves the last word to the author, scholar, and friend Christian Joerges, who is the spiritus rector and intellectual source of this new approach to supranational and transnational juridification. His creativity and his seemingly endless productivity have challenged and inspired all the contributions to this volume. Christian Joerges will continue to restlessly re-invent criticisms as well as defences of the European Project (and its transnational relatives). And, lest we delude ourselves, it needs them both.

PART I

DELIBERATIVE SUPRANATIONALISM – LAW AND DEMOCRACY IN THE POST-NATIONAL CONSTELLATION

John P. McCormick

CHAPTER 1. HABERMAS ON CONSTITUTIONAL AND SOCIAL DEMOCRACY IN THE EUROPEAN UNION*

Something of a normative and empirical fog confronts political progressives who grapple with "globalisation". The quandary has often been framed in terms of the following two questions: (A) Does increased capital mobility undercut the power of states to advance social justice on a domestic level? There is growing concern that tax-bases and regulatory capacities in post-industrial democracies have been undermined by the ability of capital to move the sites of production and corporate headquarters abroad, or by the credible threat to do so.[1] (B) Can international institutions, movements and associations advance cosmopolitan and universal schemes of rights against states that do not observe such rights with regard to minorities, women, workers, immigrants, the environment, *etc.*? Such "post-national" human rights strategies capitalise upon recent developments such as increased migration flows, changes in work-force demographics, and greater awareness of the policy implications of multi-culturalism and environmentalism.[2] However, the two questions, to some extent, stand in tension with, or work against, each other: the first is motivated by trepidation over the diminished capacity of the state in the sphere of political economy, while the other seeks to accelerate the diminution of the state's autonomy to carry out repressive political and social policies. Nevertheless, in the contemporary world, both questions assume a new status for the state.

Jürgen Habermas attempts to theorise both of these concerns in the context of the European Union (EU), which presently serves as the best test case for an analysis of post-national politics. In essays composed since the publication of his *Between Facts and Norms*, some of which have been collected in the volumes *The Inclusion of the Other* and *The Post-national Constellation*,[3] Habermas endeavours to operationalise the

* This essay draws upon Chapter 5 of my *Weber, Habermas and Transformations of the European State*, (Cambridge, Cambridge University Press, 2007). I dedicate it to Christian Joerges – mentor, friend and inspiration.

1 See, for example, Saskia Sassen, *Losing Control?: Sovereignty in an Age of Globalization*, (New York: Columbia University Press, 1998).

2 See, for example, Seyla Benhabib, *The Rights of Others: Aliens, Residents and Citizens*, (Cambridge: Cambridge University Press, 2005).

3 See Habermas, Between Facts and Norms: Contributions to a Discourse Theory of Law and Democracy, trans. W. Rehg, (Cambridge MA: MIT, 1996), herein after BFN; The Inclusion of the Other: Studies in

normative blueprint of the former work in contemporary historical-empirical circumstances often identified with globalisation. One might justly expect that, among contemporary social and political theorists, Habermas is the best equipped to confront the kind of questions raised above, given his previous efforts at combining moral-philosophical, social-scientific and historically-grounded modes of analysis. While Habermas may have rivals in each of these separate scholarly spheres, he has been a peerless practitioner of the kind of inter-disciplinary research necessary to begin even confronting a problem as multi-faceted and potentially overwhelming as globalisation. For instance, in contrast to Rawls' justifications for economic re-distribution and, more recently, global justice,[4] Habermas' efforts have seldom been entirely confined to the realm of "the ought", but have incorporated state-of-the-art knowledge of "the is" as well.[5] Habermas' "critical theory" – at its most incisive – has been characterised by concern with "an ought" that inheres immanently within the "is" – ideals that reside in reality, particularly, a constantly and often rapidly changing reality.[6]

I begin by elaborating on Habermas' account of the problems posed by globalisation which necessitate both the continued integration of Europe and the evolution of the EU; I then explicate Habermas' contradictory account of the history of the nation state, and outline his legal-discourse model of democracy in the EU. The final section uses Habermas' previous historical and empirical work, and the pre-suppositions of his present work, against the primary historical-empirical logic of recent essays, and explores the limits of Habermas' vision of the European *Sozialstaat* by juxtaposing it with the *Sektoralstaat* model of supranational governance that I suggest is emerging in the EU. The latter political configuration is comprised of both the transnational "comitological" or "infranational" policy-making that presently operates under the auspices of the European Commission; and the eventuality of "multiple-policy Europes" within the EU, a scenario in which different combinations of Member States will constitute separate energy, defence, trade, communications, welfare, and environmental regulatory regimes.

Political Theory, C. Cronin and P. de Grieff, (eds) (Cambridge MA: MIT, 1998), herein after IO; "The European Nation-State and the Pressures of Globalization", (1999) 235 New Left Review, pp. 46–59, herein after NLR; "Beyond the Nation-State?: On Some Consequences of Economic Globalization", in: E.O. Eriksen and J.E. Fossum, (eds) Democracy in the European Union: Integration Through Deliberation? (London: Routledge, 2000), pp. 29–41, herein after DEU; *The Postnational Constellation: Political Essays*, M. Pensky, (ed) (Cambridge MA: MIT Press, 2001), herein after PC; and "Warum braucht Europa eine Verfassung?" in: Habermas, *Zeit der Übergänge*, (Frankfurt aM: Suhrkamp Verlag, 2001), pp. 104–29. I cite the English translation by Michelle Everson, sponsored by the European University Institute: "So, Why Does Europe Need a Constitution?" (www.iue.it/RSC/EU/Reform02.pdf), Robert Schuman Centre, herein after RSC.

4 See John Rawls, *A Theory of Justice*, (Cambridge MA: Harvard University Press, 1971); and *The Law of Peoples: With, the Idea of Public Reason Revisited*, (Cambridge MA: Harvard University Press, 1999).

5 See Thomas McCarthy, *The Critical Theory of Jürgen Habermas*, (Cambridge MA: MIT, 1978).

6 Most explicitly in Habermas, *The Structural Transformation of the Public Sphere: An Inquiry into a Category of Bourgeois Society*, trans. T. Burger with F. Lawrence, (Cambridge MA: MIT, [1962] 1989), herein after STPS.

1. EU Democracy as a Solution to Global Problems

Habermas conceives of the EU as a post-national vehicle to preserve and advance the liberal and social democratic achievements of the European nation state; significantly, one that will abstain from the domestically- and externally-directed xenophobia and ethnocentrism to which the nation state has been susceptible in the past. The EU might constitutionally facilitate the self-government and economic equality necessary for human autonomy without the war, genocide and discrimination which renders the former impossible. Yet, Habermas' analysis of the problems posed by globalisation and potentially solved by the EU relies on an account of the historical development and the political economy of the modern European nation state, which exhibits serious tensions with, and, indeed, directly repudiates, his own earlier, but still relevant, writings.

This tension exemplifies the extent to which Habermas' understanding of historical transformation within modernity has changed from his earlier work, as well as a more recent tendency to paper-over the pathologies of the welfare state or *Sozialstaat*. Each of these "turns" renders problematical the coherence and persuasiveness of Habermas' analysis of EU supranational democracy: Habermas often describes the implications of globalisation in ways that are reminiscent of the transformation from *Rechtsstaat* to *Sozialstaat* arrangements that was the central focus of the *Public Sphere*. Moreover, the legitimation and clientalisation problems that Habermas previously identified and criticised in the Fordist state would conceivably persist and perhaps proliferate in the conduct of supranational governance. Habermas renders each of these issues subordinate to, respectively, themes of historical continuity and welfare-state efficiency in the essays under consideration. While I demonstrate that Habermas' aspirations for supranational democracy in Europe are compelling in many important respects, since his analysis of the EU abandons the sensitivity to both historical change and the constraints posed by political economy that set him apart from normative theorists in the past, I argue that the methodological approach of these essays undermines the efficacy of his normative vision today.

In the essays under consideration, Habermas flirts with the identification of globalisation as a structural transformation, then demurs from such a step, but ultimately proceeds as if it is, in fact, such a transformation, only to take a U-turn in his treatment of European integration. Unlike products manufactured in Fordist-industrial arrangements, those produced and transported via new communication technologies can be "stored and then consumed at different locations far removed from one another".[7] Consequently, the world economy is now "transnational" and no longer "international", since national boundaries have become blurred, and the political scope of states is no longer determined by "the strategic decisions of other nation-states, but by *systemic* interdependencies" among them.[8] The conduct reflective of these arrangements, and the

7 DEU, note 3 *supra*, at 31.
8 *Ibid.*, at 32.

risks entailed by them, can no longer be predicted or calculated by projecting the behaviour of strategic actors, as might have been possible in the state system.[9] Habermas is adamant that the Fordist, industrial, international state-system has been displaced and, concomitantly, so has its greatest normative achievement: globalisation "destroys a historical constellation in which, for a certain period and a favoured region, the welfare-state compromise was possible".[10] The endangered status of the post-war nation-state's social welfare functions, in what seems to be a structural transformation of the state-economy relationship, is Habermas' first concern in these essays.

Habermas equivocates on the nature and the extent of this transformation from the Fordist nation-state constellation to the new transnational one associated with globalisation, in a way which will have serious ramifications for his contemporary normative prescriptions. Certainly, Habermas' language often conjures images of structural transformation, as when he speaks of the changing "locus of control" from "space to time," and the replacement of "rulers of territory" by "masters of speed".[11] But Habermas ultimately eschews the "transformation" question:

> Whether we understand economic globalisation as the accelerated continuance of long-established trends or as a transformation to a new transnational form of capitalism, it nonetheless shares the disturbing traits common to all accelerated processes of modernization.[12]

Thus, having raised the possibility that globalisation represents a new structural transformation, Habermas then identifies it as a mere "structural adjustment", similar to others that have asymmetrically distributed social costs.[13] Nevertheless, as we will see below, this new asymmetrical redistribution of social costs and burdens seems so drastic that it signals a new historical configuration. While these essays waver over continuity and innovation, the *Public Sphere* suggested that new historical configurations require new institutional means to secure normative ideals, new or old.

But Habermas does not think that simply identifying the problems associated with globalisation suggests the institutional and cultural specifics of the solution to them in the EU, the most developed of the nascent continental regimes that he mentions. Habermas is still sufficiently sensitive to history to look at the *development* of the problems for insight into the particulars of their solution. He claims that the history of the nation-state suggests how the latter may be overcome in a salutary, rather than regressive, manner at supranational level. He states that "the institutionalised capacity for democratic self-determination, the political integration of citizens into a large scale

9 Ibid.
10 *Ibid.*, at 33.
11 PC, note 3 *supra*, at 67.
12 RSC/EUI, note 3 *supra*, at 8.
13 Ibid.

society counts among the undisputed historical achievements of the nation-state",[14] and that these functions must be preserved in supranational institutions. I will examine whether his account of this history is able to support his conclusions concerning the overcoming of the nation-state.

2. The History of the State as a Guide to the Present

Habermas claims that the "unprecedented increase in abstraction" engendered by globalisation is "merely the continuation of a process" that began with the initial development of the nation-state.[15] Just as authority accrued to a higher institutional level and extended over a wider territorial expanse in the state-building process, globalisation presently abstracts away from and beyond the local and national spheres to the regional and universal spheres. A potentially important difference between the two moments of this "continuous" dynamic are an increased integration in the former and the danger of heightened disintegration in the latter. State-building was directed by the centralised administrative authority of the newly empowered bureaucracies in tandem with market forces, while globalisation is driven by a diverse array of international actors and a global market significantly free from state direction. While the nation-state initiated "a more abstract form of social integration beyond the borders of ancestry and dialect", for social integration to continue today, this process must move to "a further abstractive step".[16] As we shall see, because Habermas understands the abstraction process of state formation to be one of trans-historical continuity, independently of whatever minor variations occur within it, he claims that we can evaluate the emergence of "post-national societies from the very historical model we are on the point of superseding".[17]

In other words, since the same process that gave rise to state dominance is contributing to its demise, the gains and losses of this outcome might be inherent to the process itself:

> Though the national state is today running up against its limits, we can still learn from its example.[18]

Habermas' main question and purpose is whether the integration of democratic citizenship previously achieved within the nation state can be carried out at a supranational level without recourse to the ethnic identity enlisted by the former in this

14 *Ibid.*, at 71.
15 IO, note 3 *supra*, at 107.
16 PC, note 3 *supra*, at 18.
17 IO, note 3 *supra*, at 107.
18 *Ibid.*, at 117.

effort.[19] He avers that attention to an ongoing historical process does not compel us, as if by fate, to re-experience the same pathologies that plagued the nation state:

> [T]here are no laws of history in the strict sense, and human beings, even whole societies, are capable of learning.[20]

Since Habermas understands social evolutionism in cognitive-adaptive, not deterministically teleological, terms, he does not resort to historical determinism, but he does think that historical trends provide road-maps to paths that may or may not be taken in the present and the future.

This ideational account of historical change has ramifications for Habermas' prognosis concerning supranational democracy, as we will see below. At this juncture, I would merely point out that these observations differ rather drastically from those presented in Habermas' *Public Sphere*, a work that (a) integrated ideas and empirical facts in the subtle transitions of history, and (b) emphasised the decidedly abrupt character of change between epochs *within* modernity, as opposed to a generalised continuity *of* modernity. The ideals of the bourgeois public sphere were conditioned by the expanded exchange of commodities in the market and the emergence of social labour. Moreover, the periodisation central to his analysis in this work was not feudal/modern, as it is in the essays under consideration, but instead, the more fine-grained distinction among feudal, absolutist, mercantilist, *laissez-faire*, and Fordist phases of modern history.

In these essays on the EU, Habermas attributes the development of the modern state to the interaction of, and tension between, formal citizenship and ethnic nationality.[21] Citizenship, based upon popular sovereignty and universal rights, justifies political participation, then socio-economic entitlement, and develops in "the communicative context of the press, and from the discursive struggle for power of political parties".[22] But Habermas suggests that this was insufficient to "mobilise" people for the domestic or international tasks of state-building, and that appeals to "nationhood" served to fill the motivational vacuum:[23]

> National consciousness owes its existence to the mobilization of enfranchised voters in the political public sphere, no less than to the mobilization of draftees in defense of the Fatherland.[24]

In other words, "democratic citizenship" was not a self-motivating phenomenon and proved necessary, albeit insufficient, for the task of social integration without the

19 Ibid.
20 IO, note 3 *supra*, at 123; See *NLR*, note 3 *supra*, at 47.
21 *Ibid.*, at 113.
22 PC, note 3 *supra*, at 102.
23 IO, note 3 *supra*, at 115.
24 PC, note 3 *supra*, at 102.

accompaniment of the unattractive politics of ethnic and cultural homogeneity. Habermas invokes his now famous notion of "constitutional patriotism"[25] as a progressive alternative which was never satisfactorily practiced outside of the "immigration nations".[26] According to this ideal, national substance was understood in terms of the interpretation of one's own constitution over time, as opposed to appeals to a pre-political identity located in either common ethnicity or even language. In this alternative account of nationalism, while admitting that political mobilisation "depends on a prior cultural integration",[27] Habermas insists that political identity is not fundamentally primordial: "peoples come into being only with their state constitutions".[28]

Nevertheless, in a supranational age, it will not be easy to carry over the substantively-formal socio-political integration associated with citizenship and constitutional patriotism. Habermas notes that contemporary cultural-circumstances entail, on the one hand, a hardening of ethnic identities, such as national majorities and minorities, but also, on the other, a fragmenting and fracturing of them to an individual level via the materialism of the global capitalist culture. He suggests that "both tendencies strengthen centrifugal forces within the nation-state, and that they will sap the resources of civil solidarity unless the historical symbiosis of republicanism and nationalism can be broken, and the republican sensibilities of populations can be shifted onto the foundations of constitutional patriotism".[29] He asks "whether here, in Europe and in the Federal Republic of Germany, a cosmopolitan consciousness – the consciousness of a compulsory cosmopolitan solidarity, so to speak –will arise".[30] This requires a tight intra-European solidarity and a weaker, but still substantive, solidarity with the peoples of other continental regimes throughout the world.

Habermas may seriously over-estimate the extent to which constitutional patriotism was ever realised *anywhere* outside of the writings of Kant, even – or *especially* – in "immigration nations" such as the United States.[31] There certainly are more than glimpses of the non-exclusionary proceduralist and deliberative aspects of nationhood in Habermas' own account of early 19th-century European civil society in *Public Sphere*. But this work is notorious for overlooking virulent nationalism, ethnic prejudice, the subjection of women, and class oppression in the bourgeois public sphere.[32] Certainly, in this work, Habermas managed to show how democratic citizenship did, in fact, serve

25 IO, note 3 *supra*, at 114.

26 See Patchen Markell, "Making Affect Safe for Democracy?: On 'Constitutional Patriotism'", (2000) 28 *Political Theory*, pp. 38–63.

27 PC, note 3 *supra*, at 64.

28 *NLR*, note 3 *supra*, at 57.

29 PC, note 3 *supra*, at 76.

30 *Ibid*., at 112.

31 See Rogers Smith, Civic Ideals: Conflicting Visions of Citizenship in U.S. History, (New Haven: Yale, 1997).

32 See Oskar Negt and Alexander Kluge, Public Sphere and Experience: Toward an Analysis of the Bourgeois and Proletarian Public Sphere, (Peter Labanyi et al., trans., Minneapolis MN: University of

as a powerful ideal immanent within historical practice, as well as the only possible rival to nationalism for putting flesh on the bones of formal constitutional liberties, universal rights and popular sovereignty.

However, Habermas insists that nationalism trumped such substantive democratic practice too often, often resulting in "the expulsion of enemies of the state" and even "the annihilation of the Jews".[33] The sheer artificiality of nationalism, in particular, makes it susceptible to manipulation by élites. Consequently, the progress of democratic citizenship could be de-railed by appeals to homogeneous identity on the part of officials who could not, or would not, facilitate social and political justice: for instance, the fact that "domestic conflicts can be neutralised by foreign military successes rests on a socio-psychological mechanism that governments have repeatedly exploited".[34] Nationalism could always be whipped up in military engagements to distract from the deficiencies of domestic policies and politicians.[35]

During the Cold War, however, such options were not available to policy élites in European nation states. Habermas gestures to a learning process through which policy élites voluntarily sought to avoid the economic mistakes of the inter-war period, which, as Polanyi pointed out, led to fascism, war and genocide.[36] He admits that these élites were actually *forced*, under novel geo-political circumstances, to facilitate democratic citizenship through more responsible domestic politics:

> Under the umbrella of a nuclear balance between the superpowers, the European countries – and not just the divided Germany – could not conduct a foreign policy of their own. Territorial disputes ceased to be an issue. Internal social conflicts could not be diverted outward but had to be dealt with in accordance with the primacy of domestic politics. Under these conditions, it became possible to uncouple the universalistic understanding of the democratic constitutional state to a large extent from the imperatives of a power politics guided by national interests.[37]

Post-war social democracy carries out this "welfare-state pacification of class antagonism" through expanded social security, reforms in education, family policy, criminal law, the penal system, data protection, etc., as well as tentative provisions for

Minnesota Press, 1993); and Habermas and the Public Sphere, (Craig Calhoun ([ed]), Cambridge MA: MIT Press, 1992).

33 PC, note 3 *supra*, at 18.

34 IO, note 3 *supra*, at 114.

35 In this sense, Habermas equivocates on the thesis associated with David Miller, *On Nationality*, (Oxford: Clarendon Press, 1997), which posits that welfare state consolidation required the undergirding of nationalism: Here Habermas suggests that nationalism *distracted* from substantive welfare issues, while later he will admit that nationalism *provided* some of the infrastructure for social democracy. His ultimate point is that political culture and redistributive politics can be sustained through an intersubjectively- not ethnically-based solidarity, see PC, note 3 *supra*, at 99.

36 PC, note 3 *supra*, at 48.

37 IO, note 3 *supra*, at 119.

gender equality.[38] Habermas asserts that "within a single generation, the status of citizens, however imperfect, was markedly improved in its legal and material substance".[39]

But Habermas' account of the welfare state here contravenes his own analyses in important earlier works such as *Public Sphere*, *Legitimation Crisis* and *Theory of Communicative Action*:[40] He now describes Fordist policies as though they "benefited the population as a whole", while he had previously emphasised their discriminatory and marginalising affects. Whereas Habermas had previously charged the mass party/corporatist state with infantilising what where once deliberating publics, in these essays he remarks that it "improved the general level of education".[41] Moreover, the following descriptions are simply not consonant with the pathologies of the welfare state diagnosed by Habermas in these earlier works:

> [C]itizens intuitively realised that they could succeed in regulating their private autonomy, and that an intact private sphere is in turn a necessary pre-condition of such political participation.[42]

All discussion of the self-defeating and intrusive public policy of LC and TCA, as well as the stultification of the populace by the plebiscitary politics of the welfare state in STPS seem to have vanished. As Habermas moves up to a supranational level, he becomes much less stringent on standards for democratic practice at national and sub-national level. For instance, is the following statement a watering down of his previous nationally-based standards for deliberative democracy, and a capitulation to localised acclamatory democracy?

> Within democratic constitutional states, the public communicative infrastructure plays the ideal-typical function of crystallizing problems of common social concerns within discourses, such that citizens are given the opportunity to orient themselves in line with equally weighted arguments and take a positive or negative stance on controversial contributions. The largely implicit and fragmented yes/no reactions to better or less well-founded alternatives are the tiny particles, which, on the one shorter-term hand, accrue to immediately influential opinions and, on the other longer-term hand, make themselves felt in underlying political attitudes and democratic electoral results.[43]

38 Ibid.

39 Ibid.

40 J. Habermas, *Theory of Communicative Action*, (Thomas McCarthy trans., Cambridge MA: Polity Press, 1984, 1987) [herein after TCA].

41 IO, *supra* note 3, at 121.

42 *Ibid.*, at 120.

43 RSC/EUI, note 3 *supra* at 19. At one point, Habermas concedes the inadequacy of post-war national politics but resorts to referenda, place-markers for deliberation translating into action, for supranational accountability: "Political decisions in polarized consensus-based democracies are notoriously intransparent. Europe must therefore consider the use of Europe-wide referenda in order to give citizens a better opportunity to influence the character of policies." See *ibid.*, at 27.

Continuing along these lines, Habermas concludes, "national economies provided a range of opportunities for redistribution that could be exploited, through wage policies and – on the side of the state – welfare and social policies, to satisfy the aspirations of a *demanding* and *intelligent* population".[44] These great achievements of the now glorified *Sozialstaat* include substantive living conditions, educational opportunities, leisure time to foster creativity, in other words, the "pre-conditions for effective democratic participation".[45]

In these writings on globalisation and the EU, Habermas repeatedly invokes the example of "a broad democracy that works reasonably well", or, at least, did so within the nation states of the post-war North Atlantic rim.[46] He identifies the welfare state, the social project achieved during the Hobsbawnian *Golden Age* of the post-war years, as "a specific culture and way of life that is today under threat".[47] Upon this basis, he poses the question: "Can this form of the democratic self-transformation of modern societies be extended beyond national borders?"[48] But before this can be answered, it must be pointed out that Habermas had not previously believed, nor does he now demonstrate, that the *Sozialstaat* operated in such a manner within national borders. Habermas may gesture to the clientalisation critique of Western welfare states by noting how they hardly encouraged "their clients to take charge of their own lives" in an unambiguous way.[49] He even invokes his former intellectual adversary, Michel Foucault, to accentuate the problems of bureaucratisation and normalisation in the *Sozialstaat*, but winds up emphasising the successes of liberalism, constitutionalism and democracy within the latter configuration.[50] In the most effusive language, he asserts that:

> [I]n the third quarter of [the 20th] century, the welfare state did succeed in substantially offsetting the socially undesirable consequences of a highly productive economic system in Europe and the OECD states. For the first time in its history, capitalism did not thwart the fulfilment of the republican promise to include all citizens as equals before the law; it made it possible.[51]

44 IO, note 3 *supra*, at 121 (emphasis added). Rather than complicit in the political apathy of *Sozialstaat* politics, in these essays, Habermas presents mass communication as progressively integrating in an almost unqualified way: "National consciousness has derived as much from the mass communication of newspaper readers as from the mass mobilisation of conscripts and voters. It has been no less shaped by public discourse on the influence and governing power of competing political parties than by the construction of proud national histories." RSC/EUI, *supra* note 3, at 17. Recall that *Public Sphere* showed mass communication to be as, or more, stultifying than it was edifying or progressively integrating.

45 RSC, note 3 *supra*, at 4.

46 *NLR*, note 3 *supra*, at 47.

47 RSC, note 3 *supra*, at 7.

48 *NLR*, note 3 *supra*, at 47.

49 Ibid.

50 DEU, *supra* note 3, at 33.

51 *NLR*, *supra* note 3, at 47.

Despite notable instances of state recalcitrance at this very moment when the state is "most overwhelmed", Habermas avers that the European nation state:

> [S]hould make the heroic effort to overcome its own limitations and construct political institutions capable of acting at the supranational level. Moreover, the latter would have to be connected to processes of democratic will-formation if the normative heritage of the democratic constitutional state is to function as a break on the at-present unfettered dynamic of globalised capitalist production.[52]

Habermas repeats that the "exemplary case" of the EU "naturally comes to mind" as the direction to be followed for "democracy functioning beyond the limits of the nation-state".[53] How does he evaluate this potential, normatively and realistically, and handicap the European "gamble on a post-national democracy"?[54] He insists that the nation-state cannot "regain its old strength by retreating into its shell".[55] It can only regain such strength by no longer operating as a state in the traditional sense, but instead by more firmly embedding itself in a continental and supranational order. But, as I suggest below, Habermas may conceive of the EU as a state writ large, rather than as a truly novel amalgamation of states.

3. Critical-Historical Limits of Habermas' Theory of EU Democracy

My immanent critique of Habermas' analysis of democracy in the EU emphasises the following three points, all of which were alluded to in previous sections: the relationship of state-integration of multiplicity and locality in the past and the tasks of supranational integration today; Habermas' retrospective romanticising of the national *Sozialstaat*; and the contradictions in, and the ramifications of, his "continuity" account of the history of the state. As we have seen, Habermas expounds a historical narrative of the nation-state according to which its gradual emergence and impending eclipse can be conceived as a progressive increase in abstraction. He presents this course as a linear development, even if he avoids designating a particular *telos*. Habermas suggests the following with the sometimes "painful" process of abstraction entailed by state-building in mind: "there is no reason to presume that such a form of civic solidarity will find its limits at the borders of the nation state."[56] The question is whether this will occur without the aforementioned "pain," or whether we can foresee what kind of "pain" that this, more precisely, will entail. However, there is a tension in these essays, which set out and then rely upon this account of the modern state: as we observed in Part (1), Habermas also describes a post-political horror-show portended by globalisation, a neo-liberal nightmare characterised by no public provision for common goods of any kind.

52 IO, *supra* note 3, at 124.
53 PC, *supra* note 3, at 88, *NLR*, *supra* note 3 at 53.
54 PC, *supra* note 3, at 88.
55 *Ibid.*, at 81.
56 RSC/EUI, note 3 *supra*, at 17–18.

When raising this very real alternative scenario, Habermas resorts to a language and logic that suggest qualitative historical change – structural transformation, if you will – that is not consistent with historical continuity in any obvious way. It is the presupposition of continuity, the dominant theme of Habermas' account in these essays, that makes plausible the robust supranational social democracy that will purportedly regulate the elusive dynamics of capitalism without the inconvenient obstacles of national borders. Yet Habermas does not reconcile these two alternative views of historical change, nor does he justify his ultimate adoption of, and reliance on, the latter, more optimistic account. He seems motivated by a professed anxiety over the intolerable nature of the former possibility, and, perhaps, too readily accepts the implications of the "global limits" argument, but does not incorporate them systematically into the historical narrative of continuity, as I explain below.

By leaving the two contradictory accounts of globalisation in these essays unreconciled – drastic qualitative change that results in apocalyptic social, political and economic outcomes *versus* continued increasing abstraction that facilitates a plausible supranational extension of the welfare state – and by failing to justify the theoretical apparatus which he employs in selecting one over the other, Habermas finds himself in a somewhat awkward position. His account aspires to a radical break with nationalism which, apparently, may not be compatible with a relatively easy extension of the *Sozialstaat*. Habermas' historical account of the dynamics of globalisation does not conclusively show why both outcomes should, or could, be expected to emerge in tandem. If globalisation can be characterised as a qualitative break, then, the first *desideratum* of overcoming nationalism could, as a novel phenomenon, be plausible, but the second one of supranational social democracy would certainly not be – at least not without further elaboration. On the other hand, if globalisation is, in fact, part of a larger historical continuity, then the second goal of welfare state transposition seems much more likely than the first, since nationalism still seems inherent in the process itself.

To be more specific, if modern history proceeds as a continuous dynamic, then capital might, indeed, prove controllable at global level. Since the nation-state managed significant, albeit never complete, regulation and re-distribution *vis-à-vis* markets, continental regimes could be expected to do so as well. But two aspects of Habermas' own work, subsidiary here and central elsewhere, raise doubts about this eventuality. Habermas' depiction of globalisation in these essays harkens back to his STPS description of the transition from *laissez-faire*/liberal to administrative/welfare state capitalism, an account in which the preservation of the normative advantages of the previous model remained decidedly precarious in the second, or, at least, required a thinking-through of alternative means to preserve them in a new historical configuration. Doubts about Habermas' model of supranational social democracy are compounded by his previous work, such as *Legitimation Crisis* and *Theory of Communicative Action*, which analysed the crisis-ridden, re-distributively insufficient and pathology-inducing qualities of the national *Sozialstaat* even as he reconstructed the model in more emancipatory ways. In the essays on the EU, the national *Sozialstaat* is supposed to serve as an unqualified, viable model for just and efficient social integration in the future. Furthermore, historical continuity in the development of the nation-state would suggest that an integrating supranational polity would also make use of exclusionary and homogenising notions of identity, rather than forsake them as Habermas hopes – at least, he does not explain why social democratic advantages should carry over through the transition to supranational arrangements while cultural disadvantages reminiscent of nationalism fail to do so.

The relatively separate state-society relationship that conditioned the emergence of the bourgeois public sphere in the 19th century *Rechtsstaat* was not sustained or extended with the emergence of the *Sozialstaat*, but was, instead, largely overcome and perhaps even extinguished by the latter. Habermas suggests that normative aspirations remained constant throughout the transformation, but that the institutions which might realise them had to change. If the phenomena associated with globalisation constitute a similar structural transformation, as his account suggests when he speaks in terms consistent with scenario (α), then, this might portend the demise of the Fordist institutional arrangements of the 20th century, rather than their extension to supranational levels. If social change within modernity entails dramatic rupture and discontinuity, as *Public Sphere* suggests,[57] then a supranational extension of the *Sozialstaat* would not be expected, and the institutions that could realise its normative goals would need more careful and specific demonstration to be rendered plausible in Habermas' present reflections.

If, on the other hand, social changes within modernity are not nearly so drastic as the one between feudalism and modernity, as suggested by Habermas' later writings such as *Communicative Action*,[58] then the more continuous and linear understanding would lend feasibility to an extension of the welfare state at a continental level. Habermas claims to "use the concept of globalisation[...]to describe a process, not an end-state".[59] But how does this viewpoint coincide with his assertion of an end of the nation-state epoch in other moments of the essays? In the latter case, globalisation would then succeed the nation state as a new, if not final, epoch. The distinction between a "process" and an "end-state" is potentially meaningless since the stateification/societalisation process led to a new epoch, that of the *Sozialstaat*, in STPS, even if Habermas never fully worked out continuity/discontinuity issues, and hence periodisations in this work. But the nation-state *is* an end-state if Habermas conceives of supranational institutions as replicating its form.

Put differently, in *Public Sphere*, Habermas could only show, with great difficulty, how the normative goals of the *Rechtsstaat* could be attained in the *Sozialstaat*,[60] but he

57 STPS, note 3 *supra*, at 9, 17–18, 78, and 224.

58 1. TCA, note 40 *supra*, at 199, 221 and 260; 2. TCA, note 40 *supra*, at 119, 174 and 178.

59 PC, *supra* note 3 *supra*, at 65.

60 See, for example, STPS, note 3 *supra*, at 208–09.

proposed socio-institutional reforms through which they might be realized the book's conclusion. Habermas ascended to the more abstract level of social and political theory in *Communicative Action* and *Between Facts and Norms*, respectively, to delineate more optimistically the emancipatory possibilities of 20th century nation states, but he could do so only by directly identifying the complex structures of the *Sozialstaat* with "modernity" itself, and by neglecting moments of qualitative change within the latter historical configuration. Yet, in re-descending from these theoretical heights to engage what, in certain moments of his account, is a *new* transformation of the state and the economy under conditions of globalisation, Habermas has not resumed historical-empirical analysis according to the same standards of *Public Sphere* – that is, not in a way that finely details the material gains and losses of the historical transformation. On the contrary, Habermas' view of the possibilities of the new scenario is purely stereoscopic: either an optimistic or pessimistic extension of some facet of the previous form of the nation-state constellation. He chooses to emphasise, perhaps arbitrarily, the general conditions that might bring about the more optimistic scenario. But this move results in a promotion of the *Sozialstaat* model at supranational level in terms rendered highly questionable by other aspects of Habermas' own efforts here, as well as by his more historical and social scientific work of the past.

Rather than a failure to consult empirical research in contemporary social science literature, I first wish to attribute these deficiencies to the unreconciled contradictions in Habermas' own account of the processes leading to contemporary circumstances and his refusal to reconsider the methodology of his earlier work, which may, in fact, be more appropriate to the present moment. In other words, in this essay, I consider this to be a conceptual or categorical problem, rather than a factual or informational one. I also consider the extent to which Habermas' *Sozialstaat*-model of EU democracy conforms with the reality of *Sektoralstaat* governance, which seems to be prevailing at supranational level. By the standards set here, Habermas should have provided better theoretical justification for abandoning his earlier views of the nature of historical change *to* the *Sozialstaat* and the limitations of political economy *within* Fordist post-war nation states.

Habermas may well have changed his mind on the worth of the kinds of normative insights provided by these earlier methods, but his famous reservations about, and lamentations over, "philosophies of history" are not sufficient to this end. Indeed, the earlier approach reflected in STPS should be acknowledged, if not integrated, into his present analysis, precisely because it was directed at a phenomenon – qualitative social change *within* rather than *to* modernity – that seems to have more in common with present circumstances than do his later writings, such as *Communicative Action* and *Between Facts and Norms*. It may be that Habermas casts modern history as continuity in the main thrust of these recent essays for the same reason that he did so in his mature social and political works: as *a direct response* to the uneasy normative conclusions of his earlier historical works, such as *Public Sphere*, that emphasised structural change. In a way potentially consistent with STPS, Habermas states that economic globalisation does not pose a threat to "functional and legitimate democratic processes as such", but rather to the nation-state as the "institutional form" in which these processes operate;[61] it only constitutes a "disempowerment" of the nation-state.[62] But, with little qualification,[63] he upholds the EU as a communicatively-sustained supranational social democracy precisely along the institutional model of the nation-state, as well as in line with the developmental logic of it.

Whatever Habermas' motives in emphasising such a temporal trajectory, historical continuity does not necessarily guarantee the sanguine results for which he hopes: if continuity governs the history of the state, then might not history be more likely to "repeat itself" than take abrupt and unexpected changes-in-course such as that entailed by the discarding of nationalism? If so, *apropos* criticisms raised at the end of the last part, it is especially alarming that Habermas provides no firmer evidence in support of the possibility of overcoming xenophobia in Europe. Why will élites confronted with the integration deficiencies of supranational politics in Europe not be tempted to appeal to substantive and exclusionary identities as their counterparts did in the earlier history of the nation-state? The infamous Huntington scenario whereby continental cultural difference leads to violent conflict may have little foundation in empirical reality.[64] But it is not ruled out by Habermas' account of the history of the state on either factual or historical grounds.

Returning to the plausibility of European social democracy in Habermas' essays – the creation of "a social Europe that can throw its weight onto the cosmopolitan scale"[65] – the status of transformations to and from the *Sozialstaat* is not the only issue at stake. Precisely *how* the *Sozialstaat* functions is also a problematical issue in Habermas' prescriptions for the EU. The state regulation of society and the economy that he once showed to be a self-contradictory and crisis-ridden operation is presented in these essays on globalisation and the EU as the paragon of re-distributive and solidarity-inducing efficiency. At certain points, he admits that the welfare-state compromise was by "no means the ideal solution" to the political-economic dilemma of capitalism, but he insists that it did succeed in keeping the social costs of capitalism down to a minimum.[66] But such statements stand in marked contrast with those found in Habermas' previous work such as *Legitimation Crisis*[67] and *The New Conservatism*.[68] Whereas the latter works grappled with the problematical relationship of capital and the state in the post-war era – a relationship rife with pathological unintended consequences in both material and

61 PC, note 3 *supra*, at 67.
62 *Ibid*., at 69.
63 See, for example, *ibid*., at 99.
64 See Samuel P. Huntington, *The Clash of Civilizations and the Remaking of World Order*, (London and New York: Free Press, 1998); which is disputed by Bruce Russett, Triangulating Peace: Democracy, Interdependence, and International Organizations, (New York: W.W. Norton and Co., 2000).
65 PC, note 3 *supra*, at 112.
66 DEU, note 3 *supra*, at 33.
67 See J. Habermas, *Legitimation Crisis*, (T. McCarthy, trans., Cambridge MA: Polity Press, 1973).
68 See J. Habermas, *The New Conservatism: Cultural Criticism and the Historians' Debate*, (S. Weber Nicholsen, trans., Cambridge MA: MIT Press, 1989).

ideological domains – this recent work fails to demonstrate how the EU would adequately address these problems nor, for that matter, the one of the flight of capitalism that he emphasises so dramatically.

If globalised capital is as slippery as Habermas' depiction in these essays suggests, then it presumably could elude regional or continental regimes as easily as it has the state. The ramifications of this are exacerbated by Habermas' retrospective romanticising of the national *Sozialstaat*: if, according to Habermas' earlier work, the national welfare state did not sufficiently control and regulate markets and compensate for their deleterious effects, despite its territorial authority, why should we expect continental regimes to do so with any efficiency? Here, Habermas remarks that the EU can "affect" or put a "break" on the dynamic of global capital, but he also intimates that the latter is a *qualitatively different* and not just *quantitatively extended* kind of capitalism; one that may not be controlled, albeit imperfectly, in the manner of classic social democracy at whatever territorial expanse. At some moments in these essays, he attributes global capital's elusiveness to what is qualitatively new in its emerging forms of production, transportation and consumption, but, generally, he understands it in terms of the expansion of a relatively similar and constant phenomenon beyond national borders.

The former understanding makes the case for a supranational welfare state exceedingly difficult, but the latter not all that easier: the former would require an unprecedented regime of regulation and re-distribution for which no previous configuration might serve as a reliable model, while the latter would be beset by the same or exacerbated inefficiencies and pathologies as the national *Sozialstaat*, perhaps to such an extent as to risk its sustainability altogether. The "global limits" logic that Habermas invokes[69] buttresses his case regarding the geographic constraints that would compel an unprecedented engagement with regulatory and re-distributive issues among continental regimes. But this pre-supposes that globalisation signals the quantitative extension of previous forms of capitalism, and not a qualitative break from them, such that territorial scope and proximity can still be translated into significant regulative capacity. In any case, Habermas does not fully explore the ramifications of both the quantitative and qualitative aspects of globalisation, and the tensions between them, which his account raises. The "global limits" argument is further undermined by the fact that Habermas never previously attributed *Sozialstaat* malfunctioning to its tendency to slough-off costs and burdens abroad. Here and elsewhere, Habermas describes the welfare state's regulative successes and failures exclusively in terms of its own internal capabilities so that any diminishing capacity to export costs should not render it any more effective at national or supranational level.

69 DEU, note 3 *supra*, at 36.

There have always been some questions about the adequacy of Habermas' analyses of the *Sozialstaat*, both in general, and for a post-Fordist scenario.[70] But this is less of a concern here than the fact that Habermas seems to completely abandon or leave unacknowledged his earlier *Sozialstaat* analysis, whatever its shortcomings. For Habermas' prescriptions to carry more weight in the context of these essays, he needs to more actively and extensively integrate such work into his present engagement with the dilemmas posed by globalisation, especially the EU – or, at least, justify why he has dispensed with the earlier approach. When a theorist such as Habermas abandons, even reverses, the analysis of one socio-political configuration at the precise moment when he is confronted by a new one, it raises the – admittedly unfashionable – issue of ideology.

The question is one of whether this dilemma is the result of, on the one hand, a permanent change in Habermas' thought towards the ideal and away from the historical – one inspired by personal predilections or career trajectory – or, on the other, is generated by the nature of the reality confronting Habermas the social scientist. In other words, does historical change cause researchers to re-evaluate previous epochs, especially the one immediately preceding the present, in a way that allows the emerging one to conform more easily with one's normative preferences? In this sense, Weber and Habermas both turn to the past to confirm a present that reflects their respective theoretical dispositions, be they pessimistic or optimistic. Habermas' stated methodological goals in these essays seem to imply that he aspires to something more than a loose application of ideal theory to contemporary circumstances. Thus, we need to look past personal predilections and the trajectory of his career and fully consider the effect of these novel circumstances on Habermas's present categories and mode of analysis.

The issue of historical methodology, as well as the spectre of ideology raised above, poses the following generalisable questions regarding Habermas' analysis in the essays under consideration here: Can any social science adequately apprehend the present by glossing over or jettisoning knowledge of the past? Many scholars of European integration, like Habermas, will project a vibrant supranational social-constitutional democracy as Europe's future. On the other hand, many other researchers who have devoted years to tracing both the deficiencies of the welfare state, *and* the imperfections of democratic accountability in liberal democratic states, now lament the demise of regulatory policy and the growing democratic deficits in supranational organisations such as the EU. This, too, is a phenomenon worth considering in greater depth if we are to take changes as vast as those affiliated with globalisation and the EU seriously, and the way we should go about analysing them.

70 See Moishe Postone, "History and Critical Social Theory", (1990) 19 *Contemporary Sociology*, pp. 170–76); Postone, "Political Theory and Historical Analysis", in: *Habermas and the Public Sphere*, note 32 *supra*, pp. 164–80.

4. Conclusion

In the immanent critique strains of this chapter, I have suggested that by minimising the traumatic nature of the previous transformations of the nation state and overestimating the accomplishments of the *Sozialstaat*, Habermas may too readily accentuate the feasibility of a kind of perfected state at European level; he may render too plausible the development of a "continental regime" to *aufheben*, as it were, or preserve, the best of the nation state, while shedding its excessive tendencies. Habermas' account of the history of the state exhibits a tension between continuity and discontinuity, which provides no clear reason why one should expect that the transition to supranational citizenship and economic regulation will be as, or any more, continuous than was the transition from the 19th century *Rechtsstaat* to the 20th century *Sozialstaat* configuration. This problem is particularly acute because the more pessimistic possibility outlined by Habermas conforms with a conception of historical change reminiscent of Habermas' earlier and more empirically-grounded work such as *Public Sphere*; work that analysed the previous transformation in terms of large-scale historical discontinuity. Yet without substantive justification, Habermas chooses to carry out the bulk of his analysis in these essays on the EU with the conceptual apparatus that he developed in his later work, such as *Communicative Action*, which biases his account in favour of less wholesale, less drastic, and potentially less intimidating historical change within modernity.

By setting out something less than an empirically- and historically-informed normative framework for a post-national future, Habermas' work on the EU shares widespread assumptions with many theoretical engagements with the prospect of democracy in Europe. Most speculation about supranational institutions – optimistic and sceptical – tend to reify some aspect of the nation state that used to be problematical or contested, and deploy it as evidence for the development of a certain vision of socio-political arrangements under supranational developments. On the one hand, supranationalists posit something approximating a constitutional-social democracy at continental level, while, on the other, intergovernmentalists predict a persistence of state treaty negotiations as the core of future European politics. Evidence suggests, as I show in the external thrust of my critique, that European politics will look very different than what is pre-supposed by either of these models, and, instead, will resemble what I call a *Sektoralstaat*: a polity in which different policy spheres are governed by those most closely affected by, or most interested in, it, and that this will have serious ramifications for democratic rule, legal scope and material equality in Europe's future – ramifications not necessarily well-met by the Habermasian paradigm in the following ways.

The *Sektoralstaat*: (1) dismisses, or, at the very least, downgrades the participation or "say" of those *less* affected but still *concretely* affected by a policy; (2) virtually abandons the participation of, or sanctioning by, the polity at large, through either constitutional or statutory law; and (3) tolerates different levels of social protection and re-distribution throughout what, in this case, is somewhat ironically named the "Union". For these reasons, the *Sektoralstaat* model emerging in Europe raises the issue of dissonance between the functioning of multifarious policy sub-groups and the rights and interests of the larger public in a way, perhaps, never before observed in European democratic theory and practice. They highlight the way in which participation, egalitarianism and accountability, and the feasibility of their legal facilitation, will be the mission of democratic theory in Europe, and the world, in the coming century.[71]

However, I do not intend for the above analysis of Habermas' reflections on the EU to imply that we ought *not* to be hopeful about the future of democratic practices in supranational institutions, and therefore not work to attain them. I merely wish to emphasise the necessity of better attention to the historical suppositions undergirding attempts to theorise supranational democracy. In fact, on normative-empirical grounds, I would suggest that we should not place the bar for the possibility of supranational social democracy *too high*. In fact, I think that it would be a mistake to forget the leftist critique of the national *Sozialstaat* that accused the latter (i) of not going nearly far enough in re-distributing wealth, (ii) of creating social pathologies and economic crises for which solutions were never sought, let alone found, and (iii) for simply being too friendly to capital. These facts ought not to be flushed away as we evaluate contemporary standards of responsiveness, accountability, participation, equality, etc., in supranational contexts.

Despite Habermas' best intentions, democracy in a supranational age could never stand up to criteria derived from a democratic past that never existed. In short, if the theoretical and practical stakes in ascertaining the institutional requirements for supranational democracy were not so high, it would be almost amusing to hear talk of the "democratic deficit" in the EU, as if there is, or ever was, a democratic equilibrium, let alone a *surplus*, in industrial-democratic states. Social and political theorists need to compare the respective democratic deficits of the nation state and continental regimes such as the EU without recourse to illusions about the former that encourage ineffectual analyses of the institutions that comprise the latter. In the spirit of the critical theory of Habermas' *Public Sphere*, this mission demands efforts at reviving and refining our notions of both history and historical change as we approach and evaluate democracy in a supranational present and future.

71 Inspired by and responding to Christian Joerges' work on deliberative supranationalism, I develop the notion of the *Sektoralstaat* most fully in McCormick, *Weber, Habermas and Transformations of the European State*, (Cambridge: Cambridge University Press, 2007), Chapter 6. See Ch. Joerges, "Deliberative Supranationalism" – Two Defences, (2002) 8 *European Law Journal*, p. 145; Christian Joerges, "Bureaucratic Nightmare, Technocratic Regime and the Dream of Good Transnational Governance", in: *EU Committees: Social Regulation, Law and Politics*, pp. 3–17, Christian Joerges and Ellen Vos, (eds), (Oxford: Hart Publishing, 1999); and Christian Joerges, *The Law in the Process of Constitutionalising Europe*, in: *Constitution-Making and Democratic Legitimacy*, p. 13, p. 42 note 88 (Erik Oddvar Eriksen *et al.*, (eds), 2002).

Jürgen Neyer

CHAPTER 2. JUSTICE OR DEMOCRACY? POWER AND JUSTIFICATION IN THE EU AND OTHER INTERNATIONAL ORGANIZATIONS

The main task of international organisations is to provide a corrective mechanism to the normative and functional failures of the nation-state under conditions of interdependence.[1] Assessments of the legitimacy of international organisations should judge them to the degree to which they fulfil that task. This chapter submits the idea to use the concept of justice as a proxy for such an assessment. The main part of the article is devoted to identifying three major obstacles for realising justice in international politics and explains how supranational organisations help these obstacles to be overcome. The concluding section summarises the argument and discusses its relevance for the debate on the legitimacy of international organisations.

1. Beyond the Democratic Deficit

Much of the debate on the legitimacy of the EU and other international organisations is built upon the assumption of a universal applicability of the concept of democracy. Conceptions of legitimate governance are exported from standard democratic theory, and are applied to the EU without systematically investigating whether the notion of democracy is the adequate standard at all. Democracy, so the implicit argument goes, is a value that cannot be meaningfully disputed. It is a normative good in itself, and is, therefore, applicable always and everywhere, indiscriminately of whether the object under scrutiny is a city, a state, a region or an international organisation. However, this approach is difficult to justify both for theoretical and empirical reasons.

On a theoretical level, it ignores the insight that all theories are built upon abstractions and that they therefore only work under specific conditions. In positive theory, this insight is reflected in the use of scope conditions, i.e., the identification of conditions

1 Earlier versions of this chapter have been presented to the conference on "Justice and Global Democracy", Frankfurt am Main, 25–26 May 2007 and the workshop on "Transnational Standards of Social Protection: Contrasting European and International Governance", Bremen, 23–24 November 2007. The author is thankful for critical comments by the participants of both meetings, especially Andreas Niederberger and Karl-Heinz Ladeur.

which limit the range of the applicability of a certain statement. Scope conditions are of eminent importance in most positive theories, for example, in liberal intergovernmentalism or in neo-functionalism. None of these theories claims to offer a universally valid explanation, but they all limit their propositions to certain specified conditions. However, the modesty that accompanies the notion of scope conditions is sometimes lacking in normative theory. It is not clear, for example, why the logical nexus between abstract categories and the limited applicability of the theory (which is established on these categories) should not hold true for normative theory. The implication of this argument is that we should demand any normative theory of democracy to identify its analytical abstractions and to explicate to what extent they limit the range of the argument.

On an empirical level, there are likewise good reasons to be sceptical about the analytical usefulness of the notion of democracy for justifying the EU. The EU lacks all those political competences which lie at the heart of any state governance and which have historically been the most prominent resources for the provision of public order: the powers to tax, to enforce sanctions by means of coercion, and to provide security against foreign powers. The EU has none of these competencies. It does not levy taxes, it commands no police, and its defence and security policy is embryonic at the very least. In addition, even after the Treaty of Lisbon, it still is the case that the supremacy of European law is not explicitly mentioned in the law of the Union and that every Member State could, by means of simple legislation, revoke its *Anwendungsvorrang*. The EU – or any other international organisation – also has no *demos*. European-wide public discourses emerge only sporadically as responses to political scandals or soccer championships. The nation-state is still the primary *locus* of allegiance in Europe and the place where political discourse and democratic reflection take place. Democratic theory, be it in a Rawlsian, in a Habermasian or in a Dahlian fashion, emphasises that democracy necessarily entails a *demos* which identifies itself with a certain authoritative structure (even if it is only understood in the Habermasian term of *Verfassungspatriotismus*). There can be no democracy without a *demos*.

In addition, the EU lacks firm borders and a clear demarcation between insiders and outsiders. The EU is a set of policy-specific regimes Democracy is also hard to imagine without firm borders. Although many speculate about the possibility of democratic governance in functionally-specified policy networks, all established theories of democracy again underline the importance of drawing a line between those who are insiders and those who are outsiders. It makes common sense that democratic procedures are instruments for identifying and implementing the normative ideas as they are held by a people with a clear territorial and juridical distinction. If adopted, these ideas become norms and rules which apply to all the people within the demarcated territory and to no one outside that territory. The EU does not only violate this principle, but follows an entirely different logic. It does not have fixed borders but consists of a set of functionally-specified political regimes with changing memberships. Whilst some regimes, such as the CFSP, accept only governments as members, others guarantee broad rights to individuals. In addition, some regimes cover all 27 Member States of the

EU, whilst others are more exclusive. It must also be mentioned that the EU does not limit its influence to its 27 Member States, but is proud to export its norms to its neighbours and to make close co-operation dependent upon their compliance with the EU's standards of democracy, human rights and, last but not least, industrial products. In sharp contrast to any nation-state, the EU does not respect territorial boundaries, but, in the words of the Declaration of Laeken, respects "only democracy and human rights".[2] In short, most contributions to the debate on the democratic deficit of international organisations, which apply the domestic analogy and use a normative concept that is deeply rooted in the history and the structure of the nation-state, commit a categorical mistake.

2. Transnational Justice as a Right to Justification

One option, in order to avoid such a categorical mistake and to formulate politically significant ideas of legitimacy, is to ensure that the analytical categories that we are using are not only normatively introduced but also empirically explained. Normative categories should be formulated with a view to the connection between "ought" and "can" and reflect an awareness that normative requirements will only be convincing to the degree that we provide evidence that they are indeed "fit for reality". It is true, however, that such evidence is often hard to collect. Any statement about the possibility of transforming normative ideas into real-world conditions must always remain, to some degree, speculative, and can be formulated only hypothetically. Nevertheless, in order to make the criterion operational, we can consider all the normative ideas, which build upon some existing element of the empirical reality and merely expand its reach, rather than invent something completely new, to be *prima facie* fit-for-reality. This idea reflects Rawls's insight that a necessary pre-condition for a convincing normative concept is "that its major principles and instructions are practiced and can be applied to existing political and social institutions".[3] Hence, such a concept expands "the borders of what we usually consider practically-politically possible"[4] while, at the same time, remaining on solid empirical ground.

An interesting possibility, in order to move in this direction, is offered by a concept of justice which focuses upon the *right to justification*. An important advantage of switching from the democracy discourse to the justice discourse is that the notion of justice can, indeed, be applied to all political contexts. It is applicable to private settings such as in a family, to the internal organisations of a company, or even to the political

2 "The European Union's one boundary is democracy and human rights", Declaration of Laeken 2001, European Council.

3 John Rawls, *A Theory of Justice*, (Cambridge MA: Harvard University Press, 1971); and *The Law of Peoples: With, the Idea of Public Reason Revisited*, (Cambridge MA: Harvard University Press, 1999), p. 15.

4 John Rawls, *A Theory of Justice*, (Cambridge MA: Harvard University Press, 1971); and *The Law of Peoples: With, the Idea of Public Reason Revisited*, (Cambridge MA: Harvard University Press, 1999, p. 4.

system of a state or a supranational entity. In addition, justice is a normative standard which is not lower than any other standard of legitimacy. It is, in the words of John Rawls, even the prime social virtue, the most important virtue of social institutions. No other quality can substitute for a lack of justice. Only conditions that are just are acceptable, never unjust conditions. Everything which is unjust has to be rectified through practical political measures and improved upon. Democracy and justice are closely related to one another. Democracy is cherished by most of us because of its contribution to the fostering of politics that are just. We cherish democracy because is the political procedure with the highest probability of producing outcomes that are just.

According to Rainer Forst, the right to justification is not a luxury good that is provided by well-developed democracies, but must be seen as a most basic human right.[5] It is centred on the idea that any restriction of individual freedom must be justified by whoever causes the restriction in question or has the intention to do so. This argument takes the freedom of the individual from domination as a starting point and places any restriction of this freedom under the reservation of good reasons. In crafting the argumentative design of a justification, the justifying person or organisation cannot act arbitrarily, but must apply good reasons. Only the reasons are to be understood to be good reasons which fulfil the two minimum conditions of reciprocity and universality, which means that nothing more is demanded from anybody than we are willing to concede ourselves, and that the reasons apply to everybody to the same degree.

Understanding justice as the "right to justification" gives the notion of justice an intrinsically procedural and discursive character. Any question about the specific implication of justice in a specific situation is answered with reference to a normatively-demanding discursive procedure. A thus defined right to justification can well be applied to international relations. It resonates with the idea of self-determination and refers to the basic right of every society to choose, independently of foreign influence, its political status, its form of state and government and its economic, social and cultural development. As a matter of principle, restrictions of this freedom are acceptable only when a state either voluntarily complies with an international legal provision, when *ius cogens* is applicable, or when other good reasons can be articulated.

It is important to note that self-determination cannot be equated with autonomy today. The global condition of complex inter-dependence implies that one can neither pursue a successful unilateral money and currency policy, nor conduct a sensible unilateral security policy. All these policy areas are characterised by a significantly reduced ability of single states to realise their preferences independently of the actions of other states. It is a generally shared insight, therefore, that complex inter-dependence among national societies has turned a purely national organisation of politics into a problem for

5 See Rainer Forst: *Das Recht auf Rechtfertigung. Elemente einer konstruktivistischen Theorie der Gerechtigkeit*, (Frankfurt aM: Suhrkamp Verlag, 2007).

democratic governance itself: in a great number of issues areas, from environmental degradation to security affairs and migration issues, the single nation-states is increasingly inappropriate for the formulation and implementation of effective policies. The normative deficiency of the nation-state is not limited to its capacity as an effective problem-solver, however. It also applies to the related structural phenomenon that the political measures taken by individual states often have effects for other states. The decision to raise or lower the interest rates of a central bank may have the effect of making neighbouring countries more, or less, attractive to capital. The easing or restricting of national provisions for immigration will likewise re-orient the decisions of individuals seeking refuge from violence or a better income, and have an effect on the relative attractiveness of other states. The national establishment of certain requirements for legally-sold products will make it more, or less, costly for producers in foreign states to import their products, and may lead to losses or gains or employment opportunities. All these effects are structural phenomena under conditions of inter-dependence. Without being embedded in an international structure of policy co-ordination, the individual nation-state has little incentive to take the external effects of its actions seriously, i.e., to integrate them systematically as an important calculus into its own decision-making practices. The basic normative principle, that those who are affected by a decision should have a say in its making, is, therefore, systematically violated by almost all inter-dependent nation-states if they are not embedded in an international structure that fosters the internalisation of the external effects of domestic decision-making.

Thus, international organisations such as the EU, the WTO, the ILO or even the United Nations (UN) derive their legitimacy, first of all, from their function as a correcting mechanism for this systematic nation-state failure. They foster the right to justification by making inter-dependent nation-states systematically aware of one another, by helping to pool resources that are necessary for tackling pressing cross-border problems, and by providing an organisational setting, in which the responsibility to take the concerns of other states seriously is transformed into legal obligations.[6] International organisations, therefore, carry, first of all, the potential to remedy the structural shortcomings of the nation-state, and should be seen as important and necessary devices for adapting the nation-state to the condition of complex inter-dependence. Today, insisting on a traditional form of self-determination that emphasises both the right and the ability to unilateral action (sovereignty and autonomy), leads not to more freedom, but runs into the paradox of self-chosen heteronomy. A modern concept of self-determination entails participation in the political discourses and justificatory practices of international organisations and of multilateral co-operation.

6 Ch. Joerges "European Law as Conflicts of Law", in: Ch. Joerges and J. Neyer, *Deliberative supranationalism: revisited.* 20/2006 *EUI Working Papers;* Ch. Joerges, "Deliberative Supranationalism" – Two Defences, (2002) 8 *European Law Journal.*

3. Obstacles to Transnational Justice

Is the right to justification just another normative utopia without any fair chance to be realized? Or does it comply with the requirement of normative realism to explicate how the "ought" and the "is" relate to one another and how and by what means the normative idea can be fostered? This section analyses three major difficulties of realizing the right to justification.

The existence of asymmetrically distributed international power resources poses a major challenge to the idea of a transnational discourse on justification. From world trade politics to environmental politics to international security politics, we can observe that the more powerful states dominate the policy-making process, while the smaller states have to subordinate themselves to the policies agreed upon by the bigger states. Due to the unequal ability of states to transform their interests into international norms which are binding for other states, many international regimes only reflect the particular interests of a limited number of powerful states. Many international regimes produce heteronomy for weaker states, instead of international justice. Within the World Trade Organisation (WTO), for instance, the big member states, until recently, negotiated all the important agreements among themselves in a so-called "Green Room Procedure" and announced their findings to the secretary general. He then presented the outcome as a "consensus" to the rest of the member states.[7] Clearly, such a procedure leaves little scope for a justice-oriented discourse of mutual justifications.

Power asymmetries exist not only in the horizontal dimension of cross-border politics, but also in its vertical dimension. In international politics, executives have far more leeway to use their discretionary powers than in the domestic realm.[8] In democratic domestic politics, governments act as the legislature's executive organ, and are normally delegated the task of implementing its decisions. By contrast, in international politics, executives generally act as gatekeepers for political proposals, and decide which issues are discussed and which are to be dealt with at all. The legislative branch can only ask its government to put an issue on the international agenda, thereby promoting the involvement of other governments. Unlike national politics, the legislative branch has no right to set the political agenda of an international organisation or to call upon a government, or, in this case, a group of governments, actually to implement a certain legal norm. Governments are, by and large, free to set the international agenda as they wish, and to decide among themselves upon regulations. It is true that international rules concluded among executives become domestic law only after a national parliament has ratified a legal act, thereby transforming it into its national legislation. Thus, the

7 See A. Kwa (2003) *Power Politics in the WTO, Focus on the Global South*, Bangkok: Chulalogkorn University.

8 See A. Moravcsik, (1994) Why the European Community Strengthens the State: Domestic Politics and International Co-operation, (Cambridge MA: Harvard University: Center for European Studies, *Working Paper Series* 52).

legislative branches retain a veto – albeit only formally. However, at the same time, a parliamentary veto against a legal act concluded among executives is, for good reasons, very rare. Vetoing a legal act by refusing to ratify it is a massive declaration of mistrust from the parliamentary majority towards the government. This is unlikely to happen in parliamentary systems in which the government can rely on a parliamentary majority. The problem of executive empowerment through international negotiations is aggravated by the fact that executives usually possess better information about the positions and the scopes of other executives, and are, therefore, able to assess what is politically viable with greater accuracy. Through their membership in international organisations, such as the OECD, the World Bank or the IMF, they have access to a kind of specialised expertise that is not – or only with considerable effort – available to MPs. Thus, a parliament arguing against an internationally negotiated regulation and denying its ratification implicitly arrogates to itself a better knowledge of what is politically viable than the executive – despite the fact that it is less informed. A denied ratification is also improbable because it is the executives themselves who decide on which information about the positions and the scopes of other executives to pass on to the media and to parliament. Thus, the executives not only have the possibility of determining the international agenda, they are also in a strong position to influence the perception of the respective legislature (and the national public) about what is actually politically viable at all.

A third crucial obstacle relates to the non-coercive nature of the international system. Justice-oriented discourses pre-suppose that successful justification is a necessary pre-condition for implementing a certain policy and that, therefore, any failure to explain or to justify incurs costs for a policy entrepreneur. Costs, however, will only be incurred by a policy entrepreneur if the group towards whom the justificatory effort is directed has some enforcement capacity which it can exert in the event of a failure, i.e., a non-convincing justification. However, because the international system is a self-help system, the power to impose costs on other states is structurally limited to the powerful states. It is for this reason that the limited capacity of the international community to provide incentives in order to make powerful states comply with their legal commitment is often described as the *Achilles' heel* of effective global governance.[9] Some even dispute that international legal rules are proper legal rules. And, indeed, in international relations, it is only too often the case that weaker states have a formal right to some justification, explanation or even compensation, but lack any means to enforce that right. Thus, justice-oriented discourses pre-suppose that not only strong, but also weak states have access to effective enforcement capacities in order to give a significant incentive to powerful actors to take justificatory discourses seriously.

9 See Oran R. Young, 1999, *Governance in World Affairs* (Ithaca: Cornell University Press, 1999), Ch. 4.

4. Supranationalism as a New Context for Justice

The considerations above are hardly apt to form much optimism with regard to the chances of a justice-oriented transnational discourse. The international polity is a space in which horizontal and vertical power-asymmetries, and the inexistence of global coercive power, are important factors in policy outcomes. Under conditions of supranational integration, however, much of the scepticism can be relaxed. Supranational structures combine a vertical and hierarchical legal order with a horizontal and non-hierarchical coercive order.[10] They are neither state nor international politics. Supranationalism is established not on a monopoly of power, but on an oligopoly of power. All member states remain in full command of their legitimate monopoly of coercion and none of that is transferred to the supranational level. Supranationalism is, likewise, different if compared with traditional international diplomacy. Vertical legal integration ties individuals, governments and supranational organisations together into a multi-level legal structure in which the legal requirement to justify and give reasons is codified, and can be enforced by both supranational and domestic courts.[11] Law in a supranational setting is, therefore, similar to national law, in that it distinguishes between basic norms (primary or constitutional law) and secondary law (statutory law), with the former more difficult to change than the latter. Individuals are not merely subjects and affected parties as they are under international law, they are also empowered with domestically enforceable rights.

4.1. Transforming Bargaining into Legal Reasoning

A supranational context has important implications for the probability of effective justificatory discourses. In order to understand the difference that supranationalism makes, it is important to recall that power in international relations is most often exerted in the mode of intergovernmental bargaining. State preferences are treated as intrinsically legitimate reflections of domestic political processes. Most often, international negotiations are not about justifying governmental preferences, but about bargaining over the differences. Under conditions of supranationalism, i.e., in a highly legalised setting, bargaining is, in general, an inappropriate mode of interaction. Highly legalised settings such as in the European Community (EC), prescribe both material and procedural norms against which the preferences of actors are to be weighted. Complying with these norms necessitates justifying preferences by explaining how they relate to them. Legal integration forces actors to abstain from simply issuing threats and promises, and requires them to re-formulate their preferences in the language of law (by referring to material and procedural norms). Legal integration transforms bargaining into legal reasoning.

10 See J.H.H. Weiler, (1981) "The Community System: The Dual Character of Supranationalism", *Yearbook of European Law* 1: p. 267.

11 See Ingolf Pernice: "Multilevel Constitutionalism and the Treaty of Amsterdam: European Constitution-Making Revisited", in: (1999) 36 *Common Market Law Review*, pp. 703–750.

It is true that legal reasoning is not immune to power asymmetries. Good arguments are often expensive arguments, because they require good lawyers and often have to refer to technical expertise or scientific evidence. It is also true, however, that re-formulating preferences in the language of law acts as a filtering mechanism, which limits the range of preferences that can be put on the table to those preferences which can be publicly justified. In his discussion of the analytical differences between arguing and bargaining, and their effects on political outcomes, Elster refers to this effect as the "civilising force of hypocrisy".[12] In order to argue, speakers must hide base motives. However, hiding base motives requires proposals to be subjected to a number of constraints which may modify them quite substantially. The first constraint is the "imperfection constraint", which implies that proposals must show less than a perfect coincidence between private interests and impartial arguments in order to be perceived as good arguments. Arguments must also be in accordance with positions that have been formulated at an earlier point in time, and be maintained even if they no longer serve the speaker's interests (consistency constraint). Otherwise, a speaker will easily be viewed as acting opportunistically and lose his or her credibility. And, finally, arguments must abstain from making claims which can easily be shown to be incorrect (plausibility constraint). Together, all three constraints work as a filter against openly selfish claims and thus civilise interaction by forcing the disputants to engage in argumentative interaction. Legal reasoning is, therefore, a deliberative mode of interaction, which forces actors to perform in accordance with shared legal norms, even if they only have self-minded interests.

By fostering argumentation in cross-border policy-making, supranationalism implies a change in the mode of representation. In international relations, states are, in general, represented by governments. International negotiations are, in fact, intergovernmental negotiations in which the weight of an argument depends upon the power resources of the state that is represented by that government. The importance that is attached to good arguments in a supranational context significantly changes this. Under conditions of legal reasoning, it is no longer a state's vulnerability to a failure of negotiations that decides who obtains what, but the quality of the argument which the opposing sides can make. Supranationalism is, therefore, about the representation of arguments, and not about power and preferences. Under conditions of anarchy, states bargain; in supranational structures, they argue.

Although it is hardly possible to observe instances of purely legal reasoning in any real-world organisational context,[13] it is also true that most political discussions in close-to-supranational entities such as the EC, or (with even less approximation) the WTO, show significant elements of such a justificatory balancing of arguments. Articles 28 and 30 of

12 See Jon Elster: "Deliberation and Constitution Making", in: Jon Elster (ed.), *Deliberative Democracy*, (Cambridge: Cambridge University Press, 1998), pp. 104–105 and 111).

13 For an empirical research project that tried to describe instances of international arguing, see Nicole Deitelhoff and Harald Müller: "Theoretical Paradise – Empirically Lost? Arguing with Habermas", (together with Harald Müller); (2005) 31 *Review of International Studies*, pp. 167–179).

the European Community Treaty (ECT) describe the prohibition of discriminatory trade practices and list the reasons which can be brought forward in order to justify an exemption. The overwhelming majority of political disputes and decisions of the European Court of Justice (ECJ) in the EC fall under the rubric of these legal provisions. Even more importantly, most legal (and even most political science) scholars agree that the decisions of the ECJ are hardly ever motivated by the difference in the size or the wealth of the disputing parties.[14] It is arguments and justification, not preferences and power, which carry the day. Likewise, the Dispute Settlement Body (DSB) and the Appellate Body (AB) of the WTO mainly have to decide on disputes that take issue with equivalent principles of non-discrimination and reciprocity, as well as a multitude of exemptions that define and restrict the normative framework described.

It is important to reflect upon a final *caveat*: even if supranational organisations have the capacity to transform bargaining into legal reasoning, they are, nevertheless, founded on an original bargaining process and often reflect – to some degree – the outcome of an asymmetrical distribution of power. The founding of WTO is most often described as reflecting a blackmailing process in which the Northern states threatened to conclude among themselves a mini-WTO if the Southern world refused to accept the inclusion of Trade Related Intellectual Property Rights (TRIPS) and a General Agreement of Trade in Services (GATS) into the legal framework of the new WTO.[15] Thus, one is tempted to assume that even an ideal mode of transnational legal reasoning only applies the procedural and material norms which have been dictated by the powerful actors. If this were true, then legal reasoning would only perform as though it were a neutral and fair language, but, in fact, would express nothing but the hidden dominance of the powerful. However, it is also the case that the law is a living thing which adopts its own dynamics once it has been established. The practices of the ECJ and the DSB provide clear evidence that Courts are only – to a limited degree – under the control of the member states, and have some leeway in interpreting the law in a way which is compatible with shared notions of fairness. Here, Burley and Mattli have explained the incomplete political control of the member states over "their" Court, with reference to the argument that the law acts "as a mask and shield" against politics.[16] It is also worth mentioning that intergovernmental bargaining hardly ever takes place in a normatively void environment. International customary law provides a distinct normative environment that encompasses compelling formal and informal norms such as the ideas of reciprocity, sovereignty, *pacta sunt servanda*, and *ius cogens*. Thus, international law is not only the product of intergovernmental bargaining, but is also the normative frame in which negotiations are conducted.

14 See Karen J. Alter: *Establishing the Supremacy of European law: The Making of an International Rule of Law in Europe*, (Oxford: Oxford University Press, 2001).

15 See Richard H. Steinberg: "Judicial Lawmaking at the WTO: Discursive, Constitutional, and Political Constraints", (2004) 98 *The American Journal of International Law*, pp. 247–275.

16 See Anne-Marie Burley and Walter Mattli: "Europe Before the Court: A Political Theory of Legal Integration", in: (1993) 47 *International Organization*, pp. 41–76.

4.2. *Safeguarding Executive Responsiveness*

Legal integration in a supranational context is not limited to the horizontal level of intergovernmental relations but also applies to its vertical dimension. In abstract terms, vertical legal integration can be understood as connecting supranational, national and individual actors by means of legal provisions so that justifications can, and must, be exchanged. Legal integration thus is not limited to relations among supranational organisations, but, instead, covers the whole range of relevant political actors in a multi-level structure. Supranational legal integration is highly relevant for establishing the pre-conditions of transnational justificatory discourses since it has the potential to safeguard that governmental and supranational actors are compelled to comply with the requirement to justify their actions, and that their policy discretion is not expanded beyond a degree which can be justified towards their respective principles.

At member state level, legal integration can tie executive discretion to a mandate formulated by a parliamentary committee. The Danish *Folketing*, for example, exercises its control over the Danish government in European affairs by clearly outlining in advance which positions the governmental delegate may present and which go beyond its mandate. The responsible minister has to present his proposal in person to a specialised European Affairs Committee of the *Folketing* and to reach a supportive majority. The members of the committee not only vote on the proposal, but also have the right to propose amendments. The minister has no right to enter into *any* negotiations in Brussels if he or she does not convince the majority of the committee of his or her proposal. Likewise, if the negotiations in Brussels make it necessary to change the Danish position, and if the minister wants to go beyond the authorisations given by the mandate, then he or she must present new suggestions to the committee and wait for new instructions. The integration of the *Folketing* into the daily decision-making in Brussels is an important element for explaining the high political awareness toward European affairs in Denmark. European politics is not limited to executive discretion but is an essential part of domestic legislative politics. Although this awareness may, from time to time, lead to a critical stance of the public toward the EU, it is obviously highly attractive from the perspective of a justificatory discourse.

The justificatory discipline of supranational legal integration also covers relations between the EC's supranational institutions and its Member States. The delegation of competences to the Commission is almost always *only* conditional, and subject to control mechanisms. The provisions of Article 202 ECT are a typical example. The article stipulates in its first sentence that the Council delegates all competences to the Commission to implement its legislative acts. The second sentence, however, immediately adds that the Council may establish certain modalities for the execution of these competences. In practice, the second sentence has been a major reason for the huge growth of the European comitology system, which acts as a safeguard against the

Commission becoming a "run-away bureaucracy".[17] Even in an area such as external trade, where the Commission has broad competences which were already codified in the Treaty of Rome, it must justify its international policies towards the Member States. According to Article 133 ECT, the Commission can act only after it has presented recommendations to the Council of Ministers, and after these recommendations have been authorised. In addition, every international legally-binding agreement that was concluded by the Commission on the part of the EC is subject to critical scrutiny in the Council.

It is true that all of these mechanisms do not provide any guarantee for the complete lifting of vertical power asymmetries between the supranational bodies of the EU, the Member States and individuals. Organisational procedures never determine action but only provide incentives to act according to prescribed rules. It is also true, however, that the list above is far from complete and only presents selected parts of a picture which, in reality, is much more complex and imposes a much more rigid discipline than the three mechanisms imply. In addition, the very existence of these procedures provides evidence that supranational legal integration is not only a means to expand governmental discretion but also simultaneously imposes additional needs for justification. Supranationalism, therefore, does not just expand or limit governmental discretion, but also provides an argumentative discipline according to which it is to be exercised.

4.3. Healing the Achilles' Heel

It is an often cited conclusion that "almost all nations observe almost all the principles of international law and all of their obligations almost all of the time".[18] This observation has recently been re-discovered by scholars endeavouring to understand why and when international regulations are complied with.[19] According to their findings, good legal management of rules is the most important factor for eliciting compliance. Chayes and Chayes[20] have put this finding quite clearly:

> Enforcement through these interacting measures of assistance and persuasion is less costly and intrusive and is certainly less dramatic than coercive sanctions, the easy and usual policy elixir for non-compliance.

It is the power of the legitimacy of legal norms, the way legal norms work once they are established, and the smart management of cases of alleged non-compliance, which leads

17 See Mark A. Pollack, "Delegation, agency and agenda-setting in the European Community", (1997) 51 *International Organization*, pp. 99–134.

18 L. Henkin, *How Nations Behave*, (New York: Columbia University Press, 2nd ed.,1979), p. 47.

19 For an overview, see R.B. Mitchell: "Compliance Theory: An Overview", in: J. Cameron and J. Werksman and P. Roderick (eds), *Improving Compliance with International Environmental Law*, (London: Earthscan, 1996), pp. 3–28.

20 See Abram Chayes and Antonia Handler Chayes: *The New Sovereignty: Compliance with International Regulatory Agreements*, (Cambridge MA: Harvard Univerity Press, 1995), p. 205.

to compliance. The reasoning of Henkin, and Chayes and Chayes is based upon the insight that a rule which is part of a broader legal system usually has a far stronger compliance-pull than an individuated legal rule, because the former is part of a larger normative design and embodies basic principles which are generally perceived as being legitimate or just. Even in the light of explicitly opposing interests, specific international legal norms have a high probability of being observed because they are perceived by the members of the international community as being part of an encompassing normative superstructure. It is also important to underline that a well-functioning international legal system is both in the interest of weak *and* strong states.[21] For weak states, an international legal order is an important pre-condition for there to be any chance at all for their concerns to be heard and taken seriously. Weak states will only have a chance of succeeding in international negotiations against more powerful states if they have *enforceable* rights. Likewise, powerful states are normally those states which have a prime interest in the stability of an international order. Any such stability, however, depends on rules which are accepted by most, if not all, states. Acceptance for rules presupposes that they are not the product of purely arbitrary decisions, but that they are based upon commonly agreed ethical standards and form part of an overarching normative superstructure (see above). In short, stability requires law. In this sense, it is, indeed, appropriate to argue that legal rules possess a compliance-pull of their own.[22]

It follows that the more a rule is considered to be part of a legal system, or, to put it differently, the more an international organisation is legalised, the more likely compliance with the rule in question becomes. Empirical evidence is highly supportive of the legalisation hypotheses:[23] in fact, the impressive compliance record of the EC is hard to explain without referring to its character as a legal community.[24] The strongest single procedure with regard to compliance enforcement is the preliminary ruling procedure according to Article 234 ECT. It directly connects governments to the control exerted by their citizens, and instrumentalises national courts as agents of supranational law. Article 234 ECT provides that any national legal person may sue his or her government if that government has violated a legal provision of the EU and inflicted damage upon that legal person. Governments are thus not only liable to each other by means of an international legal obligation, but have also adopted responsibilities

21 See Andrew Hurrell: "International Society and the Study of Regimes. A Reflective Approach", in: Volker Rittberger (ed.): *Regime Theory and International Relations*, (Oxford: Clarendon, 1993), pp. 49–72.

22 See Thomas M. Franck: *The Power of Legitimacy Among Nations*, (New York: Oxford University Press, 1990).

23 See the contributions in the special issue on Legalization of International Organisation (54:3), and in: Joerges and Zürn (eds), *Law and Governance in Postnational Europe. Compliance beyond the Nation-State*, (Cambridge, Cambridge University Press, 2005).

24 See Michael Zürn and Jürgen Neyer: "Conclusions. The Conditions of Compliance", in: Michael Zürn and Christian Joerges (eds.), *Law and Governance in Postnational Constellations: Compliance Beyond the Nation State*, (Cambridge: Cambridge University Press, 2005).

towards their citizens.[25] A supranational legal order is thus categorically different from a merely international legal order, because individuals may use their member state's courts against political decisions taken by the government or the parliament of that state. Thus, it is not surprising that the direct linkage between the EC's supranational institutions and its citizens is often interpreted as a major constitutional step towards the establishment of a European political order *sui generis*.

5. Multi-Level Legitimacy: Justice and Democracy

This chapter began with the diagnosis of a categorical mistake often made when reflecting upon the adequate normative foundations of international organisations. International organisations have neither the capacity for state-like governance, nor will they acquire – in the foreseeable future – political competences which cover more than narrowly-defined policies. It is inadequate, therefore, to assess their legitimacy in categories taken from the analysis of democratic statehood, and is more appropriate to consider their contribution(s) to transnational justice. Although this argument seems to put primary emphasis on justice and to downplay democracy, it is ultimately oriented at explaining the relationship between national democracy and transnational justice: the normative promise of national democracy to foster self-governance will only survive globalisation if it is supplemented by an organizational layer that fosters transnational justice. And, *vice versa*, if transnational justice is to have a realistic chance, it must be established on strengthened domestic procedures of strong domestic control mechanisms, which guarantee that the executives remain closely connected to their constituencies and national parliaments. Legitimacy in the new international system can only be adequately conceptualised if it is explained as a normative multi-level structure in which the domestic and the international level are closely interwoven.

Only if interdependent national democracies are supplemented by a transnational layer of justificatory discourses can we expect them systematically to respect the external effects of their decisions as a relevant factor for domestic decision-making. Democracy entails that those who rule and who take the decisions are identical with those who are addressed by those decisions. If that standard is to be respected, i.e., if we are not ready to accept the effects of the decisions of other nation-states without having had the chance to make our concerns heard in "their" decision-making processes, and if we are not willing to make other citizenries subject to our decisions, then we have to work for a system of collective multi-level governance, in which national democracies open up to the concerns of foreigners. Under conditions of interdependence, transnational justice and national democracy mutually support and necessitate each other.

The good news of this article is that supranationalism can deliver some of the functions which we traditionally attach to democratic procedures. Supranationalism promotes the

[25] See Rs. 26/62, *van Gend and Loos* (N.V. Algemene Transport- en Expeditie Onderneming van Gend and Loos gegen Niederländische Finanzverwaltung), Urteil vom 5. Februar 1963; Slg. 1963, 1, 24.

cause of justice by providing an effective remedy to horizontal and vertical power asymmetries, as well as to the problem of non-compliance. Legal integration transforms intergovernmental bargaining into transnational deliberations by providing incentives to governments to re-formulate preferences in the language of legal reasoning. In doing so, legal integration transforms the mode of representation *from* preferences and power *to* arguments and reasons. In addition, legal integration has the capacity to provide mechanisms which safeguard against the impact of vertical power asymmetries on the justificatory discourse. Finally, legal integration exerts a compliance-pull of its own by increasing the costs of non-compliance to both powerful and weak states.

It is true that legal integration has no built-in causal connection to justice. Thus, at the end of the day, even the best procedures only provide incentives. In addition, it must be underlined that they will only be effective if the powerful actors realise that it is, indeed, in their best interest to accept the discipline that is imposed upon them by supranational legal norms. If powerful states prefer to go it alone, supranational organisations have nothing but economic and political incentives to change the courses of action of these states. Real-world supranational integration must be understood as a long-term learning process which may lead to a constitutionalisation of effective justificatory discourses. It is also true, however, that the two real-world close-to-supranational entities that we know, the EC and the WTO, are moving slowly but steadily towards that goal. Both the EC and the WTO embody some significant elements of justificatory discourses and can easily be understood as (imperfect) approximations of this ideal. They are both to be cherished for the degree to which they have walked down the road already, and to be criticised for the long way that is still ahead of them.

Ernst-Ulrich
Petersmann

CHAPTER 3. CAN INTERNATIONAL PUBLIC GOODS BE SUPPLIED WITHOUT MULTILEVEL CONSTITUTIONAL DEMOCRACY AND "CONSTITUTIONAL JUSTICE"?

1. Introduction and Summary: From Realism to Multilevel Democratic Constitutionalism in International Law

International law was developed by states using their power in order to advance the interests of their rulers. Since the emergence of constitutional democracies in the Eighteenth century, elected governments have increasingly recognised that "state interests" must be defined in terms of the constitutional rules and interests of civil society, rather than only in terms of national security and welfare of the rulers. Yet, due to the rational ignorance of most citizens *vis-à-vis* foreign policy and mutually beneficial "international public goods",[1] most areas of international law continue to be shaped by intergovernmental rules that define the pursuit of "state interests", their intergovernmental co-ordination, co-operation among states or hegemonic coercion without effective civil society participation.[2] This power-oriented, state-centred focus of international law is increasingly challenged by citizens for its failures to protect human rights, democratic peace, rule of law and other international public goods more effectively in the ever more important transnational relations beyond the state.

1 On the criteria used by economists for defining pubic goods (i.e., non-rivalry use, non-excludability), and on the "jurisdictional gap", the "participation gap" and "incentive gap" impeding a more effective supply of global public goods, see I. Kaul, I. Grundberg and M. Stern (eds), *Global Public Goods*, (Oxford: Oxford University Press, 1999).

2 See J. Goldsmith and E.A. Posner, *The Limits of International Law*, (Oxford: Oxford University Press, 2005), whose identification of "state interests" with "the preferences of the state's political leadership" (at 6) entails an authoritarian theory of international law which neither explains international legal practice in Europe (for example, the transfer of state powers to the EC) nor the constitutional limits of intergovernmental power politics. As inside constitutional democracies, these constitutional limits of state powers (for example, deriving from the worldwide recognition of inalienable human rights as *jus cogens*) offer constitutional options for the international protection of citizen interests beyond power politics.

Post-Second World War European integration has demonstrated that international law and institutions can protect the interests of citizens against the centuries-old abuses of state powers, and enable governments to protect international public goods such as a common market and democratic peace among 480 million European Union (EU) citizens. All 27 Member States of the EU, all 30 member states of the European Economic Area (EEA), and all 47 member states of the European Convention of Human Rights (ECHR) have accepted that the European Court of Justice (ECJ), the European Free Trade Area (EFTA) Court, and the European Court of Human Rights (ECtHR) review state regulations in terms of human rights, fundamental freedoms and other international rules which protect general citizen interests, such as non-discrimination, the necessity and the proportionality of governmental restrictions. All three courts interpret the ECHR and EC agreements as "constitutional instruments" which protect multilevel, democratic governance for the collective supply of European public goods. State-centred theories cannot explain this successful "constitutionalisation" of European integration. "Realism" requires the reality of "constitutional pluralism" at national and European levels be taken into account in order to explore the policy question of whether multilevel constitutionalism offers lessons also for the collective supply of *global* public goods.

Virtually all 192 United Nations (UN) member states have adopted national constitutions and human rights obligations (for example, under UN law) based upon the insight that, as stated in numerous UN human rights instruments, "recognition of ... inalienable rights of all members of the human family is the foundation of freedom, justice and peace in the world". All UN member states have also accepted one or more international "treaty constitutions" for the collective supply of certain international public goods, such as the constitutions (*sic*) establishing the International Labour Organisation (ILO) for the protection of "social justice" and labour rights, the World Health Organisation (WHO) for the protection of "the highest attainable standard of health" as "one of the fundamental rights of every human being" (WHO Constitution), the Food and Agriculture Organisation (FAO) for "ensuring humanity's freedom from hunger" (FAO Constitution), and the UN Education and Scientific Co-operation Organisation for contributing "to peace and security by promoting collaboration among the nations through education, science and culture in order to further universal respect for justice, for the rule of law and for the human rights and fundamental freedoms [...] affirmed [...] by the Charter of the United Nations" (Article I United Nations Educational, Scientific and Cultural Organisation (UNESCO) Constitution). Clearly, such limited international treaty constitutions differ fundamentally from national constitutions. Why is it that – within Europe – the inter-relationships between national constitutions and international treaty constitutions are increasingly analysed in constitutional terms, whereas – outside Europe – most economists, lawyers, political scientists and governments deny the very existence of multilevel constitutionalism?

This apparent paradox can be explained by the political reality of state-centred, intergovernmental power politics in worldwide institutions, which differs fundamentally from the citizen-oriented transformations of European common market law, competition law and human rights law. Hence, the normative question – whether constitutional approaches to international law are legally and politically necessary for the collective supply of international public goods outside Europe – is considered naïve by most academics and governments. Worldwide organisations and international courts (such as the International Court of Justice, the WTO dispute settlement bodies, investor-state arbitration tribunals) also avoid constitutional discourse in their interpretation and application of worldwide agreements (such as the UN Charter, the agreements establishing the International Monetary Fund, the World Bank Group, the WTO, and multilateral environmental agreements). Yet, is such implicit acceptance of governance failures (such as the obvious disregard for the effective protection of human rights, the reduction of poverty and parliamentary democracy in intergovernmental UN negotiations, and the neglect for general consumer welfare in intergovernmental WTO negotiations) realistic and democratic? If, after centuries of intergovernmental power politics in Europe, diverse forms of "constitutionalising" European law have proven possible (such as supranational EC law, intergovernmental EEA law, and subsidiary multilevel ECHR constitutionalism): Is it not time to examine which European experiences offer lessons for reducing the ubiquitous governance failures in the worldwide supply of international public goods? The main argument of this chapter is that the European experience – that collective supply of international public goods requires multilevel constitutional democracy and multilevel judicial protection of the rule of international law – holds true also for the collective supply of many international public goods outside Europe, notably in citizen-driven areas of international co-operation such as the worldwide division of labour.

The reality of multilevel constitutional democracy in Europe is not inconsistent with the realist claim that international law and international organisations are products of the rational self-interests of states (rather than constituting exogenous legal constraints which curtail state interests). Citizens and their democratically-elected governments have rational self-interests in promoting constitutional democracy also in multilevel governance for the collective supply of international public goods so as to limit the state-centred biases of national democracies (for example, the focus of national politicians on protecting *national* interests) in favour of the collective protection of *cosmopolitan* interests. In a globally interdependent world, multilevel constitutional democracy is as necessary for the collective supply of *international public goods* as constitutional democracy is indispensable for promoting *national public goods*. Giovanni Sartori, in his classic *The Theory of Democracy Revisited*, criticised the term "democracy" as a misleading and pompous "name for something that does not exist";[3] the existing national and international rules and institutions which promote democratic rights, democratic procedures, parliamentary, participatory and deliberative democracy fall short of the normative ideals of "governance by discussion" and "government of the people, by the people, and for the people". Yet, even if most citizens remain "rationally ignorant" of most governance problems, and "élitist democracy" has been described as

3 G. Sartori, *The Theory of Democracy Revisited: Part One*, (Chatham: Chatham House Publishers, 1987), p. 7.

the worst system of governance with the exception of all the others: the historical failures of all non-democratic governance alternatives make democracy an inconvertible, normative ideal. European law has proven that diverse forms of "transnational constitutional democracy" are politically practical, and that the four normative premises of democratic and economic constitutionalism are not limited to relations inside state borders:

First, the value premise of normative individualism (i.e., that governments can derive value only from the free and informed consent of the governed individuals) applies also to *transnational* governance and requires *international* markets no less than national markets (including both consumer-driven economic markets as well as citizen-driven political markets) as decentralized information mechanisms, without which citizens and their governments can neither know nor efficiently satisfy individual preferences.

Second, the diversity of individual preferences, the scarcity of resources and the inevitable ubiquity of conflicts – both *within* individuals (for example, between their rational egoism and social reasonableness) as well as *among* individuals (for example, in their rational pursuit of self-interests) – require constitutional and judicial restraints of the Hobbesian war of each against all in *transnational* relations just as much as *within* states. As respect for normative individualism makes consensus among citizens on the outcomes of economic and political competition impossible, human reasonableness requires the constitutional protection of a limited "overlapping consensus" on constitutional rules of justice (as reflected, for example, in the universal recognition of inalienable human rights and of national constitutions).

Third, as explained by constitutional economics,[4] worldwide division of labour based on consumer-driven market competition (as the most efficient information, allocation and co-ordination mechanism for increasing individual and social productivity and consumer welfare) depends on constitutional guarantees of the "constitutive principles" of market economies (such as freedom of contract, private property, monetary stability, freedom of profession, rule of law, legal accountability), as well as of "regulative principles" of market economies (such as competition, environmental and social rules), which empower citizens to engage in mutually beneficial market exchanges subject to rules and governmental limitations of "market failures". The lack of an international "economic constitution"[5] beyond Europe

4 See E.-U. Petersmann, Constitutionalism and the Regulation of International Markets, EUI Working Paper Law 2007/23.

5 In almost all countries, national constitutions protect a national market economy. For example, the US Constitution protects a common market, private liberty and property rights. The EC's treaty constitution protects a common market based upon constitutional market freedoms, competition law and regulatory policies. The term "economic constitution" does not necessarily refer to formal constitutional law. The basic idea is the psychological insight that rational individuals should commit themselves to legal rules of a higher rank that empower individuals *vis-à-vis* abuses of private and public power. In common law countries such as England, the common law guarantees of freedom of profession, freedom of contract and judicial protection of rule of law empower citizens to engage in effective market competition and division of labour (as described already by Adam Smith). Competition law and monetary law are examples of constitutional market rules in EC law, but are

and North America is a major reason for the unnecessary poverty and exploitation, by abuses of private – as well as public – power, of more than one billion people living without adequate access to essential goods.

Fourth, in view of the ubiquity of abuses of private and public power, "enabling constitutions" must be complemented by "limiting constitutions" which constrain the abuses of power by governmental and private actors. Just as democratic governance for the collective supply of *national* and *European* public goods has proven sustainable only in mutually-agreed frameworks of multilevel constitutional restraints, so can non-discriminatory competition in *international* markets remain effective only to the extent that market actors and market regulators are constitutionally restrained from abusing their powers. *Transnational* constitutionalism – not only in Europe but also outside – is necessary for reforming "constitutional failures" (such as harmful externalities of national interest group politics on states and citizens abroad) and for enabling governments to collectively supply *international* public goods.

The thesis of this chapter – to wit, that international public goods (such as an efficient worldwide division of labour) cannot be effectively supplied by intergovernmental power politics without multilevel constitutionalism – risks being criticised as *anti*-democratic, similar to the populist criticism of the US Constitution and of constitutional adjudication as anti-democratic limitations of majority politics.[6] Constitutional reforms of international law must be prepared by challenging the prevailing paradigms of realist power politics and "international law among states". According to J. Rawls, "in a constitutional regime with judicial review, public reason is the reason of its supreme court"; it is of constitutional importance for the "overlapping, constitutional consensus" necessary for a stable and just society among free, equal and rational citizens who tend to be deeply divided by conflicting moral, religious and philosophical doctrines.[7] In Europe, the judicial transformation of intergovernmental treaties into citizen-oriented constitutional guarantees was accepted by citizens, national courts, parliaments and governments because the judicial "European public reason" protected individual rights and European public goods more effectively. The "Solange method" of multilevel judicial co-operation "as long as" constitutional rights are adequately protected, reflects an "overlapping constitutional consensus" on the need for "constitutional justice" in European law. The power-oriented rationality of governments interested in limiting

based only upon legislation in most countries. The North American Free Trade Agreement (NAFTA) offers intergovernmental guarantees of market freedoms, property rights and rule of law that are far less supra-national than EC law.

6 On the endless American discussions of "counter-majoritarian difficulties" of constitutionalism, see G.S. Wood, *The Creation of the American Republic 1776–1787*, (Chapel Hill: University of North Carolina Press, 1969).

7 J. Rawls, *Political Liberalism*, (New York: Columbia University Press, 1993), p. 231 *et seq*. Rawls explains the Kantian distinction between the reasonable (which aims at just terms of social co-operation by basing individual actions upon universalisable principles) and the rational egoism of individuals (pursuing their individual ends without moral sensibility for the consequences of their actions on the well-being of others), p. 48 *et seq*.

their judicial accountability is increasingly challenged also in worldwide dispute settlement practices. Judicial interpretation of intergovernmental rules as protecting also individual rights may be justifiable notably in citizen-driven areas of international economic law, in which individual rights (for example, of access to courts) can enhance the mutual benefits of co-operation among citizens and self-interested, individual enforcement of rule of law. Multilevel economic, environmental and human rights governance can become more reasonable, more efficient and more lawful if national and international courts co-operate in protecting the rule of international law for the benefit of citizens (as "democratic principals" of governments) affected by arbitrary governmental violations of international legal obligations.

In his *Theory of Justice*,[8] Rawls used the idea of reasonableness for designing fair procedures that prompt reasonable citizens (as autonomous moral agents) to agree upon basic equal freedoms and other principles of justice. In his later book, on *Political Liberalism*, Rawls re-framed his theory of justice as fairness by emphasising the importance of the public use of reason for maintaining a stable, liberal society confronted with the problem of reasonable disagreement about individual conceptions for a good life and a just society. "Deliberative democracy" and cosmopolitan reasonableness require legal guarantees of basic equal rights (for example, freedoms to participate as equals in public discourse) and a democratic constitution (for example, the independent judicial protection of basic rights) as legal and institutional preconditions for public debate defining the conditions for a stable consensus on the principles of justice.[9] This contribution explains why the universal recognition of human rights and the increasing number of international courts for settling disputes "in conformity with principles of justice" and human rights (as required by the customary methods of treaty interpretation as codified in the Vienna Convention on the Law of Treaties (VCLT)) entail that judicial and democratic reasoning increasingly challenge both the power-oriented "intergovernmental reasoning" and the state-centred *opinio juris sive necessitatis* which dominate the Westphalian system of "international law among states" (Sections 2–4). In Europe, three different ways of judicial transformation of intergovernmental treaties into objective constitutional orders – i.e., the judicial "constitutionalisation" of the intergovernmental EC Treaty and of the ECHR, and, to a lesser extent, also of the EEA Agreement – succeeded because their multilevel judicial protection of constitutional citizen rights *vis-à-vis* transnational abuses of governance powers was accepted by citizens, national courts and parliaments as legitimate (Section 5). Sections 6 and 7 argue that the European "Solange method" of judicial co-operation "as long as" other courts respect the constitutional principles of justice should be supported by citizens, judges, civil society and their democratic representatives also in judicial co-operation with worldwide courts and dispute settlement bodies. Section 8 concludes that "public reasonableness" and democracy require an "overlapping consensus" on rule of law not

8 J. Rawls, *A Theory of Justice*, (Cambridge MA: Harvard University Press, 1973).

9 On these dual functions of reasonableness in Rawls' theory of justice, see J. Habermas, "Reconciliation through the Public Use of Reason: Remarks on John Rawls' Political Liberalism", in: (1995) 92 *The Journal of Philosophy*.

only within constitutional democracies, but also in the international division of labour and mutually beneficial co-operation among citizens across national frontiers. Just as "public reason" among the 480 million EU citizens has constitutionally restrained the reasoning of their 27 national governments, worldwide economic integration law (for example, in the WTO) also requires "cosmopolitan public reasoning" as a democratic foundation of the inter-state structures of international law. In a world dominated by power politics and by reasonable "constitutional pluralism", international judges may find it easier to meet their obligation to settle disputes "in conformity with principles of justice" if courts co-operate and base their "judicial discourses" on "constitutional justice", notably the judicial protection of human rights and "fundamental freedoms for all" (Preamble VCLT).

2. Cosmopolitan Reasonableness as a Requirement of UN Human Rights Law and European Law

UN human rights law proceeds from the constitutional premise that – as emphasised in the Preambles to the 1966 UN Covenants on civil, political, economic, social and cultural rights – human rights "derive from the inherent dignity of the human person" and are based upon the "recognition of the inherent dignity and of the equal and inalienable rights of all members of the human family (as) the foundation of freedom, justice and peace in the world". The Preambles make it clear that human rights precede "the obligation of states under the Charter of the United Nations to promote universal respect for, and observance of, human rights and freedoms", a general obligation universally recognised in UN human rights covenants. The Universal Declaration on Human Rights (UDHR) had already recognised that "human rights should be protected by the rule of law" (Preamble); yet, they exist today as the inherent birthright of every human being. The universal recognition by all states – in hundreds of UN, regional and national human rights instruments and national constitutions – of inalienable human rights has objectively changed the legal status of individuals as legal subjects of international law: inalienable human rights now exist *erga omnes* and require respect, legal protection and fulfilment of inalienable human rights by all governments. Due to their progressive transformation into international *ius cogens*, the fragmented, treaty-based UN human rights guarantees gradually evolve into a UN human rights constitution, which also limits the powers of international organisations.[10] As in European human rights law, international human rights serve only as a "second line of constitutional entrenchment" which respect the right of self-determination of peoples as the constitutional foundation of modern international law based upon an inalienable core of human rights.

10 See E.-U. Petersmann, "Human Rights, Markets and Economic Welfare: Constitutional Functions of the Emerging UN Human Rights Constitution", in: F.M. Abbott, C. Breining-Kaufmann and T. Cottier (eds), *International Trade and Human Rights*, (Ann Arbor: Michigan University Press, 2006), pp. 29–67.

All six major UN human rights covenants acknowledge in their Preambles the close inter-relationship between "the inherent dignity and … the equal and inalienable rights of all members of the human family". The universal recognition of human dignity as the constitutive principle for human rights suggests that a common understanding cannot be found by interpreting human dignity in the light of theological concepts of "person" (for example, the creation of man in God's image). The explicit link made in Article 1 of the UDHR between "All human beings are born free and equal in dignity and rights" (first sentence), and "They are endowed with reason and conscience and should act towards one another in a spirit of brotherhood" (second sentence), confirms that "reason and conscience" must be regarded as the defining elements of humanity and dignity.[11] The appeal to moral conduct "in a spirit of brotherhood" further indicates that "reason and conscience" are referred to not only as anthropological facts, but as sources for moral reasoning which enable mankind to secure universal equal rights as the legal "foundation of freedom, justice and peace in the world" (Preamble UDHR) and of enjoyment by everybody of "an existence worthy of human dignity" (Article 23 UDHR).

Human dignity is also recognised as constitutive principle in Article 1 of the EU Charter of Fundamental Rights proclaimed by the European Parliament, the EU Commission and the EU Council in December 2000,[12] and incorporated into the 2004 Treaty establishing a Constitution for Europe, as well as into the 2007 Treaty of Lisbon. Some national constitutional systems (for example, in Germany, India, Israel and South Africa) and regional constitutional systems (such as EC law, as protected by the EC courts, and the ECHR, as protected by the European Court of Human Rights) explicitly recognise human dignity as a constitutional value underlying human rights (for example, the ECHR), or as a human right (for example, as protected in EC law by the EC Court of Justice). Yet, political and legal conceptions of human rights continue to differ dependent on how human dignity is conceptualised. For instance, while the EC Court and the EU Charter of Fundamental Rights protect "market freedoms" guaranteed in the EC Treaty as conferring "fundamental rights" to individuals, Anglo-Saxon human rights lawyers from common law countries without constitutional guarantees of comprehensive liberty rights often disregard constitutional traditions of protecting liberty rights in the economy; some claim that market freedoms are not directly rooted in human dignity and that they are fundamentally different from the

11 See K. Dicke, "The Founding Function of Human Dignity in the Universal Declaration of Human Rights", in: D. Kretzmer and E. Klein (eds), *The Concept of Human Dignity in Human Rights Discourse*, (Oxford: Oxford University Press, 2002), pp. 111 and 117.

12 The text of this Charter is published in the Official Journal of the EC, C 364/1–22 of 18 December 2000. On the controversy over whether Article 1 recognises a fundamental right to human dignity or merely an objective constitutional principle, see the commentary on Article 1 of the Charter by Borowsky in: J. Meyer (ed), *Kommentar zur Charta der Grundrechte der EU*, (Baden-Baden: Nomos Verlag, 2002), pp. 45 *et seq.*

human rights and the "fundamental freedoms" protected by UN human rights law.[13] Regardless of whether human dignity is recognised as the most fundamental human right from which all other rights flow (as, for example, in German and Israeli constitutional law), or whether human dignity is viewed only as a constitutional principle, both legal traditions recognise respect for the moral and rational autonomy of individuals as the normative source of inalienable human rights which require democratic self-government based upon "public reasoning" (as protected by freedom of opinion, freedom of the press, freedom of religion, rights to democratic governance, *etc.*) and entail obligations by governments to respect, protect and promote human rights "in a spirit of brotherhood" (Article 1 UDHR) and in the context of "an effective political democracy" (Preamble ECHR).

3. Citizen-oriented Reasonableness as a Requirement of Constitutional Justice in International Law

A second source of public reason as a constitutional principle of international law derives from the customary law requirement of protecting "constitutional justice" as a general principle of international law. Denial of justice is one of the oldest principles of state responsibility in international law. Under the customary international law rules for the protection of aliens, the international minimum standard with regard to the duties of states to provide justice to foreigners focused on procedural due process of law and the duty of states "to create and maintain a system of justice which ensures that unfairness to foreigners either does not happen, or is corrected";[14] state responsibility for denial of justice depended on proof of a systemic failure in the national administration of justice, either by a miscarriage of justice by the judiciary, or by non-judicial authorities (for example, if they prevented the judiciary from administering justice in a fair manner). The universal recognition – in regional and worldwide human rights conventions, as well as in national laws – of human rights of access "to a fair and public hearing within a reasonable time by an independent and impartial tribunal established by law" for the "determination of civil rights and obligations or of any criminal charge" has re-inforced the intergovernmental prohibition of a denial of justice by individual rights of access to justice.[15] The progressive extension – by an ever larger number of other international

13 On this controversy, see, for example, E.-U. Petersmann, "Taking Human Dignity, Poverty and Empowerment of Individuals More Seriously: Rejoinder to Alston", in: (2002) 13 *European Journal of International Law (EJIL)*, pp. 845–851; *idem*, Human Rights and "International Trade Law: Defining and Connecting the two Fields", in: T. Cottier *et al.* (eds), *Human Rights and International Trade*, (Oxford: Oxford University Press, 2005), pp. 29–94.

14 See J. Paulsson, *Denial of Justice in International Law*, (Oxford: Oxford University Press, 2006), pp. 7 and 36.

15 See Article 6 European Convention on Human Rights and similar guarantees in other regional human rights conventions (for example, Article 8 American Convention on Human Rights), UN human rights conventions (for example, Article 14 International Covenant on Civil and Political Rights) and other UN human rights instruments (for example, Article 10 Universal Declaration of Human Rights), which have given rise to a comprehensive case law clarifying the rights of access to courts and related guarantees of due process of law (for example, justice delayed may be justice denied, see D. Shelton,

treaties, notably in the field of international economic and environmental law – of individual rights of access to courts and to effective legal remedies increasingly confronts judges with a "constitutional dilemma":

- On the one hand, foreigners and their home states increasingly invoke specific treaty obligations (for example, relating to human rights of access to justice, labour rights, intellectual property rights, investor rights, trading rights, fishing rights and other freedoms of the sea, *etc.*) rather than general international law rules on denial of justice in cases of unfair treatment of foreigners.
- On the other hand, most intergovernmental treaties on the protection of human rights and other individual rights do not offer effective legal and judicial remedies to the individual;[16] hence, national and international judges are increasingly confronted with legal claims that intergovernmental treaty rules on the protection of individual rights (for example, in UN human rights conventions, World Intellectual Property Organisation (WIPO) conventions on intellectual property rights, ILO conventions on labour and social rights, WTO rules and regional trade agreements on individual freedoms of trade, investment treaties protecting investor rights) should be legally protected by judges as constituting *individual rights* and legal remedies.

The UN Charter (Article 1) and the VCLT recall the general obligation under international law "that disputes concerning treaties, like other international disputes, should be settled by peaceful means and in conformity with the principles of justice and international law", including "universal respect for, and observance of, human rights and fundamental freedoms for all" (VCLT, Preamble). The functional inter-relationships between law, judges and justice are reflected in legal language from antiquity (for example, in the common core of the Latin terms *jus, judex, justitia*) up to modern times (see the Anglo-American legal traditions of speaking of courts of justice, and giving judges the title of *Mr. Justice*, *Lord Justice*, or *Chief Justice*). Like the Roman god *Janus*, justice and judges face two different perspectives: their "conservative function" is to apply the existing law and protect the existing system of rights so as "to render to each person what is his [right]". Yet, laws tend to be incomplete and are subject to change. Impartial justice may require "reformative interpretations" of legal rules in response to changing social conceptions of justice. This is particularly true following the universal recognition – by all 192 UN member states – of inalienable human rights, which call for citizen-oriented interpretations of the power-oriented structures of international law.

Remedies in International Human Rights Law, (2nd ed.)(Oxford: Oxford University Press, 2005), p. 113 *et seq.*; F. Francioni (ed), *Access to Justice as a Human Right*, (Oxford: Oxford University Press, 2007).

16 See J. Dugard, First Report on Diplomatic Protection (International Law Commission UN Doc. A/CN.4/506, 2000), para. 25: "To suggest that universal human rights conventions, particularly the International Covenant on Civil and Political Rights, provide individuals with effective remedies for the protection of their human rights is to engage in a fantasy which, unlike fiction, has no place in legal reasoning. The sad truth is that only a handful of individuals, in the limited number of States that accept the right to individual petition to the monitoring bodies of these conventions, have obtained or will obtain satisfactory remedies from these conventions." On the dual meaning of remedies (for example, in terms of access to justice and substantive redress), see D. Shelton note 15 *supra*, p. 7 *et seq.*

Former UN Secretary-General Kofi Annan, in his final address as UN Secretary-General to world leaders assembled in the UN General Assembly on 19 September 2006, criticized the power-oriented UN system as "unjust, discriminatory and irresponsible" in view of its failures to respond effectively to the three global challenges to the United Nations: "to ensure that globalisation would benefit the entire human race; to heal the disorder of the post-Cold War world, replacing it with a genuinely new world order of peace and freedom; and to protect the rights and dignity of individuals, particularly women, which were so widely trampled underfoot." According to Kofi Annan, these three challenges – "an unjust world economy, world disorder and widespread contempt for human rights and the rule of law" – entail divisions that "threaten the very notion of an international community, upon which the UN stands".[17] Under what conditions may national and international judges respond to this "constitutional dilemma" by interpreting "principles of justice and international law" from citizen-oriented, human rights perspectives, as opposed to the state-centred perspectives of governments, whose representatives all too often pursue self-interests in limiting their personal accountability by treating citizens as mere objects of international law and of discretionary foreign policies?

4. International Courts as Guardians of Public Reason in Modern International Law

The functions of judges are defined not only in the legal instruments establishing courts. Since legal antiquity, judges also invoke inherent powers deriving from the constitutional context of the respective legal systems (such as constitutional safeguards of the independence of courts in the *Magna Carta* and in the US Constitution), often in response to claims to impartial, judicial protection of "justice". Article III, sect. 2 of the US Constitution provides, for example, that the "judicial Power shall extend to all Cases, in Law and Equity, arising under this Constitution, the Laws of the United States, and Treaties made... under their Authority" (*etc*). Based upon this Anglo-Saxon distinction between statute law and equity, which limits the permissible content of governmental regulations, courts and judge-made law have assumed a crucial role in the development of "equity law" and "constitutional justice" in many countries.[18] In international law, too, international courts invoke inherent powers to protect procedural fairness and the principles of reciprocal, corrective and distributive justice, for example, by using principles of equity for the de-limitation of conflicting claims to maritime waters and to the underlying seabed.[19] Since the democratic constitutions of the 18th century, almost all UN member states have adopted national constitutions and international agreements that have progressively expanded the power of judges in most states as well as in

17 The speech of Kofi Annan is reproduced in UN document GA/105000 of 19 September 2006.

18 See T.R.S. Allan, *Constitutional Justice. A Liberal Theory of the Rule of Law*, (Oxford: Oxford University Press, 2001).

19 See the examples given by T. Franck, *Fairness in International Law and Institutions*, (Oxford: Oxford University Press, 1997), Chapters 3 and 10.

international relations.[20] The constitutional separation of powers provides for ever more comprehensive legal safeguards of the impartiality, integrity, institutional and personal independence of judges.[21]

Alexander Hamilton, in the "*Federalist Papers*", described the judiciary as "the least dangerous branch of government" in view of the fact that courts dispose neither of "the power of the sword" nor of "the power of the purse".[22] In modern, multilevel governance systems based upon hundreds of functionally-limited, intergovernmental treaty regimes, courts remain the most impartial and independent "*forum* of principle" and "exemplar of public reason".[23] For example, fair and public judicial procedures and "*amicus curiae* briefs" may not only enable all the parties involved to present and challenge all the relevant arguments, they may also require more comprehensive and principled justification of judicial decisions, in comparison with political and administrative decisions. As all laws and all international treaties use vague terms and incomplete rules, the judicial function goes inevitably beyond being merely "la bouche qui prononce les mots de la loi" (Montesquieu). By choosing from among the alternative interpretations of rules, "filling gaps" in the name of justice, and by protecting the general principles underlying the hundreds of specialised treaty regimes, judicial decisions interpret, progressively develop, and complement legislative rules and intergovernmental treaties in order to settle disputes "in conformity with principles of justice". The multilevel judicial protection of constitutional citizen rights in Europe (see Section 5 *infra*) illustrates that the independence and impartiality of national and international judges makes them the most effective guardians of the "constitutional essentials" and "overlapping consensus" (J. Rawls) underlying national and international human rights law as the constitutional foundation of democratic self-government. Both positivist-legal theories and moral-prescriptive theories of adjudication justify such judicial clarification and progressive development of indeterminate legal rules (for example, general human rights guarantees) on the grounds that independent courts are the most principled guardians of constitutional rights and of "deliberative, constitutionally limited democracy", of which the public reasoning of courts is an important part.[24] For example, the judicial protection of equal treatment for children of different colour by the US Supreme Court in the celebrated case of *Brown* v. *Board of Education* in 1954 – notwithstanding earlier denials by the law-maker and by other courts of such a judicial reading of the US Constitution's safeguards of "equal protection of the laws" (Fourteenth Amendment) – was democratically supported by the other branches of government and is today celebrated by civil society as a crucial contribution

20 See C. Guarnieri and P. Pederzoli, *The Power of Judges*, (Oxford: Oxford University Press, 2002).

21 See A. Sajo (ed), *Judicial Integrity*, (Leiden: Nijhoff Publishers, 2004).

22 A. Hamilton, The Judiciary Department, The Federalist Papers No. 78, in: A. Hamilton, J. Madison and J. Jay, *The Federalist Papers*, (New York: Bantam Publishers, 1789/1989).

23 On supreme courts as "exemplar of public reason", see J. Rawls note 7 *supra*, p. 231 *et seq.*

24 For a justification of judicial review as being essential for protecting and promoting deliberative democracy, see C.F. Zurn, *Deliberative Democracy and the Institutions of Judicial Review*, (Cambridge: Cambridge University Press, 2007).

to protecting the goals of the US Constitutions (including its Preamble objective "to establish justice and secure the blessings of liberty") and human rights more effectively.

In its Advisory Opinion on Namibia, the International Court of Justice (ICJ) emphasised that – also in international law – legal institutions ought not to be viewed statically and must interpret international law in the light of the legal principles prevailing at the moment that legal issues arise concerning them:

> An international instrument has to be interpreted and applied within the framework of the entire legal system prevailing at the time of the interpretation.[25]

International human rights courts, such as the European Court of Human Rights (ECtHR), just as economic courts, such as the EC Court, have often emphasised that effective protection of human rights and of non-discriminatory conditions of competition may require "dynamic interpretations" of international rules with due regard to changed circumstances (such as new risks to human health, competition and the environment). As in domestic legal systems, intergovernmental and judicial rule-making are inter-related also in international relations: as all international treaties remain incomplete and build upon general principles of law, the judicial interpretation, clarification and application of international law rules, like judicial decisions on particular disputes, inevitably influence the dynamic evolution and clarification of the *opinio juris* voiced by governments, judges, parliaments, citizens and non-governmental organisations (NGOs) with regard to the progressive development of international rules. The universal recognition, by all 192 UN member states, of "inalienable" human rights deriving from respect for human dignity, and the ever more specific legal obligations to protect human rights entail that citizens (as the "democratic owners" of international law and institutions) and judges (as the most independent and impartial guardians of "principles of justice" underlying international law) can assert no less democratic legitimacy for defining and protecting human rights than governments that often dislike empowering citizens in international relations in order to limit the legal and judicial accountability of governments. From the perspective of citizens and "deliberative democracies", active judicial protection of constitutional citizen rights (including human rights) is essential for "constitutionalising", "democraticising" and transforming international law into a constitutional order, as is emerging for the more than 800 million European citizens who benefit from the human rights and fundamental freedoms protected by the ECtHR, and especially for the 480 million EU citizens who have been granted – by EU law and by European courts – constitutional freedoms and social rights across the EU that national governments had never protected before. The inalienable *jus cogens* and *erga omnes* core of human rights, and the judicial obligation to settle disputes "in conformity with principles of justice and international law", are of constitutional importance for protecting "constitutional justice" in international law in the 21st century.

25 ICJ Reports, 1971, p. 31, para. 53.

5. Constitutional Pluralism: Three Different Kinds of Multilevel Judicial Protection of Citizen Rights in Europe

An ever larger number of empirical political science analyses of the global rise of judicial power, and of "judicial activism" by supreme courts and international courts in Europe, confirm the political impact of judicial interpretations on the development of national and European law and policies.[26] This section argues that the multilevel judicial protection of European law – for instance, by the EC courts, the European Free Trade Area (EFTA) Court, the ECtHR and national courts – was a pre-condition for the multilevel, democratic supply of European "public goods", and was supported as reasonable and "just" by judges, citizens and parliaments because it enlarged the constitutional rights of EU citizens. Sections 6 and 7 explain why the European "Solange method" of judicial co-operation – "as long as" other courts respect constitutional principles of justice – deserves support by citizens, judges, civil society and their democratic representatives as the most reasonable basis for judicial co-operation, judicial dialogues and "judicial competition" also in international relations beyond Europe. Section 8 concludes that – in a world dominated by power politics and by reasonable "constitutional pluralism" – it is easier for international judges to meet their obligation to settle disputes "in conformity with principles of justice" if courts co-operate in the protection of rule of law and base their "judicial discourses" upon "public reason" and the judicial protection of the constitutional principles underlying human rights law.

Judicial protection of human rights derived from respect for human dignity as the "foundation of freedom, justice and peace", and the multilevel judicial protection of equal liberty rights in the European economy as in the polity, were the driving forces in the progressive transformation of the intergovernmental EC treaties and the ECHR into constitutional instruments which protect citizen rights and community interests (such as the EC's common market and multilevel democracy) across national frontiers

26 A. Stone Sweet, *Governing with Judges. Constitutional Politics in Europe*, (Oxford: Oxford University Press, 2000) describes how much third-party dispute resolution and judicial rule-making have become privileged mechanisms of adapting national and intergovernmental rule-systems to the needs of citizens and their constitutional rights. In his book on *The Judicial Construction of Europe*, (Oxford: Oxford University Press, 2004), Stone Sweet, analyses the judicial "constructing of a supra-national constitution" (Chapter II) as a self-reinforcing system driven by self-interested private market actors, litigators, judges, European parliamentarians and academic communities. The former EC Court judge P. Pescatore confirmed that – when deciding the case *van Gend and Loos* – the judges had a certain idea of Europe, and that these judicial ideas – "and not arguments based on legal technicalities of the matter" – had been decisive (P. Pescatore, "The Doctrine of Direct Effect", in: (1983) 8 *European Law Review*, p. 157). On the criticism of such "judicial law-making", see T. Mähner, *Der Europäische Gerichtshof als Gericht*, (Berlin: Duncker and Humblot, 2005), who criticises the inadequate democratic legitimacy of the ECJ's expansive case-law limiting national sovereignty in unforeseen ways (for example, by judicial recognition of fundamental rights as general principles of Community law). From the point of view of "deliberative democracy", however, the ECJ's case-law has been approved by EC Member States, parliaments and citizens.

by three different kinds of "multilevel judicial governance" and of "multilevel constitutionalism":

- The multilevel judicial governance in the EU among national courts and European courts remains characterised by the supranational structures of EU law and the fact that the fundamental freedoms of EU law and related social guarantees go far beyond the national laws of EU Member States (*infra* 1).
- The multilevel judicial governance of national courts and the ECtHR in the field of human rights differs fundamentally from the multilevel judicial governance in European economic law: Both the ECtHR and the ECHR assert only subsidiary constitutional functions *vis-à-vis* national human rights guarantees and respect the diverse democratic traditions in the 47 countries that have ratified the ECHR (*infra* 2).
- The multilevel judicial governance among national courts and the EFTA Court has extended the EC's common market law to the three EFTA members (Iceland, Liechtenstein and Norway) of the European Economic Area (EEA) through intergovernmental modes of co-operation, rather than by using the EC's constitutional principles of legal primacy, direct effect and the direct applicability of the EC's common market law. This different kind of multilevel judicial co-operation (for example, based upon voluntary compliance with legally non-binding preliminary opinions by the EFTA Court) confirms the legitimacy of constitutional pluralism: citizens in third countries can effectively benefit from the legal "market freedoms" and social benefits of European integration law without full membership in the EC (*infra* 3).

5.1. *Multilevel Judicial Protection of EC Law has extended the Constitutional Rights of EC Citizens*

A citizen-driven common market with free movement of goods, services, persons, capital and payments inside the EU can work effectively only to the extent that the common European market and competition rules are applied and protected in coherent ways in national courts in all 27 EU Member States. As the declared objective of an "ever-closer union between the peoples of Europe" (Preamble to the EU Treaty) was to be brought about by economic and legal integration requiring additional law-making, administrative decisions and common policies by the European institutions, the EU Treaty differs from other international treaties by its innovative judicial safeguards for the protection of rule of law - not only in intergovernmental relations among EU Member States, but also in the citizen-driven common market as well as in the common policies of the European Communities. Whereas most international jurisdictions (like the ICJ, the Permanent Court of Arbitration, the Law of the Sea Tribunal, and WTO dispute settlement bodies) remain characterised by intergovernmental procedures, the EC Treaty provided unique legal remedies not only for the Member States, but also for EC citizens and EC institutions as the guardians of EC law and of its "constitutional functions" for correcting "governance failures" at national and European levels:

- The citizen-driven co-operation among national courts and the ECJ in the context of preliminary rulings procedures (Article 234 EC) has uniquely empowered national and European judges to co-operate, at the request of EU citizens, in the multilevel judicial protection of citizen rights protected by EC law.

- The empowerment of the European Commission to initiate infringement proceedings (Article 226 EC) rendered the ECJ's function as an intergovernmental court much more effective than would have been possible under purely inter-state infringement proceedings (Article 227 EC).
- The Court's "constitutional functions" (for example, in cases of actions by Member States or EC institutions for the annulment of EC regulations), as well as its functions as an "administrative court" (for example, protecting private rights and rule of law in response to direct actions by natural or legal persons for the annulment of EC acts, failure to act, or actions for damages), offered unique legal remedies for maintaining and developing the constitutional coherence of EC law.
- The EC Court's teleological reasoning based upon communitarian needs (for example, in terms of the protection of EU citizen rights, consumer welfare, and of undistorted competition in the common market) justified constitutional interpretations of "fundamental freedoms" of EU citizens that would hardly have been acceptable in purely intergovernmental treaty regimes.

The diverse forms of judicial dialogues (for example, on the interpretation and protection of fundamental rights), judicial contestation (for example, of the scope of EC competences) and judicial co-operation (for example, in preliminary ruling procedures) emphasised the need to respect the common constitutional principles derived from the EC Member States' obligations under their national constitutions, under the ECHR (as interpreted by the ECtHR), as well as under the constitution law of the EC. This judicial respect for "constitutional pluralism" promoted judicial comity among national courts, the ECJ and the ECtHR in their complementary, multilevel protection of constitutional rights, with due respect for the diversity of national constitutional and judicial traditions. Arguably, it was this multilevel judicial protection of the common constitutional principles underlying European law and national constitutions which enabled the EC Court, and also the ECtHR, progressively to transcend the intergovernmental structures of European law by focusing on the judicial protection of individual rights in constitutional democracies and in common markets, rather than on alleged state interests in intergovernmental relations.

5.2. Multilevel Judicial Enforcement of the ECHR: the Subsidiary "Constitutional Functions" of the ECtHR

The European Convention on Human Rights (ECHR), like most other international human rights conventions, sets out minimum standards for the treatment of individuals that respect the diversity of the democratic constitutional traditions of defining individual rights in democratic communities. The 14 Protocols to the ECHR and the European Social Charter (as revised in 1998) also reflect the constitutional experiences, in some European countries (such as France and Germany), of protecting economic and social rights as integral parts of their constitutional and economic laws. For example, in order to avoid a repetition of the systemic political abuse of economic regulation prior to

1945,[27] the ECHR also includes guarantees of property rights and the rights of companies. The jurisdiction of the ECtHR for the collective enforcement of the ECHR – based upon complaints not only by Member States but also by private persons – prompted the Court to interpret the ECHR as a constitutional charter of Europe[28] for the protection of human rights across Europe as an objective "constitutional order".[29] The multilevel judicial interpretation and protection of fundamental rights, as well as of their governmental restrictions "in the interests of morals, public order or national security in a democratic society" (Article 6), are of a constitutional nature. But ECtHR judges rightly emphasise the subsidiary functions of the ECHR and of its Court:

> these issues are more properly decided, in conformity with the subsidiary logic of the system of protection set up by the European Convention on Human Rights, by the national judicial authorities themselves and notably courts of constitutional jurisdiction. European control is a fail-safe device designed to catch the breaches that escape the rigorous scrutiny of the national constitutional bodies.[30]

The Court aims to resist the "temptation of delving too deep into issues of fact and of law, of becoming the famous 'fourth instance' that it has always insisted it is not".[31] It also exercises deference by recognising that the democratically-elected legislatures in the Member States enjoy a "margin of appreciation" in the balancing of public and private interests, provided the measures taken in the general interest bear a reasonable relationship of proportionality both to the aims pursued and the effects on the individual interests affected.[32] Instead of imposing uniform approaches to the diverse human rights problems in the ECHR Member States, the ECtHR often exercises judicial self-restraint, for example:

- by leaving the process of implementing its judgments to the Member States, subject to the "peer review" by the Committee of Ministers of the Council of Europe, rather than asserting judicial powers to order consequential measures;

27 For example, the wide-ranging guarantees of economic regulation and legally enforceable social rights in Germany's 1919 Constitution for the "Weimar Republic" had led to ever more restrictive government interventions into labour markets, capital markets, interest rates, as well as to expropriations "in the general interest" which – during the Nazi dictatorship from 1933 to 1945 – led to systemic political abuse of these regulatory powers.

28 See Ireland v United Kingdom (1979), 2 European Human Rights Reports 25.

29 See the judgment of the ECtHR in *Loizidou* v *Turkey* (preliminary objections) of 23 March 1995, para. 75, referring to the status of human rights in Europe. Unlike the ECJ, the ECtHR has no jurisdiction for judicial review of acts of the international organization (the Council of Europe) of which the Court forms part.

30 L. Wildhaber, "A Constitutional Future for the European Court of Human Rights?" in: (2002) 23 *Human Rights Law Journal*, p. 161 *et seq*.

31 See Wildhaber, note 30 *supra*, p. 161.

32 See J. Schokkenbrock, "The Basis, Nature and Application of the Margin-of-Appreciation Doctrine in the Case-Law of the European Court of Human Rights", in: (1998) 19 *Human Rights Law Journal*, pp. 30–36.

- by viewing the discretionary scheme of Article 41 ECHR for awarding just satisfaction "if necessary" as being secondary to the primary aim of the ECtHR in order to protect minimum standards of human rights protection in all Convention Member States;[33]
- by concentrating on "constitutional decisions of principle" and "pilot proceedings" that appear to be relevant for many individual complaints and for the judicial protection of a European public order based upon human rights, democracy and rule of law; and
- by filtering out early manifestly ill-founded complaints because the Court perceives its "individual relief function" as being subsidiary to its constitutional function.

Article 34 of the ECHR permits individual complaints not only "from any person", but also from "non-governmental organisations or groups of individuals claiming to be the victims of a violation" of ECHR rights by one of the Member State parties. Whereas the African, American, Arab and UN human rights conventions protect human rights only of individuals and of people, the ECHR and the European Social Charter also protect the human rights of non-governmental legal organisations. The protection of this *collective dimension* of human rights (for example, of legal persons that are composed of natural persons) has prompted the ECtHR to protect procedural human rights (for example, under Articles 6, 13, 34 ECHR), as well as substantive human rights of companies (for example, under Articles 8, 10, 11 ECHR, Protocol 1)[34] in conformity with the national constitutional traditions in many European states as well as inside the EC (for example, the EC guarantees of market freedoms and other economic and social rights of companies). The rights and freedoms of the ECHR can thus be divided into 3 groups:

- Some rights are inherently limited to natural persons (for example, Article 2: right to life) and focus on their legal protection (for example, Article 3: prohibition of torture; prohibition of arbitrary detention in Article 5; Article 9: freedom of conscience).
- Some provisions of the ECHR explicitly protect also rights of "legal persons" (for example, property rights protected in Article 1 of Protocol 1).
- The rights of companies have become recognised by the ECtHR also in respect of other ECHR provisions that protect the rights of "everybody", without mentioning the rights of NGOs, notably the rights of companies to invoke the right to a fair trial in the determination of civil rights (protected under Article 6), the right to respect one's home (protected under Article 8), freedom of expression (Article 10), freedom of assembly (Article 11), freedom of religion/worship (Article 9), the right to an effective remedy (Article 13), and the right to request compensation for non-material damage (Article 41). Freedom of contract and of economic activity is not specifically protected in the ECHR, which focuses on civil and political rights; but the right to

33 See Wildhaber, note 30 *supra*, pp. 164–165.

34 See M. Emberland, The Human Rights of Companies. Exploring the Structure of ECHR Protection, (Oxford: Oxford University Press, 2006).

form companies in order to pursue private interests collectively *is* protected by freedom of association (Article 11), by the right to property (Protocol 1) and, indirectly, also by the protection of "civil rights" in Article 6 ECHR.

This broad scope of human rights protection is reflected in the requirement of Article 1 to secure the human rights "to everyone within their jurisdiction", which also protects traders and companies from outside Europe, and may even cover state acts implemented outside the national territory of ECHR Member States or implementing obligations under EC law. Yet, compared with the large number of complaints by companies brought to the EC Court of Justice, less than 3% of judgments by the ECtHR relate to complaints by companies. So far, such complaints concerned mainly Article 6:1 (the right to a fair trial), Article 8 (the right to respect for one's home and correspondence), Article 10 (freedom of expression, including commercial free speech), and the guarantee of property rights in Protocol 1 to the ECHR.

Similar to the constitutional and teleological interpretation methods used by the EC Court, the ECtHR – in its judicial interpretation of the ECHR – applies principles of "effective interpretation" aimed at protecting human rights in a practical and effective manner. These principles of effective treaty interpretation include a principle of "dynamic interpretation" of the ECHR as a "constitutional instrument of European public order" that must be interpreted with due regard to contemporary realities so as to protect "an effective political democracy" (which is mentioned in the Preamble as an objective of the ECHR).[35] Limitations of the fundamental rights of economic actors are reviewed by the ECtHR as to whether they are determined by law, in conformity with the ECHR, and whether they are "necessary in a democratic society". Governmental limitations of civil and political human rights tend to be reviewed by the ECtHR more strictly (for example, as to whether they maintain an appropriate balance between the human rights concerned and the need for "an effective political democracy") than governmental restrictions of private economic activity, which tend to be reviewed by the Court upon the basis of a more lenient standard of judicial review which allows for a "margin of appreciation" of governments.

Article 1 of Protocol 1 to the ECHR protects "peaceful enjoyment of possessions" (paragraph 1); the term "property" is used only in paragraph 2. The ECtHR has clarified that Article 1 guarantees rights of property not only in corporeal things (rights *in rem*), but also intellectual property rights, and private law or public law claims *in personam* (for example, monetary claims based upon private contracts, employment and business rights, pecuniary claims against public authorities).[36] In *Immobiliare Saffi* v *Italy*, the

35 On the Court's teleological interpretation of the ECHR in the light of its "object and purpose", see Emberland, note 34 *supra*, p. 20 *et seq.*

36 On private law and constitutional law meanings of property (as a relationship to objects of property and to other legal subjects that have to respect property rights), and on the different kinds of property protected in the case-law of the ECtHR, see A. Riza Coban, *Protection of Property Rights within the European Convention on Human Rights*, (Aldershot: Ashgate, 2004), Chapters 2 and 6.

Court also recognised positive state duties to protect private property, for example, to provide police assistance in evacuating a tenant from the applicant's apartment; the lack of such police assistance for executing a judicial order to evacuate a tenant was found to constitute a breach of the applicant's property right.[37] The inclusion of the right to property into the ECHR confirms that property is perceived as a fundamental right that is indispensable for personal self-realisation in dignity.[38] As the moral justifications of private property do not warrant absolute property rights, Article 1 recognises – in conformity with the constitutional traditions of many national European constitutions which emphasise the individual, as well as the social, functions of property (for example, in Article 14 of the German Basic Law) – that private property can be restricted for legitimate reasons. The case law of the ECtHR confirms that such restrictions may include, for example:

- taxation for the common financing of public goods (including re-distributive taxation if it can be justified upon grounds of reciprocal benefit, the correction of past injustices or re-distributive justice);
- governmental control of harmful uses of property (for example, by police power regulations designed to prevent harm to others); as well as
- governmental taking of property by power of eminent domain, whose lawful exercise depends on the necessity and proportionality of the taking for realising a legitimate public interest and – especially if the taking imposes a discriminatory burden only on some individuals – may require the payment of compensation for the property taken.

Even though the ECtHR respects a wide margin of appreciation of Member States to limit and interfere with property rights (for example, by means of taxation) and to balance individual and public interests (for example, in cases of a taking of property without full compensation), the Court's expansive protection – as property or "possessions" – of almost all pecuniary interests and legitimate expectations arising from private and public law relationships reveals a strong judicial awareness of the importance of private economic activities and economic law for the effective protection of human rights and personal self-realisation in the economy and civil society. The Court's review of governmental limitations of, and interferences with, property rights is based on "substantive due process" standards that go far beyond the "procedural due

37 *Immobiliare Saffi* v *Italy*, Reports 1999-V (2000), 30 EHRR 756.

38 On the moral foundations of market freedoms, see Petersmann, note 10 *supra*, p. 29 and 48 *et seq*. Coban, note 36 *supra*, Chapter 3, justifies property rights as *prima facie* human rights upon the basis of four arguments: (1) both the use value and the exchange value of property are essential for private autonomy; (2) a system of private property is also essential for personal self-fulfilment; (3) respect for individual autonomy requires respect for the entitlement of people to the fruits of their labour as well as respect for the outcome of peaceful, voluntary co-operation (for example, in markets driven by consumer demand and competition); and (4) a system of private property further encourages fruitful initiative and an autonomy-enhancing society based upon welfare-increasing competition, division of labour and satisfaction of consumer demand.

process" standards applied by the US Supreme Court since the 1930s.[39] In the different European context of creating an ever broader "social market economy" across the 47 member states of the Council of Europe, the ECtHR's constitutional approach to the protection of broadly defined property rights and fundamental freedoms, including those of companies, appears reasonable.

5.3. *The Diversity of Multilevel Judicial Governance in Free Trade Agreements (FTAs): the Example of the EFTA Court*

The 1992 Agreement between the EC and the EFTA states (Iceland, Liechtenstein and Norway) establishing the European Economic Area (EEA)[40] is the legally most developed of the more than 250 FTAs (in terms of GATT Article XXIV) concluded after World War II. The EFTA Court illustrates the reasonable diversity of judicial procedures and approaches to the interpretation of international trade law and confirms the importance of "judicial dialogues" among international and domestic courts for the promotion of rule of law in international trade. In order to ensure that the extension of the EC's common market law to the EFTA countries would function in the same manner as in the EC's internal market, the 1991 Draft Agreement for the EEA had provided for the establishment of an EEA Court, composed of judges from the ECJ as well as from the EFTA countries, and for the application by the EEA Court of the case law of the EC Court. In *Opinion 1/1991*, the EC Court objected to the structure and competences of such an EEA Court on the grounds that its legally-binding interpretations could adversely affect the autonomy and exclusive jurisdiction (Articles 220, 292 EC) of the EC Court (for example, for interpreting the respective competences of the EC and EC Member States concerning matters governed by EEA provisions).[41] Following the Court's negative Opinion, the EEA Agreement's provisions on judicial supervision were re-negotiated and the EEA Court was replaced by an EFTA Court with more limited jurisdiction, and composed only of judges from the EFTA countries. In a second Opinion, the EC Court confirmed the consistency of the revised EEA Agreement,[42] subject to certain legal interpretations of this agreement by the EC Court.[43] In order to promote legal homogeneity between EC and EEA market law, Article 6 of the revised

39 The US Constitution (Amendments V and XIV) includes strong guarantees of private liberty and property rights against takings without "due process of law" and "just compensation". Up to the late 1930s, the US Supreme Court frequently overturned legislation on the grounds that it violated economic liberties. Yet, when the Democrats took over the US Supreme Court in 1937, the Court had limited judicial protection of "substantive due process of law" essentially to civil and political rights; in the economic field, the Court introduced a constitutional presumption (in the famous *Carolene Products* case of 1938, 304 U.S. 144) that legislative restrictions of private property are presumed to be lawful and no longer subject to judicial review of "economic due process of law". The commerce clause in the US Constitution does not guarantee individual economic liberties as in the EC Treaty, but merely gives regulatory authority to the US Congress.

40 Signed on 2 May 1992 and in force as of 1 January 1994, OJ EC 1994, L 1/3.

41 Opinion 1/91, *Agreement on the EEA*, ECR 1991 I-6079, paras. 31 *et seq.*

42 See Official Journal EC 1994, L 1/3.

43 See Opinion 1/92, *Agreement on the EEA*, ECR 1992 I-2821.

EEA Agreement provides for the following principle of interpretation and judicial cooperation:

> Without prejudice to future developments of case law, the provisions of this Agreement, in so far as they are identical in substance to corresponding rules of the [EC Treaty and the European Coal and Steel Community Treaty (ECSC)] and to acts adopted in application of these two Treaties, shall, in their implementation and application, be interpreted in conformity with the relevant rulings of the Court of Justice of the (EC) given prior to the date of signature of the agreement.[44]

According to the 1994 Agreement between the EFTA member states on the Establishment of a Surveillance Authority and a Court of Justice (SCA),[45] the Court has jurisdiction for infringement proceedings by the EFTA Surveillance Authority against an EFTA state (Article 31), actions concerning the settlement of disputes between EFTA states (Article 32), advisory opinions on the interpretation of the EEA Agreement (Article 33), review of penalties imposed by the EFTA Surveillance Authority (Article 35), as well as jurisdiction in actions brought by an EFTA state or by natural or legal persons against decisions of the EFTA Surveillance Authority (Article 36) or against failure to act (Article 37). Out of the 62 cases lodged during the first ten years of the EFTA Court, 18 related to direct actions, 42 concerned requests by national courts for advisory opinions, and 2 related to requests for legal aid and the suspension of a measure.[46]

In its interpretation of EC law provisions that are identical to EEA rules (for example, concerning common market and competition rules), the EEA Court has regularly followed ECJ case law, and has fulfilled the homogeneity objectives of EEA law in terms of the outcome of cases, if not in terms of their legal reasoning. In its very first case, *Restamark*,[47] the EFTA Court interpreted the notion of court or tribunal (in the sense of Article 34 SCA, regarding requests by national courts for preliminary opinions) by proceeding from the "six factor test" applied by the ECJ in its interpretation of the corresponding provision in Article 234 EC: the referring body must, in order to constitute a "court or tribunal", (1) be established by law (rather than by private agreement, as in the case of commercial arbitration); (2) be permanent; (3) have compulsory jurisdiction for legally-binding decisions on issues

44 The limitation to prior case law was due to the refusal by EFTA countries to commit themselves to unforeseeable, future case law of the EU courts on which they are not represented. V. Skouris, "The ECJ and the EFTA Court under the EEA Agreement: A Paradigm for International Cooperation between Judicial Institutions", in: C. Baudenbacher, P. Tresselt and T. Orlygsson (eds), *The EFTA Court. Ten Years On*, (Oxford: Hart Publishing, 2005), p. 123 *et seq.*, concludes, however, that "it does not seem that the EFTA Court has treated the ECJ case law differently depending on when the pertinent judgments were rendered" (p. 124).

45 Official Journal EC 1994, L 344/1.

46 See H.P. Graver, "The Effects of EFTA Court Jurisprudence on the Legal Orders of the EFTA States", in: C. Baudenbacher, P. Tresselt and T. Orlygsson, note 44 *supra*, p. 79 *et seq.*

47 Case E-1/94, EFTA Court Reports 1994–95, 15.

of a justiciable nature (*res judicata*); (4) conduct *inter-partes* procedures; (5) apply rules of law and evidence; and (6) be independent. Notwithstanding this, the EFTA Court considered the request admissible even if, as frequently occurs in administrative court proceedings in Finland and Sweden, only one party appeared in the proceedings. In the EC Court judgments in cases *Dorsch Consult* of 1997[48] and *Gabalfrisa* of 2000,[49] the ECJ followed suit and acknowledged that the *inter-partes* requirement was not absolute. The case law of the EFTA Court on questions of the *locus standi* of private associations to bring an action for the annulment of a decision of the EFTA Surveillance Authority offers another example of liberal interpretations of procedural requirements by the EFTA Court.[50]

The EC Court, in its Opinion 1/91, held that the Community law principles of legal primacy and direct effect were not applicable to the EEA Agreement and were "irreconcilable" with its characteristics as an international agreement which conferred rights only on the participating states and the EC.[51] The EFTA Court, in its *Restamark* judgment of December 1994, followed from Protocol 35 (on achieving a homogenous EEA based upon common rules) that individuals and economic operators must be entitled to invoke and to claim at national level any rights that could be derived from precise and unconditional EEA provisions if they had been made part of the national legal orders.[52] In its 2002 *Einarsson* judgment, the EFTA Court further followed from Protocol 35 that such provisions with quasi-direct effect must take legal precedence over conflicting provisions of national law.[53] In 1998, in its *Sveinbjörnsdottir* judgment, the EFTA Court had already characterised the legal nature of the EEA Agreement as an international treaty sui generis that had created a distinct legal order of its own; the Court therefore found that the principle of state liability for breaches of EEA law must be presumed to be part of EEA law.[54] This judicial recognition of the corresponding EC law principles was confirmed in the 2002 *Karlsson* judgment, in which the EFTA Court further held that EEA law – while not prescribing that individuals and economic operators be directly able to rely on non-implemented EEA rules before national courts – required national courts to consider EEA rules as relevant, whether implemented or not, when interpreting international and domestic law.[55]

48 Case C-54/96, ECR 1997 I-4961.

49 Cases C-110/98 to C-147/98, ECR 2000 I-1577.

50 See C. Baudenbacher, "The EFTA Court Ten Years On", in: Baudenbacher *et al.*, note 44 *supra*, p. 13 *et seq.*, and p. 24 (who mentions that this liberal tendency might be influenced by the fact that the EFTA Court, unlike the ECJ, is not overburdened).

51 Opinion 1/91, *EEA Agreement*, ECR 1991 I-6079, para. 28.

52 Case E-1/94, EFTA Court Reports 1994–95, 15.

53 Case E 1/01, EFTA Court Reports 2002, 1.

54 Case E 7/97, EFTA Courts Reports 1998, 95.

55 Case E 4/01, EFTA Court Reports 2002, 240 (para. 28).

6. Lessons from the European 'Solange Method' of Judicial Co-operation for Worldwide Economic and Human Rights Law?

From the perspectives of economics and international law, FTAs are sometimes viewed as being sub-optimal compared with the rules of the World Trade Organisation (WTO) for trade liberalisation, rule-making and compulsory dispute settlement at worldwide levels. For example:

- As most FTAs only provide for *diplomatic* dispute settlement procedures (for example, consultations, mediation, conciliation, panel procedures subject to political approval by the member states) without preventing their member countries from submitting trade disputes to the *quasi* judicial WTO dispute settlement procedures, the compulsory WTO dispute settlement system may offer comparatively more effective legal remedies. This is illustrated by the fact that most intergovernmental trade disputes among the 3 member countries of the North American Free Trade Agreement (NAFTA) have been submitted to the WTO dispute settlement system, rather than to the legally weaker dispute settlement procedures of Chapter 20 of the NAFTA Agreement.[56]
- The submission of trade disputes among FTA member countries to the WTO has only rarely given rise to legal problems, for example, if the respondent country could not invoke, in the WTO dispute settlement procedures, legal justifications based upon FTA rules[57] or on FTA dispute settlement procedures.[58] The rare instances of successive invocations of FTA and WTO dispute settlement procedures which challenged the same trade measure[59] did not amount to "abuses of rights", for WTO members have rights to conclude regional trade agreements with separate dispute settlement procedures, as well as rights to the *quasi* automatic establishment of

56 See W.J. Davey, "Dispute Settlement in the WTO and RTAs: A Comment", in: L. Bartels and F. Ortino (eds), *Regional Trade Agreements and the WTO Legal System*, (Oxford: Oxford University Press, 2006), pp. 343–357. There have been only 3 intergovernmental disputes under Chapter 20 since NAFTA entered into force in 1994. On the other six NAFTA dispute settlement procedures and their very diverse records, see A. de Mestral, "NAFTA Dispute Settlement: Creative Experiment or Confusion?" in: L. Bartels and F. Ortino, pp. 359–381.

57 For example, in the WTO dispute between the USA and Canada over Canadian restrictions on "split-run periodicals" (WTO Panel Report, *Canada-Periodicals*, WT/DS31/R, adopted 30 July 1997), Canada did not consider it was entitled to justify in the WTO its violation of GATT Article III by invoking Article 2106 NAFTA permitting preferential measures in favour of cultural industries, see de Mestral, note 56 *supra*, pp. 364–365.

58 For instance, the WTO Appellate Body report on *Mexico-Tax Measures on Soft Drinks*, (WT/DS308/AB/R, adopted in May 2006) upheld the WTO Panel's conclusion that the Panel had no discretion "to decline to exercise its jurisdiction" based upon the existence of a NAFTA dispute on an allegedly related matter (see paras. 44–53).

59 Examples would include challenges of US import restrictions on Canadian lumber in both NAFTA and WTO panels, challenges of EC import restrictions on bananas and genetically modified organisms in the ECJ and in the WTO, challenges of Argentine import restrictions on cotton and of Brazilian import restrictions of retreaded tyres in both Mercosur and WTO dispute settlement proceedings; see K. Kwak and G. Marceau, "Overlaps and Conflicts of Jurisdiction between the WTO and Regional Trade Agreements", in: Bartels and Ortino, note 56 *supra*, pp. 465–485.

WTO dispute settlement bodies to examine complaints in the WTO on the different legal basis of WTO law.

Yet, from the perspective of citizens and their economic rights as protected by courts in Europe, the EC and EFTA courts offer citizens direct access and judicial remedies that appear economically more efficient, legally more effective, and democratically more legitimate than politicised, intergovernmental procedures among states for the settlement of disputes involving private economic actors. The fact that the EC Court has rendered only three judgments in international disputes among EC Member States since the establishment of the ECJ in 1952 illustrates that many intergovernmental disputes (for example, over private rights) could be prevented or settled by alternative dispute settlement procedures if governments granted private economic actors more effective legal and judicial remedies in national and regional courts against governmental restrictions. Unfortunately, national and international judges often fail to co-operate in their judicial protection of the rule of law in international relations beyond the EC and ECHR, for example, because they perceive international and domestic law as being based upon mutually conflicting conceptions of justice. For instance, US courts claim that WTO dispute settlement rulings "are not binding on the US, much less this court";[60] similarly, the EC Court has long since refrained – at the request of the political EC institutions which have repeatedly misled the ECJ about the interpretation of WTO obligations in order to limit their own judicial accountability[61] – from reviewing the legality of EC measures in the light of the EC's GATT and WTO obligations. WTO law tends to be perceived as intergovernmental rules, which governments and domestic courts may ignore without legal and judicial remedies by their citizens adversely affected by welfare-reducing violations of WTO guarantees of market access and rule of law.[62] Both the EC and US governments have requested their respective domestic courts to

60 US Court of Appeals for the Federal Circuit, judgment of 21 January 2005 (*Corus Staal*), available at: www.fedcir.gov/opinions/04-1107.pdf). In the *Corus Staal* dispute, the US Supreme Court denied petition for *certiorari* on 9 January 2006 (www.supremecourtus.gov/docket/05-364.htm), notwithstanding an *amicus curiae* brief filed by the EC Commission supporting this petition ("We argue that the Federal Circuit went too far by construing the Uruguay Round Agreements Act to make considerations of compliance with international obligations completely irrelevant in construing a Department of Commerce anti-dumping determination, and further argue that the Department's 'zeroing' methodology – held invalid by both a WTO Appellate Body and a NAFTA Bi-national Panel – is not entitled to Chevron deference because it would bring the United States into non-compliance with treaty obligations." (available at: www.robbinsrussell.com/pdf/265.pdf).

61 See P.J. Kuijper, WTO Law in the European Court of Justice, (2005) 42 *Common Market Law Review*, p. 1313, who claims (p. 1334) that "it is difficult to point out one specific moment at which it can be established beyond doubt that WTO rules have been breached, even after a decision of a panel or report of the Appellate Body", and "that it is rarely or never possible to speak of a sufficiently serious breach of WTO law" by the political EC institutions justifying the EC's non-contractual liability for damages pursuant to Article 288 EC Treaty.

62 See, for example, the criticism by the EC's legal advisor Kuijper (note 61) of the ECJ's "Kupferberg jurisprudence" on the judicial applicability of the EC's free trade area agreements at the request of citizens as politically "naïve" (p. 1320).

refrain from applying WTO rules at the request of citizens or of NGOs;[63] in order to limit their own judicial accountability, they have repeatedly encouraged their respective courts to apply domestic trade regulations without regard to WTO dispute settlement findings on their illegality.[64] The simultaneous insistence, by the same trade politicians, that WTO rules are enforceable at their own request in *domestic courts vis-à-vis* violations of WTO law by states within the EC or within the US, illustrates the political, rather than legal, nature of such Machiavellian objections against judicial accountability for violations by trade bureaucracies of the international rule of law.

This contribution began by arguing that the universal recognition of inalienable human rights requires national and international courts to review whether – in their judicial settlement of "disputes concerning treaties, like other international disputes,[...] in conformity with the principles of justice and international law" (Preamble VCLT) – human rights and other principles of justice (such as due process of law) justify judicial application of international guarantees of freedom, non-discrimination, rule of law and social safeguard measures for the benefit of citizens. Section 5 described the citizen-driven, multilevel judicial protection of the EC, EEA and ECHR guarantees of freedoms, fundamental rights and rule of law as models for decentralising and transforming intergovernmental rules and dispute settlement procedures for the benefit of citizens. Sections 6 and 7 suggest that the "Solange method" of conditional co-operation by national courts with the EC Court "as long as" (which means "*Solange*" in German) the ECJ protects the constitutional rights of citizens (below 6.1), as well as the judicial self-restraint by the ECtHR *vis-à-vis* alleged violations of human rights by EC institutions "as long as" the EC Court protects the human rights guarantees of the ECHR (below 6.2), should serve as a model for "conditional co-operation" among international courts and national courts also in international economic law, environmental law and human rights law beyond Europe. Section 8 concludes by asking whether the judicial function to settle disputes in conformity with principles of procedural and substantive justice

63 On the exclusion of "direct applicability" of WTO rules in the EC and US laws on the implementation of the WTO agreements, see E.-U. Petersmann, *The GATT/WTO Dispute Settlement System*, (The Hague: Kluwer, 1997), p. 19 *et seq.* At the request of the political EC institutions, the EC Court has refrained long since from reviewing the legality of EC acts in the light of the EC's GATT and WTO obligations; the Court refers only very rarely to WTO rules and WTO dispute settlement rulings in support of the ECJ's interpretations of EC law. In the US, courts are barred by legislation from challenging the WTO-consistency of US federal measures.

64 See J.A. Restani and I. Bloom, "Interpreting International Trade Statutes: Is The Charming Betsy Sinking?" (2001) 24 *Fordham Int'l L J.*, p. 1533. On the controversial relationship between the "Charming Betsy doctrine" of consistent interpretation and the "Chevron doctrine" of judicial deference, see, A. Davies, "Connecting or Compartmentalizing the WTO and United States Legal Systems? The Role of the Charming Betsy Canon, (2007) 10 *Journal of International Economic Law*, pp. 117–149.The European Court of Justice has a long history of ignoring GATT and WTO rules at the request of political EC bodies which have often misinformed the EC Court on the meaning of GATT/WTO rules and dispute settlement reports (for example, in Case 112/80, *Dürbeck*, ECR 1981, 1095, the Commission misinformed the EC Court on an unpublished GATT dispute settlement finding against the EC, and the Court relied on this information without verifying the obviously wrong information submitted to the Court).

can assert democratic legitimacy in international relations which – beyond rights-based European integration law – continue to be dominated by power politics. It is argued that the legitimacy of judicial co-operation, self-restraint, "judicial competition" and "judicial dialogues" among courts derives from their protection of constitutional citizen rights as a constitutional pre-condition for individual and democratic self-development in a constitutionally-protected framework of "participatory", "deliberative" and "cosmopolitan democracy". Citizens and courts have reason to support the multilevel, judicial protection of citizen rights in European law, and to challenge international judges (for example, in worldwide and non-European institutions) if they perceive themselves as mere agents of governments and disregard the constitutional obligation of judges to settle disputes in conformity with human rights.

6.1. The "Solange method" of Judicial Co-operation among the German Constitutional Court and the EC Court in the Protection of Fundamental Rights

The EC Court, the EFTA Court and the ECtHR have – albeit in different ways – interpreted the intergovernmental EC, EEA and ECHR treaties as objective legal orders which also protect *individual rights* of citizens. All three courts have acknowledged that the human rights goals to empower individuals and effectively protect human rights, like the objective of international trade agreements to enable citizens to engage in mutually beneficial trade transactions under non-discriminatory conditions of competition, call for "dynamic judicial interpretations" of treaty rules with due regard to the need for the judicial protection of citizen interests in economic markets and constitutional democracies. These citizen-oriented interpretations of the EC and EEA Agreements were influenced by the long-standing insistency by the German Constitutional Court on its constitutional mandate to protect fundamental rights and constitutional democracy also *vis-à-vis* abuse of EC powers affecting citizens in Germany. The "*Solange* jurisprudence" of the German Constitutional Court, akin to similar interactions between other national constitutional courts and the EC Court,[65] contributed to the progressive extension of the judicial protection of human rights in Community law:

- In its *Solange I* judgment of 1974, the German Constitutional Court held that "as long as" the integration process of the EC did not include a catalogue of fundamental rights corresponding to that of the German Basic Law, German courts could, after having requested a preliminary ruling from the EC Court, also request a ruling from the German Constitutional Court regarding the compatibility of EC acts with fundamental rights and the German Constitution.[66] This judicial insistence on the then higher level of fundamental rights protection in German constitutional law was

[65] See F.C. Mayer, "The European Constitution and the Courts", in: A. v. Bogdandy and J. Bast (eds), *Principles of European Constitutional Law*, (Oxford: Hart Publishing, 2006), pp. 281–334.

[66] BVerfGE 37, p.327.

instrumental for the ECJ's judicial protection of human rights as common, yet unwritten, constitutional guarantees of EC law.[67]

- In view of the emerging human rights protection in EC law, the German Constitutional Court held – in its *Solange II* judgment of 1986[68] – that it would no longer exercise its jurisdiction for reviewing EC legal acts "as long as" the EC Court continued, generally and effectively, to protect fundamental rights against EC measures in ways comparable to the essential safeguards of German constitutional law.
- In its *Maastricht* judgment (*Solange III*) of 1993, however, the German Constitutional Court re-asserted its jurisdiction to defend the scope of German constitutional law: EC measures exceeding the limited EC competences covered by the German Act ratifying the EU Treaty ("*ausbrechende Gemeinschaftsakte*") could not be legally-binding and applicable in Germany.[69]
- Following GATT and WTO dispute settlement rulings that the EC import restrictions on bananas violated WTO law, and in view of an ECJ judgment which upheld these restrictions without reviewing their inconsistencies with WTO law, several German courts requested the Constitutional Court to declare these EC restrictions to be *ultra vires* (i.e., exceeding the EC's limited competences) and to restrict the constitutional freedoms of German importers illegally. The German Constitutional Court, in its judgment of 2002[70] (*Solange IV*), declared the application inadmissible on the grounds that it had not been argued that the required level of human rights protection in the EC had *generally* fallen below the minimum level required by the German Constitution.
- In its judgment of 2005 on the German act implementing the EU Framework Decision (adopted under the Third Pillar of the EU) on the European Arrest Warrant, the Constitutional Court held that the automatically binding force and mutual recognition in Germany of arrest orders from other EU Member States were inconsistent with the fundamental rights guarantees of the German Basic Law.[71] The limited jurisdiction of the EC Court for Third Pillar decisions concerning police and judicial co-operation might have contributed to this assertion of national constitutional jurisdiction for safeguarding fundamental rights *vis-à-vis* EU decisions in the area of criminal law and their legislative implementation in Germany.

The progressively expanding legal protection of fundamental rights in EC law in response to their judicial protection by national and European courts illustrates how judicial co-operation has been successful in Europe far beyond economic law. Judge A.

67 The ECJ's judicial protection of human rights since 1969 (Case 29/69, *Stauder* v *City of Ulm*, ECR 1969, 419; Case 11/70 *Internationale Handelsgesellschaft*, ECR 1970, 1125; Case 4/73, *Nold*, ECR 1974, 491) continues to evolve.

68 BVerfGE 73, 339, at p.375.

69 BVerfGE 89, p.115.

70 BVerfGE 102, p.147.

71 BVerfGE 113, p.273.

Rosas[72] has distinguished the following five "stages" in the case law of the EC Court on the protection of human rights:

- In the supra-national, but functionally-limited European Coal and Steel Community, the Court held that it lacked the competence to examine whether an ECSC decision amounted to an infringement of fundamental rights as recognised in the constitution of a member state.[73]
- Since its *Stauder* judgment of 1969, the EC Court has declared, in a series of judgments, that fundamental rights form part of the general principles of Community law binding the Member States and EC institutions, and that the EC Court ensures their observance.[74]
- Since 1975, the ever more extensive case law of the EC courts explicitly refers to the ECHR and protects ever more human rights and fundamental freedoms in a wide array of Community law areas, including civil, political, economic, social and labour rights, drawing inspiration "*from the constitutional traditions common to the Member States and from the guidelines supplied by international treaties for the protection of human rights on which the Member States have collaborated or of which they are signatories*".[75]
- Since 1989, the ECHR has been characterised by the EC Court as having "special significance" for the interpretation and development of EU law[76] in view of the fact that the ECHR is the only international human rights convention mentioned in Article 6 EU.
- In the 1990s, the EC courts began to refer to individual judgments of the ECtHR,[77] and have clarified that – in reconciling economic freedoms guaranteed by EC law with human rights guarantees of the ECHR that admit restrictions – all interests involved have to be weighed "*having regard to all circumstances of the case in order to determine whether a fair balance was struck between those interests*", without giving priority to the economic freedoms of the EC Treaty at the expense of other fundamental rights.[78] The EC courts have also been willing to adjust their case law

72 A. Rosas, "Fundamental Rights in the Luxembourg and Strasbourg Courts", in: C. Baudenbacher, P. Tresselt and T. Orlygsson, note 44 *supra*, p. 163 and 169.

73 Case 1/58, *Storck* v *High Authority*, ECR 1959, 43.

74 See the cases cited in note 67 *supra*.

75 See, for example, Opinion 2/1994 on the ECHR, ECR 1996 I-1759, para. 33.

76 Joined Cases 46/87 and 222/88, *Hoechst*, ECR 1989, 2859, para.13.

77 See Case 13/94, *P* v *S*, ECR 1996 I-2143, para.16.

78 See Case C-112/00, *Schmidberger*, ECR 2003 I-5659. The Court began by examining the EC's economic freedom, as requested by the national court, and observed that "since both the Community and its Member States are required to respect fundamental rights, the protection of those rights is a legitimate interest which, in principle, justifies a restriction of the obligations imposed by Community law, even under a fundamental freedom guaranteed by the Treaty such as the free movement of goods"; "unlike other fundamental rights enshrined in that Convention, such as the right to life or the prohibition of torture and inhuman or degrading treatment or punishment, which admit no restriction, neither the freedom of expression nor the freedom of assembly guaranteed by the ECHR appears to be absolute but must be viewed in relation to its social purpose" (para.80). The judicial balancing by the ECJ refutes the claim that the ECJ gives priority to economic freedoms at the expense of other human rights.

to new developments in the case-law of the ECtHR,[79] and to differentiate – as in the case law of the ECtHR – between judicial review of EC measures,[80] state measures,[81] and private restrictions of economic freedoms in the light of fundamental rights.[82]

6.2. *"Horizontal" Co-operation among the EC Courts, the EFTA Court and the ECtHR in Protecting Individual Rights in the EEA*

Judicial co-operation between the EC courts and the EFTA Court was legally mandated in the EEA Agreement (for example, Article 6) and facilitated by the fact that the EEA law to be interpreted by the EC and EFTA courts was largely identical with the EC's common market rules (notwithstanding the different context of the EC's common market and the EEA's free trade area). The EC Court of First Instance, in its *Opel Austria* judgment of 1997, held that Article 10 of the EEA Agreement (corresponding to the free trade rules in Articles 12, 13, 16 and 17 EC Treaty) had direct effect in EC law in view of the high degree of integration protected by the EEA Agreement, whose objectives exceeded those of a mere free trade agreement, and required the contracting parties to establish a dynamic and homogenous EEA.[83] In numerous cases, EC court judgments referred to the case law of the EFTA Court, for example, by pointing out "that the principles governing the liability of an EFTA state for infringement of a directive referred to in the EEA Agreement were the subject of the EFTA Court's judgment of 10 December 1998 in *Sveinbjörnsdottir*".[84] In its *Ospelt* judgment, the EC Court emphasised that:

79 In Case C-94/00, *Roquette Frères*, ECR 2002 I-9011, para. 29, for example, the ECJ referred explicitly to new case-law of the ECtHR on the protection of the right to privacy of commercial enterprises in order to explain why – despite having suggested the opposite in the ECJ's earlier judgment in *Hoechst* – such enterprises may benefit from Article 8 ECHR: "For the purposes of determining the scope of that principle in relation to the protection of business premises, regard must be had to the case-law of the European Court of Human Rights subsequent to the judgment in *Hoechst*. According to that case-law, the protection of the home provided in Article 8 of the ECHR may in certain circumstances be extended to cover such premises (see, in particular, the judgment of 16 April 2002 in *Colas Est and Others* v *France, not yet published in the Reports of Judgments and Decisions*) and second, the right of interference established by Article 8(2) of the ECHR might well be more far-reaching where professional or business activities or premises were involved than would otherwise be the case."

80 See, for example, the ECJ cases listed in note 67 *supra*.

81 See, for example, the *Omega* Case C-36/02, ECR 2004 I-9609, in which the ECJ acknowledged that the restriction of market freedoms could be necessary for the protection of human dignity despite the fact that the German conception of protecting human dignity as a human right was not shared by all other EC Member States.

82 See Emberland (note 34 *supra*) and Cases C-341/05, *Laval*, ECR 2007 I-11767, and C-438/05, *Viking*, ECR 2007 I-10779, in which the ECJ recognized that trade unions are legally bound by the EC's common market freedoms, and that the private plaintiffs in these cases can rely directly on the EC Treaty in their judicial challenge of restrictions imposed on market freedoms by trade unions invoking their social rights to strike (for example, in order to prevent relocation of *Viking Line* to another EC Member State).

83 Case T-115/94, ECR 1997 II-39.

84 Case C-140/97, *Rechberger*, ECR 1999 I-3499, para. 39.

> [O]ne of the principal aims of the EEA Agreement is to provide for the fullest possible realisation of the four freedoms within the whole EEA, so that the internal market established within the European Union is extended to the EFTA states.[85]

The case law of the EFTA Court evolved in close co-operation with the EC courts, national courts in EFTA countries and with due regard also to the case law of the ECtHR. In view of the intergovernmental structures of the EEA Agreement, the legal homogeneity obligations in the EEA Agreement (for example, Article 6) as well as in the Agreement between the EFTA States on the Establishment of a Surveillance Authority and a Court of Justice (for example, Article 3) were interpreted only as *obligations de résultat* with regard to the legal protection of market freedoms and individual rights in EFTA countries. Yet, the EFTA Court effectively promoted "*quasi*-direct effect" and "*quasi*-primacy" (C. Baudenbacher), as well as full state liability and the protection of individual rights of market participants in national courts in all EEA countries.[86] In various judgments, the EFTA Court followed the ECJ case law also by interpreting EEA law in conformity with the human rights guarantees of the ECHR and the judgments of the ECtHR (for example, concerning Article 6 ECHR on access to justice, and Article 10 on freedom of expression). In its *Asgeirsson* judgment, the EFTA Court rejected the argument that the reference to the EFTA Court had unduly prolonged the national court proceeding in violation of the right to a fair and public hearing within a reasonable time (Article 6 ECHR); referring to a judgment by the ECtHR in a case concerning a delay of two years and seven months due to a reference by a national court to the ECJ (pursuant to Article 234 EC), the EFTA Court shared the reasoning of the ECtHR that adding the period of preliminary references (which was less than 6 months in the case before the EFTA Court) could undermine the legitimate functions of such co-operation among national and international courts in their joint protection of the rule of law.

The ECtHR has frequently referred, in its judgments, to provisions of EU law and to judgments of the ECJ. In *Goodwin*, for example, the ECtHR referred to Article 9 of the EU Charter of Fundamental Rights (the right to marry) in order to back up its judgment that the refusal to recognise a change of sex for the purposes of marriage constituted a violation of Article 12 ECHR.[87] In *Dangeville*, the ECtHR's determination that interference with the right to the peaceful enjoyment of possessions was not required in the general interest took into account the fact that the French measures were incompatible with EC law.[88] In joined cases *Waite and Kennedy* v *Germany*, the ECtHR

85 Case C-452/01, ECR 2003 I-9743, para. 29.

86 See the EFTA Court President C. Baudenbacher, "The EFTA Court Ten Years On", in: Baudenbacher *et al.* (note 44), and H.P. Graver, note 46 *supra*, p. 97: "Direct effect of primary law, state liability and the duty of the courts to interpret national law in the light of EEA obligations have been clearly and firmly accepted in national law by Norwegian courts."

87 *Goodwin* v *United Kingdom*, judgment of 11 July 2002, Reports of Judgments and Decisions 2002-VI, paras. 58 and 100.

88 *SA Dangeville* v *France* judgment of 16 April 2002, Reports of Judgments and Decisions 2002-III, paras. 31 *et seq.*

held that it would be incompatible with the purpose and object of the ECHR if an attribution of tasks to an international organisation or in the context of international agreements could absolve the contracting states of their obligations under the ECHR.[89] In the *Bosphorus* case, the ECtHR had to examine the consistency of the impounding of a Yugoslavian aircraft by Ireland upon the legal basis of EC regulations imposing sanctions against the former Federal Republic of Yugoslavia; the ECtHR referred to the ECJ case law, according to which respect for fundamental rights is a condition of the lawfulness of EC acts, as well as to the ECJ preliminary ruling that "the impounding of the aircraft in question[...] cannot be regarded as inappropriate or disproportionate"; in its examination of whether compliance with EC obligations could justify the interference by Ireland with the applicant's property rights, the ECtHR proceeded upon the basis of the following four principles:[90]

- "A Contracting Party is responsible under Article 1 of the Convention for all acts and omissions of its organs regardless of whether the act or omission in question was a consequence of domestic law or of the necessity to comply with international legal obligations."
- "State action taken in compliance with such legal obligations is justified as long as the relevant organisation is considered to protect fundamental rights, as regards both the substantive guarantees offered and the mechanisms controlling their observance, in a manner which can be considered at least equivalent to that for which the Convention provides."
- "If such equivalent protection is considered to be provided by the organisation, the presumption will be that a state has not departed from the requirements of the Convention when it does no more than implement legal obligations flowing from its membership of the organisation."
- "However, any such presumption can be rebutted if, in the circumstances of a particular case, it is considered that the protection of Convention rights was manifestly deficient. In such cases, the interest of international co-operation would be outweighed by the Convention's role as a 'constitutional instrument of European public order' in the field of human rights."

After examining the comprehensive EC guarantees of fundamental rights and judicial remedies, the ECtHR found that:

> the protection of fundamental rights by EC law can be considered to be, and to have been at the relevant time, 'equivalent'... to that of the Convention system. Consequently, the presumption arises that Ireland did not depart from requirements of the Convention when it implemented legal obligations flowing from its membership of the EC.

89 *Waite and Kennedy* v *Germany*, judgment of 18 February 1999, Reports of Judgments and Decisions 1999-I, para. 67.

90 *Case of Bosphorus Hava Yollari Turizm* v *Ireland*, judgment of 30 June 2005, European Human Rights Reports 42 (2006) 1, paras. 153 *et seq.*

As the Court did not find any "manifest deficiency" in the protection of the applicant's Convention rights, the relevant presumption of compliance with the ECHR had not been rebutted.[91]

7. Conditional "Solange-cooperation" among International Trade and Environmental Courts Beyond Europe?

The plurality of national constitutions and of complementary international treaty constitutions recognising inalienable human rights entail that national and international courts must carefully examine the conditions under which the judicial interpretation and the application of intergovernmental rules remains consistent with the constitutional principles applicable in the respective jurisdiction. Many rules of the Westphalian "international law among states" reflect power politics, rather than respect for human rights and democratic governance. Competing multilateral treaty and dispute settlement systems with "forum selection clauses" enabling governments to submit disputes to competing jurisdictions (with the risk of conflicting judgments) continue to multiply also outside economic law and human rights law, for example, in international environmental law, maritime law, criminal law and other areas of international law. Proposals to co-ordinate such overlapping jurisdictions through hierarchical procedures (for example, preliminary rulings or advisory opinions by the ICJ) are rightly opposed by most governments. Agreement on exclusive jurisdiction clauses (as in Article 292 EC Treaty, Article 23 DSU/WTO, Article 282 Law of the Sea Convention) may not prevent the submission of disputes involving several treaty regimes to competing dispute settlement *fora*. For example, in the dispute between Ireland and the United Kingdom over radioactive pollution from the MOX plant in Sellafield (UK), four dispute settlement bodies were seized and used diverging methods for co-ordinating their respective jurisdictions:

7.1. The OSPAR arbitral award of 2003 on the MOX Plant dispute

In order to clarify the obligations of the United Kingdom to make available all information "on the state of the maritime area, on activities or measures adversely affecting or likely to affect it" pursuant to Article 9 of the Convention for the Protection of the Marine Environment of the North-East Atlantic (OSPAR), Ireland and the United Kingdom agreed to establish an arbitral tribunal under this OSPAR Convention. Even though Article 35, para. 5a of the Convention requires the tribunal to decide according to "the rules of international law, and in particular those of the Convention", the tribunal's award of July 2003 was based only upon the OSPAR Convention, without taking the relevant environmental regulations of the EC and of the 1998 Aarhus Convention on Access to Information, Public Participation in Decision-making and Access to Justice in Environmental Matters (ratified by all EC member states as well as by the EC) into account. The OSPAR arbitral tribunal decided in favour of the United

91 Case of Bosphorus Hava Yollari Turizm v Ireland, note 90 supra, paras. 165–166.

Kingdom that the latter had not violated its treaty obligations by not disclosing the information sought by Ireland.[92]

7.2. *The UNCLOS 2001 provisional measures and 2003 arbitral decision in the MOX Plant dispute*

The UN Convention on the Law of the Sea (UNCLOS) offers parties the choice (in Articles 281 *et seq.*) of submitting disputes to the International Tribunal for the Law of the Sea (ITLOS), the ICJ, arbitral tribunals or other dispute settlement *fora* established by regional or bilateral treaties. As Ireland claimed that the discharges released by the MOX Plant contaminated Irish waters in violation of UNCLOS, it requested the establishment of an arbitral tribunal and – pending this procedure – requested interim protection measures from the ITLOS pursuant to Article 290 UNCLOS. The ITLOS order of December 2001, after determining the *prima facie* jurisdiction of the Annex VII arbitral tribunal to decide the merits of the dispute, requested both parties to co-operate and consult with regard to the emissions from the MOX plant into the Irish Sea, pending the decision on the merits by the arbitral tribunal. The arbitral tribunal suspended its proceedings in June 2003 and requested the parties to clarify whether, as claimed by the United Kingdom, the EC Court had jurisdiction to decide this dispute upon the basis of the relevant EC and EURATOM rules, including UNCLOS as an integral part of the Community legal system.[93]

7.3. *The EC Court judgment of May 2006 in the MOX Plant Dispute*

In October 2003, the EU Commission started an infringement proceeding against Ireland on the grounds that – as the EC had ratified and transformed UNCLOS into an integral part of the EC legal system – Ireland's submission of the dispute to tribunals outside the Community legal order had violated the exclusive jurisdiction of the EC Court under Article 292 EC and Article 193 of the EURATOM Treaty. In its judgment of May 2006, the Court confirmed its exclusive jurisdiction on the grounds that the UNCLOS provisions on the prevention of marine pollution relied on by Ireland in its dispute relating to the MOX plant "are rules which form part of the Community legal order".[94] The Court followed from the autonomy of the Community legal system and from Article 282 UNCLOS that the system for the resolution of disputes set out in the EC Treaty must, in principle, take precedence over that provided for in Part XV of UNCLOS. As the dispute concerned the interpretation and application of EC law within the terms of Article 292 EC, "Articles 220 EC and 292 EC precluded Ireland from

92 See T. McDorman, Access to Information under Article 9 OSPAR Convention (*Ireland* v *UK*), Final Award, in: (2004) 98 *American Journal of Int'l Law*, p. 330 *et seq*.

93 See Y. Shany, "The First MOX Plant Award: The Need to Harmonise Competing Environmental Regimes and Dispute Settlement Procedures", in: (2004) 17 *Leiden Journal of International Law*, 815 *et seq*.

94 ECJ Case C-459/2003, *Commission* v *Ireland* ECR (2006) I-4635, para. 121.

initiating proceedings before the Arbitral Tribunal with a view to resolving the dispute concerning the MOX plant".[95] By requesting the arbitral tribunal to decide disputes concerning the interpretation and application of Community law, Ireland had violated the exclusive jurisdiction of the Court under Article 292 EC, as well as the EC Member States' duties of close co-operation, prior information and loyal consultation of the competent Community institutions as prescribed in Article 10 EC.

7.4. *The 2004 IJzeren Rijn Arbitration between the Netherlands and Belgium*

The *IJzeren Rijn* arbitration under the auspices of the Permanent Court of Arbitration concerned a dispute between Belgium and the Netherlands over Belgium's right to the use and the re-opening of an old railway-line leading through a protected natural habitat and the payment of the costs involved.[96] The arbitral tribunal was requested to settle the dispute upon the basis of international law, including – if necessary – EC law, with due respect to the obligations of these EC Member States under Article 292 EC. The Tribunal agreed with the view shared by both parties that there was no dispute within the meaning of Article 292 EC because its decision on the apportionment of costs did not require any interpretation of EC law (for example, the Council Directive on the Conservation of Natural Habitats).

7.5. *The "Solange method" as Reciprocal Respect for Constitutional Justice*

The above-mentioned examples for competing jurisdictions for the settlement of environmental disputes among European states raise questions similar to those regarding overlapping jurisdictions for the settlement of trade disputes, human rights disputes or criminal proceedings in national and international criminal courts. The UNCLOS provisions for dispute settlement upon the basis of "this Convention and other rules of international law not incompatible with this Convention" (Article 288) prompted the ITLOS to affirm *prima facie* jurisdiction in the *MOX plant* dispute. The Annex VII Arbitral Tribunal argued convincingly, however, that the prospect of resolving this dispute in the EC Court upon the basis of EC law risked leading to conflicting decisions which, bearing in mind considerations of mutual respect and comity between judicial institutions and the explicit recognition of mutually agreed regional jurisdictions in Article 282 UNCLOS, justified suspending the arbitral proceeding and enjoining the parties to resolve the Community law issues within the institutional framework of the EC.

WTO law recognises similar rights of WTO members to conclude regional trade agreements with autonomous dispute settlement procedures; however, the lack of a WTO provision corresponding to Article 282 UNCLOS, and the WTO rights to the

95 ECR (2006) I-4635, para. 133.

96 See N. Lavranos, "The *MOX Plant* and *IJzeren Rijn* Disputes: Which Court is the Supreme Arbiter? in: (2006) 19 *Leiden Journal of International Law*, pp. 1–24.

quasi automatic establishment of WTO dispute settlement panels entail that WTO dispute settlement bodies must respect the right of WTO members to receive a WTO dispute settlement ruling on the WTO obligations of the members of FTAs, even if the respondent WTO member would prefer to settle the dispute in the framework of the FTA procedures. The EC Court's persistent refusal to decide disputes upon the basis of the WTO obligations of the EC and its Member States offers an additional argument for WTO dispute settlement bodies to respect the rights of WTO members (including EC Member States) to WTO dispute settlement rulings on alleged violations of WTO rights and obligations (for example, by the EC Council's import restrictions on bananas), notwithstanding the exclusive ECJ jurisdiction for settling disputes over WTO law inside the EC as an integral part of the Community legal system: "as long as" the EC Court continues to ignore the WTO obligations of the EC in its dispute settlement practices, and offers EC Member States no judicial remedy against EC majority decisions violating WTO law, WTO dispute settlement bodies may see no reason to exercise judicial self-restraint in WTO disputes over violations by the EC of its WTO obligations *vis-à-vis* EC Member States.[97] The lack of a treaty provision similar to Article 282 UNCLOS might also have prompted the OSPAR arbitral tribunal to decide on the claim of an alleged violation of the OSPAR Convention, without any discussion of Article 292 EC, and without prejudice to future dispute settlement proceedings in the EC Court based upon EC law (which, arguably, includes more comprehensive information disclosure requirements). The *Ijzeren Rijn* arbitral tribunal examined, as requested by the parties, the legal relevance of Article 292 EC and decided the dispute without prejudice to EC law.

The "Solange principle" conditions the respect for competing jurisdictions with respect for the constitutional principles of human rights and rule of law. It has also been applied by the EC Court itself, for instance when – in its Opinion 1/91 on the inconsistency of the EEA Draft Agreement with EC law – the EC Court found the EEA provisions for the establishment of an EEA Court to be inconsistent with the "autonomy of the Community legal order" and the "exclusive jurisdiction of the Court of Justice" (for example, in so far as the EEA provisions did not guarantee legally-binding effects of "advisory opinions" by the EEA Court on national courts in EEA member states).[98] The "Solange principle" can explain the jurisprudence of both the EC Court,[99] as well as the EFTA

97 Such challenges in the WTO by EC Member States of EC acts violating WTO law have never occurred so far. Most Community lawyers (such as Lavranos, note 96 *supra*, pp. 10–11) argue that not only from the point of view of Community law, but also "from the point of view of international law, the supremacy of Community law within the EC and its member states must be accepted" (pp. 10–11). Yet, it is arguable even from the point of view of Community law that the duty of loyalty (Article 10 EC) applies only "as long as" the ECJ offers effective judicial remedies against obvious violations by EC institutions of their obligations (for example, under Articles 220, 300 EC) to respect the rule of law and protect EC Member States from international legal responsibility for EC majority decisions violating mixed agreements.

98 ECJ Opinion 1/91, *EEA Draft Agreement* ECR 1991 I-6079.

99 Case C-125/2004, *Denuit/Cordenier* v *Transorient*, ECJ judgment of 27 January 2005.

Court,[100] which voluntarily agreed that private arbitral tribunals are not recognised as courts or tribunals of Member States (within the meaning of Article 234 EC and Article 33 SCA) entitled to request preliminary rulings by the European courts. The fact that international arbitral tribunals (such as the OSPAR and *IJzeren Rijn* arbitral tribunals mentioned above) are likewise not entitled to request preliminary rulings from the European Courts, may justify judicial self-restraint and deference to the competing jurisdiction of European courts in disputes requiring the interpretation and the application of European law. To the extent that conflicts of jurisdiction and conflicting judgments cannot be prevented by means of exclusive jurisdictions and hierarchical rules,[101] international courts should follow the example of both national civil and commercial courts and European courts, and resolve conflicts through judicial co-operation and "judicial dialogues" based upon principles of judicial comity and judicial protection of constitutional principles (such as due process of law, *res judicata*, human rights) underlying modern international law. The horizontal co-operation among national and international courts with overlapping jurisdictions for the protection of constitutional rights in Europe reflects the constitutional duty of judges to protect "constitutional justice"; it should serve as a model for similar co-operation among national and international courts with overlapping jurisdictions in other field of international law,[102] notably, if the intergovernmental rules protect co-operation among citizens across national frontiers, such as the settlement of transnational trade, investment and environmental disputes. In other areas of intergovernmental regulation where states remain reluctant to submit to review by international courts (for example, as in the Second and Third Pillars of the EU Treaty), *national courts* must remain vigilant guardians in order to protect citizens and their constitutional rights from inadequate judicial remedies at the international level of multilevel governance in order to guarantee the collective supply of international public goods demanded by citizens.

8. Multilevel Judicial Protection of Constitutional Rights as Pre-condition for International Rule of Law and Democratic Supply of 'International Public Goods

European integration suggests that multilevel legal and judicial protection of constitutional rights is a pre-condition for the transformation of the power-oriented "international law among states" into citizen-oriented international rules which protect international public goods (such as democratic peace in Europe). Rule of international

100 See note 46 *supra*.

101 See Lavranos, note 96 *supra*, p. 20: "the key to all solutions is hierarchy".

102 See N. Lavranos, "Towards a *Solange*-Method between International Courts and Tribunals?" in: T. Broude and Y. Shany (eds), *The Allocation of Authority in International Law. Essays in Honour of Prof. R. Lapidoth* (2008): "if the *Solange* method would be applied by all international courts and tribunals in case of jurisdictional overlap, the risk of diverging or conflicting judgments could be effectively minimised, thus reducing the danger of a fragmentation of the international legal order... One could argue that the *Solange*-method, and for that matter judicial comity in general, is part of the legal duty of each and every court to deliver justice."

law must remain consistent with the legitimate plurality of constitutional principles and constitutional rights. The European "Solange jurisprudence" rightly challenges the prevailing perception and authoritarian premises of the "international law among states" as foreign policy instrument for advancing *state* interests as defined by governments. For example, state-centred lawyers and power-oriented diplomats argue that effective international tribunals must remain "dependent" tribunals staffed by *ad hoc* judges closely controlled by governments (for example, through their power of re-appointment and threats of retaliation). Independent international courts are perceived with suspicion because independent judges risk allowing moral ideals and interests of third parties to influence their judgments. The domestic ideal of rule of law is seen as inappropriate for the reality of international power politics:

> Dependent tribunals are more likely to render judgments that reflect the interests of the states at the time that they submit the dispute to the tribunal.[103]

In support of such power-oriented conceptions of international judges as the agents of the governments which appoint them, reference is also made to the empirical voting patterns of *ad hoc* judges (for example, in the ICJ and arbitral tribunals) who side much more often with the legal claims of the government nominating the judge than with the legal claims of the other party to the dispute.[104] From such state-centred, rather than citizen-oriented, perspectives, intergovernmental trade and economic rules are perceived and applied as intergovernmental commitments about reciprocal market access without private rights of action.[105]

Citizen-oriented constitutional approaches, in contrast, emphasise the "constitutional functions" of international law for correcting governance failures at national levels and for enabling citizens to supply collectively private and public goods beyond what is possible through national power politics. The more citizens live and co-operate not only in local and national, but also in transnational communities (for example, as EC citizen, migrant worker protected by ILO conventions, refugees protected by UN human rights and humanitarian assistance, researchers protected by UNESCO and WIPO conventions), the more the universal recognition of inalienable human rights calls for citizens to be provided with effective legal and judicial remedies for the decentralised enforcement of citizen interests across national frontiers. Empirical evidence confirms that most national parliaments do not effectively control intergovernmental rule-

103 See E. Posner and J.C. Yoo, "Judicial Independence in International Tribunals", (2005) 93 *California Law Review*, p. 6, who define the function of international tribunals as providing states with neutral information about the facts and the law in a particular dispute.

104 See E.A. Posner and F.P. de Figueiredo, "Is the International Court of Justice Politically Biased?" (2005) 34 *Journal of Legal Studies*, pp. 599–630.

105 See A.O. Sykes, "Public versus Private Enforcement of International Economic Law: Standing and Remedy", (2005) 34 *Journal of Legal Studies*, p. 631.

making in worldwide organisations;[106] hence, parliamentary democracy must be supplemented by more decentralised forms of participatory, rights-based democracy which empower self-interested individuals to co-operate across frontiers. The ideal of "deliberative democracy" – i.e., that all rules and governance powers be justified through a fully inclusive, informed discourse among all persons affected by the rules – remains utopian in view of the rational ignorance of individuals, their limited cognitive capacities, and the inevitable "discourse failures" (for example, due to asymmetries of power and knowledge).[107] Rights-based "cosmopolitan justice" and independent, impartial courts settling disputes in conformity with principles of justice and international law offer horizontal and vertical "checks and balances" that limit abuse of power without relying on unrealistic idealisation of citizens, civil society, organisations and rulers.

The *jus cogens* core of inalienable human rights, the ever increasing number of international "treaty constitutions" limiting national policy discretion by collective rule-making and international adjudication, the proliferation of international courts, their conditional co-operation ("as long as" other jurisdictions respect essential constitutional principles) in the judicial protection of rule of law continue to transform the intergovernmental structures of European law by procedural, as well as substantive, "constitutional restraints". Multilevel constitutionalism and rights-based "constitutional justice" have become a reality for ever more European citizens thanks to the multilevel co-operation of judges in European integration. Disputes among European states have become rare in the EC Court, the EFTA Court, in the ECtHR, as well as in worldwide courts (for example, the ICJ) and in other dispute settlement bodies (such as the WTO). The ever closer networks of independent regulatory agencies and other multilevel governance institutions in Europe, and the rare recourse to the "horizontal" enforcement mechanisms of international law (such as inter-state sanctions) in relations among European democracies, confirm that "state sovereignty" is "disaggregating" in Europe.[108] Constitutional rights and principles of justice have been protected more effectively by means of the "*Solange*-method" of multilevel judicial co-operation in transnational relations among European states than at any previous time during the centuries of intergovernmental power politics.

In Europe, the "public reasoning" and multilevel co-operation of independent and impartial judges has become an important constitutional constraint on

106 On the inadequate parliamentary control of intergovernmental rule-making in the WTO, see, for example, the following two publications by the European Parliament: *Role of Parliaments in Scrutinising and Influencing Trade Policy* (European Parliament Study December 2005, DV/603690. doc); *The Parliamentary Dimension of the WTO* (2006).

107 See G. Pincione and F. Teson, Rational Choice and Democratic Deliberation: A Theory of Discourse Failure, (Cambridge: Cambridge University Press, 2009); A. Kuper, Democracy Beyond Borders. Justice and Representation in Global Institutions, (Oxford: Oxford University Press, 2004).

108 More generally on "disaggregated sovereignty", see A.-M. Slaughter, *A New World Order*, (Princeton: Princeton University Press, 2004), at 266 *et seq.*

intergovernmental power politics and one-sided government efforts to avoid judicial accountability for violations of international law. Multilevel judicial governance has become one of the most "principled" parts of constitutional democracy in Europe. The limited role of European courts in the common foreign and security policies of the European Union, as well as the limited co-operation among European and worldwide courts (such as the ICJ and the Appellate Body of the WTO) illustrate the political limits of international courts also in Europe, notably in areas of national security and foreign policy disputes over the distribution of power or the legitimacy of international law rules. Beyond Europe, international relations remain dominated by power politics, refusal by most UN member states to submit to the compulsory jurisdiction of the ICJ, insistence on state sovereignty and introverted "constitutional nationalism" which impedes the collective supply of global public goods.[109] Proposals for extending European "multilevel constitutionalism" to worldwide organisations (such as the UN and the WTO) are opposed by most states outside Europe (including the United States) in view of their different constitutional and democratic traditions and power-oriented foreign policies. The more intergovernmental networks and worldwide organisations evade parliamentary and democratic control, and the more legislators fail to correct the ubiquitous "market failures" and "governance failures" in international relations, the more citizens – as the legal subjects of international law and the "democratic principals" of government agents – have reason to appeal to the "public reasoning" of independent and impartial courts mandated to protect constitutional rights and rule of law "in conformity with principles of justice".

If democratic institutions are perceived as instruments for protecting the constitutional rights and self-governance of citizens against abuse of power (including majoritarian abuse of parliamentary powers), then the multilevel judicial protection of the fundamental freedoms of citizens can be justified as a necessary pre-condition for constitutional democracy in a globally-integrated world. The risk of paternalist abuses of judicial powers must be countered by "deliberative democracy" and "public reasoning". Rights-based "judicial discourses" which focus on the "principles of justice" tend to be more precise and more rational than political promises to protect vaguely-defined state interests. Similar to European courts, national constitutional judges and international courts outside Europe increasingly argue that constitutional democracies must be premised on "active liberty"; hence, the exercise of rights to individual and democratic self-government (in citizen-driven "political markets" as well as in consumer-driven economic markets) may serve as a "source of judicial authority and an

[109] On this "globalisation paradox" (i.e., needing multilevel governance for the collective supply of international pubic goods, but fearing and opposing such governance), see Slaughter, note 108 *supra*, p. 8 *et seq*. On the need for "multilevel constitutionalism" as a necessary legal framework for collective, democratic supply of an efficient world trading system, see E.-U. Petersmann, "Multilevel Trade Governance Requires Multilevel Constitutionalism", in: Ch. Joerges and E.-U. Petersmann (eds), *Constitutionalism, Multilevel Trade Governance and Social Regulation*, (Oxford and Portland OR: Hart Publishing, 2006), pp. 5–57.

interpretative aid to more effective protection of ancient and modern liberty alike".[110] Judicial determination of the international *opinio juris sive necessitatis* must insist that legitimacy is no longer derived from (inter-)governmental *fiat*, but from democratic and judicial justification of the relevant rules as being reasonable and *just*.[111] The independence, impartiality and constitutional function of judges to protect constitutional rights against abuse of power legitimise adjudication as a necessary component of constitutional democracy. Citizens must hold judges more accountable for meeting their constitutional obligation to protect "constitutional justice" in terms of justifying legal interpretations and judicial decisions in conformity with the human rights obligations of government institutions and the constitutional rights of citizens. The increasing cross-references in ECJ and EFTA judgments to their respective case-law, as well as to other European and international courts (such as the ECtHR, WTO dispute settlement rulings, and the ICJ), should serve as models for co-operation also among other international courts in order to co-ordinate better their respective jurisprudence upon the basis of common legal principles.[112]

Civil society and its democratic representatives rightly challenge traditional conceptions of international justice shielding an authoritarian "international law among states" as being inconsistent with the universal recognition of inalienable human rights, which call for constitutional conceptions of justice as a shield of the individual and of his or her human rights against abuse of power. As long as world governance for the collective supply of the ever more needed "global public goods" remains as deficient as it is, the legal and judicial protection of constitutional rights in transnational relations "in conformity with principles of justice and international law" are essential for the protection of human rights through pragmatic piecemeal reforms of international legal practices. It is to be welcomed that ever more international dispute settlement bodies (for example, in the WTO and investor-state arbitration) – by admitting *amicus curiae* briefs – are willing to listen to the public reasoning of citizens, whose *opinio juris* – as the "democratic principals" of government agents – may be relevant for judicial limitations of abuse of government powers (for example, if concession contracts with non-democratic rulers are influenced by corruption). Just as multilevel constitutionalism

110 See US Supreme Court Justice S. Breyer, *Active Liberty: Interpreting Our Democratic Constitution*, (New York: Knopf, 2005).

111 On the diverse (for example, rational Kantian, contractarian Rawlsian and discursive Habermasian) methodological approaches to identifying just rules see, for example, C.S. Nino, "Can there be Law-abiding Judges?" in: M. Troper and L. Jaume (eds), *1789 et l'invention de la constitution*, (Brussels: Bruylant, 1994), p. 275 and 286 *et seq.* On "justice as fairness" and "first virtue of social institutions", see J. Rawls, *A Theory of Justice*, (revised edition, Cambridge MA: Harvard University Press, 1999), p. 3. See, also, R. Forst, *Das Recht auf Rechtfertigung*, (Frankfurt aM: Suhrkamp Verlag, 2007), who infers from the Kantian idea of reason based upon universalisable principles that individuals can reasonably claim moral and legal rights to participation in decision-making which affects them, as well as to receive a justification of restrictions of individual freedoms.

112 A. Rosas, "With a Little Help from My Friends: International Case Law as a Source of Reference for the EU Courts", in: *The Global Community Yearbook of International Law and Jurisprudence 2005*, Vol. I (Leiden: Kluwer Publishers, 2006), pp. 201–230.

in Europe was promoted by the intergovernmental creation and judicial protection of common markets and of rights-based, transnational communities (rather than by "Wilsonian liberalism" projecting national democratic institutions to the worldwide level), so will the needed "constitutionalisation" of intergovernmental power politics and "cosmopolitan peace" crucially depend upon the vigilance of democratic citizens and upon both the wisdom and the courage of judges supporting citizen-oriented reforms of international law and the judicial protection of constitutional rights in the peaceful co-operation among citizens across national frontiers.

Alicia Cebada Romero

CHAPTER 4. THE EUROPEAN UNION AND "OTHERNESS": CAN THE EUROPEAN UNION REINFORCE GLOBAL JUSTICE? A VIEW FROM INTERNATIONAL LAW

1. Introductory Remarks

One of the central ideas on which Christian Joerges' approach to the European Union pivots is that the European Union, as a supranational body, serves to alleviate the democratic deficits of constitutional nation state democracies ("compensating the shortcomings of constitutional nation-states"[1]). According to Christian Joerges, "we should stop complaining about the democracy deficits of the EU and, instead, turn our attention to the democracy failures of the constitutional national State".[2] This particular way of looking at the legitimacy of the European Union echoes the Habermas approach to the legitimacy of law.[3] In this vein, the European Union is portrayed as a supranational framework in which each Member State is compelled to take into consideration the interests of the other Member States. In his contribution to this volume, Jürgen Neyer sustains that, as a result, transnational justice is strengthened.[4]

There exists little doubt that the European Union has already contributed notably to fuel regional (or intra-regional) transnational justice, but is it really re-inforcing transnational justice as well? The sceptics might answer that the (re-) distribution of welfare among comparatively wealthy Member States that takes place within the European Union, appears to be a rather negligible contribution to transnational justice. However, I will try to demonstrate that the European contribution is not as negligible as it might seem at first sight.

1 Ch. Joerges "European Law as Conflicts of Law", in: Ch. Joerges and J. Neyer, *Deliberative supranationalism: revisited.* 20/2006 *EUI Working Papers, Law* 21.

2 Ch. Joerges "European Law as Conflicts of Law" *op. cit.* at p. 22.

3 Jürgen Habermas "On the internal relation between the rule of law and democracy", (1995) 3 *European Journal of Philosophy*, p. 12.

4 See, in this volume, Jürgen Neyer: "Justice or Democracy? Power and Justification in the EU and other International Organizations", *supra* Ch. 2.

It is the thesis of this chapter that the European Union is, indeed, a suitable framework when it comes to propel transnational justice as embodied in the multilateral agenda. Nevertheless, in order to sustain this contention, further explanation is needed. If we only refer to the inclusion of more of those States that might be affected by European policies in the decision-making process, we will fail to understand why the European Union may exert such a positive influence. In fact, the analysis of the way in which the European Union operates on the world stage casts many doubts on whether the "compensation effect" described by Christian Joerges suffices to vest legitimacy upon it. The contention that more of those affected by the European policies are included in the decision-making process seems to be almost sarcastic when applied to the realm of the common agricultural policy. And it would not be difficult to adduce further evidence pointing in the same direction. At first glance, it might seem that Professor Joerges' optimistic approach to the legitimacy of the European Union has a Euro-centric bias. Furthermore, when a broader lens is applied, it could even be contended that the democratic shortfalls of the constitutional state democracies are just being transplanted onto the European Union, so that the legitimacy of the latter is undermined, rather than strengthened. In my view, when it comes to tracking a possible positive European influence on transnational justice, the crucial point should not be to highlight that, within the European Union, the members of the community take part in the decision-making process, but rather to determine whether the interests of the non-members are also taken into account – and to what extent–, even if, as non-members, they are granted some kind of access to the decision-making process. On a closer look at the performance of the European Union as an international actor, there are reasons to support the idea that the EU might be characterised by its openness to the "otherness".

Thus, in the subsequent sections of this chapter, I will make an attempt to prove that the European Union, operating as a "civilian power"[5] on the world stage, is more responsive than the Member States of which it is composed to the interests of those that might be, or are, affected by its policies. And, furthermore, it will also be sustained that it is in the interest of the European Union itself to be more open to "the others" because its very legitimacy is strengthened as a result. Should the European Union fully develop the civilian power paradigm, it would make a remarkable contribution to transnational justice. However, this is not an easy assignment, as will be explained later on in this chapter.

5 B. Hettne and F. Söderbaum. "Civilian Power or soft imperalism: the EU as a global actor and the role of interregionalism", (2005) 10 *European Foreign Affairs Review*, p. 536. The European model has also been called "liberal internationalism" by Söderbaum: "The EU's external relations objectives with a strong emphasis on the human benefits of economic interdependence, democracy, human rights and the principles of sustainable and participatory development, are often referred to as a 'liberal internationalist' approach to international relations." Fredrik Söderbaum, Patrik Stalgren and Luk van Langenhove. "The EU as a global actor and the dynamics of inter-regionalism: a comparative analysis", (2005) 27 *European Integration*, p. 368.

2. The European Union as an "Open" Community

Christian Joerges' approach, which centres on the "compensation of Constitutional Nation-States democracy failures-effect",[6] should be read alongside the "new sovereignty" approach developed by Abram and Antonia Chayes.[7] Both ideas (the compensation for the democratic deficits of states, and new sovereignty) seem to be applicable not only to supranational structures, but also to any non-supranational multilateral institutional structure. Moreover, according to what has been stated in the previous section, it might seem that, the more multilateral an international institutional framework becomes, the closer it might come to the idea of a "global community" in which the interests of every member are somehow represented. Nonetheless, in the following lines, it will be shown that the way in which the interests of the members are represented in a supranational framework clearly differs from the way in which they are represented in a non-supranational multilateral framework.

So, what are the particularities of the European Union, as a supranational institutional framework? First of all, the willingness of the leaders to take the interests of the weaker Member States into consideration is clearer in the case of a supranational structure, because in this kind of framework where the idea of solidarity is clearly embedded, the Member States are structurally bound to take these interests into account. In contrast, within other international institutional frameworks, this is more a question of political willingness (consider the difficulties to culminate the WTO Doha Round in a successful agreement as an example). In his contribution to this volume, Jürgen Neyer hints at this idea when he points out that "Legal integration therefore aims to transform bargaining into legal reasoning". Clearly, we must not lose sight of the fact that, as Neyer also contends, "even if supranational institutions have the capacity to transform bargaining into legal reasoning, they are, nevertheless, founded on an original bargaining process, and often reflect, to some degree, the outcome of an asymmetrical distribution of power". From the perspective of the "new sovereignty", it is easier to see how, within non-supranational international institutional frameworks, the chance for the least well-off members to participate in the decision-making as well as to make their voices heard and receive adequate responses to their claims is more theoretical than real. (Here, it is worth mentioning the sharp critical analysis of current international institutions accomplished by Chimni[8] or Pogge[9], among others).

6 Ch. Joerges "European Law as Conflicts of Law", in: Ch. Joerges and J. Neyer *Deliberative supranationalism: revisited*, 20/2006 *EUI Working Papers, Law* 21.

7 Abram Chayes and Antonia Chayes, *The new Sovereignty*, (Cambridge MA: Harvard University Press, 1995).

8 B.S. Chimni "International Institutions today: an imperial global State in the making", (2004) 15 *Eur. J. Int'l L, p. 1–37.*; B.S. Chimni. "The World Trade Organization, democracy and development: a view from the South", (2006) 40 *JWT*, p. 5–36.

9 Thomas Pogge "Recognized and Violated by International Law: The Human Rights of the Global Poor", (2005) 18 *Leiden Journal of International Law*, p. 717.

The "compensation effect" taking place within the European Union may be better understood if we refer to the concept of "community". In this regard, and in order to keep expectations at bay, it must be borne in mind that the European Union is not a "global" community, and therefore it will always be possible to differentiate between the consideration given to the interests of the Member States and the attention paid to the interests of the non-Member States. According to Dworkin, a "community" might be defined as follows:

> Membership in a collective unit of responsibility involves reciprocity: a person is not a member of a collective unit sharing success and failure unless he is treated as a member by others, and treating him as a member means accepting that the impact of collective action on his life and interests is as important to the overall success of the action as the impact on the life and interests of any other member.[10]

The reference to this conception of community is very enlightening, for it makes clear that only the interests of those who are recognised as full members of the community will be fully taken into account. Nevertheless, it also holds true that a given community may be more or less responsive to the interests of non-members. As already advanced, if we engage in the analysis of the performance of the European Union as an international actor, we will see that there are reasons to maintain that the European Union is more open to the "otherness" than other hegemons use to be, even though there are, of course, also numerous black holes of inconsistency undermining European Union's legitimacy.

The openness of the European Union is illustrated by its attitude towards third states (if the analysis were extended to encompass the policies for the admission of individuals as well, the account would be completely different, though). In this vein, it has become commonplace nowadays to refer to the European Union as an advanced illustration of open regionalism.[11]

The European Consensus on Development illustrates the intention of the European Union to give adequate responses to the needs of third countries. In this document, the commitment to responding to the needs of partner countries is spelled out.[12] And it is worth underlining that the goal here is not only to set up a development co-operation policy tailored to the needs of developing countries, but also to increase the consistency between this policy and others (trade or environmental policies are clear examples)

10 Ronald Dworkin "Equality, Democracy and Constitution: We the People in Court", (1990) 28 *Alberta Law Review*, p. 324, at 339.

11 For a critical approach to open regionalism, see M. Shiff and L. Winters, *Regional Integration and Development*, (Washington: World Bank, 2003), p. 244: "open regionalism is a slogan rather than an analytical term."

12 "Joint Statement by the Council and the representatives of the Governments of the Member States meeting within the Council, the European Parliament and the Commission on European Union Development Policy: 'The European Consensus'", Council of the European Union, Brussels, 22 November 2005, 14820/05, Section 3.

whose objectives may clash with those that inspired the development co-operation agenda.

The openness is also illustrated by the fact that the European Union is linked to many third states through international agreements. These agreements might be seen as a response to the need to conciliate on the one hand, the acceptance of geographical limitations (inherent to the idea of a "regional" community), with the parallel need to offer, at least to some countries, a chance to participate in the benefits resulting from the European regional integration process, on the other. The responsiveness of the European Union to the claims of third states is expressed in the association and co-operation agreements signed not only with third states, but also with other regional *blocs*.[13] Even though I cannot go in depth into the subject, it is worth mentioning that, in this vein, the efforts on the part of the EU to set up a special and privileged framework for the relations with neighbouring countries are particularly remarkable. The Neighbourhood Policy is being designed upon a bilateral basis and is, therefore, better adapted – at least potentially – to the particular interests of the EU's partners.[14] The comprehensive relationship with Russia could also be mentioned.

It is sufficient to examine the extensive network of agreements to see the extent to which the European Union can be characterised by its openness. On the other hand, the intensity with which the European Union has implemented its *ius contrahendi* can be taken as proof of its vitality as an international actor. It might also be of interest to underline that these agreements are multi-dimensional themselves. Within the "multi-dimensional" relationship arising from these treaties, the interests and claims of both parties might be better accommodated.

Finally, I briefly wish to mention here the other clear expression of the EU's openness, which pertains to the enlargement of the community itself through the admission of new Member States. Notwithstanding this, the enlargement of a regional community has its limits, and the European Union is currently striving to de-limit its borders. For this chapter, the important point is that the fact that the EU has gone through 6 enlargement processes (or 5 +) and has established enhanced relations not only with neighbouring countries, but also with other countries and regional *blocs* across the world, are reflective of its openness.

13 "The EC responds to outside pressures related to the impact of the internal market and its policies by expanding membership to applicants; offering association and preferential trade accords, development assistance, partnerships and dialogues with other regional blocs". R.H. Ginsberg, "Conceptualizing the EU as an international actor: narrowing the theoretical capability-expectations gap", (1999) 37 *Journal of Common Market Studies*, p. 429, at 437.

14 R. Dannreuther, "Developing the alternative to enlargement: the European neighbourhood policy", (2006) 11 *EFAR*, p. 183, at 183–184.

3. The Ways in Which the EU, as an International Actor, Can Propel Transnational Justice Forward: The Characterisation of the EU as a "Smart" Civilian Power

It is commonplace to characterise the European Union as a civilian power (soft power). There has been a long-lasting debate about the viability of this model and about the success achieved by the European Union in its implementation. In fact, the question might be asked as to whether the model is itself currently going through a substantial transformation.[15] There is an interesting piece of research work written by Chaban, Elgstrom and Holland, whose main goal was to identify – upon the basis of personal interviews and opinion polls – the image that the European Union projects externally.[16] And it is striking to ascertain that, according to this work, the European Union is still seen as a prospective (possible) leader, rather than as a real one. It seems that the people interviewed were not confident that the European Union might play an influential role in the world by implementing a civilian power paradigm (based upon acceptance, linked to reputation and authority) instead of by following the model that has been traditionally applied by hegemons, one that would, instead, be based upon imposition, linked to power, including military coercion. This work (Chaban *et al.*) pointed to the fact that the European Union is still fully expected to develop a military dimension. In my opinion, attention should be drawn to the fact that, should this development actually take place, it might end up displacing the European Union from the civilian paradigm to the more traditional one. Rather than to point to the need of making progress in the development of the military dimension of the European Union, the work of Chaban *et al.*, demonstrates the failure of the European Union to persuade the world of the viability of the civilian power model.

It was Benita Ferrero, the former External Relations Commissioner, who declared that "those who believe the EU is still principally a soft power are behind the times".[17] And she added:

> For over a decade, the EU's foreign policy has been adding more tools to its repertoire, including, crucially, a military dimension and crisis management functions.

In the same address, she re-named the paradigm applicable to the EU's external action as "smart power". Although the progress accomplished over the last years within the realm of the European defence policy is undeniable, I do not think it can be contended that it has led to a change in the nature of EU power. In contrast to the analysis that

15 The progress within the area of security policy could be read in this direction.

16 Natalie Chaban, Ole Elgström and Martin Holland. "The EU as others see it", (2006) 11 *EFAR*, pp. 245–262.

17 Speech by Benita Ferrero: "The European Union and the World: a hard look at soft power", given at Columbia University (New York), on 24 September 2007. Available at: www.europa-eu-un.org/articles/en/article_7330_en.htm.

points to military weakness as the reason for the poor image that the European Union projects externally, it could also be sustained that, in reality, the weaknesses of the European Union as an international actor might be a consequence of its own inconsistencies in the implementation of the civilian power paradigm. In this vein, the challenge should be for the European Union to prove that it is possible to reach a hegemonic position even without a fully developed military dimension. In other words, without renouncing to be a "soft power".[18] There can be little doubt that this is not an easy task.[19] In fact, it has been sustained that the civilian power paradigm is a *contradictio in terminis*, that it is unviable.[20] I prefer to side with those who, in contrast, contend that it is something new, not a contradiction in terms, but an oxymoron.[21]

What, then, are the axes of the civilian power paradigm? One of the keys – as has been already said – is that it does not rest on military coercion. This is not tantamount to say that the military dimension cannot be developed; on the contrary, it can exist and can be strengthened, but it should not become the central point of the external action of the EU. In this sense, we have to bear in mind that an external action which pivots on security issues would fall closer to the traditional paradigm and might become a way for the Member States to regain control over the EU's external action. In contrast, should the military dimension be implemented in full respect of the European commitment to multilateralism, the progress in this field would perfectly fit into the "civilian power" paradigm. In this vein, EU military missions, as the ones deployed in

18 B. Hettne and F. Söderbaum, "Civilian Power or soft imperialism: the EU as a global actor and the role of interregionalism", (2005) 10 *European Foreign Affairs Review*, pp. 535–582, at 536. Jurgen Habermas and Jacques Derrida, "What Binds Europeans Together: A Plea for a Common Foreign Policy, Beginning in the Core of Europe", (2003) 10 *Constellations*, p. 291. See, also, Jürgen Habermas, "Why Europe needs a Constitution", (2001) 11 *New Left Review*, p. 5, at 12. It is of interest to notice that, within the USA, a shift from the hard power to the "smart power" paradigm is also being advocated. See, for example, the work of the Center for Strategic and International Studies (CSIS) Commission on Smart Power, with the motto: "a smarter, more secure America." Available at: www.csis.org/smartpower/. These words of Professor Nye are illustrative of the scope of this Commission: "Rich and I and the rest of the commission are looking at how America wields power in the world and what type of posture is most effective. Hard power – basically military and economic might (coercion and payments) – is a vital element, but as we've seen over the past few years, it doesn't necessarily translate into influence in today's world. Smart power is about tapping into diverse sources of American power, including our soft power, to attract others. It is about how we can get other countries to share our goals without resorting to coercion, which is limited and inevitably costly". See the rest of the interview at: www.the-american-interest.com/ai2/article.cfm?Id=346&MId=16.

19 M. Farrell, "EU External Relations: exporting the EU Model of Governance?", (2005) 10 *European Foreign Affairs Review*, p. 451, at 453: "As much as American unilateralism renews the legitimacy of power politics on the world stage, the normative approach in the European management of international relations sustains the relevance of the very notion of global governance."

20 Hedley Bull, "Civilian Power Europe: a contradiction in terms", (1982) 12 *Journal of Common Market Studies*, p. 149.

21 K. Nicolaides and R. Howse, "This is my EUtopia…: Narrative as power", (2002) 40 *JCMS*, p. 767.

Chad and the Central African Republic following the United Nations mandate,[22] do not call the nature of the EU power into question.

Civilian power might be also characterised by the way in which it approaches international law, a particular approach that might further propel both a "humanised" reading of, and a multilateral approach to, international rules. At first sight, it might seem that the European Union utilises international law as the hegemons have traditionally done. As Nico Krisch has already explained, the latter oscillate between submission to international law as a way of gaining legitimacy and the infringement of international rules whenever it is necessary for them to pursue short-term self-interests.[23] Even though this oscillation is also visible in the case of the European Union, there still exists a major difference between the way in which the European Union interacts with international law and the way in which powerful states do. What are the particularities in the case of the European Union?

Firstly, it is worth stressing that the European Union – like every international organisation[24] – defines itself through discourse, going beyond what it is formalized in the foundational treaty.[25] In the case of the European Union's discourse (partly enshrined in legal rules: primary and secondary), the commitment to international law and multilateralism occupies a prominent place. This multilateral orientation is even more valuable because it is rather rare to find this kind of commitment in the case of powerful actors (the USA has joined the EU recently with the move from the G. W. Bush's preference for unilateralism to the B. Obama's pledge to multilateralism).[26] Indeed, the European Union's leverage in the world is certainly greater than that of the vast majority of the international actors typically interested in supporting multilateralism. This is beneficial for multilateralism itself and for the multilateral

22 UN Security Council Resolution 1778 (2007); Council Joint Action 2007/677 CFSP of 15 October 2007, on EU military operation in the Republic of Chad and the Central African Republic; see http://euobserver.com/9/24603.

23 Nico Krisch, "International Law in times of hegemony: unequal power and the shaping of the international legal order", (2005) 16 *Eur. J. Int'l L.*, p. 369.

24 In contrast to States, which see how the content of their international subjectivity is defined by General International Law, the content of the subjectivity of international organisations is determined on a case by case basis, according to what has been established in the Founding Treaty as well as what has been expressed in the implementation thereof through the enactment of secondary rules by the Institutions of the Organisation.
It could be contended that the categorisation of the European Union as an international organisation is outdated. In my opinion, if we consider the European Union as an international actor, it has to be conceptualised as an international organisation, albeit a "unique" one. Actually, within the international organisations landscape, the "uniqueness" of the European Union becomes one of its defining features. To say that it is an international organisation only means it has been created by a founding international treaty and it has a permanent international structure and legal personality.

25 Fastenrath. "Relative normativity in International Law", (1993) 4 *EJIL*, p. 336.

26 Fassbender sustains that the European Union is intrinsically bound to promote multilateralism: Fassbender, "The better peoples of the United Nations? Europe's Practice and the United Nations", (2004) 15 *EJIL*, p. 857.

agenda. From the European discourse, high expectations arise with regard to its commitment to development co-operation, the promotion and the protection of human rights, the protection of the environment, and so forth.

On the other hand, it is well-known that, within the European Union, the member states have gone the furthest in the transfer of competences to a supranational institutional body. This unprecedented sovereignty transfer endows the European Union with an exceptional multidimensionality (it becomes an advanced expression of the so-called "new regionalism"[27]) which places it in an ideal position to pursue many of the goals that make up the rather fragmented multilateral agenda. This goes hand in hand with the already mentioned firm European commitment to multilateralism.

It is also remarkable that the European Union is built upon the idea of regional solidarity, articulated through social and regional cohesion tools. Although it is clear that the European Union is not a model that might just be transplanted to other areas of the world, nobody would deny that the European Union is influencing, sometimes in a subtle way, the creation and implementation of other regional integration experiences throughout the world.[28] Here, mention could be made of the efforts on the part of the European Union to persuade other countries that solidarity and social cohesion must be a necessary component of any integration process. This aspect will be further developed in the next section of this chapter. Should the EU succeed in the promotion of solidarity, the result could be beneficial for transnational justice. This is one reason for welcoming the EU's efforts to promote regional integration as such. In this line, it is remarkable that the EU not only supports existing regional processes, but also encourages third countries to engage in new regional integration adventures (the association and stabilisation agreements with Balkan countries provide a good example of this).

The last idea that I wish to offer with a view to explaining why the position of the European Union, *vis-à-vis* international law, differs from the traditional position of the powerful states is that the acceptance of the fundamental general principles (and values) upon which international law is based, as embodied in the concept of *ius cogens*, is a constitutive feature in the case of the European Union. While the existence of a state does not depend at all on its attitude towards international law, the European Union –

27 On the various models of regionalism, see Andrew Hurrell, "The regional dimension in International Relations Theory", in: M. Farrell, Björn Hettne and Luk van Langenhove, *The Global Politics of Regionalism. Theory and Practice.* (London: Pluto Press, 2005), pp. 38–53. See, also, Mario Telo, (ed). *European Union and new regionalism. Regional actors and global governance in a post-hegemonic era*, (Aldershot: Ashgate, 2001).

28 Rainer Nickel, "¿El futuro inevitable del MERCOSUR? "Gobernanza, democracia y control judicial en la Unión Europea como modelo de institucionalización supranacional", in: A. Ferraro, *En busca del buen gobierno: nuevas perspectivas sobre políticas y gestión del Estado en América Latina*, (Barcelona: Edicions Bellaterra, 2007), p. 19. He brings attention to some features of the European integration process that should not be emulated, in particular, to the problem from which the European governance is suffering: "carencia de una estructura jurídica coherente e integral", at p. 47.

like every International Organisation – is founded upon an international treaty, and is, consequently, bound to abide by peremptory rules, according to Article 53 of the Vienna Convention on the Law of the Treaties. Nevertheless, it is necessary to bear in mind that different conceptions of international law are reflected in the general principles, so that when one talks about the contribution of the European Union to transnational justice, it is not only important to ascertain that it adheres (even structurally) to these principles, but also important to stress that it advocates a special informal hierarchy among principles, in which precedence is granted to those that come closer to a humanised and multilateral-oriented account of the international legal order. In this regard, the clear commitment to the protection of human rights and the central position occupied by the individuals within the European Union legal order are of the utmost importance.

To sum up, civilian power maintains a particular relationship with international law, one in which commitment to multilateralism and solidarity occupies a prominent position, one that could further propel the process of the "humanisation" of international law, and, eventually, advance transnational justice. In their search to increase their standing in the world, the hegemons are striving to find the right combination between hard and soft power. It is in this vein that the term "smart power" has been coined.[29] And I am convinced that the smarter option for the European Union is to stick to its civilian power paradigm.

4. The Subtle Influence of the European Union – the Pledge for Solidarity

The solidarity principle has been developed within the European Union in two main dimensions: inter-territorial solidarity and social cohesion.

In spite of the reluctance on the part of the member states to bestow the European Union with competence in the realm of social policy, the European Union has not been prevented from developing a "social agenda", structured firstly according to the Lisbon strategy and secondly by the so-called post-Lisbon strategy, laid out recently as a response to the financial and economic crisis. It is well-known that, from the very outset of the EU, EU action within the field of social policy was confined to the regulation of the free movement of workers and of gender equality with regard to working conditions. Over the years, the perception that the progress in the integration process should be coupled with advances in the social field has steadily been increasing. Encouraged, maybe, by the progress attained at multilateral level (the UN Copenhagen Summit on Social Development of 1995 could be mentioned as an example), the EU launched its Lisbon strategy (2000), which focused on the social dimension of the integration process. It was acknowledged there that, even in the European Union, there was an unacceptable amount of population living in poverty, or close to the poverty

[29] See note 21 *supra*.

line.[30] Within the Lisbon Strategy, the proclaimed main goals were to create employment ("decent work for all" is the motto repeatedly used by the European Institutions in line with the International Labour Organisation (ILO)), as well as to favour social integration by both protecting minorities properly and guaranteeing an improved access to basic services, such as education and health. I have already mentioned the EU's multi-dimensionality,[31] which basically means that the European process embraces not only economic, but also political and social, domains. When designing regional solidarity schemes, the deployment of an extensive array of tools is required: social, economic, political, environmental and so forth. In a certain way, it could be said that the new regionalism as incarnated in the European Union, seems particularly adapt to face problems such as social exclusion and poverty, which are multidimensional in themselves.

The mechanism that was enshrined in the Lisbon strategy, in order to proceed within the social field, was the so-called open method of co-ordination (OMC).[32] In short, it basically consisted of agreeing upon common goals to be pursued by all the EU member states, leaving the latter with the freedom to select the tools through which those common goals were allegedly to be attained. The member states were called upon to announce their national strategies (in the so-called national action plans). The OMC also comprised a peer review mechanism (the member states were required to deliver a biannual report on the progress accomplished). Through the application of this mechanism, a considerable amount of information was gathered not only with regard to the formulae applied in each country but also with regard to the results achieved. There existed a mutual learning process, which basically took place through the sharing of good practices. The European Commission and the Council both played an important role as monitoring bodies.

30 There are some estimates in this regard. http://europa.eu.int/comm/employment_social/international_cooperation/docs/seminar_13jan05/farrell_%20speech_en.pdf.

31 J.H. Jackson, "Perspectives on regionalism in trade relations", (1996) 27 *Law & Pol'y Int'l Bus.*, p. 873. See, also, Mary Farrell, "The Global Politics of Regionalism: an introduction", in: M. Farrell, B. Hettne and Luk van Langenhove, *Global Politics of Regionalism*, (London: Pluto Press, 2005), p. 8. It should be said that this multi-dimensionality can be traced in every regional scheme. Even in such projects as the Free Trade Area of Americas, which is primarily oriented towards trade, other dimensions are also being considered. Adelle Blackett, for example, pleas for the re-inforcement of social dimension within the framework of regional integration schemes in America. "Toward social regionalism in the Americas", (2002) 23 *Comp. Lab L & Pol'y J.*, p. 901.

32 For a description of the OMC, see: "When do policy innovations spread? Lessons for advocates of lesson drawing", (2006) 119 *Harvard Law Review*, p. 1467; Maurizio Ferrera, Manos Matsaganis and Stefano Sacchi, "Open Co-ordination Against Poverty: The New EU Social Inclusion Process", (2002) 12 *J. Eur. Soc. Pol'y*, p. 227; See Jean-Claude Barbier, "The European Employment Strategy, A Channel for Activating Social Protection?" in: Jonathan Zeitlin and Philippe Pochet (eds) *The Open Method of Co-ordination in Action: The European Employment and Social Inclusion Strategies*, p.417, at 419–25 (Brussels: Peter Lang Publisher, 2005); *Research Forum on the Open Method of Coordination*: http://eucenter.wisc.edu/OMC.

In spite of the existence of some progress, the truth is that the Lisbon strategy disappointed expectations, which was particularly clear after the outbreak of the financial and economic crisis. The "soft" tools of cooperation designed in the framework of the Lisbon strategy were not sufficient to overcome the crisis and the need to design a post-Lisbon strategy was presented as one of the priorities of the Spanish Presidency. The Europe 2020 Strategy has just been presented ("A European Strategy for smart, sustainable and inclusive growth"), it is focused on employment and growth and has a clear priority: to lead a successful exit from the crisis.[33] One of the pillars of the new strategy is stronger economic governance.

The second dimension of the solidarity principle that can be found within the European regional integration process is inter-territorial solidarity, which has been crucial for enhancing internal cohesion and ultimately for the re-inforcement of the organisation itself (it gives substantial content to the idea of community). European Union has been deeply affected by the crisis, but economic, social and territorial cohesion will remain at the heart of the Europe 2020 Strategy. Usually, it is at state level that these schemes implementing territorial solidarity can be found, although, of course, it is also necessary to acknowledge that there exist numerous states whose territories and populations are suffering from the lack of such schemes. To date, this has been particularly the case of Latin American states,[34] although they are gradually becoming aware of the need to work in this direction.[35]

It is less common to have regional solidarity mechanisms working effectively beyond the framework of the member states, but this is precisely what we find within the European Union. In the EU, regional solidarity tools have been implemented quite successfully, such as the structural funds and cohesion funds which finance the regional policy.

Solidarity, as approached by the European Union, has an external side as well. And both sides – external and internal – have been brought together within the enlargement process.[36] The ongoing debate on the limits to the geographical expansion of Europe is

33 Communication from the Commission: Europe 2020: www.youtube.com/watch?v=HgjQGGZiyk&feature=related. The Strategy has been endorsed by the European Council: EUCO 7/10, 25–26 March 2010.

34 In the XXXI session of the ECLAC Economic Commission for Latin America and Caribbean (ECLAC), on 22 March 2006 in Montevideo, it was stressed that "the LAC countries should re-assess the role of the state in fighting inequalities and that economic policies can hide the reality in Latin America: a region rich in natural resources but with great social inequalities". Background paper. High Level Conference: promoting social cohesion: the European Union – Latin America and Caribbean experiences. Brussels, 27–28 March 2006: http://europa.eu.int/comm/world/lac-vienna/events/idb_ec_background_230306.pdf.

35 Fourth Summit of the Americas, Declaration of Mar Del Plata: "Creating jobs to fight poverty and strengthen Democratic Governance", 5 November 2005.

36 Marise Cremona, "EU enlargement: solidarity and conditionality", (2005) 30 *European Law Review*, p. 3.

related to the limits for the solidarity effort which is required from the member states.[37] Regional solidarity enhances internal cohesion, but when the solidarity effort required is excessive, internal cohesion might be put at risk.[38]

At the external level, solidarity is advocated by the European Union both within the framework of bilateral and inter-regional relations and within international organisations. In this way, the openness of the European Union represents a unique opportunity for it to spread various features of its model across the world, a model in which solidarity occupies a central position.

The fact that the European Union has little room for manoeuvre within the social realm makes its performance on the international arena even more valuable. The efforts of the European Union in this area might also be more generally read as an illustration of its commitment to the promotion of solidarity. The greater the success of the European Union in strengthening solidarity as a general principle of international law, the closer it (the EU) will come to the compensation of the drawbacks of state constitutional democracies. In this vein, the need to improve social cohesion in developing countries has been repeatedly underlined by the European Union at multilateral, as well as at bilateral, level. At multilateral level, the intention on the part of the European Union to link the Lisbon strategy to the Copenhagen process, implemented under the auspices of the United Nations, might be underscored. At bilateral level, I would focus on the relationship with Latin-American countries within which the EU is conferring remarkable relevance to social cohesion. It might be said that the European experience in the social field is influencing, albeit in a very subtle way, the design of the regional mechanisms designed to foster social cohesion in Latin-America.

4.1. The External Side of the European Union's Social Agenda

Let us go into the external projection of the social dimension of the European integration process in greater depth.[39] It might be advanced that the results might not be spectacular, but they are more valuable if we keep sight on the fact that – as already underlined – the social field is the one in which the member states have been highly reluctant to yield decision-making to the European institutions, thereby hindering the inception of European policies.[40]

37 Benita Ferrero has recently declared in a speech in Stockholm that it is clear that the European Union "cannot enlarge *ad infinitum*": http://europa.eu.int/rapid/pressReleasesAction.do?reference=SPEECH/06/149&.

38 M. Teló, "Globalization, new regionalism and the role of the European Union" in: Teló(ed) *European Union and new regionalism. Regional actors and global governance in a post-hegemonic era.* (Aldershot: Ashgate, 2001), pp. 21–37.

39 COM (2005) 33 final Communication on the Social Agenda, at p. 5: the main goals are: the incorporation of the European social model into external dialogue and measures at bilateral, regional and multilateral level; and the promotion of decent work as a global objectives at all levels.

40 T. Atkinson, "Social inclusion and the European Union", (2002) 40 *Journal of Common Market Studies*, p. 625. On the (in)existence of a European social model, see W. Schelkle, "Can there be a European

At multilateral level, the European Union advocated the feasibility of using the OMC within the 43rd session of the United Nations (UN) Commission for Social Development (CSD) – held in New York, in February 2005.[41] The scope of this session was to review the Copenhagen Declaration on Social Development drawn up in that city 10 years before. The three over-riding issues addressed within the CSD Summit were the usual topics included in the multilateral social agenda:[42] the eradication of poverty, the promotion of full employment and social integration, including the human rights perspective, the call for the improvement in the access to basic services, such as education and health, and the promotion of gender equality. At the end of that session of the Social Development Commission, a report was issued, within which it is possible to find some references which echo the OMC.[43] In the following session of the Commission for Social Development, in 2006, the central topic was the eradication of poverty, and the importance of the implementation of the African Peer Review mechanism to advance in the social dimensions of the New Partnership for Africa's Development was emphasised.[44]

There are other examples of the action undertaken by the European Union at multilateral level, which could be associated with its effort to project its social agenda externally. Its discourse is articulated in various multilateral frameworks. For instance, the EU is engaged in the promotion of social cohesion in Latin-American countries in co-operation with other international organisations. Mention could be made of the Summit on Social Cohesion in Latin-American countries held in Washington in May 2005, in which the European Commission participated along with the IMF, the World Bank and the Inter-American Development Bank (IDB).[45] At this Summit, the parties

social model?" in: Joerges, Eriksen and Rödl (eds) *Law and Democracy in the Post-national Union.* 1/2006 ARENA Report 233. In the same volume, see F. Rödl, "Constitutional integration of labour Constitutions", p. 289.

41 See the reference to the OMC in the Commissioner Spidla's Statement to the Comission on Social Development at the United Nations, 2005. The open method of coordination has been adopted by the CSD as a working method, see: CSD 48 session (3–12 February 2010), E/CN.5/2010/4, p. 9.

42 On the incorporation of the social domain into the Multilateral Agenda on Development, see Kerry Rittich, "The future of Law and development: second generation reforms and the incorporation of the social", (2004) 26 *Mich. J. Int'l L.*, p. 199.

43 For example, with regard to the review of the implementation of the Copenhagen Declaration, it is stated that "the Commission should emphasise increased exchange of national, regional and international experiences, focused and interactive dialogues among experts and practitioners, and sharing of best practices and lessons learned" Page 7 of the Report: Draft Resolution III: Future Organisation and methods of work of the Commission for Social Development, paragraph 4. Similar reference can be found at paragraph 32 of Draft Resolution III on promoting social integration, 2010 Session, E/2010/26; E/CN.5/2010/9.

44 E/2006/26; E/CN.5/2006/6, at 7, para 5. Available at: http://daccessdds.un.org/doc/UNDOC/GEN/N06/288/49/PDF/N0628849.pdf?OpenElement.

45 Just after this Summit, the IDB delivered its Report on "the Millennium Development Goals in Latin American and the Caribbean: progress and priorities and IDB Support for its implementation", August 2005. From 2002, the European Commission and the IDB are linked through a Memorandum of Understanding addressed to the development of common initiatives within which social cohesion is given the highest priority (www.europa.eu.int/comm/external_relations/la/doc/memo05_02.htm) The

decided to set up a joint technical working group with a view to exchanging experiences in social cohesion.

The social dimension is one of the three pillars of sustainable development,[46] which embraces concerns about employment, as well as social and environmental policies. With regard to employment, the EU underscores the need to promote decent work for all in line with the International Labour Organisation (ILO). Other over-riding concerns in this regard include the provision of support for fair trade and encouraging European companies to adhere to the principles of corporate social responsibility.

With all this multilateral action in sight, it might be contended that, rather than a "European social agenda", what we actually have is the European Union "importing" the social multilateral agenda. But even if this holds true, the important point is that, once this multilateral agenda has been properly internalised at European level, it is also externally promoted by the European Union. In a way, the European experience in this field is an excellent illustration of the already highlighted ability of the EU to propel the multilateral agenda.

The external dimension of the social agenda is also implemented within the relationship between the European Union and third countries (at either bilateral or inter-regional level).

As an illustration of the relevance granted to the promotion of social standards, attention could be brought to the Cotonou Agreement, particularly Article 1 and Article 9.[47] In the democratic clause enshrined in this Agreement, the social rights are considered to be an essential element of it. The Agreements concluded by the European Community and its Member States with Latin-American countries also include democratic clauses of the kind. If we look at the last of the Association Agreements concluded with Latin-American countries – the Agreement with Chile[48] – we can see that "social development" is conceived of as a "guiding principle" for the implementation of the Agreement.

In addition to the bilateral agreements, the EU also contributes to promoting the implementation of social rights through unilateral tools such as the Generalised System of Preferences Scheme (GSP). Under this new scheme which has been fully applied since

"shared priorities for collaboration" are: the consolidation of democracy on human rights issues, social equality and poverty reduction, regional integration and development of information technologies and shared knowledge society.

46 COM (2005) 311 final. "An European Consensus on development policy."

47 In the last revision (2010) of the Agreement, a reference to the Millenium Development Goals has been included in the first paragraph of Article 1: http://ec.europa.eu/development/icenter/repository/second_revision_cotonou_agreement_20100311.pdf.

48 The text of the Agreement can be found at: http://europa.eu.int/comm/trade/issues/bilateral/countries/chile/euchlagr_en.htm.

2006, within the framework of the so-called GSP Plus, enhanced preferences are granted to the countries that have ratified and implemented the core ILO and UN Conventions on human rights and labour rights listed in part A of Annex III.[49] Furthermore, a "negative conditionality" mechanism is set up in Article 16 of the Regulation, under the heading "temporary withdrawal". This withdrawal may be decided by the European Community as a response to serious and systematic violations of the principles laid down in the Conventions listed in Part A of Annex III by one of the GSP beneficiaries, which, as stated above, comprises the main human rights and labour rights of the UN and ILO Conventions. To date, the negative conditionality has only been applied in a very few cases, such as Burma/Myanmar (1997) or Belarus (2006).[50]

4.2 *Examples of the Influence of the European Union: the Latin-American Case*

The concern with social cohesion is present in the relationship between Europe and Latin-America from the 1990s, at least; although it is primarily since the beginning of the new millennium that this concern has been prioritised in the inter-regional agenda, first by Commissioner Patten,[51] and then by his successor, Benita Ferrero. Fighting social inequalities in order to bring about a more inclusive society with more equal opportunities for all is conceived of as a first priority within the region with the highest average level of inequality in the world.[52] Despite the political progress achieved in Latin American on its way towards democratisation, it is acknowledged that this progress had not been translated into a substantial improvement in living conditions.

Latin-America has also a long record with regard to regional integration. Over the years, the regional integration processes there have evolved into "new regionalism" incarnations. Thus, it could be held that the conditions for the creation and implementation of mechanisms expressing regional solidarity already exist.

49 See Council Regulation n. 980/2005.

50 Yaraslau Kryvoi, "Why European Union trade sanctions do not work?", 4/2007 *Harvard European Law Working Paper*, available at: http://papers.ssrn.com/sol3/papers.cfm?abstract_id=1007387.

51 See, for instance, this speech by Patten in 2002: www.europa.eu.int/comm/external_relations/news/patten/sp02_447.htm or this intervention at the Rio Group ministerial meeting in 2003: www.europa.eu.int/comm/external_relations/news/patten/sp03_160.htm.

52 Inter-American Development Bank. "Social cohesion in Latin America and the Caribbean: analysis, action and co-ordination": "Latin America is the most unequal region in the world. There are vast inequalities in the distribution of income, assets, and services, including education and access to credit. These are detrimental to the development prospects of the region. While the average Gini coefficient for Latin America is 0.51, that of Eastern Europe is 0.29, and the Gini coefficients corresponding to developed countries, Southeast Asia, and Africa are 0.33, 0.37, and 0.46, respectively (see next section). Inequalities are exacerbated by the exclusion of certain population groups that are targets of discrimination on the basis of ethnicity or race, gender, physical disability, and/or age, or because of their geographic isolation.
Therefore, in order to attain the social cohesion necessary for sustainable development, the region needs to overcome major challenges related to inequality." Document available at: www.iadb.org.

Before going into the analysis of some cases in order to illustrate the Latin-American experience, I want to refer generally to the emphasis placed by the EU on the need to go further in the attainment of social cohesion in Latin-America. Social (regional) cohesion was one of the pivotal ideas in the Guadalajara EU/LAC Summit (2004[53]) and of the primary issues tackled in the Vienna Summit (May, 2006),[54] In Vienna, the decision was taken to organise Social Cohesion Fora on a periodical basis with a view to fostering the dialogue and co-operation between the two regions on equality, the fight against poverty and social inclusion. The first Forum was held on 23–25 September 2007 in Santiago de Chile. The thrust of this meeting was the need to co-ordinate social and economic policies. Solidarity is proclaimed anew as the guiding principle for health care and social security policies.[55] The exchange of experience, know-how and good practices is presented as a key element of the co-operation between the two regions in this field. It is of interest to highlight that both parties agree that the European Union has a record of successful experience in reducing disparities, not only economic and social, but also territorial. In 2006, the Third European-Latin American/Caribbean social civil forum was held prior to the Vienna Summit,[56] and it was remarkable to see that, within this framework, the inconsistencies of the European Union were clearly denounced by its Latin-American counterparts.

Let us move on now to explore some of the Andean Community's (AC) most recent experiences in this regard. Within this region, there is a regional mechanism whose functioning resembles the European open method of co-ordination. It is the so-called Integral Plan for Social Development[57] set up by Decision 611 of the Andean Community Foreign Affairs Council.[58] The proclaimed goals under this plan replicate the Millennium Development Goals exactly: employment, the reduction of poverty, and social integration. The scopes upon which the Andean countries agreed might be considered to be excessively general. As a matter of fact, it is hard to see what is the added value associated with acting at regional level if the countries within the region are unable to reach a more tailored definition of their goals. The designation of the common objectives should have been further adapted to the particular situation of the Andean region. In other words, greater effort should be required from the Andean

53 Http://europa.eu.int/comm/world/lac-guadal/00_index.htm See, also, COM (2004) 220 final where the Commission's goals are defined.

54 Http://europa.eu.int/comm/world/lac-vienna/.

55 The Conclusions of Chile Forum: http://ec.europa.eu/external_relations/la/doc/07_conclusions_en.pdf.

56 Http://ec.europa.eu/world/lac/events/civil_society/declaration_en.pdf. It is a dialogue organised by the Commission and is open to the participation of non-governmental organisations, trade unions, universities, employers' associations, consumers' organisations, and other representatives of civil society.

57 The final Declaration drawn up with occasion of the last Summit EU/Andean Community, held in Luxembourg in May 2005, acknowledged that this Plan is a useful tool for fostering social cohesion within the region: http://europa.eu.int/comm/external_relations/andean/doc/lux_ministerial.pdf, at p. 3.

58 Www.comunidadandina.org/normativa/dec/D601.htm.

countries with a view to agreeing on more specific goals. The working method laid out in the AC's Integral Plan resembles the EU's OMC. The European Commission had already underscored the feasibility of using the open method of co-ordination within the Latin American context.[59]

Within the framework of the Andean Community's Plan, three courses of action were established: 1) technical co-operation on social policy, including the exchange of good practices; 2) regional monitoring of the implementation of the Millennium Development Goals; and, 3) the implementation of individual projects selected at regional level (the projects may involve one or more countries within the region). Thus, the presence of the three basic components of the OMC can be easily traced: the common definition of goals, peer review, and the mutual exchange of practices conducive to mutual learning.

On the other hand, and with a view to providing some remedy to the inequalities between countries and regions within the Andean area, the possibility of creating a "financial instrument destined to fund some social cohesion programmes and projects" was also debated. This proposal was launched upon the basis of the Quirama Declaration issued within the framework of the XIV Andean Presidential Council Summit (2003), which called for the creation of new financing mechanisms specifically addressed to the entrenchment of democratic governance as well as to fighting poverty.[60] This project is similar to the European Cohesion Funds.

In Mercosur, and more in line with the idea of inter-territorial solidarity, a Convergence Structural Fund has already been created.

> Mercosur has just agreed to set up a Convergence Structural Fund (FOCEM) to promote structural adjustment between Mercosur members, focusing on the poorest territories and citizens. The fund will support added-value generating projects in the fields of infrastructure,

59 In this vein, reference might be made to the 2004 Communication on the goals in the relationship with Latin-America within which the improvements in social cohesion are defined as an over-riding priority, and where, with regard to to the application of the OMC in particular, the Commission declared: "In deciding how to develop a European perspective on issues of poverty and social exclusion, the Lisbon European Council chose to draw on the experience of the European strategy for employment which has been in place since 1997. It thus adopted what is known as an Open Method of Co-ordination. This method allows for dialogue, exchange of experience, the establishment of common objectives and evaluation of policies in areas relevant for fighting exclusion. The Commission encourages the countries of Latin America to launch a regional process which will create a new dynamic for dialogue and exchanges between countries of the region, allowing them to learn from each other's successes and failures. If the countries of Latin-America were to decide to establish such a mechanism, the Commission would be willing to provide and finance technical support. In this context it is also worth noting the importance of social dialogue." COM (2004) 220 final: www.europa.eu.int/comm/world/lac-guadal/docs/com2004_220_en.pdf.

60 See: Secretaria General, Comunidad Andina: SG/SM.ECSFSA/INFORME 26 September 2005: Seminario Subregional andino "Hacia una estrategia comunitaria de cohesión social y la constitución de un Fondo Social andino".

productive investment, fight against poverty and employment promotion and finally capacity building of the Mercosur administrations.[61]

This Fund was set up by the Decision Consejo Mercado Común N° 45/04. Subsequently, the Decision 18/05 set forth a Social Cohesion Programme[62] along with another three Programmes (Convergence Structural, Enhanced competitiveness, and the strengthening of the institutional structure and the integration process) to be implemented within the framework of the Fund. The funds come from the states, with Brazil bearing the lion's share of the cost (70%).[63]

It is not my intention to affirm here that, with these developments, Mercosur as well as the Andean Community are consciously following the European path, but this path is there, presented as an unprecedented successful formula,[64] so the European influence is, to some extent, unavoidable.[65]

It should be noticed that the open method of co-ordination has been subject to heavy criticism in Europe, but when this formula was applied within Latin-America, it looked like a remarkable achievement. It is true that it could also be said that it is the European Union that is adopting a practice (OMC) that seems better suited for multilateral *fora* than for a supranational body. Nevertheless, from my point of view, the fact that the European Union is directly involved in the mutual learning process, considering its successful experience concerning the implementation of the solidarity principle, is good in itself.

61 Background paper. High Level Conference: promoting social cohesion: the European Union – Latin-America and Caribbean experiences. Brussels 27–28 March 2006, p. 11: http://europa.eu.int/comm/world/lac-vienna/events/idb_ec_background_230306.pdf.

62 "Los proyectos del Programa III deberán contribuir al desarrollo social, en particular, en las zonas de frontera, y podrán incluir proyectos de interés comunitario en áreas de la salud humana, la reducción de la pobreza y el desempleo." www.mrree.gub.uy/Mercosur/ConsejoMercadoComun/Reunion28/AnexoII/DEC18-05.htm.

63 Argentina bears 27%; Uruguay (2%); Paraguay (1%). The total amount is $ 100 million. It is very interesting to see that the regulation of the distribution of the funds is reflective of the concept of regional solidarity, with 80% of the funds bound to Paraguay and Uruguay, whereas only 20% of the funds to be devoted to projects submitted by either Brazil or Argentina. After the inception of this Fund, it has been contended that a "new Mercosur" is born: A.E. Monsanto, *El Nuevo MERCOSUR: Fondos estructurales, sociedad civil y desarrollo juridico-institucional*: www.unr.edu.ar/internacional/catedra-andres-bello/downloads/elnuevomercosur.pdf.

64 For instance, within the Report issued in 2004 by the ILO World Commission on the social dimension of globalisation, the role of the Eureopean Union in promoting the social model is acknowledged www.ilo.org/public/english/wcsdg/docs/report.pdf, paragraphs 313–334.

65 For a critical account, see W. Matiaske, H. Brunkhorst, G. Grözinger, M. Neves (eds.), *The European Union as a Model for the Development of Mercosur?* (Augsburg: Hampp, 2007).

5. The Problems of the European Union to Stick to its Civilian Power Paradigm

The European Union is probably the international actor that together with United Nations, has contributed the most to disseminate the human rights "culture", and, consequently, to propel the idea of human rights as an essential component of a possible international Constitution. In this way, it is contributing to shape a "substantial" conception of such a Constitution. As underlined in the preliminary remarks, the European Union is in a perfect position to propel the good evolution of the international legal order, by contributing to the delineation of both the contours and the content of the slippery notion of *ius cogens*. However, this is not an easy task, and sometimes the European Union shows a rather hesitant face. In fact, we will see how, even within the realm of human rights protection, the European inconsistency emerges.[66]

In fact, it might be that the European institutions are not fully aware of the extraordinary influential role that the European Union may play in this regard.[67] At this point, mention can be made of the Court of First Instance (CFI) jurisprudence on the EU's implementation of United Nations Security Council Resolutions imposing sanctions on individuals, who are held responsible for being associated with Bin Laden or Al Qaida.[68] Although an in-depth examination of these judgments is beyond the scope of this contribution, I cannot avoid offering some general remarks about them. In this jurisprudence, it was recognised that international organisations are intrinsically bound to abide by *ius cogens*, according to Article 53 of the Vienna Convention on the Law of Treaties. Nevertheless, in spite of the relevance of the recognition of this "constitutive" submission to *ius cogens*, the CFI's pronouncements were disappointing, for the Court developed a restrictive approach to human rights protection, opting for an interpretation of international law in which the interest in security prevails over the interest to protect the fundamental rights of the individuals adequately. The CFI did not acknowledge the unprecedented development of the international law on human rights that has taken place in Europe, a reference that might have driven it to examine the possible existence of a European (regional) *ius cogens* within this particular field. Instead, what we found was the recognition of the primacy of the United Nations Charter, and consequently of the Security Council resolutions, over EC law, according to the same parameters upon which the primacy of EC law over domestic law is articulated.[69] The result is a rather

[66] A. Cebada Romero, "La cláusula democracia/derechos humanos como instrumento de condicionalidad en las relaciones exteriores de la CE" in: *XIX Jornadas de la AEPDIRI* (Madrid, BOE; Universidad de Cantabria; AEPDIRI, 2003), pp. 86–105.

[67] CFI, Judgments 21 September 2005, T-315/01 and T-306/01; Judgment 12 July 2006, T-253/02. On this jurisprudence, see I. Blázquez and C. Espósito, "Los límites al control judicial de las medidas de aplicación de la política exterior en los asuntos Ahmed Ali Yusuf/Al Barakaat International Foundation y Yassin Abdullah Kadi", (2006) 17 *Revista Española de Derecho Europeo*, p. 123.

[68] The reference to the CFI was appropriate at the moment in which the Workshop, where this paper was presented, was held (2007). As it is acknowledged below (see footnote 70) this CFI jurisprudence has fortunately been overcome by a decision of the European Court of Justice (ECJ).

[69] See, for example, Judgment 21 September 2005, T-315/01, p. 224.

simplistic construction, in which regard is not paid to the fact that the Court of First Instance, when it comes to the implementation of Security Council resolutions, is in the position that was occupied by the Constitutional Courts when the definition of the relationship between the national Constitutions and the European legal order came into play. Moreover, the European Court of First Instance did not take into account that it was precisely the Constitutional Court's reluctance to accept the primacy of EC law with regard to the national constitutional rules enshrining human rights protection, that pushed the European Court to accept a gradual opening of the European legal order to the values enshrined in the national Constitutions, giving rise to a process in which the humanisation of EC law was propelled forward. No consideration was given by the CFI to the fact that, in contrast to the existence of a judicial mechanism within the European realm, there is not any institutional mechanism charged with the task of monitoring the "legality" of the Security Council's action. Fortunately, the European Court of Justice, which had the last say,[70] delivered a decision reversing the CFI judgments, contributing in this way to propel still forward, instead of reversing, the process of the humanisation of international law.[71]

And, of course, talking about the incoherence which seriously hinders the implementation of the civilian power model, and, thus, undermines the EU's legitimacy, some of the areas that have to be mentioned include trade as well as immigration and asylum. In both fields, it is easy to trace further evidence of the inconsistencies of the European Union; the list would be long - undoubtedly - but I cannot go into any of them in depth here. With regard to the immigration policy, it could be advisable, for the sake of consistency, for the European Union to stay focused on designing integration policies based upon the idea of cultural diversity.[72] But what we are, instead, witnessing is how the European Union appears more focused on tightening border control (family re-union and asylum are clear examples[73]). The same European Union from which the neighbourhood policy comes out,[74] is also developing a rather restrictive approach

70 The cases have been brought before the ECJ in appeal: C-402/05; C-415/05.

71 After this chapter had been presented at the EUI Workshop, the ECJ delivered, on 3 September 2008, a judgment reversing the decision of the Court of First Instance: cases C-402/05 and 415/05. I analyzed this judgment in: Alicia Cebada Romero, La Unión Europea: ¿una acción exterior inteligente?, (Madrid: Iustel, 2008).

72 I am grateful to Professor Armin von Bogdandy for sharing with me his knowledge about the European Union approach to cultural diversity as well as for drawing my attention to the relevant role that the EU is playing with regard to the re-inforcement of cultural diversity as a principle within the international legal order.

73 A. Cebada Romero, "The coherence of the European Union as an International actor: facing the challenge of Immigration and Asylum" 7/06 *Jean Monnet Working Paper*, available at: www.jeanmonnetprogram.org/papers/index.html.

74 Roberto Aliboni,. "The geopolitical implications of the European neighbourhood policy", (2005) 10 *European Foreign Affairs Review*, p. 1; Raffaella Del Sarto and Tobias Schumacher, "From EMP to ENP: What's a stake with the European Neighbourhood Policy towards the Southern Mediterranean?", (2005) 10 *European Foreign Affairs Review*, p. 17.

towards the admission of individuals.[75] And, of course, it is not easy to keep a balance between these two courses of action.[76]

6. Concluding Remarks

With respect to the task of defining a model of external action, it would be essential for the European Union to maintain the civilian power paradigm. Should it be fully developed, the European Union would make a remarkable contribution to transnational justice. As already stated, the legitimacy of smart power depends on recognition, linked to reputation and authority, and this is something that may be only achieved by taking into account the interests of those whose recognition is needed. And, in the case of the European Union, recognition does not come exclusively from the constituent member states, but it also comes from its citizens and from third countries and their citizens. In this sense, there appear to be two distinct options available for the European Union:

Option one: It can continue to strive to persuade the rest of the world that the civilian power paradigm is plausible and viable, by fully implementing it. Should the European Union take this course of action, it would find some relief for the shortcomings inherited from the member states.

Option two: It can renounce this paradigm, blur its contours through continuous incoherence, and eventually switch to a more classic hegemonic paradigm. And, at this point, it is unnecessary to stress that, in my view, choosing this option would not only be imprudent ("unsmart"), but also detrimental for the European Union itself, as well as for the international community and its legal order.

75 Charlotte Bretherton and John Vogler, *The European Union as a Global Actor*, (New York: Routledge, 1999), p. 236. They talk about the "exclusionary dimension of self-identity determination".

76 Sara Dillon, "Looking for the progressive empire: Where is the European Union's Foreign Policy?", (2004) 19 *Connecticut Journal of International law*, p. 275.

John Erik Fossum

CHAPTER 5. ON "EUROPE'S AMERICAN DREAM"

1. Introduction

The last years have seen deep transatlantic rifts. But the presence of rifts should not deceive us into ignoring the great attraction that the United States has exerted, and continues to exert, on Europeans. There are deep ideational and historical bonds between Europeans and Americans; these are sustained and re-enforced through immigration and close contact, given direct social-institutional and even constitutional sustenance (consider America's central role in Europe's post-war reconstruction, and the transfer of the central features of its constitutional model to Germany). Ideational and emotional bonds are maintained by a wide range of direct transatlantic links. Europeans have not only been *influenced* by America, as a kind of external presence or force, but the American presence is also deeply embedded in the very way in which Europeans perceive themselves. To many Europeans, Americans are not "them", but "us" – a fact which is re-enforced by the commonalities embedded in the notion of "the West".[1]

Europeans even set the U.S. up as a mirror of themselves:

> Observation of the American social experiment has always been a cause of reflection and self-interpretation concerning European identity.[2]

* A previous version of this contribution has appeared under the title "Europe's 'American Dream'" in (2009) 12 *European Journal of Social Theory*, pp. 483–504.

1 "The idea of Europe during the greater part of the Twentieth century was subordinated to the notion of the West." (G. Delanty, *Inventing Europe – Idea, Identity, Reality*, (London: MacMillan, 1995), p.115.

2 See C. Offe, *Reflections on America – Tocqueville, Weber, and Adorno in the United States* (Cambridge MA: Polity Press, 2005), p. 4.

European scholars have discussed the potentials and pitfalls of "American exceptionalism",[3] and have discussed what is more probable and preferable: the Americanisation of Europe or the Europeanisation of America.[4]

Given this historical propensity for Europeans to discuss the U.S. as a possible model for Europe, it would only be logical that Europeans – now steeped in their greatest ever peaceful experiment in fashioning a continent-wide system of governance – were to look closely at how Americans first managed to establish a continent-wide system, and subsequently extend its influence to near-global proportions.

How prominently, then, does the U.S. figure as a model for the *European Union*? The U.S. certainly serves as a key comparative reference for students of the EU.[5] The U.S. may even be the most widely-cited *state* that people want the EU to emulate. Simply consider the frequent invocation of the notion of "United States of Europe".[6] Such pleas for emulation also appear quite unidirectional: there are few on either side of the Atlantic that urge the U.S. to emulate the EU.[7] Many of those who underline that there

3 See, especially, S.M. Lipset, *American Exceptionalism – A double-edged Sword*, (New York, Norton & Company, Inc., 1996), who describes the American creed in the following terms: liberty, egalitarianism, individualism, populism, and *laissez-faire*. The religious dimension is also stressed: "Tocqueville noted, and contemporary survey data document quantitatively, that the United States has been the most religious country in Christendom."(19).

4 See C. Offe, note 2 *supra*.

5 For a brief selection of contemporary sources, consider K. Nicolaidis and R. Howse, (eds), *The Federal Vision: Legitimacy and Levels of Governance in the United States and the European Union*, (Oxford: Oxford University Press, 2001); G. Majone, *Dilemmas of European Integration: The Ambiguities and Pitfalls of Integration by Stealth*, (Oxford: Oxford University Press, 2005); see, also, contributions to "Altneuland: The Constitution of Europe in an American Perspective", 28–30April 2004, at: www.jeanmonnetprogram.org/conference_JMC_Princeton/index.html.

6 The name United States of Europe is highly evocative: Jean Monnet, one of the founders of the EU, wrote: "Little by little the work of the Community will be felt… Then the everyday realities themselves will make it possible to form the political union which is the goal of our Community and to establish the United States of Europe… [T]he idea is clear: political Europe will be created by human effort, when the time comes, on the basis of reality…" Cited in M. Holland, "Jean Monnet and the federal functionalist approach to European Unity", in: P. Murray and P. Rich (eds), *Visions of European Unity*, (Boulder CA: Westview Press, 1996), p. 97.

7 The debate that Robert Kagan, "Power and Weakness", (2002) *Policy Review*, no. 113, *idem*, *Paradise and Power: America and Europe in the New World Order*, (New York: Knopf, 2003), sparked was set off precisely to underline the differences between the EU and the U.S. The many analysts that see the EU as a kind of international organisation (see A. Moravcsik, *The Choice for Europe*, (London: University College Press, 1998), and A.S. Milward, *The European Rescue of the Nation State*, (London: Routledge, 1992), transnational entity, and the non-state system of multilevel governance, explicitly or implicitly stress the differences between the EU and the U.S. Exceptions include J. Rifkin's *The European Dream*, (Cambridge MA: Polity Press, 2004), in which he argues that Americans should look to the EU for a better future, and Manners' conception of "normative power Europe" (see I. Manners, "Normative European Power – A Contradiction in Terms?", in (2002) 13 *Journal of Common Market Studies*, pp. 235–58, *idem*, "Normative power Europe reconsidered: beyond the crossroads", (2006) 13 *Journal of European Public Policy*, pp. 182–199) which is also, to some extent, a plea for others/the U.S. to emulate the EU.

is a deep gap between the EU and the U.S. insist that the gap can best be bridged by the EU becoming similar to the U.S.[8]

The European Union is often thought of as an *experiment* – both in governance and in polity terms. Europe, once the cradle of the Westphalian state system, is today held up as the place where the nation-state as an organisational form and mode of community is experiencing its greatest transformation.[9] The EU re-ignites and gives added weight to the question of the normative viability and empirical salience of the Westphalian state system as the key which structures the legal-political meta-frame. This system has framed our thinking on political organisation and mode of community for centuries.[10] Through the core concepts, the normative principles and the attendant institutional-constitutional arrangements, this system has offered a ready-made set of interpretations, conceptions of appropriate organisational arrangements, and systems of meaning in order to make sense of, and structure, a complex and dynamic political reality. As the most powerful state today, the U.S. serves not only as the embodiment of the core traits of this meta-frame,[11] but, through situational definitions and actions, it also sustains this frame.[12] The issue is, therefore, whether the EU will conform to this frame, or whether the EU might become a – stable and normatively viable – alternative to it.

The purpose of this article is threefold. First, I seek to uncover the normative assumptions that underpin the U.S. as an exemplar for the EU, as seen *from a European perspective*. This is not intended as an assessment of the U.S. What I am doing is to try to (re)construct a credible European viewpoint. For the reconstruction to be considered credible, it must be rooted in a coherently articulated European viewpoint, or, barring that, a European discourse. With the complexity of Europe in mind, it must be conceded that it is not likely to offer anything that remotely resembles a complete representation of the European position(s).

8 See R. Kagan, "Power and Weakness", (2002) *Policy Review*, no 113, available at: www.policyreview.org/jun02/.

9 Note that by transformation is meant the change into some other form of political entity, as distinct from the withering-away of distinctive political forms which some hyper-globalists claim is taking place.

10 With the modern European nation-state emerged a vocabulary and a set of normative principles that greatly contributed to its sustenance and legitimacy (See M. Oakeshott, "The vocabulary of the modern European State", (1975) 2 *Political Studies*, pp. 319–341, *ibid.*, 4 *Political Studies*, pp. 409–415, and A. Linklater, *The Transformation of Political Community*, (Cambridge MA: Polity Press, 1998), p. 29) This vocabulary glossed over logical contradictions and ambiguities – terms such as nation "which purport to disclose conditions of association but which specify no mode of association". (See Oakeshott, note 10 *supra*, at 338).

11 This goes beyond the debate on American exceptionalism. S.M. Lipset, note 3 *supra*, one of the foremost proponents of American exceptionalism, speaks of the distinctive traits of the U.S. *as a state*. His argument does not touch upon the state at the level of an organising meta-frame.

12 Consider how the U.S. frames its onslaught on terror in statist terms: as a war on terror; terror as propounded by states (the axis of evil); and as upheld by state-based regimes in Afghanistan and Iraq.

The reconstruction avails itself of *constitutive frames*.[13] Key to this is the notion of *polity model*, which refers to how a set of principles is reflected in a given institutional-constitutional form. It seeks to offer a guide to how normative principles have been imagined to inform institutional and political reality within a given political setting. It consists of four elements: constitutive principles; core values; a set of institutional arrangements; and a view on their capability or ability to persist over time. Europeans should, accordingly, find the U.S. an attractive polity model.[14] My starting assumption is that Europeans have, historically speaking, come to associate the U.S. with a set of important normative principles (such as individual autonomy), with a set of basic values (such as democracy), with a set of attractive institutional-constitutional features, and with successful performance (relevant factors could be economic efficiency, affluence, politico-military global presence, *etc.*).

Second, I briefly consider whether the traits that Europeans find attractive about the U.S. as a polity model have much real bearing on the EU, not in terms of how Europeans would want the EU to be, but in terms of how the EU presently *is*. The aim is to obtain a sense of the *empirical* distance that Europeans would have to travel if they were to transpose what they find attractive about the U.S. to the EU. Are the features which Europeans hold to be attractive about the U.S. also available in Europe? Or do they make it clear how different the two entities actually are? To clarify this, I consider how the EU fits in with the dimensions that were singled out for the U.S. I also discuss whether the traits that characterise the EU sum up to anything resembling a coherent EU polity model.

These two undertakings set the stage for the third, and most original, endeavour, which is to consider whether there are entities that are more compatible with what we currently find in Europe. The case that I have singled out is *another American* state, namely, Canada. A clarification and critical assessment of what I refer to here as "Europe's American Dream" is intended to serve as a kind of mirror for Europeans to clarify whether the European project is (a) one of emulating the U.S.; (b) a unique experiment; or (c) an EU that is closer to Canada than to the U.S.? If the reality of Canada is more proximate to the reality of the EU, should, then, Canada serve as "Europe's American Dream", instead?

2. The "Dream"

The U.S. played a central role in the forging of the EU. It has also offloaded the EU through the security guarantee within the NATO framework. European policy-making

13 See E. Goffman, *Frame Analysis: An Essay on the Organization of Experience* (Cambridge MA: Harvard University Press, 1974) initially developed the notion of frame analysis, which spurned a comprehensive body of literature. I here draw foremost from M. Rein and D. Schön, "Reframing Policy Discourse", in: F. Fisher and J. Forrester (eds), *The Argumentative Turn in Policy Analysis* (Durham NC: Duke University Press, 1993), pp. 145–66.

14 Consider Tocqueville's presentation of American democracy as an ideal for Europe to emulate.

has also drawn heavily on the U.S.[15] Thus, there are important empirical grounds for students of the EU to direct their attention to the U.S. This is, if anything, amplified by the dominant role American scholars played in analysing, and thus also affecting, European integration.[16] All these and numerous other factors relate to what amounts to a particularly strong contemporary European exposure to, familiarity with, and influence by America and Americans – in standards, in ideas and in experiences.

Nevertheless, despite this strong *exposure*, it is not indisputable that Europeans should draw on the U.S. as the model for the EU's own development. The EU, after all, has its roots in an international organisation and is formed on top of states, each of which has sought to emulate the U.S. in one way or the other, while, in contrast, the EU itself does not share many institutional or other traits with the U.S.[17] The EU is neither a state, nor is it a nation; hence, any "natural" propensity on the part of Europeans to draw on the U.S. needs further explanation.

I have singled out three features of the U.S. that I believe to appeal to Europeans. These mutually appear to re-enforce one another to form a coherent polity model:

2.1. A New Beginning: The U.S as Polity Model

2.1.1. Brief Description of the Phenomenon

The U.S. as an independent state was born through revolution. This was a revolution in a political, as well as in a constitutional, sense. The revolutionary beginning of the U.S. has left an indelible mark on it.[18] Politically, through the revolution, it sought to free itself from oppressive British rule and colonialism. The founding of the U.S. thus entailed the act of severing the link to its European origin: to be free and independent, Americans had to rid themselves of the shackles of their oppressive European past. This was done through two steps: emigration and the Declaration of Independence – and revolutionary

15 During the 1980s and 1990s, for instance, the U.S. became a model for Europeans bent on down-sizing the state, through New Public Management and numerous other reforms which also fed into the European integration process (consider for instance the Single European Act (SEA), 1986).

16 Consider the central role of the founding generation of Europeanists such as Ernst Haas, Karl Deutsch, Stanley Hoffmann, Leon Lindberg, and, last, but not least, Eric Stein, who invited Europeans to the U.S. and trained them in European law. More recent scholars include Andrew Moravcsik, Alberta Sbragia and Jeff Checkel – together with "Americanised Europeans" or Europeans with legs in both the American and the European scholarly community, such as Phillippe Schmitter and Joseph Weiler.

17 This is certainly the case in macroscopic terms; but varies at the level of specific institutions and policy options. Majone, for instance (1996), shows the relevance of the so-called American-style regulation also for the EU.

18 See S.M. Lipset, *The First New Nation* (New York: Norton & Company, Inc., 1979), idem, *Continental Divide – The Values and Institutions of the United States and Canada* (New York: Routledge, 1990), idem, *American Exceptionalism – A double-edged Sword* (New York: Norton & Company, Inc., 1996), and A. Stephanson, *Manifest Destiny, American Expansion and the Empire of Right* (New York: Hill and Wang, 1995).

war. This revolutionary beginning has become an intrinsic part of the U.S. founding *rationale*. The American Revolution was justified by universal principles – and many of those very same normative ideals subsequently came to inform the French Revolution.

The American Revolution also heralded in a new revolutionary constitutional tradition.[19] The constitution founded a new political order, and thus instituted a rupture or a break with the past.

> With this, constitution becomes an *exclusive* concept: it is striking that certain forms of order are now no longer labeled as faulty or wrong constitutions; rather, their claim to be constitutions at all is denied.[20]

The American constitution thus helped to establish a set of benchmarks for what counts as a constitution in the first place. The critical component here was not its formal and written character; instead, what was critical was the focus on individual freedom, which underpinned its democratic character.

The new political system was equipped with an institutional structure that entrenched democracy and thus differed from its contemporaries. America re-invented federalism, in such a way as to turn statism on its head. Whereas Bodinian statism pre-supposed "a single sovereign in a highly centralized state striving for homogeneity and self-sufficiency … American federalism, by contrast vested sovereignty in the people to prevent the development of a centralized, reified state by making all governments no more than governments of delegated powers whose scope the people could define and change as they pleased through a constitutional system".[21] This political system permitted the forging of a new nation: one based upon the embracing of democratic egalitarianism, achievement, and the explicit abolition of European status hierarchies.[22] Over time, what was forged was a new kind of, and sense of, community: the inclusive nation, or the "melting-pot".

19 See B. Ackerman, *We the People: Foundations*, (Cambridge MA: The Bellknap Press of Harvard University Press, 1991), C. Möllers, "The Politics of Law and the Law of Politics: Two Constitutional Traditions in Europe", in: E.O. Eriksen, J.E. Fossum and A.J. Menéndez (eds), *Developing a Constitution for Europe*, (London: Routledge, 2004), pp. 129–139, and H. Brunkhorst, "A Policy without a State? European Constitutionalism between Evolution and Revolution", in: *ibid.*, pp. 88–105.

20 See C. Möllers, note 19 *supra*, p. 130.

21 See D.J. Elazar, "The United States and the European Union: Models for their Epochs", in: K. Nicolaidis and R. Howse (eds), *The Federal Vision: Legitimacy and Levels of Governance in the United States and the European Union*, (Oxford: Oxford University Press, 2001), pp. 31–53.

22 S.M. Lipset, (1979) note 18 *supra*, labels the U.S. as the first new nation, because it was the first colony that successfully revolted against colonial rule.

2.1.2. Justification for Why Europeans Would See This as Relevant to the EU

The revolutionary democratic beginning of the U.S. attracts Europeans. The American Revolution was not only seen as a rejection of the oppressive and destructive aspects of the European past, the commitment to democracy also promised to herald in a new and unique opportunity. Tocqueville's project was to draw lessons for Europe from the American idea of, and experience with, democratic equality. His aim was *precisely* to probe the notion of the U.S. as a democratic polity model:

> I admit that I saw in America more than America; it was the shape of democracy itself which I sought, its inclinations, character, prejudices and passions...[23]

The European integration process entices Europeans to invoke the same spirit of breaking with the shackles of *their* European past, which is one of aggressive nationalism in a Europe divided into distinctive national entities. There are some clear parallels here between Europe and the U.S. that feed this attractiveness. First, the forgers of the EU could argue that it represented a rejection of Europe's war-prone past, a past which was extremely destructive, oppressive and divisive, precisely because Europe's past was based upon national sovereignty and not federalism.[24] Second, they could use the EU to embark on a new future of all-European democracy. Third, they could join the Americans in justifying their actions in those very same universal values that had been used to justify the American (and French) Revolutions.[25] For these and other reasons, the initial movers and shakers of European integration sought to replicate American federalism in Europe through a United States of Europe, a European federation following the American model.[26]

Many saw the recent process of constitution-making in Europe as a new chance to re-launch the EU on a course more similar to that of the U.S. The very use of the term Convention evoked images of the Philadelphia Convention, and explicit parallels were drawn between the two, even by the Convention Chair, Valery Giscard d'Estaing.[27]

From a polity model perspective, the U.S. was a pioneer, in that it appealed to universal principles and was the first to entrench such principles in explicit constitutional form.

23 A. de Tocqueville, *Democracy in America*, 2 Vols, (New York: Harper & Row Publishers, 1969), p 19.

24 Consider Ernesto Rossi and Altieri Spinelli "The Ventotene Manifesto", August 1941; Jean Monnet, "Algiers Memorandum", August 1943. Collected in: T. Salmon and W. Nicoll, *Building European Union – A documentary history and analysis*, (Manchester, Manchester University Press, 1997).

25 The Laeken Declaration explicitly addresses these three dimensions.

26 See D.J. Elazar, note 21 *supra*, p. 36. As early as in 1923, Coudenhove-Kalergi, in his "Pan-Europe", said that: "The crowning act of pan-European efforts would be the constitution of the United States of Europe on the model of the United States of America."(cited in Salmon and Nicoll, note 24 *supra*, p. 9).

27 In the context of the European Convention, its chair, Valery Giscard d'Estaing even proposed the United States of Europe as one possible name for the new entity.

There is thus a great attraction in linking up to this aspect of the American experience. Given the strong normative-conceptual status of the American constitution, that is, as a benchmark for what counts as a democratic constitution, evoking this standard can lend great credence and legitimacy to the European undertaking.

As is even acknowledged by sceptics, there appears to be a kind of inevitability here, which can be summed up as follows: in a modern democratic context, once you embark on the constitutional exercise, to establish a formal, democratic constitution, you are almost compelled by nature to go down the American path. Is there really a viable alternative or alternative way to go than precisely that of the U.S.?

2.2. The "City on the Hill"

2.2.1. Description of the Phenomenon

This notion relates to the American propensity – from the very outset – to portray itself as *exceptional* from a moral point of view. There are two dimensions to American exceptionalism, which are particularly relevant here. The first is the puritan roots which go back especially to English Protestantism; he puritans who went to America broke with English Protestantism because they found it to be deficient – infected by Catholicism. To them, America offered the prospect of a new beginning.[28] It was the special responsibility that accompanied this that John Winthrop expressed in his famous sermon, the *Arbella Covenant* (1630), in which he said that "[...] for we must consider that we shall be as a city upon a hill, the eyes of all people are upon us [...]".[29] This was later interpreted as instantiating the notion of *Manifest Destiny.* The U.S. was to carry on God's mission and set a shining example for the rest of the world. This puritan theme has resonated throughout American history.[30]

Second, American exceptionalism represents a particular fusion between Puritanism and Nationalism (which is such a central concept to Europe).[31]

> Visions of the United States as a sacred space providentially selected for divine purposes found a counterpart in the secular idea of the new nation of liberty as a privileged 'stage' ... for

28 See A. Stephanson, note 18 *supra.*

29 Www.csustan.edu/english/reuben/pal/append/axt.html.

30 "Of course, it was Ronald Reagan who perhaps most often and most dramatically cited Winthrop in his political career. Throughout his campaigns and his presidency, Reagan loved to talk about 'the shining city on the hill'." In his farewell address to the nation at the 1992 Republican Convention, Reagan said, "The phrase comes from John Winthrop, who wrote it to describe the America he imagined...In my mind, it was a tall, proud city, built on rocks stronger than oceans, windswept, God-blessed...That's how I saw it, and see it still." Paul S. Sawyer, "The City on the Hill", 8 August 2004, www.firstparish.org/sermons/2004-08-08.html.

31 "The Puritan break would then eventually serve to invest American nationality with a 'symbology' of exceptionalism or separateness that has survived remarkably intact." (Stephanson, note 18 *supra*, p. 4).

> the exhibition of a new world order, a great 'experiment' for the benefit of humankind as a whole.[32]

Richard Hofstadter has noted that: "It has been our fate as a nation not to have ideologies, but to be one."[33] Lipset also refers to Abraham Lincoln, who spoke of his country's political religion. In that sense, to become an American is "a religious, that is, ideological act".[34]

Americans have come to see themselves as chosen for greater tasks, not only domestically, but also internationally – to propound the central principles of their political system to the rest of the world, in the service of God. To many Americans, the image of the US as "*The City on the Hill*" was one that should also inform U.S. foreign policy and the role of the U.S. throughout the world. The U.S. had a special *obligation* to ensure democracy and human rights worldwide. This is the hallmark of the Wilsonian school of American foreign policy.[35] But even Wilson's civilisational project had a strong religious tenor, as, for him, Christianity was a vital component of civilisation.

2.2.2. Justification for Why Europeans Would See This as Relevant to the EU

For integration-friendly Europeans, to inject a spirit similar to the U.S. notion of the "*City on the Hill*" and *Manifest Destiny* into the European Union, would rectify one of the European Union's main deficiencies, its lack of a clear *telos*.[36] A European Union imbued with a sense of *Manifest Destiny* would lend a sense of inspiration and direction, as well as a deeper justification for the entire integration project. It could, then, also help to restore the centuries-old image of Europe as the centre of the world and as its source of modern civilisation.[37] Such a vision of Europe's past was apparent in the preamble of the defunct Constitutional Treaty which stated that:

> DRAWING INSPIRATION from the cultural, religious and humanist inheritance of Europe, have developed the universal values of the inviolable and inalienable rights of the human person, freedom, democracy, equality and the rule of law[...] [original capitals]

32 See A. Stephanson, note 18 *supra*, p. 5.

33 Cited in Lipset, note 3 *supra*, p. 18.

34 Ibid.

35 See W.R. Mead, *Special Providence – American Foreign Policy and How it Changed the World* (London: Routledge, 2002).

36 See J.H.H. Weiler, *The Constitution of Europe: "Do the new clothes have an Emperor?" and other essays on European Integration*, (Cambridge: Cambridge University Press, 1999), and, *idem*, "Federalism without Constitutionalism: Europe's *Sonderweg*", in: K. Nicolaidis and R. Howse, (eds), *The Federal Vision: Legitimacy and Levels of Governance in the United States and the European Union*, (Oxford: Oxford University Press, 2001).

37 For Europe as the cradle of civilisation, see G. Delanty, *Inventing Europe – Idea, Identity, Reality* (London: MacMillan, 1995).

If we take the notion that these values emerged in Europe literally, then the U.S. notion of *Manifest Destiny* represents an appropriation of these values by the U.S. to serve its own aims (a notion that would be greatly amplified through American unilateralism). Only by instilling a similar sense of purpose would Europe then be able to regain possession of its rightful moral leadership. Thus, there are reasons pertaining to both the European Union's internal and external dimension that could entice Europeans to *Manifest Destiny*. The internal dimension addresses a common purpose and justification for the still highly-contested integration project; the external dimension addresses Europe's restoration of its centuries-long and – it is widely held, "rightful" role as the centre of the world.[38] But in order to do so, it would also require the necessary means; those that the U.S. might possess. Emulating the U.S., in this respect, constitutes the third part of the "European Dream".

2.3. *The "Words of Power"*

2.3.1. Description of the Phenomenon

After the end of the Cold War, the U.S. ascended to the role of the sole global superpower. "The United States possesses unprecedented – unequalled – strength and influence in the world..."[39] At the turn of the millennium, it was deemed to be so powerful that former French foreign minister Hubert Védrine no longer found the notion of superpower adequate; hence, he coined a new term: *hyperpower*.[40] Other analysts also considered U.S. power "systemic" in the sense that the U.S., while formally a state, would no longer – like any other state – be reined in by the constraints built into the system of states, or international institutions for that matter (hence, the frequent references to empire and hegemony).

> The peculiarity of the United States is that, because of its global presence and power, it is able to demand a kind of external sovereignty and monopoly of decision-making, which, in cases of conflict, are not seriously hampered by the restrictions of supranational regulations and factual constraints that apply to all other states.[41]

38 The Laeken Declaration asks: "Does Europe not, now that is finally unified, have a leading role to play in a new world order, that of a power able both to play a stabilising role worldwide and to point the way ahead for many countries and peoples? Europe as the continent of humane values, the *Magna Carta*, the Bill of Rights, the French Revolution and the fall of the Berlin Wall; the continent of liberty, solidarity and above all diversity, meaning respect for others' languages, cultures and traditions. The European Union's one boundary is democracy and human rights."

39 The Bush Administration's 2002 *National Security Strategy* cited in: I.H. Daalder, "The End of Atlanticism", in: T. Lindberg (ed), *Beyond Paradise and Power*, (New York: Routledge, 2005), p. 44.

40 See P. Boniface, "Reflections on America as a World Power: A European View", in: (2000) 29 *Journal of Palestine Studies*, pp. 5–15.

41 C. Offe, note 2 *supra*, p. 98.

According to the Reagan and Bush administrations (I and II), its might and democratic conviction enabled it to stand up to, and eventually win, the global value-battle against Soviet Communism (Reagan's *Evil Empire*). Its power has given it a degree of freedom to act that is quite unprecedented. This freedom, it is claimed, has been used in the global fight against evil (and now also terrorism), a fight wherein the U.S. actively propounds its values, culture, and sense of community.

2.3.2. Justification for Why Europeans Would See This as Relevant to the EU

The obvious attraction is inherent to the unique ability that the U.S. has acquired to pursue its values and convictions over and beyond international, institutional and state systemic constraints. The attraction is two-faceted: the first is for the EU to equip itself with the necessary tools to fulfil Europe's destiny in the world, in a way similar to that of the U.S. Power, then, serves to ensure that Europe is able to operate as another "*City on the Hill*". It should be note that this has a significant restorative dimension: to *recover* Europe's previous role as the centre of the world. Here, there is, of course, also an explicit "realist" side, in the sense that it presumes that ideas do not succeed unless they are backed by power: it evokes the all-too-familiar notion that, only through might, can we be sure that we will be able to pursue our convictions and fulfil our objectives.

When stripped of its idealist overtones, the second facet is for Europe to *match* U.S. hegemony and power.[42] This can be given a co-operative and a competitive twist. On the former, Tony Blair noted that:

> [A] single-power world is inherently unstable. I mean, that's the rationale for Europe to unite. When we work together, the European Union can stand on par as a superpower and a partner with the U.S.[43]

On the latter, the U.S. can also be seen as representing both a potential threat and an obstacle to European ambitions. The previous U.S. administration (George W. Bush II) sees military might as an intrinsic part of *Manifest Destiny*. Many Europeans have argued that this sets the U.S. on a dangerous course, with the implication that the EU should amass strength in order to thwart such U.S. ambitions.

42 For references to the US as a hegemon, see R. Keohane, "The Theory of Hegemonic Stability and Change in International Economic Regimes", in: O. Holsti, R.M. Siverson and A. George (eds), *Change in the International System*, (Boulder CA: Westview Press, 1980); R, Gilpin, *War and Change in World Politics*, (Cambridge: Cambridge University Press, 1981), *idem*, *The Political Economy of International Relations*, (Princeton: Princeton University Press, 1987). A major US consideration that also motivated the second George W. Bush administration was to avoid imperial decline.

43 T.R. Reid, *The United States of Europe*, (New York: The Penguin Press, 2004), p. 4.

2.4. A Coherent Model?

Do these factors sum up to a coherent polity model which Europeans can emulate? This would appear to be so: the U.S.'s revolutionary beginning was founded upon a commitment to human rights, which helped to equip the ensuing American nationalism with a universal orientation. This became wedded with a communal sense of purpose or even *telos* through the notion of *Manifest Destiny.* The eventual U.S. status as a so-called *hyperpower* has equipped it with the military, political and even economic means of power to propound its values – without having to tie itself down to multilateral or other restrictions. These factors address an apparent mutually re-enforcing combination of motivation, moral justification, and physical ability to perform the tasks.

But, when considered more closely, we shall see that these elements are not as mutually re-enforcing as they might appear. Furthermore, the reality of the EU is quite far from any one of them.

First, the core principles that inform the U.S. revolutionary constitution are universal. One core normative issue is whether these principles can be properly entrenched in the state form. Another is how they sit with nationalism. Furthermore, U.S. power is sustained by the U.S. state (some label it as a warrior state: see Smith 2004), whose *raison d'être* is as much that of self-preservation and autonomy, as human rights and democracy. America's domestic, and, even more so, international, pursuit of the universal constitutional principles is affected by an American national identity with a distinctly religious – Christian – tenor, which infringes upon all aspects of their universal orientation.

Second, *Manifest Destiny*, understood as a particular fusion of religion and nationalism, is not merely a cultural and ideational phenomenon; it has also become deeply institutionalised. Oddly enough, this has a constitutional basis, entrenched, as it has become, in the very separation of state and church. In some contrast to Europe, the separation of state and church in the U.S. was understood to *protect religion from state power.* This has been re-enforced by another feature of the U.S. Constitution: it protects individuals against the state, but offers limited protection from the damage inflicted on individuals by *other societal actors*, hence, placing obstacles in the way of public social protection. Claus Offe has noted that:

> The suspicion of any social service provided by the state is nourished by the constitutional order and is constantly renewed in its virulence; and it means that, from the beginning and still today, political elites have felt obliged to represent the identity of the American nation as a community of free communities in 'God's own country', by means of official symbols ('God bless America', 'In God we trust', 'City on the Hill') and gestures of deference towards the religious life[...][44]

[44] C. Offe, note 2 *supra*, p. 36.

America's institutional-constitutional structure helps to sustain the religious dimension; it also contributes to crowd out alternative, entirely secular, sources of allegiance. By virtually prohibiting the development of an American welfare state, which could serve as a source of social solidarity, it renders policy stances highly susceptible to the influence of organised religion.[45]

Third, if U.S. power is to serve as a viable instrument for propounding core constitutional principles, there has to be a coherent line in U.S. foreign policy. Instead of *one* coherent line, Mead notes that U.S. foreign policy has been marked by a centuries-old struggle among *four different* schools, labelled as Madisonians, Jeffersonians, Wilsonians and Jacksonians.[46] A somewhat different reading of the past would claim that the cyclical changes between the deep international engagement and isolationism that run through the centuries of American foreign policy still resonate with the notion of *Manifest Destiny*, as they reflect a tension between a dominant impulse to serve as "an exemplary state *separate* from the corrupt and fallen world... [and a countervailing desire] to push the world along by means of regenerative *intervention*".[47] This latter position would address a closer relationship between the two latter attractions (*Manifest Destiny* and *World Power*), but without any obvious connection to the basic principles informing the first, constitutional, one. The use of power, then, easily ends up by becoming simply a self-serving act.

The different attractions reside in different conceptions of polity model. There is greater tension than what might initially have been expected between the kind of polity model that we can discern from the core American principles on the one hand, and how the U.S. operates on the other.

3. The European Union

3.1. Constitution-making European Style

The European Union is based upon many of the same universal principles that inform the model conception of the democratic constitutional state, as well as the actual U.S. Constitution.[48] But the European constitutional situation is very different from that of the U.S. Some would argue that the main difference is that the U.S. has a constitution, whereas the EU does not. But this is only partly true, as the EU *has* a constitutional

45 Fred Block (2007) points out how the development of tight links between the American business community and the Religious Right began in the 1970s, an alliance which the religious groups came to dominate in the 1990s. The growing importance of the Religious Right was an important instigator of the Bush Administration's foreign policy of unilateralism.

46 See W.R. Mead, note 35 *supra*.

47 See A. Stephanson, note 18 *supra*, p. xii.

48 Article 6 TEU asserts that: "The Union is founded on the principles of liberty, democracy, respect for human rights and fundamental freedoms, and the rule of law, principles which are common to the Member States."

arrangement, which predates the Laeken and Lisbon reform failures. It does not qualify as a formal, but rather as a material, constitution,[49] and it lacks explicit democratic sanction. Thus, it does not qualify as a *democratic* constitution on a par with the U.S. Constitution. This does not preclude the European Union's constitutional arrangement from acquiring democratic sanction at a future point in time. The EU has been involved in constitution-making for decades already, and this is a process that is distinctly different from U.S. constitution-making. The forging of the EU's material constitutional construct has taken place in a setting of *already constitutionalised entities*. This process, to be legitimate, had to relate to the already justified norms that were embedded in the national constitutional orders. The European process *could not* replicate the revolutionary impetus of its American counterpart; nor could it obtain the same democratic dignity. Thus, its greatest constitutional dignity would come not from its novelty, but from the extent to which it would succeed in forging a viable *synthesis* of the constitutional traditions common to the Member States.[50] Despite the difference in process, then, if this thrust can be sustained, it will channel European constitution-making in a state-based constitutional direction. But how far this will be able to go is not easy to tell, because of other distinct features of EU constitution-making, the most notable among which is the presence of *multiple constitutional publics*. This is directly reflected in the formal procedure for treaty change, which is conducted by the heads of state and government, in which each Member State enjoys a veto. The European process thus cannot be reduced to the image of the constitutional moment in which the will of a pre-constituted *people* is enshrined into the law in one single stroke.

The diversity of the European constitutional setting requires an alternative conception of constitution-making. Precisely because every effort to forge a formal democratic constitution for Europe will have to run up against the risk of twenty-seven national vetoes, the threshold for striking a constitutional accord is very high. One possibility is to think of European constitution-making not foremost as a process that ends up in a contractual arrangement that is established or given *at a particular point in time*, but rather as an ongoing process.[51] This could also have implications for the very conception of the constitution. It would neither be a mere contractual arrangement nor a founding pact between the citizens, but a set of procedures and rights that could accommodate an ongoing process of discursive validation of the structure in place. *Reflexive* constitution-making might be an apt term to call this.[52]

49 For this notion, see A.J. Ménendez, "Three Conceptions of the European Constitution", in: E.O. Eriksen, J.E. Fossum and A.J. Ménendez, (eds), *Developing a Constitution for Europe*, (London: Routledge, 2004).

50 See J.E. Fossum and A.J. Ménendez, "The Constitution's Gift? A Deliberative Democratic Analysis of Constitution Making in the European Union", (2005) 11 *European Law Journal*, pp. 380–410, and A.J. Ménendez, "Is European Union law a pluralist legal order?", in: J.E. Fossum and A.J. Ménendez, (eds), *The Post-Sovereign Constellation*, ARENA Report, No 4/08.

51 See. S. Chambers, "Contract or Conversation. Theoretical Lessons from the Canadian Constitutional Crisis", in (1998) 26 *Politics and Society*, pp. 143–72.

52 See J. Bowman, "Constitution Making and Democratic Innovation: The European Union and Transnational Governance", in: (2004) 29 *European Journal of Political Theory*, pp. 315–337.

The end result is that the European constitution-making experience has so many distinctive traits that set it apart from the American one that our effort is best expended on clarifying the distinctive character of the European exercise, or through looking for more appropriate contemporary examples.

3.2. *Not the City for Europe*

Europeans picked up on the American notion of *City on the Hill* and *Manifest Destiny* early on, but, even then, far from all endorsed it totally or perhaps even partially.[53] Today, many Europeans are more likely to see the *City on the Hill* and *Manifest Destiny* as justifications for American expansionism and aggrandisement than as vehicles to foster democracy and liberty.

Nevertheless, there is no doubt that part of the European integration process is a search for a normative *telos*. But this search takes place in a setting of deeply entrenched, national communities, which has largely prevented the quest for a unifying *telos* from espousing and entrenching a distinctive European community identity. This has not prevented efforts from being made to entrench a thicker sense of community, even with a religious imprint. During the Laeken constitutional process, for instance, the Pope, the Member States, political parties and other organisations sought to insert a Christian reference into the Constitutional Treaty. Their efforts were successfully rejected by a strong secularist front, with France in the lead. This has served to clarify that the European Union is a secular organisation, and one that cannot draw upon religious imagery in its search for a common purpose.

The European Union is officially justified with reference to (a) general principles such as democracy, human rights and respect for the rule of law, and (b) respect for difference and diversity. The projected mode of allegiance that we can discern from the Treaties is not only thinner than nationalism, it is also often presented as an explicit rejection of nationalism.

The American approach to the fostering of community could draw on the *City on the Hill* image in order to justify the so-called melting-pot model. Europeans recognised, from the EU's very beginnings, the problems in transposing the U.S. notion of the melting-pot to Europe: they rejected both its assimilationist assumptions and its foundation in nationalism. Indeed, some analysts have referred to the Union as being

53 Alexis de Tocqueville, for one, warned of the dangers of American exceptionalism when, in 1833, he wrote that, "It has been constantly repeated to the inhabitants of the United States that they form the only religious, enlightened, and free people. They see that up to now, democratic institutions have prospered among them; they therefore have an immense opinion of themselves, and they are not far from believing that they form a species apart in the human race". See www.firstparish.org/sermons/2004-08-08.html.

based upon constitutional tolerance; others have highlighted the EU as a Union of Deep Diversity.[54]

Many Europeans have also been deeply critical of the manner in which the previous U.S./George W. Bush administration pursued democracy and American values abroad. Thus, the U.S. appears not as a cosmopolitan guarantor of democracy and human rights, but as a national defender of sovereignty – in classical Westphalian fashion (albeit a nation-state that is not prepared to respect the sovereignty of other states).

In summary, the American notion of the *City on the Hill* (and *Manifest Destiny*) is not the bridge to the future that Europeans have yearned for. Indeed, its nationalist and religious orientation might, instead, serve to remind Europeans of what they have sought to leave behind.

3.3. *The "Power of Words"*

The European Union has very limited recourse to military power. Military and security matters are still decided by the Member States and/or under the *aegis* of NATO. Nevertheless, the EU's external presence has increased in the last decades, as the EU has taken on an increasingly important role in conflict prevention, including the establishment of a new European Defence Agency and Battle Groups.[55] With this have come renewed efforts to define, explain and justify the EU's role in the world.

The prevailing image of the EU has been one of a Civilian Power Union,[56] which was long on economic power, and short on military power, it relied on diplomacy in the handling of international conflicts and problems, and was willing to submit to legally-binding supranational institutions. Ian Manners, in his recent work, has labelled the EU a normative power:

54 As Joseph Weiler notes with regard to the EU: "the Union ... is to remain a union among distinct peoples, distinct political identities, distinct political communities... The call to bond with those very others in an ever closer union demands an internalisation – individual and societal – of a very high degree of tolerance."(J.H.H. Weiler, "Federalism without Constitutionalism: Europe's *Sonderweg*", in: K. Nicolaidis and R. Howse, (eds), *The Federal Vision: Legitimacy and Levels of Governance in the United States and the European Union*, (Oxford: Oxford University Press, 2001), p. 68) For the notion of the EU as a Union of Deep Diversity, see J.E. Fossum, "The European Union – In search of an Identity", (2003) 2 *European Journal of Political Theory*, pp. 319–340.

55 On the European Defence Agency, see: www.eda.europa.eu/ On the European Battle Groups, see: www.euractiv.com/en/security/eu-battlegroups-archived/article-150151.4.

56 See F Duchêne, "Europe's role in world peace", in: R. Mayne (ed), *Europe Tomorrow: Sixteen Europeans Look Ahead*, (London: Fontana/Collins, 1972), pp. 32–47, and *idem*, "The European Community and the uncertainties of interdependence", in: M. Kohnstamm and W. Hager (eds), *A Nation Writ Large? Foreign-Policy Problems Before the Community*, (London: MacMillan, 1973), pp. 1–21.

> [T]he central component of normative power in Europe is that it exists as being different to pre-existing political forms, and that this particular difference predisposes it to act in a normative way.[57]

To Manners, this normative propensity stems from the particular historical context within which it was forged, which highlighted the need to entrench *peace* and move beyond aggressive nationalism, its hybrid, less bounded and more permeable post-Westphalian form, and its legal constitution, which highlights human rights. The presumption is that the EU, as an organisation, is set up so as to be able to change the international system. Furthermore, this implies that it actually *also* acts to change this system, and, finally, that it *should* act in this manner.

The notion of European normative power is contested. However, whatever designation is chosen, it is quite clear that the EU places far more *onus* on legally-binding international co-operation than the U.S. does (certainly the previous U.S. George W. Bush administration) did. This, combined with its very limited military capacity, makes the European Union rely on "the power of words", and not the words of power in its external dealings.

To sum up thus far, the EU is a case not of new revolutionary beginnings, but of polity formation within a setting of established democracies. The challenge facing the European Union is to establish a type of polity that is able to resolve the problems and challenges that each state is not able to do on its own; based in a set of institutions that are in compliance with established normative principles, that foster both a sense of solidarity and a sense of belonging that is strong enough to sustain the entity, and is simultaneously not so strong as to raise doubts about the entity's respect for all relevant forms of difference and diversity. The U.S. has faced some of these challenges, but did so in a different period, at a time when the state system was still deeply entrenched. The European Union is trying to grapple with these challenges at a point in time when the Westphalian state system is undergoing profound changes.

4. Canada – Closer to Europeans' American Dream?

4.1. From Counter-Revolution to Charter Revolution

Analysts have long spoken of the important difference in the American and Canadian formative moments:

> Americans do not know but Canadians cannot forget that two nations, not one, came out of the American Revolution… One celebrates the overthrow of an oppressive state, the triumph of the people, a successful effort to create a type of government never seen before. The other

57 See I. Manners, note 7 *supra*.

> commemorates a defeat and a long struggle to preserve a historical source of legitimacy: government's deriving its title-to-rule from a monarchy linked to church establishment.[58]

But Canada's formal patriation of the Constitution from the UK in 1982 – notably the Charter of Rights and Freedoms – has brought Canada's constitution closer to its American counterpart. This act of patriation represented the first explicit effort on the part of the Canadians to found themselves as a people.[59] Since then, "...Canadians have experienced a Charter revolution. The Charter has given birth to a vigorous rights-oriented discourse and a dramatic increase in the propensity to litigate".[60]

But although these traits sit well with the U.S. experience, there are also important differences which set Canada apart from its American counterpart, notably Canada's attempt to combine individual rights with a significant recognition of group-based rights. The Charter also contributed to a political mobilisation of women's groups, aboriginals, and a wide range of ethno-linguistic groups.[61] The Charter Revolution has clear traits of *cathartic constitution-making*: the high-stakes politics has resulted in a re-configured conception of justice, in which weak disenfranchised groups have been given special constitutional recognition. This has manifested itself in a range of progressive policies, such as policies on aboriginal self-government, and same-sex marriage.

Another important difference to the U.S. is that there is still no constitutional agreement in Canada (the province of Quebec has not signed the Constitution Act of 1982), but it should also be added that Canadians are no less law-abiding than their U.S. counterparts. This adds up to an important *similarity* between the EU and Canada, because Canadian constitution-making must also respond to multiple constitutional publics. This has been extended to a *de facto* veto on constitutional change for each province.

Both the EU and Canada have also sought to democratise and open up the closed intergovernmental procedures for constitution-making, but neither has succeeded in obtaining constitutional agreement from these attempts.

58 See S.M. Lipset, (1990) note 18 *supra*, p. 1.

59 See P.H. Russell, *Constitutional Odyssey: Can Canadians become a Sovereign People?*, 2nd edition, (Toronto: University of Toronto Press, 1993).

60 See A.C. Cairns, "The Canadian experience of a Charter of Rights", in: E.O. Eriksen, J.E. Fossum and A.J. Menéndez (eds), *The Chartering of Europe: The Charter of Fundamental Rights and its Constitutional Implications*, (Baden-Baden: Nomos, 2003), pp. 93–111, at 105, and, for the notion of "Charter Revolution", see, also, F.L. Morton and R. Knopf, *The Charter Revolution and the Court Party*, (Peterborough, O.N.: Broadview Press, 2000).

61 This has been dealt with extensively in the literature. See the writings of Alan Cairns, Rainer Knopff, Ted Morton, Janet Hiebert, Miriam Smith and a host of others. For the citizenship implications, consider, in particular, W. Kymlicka, *Multicultural Citizenship. A Liberal Theory of Minority Rights*, (Oxford, Clarendon Press,1995), and *idem*, *Finding our Way*, (Oxford: Oxford University Press, 1998).

Canadians share with Europeans a complex conception of constitution: both seek to grapple with deeply-entrenched forms of difference and diversity; both are marked by ongoing processes of élite-run constitution-making; and their constitutional arrangements are neither agreed-upon contractual arrangements, nor founding pacts between the citizens. In both cases, however, there are procedures and rights that can accommodate an ongoing process of discursive validation of the structure in place. Agreement is notoriously difficult to achieve because this process deals with issues that are unlikely to find permanent resolutions, and, instead, require ongoing handling and balancing off.

4.2. Canada – EU: Towards Post-National Convergence?

Canada has, historically speaking, figured as a rather unlikely polity model, notably because many have portrayed it as a failed nation-state. The notion that Canada was made up of *two founding nations* has made it impossible to agree on a Canadian nation based upon the normal markers of nationalism (common language, *etc.*) Instead, *managing diversity* has become a key trait of Canada's self-understanding. This is also apparent in the general principles that are used to depict Canada: cultural and linguistic tolerance, inclusive community, federalism, inter-regional sharing, democracy, rule of law, and equality of opportunity, as well as respect for, and accommodation of, difference.

In a post-Westphalian context, where the nation-state is being called into question, Canada's initial "failure" to comply with the nation-state mould may be an advantage today, as it can now pose as a kind of vanguard in managing diversity:

> Canada is a world leader in three of the most important areas of ethnocultural relations: immigration, indigenous peoples, and the accommodation of minority nationalisms. Many other countries have one or more of these forms of diversity, but very few have all three, and none has the same wealth of historical experience in dealing with them.[62]

Canada's diversity has long been officially recognised through aboriginal self-government, bilingualism and multiculturalism.[63] Multiculturalism *as a doctrine* is premised on the notion of integrating immigrants from diverse cultural backgrounds into society – *without* eliminating their characteristics. It seeks to avoid the twin evils of assimilation and ethnic separation or ghettoisation. It is also an ideology that

62 W. Kymlicka, *Finding our Way*, (Oxford: Oxford University Press, 1998), p. 1 and pp.2–3, and *idem*, *Multicultural Odysseys*, (Oxford: Oxford University Press, 2007).

63 The Canadian multiculturalism policy was introduced in 1971, and, in 1988, it became officially enshrined in the Multiculturalism Act. The policy had four objectives: "to support the cultural development of ethnocultural groups; to help members of ethnocultural groups overcome barriers to full participation in Canadian society; to promote creative encounters and interchange among all ethnocultural groups; and to assist new Canadians in acquiring at least one of Canada's official languages." (Kymlicka 1998, note 61 *supra*, p. 15).

addresses inter-ethnic tolerance and the benefits that a society accrues *from* its diversity.[64] This doctrine is premised on the notion that the integration or incorporation of people from different backgrounds is a two-way process, which places requirements on those that integrate, but also on those who are already there. It can heighten social inclusiveness as well as self-reflection on the part of both the arriving minority(ies) and the receiving majority, in order to foster a process of mutual accommodation and change. Analysts find that the Canadian multiculturalism programme has been informed by these notions, although it is contested how well it has done.

Multiculturalism's approach to socialisation and incorporation differs from nationalism, which is far more attuned to integrating people into a set mould, or into a community with a clear sense of both itself and its national identity.

A trait that also sets Canada apart from the U.S. is that, in Canada, ethnic diversity is dealt with through publicly sustained welfare. Some analysts hold the American experience up as a kind of "master narrative" to the effect that ethnic diversity erodes redistribution.[65] In this light, Canada can be seen as a kind of "counter-narrative":

> [T]he evidence to date about public attitudes in Canada stands as a challenge to assertions that ethnic diversity inevitably weakens support for social programs; and the evolution of Canadian politics suggests that immigration, multiculturalism policies and social redistribution can represent a stable political equilibrium.[66]

We can understand Canada as an experiment in devising a particular balance of social solidarity and accommodation of difference – within a communal frame with a *post-national* orientation. This might suggest a certain post-national convergence between the EU and Canada.

4.3. Canada – also Propounds the "Power of Words"

Canada is no major military power and it mainly depends on favourable geography and the U.S. and NATO for its security. Like the EU, Canada is a strong supporter of international co-operation and self-binding legislation through legal provisions (it did not support the 2003 invasion of Iraq, for example). It has also been one of the foremost international peacekeepers, and has also been a key proponent of a foreign policy based

64 See W. Norman, "Justice and Stability in Multination States", in: A. Gagnon and J. Tully, *Struggles for Recognition in Multinational Societies*, (Cambridge: Cambridge University Press, 2001).

65 See D. Goodhart, "Too Diverse?", (2004) *Prospect*, pp. 30–37. available at: www.prospect-magazine.co.uk/article_details.php?id=5835.

66 See K.G. Banting, "Canada as counter-narrative, Multiculturalism, Recognition and Redistribution", paper presented at the seminar *The Ties that Bind: Accommodating Complex Diversity in Canada and the European Union*, (Brussels, Belgium 17–19 November 2005), p. 11.

upon *human security*.[67] This specific commitment has waned, although the core aims of Canadian foreign policy since the 1990s still remain to project Canadian values and culture abroad, through "respect for democracy, the rule of law, human rights, and the environment".[68] Canadians believe that their centuries-long experience with managing internal diversity provides them with a special acumen for handling international tension and conflicts. Thus, Canada also enjoys a very high international reputation for international co-operation and for its contribution to conflict handling (although researchers also find a clear discrepancy between high-minded rhetoric and practical pragmatism).

Canada's approach to conflict management, similar to that of the EU, relies not on force, but on "the power of words", the *onus* being on bringing the parties together in order to seek ways of resolving issues.

5. Concluding Reflections

This article has discussed the polity model that we can discern from the U.S., and has briefly considered it in relation to the reality of the European Union. When we disentangle the components of the U.S. understood as a polity model, we find a significant tension between moral universalism and ethical-religious and national difference. The American Constitution enjoys unique status as the pioneering edifice of the modern democratic state, but this democratic constitution was framed when the state system was consolidating, and was framed to suit the spirit of nationalism. The strong religious influence on American politics has variously given licence to international institution-building (the Wilsonian tradition) and to the recent American unilateralism.

Europe of today cannot echo the American constitutional process. European constitution-making takes place within a setting of already constitutionalised entities. These have all been inspired by the basic principles that inform the U.S. Constitution, and now also feed into the European constitutional edifice; hence, there appears to be no need for Europe to abandon the normative standards that the U.S. Constitution played such a central role to propagate. But today's challenge is, nevertheless, different, namely, to entrench these principles properly in a post-Westphalian political entity. To this, the other two components that I singled out as attractive about the U.S. do not offer much instruction, as they are accompanied by strong national, and even religious, overtones. A similar tension is seen in the U.S.'s global role: the U.S. was essential in

67 Department of Foreign Affairs and International Trade "Human Security Programme". www.humansecurity.gc.ca/psh-e.asp, 16.07.02. Canada was active in the development of ICC. The president of the International Criminal Court and its chief architect, Phillippe Kirsch is also a Canadian.

68 Canada, *Canada in the World: Government Statement*, (Ottawa, 1995). See, also, Nossal, "The World we want? The Purposeful Confusion of Values, Goals, and Interests in Canadian Foreign Policy (2003); available at: www.cdfai.org/PDF/The%20World%20We%20Want.pdf.

establishing the components of cosmopolitan law,[69] yet it has veered from cosmopolitan self-binding to moralistic unilateralism in defiance of those very rules. In this sense, the U.S., steeped, as it still is, within a Westphalian frame, is hardly the most suitable polity for the EU to emulate – partly because it is too much of a state (in its external role) and partly because it is too little of a state (in its internal, social role)

The EU represents the most explicit attempt to date to break out of the nationalist mould and to foster a different – post-national – sense of allegiance within a structure that is more permeable and reflexive than any nation-state. The question is whether this sets the EU apart from the rest of the world, as an idiosyncrasy and as a reflection of unique European patterns, or whether European developments resonate with developments elsewhere. Clearly, if we talk about the prospects for changes in constitutive frames, then isolated developments in one corner of the world need not amount to much.

In this article, I have looked at *the "other" of North-America* as a possible parallel to the EU. Somewhat paradoxically, given the inability to reach agreement on a made-in-Canada Constitution, Canada's commitment to the rule of law – both in its internal and in its external orientations – reflects a more "cosmopolitanised state". Such a state seeks to uphold core democratic principles, both internally and externally, has lower thresholds between its internal and external orientations, and seeks to foster a post-national and thinner-than-nationalism mode of allegiance. Such an internationally permeable state has traits in common with the EU. Both Canada and the EU share certain promising features in terms of fostering new constitutive frames. The really important challenge is to find out if these traits are more than just isolated components.

However, to argue that Canada fulfils Europe's "American Dream" would be to overstate the case. But Canada should figure here. Europeans might usefully set up Canada as a mirror of themselves, as Canada is the state that comes closest to the EU in several critical respects. Canada might be a useful mirror also because it addresses how far we can "stretch" the state form in diversity accommodation terms. If Canada can demonstrate that the state form is so flexible and so accommodating of difference, and still manages to retain a fundamental commitment to rights and democracy, then this suggests that the state form of political organisation could still work for Europe. Then, a further and equally demanding challenge could be addressed, whether a cosmopolitanised state could uphold the sanctioning force of the law, internally and externally. What matters today, it seems, is to establish *how* we might wed the great ideals espoused by the American Revolution with the experiences and efforts that Canada and the EU are going through.

69 See J. Habermas, "America and the World – A Conversation with Jürgen Habermas", with Eduardo Mendieta, in: *Logos* 3.3 (summer 2004), available at: www.logosjournal.com/habermas_america.htm.

Michelle Everson

CHAPTER 6. EUROPEAN CITIZENSHIP AND THE DISILLUSION OF THE COMMON MAN

1. Introduction

Almost 20 years ago, the European Union was born, and with it, the European citizen.[1] Today, we may have grown used to the concept of a European citizen; but, in the heady days following the dedication of a, once, European (Economic) Community to a, forever, "closer union of the peoples of Europe", the novel concept of supranational citizenship drew a host of excited comment. But where was it to be located amongst the sliding range of communitarian, republican and identity-based theories of citizenships, and could it be deployed to give voice to traditionally marginalised constituencies?[2] Alternatively, should it be dismissed as impossible on its own terms - after all, when have we ever seen a citizenship without a state? - and, accordingly, treated as a veiled, but nonetheless usurping, threat to the sovereignty of the Member States.[3] Or, was it simply a chimera, which, with its paltry catalogue of political rights, merely masked the essential character of the European as *homo economicus*; a pale modern echo of Bismarck's *Wirtschaftsbürger*, and a vehicle for the creation of an irredeemably neo-liberal European market as the ill-conceived precursor to the forced creation of a European state *grand goût*?[4]

Today, both overly optimistic and menacingly apocalyptic visions of the European citizen might appear to have been misplaced. Notwithstanding all this, we have not witnessed the emergence of a new, instantly recognisable, post-modern European citizen, armed with the necessary rights to forge his or her own identity against the once

1 Treaty on European Union, Articles 17–21.

2 Jo Shaw, "The Many Pasts and Futures of Citizenship in the European Union", (1997) 22 *European Law Review* p. 554. U.K. Preuß, "Problems of a Concept of European Citizenship", (1995) 1 *European Law Journal*.

3 Preuß, note 2 *supra*.

4 M. Everson, "The Legacy of the Market Citizen", in: J. Shaw and G. More (eds), *New Legal Dynamics of European Union*, (Oxford: Clarendon, 1995), pp. 73–89.

unyielding backdrops of "imagined" (national) collectivities;[5] nor have we seen the creation of the State of Europe, neo-liberal or otherwise. Instead, and all grand, but failed, constitutional aspirations apart, the legal vehicle of citizenship would appear to share this much with all European mechanisms of potential constitutional renewal: legal evolution is not so much a child of minutely-planned conceptual revolution, but, rather, a matter of incremental pragmatism, whereby citizenship is unfolded by means of judicial response to instances of the assertion of individual right. European citizenship has thus proceeded slowly to recognise the free-standing (non-economic) right of free movement (*Martinez Sala*[6]), to establish an essential link between the acquisition of "derivative" rights of citizenship and human rights (*Chen*[7]), and to concede a measure of transnational solidarity (*Grzelcyk*[8]).

Is this, then, the end of the story of European citizenship? Might we accordingly be satisfied that the incremental legal evolution of Articles 17–21 of the European Treaty will provide us with an appropriate vehicle of self-recognition and self-projection for the individual European? The following pages argue that this question must be answered with a resounding "'no". Things are now far from well in the world of European citizenship. The initial impetus for this negative assessment is drawn from a discipline foreign to legal science, and, above all, from Neil Fligstein's recent sociological-empirical finding that economically-driven processes of European integration only have the full support of a very small and financially very privileged group of Europeans (10–15% of the European population).[9] However, the lesson that the entire project of European integration is now threatened by its own fatal disregard for the historical core of citizenship – the binding together of disparate and *antagonistic* classes within a community of fate – is one that is drawn specifically for legal science; and, above all, in promotion of a form and rigorous method of legal scholarship that has, all Europeanised temptation apart, retained its primary respect for the achievements of the post-war national constitutional settlement, but which has, likewise, never failed to pay due note to its historically-conditioned failings.[10]

2. Maastricht: The False Promise of the Homo Economicus?

Making an initial and brief historical detour, it is worth recalling exactly why the original concept of European citizenship was subject to such suspicion when viewed through the lenses of a historical citizenship theory.[11] In this view, the European scheme

5 M. Everson and J. Eisner, with reference to the pluralist tradition, The *Making of a European Constitution*, (Oxford and New York: Routledge-Cavendish, 2007).

6 Case C-85/96, *Maria Martinez Sala* v *Freistaat Bayern* [1998] ECR I-2691.

7 Case C-200/02 *Zhu and Chen* [2004] ECR I-9925.

8 C-184/99 Grzelcyk v Centre Public d'aide sociale d'Ottignies-Louvain-la-Neuve, [2001] ECR I-6193.

9 N. Fligstein, Euro-Clash: The EU, European Identity and the Future of Europe, (Oxford: Oxford University Press, 2008).

10 In short, the legal science pursued by Christian Joerges (see, below, Section V).

11 I refer primarily to my own analysis, M. Everson (1995).

whereby the existence of the European citizen was boldly declared, was linked with the nationality law of the Member States, and was further elaborated with specific reference to a restricted set of (European) political rights and rights of consular representation, was not merely to be doubted with regard to its lack of an independent genesis for European citizenship. It was, instead, to be decried for its seeming failure to establish "allegiance", or to ensure that European citizens would be "bound to one another by the personal bond of fellow-membership of one body".[12]

Thus, critique did not focus upon the lack of a pre-political, or communitarian, wellspring for European "being" within a common European language, religion or race.[13] Nor, importantly, did it descend into a republican-liberal reverie to dream of a common illiberal European enemy and thus to bemoan the lack of concomitant citizenship duties (military service), whose exercise might accordingly unite the body of imagined Europeans through shared adversity.[14] Instead, the homily that nationality is merely "the other side of the citizenship coin" to rights[15] was placed within its historical-industrial context to breathe new comparative force into T.H. Marshall's seminal narrative of the evolution of citizenship.[16] The vital question then posed was one of whether European citizenship had been consciously developed in order to compensate for the inequalities of the emerging European market, and thus to ensure the continuing loyalty of Europeans to the project of Europe, even if its market should be experienced in a negative light.

Outside the communitarian perspective, the acquisition of European citizenship by virtue of possession of the nationality of one of the Member States does not preclude the establishment of reciprocal loyalty between individual Europeans. Instead, with an eye to contractual theories of the establishment of *res publica*, T.H. Marshall tells us the stirring concrete story of the evolution of industrial citizenship within the United Kingdom – and similarly lays the fundaments for the telling of the abstract tale of the creation of allegiance to the alienating state of modernity and the modern mass economy – with recourse to rights rather than nation. Citizenship is a historical and a violent happening, which both creates and tames the market and the state: civic rights – including, most importantly, the right to contract – are medieval artefacts whose post-Black Death development shattered the feudal system and elevated the feudal subject to the status of a contractual party, who might then forge a new market-based economy; political rights are the child of the 17th century and the struggle by market burghers to assert their growing economic power by means of violent struggle for a share in the political powers of the sovereign; social rights are corrective, status-based, mechanisms, politically hard-fought-for by the industrial classes of the 19th and 20th centuries in

12 J.W. Salmond, "Citizenship and Allegiance", (Part II), (1902) 17 *LQR*, pp. 49–63.

13 See, for explanation of communitarian visions of acquisition of citizenship, note 2 *supra*.

14 For a disturbing example of this tendency, see Ulrich Haltern, "On Finality", in: A. von Bogdandy and J. Bast (eds), *Principles of European Constitutional Law*, (Oxford: Hart Publishing, 2006), pp. 373–403.

15 Preuß, note 2 *supra*.

16 T.H. Marshall, (1953) *Citizenship and Social Class*, (Pluto Press: London, 1992).

response to the necessary functional differentiations of the mass economy, as well as the abject indifference of a *bourgeois* state to the inequalities of class. From subjecthood, to contract, to status, the historical antagonisms captured within the concept of citizenship are then, in turn, seemingly reconciled, as – following the formula given by Ralph Dahrendorf[17] – civic, political and social rights are concentrically constitutionalised within the post-war national settlement, furnishing each such reborn nation with a normative concept of citizenship, which both recognises its own historical class struggle, and holds it in permanent equilibrium; a concept of citizenship which guarantees, not only the market, with its myriad inequalities, but also the means of its social correction within a politically-inclusive state.

Citizen is brother to citizen, and all citizens have reason to be loyal to their state. What then of the rights of the European Union citizen? Herein, the critique of the Maastricht citizen is to be found: clearly, rights to vote and stand in European and local elections, together with the right to petition the European ombudsman, as well as the right to consular protection, were not born out of portentous European class struggle, nor do they represent a genuine European effort to reproduce the normative, concentric scheme of Dahrendorf's "allegiance-inducing" civic, political and social rights. More tellingly still, the core and unique right of the Union citizen, the right to move and reside freely within the borders of the EU, appeared, in the Maastricht Treaty at least, to be qualified, exercisable only "subject to the limitations and conditions laid down in this Treaty and by the measures adopted to give it effect" (now, Article 18(1) European Treaty). Alternatively, Article 18 explicitly related the new Union Citizenship to older provisions of European law, and, more particularly, to the existing right of free movement for European workers now laid down in Article 39 EC; one of the quartet of European rights of labour movement, establishment (Article 43), service provision (Article 49) and capital movement (56), commonly known as the "four freedoms".

With this irresistible reminder of the economic antecedents of European integration, the TEU's chapter on citizenship itself placed renewed emphasis upon an existing vision of the individual European as *homo economicus*; the economically active and pro-active European economic citizen, who, in the manner of Bismarck's *Wirtschaftsbürger*, would be the primary instigator – *creatur ex nihilo* – of a European market, asserting European economic rationality and, where necessary, setting the obstructions of national regulatory provisions aside. Was this, then, the true face of European citizenship, a face of naked entrepreneurial endeavour? Given the weak nature of the political rights within the Treaty of Maastricht, the absence of a normatively-stated social commitment to the correction of market inequalities at European level, and the proven juridical strength of the four freedoms, the European *homo economicus* was undoubtedly still predominant. Furthermore, lacking even the paternalistic (anti-democratic) framework of social provision and control within which Bismarck sought to neutralise the individualism (inherent cosmopolitanism) of his *Wirtschaftsbürger*, the European economic citizen could surely not be other than a selfish being; a contractual party

17 R. Dahrendorf, (1992): *Der moderne soziale Konflikt*, (Stuttgart: Deutsche Verlagsanstalt, 1992).

dedicated by European right to personal profit, a cosmopolitan dismissive of the feudal confines of the nation state, a solipsist utterly without loyalty to his or her fellow Europeans, and also – where no individual profit was to be made – without status within, or allegiance to, any common European project.

3. The End of Nation and History within European Citizenship

That was then, and now is now. The European Court of Justice has since pronounced repeatedly upon the notion of the European citizen. Further, responding to the pragmatic problems thrown up by integration processes, the ECJ has surprised and confounded traditional citizenship theory. The primary European "bolt from the blue" was to come in the seminal case of *Martinez Sala* in 1998,[18] which severed the existing link between free movement and economic activity. Thereafter, judicial inventiveness was fundamentally to refashion all accepted understandings of the nature of citizenship: on the one hand, allowing for the derivation of a right to citizenship, not from nationality, but from human rights; and, on the other, extending rights of solidarity across the once wholly-impermeable borders of national solidarity collectivities – and this in disregard of the wishes of the Council. With this, it might, accordingly, be argued that European citizenship is evolving, not as an unconscionable assault upon traditional citizens, but rather as a promising solution to the inherently exclusionary nature of the historical citizen.

Thus, the case of *Sala* – confirming that Article 18 EC Treaty was a free standing Treaty right, and was not qualified by Article 39 EC Treaty – was revolutionary in its effects, not simply since it expanded the *dramatis personae* of the European integration stage to include persons moving across frontiers for non-economic reasons, but also, since it laid the foundations for a series of subsequent cases,[19] which can be viewed as divorcing the legal vehicle of Union citizenship from notions of nationality, locating its *genus* within human rights, instead. Citizenship, it should never be forgotten,[20] matches its own inclusionary aspirations with its own exclusionary impact: even in its republican/

18 See note 6 *supra*. For details of the extraordinary and immediate resonance of this case, see S. O'Leary, "Putting Flesh on the Bones of European Citizenship", (1999) 24 *European Law Review*, p. 68.

19 There is very little room here to detail all the cases and commentary on a complex area of European law. Interested readers should refer to: A. Tryfonidou, "Jia or 'Carpenter II': the edge of reason", (2008) 32 *European Law Review*, p. 908; E. Drywood, "Giving with one hand, taking with the other", (2007), 32 *European Law Review*, p. 369; O. Golynker, "Student loans: the concept of social justice according to Bidar", (2006) 31 *European Law Review*, p. 390; Ch. Hilson, "What's in a right? The relationship between Community, fundamental and citizenship rights in EU law", (2004) 29 *European Law Review*, p. 636; S. Peers, "Implementing equality? The Directive on long term resident third-country nationals", (2004) 29 *European Law Review*, p. 437; R.C.A. White, "Conflicting competences: free movement rules and immigration laws", (2004) 29 *European Law Review*, p. 385.

20 See U.K. Preuß and M. Everson, "Concepts, Foundations and Limits of European Citizenship", ZERP-Diskussionspapier 2/95, ZERP an der Universität Bremen (1995); P. Tuitt, *Race, Law, Resistance*, (London: Glasshouse Press, 2004); D. Heater, *Citizenship: The Civic Ideal in World History and Politics*, (London: Longman, 1990).

contractual variant, which rejects all pre-political notions of belonging, to include citizens within the state by means of rights, the legal vehicle of nationality – typically *ius soli* based – draws an exclusionary line, in fact, if not in theory,[21] based solely upon the accident of birth. Nationality is the gateway to citizenship. An exclusionary feature of citizenship that has long haunted the enlightenment ideal of a universal brotherhood of man, the gate of nationality has, nonetheless, been prised open by an ECJ, which has collapsed the distinction between "the rights of man and the rights of the citizen", extending derivative rights of European citizenship to individuals who are not nationals of a Member State. The exemplary case here is that of *Chen.*[22] Master Chen, at the planned instigation of his Chinese parents, was born in Northern Ireland, becoming a citizen of the Irish Republic by virtue of *ius soli* and,[23] thus, a European citizen by virtue of Article 17(2) EC. Accordingly, Master Chen could exercise his Article 18 EC right of free movement to re-locate to London. But, what of his Chinese mother? Surely, the UK Home Office could exercise its right to exclude a Chinese national? Not so, said the ECJ: human rights, particularly the right to the enjoyment of family life, would determine that Mrs Xhu, as the primary carer, could move with her son.

The derivative exercise of a European right of free movement by a Chinese national, may not initially appear to be such a momentous evolution, being qualified, as it is, by the need to establish a relational connection between a non-EU mother and an EU child. However, the core sociological-empirical element within the judgment – the ECJ's recognition of a need to deal pragmatically with a simple human happening, the birth of a child[24] – and its use of human rights to imbue the particularist/exclusionary vehicle of citizenship with a measure of universal humanity, further gains in significance if read in the light of the ECJ's recent and notable efforts to expand the addressees of national solidarity collectives to include the figure of the impecunious, but needy, stranger. Article 18 EC and the free-standing (non-economic) European right of movement, thus sets its own limits on its exercise by European citizens, reserving to the Council a right to determine the conditions under which it will be exercised (Article 18(2) EC). Predictably, Council action to implement the right of free movement within the Union has seen the re-emergence of economic qualifications within the concept of European citizenship, this time, with regard to the assertion of the primacy of the national solidarity collective. Most recently, then, Directive 2004/38[25] on free movement re-emphasises the closed nature of the national solidarity collective – or the exclusionary

21 In its original revolutionary form, the French Constitution offered French citizenship to all who professed to share in the ideals of the Republic; French-speaking slaves within the Caribbean foolishly relied upon this sentiment, only to be bloodily suppressed by the young Republic: see Heater note 20 *supra*.

22 See note 7 *supra*.

23 The Republic extends its *ius soli* rule to include all persons born within the island of Ireland.

24 Even in the face of suggestions that the situation had been contrived by the parents. See, however, an opposite finding in *Akrich* (Case C-109/01 ECR I-9607), where the "misconduct" of the applicant defeats the claim to derivative citizenship.

25 [2004] O.J. L158/77.

notion that the re-distributive social benefits of citizenship are reserved for members of the nation alone – by granting EU citizens and their family members a right of residence throughout Europe only "as long as they do not become an unreasonable burden on the social assistance system of the host Member State" (Article 6).

The operative word here, the measure of the willingness of the Member States to open up national solidarity to afford real succour to the indigent Union citizen, is to be found in the word "unreasonable";[26] and it is here, too, that the determination of the ECJ to pry open that door further is demonstrated. Prior to the implementation of Directive 2004/38, the Court had already firmly signalled its universalist welfare aspirations in cases such as *Grzelczyk*, accordingly stating that the fact that Directive 93/96[27] regulating movement of students did not provide for benefits for students, similarly did not preclude the extension of national benefits to EU students where such students found themselves in the same needy circumstances as national students. In *Baumbast*, where a German national had not satisfied UK requirements that he maintain sufficient sickness insurance for himself and his family, the Court accordingly declared that national legislation implementing Directive 2004/38 must be "proportionate". As has been cleverly noted,[28] the imposition of the community principle of proportionality to national implementing legislation thus also amounted to a "constitutional review" of the efforts of the Council to set the legislative limits to national solidarity through the judicial frontline assessment of the impact of a notion of "unreasonable burden" in the light of every-day-cases in individual Member States.

Naturally, this constitutionally-oriented aspiration to review the actions of the Council in setting limits to national solidarity collectives has also inexorably implicated the ECJ in a series of intricate judgments, concerning the intimate tax, benefits and financial dealings of a host of EU citizens from students to pensioners.[29] Nonetheless, such painstaking judicial labour has also brought with it immense benefits in terms of the pursuit of the Court's dedicated campaign to re-orient Union citizenship in line with common understandings of the simple humanity that is due from man to man under circumstances of real human want. Abstracting to the level of political theory, the Court's very real materiality, its willingness to engage with an "other" within the immediacy of needy circumstances, is reborn as a pragmatic, empathetic and reflex-driven reproach to Hannah Arendt's eternally sorrowful observation of the human condition and the imperative need to "locate" humanity – the recognition of the human by humans as a human – within time and within "space".[30] Temporality and spatiality

26 M. Dougan, "The constitutional dimension to the case law on Union citizenship", (2006) 31 *European Law Review*, p. 613.

27 [1993] OJ L317/59.

28 M. Dougan (2006).

29 Here, it suffices to note only Case C-258/04 *Ioannidis* [2005] ECR I-8275, in which the Court continued to struggle to identify "an effective and genuine link" between the applicant and the host state.

30 H. Lindahl, "Finding a place for freedom, security and justice: The European Union's claim to territorial unity", (2004) 29 *European Law Review*, p. 461; A. Somek, "Solidarity decomposed: being

are the measure of the traditional concept of citizenship: Mrs Xhu's maternal pre-occupations are wholly irrelevant to a republican nation which demands individual philosophical concordance with revolutionary principles born out of, and reified within, bloody history; contractual citizenship and solidarity, invigorated by a shared geographical experience of class struggle and re-distributive resolution, is utterly blind to Mr Baumbast's, or the geographical stranger's, need for immediate medical care for his family.

This need not be so, intones the ECJ: the measure of recognition and solidarity within Europe is certainly not to be negated by spatially-bounded history; still less, is it to be found within a simple reciprocal display of solidarity between and beyond actuarial national calculations of the costs and benefits in social provision.[31] Instead, a "wonder" of extra-European recognition is invoked into being as the Court's very post-modern act of observing and responding to the personalised need situation of a non-European subject is conjoined with the modern legal instrument of human rights, in order to recall, and, importantly, to juridify the pre-modern emotions of universal empathy and brotherhood. By the same token, a once technical yardstick of procedural legal review, "proportionality", is transformed into a far more indistinct realm of substantive adjudication, open to an emotionally-founded *interposito auctoritas*, within which a "miracle" of European solidarity is born – a miracle of unbounded love[32] – as the ECJ forensically interrogates the wants of individual citizens, requiring the national solidarity collective to be prised open in response to, and in sympathy with, the facts of the individualised situational context.

The notable degree of comment, controversy and puzzlement about the ECJ's jurisprudence on Union citizenship is thus explained:[33] a post- and pre-modern process whereby the identity of European citizens and, thus, Europe itself, is negotiated in reflexive confrontation (or emotional reflex) with a concrete other, is not easily explained in formal legal categories; still less is it easily recognised within a proceduralist legal paradigm – how can a collective national expression of shared love ever be "proportionally" balanced against the "miracle" of universal and unbounded solidarity? Instead, European legal evolution is lead by the emotions of European judges. Nonetheless, the pre-/post-modern stripping away of the history and geography of

and time in European citizenship", (2007) 32 *European Law Review*, p. 787. I am immensely grateful to each of these authors for their insights.

31 Both Dougan (2006) and Somek (2007) confirm – each in their own way – that the ECJ has moved beyond simple notions of reciprocity to justify its creation of European solidarity. In Somek, this idea is to be found in the notion that European solidarity is a "miracle" drawn forth by virtue of empathetic empirical observation; within Dougan, the constitutional review of the actions of the Council, a European figure, provides us with a distinct European (i.e., not nationally reciprocal) form of solidarity.

32 Somek (2007) recalling Unger's description of social solidarity as an irrational act of collective love: *Law in Modern Society*, (New York and London: Free Press, 1975).

33 See, in particular, Somek's musings on the complex differences in the treatment of students, pensioners and what-have-you (2007).

Europe, and the pragmatic juridical preparedness to consider each individual in his or her situational context, not only seems to echo and to embody the political/constitutional aspirations of the Union to give normative voice to identity-oriented concepts of citizenship, particularly in the sphere of non-discrimination,[34] but also, it might be argued, furnishes Union citizenship with an inspirational quality to match the antagonistically reconciling history of industrial citizenship. Following the judicial execution of nation and history in Europe, has European citizenship, finally and, indeed, remarkably, overcome the destructive problems of spatiality, temporality and exclusion?

4. Union Citizenship Fallito (1): Nation and History Bite Back

Hans Lindahl has reminded us of just how powerful Arendt's concept of spatiality is.[35] The notion of space is:

> [N]ot merely a geographical term. It relates not so much, and not primarily, to a piece of land as to the space between individuals in a group whose members are bound to, and at the same time separated and protected from, each other by all kinds of relationships, based on a common language, religion, a common history, customs, and laws.

Writing against the post-war backdrop of Europe's proven moral turpitude, its utter failure to secure the most basic of rights of the millions of murdered dead, who had seen their citizenship and concomitant protection negated, its continuing complicity in the mass displacement of the millions of individuals who had found themselves on the wrong side of re-drawn borders, Arendt's sorrowful observation that "[F]reedom, where it existed as tangible reality, has always been spatially limited",[36] her assertion that human security can only be found within time and place, was no intentionalist statement of sovereign exclusion. Instead, it was a highly ambivalent recognition that freedom is only ever secured within a substantive realm of collective nation and history – which contemporaneously and inexorably imperils freedom – and it is this ambivalence which has likewise led Hans Lindahl to conclude that, with its constitution of a legal space of European values, the EU has also re-asserted, with all its negative connotations, a *place* of European nation and history, a European *place* of exclusion.

In other words, and for all the brave efforts of the ECJ, a curiously differentiated European regime, whereby Union citizens are afforded rights, third country nationals

34 And here, the reference is to Articles 141 and 13 EC Treaty and the Union's seeming desire to extend its highly successful sex equality provisions to cover fields of race, religion, age, disability and gender.

35 Hannah Arendt (1963), *Eichmann in Jerusalem: A Report on the Banality of Evil*, (Penguin: London, 1994), p.262. See, also, Hannah Arendt, *The Human Condition*, (Chicago: Chicago University Press, 1958), p.52. Cited by Lindahl (2007).

36 Hannah Arendt, *On Revolution*, (London: Penguin Classics,1990).

are afforded limited recognition,[37] and asylum-seekers are subject to a common framework of control,[38] does not end exclusion in Europe, but rather re-inforces it within a binary legal code, whereby the "legally-resident" take their stratified place within a European space, which protects individual Europeans, one from the other, and Europeans from *the* other, so that "the illegal", both within Europe and without, are left bereft, knocking at the firmly closed doors of recognition and solidarity. The European other dies daily in the waters of the Mediterranean, just as the draft European Constitution promises its citizens "an area of freedom, security and justice without internal frontiers" (Article 3(2)). Spatiality and temporality inexorably return to haunt Europe and, with them, the pressing questions of which are the narratives of history, and which are the narratives of nation, that are unfolding within our common realm of legal place? We have already observed the ECJ's liberating "blindness" to history and to nation within its jurisprudence, but we must now ask, by means of disruptive eversion (*Umstülpung*), whether blindness is, itself, only a mask for the construction of a sanitised narrative of European history, for the assertion of a European nation that ignores the antagonisms that exist between individual Europeans and between Europeans and their other; antagonisms that must, nevertheless, be revealed and reconciled (also within European citizenship) if Europe is to endure and not merely to founder within the empty promises of the *ius publicum europaeum*, and its simple veneer of occidental rationalism.[39]

The deconstructive quest for this veiled narrative of history and nation focuses on two cases that may, initially, seem quirkily distanced from one another: the case of *Lechourito*, on the one hand, where the ECJ held that a 1943 retaliatory massacre committed by German armed forces within Greece did not fall within the *ratione materiae* of the 1968 Brussels Convention, since the massacre concerned the exercise of public, rather than civil, powers;[40] and the case of *Commission* v *Austria*, on the other, where the "open-door" policy of university entry within Austria, which guarantees university admission to all Austrians holding a high school diploma, regardless of grade, was held to be indirectly discriminatory against non-Austrian EU-nationals, who were required to qualify themselves for admission in-line with their own national practices.[41] What, then, unites these utterly disparate cases? The answer is the potential for the recognition of emotion and irrationality within European law, for the acknowledgment of uncomfortable history and acts of social love within the *ius europaeum*. As Carol Lyons notes, above all, in her treatment of Advocate General Ruiz-Jarabo Colomer's

37 As family members under Directive 2004/38 and long term residents under the Long Term Residents Directive 2003/109EC.

38 See, C. Barnard, *The Substantive Law of the EU: The Four Freedoms*, (Oxford: Oxford University Press, 2004), for comprehensive details on the disturbing differentiated categorisation of individuals in Europe.

39 The echo of Carl Schmitt is wholly intentional, see C. Schmitt (1932), *Der Begriff des Politischen*, (Berlin: Dunker & Humblodt, 2001).

40 Case C-292/05 *Lechouritou* v *Germany* [2007] OJ C82/85.

41 Case C-147/03 Commission of the European Communities v Republic of Austria [2005] ECR I-5969.

sensitive efforts to address "the other country of [Europe's] past",[42] *Lechouritou* concerned memories of European trauma that will not die, and, further, implicates the European Court in an act of "listening rather than answering",[43] of responding empathetically to enduring human emotion rather than immediate legal right. By the same token, as Alex Somek asserts,[44] the facts of *Austria* v *Commission* also encompass a measure of irrationality, or social love, a diffuse but collective decision that "everyone who has made it through school [should be] rewarded with a fresh start";[45] a measure of national empathy, with very real socially redistributive consequences, which closes the space of Austrian education to non-Austrians, just as it makes inclusive reparation for jointly-experienced memories of adolescent self-discovery and academic under-achievement.

As noted, within the legal technical term of proportionality – at least, as it applies to reciprocity between schemes of social assistance – the ECJ has opened up potential for itself to respond to the facts of European integration within an emotionally-founded *interposito auctoritas.* The robed, if not be-wigged, European Justice is undoubtedly, and perhaps sometimes usefully so, judge-king[46] within Europe, with the freedom to adapt the normative framework of European law to the factual demands thrown up by integration processes, in line with his or her own emotional processes of recognition and empathy. But what of the European judge-king's preparedness to respond to the emotions and irrationalities of the European publics? Here, however, a façade of occidental rationalism is decisively re-established within the law as: 1) in *Lechouritou*, the Court perhaps takes the Advocate General's exhortation to exercise its judicial role in a "restrained" manner – that is, "without sentiment" – too much to heart, dismissing the AG's opinion in its entirety and treating the matter before it solely within the rationality language of the self-referential jurisdiction of civil matters;[47] and 2) all issues of emotional solidarity with the under-achieving teenager of our pasts are simply swept aside as the Court "gives Austria the unsolicited [but brutally rational] advice to establish 'entry examinations or the requirement of a minimal qualification to avoid the system's collapse'".[48]

History and nation are, indeed, dead within the minds of the ECJ as reparation in its historical and cultural contexts is not even addressed within the language of the Court, much less allowed to contaminate the implementation of European law. Or is it?

42 Carol Lyons, "The persistence of memory: the *Lechouritou* case and history before the European Court of Justice", (2007) 32 *European Law Review*, p. 563.

43 *Ibid.*

44 Somek, note 30 *supra.*

45 Somek also notes the potentially regressive social impacts of the decision: Are those failing to obtain a grammar school education (typically, from the less-advantaged Austrian classes) to be excluded from Austrian educational life?

46 E. Ehrlich, (reprint from 1903), *Freie Rechtsfindung und freie Rechtswissenschaft*, (Aalen: Scientia, 1987).

47 Lyons, note 42 *supra.*

48 Somek, note 30 *supra.*

Certainly, in terms of Arendt's eternally ambivalent notion of spatiality, *Lechouritou's* utter failure to re-focus European minds – however symbolically – on the other of our own bloody past, must be decried as an instance of historical blindness, which inevitably contributes to the process whereby the modern European mind is stripped of empathy for, and inured to, the sufferings of the European other that languishes nightly in Mediterranean death-traps, or daily in the asylum detention-centres that *border* our "area of freedom, security and justice without internal frontiers". At the same time, however, the language of legal rationality must also be recognised to be a re-assertion and affirmation of the emotionally-denuded narrative of occidental rationalism that has, ever since the Enlightenment, presented and justified European expansion and self-profligation upon the world stage within an argument of evolutionary superiority and logical inevitability: a history of logical rationalism, which swamps and displaces a bloody history of slavery and European colonial expansion – as well as, continuing post-colonial dominance – relieving us of our enduring historical responsibility for the European other; and – once again in Arendt's terms – which disguises and neuters the antagonistic class relations that lie behind our constitutional frameworks of civic, social and political rights, voiding our memories of feudal, *bourgeois* and industrial conflagration and laying us open to the rational colonisation and perversion of a *ius publicum europaeum*, which, through its self-referential placement in a sphere beyond politics (and emotional history), undermines its own socially-reconciling promise.[49]

5. Union Citizenship Fallito (2): Class Bites Back

5.1. *The Empirical Traces of Class Exclusion*

Returning, then, to our notion of industrial citizenship, the case of *Commission* v *Austria* may also be treated in explicitly class-oriented terms. For all of Somek's doubts about the socially-regressive impact of the legislation in question – which rewards a *per se* middle class failure to achieve outstanding results within the Austrian system of grammar schools with a university education – the refusal to establish an exclusionary *numerus clausus* within continental universities has generally been motivated by corrective concern about the stubborn persistence of structural class inequalities within the education system. Seen in this light, ECJ's jurisprudence might accordingly be regarded as rewarding the middle class success of Polish, Portuguese and Greek students at the price of the working-class failure of their Austrian counterparts. This, in its turn, raises the highly uncomfortable question of whether processes of European integration

49 The initial congruence between Arendt's (that is, our heroine's) negative evaluation of European republicanism and Schmitt's (our universal fiend's) dismissal of plural constitutional settlement is one that disturbs many a political theorist. However, Schmitt's binary friend-enemy distinction, which justifies the sovereign colonisation of political power must be starkly contrasted, in its theoretical-political impact, with Arendt's spatial ambivalence and consequential recognition of the normative primacy of enduring antagonism.

have – in fact, rather than in the esoteric terms of allocational economic theory – been detrimental to the interests of a European working class.

Arendt herself was highly pessimistic:[50] the predominantly economic nature of the founding European Treaties would only aggravate the inherent failings of the European, rather than the American, republican revolution – namely, its tendency to subdue the confrontational class politics that was deemed to have to have explosively expressed and, thus, ended itself within the revolutionary moment, its promotion of a history-denying, history-displacing and history-creating rationality, as well as its assertion of a self-deluding, normative narrative of evolutionary progress.[51] A European working-class might only forge a Europe that would be responsive to its needs were it to end the constitutionally-conditioned *bourgeois* monopoly over European (non-) politics. However, that was then, and now is now, and, furthermore, the past thirty years of European integration have been wholly dominated by a normative-descriptive narrative of the *telos* of European integration, which has no room for class analyses or, indeed, for any empirical analysis at all.[52] Is it now at all possible to ascertain properly the differentiated class impact of processes of European integration?

Certainly, the traces of a differentiated class impact can be identified within the very dissimilar self-perceptions of European identity maintained by different social classes within Europe, and which, more particularly, have recently been so identified by the American sociologist, Neil Fligstein, in his timely book, *Euro-clash*.[53] For *Euro-clash* read "a clash of European social classes" and an embarrassment for European politicians and academics alike: Why has it taken an American to reveal the obvious to us, that, as a simple matter of course, an integration process, which is primarily economically-driven, is perceived to be of great benefit to a small élite of Europeans (10–15%) who will accordingly give it their full support at all times, is thought to be of occasional benefit to a middle group (40–50%), whose "European-ness" is, by the same token, necessarily contingent, but is, likewise perceived as a very real threat to a final set of Europeans (40–50%), who remain inexorably trapped within national paradigms of consciousness and self-protection.[54]

50 Her general concerns about the European constitutional settlement are explicitly related to the European Communities in M. Walzer, *Exodus und Revolution*, (Frankfurt: Fischer Taschenbücher, 1995).

51 Hannah Arendt, *On Revolution*: the European republic was beholden to European rationalism rather than pragmatic politics.

52 See M. Everson and J. Eisner (2007), Chapter 2, note 5 *supra*; G. Majone, *Dilemmas of European Integration*, (Oxford: Oxford University Press, 2006): the point being that, in its efforts simultaneously to describe and legitimate European processes of integration, European scholarship has often failed to take proper empirical note of what is happening in a real world of European integration, fatally pre-empting any systematic empirical analysis as facts are viewed through normative lenses.

53 Fligstein, Euro-clash: the EU, European identity and the future of Europe, (Oxford: Oxford University Press, 2008).

54 *Ibid.*, Chapter 8.

Fligstein accordingly presents us with the shocking, but, surely, not too surprising fact that socio-economic variables furnish us with an exact prediction of the degrees of European identity formation amongst European individuals.[55] Persons will identify themselves as more or less European in direct correlation to their mobility, levels of civic association (business, professional, NGO-related, tourism-related, *etc.*), levels of education and levels of (higher) cultural interaction. At one level, this seems a self-obvious conclusion, dictated to us by common sense, but does Fligstein, the empirical sociologist, tell us more? Does he tell us whether this brave new European world of re-invigorated class and differentiated identities is merely a matter of perception or, by stark contrast, is one of brutal fact?

Fligstein's orienting thesis is taken from Karl Deutsch and is, thus, also flavoured by centuries of European history (of class struggle and nation formation). Reviewing the wide range of sociological theories, historically centred on the nation state, which help to explain why groups of individuals with very divergent life experiences, as well as interests, are prepared to give their undivided loyalty to one political-legal entity, Fligstein plumps for Deutsch's exhortation that:

> the historical 'trick' to the rise of a nation state will be to find a horizontal solidarity for the existing [class] stratification and a rationale that using a state apparatus to protect the nation makes sense.[56]

In Arendt's politically-centred view, both Deutsch and Fligstein may initially appear to be a mite cynical within a Bismarckian semantic: identity, loyalty and the feeling that the search for a common fate is the best bet for self-protection (against forces both internal and external to the nation), are not to be won through the final overcoming of "stratification", but are, instead, to be bought through the establishment of a common culture (through shared national institutions such as church, army and educational establishments), which, continuing stratification notwithstanding, give a diffuse sense of common purpose and protection. Nonetheless, to the degree that the various joint institutions of national life are themselves centres for the reproduction and the reconciliation of the antagonistic class politics that simultaneously undermine and build the nation, which are the institutions of European life that might permit the reproduction and the reconciliation of a purging European class conflict?

And it is here that Fligstein begins to sketch out a reality – not a perception – of European life that segregates European classes and denies them access to antagonistically-reconciling politics. European integration is now, and has always been, a response to economic realities; in a first integrationist wave, with an eye to the need to rebuild the shattered economies of European nation states (and empires); and, in a second stage, as an answer to the pressures of globalisation and the need to reform

55 *Ibid.*, p. 140.
56 *Ibid.*, p. 130.

(protect) European economies, in order to meet the competitive pressures of a global market. In turn, however, economic processes of integration within the European market are themselves, and also give rise to, specific "fields of interaction" between individual Europeans,[57] which then determine the make-up of a European society, and also create opportunities for, and place constraints upon, European politics.

This process of economically-bounded interaction should never be mistaken for integrative "spill-over". Quite to the contrary: taking care empirically to dissect the exact nature of economic integration, globalisation, social interaction and political constraints/ opportunities, Fligstein demonstrates that integration has not evenly and smoothly diffused its impact across the whole of a European society. Instead, the initial process of integration, though often blocked by nationally-oriented Member States, nevertheless gave birth to powerful economic élites, with lobbying capacities at European level. By the same token, globalisation pressures and economic reforms have likewise enabled Europeanised élites to strengthen their presence within the higher – ownership – strata of the increasingly integrated European market. In socio-economic terms, the élite or ownership class now experiences a daily reality of Europeanisation within the workplace and within social life. Equally, the European élite has long found its political voice in Brussels, perceives Europeanisation to be in its interests (i.e., to act as a bulwark against globalisation), and will, therefore, place political pressure upon Member State governments to deepen the integration process at both national and European levels, no matter how resistant such governments may be. By contrast, at national level, political pressure – the need constantly to re-assert the core measure of national life – has also determined that national frameworks of property and labour law have been maintained and that market integration, in wide-scale industrial sectors, such as defence and telecommunications, has been effected, not through the establishment of conspicuously European firms, but through mergers, joint ventures and jointly-owned subsidiaries; an integration model that leaves the concrete impression that economic life is still national and not European in nature (ironically, even where ownership is American).[58] This, in turn, determines that the mass of industrial workers experience their daily lives wholly within the national context. In contrast to a middle class, which may have a more diffused understanding of Europeanisation processes, and which, at the very least, experiences Europeanisation – and, importantly, interacts with other Europeans – through the benefits of culturally-oriented tourism (i.e., *not* mass package tourism), a working class is never socialised within joint institutions of European life.

The site of politics for the European working class is, primarily, a national one. Furthermore, at national level, the European working class confronts a national political leadership, which is itself beholden to the Europeanised interests of an ownership élite,

57 *Ibid.*, pp. 9–10.

58 The one exception being the UK, where ownership passes easily to non-UK companies. Equally, the UK labour market is heavily Europeanised.

and which is also uncertain of the degree of nationalised support that it will receive from a mass of middle-class workers, whose political sentiments often prove to be as unpredictable as their partially-Europeanised daily life. In political terms, then, the European working-class is doubly excluded from reconciling process of antagonistic European class expression, on the one hand, as they neither experience a site or institution of joint European political interaction, and, on the other, since they might never win the undivided (national) attentions of their own political leaders.

5.2. *The Legal Consolidation of Class Exclusion*

To the degree that economic processes of European integration have isolated the working-classes of Europe within national paradigms of protective politics, where they cannot but fight, the one against the other, rather than join together to contest *bourgeois* economic might, recent non-votes against the draft European Constitution or draft Treaty of Lisbon are even less to be dismissed as the result of the European populace's unfortunate ignorance about, and lacking understanding of, the workings of European institutions. Instead, hostility is a highly rational phenomenon, both amongst the social class to whom integration is most threatening and amongst the better placed group of "occasional" Europeans, whose support is given either to the nation state, or to the EU, in line with a considered calculation as to which body is better placed to provide social cohesion at any one time. Indeed, the "no" vote was potentially the only site of European politics within which class antagonisms might, at least, be jointly aired.

Given this conclusion, the analysis now finally returns to its starting point in order to ask whether adjudicative European law – the confounding *Janus* that engages in acts of emotional irrationality, just as it draws a veil of rationalism over its activities – has made its own particular contribution to the exclusion of the common European man from the core sites of antagonistic European class conflict; whether it, too, and not just a diffuse process of economic differentiation, is actively engaged in the *bourgeois* colonisation of the normative framework of European law, a process of colonisation, which, by means of its negation of the European nation and its history of class struggle, has undermined the core of European citizenship? The response to this question, however, is found relatively easily, and must now be a resounding "yes".

The recent European cases of *Viking*, *Laval* and *Rüffert* have thus become pivotal within this context,[59] not simply since they have, quite remarkably, rejected the warnings given by Marx and, more recently, by Polanyi,[60] about the dire consequences of forcing a working-class into wage competition with itself – and that in the name of "social

59 Case C-438/05, International Transport Workers' Federation, Finnish Seamen's Union v. Viking Line ABP, OÜ Viking Line Eesti (Judgment of 11 December 2007; Case C-341/05); Laval un Partneri Ltd v. Svenska Byggnadsarbetareförbundet, Svenska Byggnadsarbetareförbundet, avd. 1, Svenska Elektrikerförbundet (Judgment of 18 December 2007); Case C-346/06, *Rechtsanwalt Dr. Dirk Rüffert v. Land Niedersachsen (*Judgment of 3 April 2008).

60 Karl Polanyi (1944), *The Great Transformation*, (New York: Beacon Press, 2001).

justice",[61] but rather, since they have also, with the aid of our old adjudicative friend "proportionality", once again excluded a European working-class from any possible site of political contestation, within which its antagonistic interests might be presented and asserted. The adjudicative interplay between a Posted Workers Directive,[62] purportedly introduced by the Council in order to regulate potential social dumping within the European market, and European rights of establishment and service-provision, as well as the primary provisions of European state aid law have thus led in European law to: 1) the creation of an absolute judicial prohibition against an international seaman's strike (and *all* international solidarity strikes) called in solidaristic opposition to the re-flagging of a vessel, in order to allow for the hiring of cheaper foreign labour (*Viking*); 2) the imposition of a judicial value of "proportionality" upon *all* national strikes called in defence of local bargaining agreements (*Viking* and *Laval*); and 3) the establishment of a final prohibition on the democratically-legitimated enforcement of *all* local bargaining agreements, as local and national authorities are precluded by the provisions of the state aid law from tailoring their tenders to respect such agreements, and Article 3(1) of the Posted Workers Directive is deemed to give European protection only to *universal* provisions of national labour law, such as minimum wage requirements, working hour legislation and health and safety regulation, which apply to *all* workers in a Member State (*Laval* and *Rüffert*).

Not surprisingly, such judgements have drawn a host of outraged comment from commentators, not least since the European Court appears thus to have drawn a coach and horses through the social constitutional settlements of countries, such as Sweden, which, historically, have not maintained minimum wage legislation, but have, instead, reconciled antagonistic class struggle by means of governmental enforcement of union-employer negotiated-bargaining agreements. At this one level, the ECJ would thus seem to have confirmed that the corporatist model of economic organisation within Europe is dead, and declared – the somewhat untimely – sovereignty of an Anglo-Saxon model of universal welfare provision.[63] However, the interventionist impact of the Court just as surely extends far beyond the misconceived negative constitutional juxtaposition of the Anglo-Saxon model with continental models of social organisation, in order to effect the *bourgeois* colonisation of the framework of European law, instead.

The clear, but shocking, historical analogy is the case of *Lochner* v *New York*, decided by the US Supreme Court in 1905,[64] whereby the democratic right of the state of New York to set its own working conditions (including the rights of workers to strike) was overturned with reference to the US Constitution's absolute guarantee for property. Presented by the majority of the Court as a formalistic inevitability, driven simply by

61 See below.

62 Directive 96/71/EC, OJ L 18/1996, 1.

63 See the relevant references in, Ch. Joerges and F. Rödl, "Informal Politics, Formalised Law and the 'Social Deficit' of European Integration: Reflections after the Judgments of the ECJ in Viking and Laval", (2009) 15 *European Law Journal*, pp. 1–19.

64 *Lochner* v *New York*, 198 U.S. 45 (1905).

the hierarchical precedence of the Constitution over state legislation, the cracked veneer of formalist rationality within the Court was, nonetheless, readily exposed, as the dissenting Judge, Justice Holmes, laconically observed that the democratic right of the states to legislate in this area was guaranteed also by the Constitution.[65] The *bourgeois* sentiments of the US Supreme Court are readily identified; and so, too, are the *bourgeois* sentiments of European judge-kings who, once again, engage in an ill-advised, emotionally-driven *auctoritas interposito*, giving voice to their own perceptions of the social justice due to Eastern European workers, but, at the same time, denying the European working-class as a whole the opportunity to assert its antagonistic interests against a *bourgeois* European economy. The ECJ need not have decided as it did.

Eastern enlargement and the failure of Western Europe to afford a measure of democratically-legitimated redistributive justice to its recently-liberated eastern cousins is the backdrop against which the cases were decided, and it is also the backdrop against which the formalistically-flavoured *choice* of the Court to assert – under the veil of occidental rationalism – the hierarchical precedence of Articles 43, 49 and 87 EC Treaty above the constitutional traditions and democratic processes of the Member States was taken. For all his talk of the creation of a European social constitution, the measure of AG Maduro's notion of social justice in modern Europe is to be found in his promotion of social constitutionalism within a dominant European economic model of "allocative efficiency"; an ill-timed and emotional *auctoritas interposito*, which reacts to the clearly disadvantaged position of Eastern European workers with a notion of "social justice" that will see them work for less than western workers, and western workers denied access to their own jobs. Worse still, this false individual sentiment affects the Court as a whole, as the useful precedents of a series of social insurance cases are rejected,[66] and the hands of national courts are tied, as proportionality becomes the impossible yardstick against which social antagonism must be measured.

Within the social insurance cases – primarily concerning professional "trade agreements", rather than the industrial bargaining agreements commonly concluded by the mass trades union movement – the core decision was one that such restrictive practices were *per se* legitimate mechanisms of social policy, and might only be reviewed under the European competition regime (Article 81 EC), with an eye to a procedural principle of proportionality, whereby such private arrangements would be reviewed by national courts in order to ensure that they were fair and not abusive in their composition and rates.[67] Such a procedural resolution was also conceivable in the case of collective bargaining agreements; here, however, the formula is reversed. Collective bargaining agreements are *per se* restrictions on European rights; strikes will be

65 *Lochner* v *New York*, 198 U.S. 45 (1905.

66 Joined Cases *Poucet and Pistre* C-180/98 to C-184/98 [2000] ECR I-6451; Joined Cases *Albany* C-115/97, C-117/97, C-210/97, [1999] ECR I-6025 and [1999] ECR I-6121; Joined Cases, *Pavel Pavlov*, C-180/98 to C-184/98 [2000].

67 See, M. Everson, "Social Pluralism and the European Court of Justice. A Court between a Rock and a Hard Place", (2003) 8 *The Journal of Legislative Studies*, pp. 98–116.

contested in national courts to ascertain whether they are proportionate with those rights, in their substance, and not in their conduct.

And, thus, false sentiment is unveiled as *bourgeois* might. A strike, the withdrawal of labour, is never substantively proportionate. Certainly, it may be illegally conducted, and, here, proportionality may have a real legal meaning, allowing courts to review whether strike votes were properly held. Beyond that, however, the strike is an irrational and disproportionate act, a concrete political expression of antagonistic class conflict, a modern continuation of the struggle that creates and undermines both our market and our state, a necessary site of reconciling conflict between antagonistic European classes, and a necessary site of conflict that the European Court has decisively foreclosed.

6. The Responsibilities of Legal Method in European Law

The consequences of the *bourgeois* colonisation of European law under current conditions of extreme economic decline are potentially catastrophic and may lead us blindly into a revolution ending in the very destruction of Europe. Wildcat strikes within the UK against contracted labour from other European states, the prospect that continental unions will take legal action to ask their constitutional courts to set European law aside, are all the more shocking for the manner in which they have been represented within both the national and the European media.[68] In a highly unfortunate clash between identity-based notions of citizenship and industrial conceptions of the citizen, workers are dismissed as "xenophobic" and "racist", are denied political voice as the mere representatives of the dinosaur of industrial self-interest. Contracted workers are viewed as the victims of the strikers, rather than as the victims of a *bourgeois* European economy, which has no proper redistributive provisions. Worker is set against worker as national governments, in thrall to the interests of the European ownership élite, are deaf to their protests; worker is set against worker as national courts are closed to them as sites of political contestation. The worker is eradicated from the stage of European politics and becomes easy prey for extremist organisers both from the left and from the right.

The time then has surely come to end the complacency of a European scholarship, which has lauded processes of supposed deliberation within, say, the European Convention and Open Method of Co-ordination, has been blind to the real assertion of social interest within Europe, dismissing no-votes as being reflective of the ignorance of individual Europeans and has thus located itself within a European élite[69] that is inured

68 *The Times* Comment (30 January 2009): "For many, complaints about foreign workers coming here and taking their jobs are disturbingly reminiscent of the atmosphere whipped up in Britain's cities during the 1960s and 1970s, when the backlash against Commonwealth immigration was reflected both in the ballot box – in support for extreme right-wing parties – and, in many cases, in street violence. As unemployment starts to edge up to levels last seen in the mid-1980s, the hunt is on for scapegoats."

69 Fligstein highlights the role of the European academic in the creation of the European élite (Fligstein 2008), Chapter 6.

to the social and political aspirations of the European people. Surely the time has now come to develop a European legal method, which is founded within history, sensitive to the dangers posed by a judge-king, and which is never fooled or perverted by a lure of European élitism? Or, has it not, by stark contrast, been there all the time? We are fortunate to have experienced this legal scholarship from the very outset. In his time at the European University Institute, European Christian Joerges has not only reminded us constantly about the ambivalence of the judge-king,[70] however well-intentioned he or she may be, he has also written repeatedly on the need to celebrate lawyers who have fought against – at great personal cost – the very real dangers of occidental rationalism, and its collapse, within the *ius publicum europaeum*.[71] He has not only repeatedly stressed the vital importance of the maintenance – within a conflict of laws logic – of the core of the national social settlement,[72] he has also powerfully intervened to oppose the forces of blind economic rationality that are now threatening the very future of Europe.[73] And, finally, with his historical sensitivity for the failings of the classical European nation state within all of its myriad legal settlements, he has just as surely primed us to maintain, at all times, our core humanity and empathy for the European other.[74]

70 In an excellent, if very difficult, seminar on legal theory.

71 "History as Non-History: Divergencies and Time Lags between Friedrich Kessler and German Jurisprudence", (1994) 42 *American Journal of Comparative Law*, pp. 163–193; "Geschichte als Nicht-Geschichte: Unterschiede und Ungleichzeitigkeiten zwischen Friedrich Kessler und der deutschen Rechtswissenschaft", in: Marcus Lutter, Ernst C. Stiefel and Michael H. Hoeflich (eds), *Der Einfluß deutschsprachiger Emigranten auf die Rechtsentwicklung in den USA und in Deutschland*, (Tübingen: Mohr & Siebeck, 1993), pp. 221–253.

72 Christian Joerges, "What is left of the European Economic Constitution? A Melancholic Eulogy", (2005) 30 *European Law Review*, pp. 461–48; "Rethinking European Law's Supremacy: A Plea for a Supranational Conflict of Laws", in: Beate Kohler Koch and Berthold Rittberger (eds), *Debating the Democratic Legitimacy of the European Union*, (Lanham MD: Rowman and Littlefield, 2007), pp. 311–327; and Jürgen Neyer, "From Intergovernmental Bargaining to Deliberative Political Processes: The Constitutionalisation of Comitology", (1997) 3 *European Law Journal*, pp. 273–299.

73 Ch. Joerges, "The 'Social Market Economy' as Europe's Social Model?", in: Lars Magnusson and Bo Stråth (eds), *A European Social Citizenship? Preconditions for Future Policies in Historical Light*, (Brussels: Lang, 2005), pp. 125–158; Christian Joerges and Florian Rödl, "The 'Social Market Economy' as Europe's Social Model?", EUI Working Paper Law No. 2004/8; Ch. Joerges and F. Rödl, "Informal Politics, Formalised Law and the 'Social Deficit' of European Integration: Reflections after the Judgments of the ECJ in Viking and Laval", (2009) 15 *European Law Journal*, pp. 1–19.

74 Erik Oddvar Eriksen, Christian Joerges and Florian Rödl (eds), *Law, Democracy and Solidarity in a Post-national Union*, (London and New York: Routledge, 2008), especially, "Working through 'Bitter Experiences' towards Constitutionalisation: A Critique on the Disregard for History in European Constitutional Theory", pp. 175–192); Ch. Joerges and Navraj S. Ghaleigh (eds), *Darker Legacies of Law in Europe: The Shadow of National Socialism and Fascism over Europe and its Legal Traditions*, (Oxford: Hart Publishing, 2003); Ch. Joerges, "Continuities and Discontinuities in German Legal Thought, The Darker Side of a Pluralist Heritage: Anti-liberal Traditions in European Social Theory and Legal Thought", (2003) 14 *Special Issue of Law and Critique*, pp. 297–308.

Ellen Vos

CHAPTER 7. ABOUT DELIBERATIVE SUPRANATIONALISM, COMITOLOGY AND OTHER HEROES

1. "Comitology is Our Hero!"

"Comitology is our hero!" This exclamation was frequently heard in many rooms of the Villa Schifanoia and at conferences held at the European University Institute and elsewhere during the 1990s, when I did my PhD thesis under the supervision of Christian Joerges. With this, Christian Joerges wanted to underline the important role that comitology played in the European integration process, and he praised it for its deliberative interaction and the emergence of an *esprit de corps* in the committee system, arguing that it "had achieved a change for the better, silently and behind the backs of the officially accountable actors".[1] While comitology had long been discussed in the institutions since the 1960s, it had also long been ignored by academic literature. Even at its inception, comitology was already an issue of legal and institutional dispute between the institutions. It was argued that it detracted from the Commission's independent right of decision and thus also from the Parliament's right of control, and, ultimately, that it distorted the EU's institutional balance of powers. In particular, the Parliament was very keen to fight for more insight and control of comitology, referring to its obscure and undemocratic character and demanding that it be treated on an equal footing with the Council, where powers had been delegated by the European Parliament and Council to the Commission under co-decision.

1 Ch. Joerges and J. Neyer, "From Intergovernmental Bargaining to Deliberative Political Processes: The Constitutionalisation of Comitology", (1997) 3 *European Law Journal* (*ELJ*), p. 299.

It was only in the 1990s that researchers, in particular Christian Joerges,[2] started to address this "low politics" of the European Union[3] concerning the preparation, shaping and implementation of decisions by comitology committees. In particular, the Bremen project led by Christian Joerges, which studied the comitology in the practice of risk regulation in the internal market,[4] revealed important insights into the practical operation of comitology, and demonstrated its enormous impact upon EU decision-making. Upon the basis of an empirical study in the food sector, Christian Joerges and Jürgen Neyer explained that:

> [T]he Commission had accepted this co-operative arrangement because it needed the resources of national administrators in order to perform the function which the 'implementation' of Community law required. The Member States accepted it because they hoped to supervise the control of the Commission's practices. No principal and no agent had planned to establish the type of deliberative problem-solving that we had observed and described.[5]

2 To be sure also G. Schaefer examined this topic; see R. Pedler and G. Schaefer, (eds), *Shaping European Law and Policy: The Role of Committees and Comitology in the Political Process*, (Maastricht: EIPA, 1996). See, for the work by Christian Joerges, for example, Ch. Joerges, "Social Regulation by the Community: the Case of Foodstuffs", in: F. Snyder (ed), A *Regulatory Framework for Foodstuffs in the Internal Market*, EUI Working Paper LAW 94/4 (European University Institute, Florence, 1994), pp. 50–56; Ch. Joerges, "Die Beurteilung der Sicherheit technischer Konsumgüter und der Gesundheitrisiken von Lebensmitteln in der Praxis des europäischen Ausschußwesens ('Komitologie')", 95/1 *ZERP-Diskussionspapier* (1995); Ch. Joerges, "Scientific Expertise in Social Regulation and the European Court of Justice: Legal Frameworks for Denationalised Governance Structures", in: Ch. Joerges, K.-H. Ladeur and E. Vos (eds), *Integrating Scientific Expertise into Regulatory Decision-Making. National Traditions and European Innovations*, (Baden-Baden: Nomos, 1997), pp. 295–323; Ch. Joerges and J. Neyer, "From Intergovernmental Bargaining to Deliberative Political Processes: The Constitutionalisation of Comitology", (1997) 3 *ELJ*, pp. 273–299; Ch. Joerges and J. Neyer, "Transforming strategic interaction into deliberative problem-solving: European comitology in the foodstuff sector", (1997) 4 *Journal of European Public Policy*, p. 609; Ch. Joerges and E. Vos, *EU Committees: Social Regulation, Law and Politics*, (Oxford: Hart Publishing, 1999); Ch. Joerges and J. Falke, (eds), *Das Ausschußwesen der Europäischen Union – Praxis der Risikoregulierung im Binnenmarkt und ihre rechtliche Verfassung*, (Baden-Baden: Nomos, 2000); Ch. Joerges, "Comitology and the European model? Towards a Recht-Fertigungs-Recht in the Europeanisation Process", in: E.O. Eriksen, Ch. Joerges and J. Neyer, (eds), *European Governance, Deliberation and the Quest for Democratisation*, (Oslo, Arena Report, 2003); Ch. Joerges, "Deliberative Political Processes Revisited: What Have we Learnt About the Legitimacy of Supranational Decision-Making", (2006) 44 *Journal of Common Market Studies*, p. 779; Ch. Joerges, "Reconceptualising the Supremacy of European Law: A Plea for a Supranational Conflict of Laws", in: B. Kohler-Koch and B. Rittberger, (eds), *Debating the Democratic Legitimacy of the European Union*, (Lanham MD: Rowman and Littlefield Publishers, 2007), p. 311.

3 T. Christiansen and T. Larsson, "Introduction: the role of committee in the policy process of the European Union", in: T. Christiansen and T. Larsson, (eds), *The Role of Committees in the EU Policy-Process*, (Cheltenham: Edward Elgar, 2007), p. 1.

4 Joerges 1995, see note 2 *supra*; Joerges and Falke 2000, see note 2 *supra*.

5 Joerges 2006, see note 2 *supra*, p. 785.

They claimed that the establishment of non-hierarchical governance structures needs to be understood as an indispensable pre-requisite for the functioning of the common market. This type of governance will depend upon persuasion, argument and discursive processes, rather than on command, control and/or strategic action.[6] It "rejects the idea of supra-national central implementation machinery headed by the Commission, and thus directly forces national governments into a co-operative venture".[7] Comitology, then, in their view, was the normatively imperfect institutionalisation of co-operative problem-solving.

This "deliberative supra-nationalism", as they termed it, needed a "constitutionalisation" of comitology, an improved legal framework that would stabilise the deliberative potential of comitology governance. With this, they tried to offer an alternative to the vision of a European "regulatory state", and the resort to independent agencies as advanced by Giandomenico Majone. This novel and challenging analysis of comitology, viewing committees as deliberative bodies that would not be confined purely to implementation issues, radically changed the traditional vision of comitology as being an instrument of intergovernmental control, generally held in the hands of the main institutional actors, the Council, the Parliament and the Commission.

Not surprisingly, Christian Joerges' analysis had, and still has, an enormous impact on academic research, which started to debate the "good" and the "bad" of comitology in this new light. Many authors were particularly sceptical of the attempt to build a theoretical justification for a positive assessment of comitology, as a forum for "deliberative politics", as a form of "deliberative supra-nationalism", thus enhancing legitimacy.[8]

In addition, others also criticised the claims of the democratic character of comitology, and accused "deliberative supra-nationalism" to favour a traditionally technocratic model of policy consultation that would not place European governance in line with the normative criteria of theories of deliberative democracy.[9] Other analyses, while acknowledging that committees may well contribute to the erosion of the crude pursuit of national interests and thus promote "deliberative problem-solving" in European governance, distinguish committees with formally weak powers (advisory) and committees with far-reaching powers (regulatory). They reveal, upon the basis of an empirical study in the field of the environment, that the latter type of committee is much more based upon "power-based pursuit of parochial interests", rather than on

6 Joerges and Neyer, 1997, see note 1 *supra*, p. 277.

7 Ibid.

8 See, for example, B. Kohler-Koch, "Die Europäisierung nationaler Demokratien. Verschleiß eines europäischen Kulturerbes?" in: M. Greven (ed), *Demokratie – eine Kultur des Westens?* (Opladen: Leske + Budrich, 1998), p. 277 *et seq.*

9 R. Schmalz-Bruns, "Deliberativer Supranationalismus: Demokratisches Regieren jenseits des Nationalstaates", (1999) 6 *Zeitschrift für Internationale Beziehungen*, p. 185. J.H.H. Weiler, "Epilogue", in: Ch. Joerges and E. Vos, (eds), *EU Committees: Social Regulation, Law and Politics*, (Oxford: Hart Publishing, 1999), p. 338 and p. 340.

promoting deliberative consensus-building.[10] Others again, although critical about the empirical underpinning of the theory, strongly supported the need for the Member States to participate in the implementing phase of EU decision-making through deliberative interaction,[11] confirmed that this mechanism makes the action of the Commission more democratic and "closer to the citizen",[12] and viewed it as complementing the limited staff resources in the Commission.[13] As they are composed of both bureaucrats and national representatives at the same time, committees have been considered as co-ordinating bodies which act between supra-national and national, and governmental and social, actors, and may (although not always) voice national viewpoints.[14]

Faced with these criticisms, Christian Joerges has defended[15] and further explained deliberative supra-nationalism as being understood as a "conflict-of-laws methodology", which is about "the recognition of foreign law, the adaptation of domestic law to the co-operative needs and legal commitments and principles furthering co-operative problem-solving".[16] He distinguished two types of deliberative supra-nationalism: DSN I, which is "a law of conflicts mediation", and DSN II, which is "a law that responds to the apparently irresistible transformation of institutionalised government into transnational governance arrangements".[17] It is the latter type that this article discusses, with a focus upon the comitology that Christian Joerges considers as being an (imperfect) example of this. It will share some new insights and developments that have taken place in the food sector – the cradle of Christian Joerges' analysis in the pre-BSE era – and examine whether and to what extent these developments and new institutional arrangements fit with Christian Joerges' model.

10 See, for example, T. Gehring, "Arguing, Bargaining and Functional Differentiation of Decision-making. The Role of Committees in European Environmental Process Regulation", in: Ch. Joerges and E. Vos, (eds), *EU Committees: Social Regulation, Law and Politics*, (Oxford: Hart Publishing, 1999), p. 206.

11 E. Vos, "The rise of committees", (1997) 3 *European Law Journal*, p. 230.

12 K. Lenaerts and A. Verhoeven, "Towards a legal Framework for Executive Rule-making in the EU? The Contribution of the New Comitology Decision", (2000) 37 Common Market Law Review, p. 664.

13 L. Allio, "The Case for Comitology Reform: Efficiency, Transparency, Accountability", in: L. Allio and G. Durand, (eds), *From Legislation to Implementation: the Future of EU Decision-making*, (Brussels: European Policy Centre, 2003), p. 39.

14 E. Vos, "The role of Comitology in European Governance", in: D. Curtin and R. Wessel, (eds), *Good Governance and the European Union-Concept, implications and applications*, (Antwerp: Intersentia, 2005), p. 107.

15 See, for example, Ch. Joerges, "Deliberative Supra-nationalism, Two Defences", (2002) 8 *ELJ*, p. 133.

16 Joerges 2006, see note 2 *supra*, p. 802. See, also, Joerges 2007, see note 2 *supra*.

17 Joerges 2007, see note 2 *supra*, p. 322.

2. DSN II, Comitology and Foodstuffs

2.1. *Comitology as a Co-operative System*

When looking at the practice of comitology, we may observe that, over the years, the decision-making involving comitology led to a more consensual and problem-solving approach to decision-making between the Commission and the committees.[18] When looking at the figures presented by the European Commission, it appears that only a few draft decisions are submitted to the Council, under the regulatory committee procedure.[19] These data clearly indicate the great importance of committee-based decision-making. Moreover, recent empirical analysis confirms the picture that emerged from the empirical research carried out by Christian Joerges and others, namely, that of a more deliberative process. According to these findings, the comitology system "instead of being exclusive and manipulated by a few, [...] seems to be more inclusive and focused on finding solutions through reasoning not bargaining, at least when compared with many national governments".[20] It is concluded that:

> [T]his is a system which uses socialisation as an important tool in making politicians, experts and interest representatives from different nations agree on issues of common interest.[21]

In comitology committees, so this study argues, the expertise of the Commission, often supported by outside expertise through interest groups and consultancies, is merged with the know-how of the experts of the Member States. In this manner, the comitology system enables the Commission and Member States to manage the extremely complex system of agriculture efficiently. Other comitology committees confront difficult and technical issues in long and tedious negotiations, which are not time-efficient but are consensus-efficient.[22] Practice, moreover, demonstrates that comitology may be extremely important, as it allows national positions also to be taken into account in the implementing phase in order to ensure the proper enforcement of, and compliance with,

18 See, for example, COM(2001) 783 final, p. 7.

19 For 2006, for example, the data produced by the Commission reveal that the number of favourable opinions delivered by regulatory and management committees amounted to 2,933 (compared with 2,582 in 2005), the number of cases in which no opinion could be obtained or an opinion was absent, amounted to 129. No unfavourable opinions were reported. Of the 3,061 draft decisions submitted to the committees, only 6 were referred to the Council under the regulatory committee procedure. In these cases, no opinion could be reached by the relevant committees on waste, genetically modified organisms (GMOs) and the Generalised System of Preferences (trade). See the Commission of the European Communities, *Report from the Commission on the Working of Committees During 2006*, COM(2007) 842 final, 20 December 2007, pp. 6–7. See, also, the List of Comitology Committees assisting the Commission of the European Communities, February 2008, available at: http://ec.europa.eu/transparency/regcomitology/docs/comitology_committees_en.pdf.

20 T. Christiansen, T. Larsson and G.F. Schaefer, "Conclusion", in: T. Christiansen and T. Larsson, (eds), *The Role of Committees in the EU Policy-Process*, (Cheltenham: Edward Elgar, 2007), p. 271.

21 Ibid.

22 *Ibid.*, p. 265.

EU decisions. Striving for more effective decision-making and better policies would thus require the Member States to be consulted in the implementing phase.[23] This is clearly demonstrated by the recent empirical study which finds that the comitology committees contribute effectively to improving the implementation and application process of EC law in, and through, the Member States. Without the comitology system, the current implementation and application deficits would be much worse.[24]

2.2. The Food Sector

For the field of foodstuffs, a slightly different picture emerges. It was this field that was the origin of Christian Joerges' analysis in the pre-BSE era. Today, more than ten years after the outbreak of the BSE crisis, the refurbished Standing Committee on the Food Chain and Animal Health absorbs the formerly existing Standing Committee on Foodstuffs and other standing committees, whilst the Scientific Committee for Food has been absorbed into the newly created European Food Safety Authority (EFSA). A few observations based upon a recent small-scale empirical study[25] seem to suggest that, in this domain, this "normatively imperfect institutionalisation of co-operative problem-solving" as Christian Joerges and Jürgen Neyer proclaimed in the pre-BSE era,[26] is "losing ground", and, indeed, challenges the concept of deliberative supra-nationalism.

Firstly, the research revealed that, today within the framework of the Standing Committee, there seems to be less deliberation and more bargaining and negotiation around representative interests than Christian Joerges and Jürgen Neyer observed in the pre-BSE era.[27] In view of the highly political and politicised character of food issues in the aftermath of BSE, particularly with regard to GM issues, this may not come as a real surprise.[28] In this manner, it is felt by various Commission officials who were interviewed that Committee members consult more often with their national ministries, and that, in some politically very sensitive areas, such as GM food or contaminants, some members tend to come to meetings with clear instructions from "home" and/or have clearly defined positions to defend. As a consequence, the meetings of the Standing Committee deliberately start in the morning so as to give members the opportunity to obtain feedback from the Member States and to allow the Commission to alter its proposal by the evening, thereby enhancing the possibility of reaching

23 See note 14 *supra*.

24 Christiansen, Larsson and Schaefer, see note 20 *supra*, p. 265.

25 For the purpose of this study, 13 persons were interviewed, of whom 9 were from DG SANCO of the Commission, 1 from the EFSA and 3 from stakeholder associations. Of the 13 interviewees, 4 were female. Both senior managers and desk officials were interviewed. The interviews took place between April and July 2005. See E. Vos and F. Wendler, "Food Safety Regulation at the EU Level", in: E. Vos and F. Wendler (eds), *Food Safety Regulation in Europe. A Comparative Institutional Analysis*, (Antwerp: Intersentia, 2006), pp. 65–138, at 116–131.

26 Joerges and Neyer 1997, see note 1 *supra*.

27 Gehring observed this situation of bargaining to take place in the area of environmental policy in the 1990s, See T. Gehring, note 10 *supra*.

28 See P. Dabrowska, *EU Governance of GMOs*, (Oxford: Hart Publishing, forthcoming 2009).

agreement on the measure in question.[29] This practice seems to be in contrast with the pre-BSE practice of the former Standing Committee on Foodstuffs, in which members appeared to be free to discuss solutions without any ministerial backing and with a formal vote rarely being taken.[30]

Secondly, discussions with stakeholders no longer take place within the comitology setting. Although the Commission had already created an Advisory Committee on Foodstuffs in the 1970s, composed of various stakeholder representatives, this Committee was no longer consulted in the 1980s. In the post-BSE era, in an attempt to overcome the crisis of confidence in EU risk regulation and to compensate for the closed science- and policy-making within the Standing Committee and EFSA's scientific Committee and Panels, we can observe the creation of separate platforms by both the Commission and the EFSA, on order to discuss more policy-oriented issues for the Commission and more science-oriented issues for EFSA with the stakeholders. As a result, today, discussions with the stakeholders take place separately with the EFSA and the Commission,[31] outside of the context of comitology.

Thirdly, we can observe an increasing scientification of food safety regulation and the Europeanisation of science in the field of foodstuffs, which seem to give Member States less influence within the context of comitology than was the case in the pre-BSE era. This is exemplified by the intensification of the relationship between the Commission and the EFSA, to the detriment of the relationship between the Commission and the national representatives within the Standing Committee. In this manner, there are the first indications that, at least for priority-setting, the Commission prefers to consult the EFSA first, instead of asking the Member States for advice within the framework of comitology, which was the general practice before the EFSA was created. Discussions on this topic now seem to take place in the comitology setting only at a second stage.[32]

These findings, nevertheless, do not encroach upon Christian Joerges' view that comitology is key to the co-ordination of viewpoints between the Commission and the Member States, and that it also operates as a conflict-of-laws rule between the EU and the Member State level in this field.[33] The empirical study indeed confirms that comitology is an essential and indispensable element of food regulation. The Commission officials of DG SANCO who were interviewed were all very much aware of the importance of collaboration with, and approval by, the Member States for their draft decisions within the framework of the Standing Committee, and that they are willing to compromise, albeit not at any cost. Moreover, national representatives were viewed as being more "EU-minded", or, to express it differently, more "compromise-oriented"

29 See Vos and Wendler, note 25 *supra*.

30 Joerges and Neyer 1997, see note 1 *supra*.

31 Commission/EFSA representatives may, nevertheless, attend meetings of the EFSA's Stakeholder Platform/the Commission's Advisory Group on the Food Chain and Animal Health.

32 Vos and Wendler, see note 25 *supra*, p. 132.

33 Joerges 2007, see note 2 *supra*.

than before. Furthermore, all interviewees favoured the comitology procedure above the normal legislative, co-decision procedure. Among some officials, it was felt that there was "no alternative" to the comitology procedure; indeed, one EFSA official considered it even to be the "most democratic procedure".[34]

Figure 7.1. Interplay of various actors within the field of food safety regulation in the post-BSE era

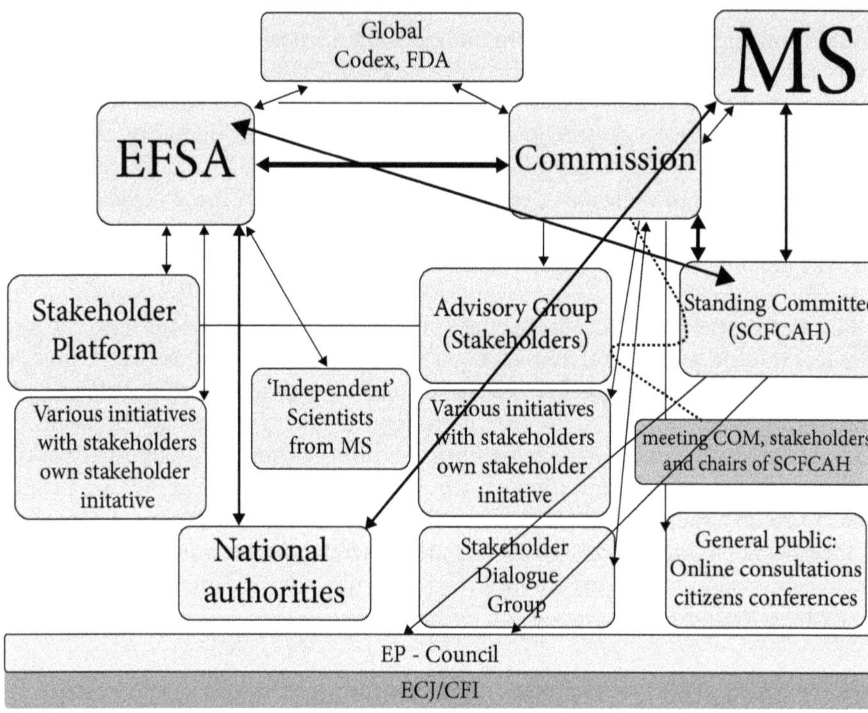

What these developments do show, however, is that the current practical reality is more diverse and complex than the model that Christian Joerges suggests (see Figure 1). Social pluralist interests are discussed outside the framework of the Standing Committee with either the Commission or the EFSA separately, without Member States representatives being present.[35] In view of the mere one-sided communication

34 Vos and Wendler, see note 25 *supra*, p. 129.

35 The stakeholders interviewed considered the Stakeholder Consultative Platform of EFSA to be very open, quite interactive and truly involving stakeholders in the choice of subjects for consultation. In contrast, the Commission's Advisory Group was seen mainly as a communication and information channel for the Commission to the stakeholders, without offering stakeholders the possibility of influencing the debate or exchanging opinions. F. Wendler and E. Vos, "Stakeholder Involvement in EU Food Safety Governance: Towards a More Open and Structured Approach?", Working Paper for Subproject 5 of the SAFE FOODS Project (Maastricht 2008).

channel within the Commission's stakeholder setting, stakeholder representatives themselves ask to be included in the meetings of the Standing Committee as it is precisely there that the decisions are being taken. Quite revolutionarily, DG SANCO seems to be willing to accommodate such wishes, and it would seem that it intends to encourage discussions between the chairs of the different sections of the Standing Committee, the Advisory Group on the Animal Food Chain and Plant Health and other stakeholders with the DG SANCO representatives,[36] thereby establishing the first step towards the creation of a public sphere on comitology, in which interested parties can voice concerns and exchange ideas with both Commission and Member State officials; this is, indeed, a development which would point towards Christian Joerges' model.

Yet, it is the third development, that of science and rationality being considered as a *panacea* to restore and secure public faith in the credibility of risk regulation, which seems to be the most important challenge to deliberative supra-nationalism. Undoubtedly, the role of science and the importance for a (regulatory administrative) committee, entrusted with the task of adapting directives to technical progress, in order to ensure expert advice was already recognised by Christian Joerges in the 1990s.[37] Thus, the European Court's judgment in the *Angelopharm* case was another "hero" of Christian Joerges, as it would transform the use of expert advice into a legal duty, and non-compliance with this duty would become a *per se* incorrect exercise of discretion in decision-making.[38] Yet, post-BSE, the pressures for the scientification of politics have become irresistible, not only due to the revelations by the *Medina Ortega Report* that the scientists on the scientific committees dealing with beef (in particular, the Scientific Veterinary Committee) had been put under a great deal of political pressure, and that the responsibilities for science and politics had been blurred,[39] but also due to global pressures for the liberalisation of trade regimes. So, we witnessed the move of science and the responsibility for scientific advice away from the framework(s) of the Commission and the committee to independent agencies, in the case of food, the EFSA. This agency plays, as we have observed above, an increasingly important role in Community decision-making, with the Commission, as a "blind driver" becoming increasingly dependent on the EFSA, as the "'directions-giving passenger".[40] Unsurprisingly, therefore, the Commission has always followed the

36 Conclusions and Actions following DG SANCO 2006 Peer Review Group on Stakeholder Involvement, *Healthy Democracy*, February 2007. See http:/ec.europa.eu/health/ph_overview/Documents/stakeholders_en.pdf. The first meeting was planned to take place in November 2007.

37 Joerges 1997, see note 2 *supra*.

38 Joerges 1999, see note 2 *supra*. See, however, the critical remarks by K.St.C. Bradley, "Institutional Aspects of Comitology: Scenes from the Cutting Room Floor", in: Ch. Joerges and E. Vos (eds), *EU Committees: Social Regulation, Law and Politics*, (Oxford: Hart Publishing, 1999).

39 European Parliament *Final BSE Inquiry Report*, Rapporteur Manuel Medina Ortega, A4-0020/97/A, 1997.

40 During one of the interviews, a Commission official depicted the relationship between the Commission and the EFSA as two people driving a car: a blind driver (the Commission) and a directions-giving passenger (EFSA). See Vos and Wendler, note 25 *supra*, p. 122.

scientific opinions of the EFSA. Another indication of EFSA's growing importance is the Commission's attitude to make use of the scientific opinions of EFSA in order to defend its own position within the Codex Alimentarius Commission (CAC) at international level.[41] At the same time, we can also observe increasing influence of science in the setting of the Standing Committee. For example, meetings of the (various sections of the) Standing Committee are regularly attended by EFSA officials, whilst it is no secret that, especially in debates on the authorisation of GMOs, both Member States and the Commission harness themselves with science-based arguments.[42] In the latter context, it is the Member States that are more often unwilling to adhere to the opinions of the EFSA, and tend to rely on their own, "nationally produced" science.

This development of scientification of politics and thus de-politicisation, leads paradoxically to the politicisation of science.[43] This can and, indeed, might lead to obscure and insensitive decision-making with the simple application of science to complex social relations, which might, furthermore, also deny its own normative underpinnings or commitment to positive values such as human health.[44] This is particularly problematical where decision-making in situations of uncertainty involving human health and/or the environment may, and often must also, be political in nature. These are the challenges that deliberative supra-nationalism would still need to deal with and which require further clarification and conceptualisation by Christian Joerges.

3. Concluding Remarks: Another Hero

This article was about Christian Joerges and his heroes. It celebrated the intellectual curiosity of a very special person. In my presentation at the workshop celebrating Christian's farewell from the European University Institute in September 2007 in Florence, I tried to demonstrate that it is not surprising that it was Christian Joerges who developed the concept of deliberative supra-nationalism, striving for the conceptualisation of the "*unitas in diversitate*" formula, with comitology as an example of this; for this would actually be inherent to him having so "many faces" (see Figures 2 and 3).

41 See M. Masson-Matthee, *The Codex Alimentarius Commission and its Standards*, (The Hague: T.M.C. Asser Press, 2007).

42 See, for the discussion held in the Standing Committee on the Food Chain and Animal Health Section: Genetically Modified Food And Feed and Environmental Risk, at http://ec.europa.eu/food/committees/regulatory/scfcah/modif_genet/index_en.htm.

43 See P. Weingart, "Scientific expertise and political accountability: Paradoxes of science in politics", (1999) 26 *Science and Public Policy*, pp. 151–161.

44 M. Everson and E. Vos, "The Scientification of Politics and the Politicisation of Science", in: M. Everson and E. Vos (eds), Uncertain Risks Regulated, (Abingdon/New York: Routledge/Cavendish Publishing, 2009), pp. 1–17.

Figure 7.2. United in Diversity: Comitology

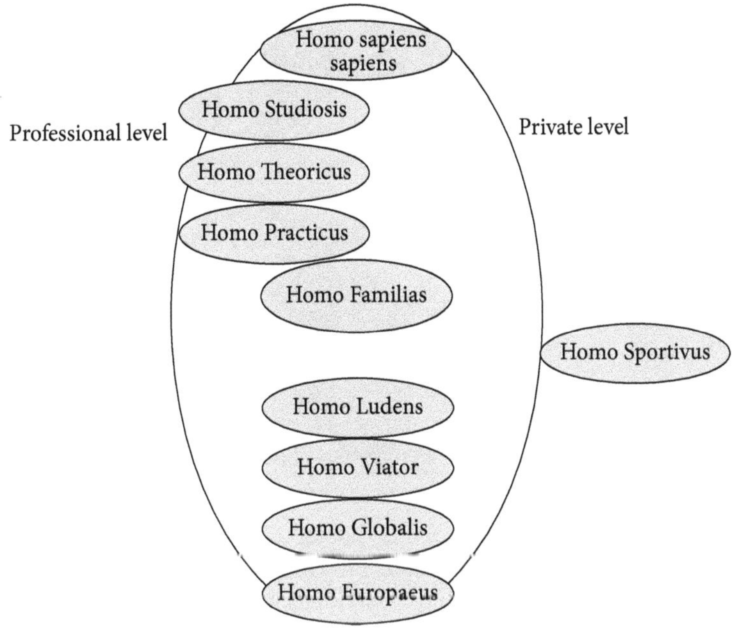

Figure 7.3. Understanding DSN

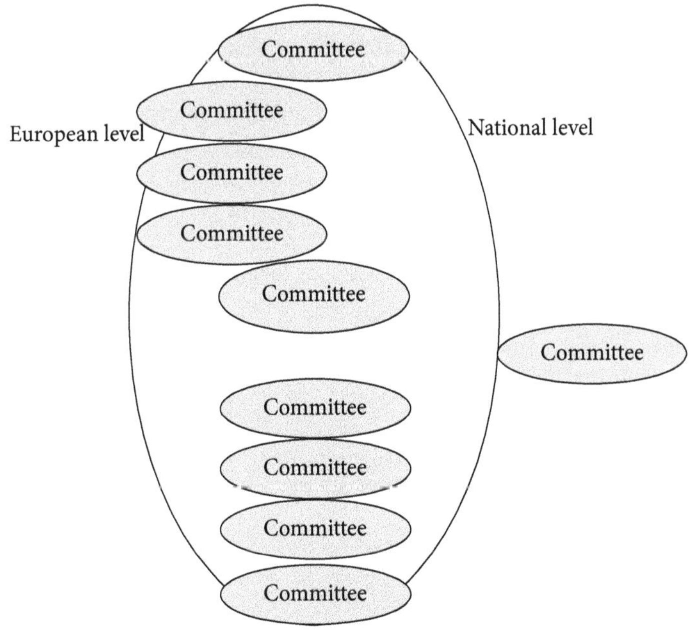

The many faces of Christian Joerges

On a more serious note, I have tried in this chapter to sketch the challenges with which the EU is faced, specifically in the food sector, but also more generally. I have argued that, first and foremost, the more global development of the scientification of politics and the politicisation of science requires further clarification and conceptualisation by deliberative supra-nationalism.

The discussions during the workshop and the articles in this book make it clear that Christian Joerges' work has had, and still has, an enormous impact on academic research and writing, not to mention institutional practice. It was foremost thanks to the work of Christian that we observe a clear shift away from a more traditional understanding of comitology as purely a mechanism of intergovernmental control in the 1970s, to a vision of comitology as more deliberative, problem-solving *fora* in the 1990s, which is still the prevailing opinion in the 2000s. Christian Joerges is an extraordinary man who has had both the ability and the patience to inspire not only his PhD researchers but also many other academics and practitioners. It is therefore safe to conclude that it is not comitology but Christian Joerges, who is our hero! Thank you, Christian.

Karl-Heinz Ladeur

CHAPTER 8. THE SIGNIFICANCE OF GENERAL ADMINISTRATIVE LAW FOR EUROPEAN ADMINISTRATIVE LAW*

1. The Development of a "Europeanised General Administrative Law"

1.1. Learning Processes between General and Specific Administrative Law on the National Plane

It is common knowledge that the Europeanisation of German administrative law has not only fundamentally re-modelled the content of administrative law, but has also buffeted national administrative law with several shockwaves, as well as putting its institutions under pressure to conform,[1] a pressure which also threatens their formative culture and their capacity to review.[2] Other metamorphoses have occurred at a more pedestrian pace through extensions to already existing systems and have only incrementally led to the development of new forms or procedural structures. This is true, for instance, in planning proceedings[3] and in the new dogmatics of balancing,

* Translation by Rory S. Brown.

1 See, from the almost countless contributions, only E. Schmidt-Aßmann, "Allgemeines Verwaltungsrecht in europäischer Perspektive", (2000) 54 *ZÖR*, p. 159; *ibid.*, "Einleitende Problemskizze", in: W. Hoffmann-Riem/*idem.*, (ed), *Strukturen des europäischen Veraltungsrechts*, (Baden-Baden: Nomos, 1999), p. 9; J. Schwarze (ed), *Administrative Law Under European Influence*, (Baden-Baden: Nomos, 1996); S. Kadelbach, *Allgemeines Verwaltungsrecht unter europäischem Einfluß*, (Tübingen: Mohr, 1999); *idem.*, "Administrative Law and the Law of a Europeanized Administration", in: Ch. Joerges and R. Dehousse (eds), *Good Governance in Europe's Integrated Market*, (Oxford: Hart Publishing, 2002), p. 167; for a comparative law perspective, see J. Bell, "Public Law in Europe: Caught Between the National, the Sub-national and the European?", in: M. van Hoecke (ed), *Epistemology and Methodology of Comparative Law*, (Oxford: Hart Publishing, 2004), p. 259, especially, p. 265 *et seq.*; K.-H. Ladeur (ed), *The Europeanisation of Administrative Law*, (Dartmouth: Ashgate, 2002).

2 See, on civil law, J. Smits, "The Europeanisation of National Legal Systems: Some Consequences for Legal Thinking in Civil Law Countries", in: M. van Hoecke (ed), (note 1 *supra*), p. 229 and 237.

3 See, only, W. Hoppe, C. Bönker and S. Grotefels, *Öffentliches Baurecht*, (Munich: Beck, 3rd ed., 2004), § 7; and, going further, M. Pöcker, "Irritationen einer Grundlage des Rechtssystems. Die Problematik des Verhältnisses von materiellem Recht und Verfahrensrecht bei Planungsentscheidungen", (2003) 56 *DÖV*, p. 980; for a European perspective, see J.B. Auby, "The Influence of European Law on Planning", (1998) 4 *EPL*, p. 45.

which have gradually emancipated themselves from the classic discretionary *credo* and have developed the new logic of the procedurally staggered decision.[4]

Similarly, in the administrative law of risk,[5] which, first, unsure of itself, provoked a limitless expansion of the procedural rationality behind the reason for decisions, until new procedural elements seeped through, which, again, adjusted the relation between information, external expertise,[6] and the specific rationality of administrative decision-making ("Concept").[7]

The overcoming of this development of the dogmatics of administrative law has allowed the mutual observation and analysis of particular administrative law in the medium of the "ordering idea" of general administrative law, and, obversely, its "preservation" in the differentiation of its systematic performance in the scrutiny of particular "reference areas".[8] This term "reference area" (used with justifiable frequency) takes the necessity of the dynamic development of general administrative law and its ineluctable dependency on various trends into consideration: general administrative law creates no rigid hierarchy to guide particular administrative law and remains untouched by the "application" of the latter in specific substantive cases. For its part, it is dependent on the observation of administrative legal practice for the variation of its terminology in the stabilisation of its general structures. Individual tasks make different demands on the system formation, and, thus, must leave an imprint.[9] The status of particular fields of substantive administrative law as "reference areas" expresses the anti-social aspect of the normative performance of administrative law, and its corresponding disjointedness and dissimilarity: general administrative law does not employ the generalisable forms that generate themselves from specific administrative fields, but, instead, distinguishes between the reference areas that produce the guiding ideas and others that are fitted to these ideas, or, alternatively, their semantic existence takes up only a peripheral role, i.e., cannot generalise, that is, direct performance.[10] The concept of the "reference area" facilitates an aperture for the observation of the temporal and physical dynamics of the

4 See Schmidt-Aßmann, (note 1 *supra*), "Problemskizze", S. 36 and 37.

5 See A. Scherzberg, "Risiko als Rechtsproblem", (1993) 84 *VerwAch*, p. 484; O. Lepsius/*idem*,, "Risikoverwaltungsrecht – Ermöglichung oder Begrenzung von Innovationen?", (2004) 63 *VVDStRL*, p. 214 and 264; and, generally, P. Th. Stoll, *Sicherheit als Aufgabe von Staat und Gesellschaft*, (Tübingen: Mohr, 2003).

6 A. Voßkuhle, Sachverständige Beratung des Staates, in: *HbStR* Bd. III, 3. Aufl., § 43.; P. Scholl, *Der private Sachverständige im Verwaltungsrecht*, (Baden-Baden: Nomos, 2005).

7 See BVerwGE 69, 37, 45.

8 Schmidt-Aßmann, *ibid.*, Kap. 1, Tz. 12f.; *idem*, *Aufgaben und Perspektiven verwaltungsrechtlicher Forschung. Aufsätze 1975 – 2005*, (Tübingen: Mohr, 2006), S. 384, 398; *idem.*, S. Dagron, "Deutsches und französisches Verwaltungsrecht im Vergleich ihrer Ordnungsideen", appears in: (2007) 67 *ZaöRV*, Ms., p. 3 and 6.

9 See C. Bumke, "Die Entwicklung der verwaltungsrechtswissenschaftlichen Methodik in der Bundesrepublik Deutschland", in: E. Schmidt-Aßmann and W. Hoffmann-Riem (eds), *Methoden der Verwaltungsrechtswissenschaft*, (Baden-Baden: Nomos, 2004), p. 73 and 109.

10 Schmidt-Aßman, (note 8 *supra*), "Ordnungsidee", Kap. 1 Tz. 12f.

changes. Not least, the increasing special legislation throws doubt on the leading role of classic police and regulatory law.

In particular, the result-orientation, thrown into relief by the focus of general administrative law on the administrative act,[11] has been altered, amongst other things, through the ascent of the procedural dimension, the differentiation of new forms of administrative authorisations, the opening of the process to the variations of the "external" participation, and the increased usage of experts.[12]

The Europeanisation of national general administrative law seems to come about in quite a different fashion: the Europeanisation of the particular national administrative fields (environmental law, for example) came about through the alteration of norms (through adaptation to guidelines[13]), and, in this way, indirectly necessitated the faster growth of the formative systemic and normative function of general administrative law.[14] Thus, for several years, the shockwave has directly – without any form of mediation by a specific legal field – hit general administrative law, and, above all, suffused with the dictate of guaranteeing "*effet utile*"[15] for specific European administrative law, we see the formative effect of the dogma of general administrative law: here, it is no longer about evaluating new systemic forms of the particular administrative laws upon the basis of their performance or their capacity to conform; instead, it is to ensure the partially stabilised statutory forms (and contrarily), that the achievement of the aims of particular European administrative laws are not hampered by the structural demands of general national administrative law. This novel challenge is especially clear in the application of the prescriptions of general administrative law to the withdrawal of administrative acts contrary to EC law:[16] with regard to the *effet utile*,

11 See O. Mayer, "Zur Lehre vom öffentlichen Vertrage", (1890) 5 *AöR*, p. 3; for criticism, see P. Laband, "Rezension", (1910) 26 *AöR*, p. 365.

12 See, generally, on the development of German administrative law in the post-war period, R. Wahl, *Herausforderungen und Antworten. Das öffentliche Recht der letzten fünf Jahrzehnte*, (Berlin: de Gruyter, 2006); see, also, G. de Cananea, "Beyond the State: The Europeanisation and Globalisation of Procedural Administrative Law", (2004) 10 *EPL*, p. 563.

13 The methods of the conforming interpretation also belong to this normative effect; see H.D. Jarass, "Richtlinienkonforme Interpretation nationalen Rechts or EG-rechtskonforme Auslegung nationalen Rechts", (1991) 26 *EuR*, p. 211; G. Ress, "Die richtlinienkonforme 'Interpretation' innerstaatlichen Rechts", (1994) 47 *DÖV*, p. 489.

14 See R. Wahl, "Die zweite Phase des öffentlichen Rechts in Deutschland. Die Europäisierung des öffentlichen Rechts", (1999) 38 *Der Staat*, p. 495.

15 See EuGH/ECJ Slg. 1990, I-2433 (*Factortame*); Slg. 2001, I-3541 (*Commission* v *Netherlands*); Slg. 1998, I-4767 (Ölmühle Hamburg); R. Streinz, *Europarecht*, (Heidelberg: Müller, 7th ed., 2005), Rn. 797.

16 See, from the expansive literature, D. Scheuing, "Europäisierung des Verwaltungsrechts. Zum mitgliedstaatlichen Verwaltungsvollzug des EG-Rechts am Beispiel der Rückforderung gemeinschaftsrechtswidriger Beihilfen", (2001) 34 *Die Verwaltung*, p. 107; D. Hanf, "Vertrauensschutz bei der Rücknahme rechtswidriger Verwaltungsakte als neuer Prüfstein für das Kooperationsverhältnis zwischen EuGH und BverfG", (1999) 59 *ZaöRV*, p. 51; J. Suerbaum, "Die Europäisierung des nationalen Verwaltungsverfahrensrechts am Beispiel der Rückforderung gemeinschaftsrechtswidriger staatlicher Beihilfen", (2000) 91 *VerwArch*, p. 169; S. Schonberg, "Legal Certainty and Revocation of Administrative Decisions: A Comparative Study of English, French and EC-Law", *Yearbook of Eur. Law* 2000, p. 257 and p. 297: as to the conflict with English law; BVerwG, (1999) 129 *BayVBl*, p. 22.

it is a concern of the ECJ, that, without a European competence for general procedural administrative law, not simply its interpretation in special circumstances, only a particular result will be pre-determined without a European competence for general procedural administrative law. To this extent, *effet utile* is more apt than the German expression "*Effektivität*", which does not adequately convey the purely pragmatic orientation, developed in the jurisprudence of the ECJ: it is irrelevant whether or not the "effect/benefit" is achieved through the non-implementation or the reconstruction of a norm of general administrative law. Consequently, EC law intervenes in a far stronger and seismic manner in national administrative law than the legal principle of consistent interpretation in national law, a principle, which in Germany, as in Italy, conveys the duty to interpret laws in line with the constitution. A similar phenomenon can be observed in civil law, where the implementation of European prescriptions in particular instances overplays the norms of the *BGB* (the German Civil Code) and even here, only mandates a certain "effect/benefit", without providing a certain form.[17] In any event, for the time being, one cannot say, either of administrative law or of civil law, that a separate general part of a European or civil law is developing; instead, it seems that the effect of particular law on the general law is purely disruptive.

1.2. Disruption through European Law?

On closer inspection, it can be seen, at least for administrative law, that the expectation of guaranteed *effet utile* is not as destructive for national general administrative law as it first might seem. Correspondingly, the legal position no longer proves to be so clear, that, for instance, §48 *Verwaltungsverfahrensgesetz* (VwVfG; Code of Administrative Procedure) is valid in its original form for the not yet Europeanised administrative law, whilst, for the Europeanised law, "hindrances" are simply moved aside. The contours of a new European general administrative law can much more easily be recognised in that a pluralisation of public law is taking place; the same can be said for procedural administrative law.[18] When one considers, in the "purely German" legal situation of a judicial review (and the administrative law claim) involving a third party, in which an administrative act has affected legally protected interests, it becomes clear, that the staying power in the triangular relationship is limited if the third party is not participating in the proceedings and the administrative act has not been communicated to him. Also, in this case, the addressee might have to anticipate *certiorari* in review proceedings or a court's decision long after the administrative act.[19] Similarly, there are

17 See C. Schmid, "The ECJ as a Constitutional and a Private Law Court: A Methodological Comparison", Zentrum für Europäische Rechtspolitik, DP 4/2006; J. Smits, (note 2 *supra*), National Legal Systems.

18 See, on this fundamentally, as to the concept of protecting the third party, M. Schmidt-Preuß, "*Kollidierende Privatinteressen im Verwaltungsrecht*", (1992), (Berlin: Duncker and Humblot, 2nd ed., 2005).

19 Par. 80a VwGO reacted to this; note the expansion of third party rights onto material or procedural law fundaments endangering the position of subjectively public law in German administrative law? See, also, S. Hölscheidt, "Abschied vom subjektiv-öffentlichen Recht? Zu Wandlungen der Verwaltungsrechtsdogmatik unter Einfluss des Gemeinschaftsrechts", (2001) 36 *EuR*, p. 376; M.

competing relationships of public interest through various German sovereigns: contestations by municipalities of the administrative measures of other municipalities,[20] or other counties or institutions of the counties against one another (the *Radio* case),[21] are not rare in the concatenated legal order of the *Bundesrepublik*. Here, again, we are met with the phenomenon of the pluralisation of public interests, which can also affect private belief in the staying power of an administrative order. The *effet utile* jurisprudence strengthens the position of the competing public and private interests in a procedure. One can, in this procedural format, draw a parallel to legal procedural protection: the Commission also has the capacity to bring claims against a Member State, for example, pursuant to Article 227 EEC, because of the awarding of a subsidy contrary to European law in a contractual dispute before the ECJ.[22] In this case – leaving the constellation of review proceedings aside – it would not seem plausible that the Member State could deploy the argument that the protection of the trust of the German citizenry could hinder the rescinding of an *ultra vires* administrative order if this argument were not available in proceedings before a German administrative court to a private party (for whom the administrative order has not come into force). An intermediary conclusion, in the light of the above considerations, is that it seems doubtful as to whether the formula of *effet utile* used by the ECJ, which national law must ensure the smooth reception of particular European administrative law, is beneficial for the development of a Europeanised general administrative law. It is, however, thoroughly compatible with a Europeanised general administrative law. Here, we have a new perspective which can be fruitful when it comes to outlining the staying power of an administrative order based upon European administrative law: less conceptual limits should be set by the thought of the redemption of legitimate expectations than by the pluralisation of public interests,[23] which are not only German interests. In the case of a subsidy contrary to European law, both the interest of the other Member States and the collective private

Ruffert, "Dogmatik und Praxis des subjektiv-öffentlichen Rechts unter dem Einfluß des Gemeinschaftsrechts", (1998) 113 *DVBl*, p. 69; see, on the expansion of the associative/group claim, H.J. Koch, "Die Verbandsklage im Umweltrecht", (2007) 26 *NVwZ*, p. 369.

20 See, on inter-municipal claims, BVerwG, (2006) 26 *UPR*, p. 216.

21 BVerwG, (1999) 113 *DVBl*, p. 615 (Claims between counties in a radio conflict).

22 See E. Schmidt-Aßmann, "Einleitung", in: *idem.*/B. Schöndorf-Haubold (ed), *Der Europäische Verwaltungsverbund*, (Tübingen: Mohr, 2005), p. 1, 10 and 20; the diffuse extension of subjective rights for purposes of compensation of community supervision is, from the point of view of system building, not unthinkable; see, critically, C.D. Classen, "Der Einzelne als Instrument zur Durchsetzung von Gemeinschaftsrecht?", (2007) 88 *VerwAch*, 645; see, also, Ruffert (note 19 *supra*), "Dogmatik und Praxis", Hölscheidt, (note 19 *supra*), "Abschied vom subjektiv-öffentlichen Recht?". The pure instrumentalisation for community supervision destroys the dogmatic rationality of the construction of individual terms in contextual relation: in the future, the only valid question is: To what end the community? That this is the central question, to which the ECJ orientates itself in the jurisprudence, is supported in a particularly spectacular case by K. Hailbronner, "'Gatoussi/Stadt Rüsselsheim' – ein neuer Schritt des EuGH zur Entmündigung der Mitgliedstaaten?", (2007) 26 *NVwZ*, p. 415 – on ECJ, (2007) 26 *NVwZ*, p. 430). The ECJ tends, with its "*effet utile*"-jurisprudence, to change the principle of individual authorisation on its head, whenever it is useful to the EC, which is almost always.

23 See, also, Schmidt-Aßmann, (note 22 *supra*) "Einleitung", p. 7.

interest of the affected branch of business are the subject of a German decision.[24] Moreover, at a secondary level, the protection of legitimate expectations is also limited: in proceedings, with the submissions of third parties affected by the administrative order, one cannot assume that their rights will be considered valid by the court, nor, conversely, of the inconsequentiality of the failure to observe competing plural public interests. Also involved here is a capitulatory (not only in terms of the factual "pressure to ensure effectiveness") interpretation of the meaning of the period in §48 Abs. 4 VwVfG.[25] Basically, one cannot rely on the protective effect of the expiration date for the withdrawal of transgressive administrative acts, because other bearers of public interests (Member States) could not use the period of gestation for themselves.

2. Europeanised Administrative Law as a Consequence of the Pluralisation of the Public Interest

2.1. Does the Principle of Effet Utile make the General Administrative Law a Quantité Négligeable?

If one accepts this notion of European general administrative law, a notion stemming from the relativisation of staying power, one can, on the other hand, not bear the recourse of the ECJ to the facticity of the *effet utile*. At this point, the reflexive and observatory capacity of the general administrative law must be specified and be used for the legal differentiation of protection. That national general administrative law must support the application of the particular European administrative law is one thing, that this must happen limitlessly and quite without consideration from the point of view of the protection of legitimate expectations is quite another. Here, proceeding from the acknowledgment of pluralised public interests, we must distinguish between certain interests, which can be permanently damaged by the guarantee of legitimate expectations favourable to private third parties: this is valid fundamentally in situations of transgressive subsidies, which distort the market.

The supposed visibility of the pluralisation of public interests, in a European legal order which comprises, in the narrow sense, both European law and national law, speaks for the consideration of the weight of these interests. However, this can be seen in certain administrative orders, which only have an indirect and distant effect on both the internal market and the competing private and public interests of other Member States. This would be the case for pollution licences contrary to EC law, or, for instance, water allowances, if the state's own population would be harmed. In such cases, the plurality of the potentially affected interests is not recognisable for the citizens of a Member State, because the assignment of the legal prescription is not transparent: for a company, too,

24 See Schmidt-Aßmann, (note 1 *supra*), "Problemskizze: Zur Pluralisierung des europäisierten Rechtsverhältnisses", p. 32 and 37.

25 See ECJ, (1998) 16 *NVwZ*, p. 833; S. Müller-Franken, "Gemeinschaftsrechtliche Fristenhemmung, richtlinienkonforme Auslegung und Bestandkraft von Verwaltungsakten", (1998) 113 *DVBl*, p. 758.

it is also not easy to differentiate between German and European norms, whilst subsidies with potentially distorting effects on the internal market are easily spotted.[26] In these constellations, the transgression must be sanctioned. Here, a process for breach of contract and, if applicable, the imposition of a fine against the state violating EC law, would be the suitable sanction; however, no theoretically satisfactory answer to the foregoing reflections has been provided. Nevertheless, in this connexion, a statement can be developed as to the formulation of Europeanised general administrative law in the multilevel system of the legal order: a general administrative law of the European Community can, pursuant to the above discussions, be based upon the specific administrative law and, conversely, not upon the subordination to the interest in building unity at central level. In this respect, we must be mindful that the general administrative law, even in a Europeanised legal order, sought for possible transfers out of the "reference areas" (of the particular European administrative law and of the law of the Member States).[27] This might well be different for the area of the general administrative law of the self-standing administration of the EC. Here, it might well come to a juxtaposition of the competence to select the applicable general law of the EC, which, however, already, due to the various legal traditions of the Member States, cannot convert the general administrative law of the Member States into a congruent body, like the administrative process laws of the country and counties in Germany. A Europeanised general administrative law cannot, paradoxically, be "European law" in the narrow sense.[28] This is decisively ruled out by the limited authorisation of primary law. This might seem to be a deficiency of European law, and the Commission, as well as the Court, seem to allow themselves, respectively, to be swayed by this assumption in their fundamentally political strategy or in individual decisions. More recent decisions of the ECJ must beg the question, given the limited competence of the EC in civil or administrative law, of whether it should, through penetratingly formulated *factual* pressures to conform, create a unified, general part of the law in the Member States. The guidelines to ensure *effet utile* can also be interpreted in this manner. Thereby, one loses focus of the peculiarity of the conflict between particular European law and national general administrative law. Ultimately, there is a problem here, structurally very different to a "vertical" conflict between different laws on the same subject, which can

26 Here, the third party protection of individuals is deployed domestically to ensure "*effet utile*". So, when the term is not used here, the concern is the same "interest in efficacy"; ECJ v. 7.1.2004 201/02, (2005) 27 *NuR*, p. 517, (obligation to carry out environmental impact assessment protects individual interests), but an attempted systematisation is not recognisable.

27 Correctly, the lack of cases and the consequent learning difficulties of EC law is noted in the English administrative law literature; see C. Harlow, "Changing the Mindset: The Place of Theory in English Administrative Law", (1994) 14 *Oxford Journal of Legal Studies*, p. 429 (a critique of J. Schwarze's "European Administrative Law"); A. Tomkins, "Of Institutions and Individuals: The Enforcement of EC-Law", in: P. Craig and R. Rawlings (eds), *Essays in Honour of Carol Harlow*, (Oxford: Oxford University Press, 2003), p. 273, who notes how little consideration the ECJ pays to the particularities of English law ("Factortame"), even if it complies with EC law in its own forms.

28 See Schmidt-Aßmann/Dagron, (note 1 *supra*), Deutsches und französisches Recht, Ms. p. 2; on private law: Ch. Joerges, "European Law as Conflict of Laws", in: *idem.*/J. Neyer, "Deliberative Supranationalism" Revisited", EUI-WP Law 2006/20, p. 15 and 23.

be overcome with the devices of "primacy"[29] of European law or the duty of consistent construction.[30]

2.2. *The Standardisation of General Administrative Law without an "Ordering Principle"?*

Frequently in its jurisprudence, the ECJ has expressly encouraged Commission legislation on the procedural law of the Member States – without success.[31] Earlier, the ECJ recognised the autonomy of the Member States in the area of administrative procedure.[32] However, later, in the judgments on *effet utile*, this principle is not mentioned even once. An English observer of this development correctly referred to the tense relationship between the use of administrative procedures for an efficient rule, which supports European law and its implementation in the practice of the administrative law of the Member States, and "individual enforcement", which aims at *effet utile*. In the *Factortame* case,[33] the Commission had already successfully used the former method to implement a new rule against Great Britain. It required absolutely no direct measures to ensure the *effet utile* in this instance. A. Tomkins correctly noted that, thereby, the fruitfulness of the self- and foreign observation of the general administrative law in the Member States was blocked. It would have been more productive, to insist more strongly on the stimulus for the formulation of rules for "good practices of administration".[34] In the German literature, the homogenisation of the administrative law system of the Member States is much more strongly emphasised, on the basis of a "shared stock of administrative law rules" in the Member States as well as in the EC.[35] Methodically, it is anything but self-explanatory that a stock of "administrative law precepts" can be extricated from the laws of the Member States, which not only structures the domestic legal order but also effects (or should effect), in exchange with the other legal orders, a standardisation measure.[36] The position of normativity in this interpretation is unclear. English authors, in particular, have criticised this concept of the development of a common European administrative law, since it is obviously (and especially) incompatible with English law.[37] Incidentally, the literature in Germany is dominated by the

29 Streinz, (note 15 *supra*), *Europarecht*, Rn. 200.

30 See note 14 *supra*.

31 A. Arnull, *The EU and Its Court of Justice*, 2nd ed., (Oxford: Oxford University Press, 2006), p. 51; Tomkins, (note 27 *supra*), "Of Institutions", p. 273 and 282.

32 ECJ, Rep. 1973, 1039.

33 See. ECJRep. 1990, I-2433 (*Factortame*); Slg. 2001, I-3541 (*Commission* v *Netherlands*); Slg. 1998, I-4767 (Ölmühle Hamburg); Streinz, (note 15 *supra*), *Europarecht*, Rn. 797.

34 Tomkins, (note 27 *supra*), "Of Institutions", p. 273 *et seq*.

35 J. Schwarze, *Europäisches Verwaltungsrecht*, (Baden-Baden: Nomos, 2nd ed., 2005), S. XLVIII; emphasising more strongly the plurality of laws, Schmidt-Aßmann/Dagron, (note 8 *supra*), "Deutsches und französisches Verwaltungsrecht", Ms. p. 3; *ibid*., (note 22 *supra*), "Einleitung", p. 7; *ibid*., (note 1 *supra*), "Problemskizze", p. 30.

36 Schwarze, *ibid*., p. CXIII.

37 Harlow (note 27 *supra*), "Changing the Mindset", p. 429; Tomkins, (note 27 *supra*), "Of Institutions", p. 273 *et seq*.

understanding of a "Europeanised general administrative law" as a medium of moulding the national general administrative law to the expectation of the European institutions through the harmonisation of the particular administrative laws, without thereby taking into account the independence of an "ordering principle" of a European general administrative law. Correctly, E. Schmidt-Aβmann sees this differently. He understands *effet utile* jurisprudence in the sense of a "duty to optimise", but at the same time, points out both the value of the variety of manifestations of European administrations, and the meaning of co-operation in a polycentric order of networks.[38] Besides, he correctly alludes to the limitations of the principle, for no orientation can be gained from the notion of completing the standardisation of an order.

2.3. The EC as an Association of States and the Need for a Novel Law of Conflicts

The peculiarity of the construction of an "association of states" is marked by the many different forms of conflict between national and supranational law; there is no general equalising formula available, such as recourse to the unity of the legal order or, as in a state, the integrative effect of a constitution. This constellation is thrown into relief where European competition law meets with national broadcasting law.[39] This conflict can, of course, happen in a purely national context, but the division of authority at national level, for example, in Germany, proceeds from the demarcation of subjects of competence, whilst, in the EC, to a great extent, the competences are determined by the *goals* of the internal market, raising the question, of whether organisations and activities such as radio can be designated as economic activity and regulated as such. Christian Joerges and Christoph Schmid[40] suggested the description "*diagonal*" for such conflicts, which expresses the particularity of conflicts in the EC. Here, neither the classic international private law, nor the conflicts provisions of administrative law for territorially-determined "horizontal" conflicts (and thereby its logic of referral) suffice. Equally insufficient are the rules of primacy for constitutional law (in Germany, pursuant to Article 31 GG) and the rules of the EC for "vertical" conflicts. What is needed here are rules (nevertheless, to be thought of as conflicts laws) of mutual agreement and co-operation, which must be determined by individual cases and not by stable demarcations.[41] This arrangement of the conflict type as "*diagonal*" proves itself, even

38 Schmidt-Aßmann, (note 1 *supra*), "Problemskizze", p. 30 and 37.

39 See K.-H. Ladeur, "Die Kooperation von europäischem Kartellrecht und mitgliedstaatlichem Rundfunkrecht", (2000) 50 *WuW*, p. 965.

40 Joerges, (note 28 *supra*), "Supranationalism", p. 26; *ibid.*, "The Impact of European Integration on Private Law: Reductionist Perceptions", (1997) 4 *European Law Journal*, p. 374; C. Schmid, "Diagonal Competence Conflicts between European Competition Law and National Regulation: A Conflict of Laws Construction of the Dispute of Book Price-Fixing", (2000) 8 *European Review of Private Law*, p. 155.

41 Traditional conflicts law and public and private law is orientated towards it; see C. Ohler, *Die Kollisionsordnung des allgemeinen Verwaltungsrechts. Strukturen des deutschen internationalen Verwaltungsrecht*, (Tübingen: Mohr, 2005); as to private law, R. Michaels, "EU-Law as Private International Law? Reconceptualizing the Country of Origin-Principle as Vested-Rights-Theory",

given the persistent limits to the staying power of bureaucratic acts in European administrative law, to be compatible: here, we may also speak of a limited overlap between general national administrative law and particular European administrative law, not that this problem can be solved by a simple rule of primacy. In truth, the duty to ensure *effet utile* is derived from the principle of co-operation (Article 10 ECT).[42] The substance of this is not in a purely instrumental duty of the effective implementation of the particular European administrative law, with the help of the national general administrative law and its forms and procedures; instead, it aims, correctly understood, to make the general forms of civil and administrative law (potentially also criminal law in the future) permeable for the fulfilment of the peculiarities of a multipolar legal order, which in the use and development of institutions of general administrative law that may not ignore, in the interpretation of "public interest", the realisation of the interests of the EC and other Member States or of the citizens of these states. An expectation of co-operation also points in the other direction, thanks to the "diagonal character of the collision", so that no primacy in favour of one or the other legal system is foreseen.[43] The expectation of co-operation is not to be understood as unidirectional; therefore, *effet utile* cannot simply be aimed at the setting aside of rules regarding the potency of administrative acts. The principle of the limited authority of a decision-maker may not be evaded by the usage of *effet utile*.

The protection of legitimate expectations is a valid base for general administrative law, which falls within the governing competence of the Member States, provided that the connected expectations of specific European administrative law are co-ordinated. In this field of co-operative co-ordination of the legitimate expectations of the implementation of EC law, and equally legitimate considerations regarding the preservation of the "ordering principle" of the particular national administrative law, there is a need for the development of related decision-making, evidentiary and balancing rules, about which the ECJ has said very little of any use.[44] This finds frequent expression in the literature on European Law, in which, systematically, three categories of general administrative law in the stratified European system are differentiated: general administrative law of the EC, national general administrative law of the Member States, and Europeanised national administrative law, which serves the implementation of particular European administrative law.[45]

(2006) 2 *Journal of Private International Law*, p. 195 and 211; R. Wai, "Transnational Private Law and Private Ordering in a Contested Global Society", (2007) 47 *Harvard International Law Journal*, p. 471 and 472; Ch. Joerges, "Europarecht als Kollisionsrecht neuen Typs", in: (2007) *FS E. Rehbinder*, p. 717.

42 See Th. Oppermann, *Europarecht*, (Munich: Beck, 3rd ed., 2005), Rn. 243.

43 See K.-H. Ladeur, (note 39 *supra*), "Kooperation von europäischem Kartellrecht und mitgliedstaatlichem Rundfunkrecht".

44 See, on the meaning of learning in the general administrative law in case material, Harlow, (note 27 *supra*) Changing the Mindset; on learning through the development of "ordering ideas" through the exchange of ideas between general and particular administrative law, Schmidt-Aßmann/Dagron, (note 8 *supra*) "Deutsches und französisches Verwaltungsrecht", Ms. S. 3, 6, 22.

45 See Kadelbach, (note 1 *supra*), *Administrative Law*.

This tendency to a schematic differentiation possibly hangs together with (a previously very productive), but, recently, an increasingly disruptive, amount of implicit options for the consolidation of the supremacy of European law with the help of systematic measures in national law.[46] Certainly, the increasing penetration of particular European administrative law (and similarly civil law) in the general legal structures of the Member States is causing collateral damage, which is increasingly difficult to manage. An example from civil law is provided by the expanding interpretation of the Product Liability Directive as a *comprehensive* rule for all claims for damages caused by products in the sense intended by the directive;[47] thus, all possible national rules expanding or extending liability are excluded from usage in cases with a European element,[48] whilst they, simultaneously, still apply to factual situations which fall exclusively within the scope of national law. This is the case, even though this potential for an expansive understanding of the directive was not conceived of at its inception.[49] The ECJ should, in civil law as in public law, observe much more attentively and further the productive side of the multipolar European legal order, and, thereby, rely, for its part, on material and procedural law co-operation from the legal orders and judiciaries of the Member States.[50] In this context, we should be mindful, above all, that the Europeanisation of law, because of its penetration into national legal orders, whose embedment in a substantial practice, in particular, due to decisions in a multiplicity of cases and the experience gained from them, is an interruption, without European law having to hand a corresponding infrastructure gathered from the knowledge of cases, procedures, and patterns of expectation, normative priority, and cognitive, evidentiary and suppositive rules.[51] The EC, due to its size and the plethora of political, cultural and legal traditions and experiences, can never meaningfully pursue the goal of becoming a European "superstate".[52] The ECJ seems to ignore this in its over-estimation of the unity of law as a canon of construction,[53] which threatens to undermine the boundaries dividing responsibility.

Based upon the contemplation of the existence of administrative orders in a Europeanised administrative law, a preliminary conclusion might be that a general European administrative law cannot be conceptualised according to the unity-building

46 See K.-H. Ladeur, "Richterrecht und Dogmatik – eine verfehlte Konfrontation?", (1996) 79 *KritV*, p. 77.

47 ECJ, Rep. 2002, I-3901 (González-Sanchez); Schmid, (note 17 *supra*), "The ECJ as a Constitutional and a Private Law Court", p. 22 *et seq.*

48 Joerges, (note 41 *supra*), "Europarecht als Kollisionsrecht", p. 736 m.w.N.

49 See, also, Schmid, (note 17 *supra*), "The ECJ as Constitutional and Private Law Court".

50 See K.-H. Ladeur, "Methodology and European Law – Can Methodology Change so as to Cope with the Multiplicity of Law?", in: van Hoecke (ed), (note 1 *supra*), p. 207; *idem*, "Flexibility and Cooperative, The Coordination of European Member States' Laws", in: G. de Burca and J. Scott (eds), *Constitutional Change in the EU: From Uniformity to Flexibility?*, (Oxford: Hart Publishing, 2000), p. 284 *et seq.*

51 See, on the necessity of learning; Schmidt-Aßmann and Dagron, (note 8 *supra*), "Deutsches und französisches verwaltungsrecht", Ms. S. 22; in an English perspective Harlow, (note 27 *supra*), "Changing the Mindset"; Tomkins, (note 27 *supra*), "Of Institutions".

52 On this danger, see J.J. Rosa, *Le second XXe siècle*, (Paris: Grasset, 2000).

53 See Schmid, (note 17 *supra*), "The ECJ as a Constitutional and a Private Law Court", p. 25.

pattern of the systematic and reflexive traditions of national general administrative law. It must be developed in the sense of the aperture of the national general administrative law to the heteronomous legal relationships in a multipolar European legal system. In this sense, a Europeanised general administrative law must observe conflict of laws principles and take a co-operative stance towards the permissiveness of national law for the realisation of the law or interests of the supranational and national levels. Such a law of conflicts no longer follows classic laws of ranking, but is, instead, orientated by the permeability of the legal orders and its disposition should be co-operative.[54]

The various conceptual approaches to business in the Member States are only partly a problem for the functioning of the Community, in so far as it could restrict transnational trade in services and goods through stabilisation with the help of the respective national laws.

However great the necessity to harmonise in particular cases becomes in the light of these competing practical interests, the variety of the cognitive processes must, in any case, also be seen as an expression of a distributed experimentation of self-organised "practical communities" and/or the state administration, and, thus, as an element of the dynamic and of the productive comparison over national borders, be valued and practically harnessed. Whether one can describe the discursive, confrontational, standardising and conforming processes, structured through comitology as "supranational deliberation",[55] might, due to the smoothing with the respective national practice and its functionally-leaning selectivity (also, therefore, the exclusion of other possibilities) seem doubtful. The cognitive rules do not derive their legitimacy from the force of the "arguments" used in their particular field, but from their "preservation" in practice, which can (and should) only partially be understood or reflected upon "discursively". Precisely as to the peculiar rationality of the "preservation"[56] in practice, and the comparison of the different logics of the generation and the stabilisation of trade-related knowledge operating with a mixture of know-how and uncertainty allows for the organisation of productive competition between institutions. Not least, this

54 See, especially, Michaels, (note 41 *supra*) "EU Law as Private International Law", p. 212 and 232; see, also, critically as to superficial expectations of convergence towards Member State law; P. Legrand, "Against a European Civil Code", (1997) 68 *Modern Law Review*, p. 40 and 45 *et seq.*; *idem*, "European Legal Systems are not converging", (1996) 45 *International and Comparative Law Quarterly*, p. 45 and 92; for the opposite position, see K.P. Sommermann, "Konvergenzen im Verwaltungsverfahrens- und Verwaltungsprozessrecht der europäischen Staaten", (2002) 55 *DÖV*, p. 133; J. Schwarze, "The Convergence of the Administrative Laws of the EU Member States", (1998) 4 *EPL*, p. 191.

55 See Joerges, Supranationalism, in: *idem.*, Neyer, (note 28 *supra*).

56 For European law, Schmidt-Aßmann, (note 8 *supra*), Aufgaben, p. 398; this fits nicely with the Anglo-American legacy of European law based upon practical experience; see O.W. Holmes, *The Common Law*, (London/New York: Macmillan, 1881), p. 1: "The life of law has not been logic; it has been experience."

occurs in comitology; therefore, it must be considered a thoroughly successful element of European "Governance"[57] beyond both the nation state *and* the supranational level.

3. Forms of a General Administrative Law of Open Government

3.1. EC Law as Conflicts Law: Transnational Administrative Acts

A further important building-block of a general European administrative law is the transnational administrative act.[58] The legal effect of the duty of mutual "recognition" of product licences, which goes back to the *Cassis* case, has, justifiably, been described as a "transnational administrative act". Whilst the effect of civil law outside of the borders of the state has long been recognised, because it was considered "apolitical",[59] until a few years ago, the recognition of the legal meaning of the transnational *factual* effect of a granting of a licence was contended,[60] because of the perceived necessity of restricting the validity of administrative acts territorially. The recognition of the factual transnational effects of an administrative act was, however, only one step on the way towards a transnational administrative act, of which we can only speak when its effects become "de-territorialised". With the *Cassis* decision of the ECJ,[61] this possibility was integrated into the form of European administrative law.[62] Thereby, the legal power of administrative orders was stretched over the borders of the state. As is well known, a pre-requisite for this is the existence of European substantive law demands on the decisions of national authorities and their concrete application in national administrative procedures. This extension of validity, as it is understood, is, logically, compensated by the possibility, under certain conditions (safety considerations), to refuse to recognise its effect; the case is then brought before the Commission.[63] Thereby, a third state has the possibility of influencing the administrative decision also in the Member State where it was taken. Here, we are concerned not only with the participatory rights of another Member State, which protects its own, but also with the interest of the EC, while, in the case of the limitation of the effect of administrative acts, the initiative, at the same time, also comes from the Commission. The crystallisation of safety standards is exemplary: here, the competition of rules and institutions takes the place of a unified definition of the public interest. This would seem sensible, since it can be assumed that, in Europe, the development of legal principles and standards is so far advanced that, what for one

57 See, on the concept, C. Möllers, "Governance: Meaning and Value of a Concept", (2006) 43 *CMLR*, p. 313; A. Gatto, "Governance in the European Union – A Legal Perspective", (2006) 12 *Columbia Journal of European Law*, p. 487.

58 M. Ruffert, "Der transnationale Verwaltungsakt", (2001) 34 *Die Verwaltung*, p. 453; Schmidt-Aßmann, (note 8 *supra*) Aufgaben, p. 408 *et seq.*

59 Michaels, (note 41 *supra*), EU Law as Private International Law, p. 232 *et seq.*

60 BVerwGE 75, 285 (Emsland).

61 ECJ, Rep. 1979, 649; 1987, 1227 (Reinheitsgebot); see, also, Streinz, (note 15 *supra*), Rn. 672 at 687.

62 See, in detail, H.C. Röhl, *Akkreditierung und Zertifizierung im Produktsicherheitsrecht, Zur Entwicklung einer neuen europäischen Verwaltungsstruktur* (Berlin: Springer, 2000).

63 See Streinz, (note 15 *supra*), Rn. 731 *et seq.*

state, for example, is not dangerous, must also be accepted as such in another, while citizens can bring their preferences to bear in the selection of products. Here, it is problematical that a generalisable logic of forms of European administrative law has faded into obscurity behind the pragmatic goal-setting of a European standardisation of mandates for Member States, particularly in product safety law.[64] In addition, the Commission clearly regards these variants of Europeanisation as a "second best" strategy, given that the "full harmonisation" (through European Standards) seems to be too difficult or impossible.[65] The dominance of the standardisation of practice has, in the field of the vision of the European institutions, obscured the necessity of the development of a distinguished theory of forms of transnational administrative acts.

3.2. *A New Supervisory Law for the Delimitation of Divergences amongst the Association of States*

A differentiated approach to the theoretical construction of the transnational administrative act and its cross-border effects could now, beyond the "central perspective" of the European institutions, much more strongly accentuate the various paths of development and the diverse bundles of interests of the Member States,[66] which, in part, are not different from those interests, which, for example, in the case of subsidies, restrict legal effects in the case of illegality. This, however, relates to the possibility of intervention of the EC institutions in national administrative law, whereas here, we are concerned with the heteronomous interests of Member States, which frequently diverge from the concerned interests of other Member States. The issuance of quasi-administrative "certificates" (for example, in social law, the recognition as an employer),[67] or reports from state educational institutions or similar, which could be a risk to the public interests of another state, which does not need to be taken into consideration in the state where the act was performed (other than for security questions that concern citizens and foreigners) but can be entirely externalised, also needs to be viewed in a similar fashion. Here, it would seem necessary to build an equivalent to the hierarchical oversight in the structure of authority in the state into transnational administrative law: in the absence of transparency, this cannot be achieved for a single administrative act (as in the case of security issues). In the case of transnational processes with built-in

64 See, on the current discussion on comitology, Ch. Joerges and E. Vos (eds), *EU-Committees – Social Regulation, Law and Politics*, (Oxford: Hart Publishing, 1999); see, also, Schmidt-Aßmann/Dagron, (note 8 *supra*), "Deutsches und französisches Verwaltungsrecht", Ms. p. 17.

65 See European Governance. White Paper from the Commission to the European Council. COM (2001) 428 final, S. 29s.; see, also, die kritischen Beiträge in: Ch. Joerges, Y. Mény and J.H.H. Weiler (eds), A Critical Appraisal of the Commission White Paper on European Governance, EUI-Jean-Monnet WP 6/2001.

66 K.-H. Ladeur and R. Prelle, "Environmental Assessment and Judicial Approaches to Legal Errors: A European and Comparative Analysis", (2001) 13 *Journal of Environmental Law*, p. 185.

67 See, generally, on the difficulty of calculating the role of the social law jurisprudence; W. Frenz, "Grenzüberschreitende medizinische Leistungen und Grundfreiheiten im Spiegel der EuGH-Rechtsprechung", (2004) 23 *MedR*, p. 296; M. Wollenschläger and S. Grimm, "Die Auswirkungen der Rechtsprechung des EuGH auf das nationale Sozialrecht", (2004) 18 *ZIAS*, p. 335.

divergences of the interests of the decision-making and the affected state, the Commission should provide for transnational oversight,[68] for example, with spot tests, which, without systematic checking of the interests of the affected states, might, possibly, not come to fruition. A diffusion of the oversight function in various legal institutions which were developed for other tasks, is, however, not acceptable.

Here, it is clear that European administrative law needs administrative oversight that corresponds to its heteronomous decision-making and procedural structure, so that transnational administrative acts can be theoretically ordered and practically utilised. This is hampered, as mentioned earlier, by the strong orientation of the EC institutions to their own interests.[69] This defective perspective towards system development and the neglect of the particularities of the pluralisation of the public interest in a heteronomous association of states,[70] in which EC institutions may only sparingly use the means of supranational legislation and decision-making for the achievement of European interests, reveals itself particularly clearly in the erratic interventions of the ECJ in social law. That there may be good grounds in social law strictly to attend to the territorial radius of the legal relationships and to put the unifying interests of the EC on a back burner is not seriously entertained. Consequently, the complex calculation of contributions and expectations of benefits, which takes place at national level, is plunged into greater uncertainty. In addition, Europeanised telecommunications law has introduced a new variant of the *ex ante* participation of authorities of other Member States in state administrative law processes.[71] The national regulating body (NRB) is obliged to consider, as far as possible, the stances of other regulating bodies. This is an intensive form of mutual binding, which is strongly influenced by the position of the Commission. Lastly, this variant of a European administration is geared towards a relatively unified decision-making practice, and can, therefore, not be informative for a multipolar European administration, however it might seem at first sight.

3.3. *Mutual Learning inside a Pluralised Administrative Legal Order*

A further variant of the pluralisation of the particular European administrative law (for example, environmental law) comes about, in that new particular procedural elements (environmental impact assessment) become connected to procedural ideas and

68 See, on oversight, also, Schmidt-Aßmann, (supra, note 22 *supra*), "Einleitung", p. 10 and 20.

69 See, on the meeting of multiple organisational principles in the European administrative co-operation, Schmidt-Aßmann, (note 8 *supra*), Aufgaben, S. 411 *et seq.*, *idem.*/Dagron, (note 8 *supra*), "Deutsches und französisches Verwaltungsrecht", Ms. p. 7.

70 BVerfGE 89, 155, 182ss.; Schmidt-Aßmann/Dagron, (note 8 *supra*), "Deutsches und französisches Verwaltungsrecht", Ms. p. 7.

71 See H.H. Trute, Der europäische Regulierungsverbund in der Telekommunikation – ein neues Modell europäisierter Verwaltung, *FS Selmer*, (Berlin: Duncker & Humblot, 2004), p. 565; G. Britz, "Vom Europäischen Verwaltungsverbund zum Regulierungsverbund?", (2006) 41 *EuR*, p. 41; K.-H. Ladeur and C. Möllers, "Der europäische Regulierungsverbund der Telekommunikation im deutschen Verwaltungsrecht", (2005) 109 *DVBl*, p. 525.

conceptions of legal protection or control standards. Thus, the meaning of connecting procedural challenges with the acceptance of a causality of mistakes for the result of decisions is different in the individual Member States.[72] Here, too, the fluctuation of the possibilities that arise out of different national procedural conceptions should not be seen as immediately problematical. This would be a one-sided viewpoint, neglectful of the value of a multipolar administration and its law. Primarily, it would be necessary, more closely to observe the various legal forms (perhaps through combinations of alternative institutional elements and their functional equivalents) anchored in the administrative law of the Member States, and not to restrict ourselves to a unified model. A Europeanised general administrative law would have to permit differences and would have to observe and evaluate their factual meaning retrospectively for the (legal) protection of interests. Should the occasion arise, a second step towards the harmonisation of implementation forms would be beneficial for a pluralised European administrative law. A Europeanised general administrative law must calibrate its theoretical constructions not only to tolerate the varieties of connections between European and national general administrative law, but also to generate a comparative perspective of the possible learning opportunities in a multipolar legal order.[73] Above all, in the Europeanised administration, the value of the conformity of decisions in Europe is not to be over-estimated, when we must also calculate that the standardised law could block the development of practical experience, without knowing whether this can be compensated on the European plane. An evening out of the practical losses of experimental knowledge "from below"[74] can hardly be achieved at the level of European institutions. Here, too, we can see the necessity to facilitate structural learning processes in the individual outposts of the administrative networks in Europe. According to the logic of multipolar thinking,[75] the European institutions could, upon the basis of these experiences, in the learning processes and the experiences collected at the level of Member States play an important moderating role, without being able to propagate or implement a standardised general European administrative law. For this variant of learning in a multipolar network, the procedural norms could also be made fruitful: this process not only serves European administrative law primarily pursuant to the old understanding of law as a guarantee of correctness, but also, and, indeed, precisely, the aperture of decision-making processes allows for a structured observation of administrations through EC institutions. The practice of the ECJ seems to tend to the application of administrative procedural law, without reference to an overarching "ordering idea", so that an *effet utile* can be aimed at.

72 Ladeur and Prelle, (note 66 *supra*), Environmental Assessment.

73 Fundamentally, see C.F. Sabel and J. Zeitlin, Learning from Differentiation: The New Architecture of Experimentalist Governance in the EU, available at: www.2.law.columbia.edu/sabel; see, also, L. Krämer, "Differentiation in the EU Environmental Policy", (2000) 9 *European Environmental Law Review*, p. 133.

74 Their value is rightly highlighted by Harlow, (note 27 *supra*), "Changing the Mindset".

75 Schmidt-Aßmann, (note 1 *supra*), "Problemskizze", p. 32 and 37.

3.4. *Differentiation through the Europeanisation of Administrative Law. The Example of the Precautionary Principle*

The jurisprudence of the ECJ, biased towards the primacy of the goals and interests of the EC, has far-reaching effects on the flexibility of general administrative law, in particular, on the (pre-)structuring of the room for manoeuvre in national administrations. This goes against the grain for a flexible administration, and its inclusion in private-public networks as well as the necessity of a transfer from an isolated decision-making practice to more complex decision-making strategies. So, in Germany, a requirement for the erection of a structure-building "concept"[76] to shape the "precaution" in environmental law has developed in the jurisprudence of the Constitutional Court, and the proportionality of the measures is made concrete through their relationship to a long term and discerning, differentiating strategy, for example, the reduction of the burden on the environment by using particular materials. The ECJ, in contrast, in *Pfizer*,[77] held that the precautionary bans of materials (in particular, penicillin in animal medicine) were permissible, even without such procedural rules, which make transparency and understanding possible. Indeed, a scientific explanation, which in the case of uncertainty on the part of the state (not uncommon when it comes to precautionary measures) does not impede the adoption of the measure. This would have been a combination which the ECJ could have reached for a comparative analysis of the various strategies of the Member States, potentially to accept a spectrum of variant concepts and to tie this comparison back into general administrative law. Instead, the Court took a blinkered view and left the Member States discretion, without making any gains for a general administrative law. In the case of *Altmark-Trans*,[78] the ECJ, in contrast, when faced with the question of the boundaries of the implementation of public aid (with a view to avoiding unlicensed aid) formulated a universal procedural structuring through guidelines for the criteria for justifications, which not only shapes the area of national discretion, but also aims for an increase in transparency within a transnational network of administrations.

76 BVerwGE 69, 37; see K.-H. Ladeur, "The Introduction of the Precautionary Principle into EC Law – A Pyrrhic Victory for Environmental and Public Health Law?", (2003) 40 *CMLR*, p. 1455; for a critique, see S. Wolf, "Risk Regulation, Higher Rationality and the Death of Judicial Self-Restraint", (2004) 41 *CMLR*, p. 1125.

77 ECJ, Rep. 2002, I-3305.

78 ECJ, Rep. 2003, I-7747.

4. The "Ordering Idea" of a "Conflicts Law": Reconstruction of a Europeanised General Administrative Law

4.1. A Practical Example for a Productive Irritation of the German Administrative Law through European "Influence"

That the co-operative factor of the Europeanisation process is not sufficiently observed, or institutionally and theoretically shored up, is the result of the tendency of the EC institutions, described above, in particular, the ECJ and the Commission, to measure the administrative law of the Member States primarily by way of the unquestioned notion of the "efficiency" of the supranational level of the European multilevel system. This also find expression in that the subsidiarity principle is prescribed in a one-dimensional manner, which is exclusively orientated towards the unified implementation of EC law, and disregards the practical possibilities of the variety and the learning in a legal order, which is understood as being decentralised.[79] The subsidiarity principle has, in the practice of the supranational institutions of the EC, practically reversed itself; it has been transformed into a presumptive rule for the *effet utile* of a uniformity of EC law. Thereby, on the side of the Member States, the potentiality of a process of development of general administrative law based upon transnational exchange is only seldom harnessed.

In particular, the German administrative law, has, in the last decades, changed, in a productive way, through the introduction of new procedural elements from the legal systems of other Member States, although theoretically, it finds itself in a defensive position *vis-à-vis* an open, plural procedural concept, whose forms (likewise returning to European influences), especially in telecommunications law (for example, the "notice and comment" procedure before the issuance of a regulatory administrative act), are also deployed, whose performance, however, has yet to bear fruit, and is, instead, barricaded in a form of "service after prescription" against the "foreign" European demands: for example, (on the initiative of VG Köln) requests for preliminary decisions, which turn on the "protection of third parties" in procedural norms of the TKG (and its interpretation, consistent with law).[80]

The development of the procedural rationality of the Europeanised administrative law, has not yet taken the step towards the brink of a new procedural conception, which would be orientated towards the model of "open governance"[81] both in a transnational and a community dimension.

79 See the sharp but direct criticism of the interpretation of the subsidiarity principle by the Commission; G. Davies, "Subsidiarity: The Wrong Idea, at the Wrong Place, at the Wrong Time" (2006) 43 *CMLR*, p. 63.

80 VG Köln, (2007) 9 *MMR*, p. 203.

81 U. Di Fabio, *Das Recht offener Staaten – Grundlinien einer Staats- und Rechtstheorie* (Tübingen: Mohr, 1998); E. Schmidt-Aßmann, "Die Herausforderung der Verwaltungsrechtswissenschaft durch die Internationalisierung der Verwaltungsbeziehungen" (2006) 43 *Der Staat*, p. 315, at 326.

Therein lies a task for a general administrative law, which is incrementally building itself into both the picture of and the foundations of variety, which could work in opposition to the increasingly visible centralising tendency of EC law in recent years. The dimension of procedure of Europeanised administrative law will be technocratically curtailed if it is tied to the easing in the "oversight" of the EC Commission over the implementation of EC law in the Member States. It must be unfolded much more pronouncedly in its horizontal and heteronomous dimension, which, in the transnational opening for the interests of other Member States, is facilitated in the iterative formulation of plural public interests and in the mutual observation of administrative strategies, especially in complex types of task (for example, in planning and environmental law, in telecommunications law, but also in social law).

It is hardly productive for the development of a "relational rationality" of the law of a European multilevel system, if, at the supranational level of the community, a narrowing begins, in which the multipolarity and multi-dimensionality of the European legal system are only viewed as a danger to the effectiveness of the transformation of particular European administrative law in the national administrative law, and the inquiry is reduced to which variations in the laws of the Member States seem to be "just about" acceptable. A Europeanised general administrative law can be neither European (in the institutional sense) alone, because it does not belong to the competences of the EC, nor a pure national general administrative law, which merely becomes adjusted to the idiosyncrasies of the "transformation" of the particular European administrative law only upon the basis of effectiveness. In the light of procedural law alone, it can only be understood as a project to be realised co-operatively,[82] which, at a minimum, partially follows the multipolar logic of "conflicts law", but, at the same time, with mutual references between the legal orders in the search of linkages, overcomes the danger of frustrating itself and others, ever hearkening to a logic of experimentation and observation.[83] Such a development is only imaginable in a perspectival crossover, in which must begin primarily at the level of the Member States, where the general administrative law will keep its seat. Secondarily, also at European level, the limitation, namely, the fixation on the national achievement of *effet utile*, must be overcome. Instead, it is better to ask how a plural network of European law, Europeanised administrative law and transnational connections between domestic legal orders can be generated.[84] Here, the ECJ can play a particular role of moderation. Unfortunately, in this regard, scepticism is shown, because the Court shows little feeling for the notion that the unity of law and of legal application is far too blunt an instrument for such a complex polity as the EC, and that, obversely, the acceptance of a differentiated legal order is not only a second best model, but that the ideal of a "complete harmony" or a statistical alignment of supranational and national orders must be abandoned.

82 See Schmidt-Aßmann/Dagron, (note 8 *supra*), "Deutsches und französisches Verwaltungsrecht".

83 Sabel and Zeitlin, (note 73 *supra*), "Learning from Differentiation"; Ladeur, (note 50 *supra*), "Methodology".

84 See Schmidt-Aßmann, (note 1 *supra*), "Problemskizze", p. 30.

4.2. *The Organisation of "Information Networks" as an "Ordering Idea" of a Europeanised Administrative Law*

E. Schmidt-Aßmann has frequently, and justifiably, emphasised that all administration of communal space is based upon "information networks".[85] This is true not only for the Europeanised administration, but is especially so in its case. Here, a small historical reminiscence might be in order, noting the ascent of the general administrative law in Germany towards the end of the Nineteenth century. The centring of German administrative law on the "administrative act" as an expression of the sovereignty of the state (O. Mayer) has been frequently drawn out of its historical context, in which it is paradoxically evaluated by virtue of its distance from the time-honoured "state scientific", purposive orientation.[86] The administrative order, which emerges from "state science" ("*Staatswissenschaft*"), and which emphasises the single decision as the system-constructing moment, is related to the autonomy of the administrative system (outside of these purposes) and constitutes therewith a new perspective on decision-making, which allows for the self-generation of connecting compulsions and possibilities through the processing of cases and from decision to decision.

From this perspective, it is no coincidence that C.F. Gerber[87] conceived of the administrative act as a "declaration of intent" of the state, which thereby (not only in the foreground) sought a connection to civil law. Similarly to private law, which is based upon declarations of intent, the modern administrative law, with its orientation on the "administrative act" as its most important building-block, releases a forward-looking decision-making process, which, through the selectivity of the case orientation and the acceptance of the pressure to decide, was intended to promote the self-generation of an entire infrastructure of knowledge-, presumptive- and evidentiary rules as well as compatible community experiences and expectations, which allow the intrinsic rationality of the administrative act to ripen. It is against this backdrop that the efforts of states to develop the cognitive infrastructure of society, the collection of knowledge, the standardisation of norms, the exchange of experience between the domestic regions, and the development of schools and universities, are to be understood; not only as a service to the community, but as a self-service, towards which the dynamic administration beyond stable purposes was directed. Such an intrinsic rationality of the administration could only come about in co-ordination with the cognitive rationality of a dynamic social knowledge base. That social knowledge system has, with technological progress and the science based- (high-) technology, fundamentally changed, and has required new state initiatives of systematisation and standardisation pursuant to a new structuring paradigm. While earlier knowledge was empirical, bound to large "practice

85 Schmidt and Aßmann, (note 22 *supra*), "Einleitung", p. 22.

86 M. Bohlender, "Metamorphosen des Gemeinwohls. Von der Herrschaft guter polizey zur Regierung durch Freiheit und Sicherheit", in: H. Münkler and H. Bluhm (eds), *Gemeinwohl und Gemeinsinn. Historische Semantiken politischer Leitbegriffe*, (Berlin: Akademie-Verlag, 2001), p. 247.

87 C.F. von Gerber, *System des Deutschen Privatrechts*, (7th ed.), (Jena: Mauke,1860).

communities" and continually developed by them, the knowledge in the industrial society is strongly dynamised:[88] The progress of knowledge advances unevenly and gives rise to corresponding "professional societies", which, for example, as a society of engineers or other professionals can formulate a "technological class", which is no longer identical to the "generally acknowledged rules" of the profession. In the post-modern society another fragmentation of knowledge generation comes about, which is driven by project based "epistemic communities". These orientate themselves more towards strategic goals, while the earlier "knowledge communities" (for example, engineers such as the VDI) aimed towards the continuing progress of the general stocks of knowledge.[89]

In the past, the state itself was always concerned that knowledge must be extended, generalised, stabilised, and distributed so that it can be useful for those other than the "discoverer" - and this also means access for the state and its decision-making practice. Not only for this reason, but also for this reason, the stocks of knowledge also have a rule-like, practical character. In a European multilevel system, a multipolar processing of knowledge is required, which can be shored up by the transnational co-operation between legal orders.

5. Synopsis

In this perspective, a general European administrative law cannot exist under the dominance of common European administrative precepts, which inform the administration of the EC Institutions and are then passed on to the Member States, and which are distilled from the varied national legal orders. A general European administrative law must be construed as a new species of "conflicts law", which renders the national, transnational and supranational components of law permeable to one another, and opens them up for co-operation. Within the association of states that forms the EC, the intrinsic rationality of national administrative law must not (only) be preserved because of the division of competences between the EC and the Member States. The European administrative legal order must be polycentric and be serviceable for the co-ordination of unity and plurality, and the ordering of the general administrative law of the domestic orders, instead of putting it under the pressure of the *effet utile*.

88 See M. Več, *Recht und Normierung in der industriellen Revolution. Neue Strukturen der Normsetzung in Völkerrecht, staatlicher Gesetzgebung und gesellschaftlicher Selbstnormierung* (Frankfurt aM: Klostermann, 2006).

89 See M. Gensollen, "Economie non rivale et communautés d'information", (2004) 124 *Réseaux*, p. 141; *idem*, "Biens informationnels et communautés médiatisées", (2003) 113 *Revue d'Economie Politique*, Special Number, p. 8.

Poul F. Kjaer

CHAPTER 9. FORMALISATION OR DE-FORMALISATION THROUGH GOVERNANCE?

1. Introduction[1]

Christian Joerges has forcefully argued that the "turn to governance" of the European Union (EU) implies a move towards de-juridification.[2] Following Joerges, especially the Open Method of Co-ordination (OMC) introduces a break with traditional forms of legally-mediated political decision-making because the production of political decisions within the framework of the OMC does not imply a simultaneous reference to legal procedures, obligations and sanctions. Hence, the OMC, at least potentially, threatens to undermine the functional synthesis (*Funktionssynthese*) between law and politics, which has been celebrated as one of the key achievements of modernity.[3]

Today, different versions of the OMC are applied within a wide range of policy areas of the EU. One group of policy areas shares the feature that public involvement at EU level is a relatively new phenomenon. This, for example, is the case for employment policy and policies related to the information society. Another cluster of policy areas share the feature that they do not fall under the Community Method (CM) while, at the same time, they possess strong interdependencies with other EU policy areas which are themselves subject to the CM. The prime example here is the co-ordination of the economic policies of the Member States (MS) and their relation to European monetary policy. A third group consists of social policy (pensions and social inclusion), and research and technological development. One shared characteristic of these areas is that earlier attempts to transfer competences from the MS to the EU failed. As a result of

1 An earlier version of this chapter was presented at the conference *Law and Society in the 21st Century: Transformations, Resistances, Futures*, Berlin, 25–28 July 2007. I would like to thank the participants of the relevant session for useful comments and discussion. Responsibility remains with the author.

2 Christian Joerges: *Integration durch Entrechtlichung? Ein Zwischenruf*, ZERP-Diskussionspapier 1, 2007.

3 Jürgen Habermas: Faktizität und Geltung. Beiträge zur Diskurstheorie des Rechts und des demokratischen Rechtssstaats, (Frankfurt aM: Suhrkamp Verlag, 1992), p. 167.

this failure, the OMC was introduced as a substitute for increased competence transfers.[4]

The latter group is particular interesting, because EU/EC policies within these policy areas have been in place for several decades. Moreover, within R & D policy, OMC-like methods such as institutionalised mutual observation and benchmarking had been in place for several decades prior to the official adoption of the OMC as a policy tool within the EU. Hence, this chapter reconstructs the evolution of the OMC in R & D. The reconstruction illustrates that soft law is, by no means, a new phenomenon within the context of European integration.[5] Moreover, due to the considerable policy efforts within the area of R & D, both before and after the introduction of the OMC, the analysis is capable of assessing the "added value" which has emerged from the introduction of the OMC. The findings indicate that the "direct effect" of the OMC is rather limited. Extrapolating from the example of R & D, it can, however, be argued that the OMC contributes to a systematisation, intensification and professionalisation of already existing modes of "pre-integration activities", understood as the kind of policy activities which were unfolded prior to formal competence transfers throughout the history of the integration process. OMC processes contribute to the construction of a "common basis" which can potentially serve as a structural basis for competence transfers at a later date. In contrast to Joerges' argument concerning a move towards de-juridification through the OMC, it is therefore possible to view OMC processes as a structural condition for the transfer of legal competences at a later date, thereby somewhat dissolving the distinction between formalised and de-formalised governance which Joerges departs from.

2. The Expansion of Knowledge

R & D policy is linked to profound societal changes, as also expressed in fashionable terms such as the "information society" and the "knowledge society". The term "information society" implies that it is possible to observe a tendency towards increased temporalisation, in the sense that the time-interval occurring between the introductions of distinctions is being continually reduced. In concrete, this means that the time that products, scientific knowledge, news, legal regulations, political decisions and other manifestations of social operations remain relevant is being continuously diminished because the pace with which they are being replaced is accelerating.[6] That is, of course, not a new phenomenon, as increased temporalisation has been a key characteristic of

4 Susana Borrás and Kerstin Jacobsson: "The open method of co-ordination and new governance patterns in the EU", (2004) 11 *Journal of European Public Policy*, pp. 185–208, at. 191.

5 David M. Trubek and Louise G. Trubek: "Hard and Soft Law in the Construction of Social Europe: the Role of the Open Method of Co-ordination", (2005) 11 *European Law Journal*, pp. 343–364.

6 Niklas Luhmann: *Soziale Systeme. Grundriß einer allgemeinen Theorie*, (Frankfurt aM: Suhrkamp Verlag, 1984), p. 253; Niklas Luhmann: "Die Knappheit der Zeit und die Vordringichkeit des Befristeten", pp. 143–164, in: Niklas Luhmann: *Politische Plannung*, (Opladen: Westdeutscher Verlag, 1971).

modernity since Kant's praise of the emerging modern states ability to pursue constant reform.[7] In this sense, we are merely experiencing an intensification of distinct modern processes. The increased temporalisation does, however, mean that all parts of society are faced with an increased demand for continued change and adaptation. Hence, the related term of "knowledge society" implies that the constant and systematic ability to produce new knowledge and, in particular, the ability proactively to use such knowledge in the development of products, decisions, regulations and so forth, is a key characteristic of present day society. But knowledge is not only being used proactively to "drive development forward", it is also being deployed reactively in order to enable adequate responses to new knowledge which are produced in other spheres of society. For example, public authorities are continuously faced with a demand to develop new knowledge in order to maintain their ability to assess the risks involved in relation to the introduction of new products on the market[8], products which are themselves the consequence of the transformation of new knowledge into new products. As a consequence hereof the ongoing transformation processes implies a move towards an increase in the societal relevance of structures with strong cognitive features, such as science, technology and the economy in relation to normatively-based structures, such as law, politics and moral forms of communication.[9]

This development means, for example, that political decision-making, legal judgments, the interpretation of events by the media, product development and so forth, are increasingly relying upon scientific knowledge and upon the advice of experts.[10] The "competitive advantage" of private and public organisations as well as cities, states and regions such as Europe is, therefore, increasingly dependent on the existence of well-developed research environments just as the strategic fostering of such environments is becoming an increasingly important activity of public organisations.

3. The Evolution of European Science Co-operation

The evolution of R & D policies in the EU is very much a reflection of the general development towards an increased reliance on knowledge in radicalised modernity. European co-operation in the broader realm of science is however having a long history which goes beyond the present focus on R & D as well as beyond cooperation within the framework of the community and the Union. The European Nuclear Research Centre (CERN) was founded in 1953 on the basis of an intergovernmental convention. The European Atomic Energy Community (EURATOM) was launched with the second

7 Gorm Harste: *Modernitet og Organisation*, (Copenhagen: Forlaget Politisk Revy, 1997).

8 For example, within the area of risk regulation. See Poul Kjaer: "Rationality within REACH? On Functional Differentiation as the Structural Foundation of Legitimacy in European Chemicals Regulation", *EUI Working Papers* (Law), nr. 18, 2007.

9 Niklas Luhmann: *Soziale Systeme. Grundriß einer allgemeinen Theorie*, (Frankfurt aM: Suhrkamp Verlag, 1984), p. 436.

10 Helmut Schelsky: Die Soziologen und das Recht. Abhandlungen und Vorträge zur Soziologie von Recht, Institution und Planung, (Opladen: Westdeutscher Verlag, 1980).

Treaty of Rome in parallel with the EEC in 1957. In 1962, the European Southern Observatory (ESO) and in 1964 The European Molecular Biology Organisation (EMBO) was established upon the basis of intergovernmental agreements. As early as in 1965 the EEC, under the impression that a "technology gap" existed *vis-à-vis* the United States, set up a committee to deal with research, science and technology policy, and the impact of the foreseen internal market on these policy areas. The committee was charged with a systematic comparison of national research activities and proposed stronger co-ordination in a whole range of research areas.[11] In 1967, the *Institut Laue-Langevin* (ILL), a European neuron science institute, was set up and in 1971 an intergovernmental framework for European Co-operation in the field of Scientific and Technical Research (COST) was established. COST was originally initiated by the EEC, but most Western European countries were included. In 1972, the Heads of State and Government of the European Community (EC) expressed their support for an increase in the co-ordination of national research policies. The European University Institute (EUI) was established the same year. In 1973, the Commission established the Directorate General for Research, Science and Education. In addition, the 1973 Action Programme of the Commission for the first time called for a harmonisation of national procedures on R & D funding, as well as for a systematic exchange of information between the MS in the area of R & D. These objectives were formulated under the first Commissioner of Research, Ralf Dahrendorf, who also launched the concept of a "single European science area", which should be achieved through the lowering of national barriers within the area of science and research.[12] As a part of these efforts, CREST (Committee on Science and Technical Research) was established in 1974. CREST is a consultative body of the Commission, which consists of MS representatives who monitor R & D polices within the MS, and serves as a platform the development of common approaches. In addition, and on the suggestion of the Commission, the European Science Foundation was established in 1974 as an umbrella structure for national research organisations. However, none of these initiatives were greeted with much enthusiasm by the MS and they did not significantly transform the national R & D systems just as no major move towards integration of those systems took place. Notwithstanding this, Intergovernmental co-operation continued to expand with the creation of the European Molecular Biology Laboratory (EMBL) in 1974 and the European Space Agency (ESA)[13] in 1975.

11 Thomas Banchoff: "The Politics of the European Research Area", *ACES Working Paper.* 2002, 3, p. 7; Yoshiko Okubo, Alvaro de Miranda and Peter Senker: *European Scientific Co-operation and its significance for new EU Member States,* Paper prepared for the 5th Triple Helix Conference, Turin, Italy, 18–21 May 2005, p. 3; Pierre Papon: "L'Europe de la researche: une réponse aux defies de l'avenir", (2006) 12 *Revue D'histoire de L'integration Européenne*, pp. 11–26, at 14; Josephine Anne Stein: "Science, Technology and European foreign policy: European integration, global interaction", (2002) 29 *Science and Public Policy*, pp.463–475.

12 Thomas Banchoff: "The Politics of the European Research Area", *ACES Working Paper*, 2002, 3, p. 8.

13 The ESA was a merger of the European Launch Development Organisation (ELDO) and the European Space Research Organisation (ESRO) which both were established in 1964.

In the 1980s, EUREKA, an intergovernmental programme for technological development was launched. In addition, the Community changed its strategy with the launching of founding schemes such as ESPRIT and RACE. These programmes were aimed at strengthening Europe's position within specific research areas by mobilising increased founding. An additional objective was to minimise the "technology gap" between the different Member States. Later on, these programmes were incorporated in the framework programmes (FP), which the Community has maintained and continuously expanded since 1984. The development of the FPs was strengthened with the SEA which, in 1987, under the condition of unanimity in the Council, granted the Community the competence to co-ordinate national R & D policies.[14] Today, the FP is the third largest budget item of the EU after the Common Agricultural Policy and the Structural Funds.

In the early 1990s, the Commission re-launched the idea of a common European science area. But, again, the attempt ran aground because of reluctance on the part of the Member States and the failure of the Commission to ensure backing from other players such as industry and the national research communities.[15] In 1993, the Treaty of Maastricht introduced co-decision within the area of R & D, but maintained the unanimity requirement in the Council. Hence, the decisional procedures became more complex because the number of institutional actors was increased at the same time as the existing barriers to decision-making in the Council were maintained. With the entering into force of the Treaty of Amsterdam in 1997, the Council switched to Qualified-Majority Voting (QMV) on R & D just as the development of an R & D policy was made an objective of the Union.[16] In parallel to the gradual communitarisation of R & D policy, intergovernmental cooperation kept expanding in the area of basic science, through, for example, the establishment of the European Synchrotron Radiation Facility (ESRF) in 1988.

4. The European Research Area

In January 2000, the Commission, under the label European Research Area (ERA) made a new attempt.[17] This time, the plan was endorsed by the European Council at the by now famous Lisbon summit in March 2000, where it was made into a cornerstone of

14 Single European Act: Title VI (Articles 130f-130q).

15 Thomas Banchoff: "Institutions, Inertia and European Union Research Policy", (2002) 40 *Journal of Common Market Studies*, pp. 1–21.

16 Chapter XVIII (Articles 163–173) of the Treaty of the European Union; Gérard Boussuat: "Les coopérations européennes pour la researche scientifique et technique", 2006, 12, *Revue D'histoire de L'integration Européenne*, pp 5–10.

17 Commission of the European Communities: Communication from the Commission to the Council, the European Parliament and Social Committee and the Committee of the Regions. Towards a European Research Area, *Com*, 18 January, 2000.

the Lisbon Process with its strategic objective of revitalising Europe through a transformation of its economy into a "knowledge based" economy.[18]

In the academic literature, the new offensive has been presented as being based upon a "whole new vision".[19] The ideas presented were, however, virtually identical to those presented 30 years before, in so far as the focus was on the establishment of a "common research space" through the increased mobility of researchers, the increased linking of national research communities, common projects and the establishment of common laboratories in specific fields.[20] In fact, the only difference to the earlier attempts seems to be in the framing of the proposal. The Commission aligned itself with the fashionable concept of the "knowledge society" just as it followed the general trend towards an increased embeddedness of public activities in economic semantics.[21] Hence, the Commission this time called for the creation of a "common market" for R & D, rather than for a common science area. The explicit objective was to achieve for the area of R & D what the SEA had achieved for the economic area. The principles of the Internal Market concerning free movement, non-discrimination and so forth, thus served as the role model for the ERA approach developed by the Commission. In addition, the change of focus from basic research towards innovation enabled the Commission to highlight the explicit economic gains which potentially can be derived from a stronger research policy.[22]

Moreover, the new framing of the old approach found support because it corresponded with ongoing reform efforts in the leading Member States, thereby creating compatibility between the Member States and European perspectives.[23] In addition, the ever increasing internationalisation of science and research started to have profound effects, thereby creating structural conditions which increased the receptibility for the Commission proposals among Member State governments and other stakeholders. But the Commission was not only riding on a wave of profound structural changes within the area of science and research, it was also acting as a central entrepreneur within the

18 Presidency Conclusion: Lisbon European Council, 23 and 24 March 2000.

19 For such an historical unfounded perspective see Álvaro de Elera: "The European Research Area: On the Way Towards a European Scientific Community?", (2006) 12 *European Law Journal*, pp. 559–574, at 563; Robert Kaiser and Heiko Prange: "A New Concept of Deepening European Integration? The European Research Area and the Emerging Role of Policy Co-ordination in a Multi-level Governance System", 2005, 3, 3, *Comparative European Politics*, pp. 289–306.

20 Commission of the European Communities (2000): Communication from the Commission to the Council, the European Parliament and Social Committee and the Committee of the Regions. Towards a European Research Area. Com (2000) 6, 18 January, p. 8; Michel André: "L'espace européen de la recherche: historie d'une idée", (2006) 12 *Revue D'Histoire De L'Integration Européenne*, pp. 131–150, at 133.

21 Poul Kjaer: "Post-Hegelian Networks: Comments on the Chapter bij Simon Deakin", in: Marc Amstutz and Gunther Teubner: *Networks: Legal Issues of Multilateral Co-operation*, (Oxford: Hart Publishing, 2009), p. 75–85.

22 This approach has also been coined a "From invention to invoice" policy.

23 Thomas Banchoff: "The Politics of the European Research Area", ACES Working Paper, 3, 2002, p. 11.

broader realm of the internationalisation processes, in so far as it, since the introduction of the Framework Programmes in the mid-1980s, has systematically used the funding programmes to open up national R & D environments. Hence, with the support of the European Parliament (EP), the Commission deployed its classic strategy for circumventing opposition from Member State governments by systematically linking up with "lower level" organisations and thereby transforming them into advocates of increased Europeanisation. For example, the number of research institutions which acted as partners in the FP was increased from 13,000 to 18,000 between 1987 and 1994,[24] thereby creating increasingly dense European networks. In addition, the Commission systematically promoted the establishment of European associations and Brussels-based representation offices within the area of science and R & D. This semantic turn from science to R & D also served to ensure full support from European business associations, which again exercised considerable pressure on Member State governments.

The efforts of the Commission in relation to the European Research Area has, moreover, been complemented by the increased expectations created through the massive increase in available funding of the 7th Framework Programme (2007–13) when compared with earlier Framework Programmes. In institutional terms, the Framework Programme has also been stabilised through the establishment of the European Research Council (ERC), which will act as a permanent funding agency, which, between 2007 and 2013 alone, will hand out 7.5 billion euro to specific projects (compared to 4 billion euro under the previous framework programme).[25] Furthermore, the outsourcing of funding activities to the ECR means that DG Research, which, in the 1980s and 1990s, was bogged down by the strong emphasis on the rather technocratic administration of the Framework Programme(s), can increasingly devote its attention to the strategic objective of building the European Research Area. With the launching of the Galileo satellite navigation project in 2003, and the signing of the Treaty establishing the International Thermo-nuclear Experimental Reactor (ITER) in 2006 between China, the EU, India, Japan, Russia, South Korea and the United States, the EU made a decisive move towards replacing the Member States as the key player in relation to the establishment of new research infrastructure and facilities.

5. The OMC in Research and Development

The adoption of the ERA concept at Lisbon also signalled the introduction of the OMC within the area of R & D. The Lisbon summit initiated the deployment of OMC tools in order to ensure the realisation of the European Research Area through the benchmarking of national practices, the facilitation of the cross-border mobility of researchers and the improvement of research infrastructures. In addition, it was agreed at the Barcelona summit in March 2002 that all Member States should increase R & D spending from

24 Thomas Banchoff: "The Politics of the European Research Area", ACES Working Paper, 3, 2002, p. 18.
25 The European Research Council website (http://erc.europa.eu/) accessed on 27 December 2007.

an average of 1.9% of GNP in 2000 (EU 15) to 3% of GNP by 2010 and that the process towards the realisation of this objective also should be achieved with OMC methods.

At the organisational level, these ambitious targets were followed up by a merger of the three Council configurations for the Internal Market, Industry, and Research into a single Competitiveness configuration in 2002, thereby strengthening the economic framing of R & D policy. Hence, the Council chose to emphasise i) human resources, ii) investment productivity, iii) impact on competitiveness, and iv) impact on employment in their attempt to concretise the process. Under these headings, the first OMC cycle within R & D was carried out from 2000 to 2003. The main focus was on the development of indicators with which national performance in R & D could be assessed. A high level working group with Member State representatives was entrusted with this task. For each of the four themes, five indicators were selected. Fifteen of the twenty indicators already existed within EUROSTAT or the OECD, and thus the process only added five additional indicators to an already well-established system. This was followed up by the establishment of five expert groups, which were respectively charged with the task of i) defining good practices, ii) the way they had been achieved, iii) the potential for transferring such practices from one Member State to other Member States, and iv) the development of policy recommendations. These groups mainly consisted of academics, who were partly appointed by the Commission and partly by the Member States. Officially, the Member State representatives did not act as national representatives.

The second cycle started with the 2002 agreement that R & D spending should be increased to 3% of GNP by 2010. The task of carrying out the OMC processes was outsourced to CREST. As noted, CREST is an advisory committee under the Commission consisting of Member State representatives, which was established in 1974 with the task of assisting the Commission in its efforts to co-ordinate national R & D policies. Thus, in practice, CREST serves as a structural coupling between Member State authorities as well as between Member State authorities and the Commission, since its function is to increase the reflexivity of these structures by increasing the level of mutual observation. Under the auspices of CREST, five working groups were established, which continue to follow the development towards the 3% target.

A third cycle was started in mid-2006. The main focus of this cycle remains the 3% target. In addition, it has been proposed that the cycle should involve areas such as "globalisation and R & D" and the use of structural funds to support this research.[26] In

26 Presidency Conclusions: Conference on "Improving Research Policies in Europe through the Open Method of Co-ordination", Brussels, 18 May 2006, p. 3; Improving Research Policies through the Open Method of Co-ordination, Speech by European Commissioner for Science and Research Janez Potočnik (SPEECH /06/311), European Commission conference on the open method of coordination in research, Brussels, 18 May 2006.

the attempt to concretise the further work, the Commission adopted a Green Paper entitled "The European Research Area: New Perspectives",[27] in the spring of 2007.

Apart from the merger of the council configurations, the evolution of the OMC within the area of R & D indicates that it is difficult to identify institutional innovations which can be said to be specific to the OMC. This is also being confirmed through the actual use of OMC tools. The Commission foresaw the deployment of the OMC within five areas: i) the "3-percent action plan", ii) human resources and mobility, iii) science and society, iv) networking of national research programmes, and v) research infrastructure.[28] In practice, however, OMC tools have been deployed in other areas as well, just as some of the five areas have only experienced a partial deployment of OMC instruments.

In addition, the overall objective concerning the establishment of the European Research Area is more than 30 years old. The introduction of the OMC has, therefore, merely led to a new framing of already existing activities and efforts. The outsourcing of the OMC processes to CREST confirms this, in so far as CREST has been carrying out OMC-like processes for the last 30 years. When the fact that the Commission and the OECD have systematically tried to benchmark best practises and to achieve convergence between national research systems since the 1960s, it is difficult to see what all the hype is about in relation to the OMC. The OMC in R & D amounts to little more than an attempt to breathe new life into old, and not particularly dynamic, structures. However, such attempts to establish increased momentum were already apparent in the launching of the idea of a European Science Area and CREST in the mid-1970s, in the launching of the Framework Programme(s) in the mid-1980s, and in the attempt to re-launch the idea of a common European Science Area in the early 1990s. These attempts, however, all ran out steam after a short period.

6. The Function of the OMC

The insight that the deployment of OMC instruments is not a new phenomenon within the context of the European integration processes makes it questionable to claim that the OMC is a "new mode of governance".[29] In addition, the modest results which have been achieved with such tools to date make the claim that such instruments possesses

[27] Commission of the European Communities: The European Research Area: New Perspectives, COM (2007) 161 final.

[28] Draft Summary Conclusions of the 288th meeting of the Scientific and Technical Research Committee (CREST) held in Iraklion, Greece, 27–28 March 2003. CREST 1203/2003, p. 7, and Åse Gornitzka (2005): "Coordinating policies for a "Europe of Knowledge". Emerging practices of the "Open Method of Co-ordination" in education and research, Arena Working Paper, 16, p. 23.

[29] Charles F. Sabel and Jonathan Zeitlin (2007): Learning from Difference: The Architecture of Experimentalist Governance in the European Union, *European Governance Papers*, No C-07–02 (www.connex-network.org/eurogov/pdf/egp-connex-C-07–02.pdf); Maria Joao Rodrigues: *European Policies for a Knowledge Economy*, (Cheltenham, Edward Elgar, 2003).

the potential to radically increase the problem-solving capacity of the EU and to act as a real alternative to the classical community method implausible. Chalmers and Lodge, in relation to the deployment of the OMC within the area of the European Employment Strategy, go so far as to claim that the OMC is nothing but a rhetorical trick, which was invented within the context of the EMU in order to assert the claim that the EU was not heedless of the social consequences of monetary union.[30]

Another and somewhat more positive possibility is to view the introduction of the OMC as a systematisation, intensification and professionalisation of "pre-integration" processes. Systematisation, because it frames the already ongoing soft law activities and links them to the overall policy objectives of the EU; intensification, because it increases the level of mutual observation between the Member States, and hence increases the reflexivity of their administrations, and professionalisation, because it somewhat formalises the already existing instruments and procedures for "soft" policy-making. Hence, as long as the OMC is not used as a substitute for the Community Method, it increases, rather than decreases, the formalisation of policy-making, just as it increases the possibility of exercising critique in so far as it renders the existing structures more visible.

The introduction of the OMC should thus be understood as a strengthening of the kind of policy conduct which tends to takes place prior to formal transfers of competences. As is well-known, one of the reasons for the emergence of the OMC was the desire of the Member States to prevent further transfers of competence to the EU level. Nonetheless, the OMC is de facto "uploading" a number of policy areas which were not subject to common European approaches before the launching of the OMC.[31] Good examples of this are unemployment and social exclusion policies. In addition, OMC instruments are mainly deployed within policy areas that fall outside the Community Method or where the Community only have supportive or complementary competences *vis-à-vis* the Member States. Furthermore, one common feature of the policy areas in which OMC tools have been deployed is that they are characterised by substantial divergences in their organisation across the Member States. Additionally, the specific ways in which these policy areas are organised, and the policy objectives that they embody, are, within national political discourses, often considered as constituent of the inner core of Member State national identities, expressing essential characteristics of these nations. Such idealisations can, of course, be easily dismissed with the observation that these regimes are evolutionary phenomena resulting from contingent and

30 Damian Chalmers and Martin Lodge: "The Open Method of Co-ordination and the European Welfare State", ESRC Centre for Analysis of Risk and Regulation, Discussion Paper No. 11, June 2003, The London School of Economics and Political Science, (www.lse.ac.uk/collections/CARR/pdf/Disspaper11.pdf), 5 January 2005.

31 Bent Greve and Susana Borrás: "Concluding remarks: New method or just cheap talk?", (2004) 11 *Journal of European Public Policy*, pp. 329–336.

uncontrollable processes.[32] In terms of political realities, nationally-embedded regimes are, however, linked to both substantial socio-economic interests and to strong ideological and emotional forces, making attempts to increase EU competences within such areas extremely difficult. It is against this background – large differences in organisational mode and policy objectives, and high levels of political sensitivity – that the deployment of the OMC should be understood. It is a subtle instrument, applied to achieve convergence between policy objectives and organisational modes in policy areas in which the political resistance and practical difficulties that stand in the way of harmonisation are substantial. From this perspective, and to the extent that it succeeds in terms of output, the OMC could provide a structural basis for increased integration through competence transfers at a later date. Political sensitivities might gradually be overcome by intensive communicative exchanges taking place at EU level, if these can provoke a change of perspective among the key actors and public opinion in favour of EU involvement in the areas in question. Systematic comparisons and evaluations can, moreover, be seen as reflexivity-increasing instruments that break down national myths concerning the superiority of national policy regimes when compared with other regimes, and hence reduce resistance to common European approaches.[33] To the extent that convergence between the different ways of prioritising and organising relevant policy areas is achieved, this is likely to provide a structural basis which will facilitate actual harmonisation. Hence, the particularity of the method lies in its focus which is to construct common European "universes" or discourses within areas in which such discourses have not existed so far. This also means that the OMC's actual impact remains difficult to assess. The OMC is not intended to produce "real" decisions, but to ensure the continued transformation of discursive structures. The main outcome of OMC processes is a common language, in the form of key concepts, classifications, indicators and a common knowledge base, which is followed up by strategic diffusion of knowledge and evaluation of results.[34] Hence, the OMC processes can also be described as being oriented towards the establishment of discursive hegemony and the "voluntary" internalisation of preferences and norms associated with these models amongst relevant actors in the Member States.[35] In other words, and bearing in mind that the vast majority of policy areas in which it is applied have only recently been "uploaded" to European level, the OMC can be characterised as an instrument for "entrepreneurial discourse building". It is a method which creates common European universes within policy areas which until now have been dominated by separate, nationally embedded discourses.

32 Niklas Luhmann: "Wohlfahrtsstaat zwischen Evolution und Rationalität", pp. 26–40, in: Peter Koslowski *et al.*, (ed), *Chancen und Grenzen des Sozialstaats*, (Tübingen: Mohr Siebeck, 1983).

33 Stijn Smismans: "Reflexive law in support of directly deliberative poliarchy: Reflexive-deliberative polyarchy as a normative frame for the OMC", pp. 99–144, in: Olivier De Schutter and Simon Deakin (eds): *Social Rights and Market Forces: Is the Open Co-ordination of Employment and Social Policies the Future of Social Europe?*, (Brussels: Bryant, 2005).

34 Kerstin Jacobsson: "Soft Regulation and the Subtle Transformation of States: The Case of EU Employment Policy", (2004) 14 *Journal of European Public Policy*, pp. 355–70.

35 Poul F. Kjaer: *Three Forms of Governance and Three Forms of Power*, pp. 23 – 43 in: Erik Oddvar Eriksen, Christian Joerges and Florian Rödl, *The Unsettled Political Order of Europe*, (Oxford: Routledge, 2008).

From the Brussels perspective, the OMC has, therefore, become an instrument that can be used to create new "fields of action". Hence, in so far as integration is narrowly defined as a conveying of legal competences to the EC institutions, the OMC can thus be characterised as "pre-integration" tool, which constructs a "common basis" within policy areas where such a basis did not previously exist.

Within the area of R & D, the kinds of efforts described above have been unfolding for many years. However, no major breakthrough in terms of legal integration has occurred to date. Hence, the use of OMC instruments in order to pave the way for "real" integration has so far only been a very modest success. Viewed over the long period, the area over R & D has, however, experienced a slow but steady increase in the level of Europeanisation. This increase might lead to significant changes in the preferences of Member State actors further down the road, and hence ensure their backing for a major integrative initiative through increased transfer of competences and the construction of an adequate constitutional framework for the area of R & D.

PART II

TRANSNATIONAL REGULATION AND SOCIETAL CONSTITUTIONALISM: CONFLICT OF LAWS OR LAWS OF CONFLICT?

Gunther Teubner

CHAPTER 10. THE CORPORATE CODES OF MULTINATIONALS: COMPANY CONSTITUTIONS BEYOND CORPORATE GOVERNANCE AND CO-DETERMINATION

German co-determination is one of the casualties of globalisation.[1] Thirty years ago, the battle for union participation in corporate boards seemed to come to a conciliatory conclusion in the historic compromise of the German co-determination law. In the meantime, the power ratios might well have altered to such an extent that the shareholders can celebrate a clear victory, whilst the trade unions are left to fight retreating battles. In company law, co-determination is being usurped by corporate governance.

Nevertheless, it is somewhat surprising that the self-same globalisation process, which pushed the German form of co-determination onto the back foot, contemporaneously forced a large number of multinationals to develop new forms of company constitutions, at a safe distance from the crossfire of corporate governance and co-determination.[2] The corporate codes of multinationals are directed neither at the interests of their shareholders, nor at the participation of the trade unions. These codes are different instances of corporate social responsibility with a potential that is hard to gauge.

The corporate codes of multinationals react to both new perils in the working environment and the disappearance of traditional actors due to the globalisation process: the worldwide inter-linking of markets, capital, and production facilitate a slackening of working conditions in developing countries and endanger the social achievements in developed industrial states, a situation in no way ameliorated by nation states policies. Hopes that traditional international organisations (particularly the International Labour Organisation) would come to rescue, have been disappointed because, although binding, their founding inter-state treaties are unenforceable. Similarly, social clauses in international trade contracts promise little. A strategy in which the pressure amassed by worldwide social conflicts, protest movements, domestic

1 Translated from the German by Rory Stephen Brown. I would like to thank Anna Beckers for her help in preparing this article.

2 See K. Abbott and D. Snidal, "Strengthening International Regulation Through Transnational New Governance", (2009) 42 *Vanderbilt Journal of Transnational Law*, p. 501.

courts, non-governmental and international organisations, coerces multinationals into adopting codes of conduct in which they assume an obligation to uphold social standards, is more likely to succeed.[3] A committed advocate of industrial democracy observes, in the relative success of the corporate code,

> [...] the inexorable result of the shift of power subsequent to globalisation. Neither states nor international organisations can notably limit the room for manoeuvre enjoyed by multinationals. The latter insist upon their freedoms, guaranteed by the principle of voluntarism, and employ them to draft their own normative registers. Even when these rules do not correspond to the traditional notion of law, they are norms for which respect is a legitimate expectation. It is imperative, therefore, that "soft law" does not remain merely cosmetic. If NGOs, the media, and perhaps also trade unions, intensify their efforts to promote an international consciousness which reflects the global civil society of the future in the world of work, then we may set our hopes high.[4]

This view is primarily interested in political strategies and their results. Legal aspects of the codes of conduct appear only at the periphery; that is to say, these codes occupy a juridical "no-man's land". As soft law, they are not enforceable; instead, they *morally* oblige companies. Everything depends on political relationships, namely, the pressure exerted by the leading actors and the mobilisation of the public.[5] It would seem salutary, to ponder as to whether or not legal phenomena manifest themselves within corporate codes, which not only alter the *gravitas* of the law-giving institutions, but also, by dint of their juridical positivity, have a knock-on effect on political and economic relationships. The thesis proposed here is that corporate codes are emergent legal phenomena in the constitutionalisation of private governance regimes. Unlike when they were first spawned, they are no longer mere public relations strategies; instead, they have matured into genuine civil constitutions – in the fashion of constitutional pluralism. In what follows, five observable trends will be sketched in support

3 L. Backer, "The Autonomous Global Enterprise", (2006) 41 *Tulane Law Journal*, p. 101 S. Picciotto, "Rights, Responsibilities and Regulation of International Business", (2003) 42 *Columbia Journal of Transnational Law*, p. 131, at 139; V. Haufler, *A Public Role for the Private Sector: Industry Self-Regulation in a Global Economy*, (Washington DC: Carnegie Endowment for International Peace, 2001); C.M. Dickerson, "Transnational Codes of Conduct Through Dialogue: Leveling the Playing Field For Developing Workers", (2001) 53 *Florida Law Review*, p. 611; H. Arthurs, "Private Ordering and Workers' Rights in the Global Economy: Corporate Codes of Conduct as a Regime of Labour Market Regulation", in: J. Conaghan, R.M. Fischl and K. Klare (eds), *Labour Law in an Era of Globalization: Transformative Practices and Possibilities*, (Oxford: Oxford University Press, 2002), p. 471; O. Boiral, "The Certification of Corporate Conduct: Issues and Prospects", (2003) 142 *International Labour Review*, p. 317; R. Jenkins "The Political Economy of Codes of Conduct", in: R. Jenkins, R. Pearson and G. Seyfang (eds), *Corporate Responsibility and Labour Rights: Codes of Conduct in the Global Economy*, (London: Earthscan, 2002), p. 13.

4 M. Weiss, "Gefangen im globalen Wettbewerb: Chancen und Grenzen des Arbeitsrecht: Internationale Organisationen, staatliche Eigeninteressen und multinationale Konzerne", (2004) 22 *Forschung Frankfurt*, p. 15.

5 Ibid.

of this contention: (1) Juridification; (2) Constitutionalisation; (3) Judicialisation; (4) Hybridisation; and (5) Intermeshing.

1. Private Juridification: Corporate Codes as Law without the State

By simply describing corporate codes as soft law, one sidesteps categorising them as law or non-law. Mindful of the grave consequences of this categorisation, such a sidestep is inadvisable. Corporate codes beg the same question as *lex mercatoria*, internet law and other global regimes in which private actors make rules, the binding nature of which is not guaranteed by state power, yet which display a high normative efficacy. Are we considering social norms or real law? For the time-being, the conclusion that we are experiencing real law has been arrived at in various vehicles of social and legal theory: legal pluralism,[6] post-modern governance,[7] social fields,[8] systems,[9] and soft-law.[10]

What we are observing here is the emergence of a legal discourse of global dimensions, the boundaries of which are drawn by the binary code of legal and illegal, and which self-perpetuates by recycling symbolic global (not national) validity. The first criterion, binary code, distinguishes global law from economic and other social processes. The second criterion, global validity, differentiates between national and international legal phenomena. Both criteria are instruments of second order observation. Thereby, law observes its own operations in the environs of national legal orders and global social systems.

Corporate codes call for differentiation. Not every formalised statement of corporate social responsibility by a multinational can be attributed legal character. Only when particular conditions are fulfilled can we talk of law in the real sense. To date, Martin Herberg has undertaken the most detailed examination of the necessary normative structures,[11] and asserts that it is the interplay between three levels of norms that

6 J. Griffiths, "What is Legal Pluralism", (1986) 24 *Journal of Legal Pluralism*, p. 1; S.E. Merry, "Legal Pluralism", (1988) 22 *Law and Society Review*, p. 869; H. Peterson and H. Zahle, *Legal Polycentricity: Consequences of Pluralism in Law*, (Aldershot: Dartmouth, 1995).

7 G. Stoker, "Governance as Theory", (1998) 155 *International Social Science Journal*, p. 17.

8 P. Bourdieu, "The Force of Law: Toward a Theory of the Juridical Field", (1987) 38 *Hastings Law Journal*, p. 808.

9 G. Teubner (ed), *Global Law Without A State*, (Aldershot: Dartmouth, 1997); J. Priban and D. Nelken, *Law's New Boundaries: The Consequences of Legal Autopoiesis*, (Aldershot: Dartmouth, 2001); G.-P. Calliess, *Grenzüberschreitende Verbraucherverträge*, (Tübingen: Mohr Siebeck, 2006), at 176 *et seq.*

10 S. Sciarra, "Social Values and the Multiple Sources of European Law", (1995) 1 *European Law Journal*, p. 60; A.E. Boyle, "Some Reflections on the Relationship of Treaties and Soft Law", (1999) 48 *International and Comparative Law Quarterly*, p. 901.

11 M. Herberg, "Private Authority, Global Governance, and the Law. The Case of Environmental Self-Regulation in Multinational Enterprises", in: G. Winter (ed), *Multilevel Governance of Global Environmental Change. Perspectives from Science, Sociology and the Law*, (Cambridge: Cambridge University Press, 2006), p. 149; *idem*, *Globalisierung und private Selbstregulierung*, (Frankfurt aM: Campus, 2007); *idem*, "Erzeugen multinationale Unternehmen ihr eigenes Umweltrecht? Bausteine zu einer Theorie transnationaler Regulative", in: G. Winter (ed), *Die Umweltverantwortung*

transforms the codes into genuine laws. Hence, codes of conduct take on legal character if:

- first, at the upper level, firm-specific self-commitments and guidelines exist, under conditions of increasing legal porosity; they are an important means for development of trust and for the discovery of legitimacy;
- second, at the central level, activities of the internal regulatory and executive organs work, partially and variably, as advisers, investigators and enforcers, and frequently as developers of valid norms;
- third, at the lower level, concrete technical and organisational rules exist, which, so to say, identify the operative core of the regulatory organs; they comprise duties and tasks, which one could not cast in this concrete form from the guidelines, and which, at times, take on the format of implicit basic rules and indices of normality.

Herberg thus puts forward a catalogue of additional features upon which the legal character of a code is contingent. It must be an inter-linking bundle of inter-related norms, rules and procedures (which typically also includes very concrete guidelines for specific situations), clearly distinguish between permissible and impermissible practices, and give its addressees a reliable means of orientation. An additional indicator is the component of factual efficacy, which comes to being, partially, by dint of the internal binding and persuasive force of the rules, and partially through instruments of surveillance and enforcement. One fundamental definitional pre-requisite is the development of specific, distinguishable organs whose central task is the maintenance and further advancement of the normative order.

To be sure, a clear legal theoretical orientation can only be developed if one can trace these combinations of features back to "secondary norm-formation processes". Contrary to several sociological or economic formulations, not every norm formation or "private ordering" is law. The indifference with regard to the legal proprium which such theories exhibit would be fatal to any socio-legal or doctrinal analysis, which *per force* concerns itself with the internal rationality and normativity of law.[12] In order to avoid the misunderstandings about a system-theoretical approach, it must be stressed that the usage of the binary code is insufficient for the identification of law. The institutionalisation of processes of secondary norm-formation is decisive. This not only recalls Herbert Hart's definition of law as the unity of primary and secondary norms,[13]

multinationaler Konzerne. Selbststeuerung und Recht bei Auslandsdirektinvestitionen, (Baden-Baden: Nomos, 2005), p. 73. These studies are primarily concerned with corporate codes relating to the environment, but are, *mutatis mutandis*, relevant to labour law.

12 J. Griffiths (*supra* note 6), at 1 *et seq.*, in his description of legal pluralism as a plethora of systems of "social control", is rather insensitive with respect to the legal proprium. As to the indifference of economic analysis of "private ordering", see A. Aviram, "A Network Effects Analysis of Private Ordering", (2003) 80 *Berkeley Program in Law and Economics Working Paper Series* 5, available at: http://repositories.cdlib.org/blewp/.

13 For the parallel attempt to Kelsen's ideas on customary international law and the Grundnorm, see A. Fischer-Lescano, "Monismus, Dualismus? – Pluralismus. Selbstbestimmung des Weltrechts bei Hans

but also goes beyond it, since it replaces structural with operational orientation. Only when institutional arrangements which systematically subordinate the first order observations to the second order observation of a legal code exist, can we speak of autonomous law (with or without the involvement of the state). A "global law without a state" should not yet be assumed upon the basis that non-state institutions judge behaviour pursuant to the normative code, but, rather, that it may be acknowledged only when processes which observe these judicial functions under the binary legal code have been institutionalised. Only then do corporate codes satisfy the structural pre-requisites of a transnational law outside of state law.

> Transnational law describes a third category of an autonomous legal system that goes beyond the traditional categories of national and international law. It is created and developed through the legislative powers of a global civil society and based upon general legal principles and their crystallisation in civil practice. Private conflict resolvers are responsible for its usage, interpretation and furtherance, and a codification – if one appears at all – will appear in the form of general principles and rules, standard contract forms, or codes of conduct, which are established by private standardising institutions.[14]

To stress this point again, in order for private ordering to qualify as genuine law, it is not sufficient that the pertinent behavioural rules are alloyed to the notion of legal or illegal. Instead, the rules must themselves be subjugated to a process, in which they are judged according to the legal code. This reflexive process requires certain institutional precautions, in particular, the development of actors or instances, who or which are responsible for the establishment, modification, interpretation and implementation of the primary norm formation. Fundamental to this is the growth of the central level of internal control and implementation organs, which mediates between the two other normative levels, thusly grounding the legal character of the corporate code.

A more exacting determination of whether corporate codes constitute law, the question of whether such self-curtailments qualify can be supported by two perspectives. From the outside, the code appears to be a contractual obligation or a unilateral public declaration, designed to transform political statements into binding legal form. From the inside, the code seems to be a corporate act, through which associative rules become binding for the organs of the company, in an internal relationship to the organs and the shareholders as well as in a labour law relation to the workers. The interplay between the company law rules and the external efficacy of these rules does merit further

Kelsen und Niklas Luhmann", in: H. Brunkhorst and R. Voigt (eds), *Rechts-staat: Staat, internationale Gemeinschaft und Völkerrecht bei Hans Kelsen*, (Baden-Baden: Nomos, 2008).

14 G.-P. Calliess, "Transnationales Verbrauchervertragsrecht", (2004) 68 *Rabels Zeitschrift*, p. 244, at 254 *et seq.*; for the terminological history of transnational law, see H.H. Koh, "Transnational Legal Process", (1996) 75 *Nebraska Law Review*, p. 181; see, further, F. Hanschmann, "Theorie transnationaler Rechtsprozesse", in: S. Buckel, R. Christensen and A. Fischer-Lescano (eds), *Neue Theorien des Rechts*, (Stuttgart: Lucius and Lucius, 2006), p. 235; P. Schiff Berman, "From International Law to Law and Globalization", (2005) 43 *Columbia Journal of Transnational Law*, p. 458.

examination. It is worthwhile drawing a parallel here between the interplay of international law covenants and unilateral governmental declarations, and the effect of the former on laws of the constitutional variety in the domestic legal order. It should, therefore, become clear that these norms, pursuant to their double-juridification, have binding legal force. Moreover, according to the argument here, they represent genuine legal norms in both the sociological and the juridical sense.

2. Civic Constitutionalisation: Elements of a Communal Constitution

Even more astonishing than their qualification as law in the formal sense, is the peculiar constitutional element exhibited by such private codifications of corporate rules. The reflexive legal standardisation, which takes place at the central level, substantiates the transposition of the corporate code from social norms into legal norms, without, however, *stricto sensu*, representing a constitutionalisation. This occurs only when the reflexive processes in the organisations are appended to reflexive legal processes – in other words, when inter-systemic linking institutions tie together secondary rule-making in the law with fundamental, rational principles of the organisation.[15] This is based upon a constitutional concept which is not limited to nation states constitutions, but which, instead requires that, under particular historical conditions, even non-state civic orders give birth to autonomous constitutionalisation. The positivisation of constitutional norms moves from the global political level to various social sectors, which, in parallel to political constitutions, produce their own constitutions of civil society.[16] Pursuant to the concept of constitutional pluralism, one can speak of a

15 See, further, on these processes of auto-constitutionalisation: G. Teubner, "Self-Constitutionalizing TNCs? On the Linkage of 'Private' and 'Public' Corporate Codes of Conduct", (2010) 17 *Indiana Journal of Global Legal Studies* (forthcoming).

16 As to the concept of "societal constitutionalism" in social theory, see D. Sciulli, *Theory of Societal Constitutionalism*, (Cambridge: Cambridge University Press, 1992), at 21 *et seq.*; *idem*, *Corporate Power in Civil Society: An Application of Societal Constitutionalism*, (New York: New York University Press, 2001), at 131 *et seq.*; G. Teubner (*supra* note 15), at 1 *et seq.*; on plural constitutionalism, see N. Walker, "The Idea of Constitutional Pluralism", (2002) 65 *Modern Law Review*, p. 317; C. Walter, "Constitutionalizing (Inter)national Governance: Possibilities for and Limits to the Development of an International Constitutional Law", (2001) 44 *German Yearbook of International Law*, p. 170; A. Fischer-Lescano, *Globalverfassung: Die Geltungsbegründung der Menschenrechte*, (Weilerswist: Velbrück, 2005), at 247 *et seq.*; H. Brunkhorst, *Solidarität. Von der Bürgerfreundschaft zur globalen Rechtsgenossenschaft*, (Frankfurt aM: Suhrkamp Verlag, 2002), at 203 *et seq.*; G.-P. Calliess, "Reflexive Transnational Law: The Privatisation of Civil Law and the Civilisation of Private Law", (2002) 24 *Zeitschrift für Rechtssoziologie*, p. 185; T. Cottier and M. Hertig, "The Prospects of 21st Century Constitutionalism", (2003) 7 *Max Planck Yearbook of United Nations Law* 261; H. Schepel, "Constituting Private Governance Regimes: Standards Bodies in American Law", in: Ch. Joerges and G. Teubner (eds), *Constitutionalism and Transnational Governance*, (Oxford: Hart Publishing, 2004), 161; C. Scott and R. Wai, "Transnational Governance of Corporate Conduct through the Migration of Human Rights Norms: The Potential Contribution of Transnational 'Private' Litigation", in: Ch. Joerges, I.-J. Sand and G. Teubner (eds), *Transnational Governance and Constitutionalism*, (Oxford: Hart Publishing, 2004), p. 287. On a global economic constitution, see H. Arthurs and R. Kreklewich, "Law, Legal Institutions, and the Legal Profession in the New Economy", (1996) 34 *Osgoode Hall Law Journal*, p. 1, at 4; D.Z. Cass, "The 'Constitutionalization' of International Trade Law: Judicial Norm-

constitution of a community outside of the domestic context, when the following conditions are fulfilled:

> (i) the development of an explicit constitutional discourse and constitutional self-consciousness; (ii) a claim to foundational legal authority, or sovereignty, whereas sovereignty is not viewed as absolute; (iii) the delineation of a sphere of competences; (iv) the existence of an organ internal to the polity with interpretative autonomy with regard to the meaning and the scope of the competences; (v) the existence of an institutional structure to govern the polity; (vi) rights and obligations of citizenship, understood in a broad sense; and (vii) specification of the terms of representation of the citizens in the polity.[17]

The expressions "polity", "governing", and "representation" may not be understood in the narrow sense of an institutionalised political system, but may, instead, also denote an "unpolitical" civic manifestation, be it economic, scientific, educational, health-related, artistic or sporting, in which the global constitutionalisation process takes place.[18]

Therefore, an autonomous, non-state, non-political, civic constitutionalisation of multinationals takes place if reflexive social processes, which concern the relationship of the multinational in its various environs, are interwoven with reflexive legal processes. Under these conditions, it makes sense to speak of elements of a genuine constitution in the corporate codes of multinationals. We can observe the typical components of a constitution: regulations about the establishment and functioning of decision-making processes (organisational and procedural rules), and the codification of the boundaries of the organisation in relation to individual freedoms and civil liberties (basic rights).

The norms of the upper level of the codes are orientated towards precisely these conditions. They concern the underlying decision-making processes of the multinational, which pertain to the organisation's relationship to its employees, whose rights it respects. The guidelines at this upper level are the genuine constitutional norms of the multinationals. By dint of their structure, these directives are neither substantive rules, such as the standards at the lower level, nor mere procedural norms such as those at the central level. Instead, they are explicit superior norms of the company constitution,

Generation as the Engine of Constitutional Development in International Trade", (2001) 12 *European Journal of International Law*, p. 39, at 40 *et seq.*; R. de Lange, "Divergence, Fragmentation, and Pluralism. Notes on Polycentricity and Unity in Law", in: H. Petersen and H. Zahle (eds), *Legal Polycentricity: Consequences of Pluralism in Law*, (Aldershot: Dartmouth, 1995), p. 103, at 112 *et seq.*

17 N. Walker, "The EU and the WTO: Constitutionalism in a New Key", in: G. de Burca and J. Scott (eds), *The EU and the WTO. Legal and Constitutional Issues*, (London: Hart Publishing, 2001), p. 31, at 33.

18 This receives special emphasis in D. Sciulli (*supra* note 16, 1992) at 21 *et seq.*; G. Teubner (*supra* note 15), at 1 *et seq.*; H. Brunkhorst (*supra* note 16), at 203 *et seq.*; A. Fischer-Lescano (*supra* note 16), at 195 *et seq.;* Ch. Joerges, H. Schepel and E. Vos, "The Law's Problems with the Involvement of Non-Governmental Actors in Europe's Legislative Processes: The Case of Standardisation under the 'New Approach'", in European University Institute (eds), *EUI Working Papers* No. 99/9 (San Domenico: Badia Fiesolana, 1999), 1 *et seq.*; L. Scott and R. Wai (*supra* note 16), at 287 *et seq.*

which are formulated as general principles, and serve both as the departure point for internal norm-generation and as the yardsticks of the internal and external reviews.

To speak of the "limits on power" due to the external effects of organisational action, as Herberg does, is not idle, but is too close to conceptions of the division of powers in a state constitution.[19] It would be more accurate to speak not only of the curtailments of freedom in situations in which economic power relations manifest themselves, but also, more comprehensively, of externally imposed self-restraint of the organisational matrix, due to its negative externalities.[20] The problem centres on the negative externalities of the profit principle, the chosen production technologies, and the formal organisation. We are not concerned here with a transfer of the rights of basic national law as a result of the exercise of power by societal actors, but, instead, with basic rights, which actively oppose the external effects of such pursuits. The constitutional question of globalised civic sectors is thoroughly reminiscent of the constitutional question of the nation state of the 18th and 19th centuries.

3. International Judicialisation: Corporate Codes in Conflict with State Laws

The juridification and constitutionalisation of multinationals through corporate codes are instances of independent law-formation, and therefore have little to do with national or international politics and law. Corporate codes produce global laws and global constitutions without a state. In the light of globalisation's tendency to differentiate between politics and law more than in the nation-state, the relation of these corporate codes to national and international law, on the one hand, and to national and international politics, on the other, need to be discussed separately.

One important condition for the success of corporate codes is their interaction with national legal systems. The effectuation of this interaction should be one of the most important tasks. But these efforts come up against the tough and enduring resistance of multinationals, which jealously guard their "sovereignty" over their corporate codes, and which are fain to avoid judicial reviews. For the implementation success of codes of conduct, their judicialisation in the national legal order will be one of the most important pre-requisites.[21] At the same time, it should be clear that their reception in national law is not a condition of the legal character or binding effect of the codes. Both are produced by the juridification and the constitutionalising processes in the company, and also in interactions with actors external to it.

19 M. Herberg (*supra* note 11).

20 For more details, see G. Teubner, "The Anonymous Matrix: Human Rights Violations by 'Private' Transnational Actors", (2006) 69 *Modern Law Review*, p. 327.

21 See the conclusions drawn by R. Zimmer from an empirical study of corporate codes in Salvador: R. Zimmer, "Menschenrechte der Arbeiterinnen werden häufig missachtet", *Frankfurter Rundschau, 12 September 2006*, available at: www.fr-online.de.

It should be equally apparent that this interaction with state law does not signify the transformation of a legal register of civil society into domestic law. The corporate codes are neither prescribed by national legislation, nor adopted, nor integrated. More pertinent is the notion of conflict of laws: the autonomous legal orders of the multinationals collide with national and international laws. In this collision between autonomous legal orders, both undergo a deep process of change. In the event, corporate codes are not subordinated to domestic law, nor is domestic law ousted by the codes, rather there is a reciprocal reconstruction of the state law in the corporate code and *vice versa*. Existing conflicts law is not equipped for such transnational and trans-institutional collisions. The problems arising here can be overcome through a new law of conflicts, which, unlike the traditional territorial jurisdictional predicates of international private law, locates itself in a plurality of national, international and corporate legal systems.[22] From the offset, a substantive law approach would be preferable, which, by virtue of the transnational and trans-institutional collisions, makes it impossible to refer the conflict exclusively to one of the colliding legal orders. Here, we are concerned with regime-transcending legal conflicts, with effects in both legal orders. The only escape route in such a case of inter-regime conflict would be for the tribunal concerned to develop its own substantive norms. Mindful of the "domestic" and the "foreign" legal order, and with one eye on the third order, trans-institutional substantive norms, following the fashion of an asymmetrical law-mélange, could be formed. The goal would be that, in such conflicts, organisational, international and national norms could jostle for position. The challenge for the relevant national, international and "private" conflict resolution tribunals is to approach the quandary in such a manner that they distil the pertinent laws from the territorial, organisational or institutional legal context, and creatively combine them to form genuine transnational norms. Each tribunal *per force* "legislates" from its own perspective, and no hierarchy of tribunals exists to rank their efforts. Thus, the most pressing task might be the organisation of mutual awareness and reciprocal acknowledgement between decentralised tribunals.

4. Regulatory Hybridisation: The Mixing of Private and Public Policy

Similar to the importance of their co-ordination with the global legal system, the success of corporate codes depends on their interaction with political regulatory bodies. A great deal hinges on whether or not political pressure leads to the subjection of autonomous corporate codes to external regulatory impulses. Here, again, collective actors outside the company – NGOs, trade unions, media, international organisations and administrative agencies – play a decisive role, in offsetting the closure tendencies of the company both in terms of the formulation of the code and also its implementation and future development.

22 With regard to these new conflicts, see A. Fischer-Lescano and G. Teubner (*supra* note 15); P. Schiff Berman (*supra* note 14); R. Michaels, "The Re-State-ment of Non-State Law: The State, Choice of Law, and the Challenge from Global Legal Pluralism", (2005) 51 *Wayne Law Review*, p. 1209.

As to the relationship between corporate codes and political normative orders, the question is not of a simple re-integration of private rules into political-state norms. The comprehensive transformation of purely voluntary codes into state-regulated and state-implemented registers is neither probable nor desirable. Instead, the hybridisation of the corporate codes is a developmental trend, in which the autonomy of the codes is preserved, but in which state agencies and international organisations are involved to the extent that they contribute to the delineation of the borders of the private code and to its implementation and regulation. Only by a complex of strategies and only with co-operation, will multinationals, international organisations, state governments, employers' syndicates, trade unions, and NGOs be able to approach the goal of the worldwide establishment of employees' rights – not only on paper but also in practice. In fact, mutual agreement between the various actors will be crucial.

5. Inter-organisational Co-operation: The Extension of the Corporate Codes into Production Networks

That corporate codes only work as the internal self-regulation of a single multinational and do not control the entire value-creating chain of production and distribution represents a grave flaw. Consequently, the key players in an industry boast relatively high labour law standards, whilst the working conditions in peripheral companies are significantly worse. Recently, a trend that counters these tendencies has been observable: the emergence of inter-company networks as an extension of the corporate code onto an entire production network. Global commodity chains have developed, which constitute neither market relationships nor integrated multinationals.[23] Instead, what we can observe are networks of independent companies, which have generated their own governance structures. Two types may be distinguished: producer-driven and buyer-driven chains. The nerve centre of the network lies either in the ambit of manufacture or in the domain of consumption.

For corporate codes, it is important that the organisational features of the network offer certain advantages, making it possible to extend the reach of the code to several inter-linking companies.[24] The over-reaching governance structures of the network facilitate – in spite of the independence of nodal companies – the centralising function of the codes as well as their unified validity in the total production chain. The role of the network's nerve centre, whose considerable influence on the other parts of the network promotes the universal usage of the code, is of imperative importance. Moreover, we can observe an interplay between factors internal to companies and inter-organisational features. Control and implementation structures developed in the nerve centre, for

23 G. Gereffi and M. Korzeniewicz, *Commodity Chains and Global Capitalism*, (Westport: Greenwood Press, 1994).

24 See, for more proofs, M. Fichter and J. Sydow, "Using Networks Toward Global Labor Standards? Organizing Social Responsibility in Global Production Chains", (2002) 9 *Industrielle Beziehungen*, p. 357.

example, a social responsibility task force or a responsible officer, spread through the network to the other companies and facilitate the co-ordination of the various internal corporate codes.

Only when these five elements - private juridification, civic constitutionalism, international judicialisation, regulatory hybridisation and inter-organisational networks - emerge simultaneously in the future, might we be justified in making cautiously optimistic prognoses for corporate codes. Finally, their success depends on a combination of political and legal constellations, which, on the one hand, allows pressure from external actors - that is to say, from NGOs, trade unions, media, international organisations, and domestic organs - to be effective, and, on the other, give impetus to a juridification of the civic norms and their interaction with state law so that the codes constitute, not a corporate fad, but permanent valid law which generates durable legal institutions, and which guarantees the preservation of high labour law standards. As demonstrated by recent empirical studies, the juridification of corporate codes, i.e., their metamorphosis into concrete rights, the transgression of which entails damages or other sanctions, represents a crucial condition to their success.[25]

25 O. Perez, "The Dynamic of Corporate Self-Regulation", (2009) 43 *Law & Society Review*, p. 593.

Neil Walker

CHAPTER 11. TAKING CONSTITUTIONALISM BEYOND THE STATE

1. Introduction

In recent years, the modernist idea that constitutional modes of government are for states, and for states alone, has been the subject both of sustained challenge and of strong defence. Anticipating our definitional discussion, we can comprehend the challenge to a state-centred constitutionalism, and the response to that challenge, as having both material and ideational dimensions. It refers, first, to the development, beyond the states, of certain levels of decision-making capacity that are normally associated with the demand for constitutional governance, as well as to certain types of transnational regulatory institutions and practices – from the emergence of charters of rights and strong regimes of judicial review to the elaboration of inter-institutional checks and balances, and developed systems of political accountability – that are normally associated with the supply of constitutional governance. These developments in both supply and demand may be found (i) in *regional* organisations such as the European Union (EU) and the North American Free Trade Association (NAFTA), (ii) in *functional* organisations as diverse in their remit and in their pedigree (public or private) as the World Trade Organisation (WTO) and the Internet Corporation of Assigned Names and Numbers (ICANN), as well as (iii) under the general *global* umbrella of the UN Charter and institutions or the international legal framework more generally.[1] The challenge to a state-centred constitutionalism refers, secondly, to the increasing tendency for such existing post-state policy capacities and related regulatory institutions and practices to be conceptualized in explicitly constitutional terms, as well as to the growth in "constitutional" imagination or sponsorship of alternative post-state regulatory institutions and practices.

1 For reasons of space, the present article does not consider the related trend towards *sub*-state constitutionalism. See, for example, Tierney (2004). See N. Walker, "The Idea of Constitutional Pluralism", (2002) 65 *Modern Law Review*, pp. 317–59, and B. Fassbender "'We the Peoples of the United Nations': Constituent Power and Constitutional Form in International Law", in: M. Loughlin and N. Walker (eds), *The Paradox of Constitutionalism: Constituent Power and Constitutional Form*, (Oxford: Oxford University Press, 2007).

The present chapter has three aims. It asks, first, why taking the idea and associated ethos and methods of constitutionalism "beyond the state" might be viewed as a significant and controversial innovation, and thus be in need of explanation and justification. This requires us to engage in some detail with the definition of constitutionalism as well as with the contestation surrounding that definition. Secondly, taking account of the various arguments that lie behind these definitional differences, the chapter attempts to develop a scheme for understanding certain key features of constitutionalism in general, and of its post-state development in particular, which is sufficiently inclusive to command broad agreement. Thirdly, and bringing the concerns of the first two sections together, it seeks to identify the key current tensions – or antinomies – surrounding the growth of post-state constitutionalism with a view to indicating what is at stake in the future career of this concept.

2. The Statist Legacy and the Problem of Definition

Given the considerable *prima facie* evidence that the demand for and supply of constitutional governance is increasingly moving beyond the state, why does such an extension of the proper domain of constitutionalism meet with strong resistance? We can identify four kinds of objections which, sometimes cumulatively, are levelled against taking constitutionalism beyond the state, each referring to a different way in which constitutionalism is implicated or invoked in contemporary social and political relations. Constitutionalism beyond the state may be rejected or challenged as *inappropriate*, as *inconceivable*, as *improbable* or as *illegitimate*. Let us briefly examine these four "*i*"s in turn.

The argument from *inappropriateness* refers to the way in which constitutional techniques and values are invoked as a form of *normative resource* in law-mediated endeavours to articulate values and objectives relevant to "good government" and to supply the institutional technology to achieve these values and objectives. From this perspective, it may be argued that, as the solutions provided within the normative arsenal of modern constitutionalism are historically tailored to the problems of states, then, notwithstanding the superficial familiarity of the regulatory techniques that have developed in the post-state domain, such solutions may remain appropriate and relevant only, or mainly, to the problems of states.[2] For instance, the historical preoccupation of modern constitutions with the separation of powers, with the independence of the judiciary, with institutional checks and balances more generally, with the federal dispersal of power and with government-constraining Bills of Rights, may be viewed not as universal precepts and techniques of good government, but as being directed against the dangers of tyranny or the arbitrariness associated with the concentration of political power, in the particular case of the modern state, with its claim to the monopoly

2 See, for example, G. Majone, "Delegation of Regulatory Powers in a Mixed Polity", (2002) 8 *European Law Journal*, pp. 319–45.

of legitimate authority over discrete territorial populations.[3] Conversely, this same unique concentration of power in the state also points to the scale and depth of its positive responsibility as the primary point of political initiative. In so doing, it focuses attention on the importance of ensuring against decision-making gridlock (through aspects of intra or inter-institutional balance and co-operation, such as majoritarian voting rules or co-decision devices) or against decision-taking inflexibility and unresponsiveness (through various methods of executive empowerment, such as expansive prerogative powers in the British example, or the development of the "political questions" doctrine in the example of the United States and other documentary constitutional traditions). In either case, the particular - and sometimes conflicting - imperatives of constraint and empowerment, and the mechanisms appropriate to their pursuit and reconciliation, are arguably peculiar to the modern state and to its highly privileged place as an exclusive or dominant repository of legal authority and political power in the global configuration. As such, these mechanisms are not directly relevant to any other type of entity with a less comprehensive depth and range of capability and responsibility.

The argument from *inconceivability* takes the case from *inappropriateness* a stage further. It holds not only that the tool-box of state constitutionalism is ill-suited or less appropriate to any other endeavour, but that the very idea of taking constitutionalism beyond the state - considered as anything more than a loose analogy to convey a continuing general commitment to "good government"- is a kind of "category error".[4] The invocation of the ideas and practices of constitutionalism involves a distinctive way of thinking about the world - an *epistemic horizon* and political imaginary that pre-supposes and refers to the particular form of the state. Various features of the modern state and its constitutional representation characterise and reflect this very particular political imaginary. These include not only the idea of a "sovereign" and so autonomous, self-contained and internally-integrated legal and political order, but also the notion that for each sovereign political order there is a distinct "society" or "*demos*", as well as a dedicated collective agency - whether "nation", "people" or even the "state" itself which is, or should be, imputed to be the ultimate authors of that order. On such a view, if these background ideas of sovereign or autonomous system, distinct society and dedicated collective agency are not in place, as arguably they are not unless in the presence of the modern state, then we cannot meaningfully characterise any candidate normative and/or institutional design as constitutional.

The argument from *improbability* refers to the way in which constitutionalism is implicated in existing relations of authority. Any constitutional order is not just the articulation of a way of thinking about the world, but also a framework for the organisation and application of political power. And since the actually existing

3 See J. Madison, A. Hamilton and J. Jay, *The Federalist Papers*, (London: Penguin, 1987).
4 See A. Moravcsik, "A Category Error", (2005) *Prospect*, July pp. 22–26, at 25.

constitutional orders tend be centred on the state, the "state system"[5] has long served as a mechanism of *authoritative pre-emption* to frustrate the pursuit of non-state constitutional initiatives, or, at least, ensuring that such initiatives remain within the delegated authority of states. In this way, the established Westphalian configuration of mutually exclusive states with mutually exclusive domains of constitutional authority, joined by an essentially state-parasitic framework of international law conceived of as a set of agreements *between* sovereigns, serves continuously to reproduce itself and to repress or marginalise any challenge to its domination.

The argument from *illegitimacy*, finally, concerns the manner in which constitutionalism is frequently invoked as an *ideological claim*, as a way of adding or detracting symbolic value from an actual or projected state of affairs upon the basis of its supposedly "constitutional" or "unconstitutional" qualities. The case here is a straightforwardly consequential one. If constitutionalism, on one or more of the three grounds considered above, can only be properly conceived of as a matter of, and for, the state, then any attempt to assume the mantle of constitutionalism beyond the state is by necessary inference illegitimate. If a claim of constitutional status is made on behalf of an entity or a set of regulatory practices in circumstances in which the tools are inappropriate to the problem, or in which the requisite underlying belief system is not in place, or in which the necessary "*de facto*" authority is absent, then that claim becomes an empty or misleading one.[6]

If we ask how the defenders of constitutionalism beyond the state respond to these sceptical perspectives, we can begin to appreciate that the key differences and points of disputation are conceptual, rather than empirical. There is no compelling "fact of the matter" or even a persuasive body of evidence available to settle the argument between the sceptics and defenders of constitutionalism beyond the state. Instead, definitional issues and the underlying differences of perspective that they expose are pivotal. We can demonstrate this by re-examining each sceptical perspective in turn.

The argument from *inappropriateness* claims that the tools of constitutionalism are the wrong type for non-state polity problems, and, in so doing, treats constitutionalism as an instrument of regulatory design. The critique of this position would begin by re-iterating that the very similarity of many non-state regulatory instruments to the state model suggests that, at least, some of the techniques of prudential reasoning and design associated with constitutional statecraft are relevant to other types of political arrangement with more limited concentrations of political power. But this immediately raises the question of whether the definition of constitutionalism can properly admit of

5 See R. Falk, *The Study of Future Worlds*, (New York: Free Press, 1975).

6 See J. Klabbers, "Constitutionalism Lite", (2004) 1 *International Organizations Law Review*, pp. 31–58, D. Grimm, "The Constitution in the Process of Denationalization", (2005) 12 *Constellations*, pp. 447–63, and J.H.H. Weiler, "In Defence of the Status Quo: Europe's Constitutional *Sonderweg*", in: J.H.H. Weiler and M. Wind (eds), *European Constitutionalism beyond the State*, (Cambridge: Cambridge University Press, 2003).

degrees, particularly in the light of the sceptics' epistemic claim, with its all-or-nothing threshold qualification.

According to this epistemic claim, the constitutional way of addressing the world is inconceivable other than in the context of the state, and thus treats constitutionalism as a limited and limiting situation and perspective from which to imagine the world. The critique of this position would begin by questioning whether those supposedly limited and limiting pre-suppositions of the constitutional imaginary – the ideas of autonomous system, distinct society and dedicated collective agency – must, indeed, be tied to the state, or whether they may possess a broader significance. Again, this is, in the end, an open conceptual question, rather than one of incontrovertible empirical fact or of essential definition. Although the relevant rhetoric of sceptical argumentation often suggests otherwise, the core ideas of system, society and dedicated collective agency posses neither the rigidity of meaning, nor do states possess the uniform distinctiveness of empirical characteristics relative to any such rigid meanings, that would be necessary to close down debate.[7] What is more, even if the relevant conceptual and empirical arguments do stack up against an expansive understanding of the non-state range of application of some or all of these core ideas, then this simply returns us to the prior definitional question considered above – whether we are simply stuck with the inimaginability of post-state constitutionalism under a pure, all-or-nothing conception, or whether we may still contemplate its moderate incidence under a more-or-less conception.

The argument from *improbability* claims that there is no state-independent source of power that is able to assume the mantle of constitutionalism, and, in so doing, it treats constitutional authority as a brute question of social and political power. The critique of this position would begin by re-iterating that, despite the historical dominance of state-based constitutionalism, there is increasing evidence of constitutional development at non-state sites. But this again immediately begs the definitional question of what actually counts as constitutional development? Does it include "subjective" claims, as in the ideological register, or must it refer only to actual or projected states of affairs – to "objective" measures and conditions – under the normative and epistemic registers?

If, lastly, we revisit the argument from *illegitimacy*, the contention that the discursive claim of constitutional character and status is not justified in any post-state context treats constitutionalism as a "speech act" or rhetorical claim, and, in this case, as a quite unsubstantiated one. Yet, the critique of this position would again begin by asserting that there is, by now, ample emergent evidence of constitutionalisation under the other three registers to rebut the charge that such a rhetorical claim is empty. And, to the extent that the "objective" evidence of the appropriateness of the so-called constitutional measures and the conceivability of the so-called constitutional pre-conditions does not

7 On the temptations and frequent tendencies towards state-centred essentialism in the academic and political debate over the constitutional status of the EU, see J.H.H. Weiler, *op. cit.*, note 6 *supra*, p. 199; ch.10.

convince, a broader critique of the argument from illegitimacy would ask whether and why the imaginative prospect and projection of constitutionalism should, in any case, be entirely in thrall to constitutionalism's achievements in modern history, rather than be considered as a self-standing and open-textured feature of the constitutional enterprise.

This encounter with constitutionalism's "politics of definition"[8] helps to clarify what is at stake in the endorsement or otherwise of each or any of the four critical perspectives, and indicates how we might set about developing a more inclusive scheme to steer our substantive discussion of post-state constitutionalism. To begin with, patently, the definition of constitutionalism and the question of whether and to what extent constitutionalism might extend to the post-state context is both controversial and complex. Such controversy and complexity indicates the need, as a basic orienting premise, to contemplate the potential range of constitutionalism in open-ended terms so as to avoid the premature exclusion of the possibility of post-state constitutionalism by definitional fiat.

Secondly, and in the spirit of that open-ended brief, we should be careful not to settle *a priori* the question of whether constitutionalism beyond the state may be understood in more-or-less, incremental terms, or whether it needs to be judged in all-or-nothing, holistic terms. To this end, it is helpful to think of how we might approach constitutionalism as something that can be parsed or disaggregated into its component parts or dimensions in such a way that, on the one hand, we, at least, possess the tools to comprehend it as a matter of degree and partial realisation, without, on the other hand, denying the possible significance of the pattern of combination of these dimensions and so the potential force of the holistic argument.

But, how, thirdly, should such a parsing exercise proceed? What key dimensions of constitutionalism can serve as a broadly endorsed checklist for its post-state variant, and how should we think of the relationship between these dimensions? To answer this question, we must appreciate that, what underlies the significance of constitutionalism *for both the sceptics and the promoters of post-state constitutionalism alike* in each of the four arenas of contestation is its character as a special form of practical reasoning pitched at a general or "meta" level of social and political organisation. That is to say, if practical reasoning, in general, is about deciding upon how to act in a context of practical choice, the special type of practical reason associated with constitutionalism is concerned with the deepest and most collectively implicated questions of "how to decide how to decide" how to act. Whether it be understood as a set of normative resources, an epistemic horizon, a locus-specific authoritative force, or an ideological claim, constitutionalism is concerned, in the broadest possible sense, with the question of *how we can, and how we should, approach the practical puzzle of developing, refining and interpreting the appropriate terms of governance of collective action.*

8 See G. Anderson, *Constitutional Rights after Globalization*, (Oxford: Hart Publishing, 2005), Chapter 6.

Accordingly, constitutionalism conceived of as this special form of practical reasoning must always strike a balance between the "can" and the "ought". One the one hand, it is not a purely idealistic discourse, concerned to name and pursue certain ends regardless of whether these ends are ones that are broadly endorsed or (relatedly) feasible to achieve. This caution pushes us towards the conventional and the historical as indicators of, and controls upon, what constitutes a plausible political enterprise, and thus to the identification of certain dimensions of constitutionalism in objective terms as socially realised, and, it follows, in the modern age primarily state-situated or, at least, state-rooted forms of organisation and practice. Yet, we cannot, on the other hand, defer entirely to modern history and convention and to their "externally" verifiable record. The "ought" dimension of practical reasoning always also suggests either an endorsement of, or a critical rejection of, existing practice, and, if the latter, the possibility of the revision of the ethical core of constitutionalism in the light of past experience and the novelty of the practical context – most notably, for present purposes, the transnational context. This brings back in the subjective and evaluative dimension – the importance of the "internal" construal of "external" developments in constitutional terms – and the idea of constitutionalism as an ethical discourse under a constant process of re-imagining and reconstruction. And, indeed, in the final analysis, the proposition that the constitutional imagination can escape the extensive legacy of modern history and the modern state is not simply a matter of theoretical faith. The fact (to be developed below) that constitutionalism also has a *pre*-modern history – a phase that pre-dated the development of the modern state as the exclusive vehicle of the constitutional ambition to provide an active and comprehensive design or blueprint for the proper government of a clearly demarcated society – suggests that, if there was nothing inevitable or essential about the relationship between constitutionalism and statehood in the past,[9] therefore, there cannot be in the future, either.

In a nutshell, in our parsing of constitutionalism as a multi-dimensional form of practical reasoning, precisely because it *is* a form of practical reasoning constitutionalism in general, and in post-state constitutionalism in particular, must tread a line between two precipices. It must avoid the twin dangers of the solipsism of excessive idealism (on

9 In an influential article, while not seeking to deny that the idea of constitution has a distinctive pre-modern history going back at least to the Latin *constitutio*, G. Sartori, "Constitutionalism: a preliminary discussion", (1962) 56 *American Political Science Review*, pp. 853–64, dismisses the relevance of the early notion to modern debate. He argues that the modern sense of constitutionalism is about the *control* of power (*jurisdictio*) in the modern state, whereas the ancient sense was concerned simply with power's efficient *exercise* (*gubernaculum*) in the emerging political forms of the classical age – a quite different, and, in some respects, opposing idea. However, as G. Maddox persuasively responds, in "A Note on the Meaning of 'Constitution'", (1982) 76 *The American Political Science Review*, pp. 805–809, that such a stipulative definition suggests the kind of critic-centred, rather than use-centred, approach that Sartori himself is at pains to deny, and ignores the fact that modern constitutionalism is an evolution from ancient constitutionalism, rather than a radical departure. In particular, neither ancient nor modern constitutionalism, for all their different emphases, focus upon either *gubernaculum or jurisdictio* in isolation. Instead, in their common basic emphasis upon the reduction of power to a legal form, both ancient and modern modes have been concerned with the balance between these two properties. See, also, C. McIlwain, *Constitutionalism Ancient and Modern*, revd. edition, (Ithaca: Cornell, 1947).

the subjective side) and the apologetics or fatalism of excessive conventionalism (on the objective side), and, in so doing, employ each dimension to modify the other.

3. The Frames of Transnational Constitutionalism

A scheme that addresses the two large methodological tensions identified above – the more-or less versus all-or-nothing question and the balance between objective and subjective factors – while respecting both the resilient floor of shared understanding of our master concept and its semantic roots, is suggested by thinking about the different dimensions of constitutionalism as a series of reinforcing frames. The idea of constitutionalism as a framing mechanism resonates closely with a minimum shared sense of constitutionalism as a special species of meta-level practical reasoning – as something concerned with the very framework within which, and in accordance with which, we engage in collective forms of practical reasoning. Furthermore, the idea of constitutionalism as a framing mechanism is already present in the etymological roots of the constitutional idea. It is visible in the early shift from the literal reference to the composition and health of the human organism to the metaphor of the "body politic" – first, in the tradition of ancient constitutionalism conceived of as a descriptor of the already "constituted" polity, and only gradually augmented by a sense of active prescription and projection of its "good working order".[10] In the modern state tradition in which this shift found its mature expression, five forms of constitutional, and, indeed, "constitutive" framing of the polity have tended, albeit with highly uneven application and variable success, to take hold and to converge. These are juridical, political-institutional, self-authorising, social and discursive frames.[11]

What typically counts, as constitutional in terms of the juridical frame is the idea of a mature rule-based or legal order – one that reaches or aspires to a certain standard both of the independent efficacy and of the virtue that we associate with legal "orderliness". What typically counts as constitutional in political-institutional terms is the presence of a set of organs of government that provide an effective instrument of rule across a broad jurisdictional scope for a distinctive polity as well as seeking a fair form of internal balance between interests and functions. What typically counts as constitutional in *self-authorising* terms is that the legal and political-institutional complex may plausibly be attributed to some *pouvoir constituant* that is both original to, and distinctive of, that polity, and is also qualified to claim a legitimate pedigree or authorial title. What typically counts as constitutional in *social* terms is a community sufficiently integrated to be the subject of legal regulation and institutional action that is both plausibly effective in terms of collective implementation and compliance, and capable of locating and tracking some meaningful sense of that community's common good. And finally, what typically counts as constitutional in *discursive* terms is both the balance of the

10 See D. Grimm, note 6 *supra*.

11 See N. Walker, "European Constitutionalism in the State Constitutional Tradition", in: J. Holder, C. O'Cinneide and C. Campbell-Holt (eds), (2006) 59 *Current Legal Problems*, pp. 51–89.

existing ideological power struggle and the ongoing normative "battle of ideas" entailed in the labelling of certain phenomena or prospects under the binary logic of constitutional/unconstitutional, with all that that implies in terms of the "constitutional" status and worthiness of the phenomena so framed.

How does this approach allow us to handle the two large methodological question of post-state constitutionalism that we have identified without prejudice? In the first place, with regard to the "more-or-less" *versus* "all-or-nothing" question, the basic criterion of internal distinction permits access to both readings. The possibility of an incremental reading is retained through the basic idea of the separability of the frames, a notion vindicated by the fact that in the state tradition the layering of the frames has tended to follow a historical trajectory of re-inforcement. This has involved the overall structure being reinforced by the later addition of the self-authorising and social frames to the original juridical and political-institutional frames, with the increasing resonance of the discursive frame reflecting and re-inforcing this gradual thickening.[12] Equally, the possibility of a holistic reading is kept open by the very structure of the framing idea. If we recall the epistemic basis of the holistic critique of post-state constitutionalism, it is found in the ideas of autonomous system, dedicated collective agency and distinct society. In each case, there is an explicit fit with one or more of our defining constitutional frames – autonomous system to the juridical and the political-institutional, dedicated collective agency to the self-authorising and distinct society to the social. Indeed, each of the three epistemic preconditions pre-supposes the very idea of integrity and boundedness implicit in the very notion of a frame. If, then, the framing notion captures both the shared affinity of the various epistemic pre-conditions with the roots of the constitutional idea and the basis upon which these preconditions complement one another, then that same framing notion poses a difficult challenge to those who would seek to disaggregate that constitutional form into its component parts and treat no part or combination as indispensable.

In the second place, with regard to the tension between objective and subjective, fact and value, apology and utopia, here the substantive content of the categories supplied by the framing criterion seeks to reflect and maintain the appropriate balance. Most obviously, the idea of a separate discursive register – a domain of "constitution talk" – provides an explicitly subjective frame to correct for the objectivity of the other four frames. In addition, even the objective frames must be understood as a mixture of fact and value, with the idea of the "good working order" of the legal, political-institutional, self-authorising and social frames of the constitution suggesting in each case, a critically evaluative benchmark to accompany the empirical accomplishment.

12 See note 11 *supra*.

4. The Five Frames Considered

Let us now look at these five framing dimensions in turn. To begin with *legal order*, this refers to the circumstances under which we may conceive of a certain domain of law *qua* legal order – as something systemic and self-contained.[13] The fine details may be viewed differently across jurisprudential schools, but the very idea of legal order is commonly understood as a necessary incident, or, at least, a pre-condition, of any constitutional system. Legal order involves a cluster of interconnected factors; in particular, self-ordering, self-interpretation self-extension, self-amendment, self-enforcement and self-discipline. The quality of self-ordering refers to the capacity of a legal system to reach and regulate all matters within its domain or jurisdiction, typically through its successful embedding of certain law-making "secondary" norms as a means to generate and validate a comprehensive body of "primary" norms.[14] The quality of self-interpretation refers to the capacity of some organ or organs internal to the legal order, typically the adjudicative organ, to have the final word with regard to the meaning and purpose of its own norms. The quality of *self-extension* refers to the capacity of a legal system to decide the extent of its own jurisdiction – often known as *kompetenz-kompetenz*.[15] The quality of *self-amendment* refers to the existence of a mechanism for changing the normative content of the legal order, which is provided for in terms of that order and which empowers organs internal to that order as the agents of the process of amendment. The quality of *self-enforcement* refers to the capacity of the legal order, through the development of a body of procedural law and associated sanctions, to provide for the application and implementation of its own norms. The quality of *self-discipline* refers to the positively evaluative and aspirational dimension of "legal order", for which the first five dimensions provide a necessary, albeit insufficient platform. Once the legal order reaches a certain threshold of certainty and reliability in its production and of comprehensiveness in its coverage of its primary norms (*self-ordering*), once it has reached a certain threshold of effectiveness in its rules of standing, justiciability and liability (*self-enforcement*), once it has obtained the capacity to adjust or "correct" its own normative structure, and provided it can guarantee sufficient autonomy from external influences in these systemic endeavours (*self-amendment*, *self-interpretation* and *self-extension*), it is then in a position to achieve two related aspects of *self-discipline*. In the first place, it can offer a certain level of generality and predictability in the treatment of those who are subject to its norms, and, in so doing, help cultivate a system-constraining cultural presumption against arbitrary rule. Secondly, and more specifically, the consolidation of a legal order with mature claims to autonomy, comprehensiveness and effectiveness provides the opportunity and helps generate the expectation that even the institutional or governmental actors internal to the legal order need not, and should not, escape the discipline of legal restraint in accordance with that mature order. Indeed, these two core ideas – of the "rule of law, not man" and of a

13 See J. Raz, *The Concept of a Legal System*, 2nd edition, (Oxford: Oxford University Press, 1980).

14 See H.L.A. Hart, *The Concept of Law*, 2nd edition, (Oxford: Clarendon Press, 1994), Chapter 5.

15 See J.H.H. Weiler, *The Constitution of Europe*, (Cambridge: Cambridge University Press, 1999), Chapter 9.

"government limited by law",[16] – provide a key element of all Western legal traditions, whether they be couched in the language of "rule of law", or *état de droit* or *Rechtsstaat*, and thus supply a cornerstone of constitutionalism understood as a value-based discourse.

Whereas this first building block of modern constitutionalism can be traced back to the Roman roots of civilian law, even though its "rule of law" characteristics developed later, the second feature was one of the distinctively novel features of the modern state as it emerged as a new form of political domination in continental Europe in response to the confessional civil wars of the Sixteenth and Seventeenth centuries. What we are concerned with here is the establishment and maintenance of a comprehensive political-institutional framework understood as a system *of specialised political rule*. This is a development that achieved an early stylistic maturity in the form of the French and American documentary Constitutions of the late Eighteenth century. For such a system, neither its title to rule, nor its ongoing purpose flows from prior and fixed economic or status attributes, or concerns (of the type that, in the constitutional thought of classical and mediaeval polities, tend to exclude some actors from the polity, or grade and degrade them within it), or from some notion of traditional or divine order external to the system itself (as in pre-modern constellations of political power generally). Instead, authority rests upon a putative idea of the individual as the basic unit of society and as the (presumptively equal) source of moral agency, with the very idea of a political domain built upon, and dedicated to, that secular premise – one that develops its own authoritative yardsticks for conflict-resolution and its own mechanisms for collective decision making.[17]

This development speaks to a new stage in the differentiation of social forms, one in which there is, for the first time, a separate sphere of the public and the political, which, in its operative logic, is distinctive both from the society over which it rules and from some notion of transcendental order. Such a specialised system has the dual attributes of immanence and self-limitation. On the one hand, it purports to be self-legitimating. The justification of the continuing claim to authority of the autonomous political domain and of the higher order rules through which that authority is inscribed rests not upon the external force and discipline of a metaphysical or a reified-through-tradition "order of things", but upon the operation of the political domain itself and the secular interests that it serves. On the other hand, as the flip-side of this, there emerges a general sphere of purely private action and freedom that lies beyond either the autonomous domain of politics or the now redundant special mixed regimes of public and private rights and obligations based upon prior forms of privilege or natural order.[18]

16 See B. Tamanaha, *On The Rule of Law: History, Politics, Theory*, (Cambridge: Cambridge University Press, 2004), Chapter 9.

17 See I. Loader and N. Walker, *Civilizing Security*, (Cambridge: Cambridge University Press, 2007), Chapter 2, and M. Loughlin, *The Idea of Public Law*, (Oxford: Oxford University Press, 2003), Chapter 3.

18 See D. Grimm, note 6 *supra*, pp 452–3, and J. Habermas, "Constitutional Democracy: A Paradoxical Union of Contradictory Principles", (2001) 28 *Political Theory*, pp. 766–81.

The regulatory structures of the new specialist political order echo its distinctive attributes. Positively, and reflecting the quality of immanence, they take the form of third order institutional rules and capacities for making (legislature), administering (executive) and adjudicating (judiciary) the second-order "legal system" norms through which the co-ordination of first-order action and the resolution of first-order disagreement within a population is secured. Negatively, and reflecting the quality of self-limitation, they take the form of checks and balances and monitoring mechanisms – of constitutionalism as "limited government" – aimed at protecting a separate sphere of private individual or group freedom, one which is safe from incursions at the third order level of public authority or infraction at the second order level of the substantive norms of the legal system.

The idea of a specialised system of political rule also carries with it certain assumptions about the kind and intensity of normative concern properly considered to be constitutional. There are again two aspects to this, which mirror those affecting the institutional dimension. On the one hand, there is the idea of the normative system providing a "comprehensive blueprint for social life"[19] – of recognising no externally imposed substantive limits to its capacity to regulate each and every areas of social policy with which it may be concerned, and to do so in a "joined-up" manner. On the other hand, there is the recognition of an *internally* imposed constraint – the protection of the very sphere of private autonomy which underpins the idea of a secular political order in the first place. In turn, this entails formal or informal catalogues of individual rights – constitutionalism as fundamental rights protection – to add substance to the institutional or structural checks referred to above.

The institutionalisation of a separate and specialist sphere of political contestation and decision and a correspondingly broad and deep political jurisdiction stands in a close relationship to the legal order dimension already considered. Indeed, it is this basic relationship that Luhmann[20] had in mind when he talked about the constitution as operating within both legal and political systems and providing a mechanism for their linking, or "structural coupling", with the institutions of the political system both dependent upon – "instituted" under – a legal pedigree and implicated as key agents in the processes of self-ordering, self-interpretation, self-extension, self-amendment, self-enforcement and self-discipline through which the legal order is sustained and developed. However, the idea of a specialised political system, still less that of an autonomous legal order, does not necessarily imply, within the third framing register of constitutionalism, a type of authorisation that claims either a democratic founding or a continuing democratic warrant. Instead, the operational autonomy, specialist nature and expansive normative scope of the political sphere may be consistent with a set of arrangements in which the original authorisation comes from beyond the system, as in

19 See C. Tomuschat, "Internation Law: Ensuring the Survival of Mankind on the Eve of a New Century, General Course on Public International Law", (2001) 281 *Recueil des Cours de l'Académie de droit international*, p. 63.

20 See N. Luhmann, *Das Recht der Gesellschaft*, (Frankfurt aM: Suhrkamp Verlag, 1993).

many of the subaltern constitutions of imperial systems:[21] or in which the original authorisation is located within the system, but is presented as a "top-down" monarchical or aristocratic grant or bequest, rather than a "bottom-up" popular claim.[22]

So, the autonomy and capaciousness of the political sphere need not imply that all those affected by the operation of the system participate or are represented in its institution or even in its subsequent homologation. It need imply merely that, within the third framing register, an understanding of political title should prevail, whether this be presented in terms of *raison d'état* or *salus populi* or some other version of the collective good which is adequate to the constitutional polity's claim and character, within the second framing register, *as* a special and encompassing sphere of political action – one in which there is no transcendental or otherwise overriding external justification, and in which there is freedom from special social or economic interests. However, the specialised system of political rule, just because it introduces the idea of a sphere of authority that must construct itself and provide for its own secular justification, cannot indefinitely avoid the very question of "how to decide how to decide", nor its even more starkly indeterminate derivative – "who decides who decides"[23] – that it brings into sharp relief for the first time. Therefore, at least in the developing state tradition, constitutionalism tends to be a precarious achievement unless and until it is joined by a claim of collective *self-authorisation*.

Within constitutional thought in the state tradition, then, this third authorising frame gradually comes to be conceived in terms of the idea of constituent power, or the ultimate sovereignty of the people.[24] Again, the documentary form that stands at the centre of modern state constitutionalism directly engages this dimension, with the canonical text typically claiming to be not only *for* the people but also *of* the people, and its drafting procedures – typically through the involvement of constituent assemblies and popular conventions – dramatising a commitment to substantiate the claim of popular authorship.[25] So prevalent, indeed, is the ethic of democratic pedigree in modern state constitutionalism – of democracy as a meta-value in terms of which other governance values are understood and articulated[26] – that debate tends to centre not on the question of its appropriateness, but only on the adequacy of its instantiation. This may manifest itself in the critique of those constitutional settlements that lack a founding documentary episode, or, at least, a plausible narrative of subsequent popular

21 See K.C. Wheare, *The Constitutional Structure of the Commonwealth*, (Oxford: Oxford University Press, 1960), and P. Oliver, *The Constitution of Independence*, (Oxford: Oxford University Press, 2005).

22 As in many of the *constitutions octroyées* of the Nineteenth century (for example, the French Charters of 1814 and 1830, the Italian *Statuto Albertino* of 1848).

23 See M. Maduro, "Europe and the Constitution: What if this is as good as it gets?", in: J.H.H. Weiler and M. Wind, *op. cit.*, note 6 *supra*.

24 See A.Kalyvas, "Popular Sovereignty, Democracy and the Constituent Power", (2005) 12 *Constellations*, pp. 223–244.

25 See A. Arato, *Civil Society, Constitution and Legitimacy*, (Lanham MD: Rowman and Littlefield, 2000).

26 See J. Dunn, Setting the People Free: The Story of Democracy, (London: Atlantic, 2005).

homologation,[27] or in the claim that the constitution has betrayed its popular foundations, or in the criticism that, for all its derivative concern with democracy in the everyday framework of government, the constitution is not autochthonous, but, instead, remains dependent upon the "constituted" power of another polity or polities.

Modern (state) constitutionalism is not only about the generation through an act and continuing promise of democratic self-authorisation of the wherewithal for the operation of a self-sufficient legal order underpinned by its own institutional complex and normatively expansive framework of secular political rule. Alongside these normative or juridical forms, given the increased emphasis upon the prescriptive over the descriptive work of the constitution that the idea of an autonomous and self-authorising political sphere inevitably brings, the modern state constitution also either pre-supposes or promises (and typically both), as a fourth framing achievement, a degree of *societal integration* on the part of the constituency in whose name it is promulgated and to whom it is directed.[28] Unless there is already in place some sense of common cause to endorse those interests or ideals that the constitutional text has identified as being well-served by being put in common, and to affirm and so vindicate the capability of the institutional means that the constitution deems instrumental to the pursuit of these common interests or ideals, then the constitution conceived of as a project of political community is in danger of remaining a dead letter. What this prior propensity to put things in common or basic sense of political community amounts to is an issue of much controversy, and in any event is something better conceived of as a matter of degree. As a basic minimum, however, it refers to a sense of common attachment or common predicament within the putative *demos* sufficient to manifest itself in three inter-related forms. It should be sufficient to ensure that most members demonstrates the minimum level of sustained mutual respect and concern required to reach and to adhere to collective outcomes that may work against their immediate interests in terms of the distribution of common resources and risks. Reciprocally, it should be sufficient to ensure that each is prepared to trust the others in order to participate in the common business of dispute-resolution, decision-making and rule-following on these same "other-respecting" terms. Finally, this web of mutual respect and trust should be strong enough to sustain a political culture that, just because of the accomplishment of its core common commitment, can acknowledge and accept difference beyond this core commitment.[29]

However, simply because it cannot supply the necessary social supports of respect and concern, trust and mutual toleration merely through normative enunciation does not mean that the constitution is incapable of influencing the measure of social integration necessary to its effective application and must passively presuppose the prior existence

27 See A. Tomkins, *Our Republican Constitution*, (Oxford: Hart Publishing, 2005).

28 See D. Grimm, "Integration by Constitution", (2005) 3 *International Journal of Constitutional Law*, pp. 191–210.

29 See M. Canovan, *Nationhood and Political Theory*, (Cheltenham: Edward Elgar, 1996), and D. Miller, *On Nationality*, (Oxford: Oxford University Press, 1995).

of the requisite measure of social integration. To begin with, its normative framework of political rule seeks to provide a settled template for living together in circumstances free from despotism or intractable conflict, and, to that extent, offers an incentive to all who are attracted by such a template to secure the floor of common commitment necessary for its effective implementation. Secondly, the act of making the constitution may have a mobilisation dividend that goes beyond agreement upon the particular text in question. The value of the process is not exhausted by its textual product,[30] but may extend to the generation or bolstering of just those forms of political identity necessary to the successful implementation of the text. Thirdly, as constitutions in the modern age are typically viewed as the expression and vindication of the constituent power of a "people", the successful making of a constitution has come to assume a special symbolic significance as a totem of peoplehood. So powerful, indeed, is the chain of signification developed under the modern banner of popular, nation state constitutionalism, that, regardless of how it came into existence, the very fact that a constitution exists is typically understood and widely portrayed as testimony to the achievement, the sustenance, or – as in the case of the new Central and Eastern European States after 1989 – the restoration of political community. Fourthly, in so far as the constitution crystallises such general common ends or values as are the subject of agreement in the constitution-making moment and as may also be already present in the pre-constitutional ethical life of the relevant social constituency, it may have a "double institutionalisation" effect.[31] The addition of the constitutional *imprimatur* may amplify the importance of, and the extent of, common subscription to these common values and ends, and in so framing and re-inforcing a common political vernacular, strengthen the societally-integrative relationship between that common political vernacular and mutual respect, concern, trust and tolerance which is indispensable to political community. Fifthly and lastly, we may look beyond the founding moment of the constitution to see how it can become an ongoing source of intensification of the social foundations necessary to its effective implementation. This operates in at least two ways. On the one hand, the constitution may function as a reminder of community. In so far as common political identity often develops alongside and feeds off the collective memorialisation of claimed common events, achievements and experiences, constitutional history provides one such stream of sanctified tradition. The constitution may thus write itself into collective history.[32] On the other hand, the constitution may provide a resilient but flexible structure for political-ethical debate, an anchor for a continuing conversation about the meaning of political community that operates in a Janus-faced manner to strengthen that political community. Looking back, it supplies a token not only of the supposed depth and extension of common experience, but also of the weight of accumulated practical knowledge Looking forward, the constitution may

30 See W. Sadurski, "Conclusions: On the Relevance ofInstitutions and the Centrality of Constitutions in Post-Communist Transitions", in: J. Zielonka (ed), *Democratic Consolidation in Eastern Europe, Vol 1 – Institutional Engineering*, (Oxford: Oxford University Press, 2001, pp. 455–72.

31 See P. Bohannan, "The Differing realms of law", in: P. Bohannan (ed), *Law and Warfare: Studies in the Antropology of Conflict*, (New York: Natural History Press, 1967), p. 45.

32 See A. Margalit, *The Ethics of Memory*, (Cambridge MA: Harvard University Press, 2002), p. 12.

be sufficiently open-ended and sufficiently understood as a work of trans-generational authorship for its structures and values to be capable of being inflected in ways which retain the symbolic *gravitas* of accumulated wisdom, and, at the same time, are adaptable to contemporary forms of political vernacular and understandings of trust, solidarity and tolerance. In other words, the constitution may provide a repository, and thus a standing corroboration of the viable ethical threshold of political community, as well as a vehicle for its continuous adaptation.[33]

Let us finally turn to "constitution talk" – and so to the discursive frame. Some aspects of this we have already considered under the "symbolic" aspect of the social dimension. Constitutional discourse is not unique in its reference to legal order, a specialised political system, extensive normative capacity, constituent power or political community, but it provides a unique imaginary frame in its potential to join these elements together in a singular discourse *about a polity*. That is to say, it is capable of proving an encompassing and self-reflexive vocabulary for imagining the polity in political-ethical terms. Of course, "constitution talk" can also be used ideologically and strategically. As we have seen in our discussion of its societal dimension, such a socially resonant discourse is constantly invoked as a way of re-inforcing particular claims and judgements, whether positive or negative – constitutional or unconstitutional – about particular political acts or practices, or categories of political acts or practices. Indeed, its ethical centrality and its susceptibility to ideological exploitation and strategic manoeuvre are two sides of the same coin – accounting for the status of constitutionalism as a "condensing symbol"[34] to whose terms a whole series of debates about how we do, and how we should live together are continuously reduced.

5. The Five Frames in Transnational Context

We can observe the growth of all five constitutional frames in the post-state context. Undoubtedly the most developed and best-known example of transnational constitutionalism is found in the European Union, a process which appeared to many to have reached its apotheosis with the Convention on the Future of Europe in 2002–3 and the signing of the EU Constitutional Treaty (CT) of 2004.[35] However, the prospect of a final constitutional settlement was subsequently thwarted by the "no" votes in the referendums in France and the Netherlands in 2005, which in turn led to the European Council's decision to abandon the constitutional project and replace it with a traditional international convention in the form of the Treaty of Lisbon 2007. Despite these recent tribulations, the EU experiment as it has unfolded both before and after the 2004

33 See J. Habermas, "On Law and Disagreement: Some Comments on 'Interpretative Pluralism'", (2003) 16 *Ratio Juris*, pp. 187–99.

34 See V. Turner, Dramas, Fields and Metaphors: Symbolic Action in Human Society, (Ithaca: Cornell University Press, 1974).

35 See J. Ziller, *The European Constitution*, (Amsterdam: Lower, 2005).

watershed has succeeded in registering across all five constitutional dimensions,[36] although in no one register do its claims go unchallenged.

The EU's most venerable and still its most intense constitutional claim is in the juridical sphere. It is based upon a legal order with many of the attributes of autonomy. The so-called *acquis communautaire* – the accumulation of 50 years of law under the Treaty framework – provides the ample fruit of the doctrines of supremacy and direct effect, with their strong self-ordering, self-interpreting, self-extending and self-disciplining elements. At the same time, the overlap between the territorial and jurisdictional claims of the EU and its Member States means that none of these accomplishments go entirely uncontested by the states themselves. Furthermore, in the case of the attributes of self-amendment – given that the Member States remain the "Masters of the Treaties" and finally responsible for their reform, and of self-enforcement – given the high reliance upon domestic legal systems for the implementation and application of EU law, the EU legal order remains in significant respects a dependent one.

The EU also boasts its own specialised and increasingly well-established political system – Council, Commission, European Parliament, European Court of Justice, *etc.* Today, that system embraces a very broad normative scope – much wider that its original market-making remit under the foundational Treaty of Rome in 1957, and, since 2000, incorporates a Charter of Rights. However, as with the legal system, the political system remains locked in a dual relationship of interdependence and competition with national systems. In many respects, moreover – in particular, with regard to popular support or recognition and with regard to decision-making capacity and the effective management of veto powers, these European institutions remain less potent than the national institutions with which they interlock.[37]

Largely in response to perceived deficiencies in the political-institutional system and (to a lesser extent) the legal system, the forming of a diversely representative Convention to provide the initial draft of the 2004 Constitutional Treaty signalled a concerted attempt on the part of integrationist interests to provide for the authority of the EU to be persuasively founded not just on the states but also directly on the "peoples" and "people" of Europe. The sponsors of the constitution sought, in other words, to assert a constituent power which was not simply derivative and aggregative of the constituent powers of its Member States. The Convention process and the promulgation of the Constitutional Treaty with its emphasis on common values, common citizenship, flags, anthems and other symbols of common attachment, was also clearly concerned with the mobilisation and amplification of the idea of a European-wide society to complement national political societies. And, finally, the same documentary constitutional process

36 See N. Walker, note 11 *supra*, and *idem*, "'Post-Constituent Constitutionalism.' The Case of the European Union", in: M. Loughlin and N. Walker (eds), *The Paradox of Constitutionalism: Constituent Power and Constitutional Form*, (Oxford: Oxford University Press, 2007).

37 See F. Scharpf, *Governing in Europe: Effecive and Democratic?*, (Oxford: Oxford University Press, 2006).

certainly stimulated the migration of transnational 'constitution talk' from the arcane world of European judges, Brussels élites and specialist university departments to much broader contexts of political deliberation. By the same token, however, although the seriousness of the documentary constitutional attempt is a telling measure of the momentum that had developed around the idea of a "thicker" constitutional frame for the EU, its ultimate failure and the alacrity and eagerness with which European élites retuned to the "not the constitutional"[38] alternative of an old-fashioned (and as yet not fully ratified) Reform Treaty at Lisbon, demonstrates a continuing skewing towards the "thinner" legal and political-institutional frames.

Elsewhere, we see the same constitutionalising trend, if, as yet, much less fully developed, and with little attempt to move beyond a combination of the thin legal and political-institutional frames and the discursive frame. Still on the regional front, the continental human rights organisations, most prominently in the case of the Council of Europe's European Convention on Human Rights, have begun to attract "constitutionalising" claims, in particular, for the normative ambition and trumping (over domestic norms) qualities of their substantive human rights provision and their emergent sense of a continental "public order" and common societal standard.[39] If we look at the functional organisations, the World Trade Organisation, to take the best-known example, has recently become the subject of an intense debate over its "constitutionalisation" in both academic, and, increasingly, in political, circles.[40] Over the last 15 years, its legal order has become more robust, particularly through the strengthening of its judicial branch or Appellate Body, and through the widening of its normative remit from the confines of the predecessor GATT jurisdiction. More generally, its political architecture has become somewhat more independent of its member states, and its defence of certain individual rights – with a particular emphasis on trading rights – against state and regional protectionist interests has become more robust and effective. Similar debates are taking place in a lower key elsewhere, not least with regard to the "civil constitutions" associated with traditionally non-state and non-public sectors such as the internet and the organisation of sports.[41]

38 See N. Walker, "Not the European Constitution", (2008) 15 *Maastricht Journal of European and Comparative Law*, pp. 135–141.

39 See S. Greer, "Constitutionalizing Adjudication under the European Convention on Human Rights", (2003) 23 *Oxford Journal of Legal Studies*, pp. 405–33.

40 See J.L. Dunoff, "Constitutional Conceits: The WTO's 'Constitution' and the Discipline of International Law", (2006) 17 *European Journal of International Law*, pp. 647–70, R. Howse and K. Nicoladis, "Legitimacy and Global Governance: Why the WTO is a Step Too Far", in: R.B. Porter, P. Suave and A. Subramian (eds), *Efficiency, Equity, Legitimacy and Governance: The Multilateral Trading System at the Millenium*, (Washington: Brookings Institute, 2001), J. Trachtman, "The Constitutions of the WTO", (2006) 17 *European Journal of International Law*, pp. 623–46, and E.-U. Petersmann, "The WTO Constitution and Human Rights", (2000) 3 *Journal of International Economic Law*, pp. 19–25.

41 See G. Teubner and A. Fischer-Lescano, "Regime-Collisions: The Vain search for Legal Unity in the Fragmentation of Global Law", (2004) 25 *Michigan Journal of International Law*, p. 999.

At global level, the constitutional debate is less new, but its recent growth has arguably been more exponential than in any sector other than the EU. Since the Second World War and the birth of the UN Charter, there has been an intensified interest in the idea of the international legal and institutional order as a constitutional system, one which was never entirely extinguished by the *realpolitik* of the Cold War. Today, the combination, positively, of the post-war resilience of the UN and its institutions (as opposed to its inter-war League of Nations predecessor) and, negatively, of the new threats to *any* notion of a multilateral global order posed by American exceptionalism and neo-imperialism on the one hand and the rise of fundamentalist challenges to the pluralist premises of contemporary cosmopolitanism on the other, has created the conditions for a renewed interest in the discourse of constitutionalism. Jürgen Habermas is, perhaps, the most prominent thinker[42] to have argued for a new overarching global authority, at least in certain narrow, but vital, areas of the global public good – war, security and human rights – organised around the reform of the UN in general, and its Security Council in particular. In so doing, he has built upon a significant tradition of (strongly German influenced) thinking on an idea of global constitutionalism pivoting upon the common interest of the "international community"[43] and underwritten by those *ius cogens* norms and *erga omnes* obligations that emphasise universal values over multilateral or bilateral negotiations.[44] What is perhaps most strikingly distinctive about this global strain of constitutionalism is the extent to which the discursive frame is to the fore. Whereas at every other post-state site including the EU,[45] the constitutional idea – at least, in the early phase of its articulation – tends to follow from, and react to, events – to objective changes in the other constitutional frames, this priority has tended to be reversed at global level. Here, from the outset, constitutional discourse seems to have been more focused, on the one hand, upon a general reconceptualisation of an established legal and institutional domain (regardless of – or with less emphasis upon – changes in that domain), and, on the other, on the provision of a legitimating rhetoric for an explicit agenda of reform.

6. The Antinomies of Transnational Constitutionalism

In this final section, we pull together the strands of the conflicted career of constitutionalism beyond the state by examining three sets of interrelated oppositional forces, or antinomies, in the current moment of development. The first is between *consolidation* and *contestation*. The second is between *diffusion* and *defusion*. The third

42 See J. Habermas, *The Divided West*, (Cambridge MA: Polity Press, 2006).

43 See, for example, B. Fassbender, "The United Nations Charter as the Constitution of the International Community", (1998) 36 *Columbia Journal of Transnational Law*, pp. 529–620, B. Simma, "From Bilateralism to Community Interest in International Law", (1994) 250 *Recueil des Cours de l'Académie de droit international*, p. 6, C. Tomuschat, note 17 *supra*, and A. von Bogandy, "Constitutionalism in International Law: Comment on a Proposal from Germany", (2006) 47 *Harvard International Law Journal*, p. 233.

44 See E. de Wet, "The International Constitutional Order", (2006) 55 *International and Comparative Law Quarterly*, pp. 51–76.

45 See J.H.H. Weiler, *The Constitution of Europe*, (Cambridge: Cambridge University Press, 1999), Chapter 1.

is between *intensification* and *incoherence*. In what sense are these properly conceived of as oppositional tensions? Are these tensions inescapable, and, if so, need they be unproductive? These are difficult questions, and matters of projection as much as current and historical analysis. All we can do is sketch the contours of each tension and draw some indicative conclusions.

The most profound irony of transnational constitutionalism is that just at the moment of its consolidation in the legal (and to a lesser extent) political vernacular – when it has reached a point of discursive "no return", it has also plumbed unprecedented depths of contestation. Again, the EU provides a key case in point. The political élites of the Member States may have been eager to re-embrace the familiar form of an international treaty after the documentary Constitution of 2004 became irretrievably bogged down in ratification difficulties, but it is hard to see the constitutional debate being quietly laid to rest in the longer-term. There is sufficient dissatisfaction with the classically indirect state-centred discourse of EU constitutionalism – one that continues to rely on the traditional tropes of national sovereignty, internationalism and state delegation as the standard structuring devices of regional political community notwithstanding the qualitative shift of political and economic power and of associated regulatory forms away from the state – to ensure that even if there is no consensus on the optimal "constitutional" form of a new order, a powerful critique of the anachronism of a purely state-centred "misframing"[46] will remain within the political culture.

But this discursive strengthening of constitutionalism remains problematical in at least two senses. First, while it may be potent enough to destabilise the state-centred view and challenge its presumptive authority, the failure of the Constitutional Treaty suggests that it does not carry sufficient momentum to resolve in an affirmative manner the second order debate about whether the EU should indeed have constitutional status. Instead, the view that "thick" documentary constitutions should remain an affair exclusively or primarily of states continues to hold significant sway. Secondly, there are those who believe, from the other flank, that the discourse of EU constitutionalism, far from being too heterodox a departure, may constitute an insufficiently radical break with the epistemic and normative properties of the Westphalian frame (Tully 2007a, Watkins, 2005);[47] that in borrowing from the state tradition it also endorses a set of assumptions about the autonomous, top-down, centralised, law-fetishising, self-contained, exclusionary and presumptively imperialising polity that has blighted that state tradition.

And if the second-order debate – constitutional framing or not – remains unresolved – the danger is that we are left in a state of constitutional limbo. The inability to find a constitutional settlement is eloquent testimony to the problem of legitimising the post-

46 See N. Fraser, "Reframing Justice in a Globalizing World", (2005) 36 *New Left Review*, pp. 69–88.

47 See J. Tully, "A New Kind of Europe? Democratic Integration in the European Union", (2007) 10 *Critical Review of International Social and Political Philosophy*, pp. 71–86, and S. Watkins, "Constitutional Tremors", (2005) 33, *New Left Review*, pp. 5–21.

national or supranational order, but the similar lack of consensus on the continuing adequacy of a non-constitutional settlement shows that there is no longer an uncontentious second-order statist default position, whatever the fate of particular constitutional initiatives.[48] And although the debate is not so well advanced anywhere else, arguably, we are approaching deep second-order contestation in other contexts, too – whether the WTO, the regional human rights organisations or, increasingly, the UN and the global order – with some criticizing constitutionalism as an illegitimate grab for power that properly should remain with the states,[49] others treating constitutionalism as the key to breaking the Westphalian frame, and others still sharing the constitutionalists' dissatisfaction with the *status quo* but inclined to view constitutionalism itself as the continuation of a familiar structure of power by other means.

In turn, the exploration of the second-order debate reveals a more detailed level of contestation over the first-order meaning of constitutionalism in terms of the significance or otherwise of the dimensions set out earlier. In so doing, it demonstrates the resilience of the division between incremental and holistic understandings of constitutionalism. For some, the thick state-derivative frame, with all five dimensions in place, remains the non-negotiable *sine qua non* of constitutional status. Unless a polity boasts an autonomous legal order, a distinctive institutional architecture of legislative, executive and judicial powers and a wide normative ambit, a democratic founding and a resilient democratic pedigree, a political community of common attachment and commitment and a lively discourse of constitutional critique and self-interrogation, then it is at best a form of "constitutionalism-lite"[50] and at worst a fraud. For others, a more selective approach to constitutional status should not be viewed pejoratively as constitutional defusion, but should instead be seen as the potentially healthy diffusion of the constitutional idea. So it may be argued that it is neither feasible nor necessary for many transnational organisations to have the democratic foundations or the level of societal integration or the broad normative scope of national constitutions. Some exponents of WTO constitutionalism, for example, concentrate largely on its capacity to offer secure forms of protection of the private sphere of economic rights.[51] Some exponents of the global constitutionalism of the UN concentrate on the universal and so polity- and society-unspecific claim of the UN legal order and political system.[52] Some exponents of a relatively thin constitutionalism for the EU also concentrate on the virtue of its insulation from the policy inefficiencies and potential rights-abuses of a

48 See N. Walker, "A Constitutional Reckoning", (2006) 13 *Constellations*, pp. 140–150.

49 See W. Schneiderman, "Constitution or Model Treaty? Struggling over the interpretive authority of NAFTA", in: S. Choudhry (ed), *The Migration of Constitutional Ideas*, (Cambridge: Cambridge University Press, 2006), pp. 294–315.

50 See J. Klabbers, note 6 *supra*, Grimm, note 6 *supra*, and J.H.H. Weiler, note 6 *supra*.

51 See E.-U. Petersmann, note 40 *supra*.

52 See B. Fassbender, "We the Peoples of the United Nations": Constituent Power and Constitutional Form in International Law", in: M. Loughlin and N. Walker (eds), *The Paradox of Constitutionalism: Constituent Power and Constitutional Form*, (Oxford: Oxford University Press, 2007), pp. 269–290.

democratically volatile policy process,[53] or on the compensating virtues of an "output legitimacy"[54] garnered through the aggregate benefits of policy outcomes rather than the responsiveness of such policies to a full range of popular input.

To complicate matters further, there are those both on the sceptical side and on the pro-constitutional side, who would draw a clear distinction between the constitutional requirements and potential of the "in-between" EU, with its more state-like capacity and regulatory structure, and those of other less mature post-national sites. On this view, the level of development of the EU uniquely allows of no half-measures, but simply demands a thicker form of constitutional legitimation than other post-state sites. The prospect of this thicker form of legitimation is then either dismissed (by the sceptics) as simply implausible given the resilient location of political and social identity at the state level, thus throwing into doubt the general legitimacy of the EU in its current expansive form, or urged (by the enthusiasts) as a possibility born of necessity.[55]

Regardless of differences both over the basis of the claims to the virtue of partial constitutionalism and over whether these partial claims should apply generally, or only, to the less mature post-national sites, the argument typically runs that not only is it not plausible to look for full-pedigree constitutionalism at the post-national level, but that we would not even like it if we found it; that the virtues of political community are not always reducible to democratic will and popular implementation, but can lie in certain matters of the right or the good being insulated from politics, in policy being developed by experts, or in rules being better implemented in interested and knowledgeable communities of practice.[56] In this vein, we can see quite graphically how constitutionalism serves as a "subjective" and dynamically evolving register of debate about the optimal political resolution of collective action problems, rather than as an "objectively" decisive and unchanging resource in its resolution.

This brings us to the final antinomy – between intensification and incoherence. The simultaneous development of various post-national constitutional initiatives both reflects and reinforces a very uneven and untidy global scenario of transnational legal relations. It announces or portends a multi-dimensional configuration of overlapping and variously and partially constitutionalised polities. This is quite different from the post-Westphalian world system of modernity – a one-dimensional system of mutually exclusive and uniformly and comprehensively constitutionalised polities. Clearly, this was always a stylisation, a template that operated within the imperial world centred on

53 See G. Majone, note 2 *supra*, and A. Moravcsik, note 4 *supra*.

54 See F. Scharpf, note 37 *supra*.

55 See N. Walker, note 11 *supra*.

56 See G. Majone, note 2 supra, Ch. Joerges, "What is left of the European Constitution? A melancholic eulogy", (2005) 30 European Law Review, pp. 461–489, P. Mair, Democracy beyond Parties, (Paper 05-06, Center for the Study of Democracy, University of California, Irvine. Available at: http://repositories.cdlib.org/csd/05-06, and P. Pettit, "Depoliticizing Democracy", (2004) 17 *Ratio Juris*, pp. 52–65.

Western Europe rather than across imperial-subaltern relations.[57] There was, nevertheless, a coherent imaginary of legal authority at work – a singular "order of orders";[58] that divided the world into the domestic constitutional law of sovereigns (and, ideally, of democratically endorsed sovereigns) and international law (however unstable) between sovereigns. Every place on the Westphalian map, at least, in terms of its official legend, was the subject of a singular and determinate set of juridical relations. Legal pluralism was a purely external pressure – the occasional incursions of alternative regulatory logics, of local or trans-local customary law and the like. Under the new order, pluralism is internal – written into the emergent frame itself. We see this, for example, in the relations between state orders and the EU, or between the EU and the WTO, or, between state or regional bodies and various UN Charter organs and global treaty regimes.[59]

The problem of incoherence, of there being opposite or unclear messages at work within the global juridical framework with its proliferation of authority sources, moreover, is not just one of the relational margins – of the occasional boundary dispute. For just as there is no agreement on the meaning of constitutionalism – diffuse or defused – or even on the justification, in principle, of its migration beyond the political agency of the state, so there is no meta-agreement on how the various more or less agreed parts of the post-Westphalian jigsaw should fit together. Rather, there are an increasing range of meta-agreements vying for ascendancy – a new "disorder of orders".[60] Can we imagine, as one such meta-agreement, a polyarchy of regions and strong states? Or can we imagine, with Habermas,[61] a narrow and modest global peak, underpinned by new regional sites of "global domestic policy" and with the base continuing to be made up of states? Or must we fear the *ersatz* liberal internationalism of a world under the constitutional, as well as the military, shadow of American unipolarity? Or can we envisage a horizontal rather than a vertical principle of coherence, one based upon values other than hierarchy, as in some forms of "multi-level constitutionalism",[62] and, indeed, of many new forms of cosmopolitanism.[63] And, if so, where is the guarantee of the genuine rather than hegemonic universality of the values?[64] And if not, are we not simply left with a fragmented post-national legal order, where the attempt to track

57 See G. Anderson note 8 *supra*, and J. Tully, The Imperialism of Modern Constitutional Democracy", in: M. Loughlin and N. Walker (eds), *The Paradox of Constitutionalism: Constituent Power and Constitutional Form*, (Oxford: Oxford University Press, 2007), pp. 315–338.

58 See N. Walker, "Beyond Boundary Disputes and Basic Grids: mapping the Global Disorder of Normative Orders", (2008) 6 *International Journal of Constitutional Law*, pp. 273–296.

59 See M. Koskenniemi, "The Fate of Public International Law: Between Technique and Politics", (2007) 70 *Modern Law Review*, pp. 1–30.

60 See N. Walker, note 58 *supra*.

61 See J. Habermas, note 42 *supra*, at Chapter 8.

62 See I. Pernice, "Multi-Level Constitutionalism and the Treaty of Amsterdam: Constitution-making Revisited?", in: (1999) 36 *Common Market Review*, p. 703.

63 See D. Held, Global Covenant: The Social Democratic Alternative to the Washington Consensus, (Cambridge MA: Polity Press, 2004).

64 See M. Koskenniemi, note 59 *supra*.

fugitive political power in post-national legal arrangements, leads – to embellish Michael Walzer's famous phrase[65] – to countless "petty juridical fortresses", with no principle of mutual coherence? Or does such a radical pluralism of overlapping polity forms have the potential to provide its own power-levelling virtues?[66] Constitutionalism, including the relationship between state and transnational constitutionalism, clearly plays quite differently in the construction of these rival candidate meta-agreements. As we have seen most starkly in the case of the EU, on the one hand, and global constitutionalism, on the other, constitutional discourse in such conditions of deep uncertainty and incoherence becomes much more emphatically a question of imaginative and, more or less, persuasive *projection* – a gambit in the symbolic futures market, rather than a confident investment in established stock.

Transnational constitutional discourse, in conclusion, appears to capture both the open-ended possibilities and the deracinated quality of the new political imaginary. Its authoritative, ideological, normative and epistemic power – its capacity to compel, to persuade, to intervene effectively and even to "make sense" – is rooted in its statist origins. Yet, transnational constitutionalism is increasingly attenuated from these roots, and is increasingly implicated in attempts to re-order an ever less settled map of transnational legal relations. At the same time, state-centred constitutionalism, while no longer hegemonic, provides a powerful continuing counterpoint to transnational constitutionalism at the authoritative and ideological level, one with the accumulation of practice and tradition very much on its side, as well as a distorting influence at the epistemic and even the normative level. If constitutionalism offers a route to a new state-decentred framework of legal authority, it must perforce continue to contend with heavy traffic from the direction of the state.

65 See M. Walzer, *Spheres of Justice: A defence of pluralism and equality* (Oxford: Blackwell, 1983), p. 39.

66 See N. Krisch, "The Pluralism of Global Administrative Law", (2006) 17 *European Journal of International Law*, pp. 247–278.

Rainer Nickel

CHAPTER 12. TRANSNATIONAL BORROWING AMONG JUDGES: TOWARDS A COMMON CORE OF EUROPEAN AND GLOBAL CONSTITUTIONAL LAW?

1. Introduction

The European Commission for Democracy through Law, better known as the Venice Commission, is the Council of Europe's advisory body on constitutional matters. Established in 1990, the commission has played a leading role in the adoption of constitutions that conform to the standards of Europe's constitutional heritage. Initially conceived as a tool for emergency constitutional engineering, the commission has become an internationally recognised independent legal think-tank. It contributes to the dissemination of the European constitutional heritage, based on the continent's fundamental legal values while continuing to provide "constitutional first-aid" to individual states. The Venice Commission also plays a unique and unrivalled role in crisis management and conflict prevention through constitution building and advice. The work of the European Commission for Democracy through Law aims at upholding the three underlying principles of Europe's constitutional heritage: democracy, human rights and the rule of law – the cornerstones of the Council of Europe. Accordingly, the Commission works in the following four key-areas: Constitutional assistance, elections and referendums, co-operation with constitutional courts, and transnational studies, reports and seminars.[1]

1 This self-description of the Venice Commission, or European Commission for Democracy through Law, can be found at www.venice.coe.int/site/main/presentation_E.asp?MenuL=E#1. The text suggests that European constitutionalism is a necessary and legitimate gift to mankind, embodied in "Europe's constitutional heritage", which consists of democracy, human rights, and the rule of law. This self-assured attitude may be taken as a clear sign of the short range of human memory. For a different account of the recent history of Europe, see Tony Judt, *Postwar. A History of Europe since 1945*, (London: William Heinemann, 2005), and for a profound historical-legal analysis of the European project Ch. Joerges and N. Singh Ghaleigh (eds), *Darker Legacies of Law in Europe*, (Oxford: Hart Publishing, 2003). – The Venice Commission is a sub-commission of the Council of Europe (CoE), www.coe.int. It has nothing to do with the European Commission or the European Union.

European and global constitutionalism is on the rise. This is valid in two respects: Firstly, we can observe an extensive, engaged and on-going theoretical discussion in philosophy, political sciences and law about the promises and perils of the cosmopolitan ideal (mostly based upon I. Kant's *Zum Ewigen Frieden*, 1795) and its practical implementation.[2] Secondly, after its sweeping victory in the domestic realm, the idea and the concept of constitutionalism is more and more often applied to legal orders, arrangements and "condensed" treaty constellations beyond the nation state and its borders, sometimes cautiously,[3] and sometimes vigorously.[4]

With the rise of supra- and transnational constitutionalism comes a growing unease about its structures, actors, and effects.[5] It raises numerous concerns about a biased and hegemonic project of constitutionalism, and the European Commission for Democracy through Law, with its seemingly self-assured, missionary attitude, may thus represent the spearhead of a Kantian movement that will sweep away local knowledge and "odd local details",[6] resulting finally in one uniform global constitutional law machinery.

In the U.S., the idea of such a global constitutional compound has been greeted with deep scepticism by many politicians and legal scholars alike. The development towards a global understanding of contemporary international law as a kind of transnational[7]

2 From the vast literature, see only J. Habermas, "Does the Constitutionalisation of International Law Still Have a Chance?", in: *ibid.*, *The Divided West*, (Cambridge MA: Polity Press, 2006), 115–193; H. Brunkhorst, *Solidarity. From Civic Friendship to a Global Legal Community*, (Cambridge MA: MIT Press, 2005); J.L. Cohen, "Rethinking Human Rights, Democracy and Sovereignty in the Age of Globalization", (2008) 36 *Political Theory*, pp. 578–606; Bardo Fassbender, "The United Nation's Charter as Constitution of the International Community", (1997) 36 *Columbia Journal Of Transnational Law*, p. 575; and the contributions to Vol 10 no 1 (2009) of the *German Law Journal*, www.germanlawjournal.com.

3 For tentative explorations, see the contributions in: Ch. Joerges and E.-U. Petersmann (eds), *Constitutionalism, Multilevel Trade Governance and Social Regulation*, (Oxford: Hart Publishing, 2006, 2nd edition 2010).

4 For a 'constitutional' understanding of WTO trade law, see E.-U. Petersmann, "Multilevel Trade Governance Requires Multilevel Constitutionalism", in: C. Joerges and E.-U.Petersmann (eds), note 3 *supra*, pp. 5–57.

5 See, for example, E.A. Young, "The Trouble with Global Constitutionalism", (2003) 38 *Texas International Law Journal*, p. 527.

6 Günther Frankenberg, "Comparing Constitutions – Toward a Layered Narrative", in: (2006) 4 *I.CON*, pp. 439–459, underlines the important function of – often historically determined – "odd details" in national constitutional texts.

7 Philip Jessup is said to have coined the idea of "transnational law": "I shall use, instead of 'international law', the term 'transnational law' to include all law which regulates actions or events that transcend national frontiers. Both public and private international law are included, as are other rules which do not wholly fit into such standard categories." Philip Jessup, *Transnational Law*, (New Haven: Yale University Press, 1956), p. 136. For a discussion of the term, see C. Scott, "'Transnational Law' as Proto Concept: Three Conceptions", (2009) 10 *German Law Journal*, pp. 860–876, www.germanlawjournal.com. Scott calls transnational law "a kind of fuzzy or suggestive proto concept".

constitutional[8] law in the making, a law which is supreme to domestic law, is despised and feared at the same time: for example, even the most cautious attempts to acknowledge "foreign" constitutional law and practices as a source of inspiration, or guideline, for decisions on domestic constitutional issues have led to a heated debate about the legitimacy of such a practice in the United States. References to "foreign" legal positions and attitudes in a number of recent U.S. Supreme Court cases (*Atkins* v *Virginia*, *Roper* v *Simmons*, or *Lawrence* v *Texas*) have provoked sharp criticism from both inside and outside the Court.[9] But also in other parts of the world, we can find reservations against a global legal order and accompanying concepts of human rights that are imposed upon, rather than independently established by, "third world" countries, such as India.[10] Can we thus assume and hope that the U.S. (and its constitutional "originalists") will defend national constitutionalism against the European Constitutionalist Empire? And what exactly are these mechanisms that promulgate and disseminate supra- and trans-national constitutionalism?

The central topic of this contribution is not simply the spread of constitutionalism as such (this has been commented upon abundantly[11]), but rather the mechanisms and consequences of an enhanced constitutional dialogue, and the emergence of a trans- and supranational constitutionalism as a *discoursive practice*. It will disregard difficult methodological questions of comparative law in general, questions such as whether legal transplants – the transfer of conceptual parts of one legal system into another legal system – are possible and useful, or whether, instead, they are undesirable and destructive, or the question of whether legal systems around the world converge or not. These are important issues, but the discussion of which often suffers from the normative bias of the authors (for or against cosmopolitanism),[12] and they only have little to say about the actual mechanisms of existing constitutional discourse worlds.

8 For an early account, see Eric Stein, "Lawyers, judges, and the making of a transnational Constitution", (1981) 75 *American Journal of International Law*, pp. 1–27.

9 See the recent debate between Posner and Sunstein and Rosencrantz: E.A. Posner and C.R. Sunstein, "The Law of Other States", (2006) 59 *Stanford Law Review*, p. 131 (defending the practice of references to other legal systems and their legal practices); N.Q. Rosencrantz, "Condorcet and the Constitution: A Response to The Law of Other States", (2007) 59 *Stanford Law Review*, p. 1281; and Posner and Sunstein, "On Learning from Others", (2007) 59 *Stanford Law Review*, p. 1309, responding to Rosencrantz' critique.

10 B.S. Chimni has stated that a "transnational capitalist class" is "in the process of congealing and establishing a global state", "International Institutions Today: An Imperial Global State in the Making", (2004) 15 *European Journal of International Law*, pp. 1–37, at 4.

11 A. Stone Sweet, *Governing with Judges*, (Oxford: Oxford University Press, 2000), diagnoses a "judicialisation" of politics.

12 Compare P. Legrand, "On the Singularity of Law", (2006) 47 *Harvard Journal of International Law*, pp 517–530 (denying any meaningful convergence and criticising a "fixation with monistic thought", *ibid.*, p. 522) and Alan Watson, *Legal Transplants* (Atlanta: Univ. of Georgia Press, 2nd ed. 1993 [1st ed. Edinburgh, 1974], who holds that "the transplanting of individual rules or of a large part of a legal system is extremely common" and that "transplanting is, in fact, the most fertile source of development", p. 100.

In this contribution, I will first characterise the U.S. discussion as a rather singular and deviant – and consequently, distracting – interlude (see Section 2). Most parts of the world, and especially the European part of the world, have already moved on. A global practice of mutual observation, information, and strategic interaction, in short, of *Comparative Constitutional Borrowing* is well under way (Section 3). The result is a densely woven carpet of constitutionalism. European constitutionalism represents the most advanced practice in this regard; it has developed into a complex web of hierarchies and heterarchies (Section 4). This effect is reflected in both large and small cases, and they also reveal the paradoxes of this growing constitutionalisation (Section 5). In absence of clear hierarchies, supra- and trans-national constitutional conflicts cannot be resolved authoritatively and *ex cathedra*. A concept of "constitutional conflicts law" is needed. It should combine respect for the legal traditions which have grown over time, and to "odd" details contained in them, with a necessary sense of the promises of constitutionalism (Section 6).

2. The U.S. Sonderweg: Parochialism, or the Fight against 'Juristocracy'?

The triumph of constitutionalism in the second half of the Twentieth century is already a common place, and the proliferation of constitutionalism in the new countries of the former Eastern *Bloc* has been thoroughly documented as well.[13] What is new is a sense and a concept of similarity and comparability, of an iteration loop, of an ever-denser textual web of "higher law", all of which is progressing on a regional and global scale.

Two terminological *caveats* have to be mentioned here: The term "constitutionalism" is often used in this context in a modified sense. Firstly, it is uncoupled from its origin as a characteristic of a state constitution. The term "constitution", as a foundational political document of a political community which is clearly defined by its borders, its members, and its state monopoly of power,[14] has been de-contextualised as well.[15] As the "disaggregated state" (A.-M. Slaughter[16]) of the presence has moved away from this original concept of the Westphalian age, it is well-justified to speak about a supra- and trans-national "constitutionalisation",[17] notwithstanding this difference with the

13 For an assessment of the role of constitutional courts in Central and Eastern Europe, see Wojciech Sadurski, *Rights Before Courts. A Study of Constitutional Courts in Postcommunist States of Central and Eastern Europe*, 2nd. ed. (Dordrecht: Springer, 2008).

14 These are the three elements of Jellinek's famous definition of statehood, G. Jellinek, *Allgemeine Staatslehre*. (Berlin: Springer, 3rd ed. 1921), p. 394.

15 See, for example, the discussion about a 'constitutionalisation' of the WTO: D. Cass, *The Constitutionalisation of the WTO*, (Oxford: Oxford University Press, 2004). – G. Teubner suggests an even wider concept: "Societal Constitutionalism: Alternatives to State-Centred Constitutional Theory?", in: Ch. Joerges, I.-J. Sand and G. Teubner (eds), *Transnational Governance and Constitutionalism*, (Oxford: Hart Publishing, 2004), pp. 3–28.

16 A.-M. Slaughter, *A New World Order*, (Princeton: Princeton University Press, 2004).

17 J. Habermas, for example, uses the term to describe and to demand a transformation of international law: "Does the Constitutionalisation of International Law Still Have a Chance?", in: J. Habermas, *The Divided West*, (Cambridge: Polity Press, 2006), pp. 115–210.

traditional nation-state constitutionalism. Secondly, "constitutionalism" is often used in contexts in which it basically means *human rights adjudication*. This signals a double reduction: constitutionalism is bared of the concept of democracy, and of the institutional arrangements of modern democratic nation-states, including its system of a separation (or balance) of powers. These reductions pose additional challenges to the legitimacy of such an operation, but human rights or fundamental rights, and judicial review, are, nonetheless, essential elements of modern constitutionalism. As Stone Sweet[18] correctly observes, discursive practices and techniques of constitutional adjudication come to structure the work of governments, parliaments, judges, and administrators, with constitutional courts as authoritative interpreters of the constitutional law, and especially of human rights provisions. On the supra- and trans-national level, the two other balancing factors of a democratic society under the rule of law, namely, democratic institutions and an executive which can be held accountable, are absent. Thus, courts move into the centre of constitutionalism.

There are a number of reasons why we should fear global constitutionalism. Not long ago, Philipp Allott, in an article entitled "The Emerging International Aristocracy", warned us that "we must face a new global social reality, the total social reality, a reality dominated by a new version of an age-old social phenomenon, an emerging international aristocracy, an oligarchy of oligarchies", and that this new total social reality will entail "the end of democracy".[19] Allott refers to those actors that shape the juridification of transnational societal relations: government bureaucrats, private actors, and judges. A recent book by Ran Hirschl uses this train of thought for an even more drastic description of the constitutional review revolution after the Second World War; in Hirschl's view, this trend culminates in a new class rule, a "juristocracy".[20] Thus, with global constitutionalism, we may reach an additional, new stage of oligarchism: a *global constitutional juristocracy*.

There are, indeed, clear signs pointing at such a development. Two aspects may underline this presumption: firstly, we have already stated that an important global transformation has taken place after the Second World War; post-war and post-cold war developments have led to a worldwide expansion and deepening of judicial review in constitutional matters. Of the 191 member states of the UN, only five countries, a recent survey

18 A. Stone Sweet, note 11 *supra*.

19 Philip Allott, "The Emerging International Aristocracy", (2003) 35 *New York University Journal of International Law and Politics*, p. 309.

20 Ran Hirschl, *Towards Juristocracy. The Origins and Consequences of the New Constitutionalism*, (Cambridge MA: Harvard University Press, 2004). Hirschl argues from an anti-bourgeois perspective that bears resemblance to the classical Marxist critique of law as a mere *Überbauphänomen*. For an instructive discussion of materialistic approaches to and criticisms of International Law in general, and criticisms of post-national constitutionalism in particular (which are mainly of a fundamental nature), see S. Marks, "International Judicial Activism and the Commodity-Form Theory of International Law", (2007) 18 *European Journal of International Law*, pp 199–211; and for a profound critique of Hirschl's neoliberal- juristocracy- thesis, see M. Kende, *Constitutional Rights in Two Worlds - South Africa and the United States*, (Cambridge: Cambridge University Press, 2009), pp. 286 *et seq.*

suggests,[21] remain without a system of constitutional review, or of judicial review in a constitutional sense: the United Kingdom and the Netherlands in Europe, and Lesotho, Liberia, and Libya in Africa. It must be added, however, that the UK is well on its way to joining the Supreme Court club.[22] Secondly, we can observe an ongoing proliferation of methods and techniques of constitutionalism and constitutional review throughout the world. The Venice Commission is a major player and an excellent example for strategies of promoting both constitutionalism and, in particular, constitutional review managed by constitutional courts.[23] It is an especially apt example because it actively promotes a distinct European way of constitutionalism and constitutional review – as became clear from the quotation at the beginning of this contribution.

Thus, we must ask ourselves whether the conservative wing of the U.S. Supreme Court and its academic adherents are correct to reject any kind of involvement in a supra- and trans-national discourse on the shape, contents and limits of fundamental rights? A closer look at the controversy reveals that ideological reasons are the main driving forces behind the categorical rejection of any kind of transnational constitutional discourse, and not a more sophisticated legal philosophy which tries, for example, to preserve a legitimate legal pluralism. Susan Marks reports on a speech by Michael Chertoff, the former US Secretary of Homeland Security:

> On 17 November 2006 the United States Secretary of Homeland Security, Michael Chertoff, made a speech at the Annual Lawyers Convention of the Washington DC based Federalist Society, in which he addressed the subject of international law. [... H]e recalled the shift that had occurred in United States judicial policy since he first began his career in the 1970s. A backlash had occurred against the 'judicial activism' of the 1960s and 1970s, and an ethos of 'judicial restraint' – a greater sensitivity to the limits of the judicial function, a more modest approach with respect to the decisions of democratically elected legislators – had come to prevail in the Supreme Court. Chertoff noted that this was in no small measure due to the efforts of people like the members of the Federalist Society, but he said there was no room for

21 The author A. Mavčič has analysed and classified different models of constitutional review around the world. See the overview at www.concourts.net/tab/tab1.php?lng=en&stat=1&prt=0&srt=0.

22 In 2004, the UK government has lodged an initiative to establish a US-style UK Supreme Court, see the contributions in Andrew LeSueur (ed), *Building a New UK Supreme Court*, (Oxford: Oxford University Press, 2004). The House of Lords has been renamed since then: The *Supreme Court of the United Kingdom* was established in law by Part III of the Constitutional Reform Act 2005. It began its work in October 2009. Although the old House of Lords as well as the new UK Supreme Court lack the power to nullify legislation, see Chapter 4 subsection 4 and 6 of the Human Rights Act of 1998, the introduction of the Human Rights Act has dramatically changed the legal landscape of the UK.

23 The author of this contribution has also took part in this enterprise (if only, in hindsight, somewhat unknowingly) as an agent of this form of constitutional promotion: 1998 in Yerevan and Vanadzor/Armenia (in the framework of the PHARE programme of the Council of Europe, on fundamental rights and their judicial protection), 2000 in Sarajevo (for the German Society for International Legal Co-operation, on procedural rules guiding the access to constitutional courts and the ECHR), 2001 in Albania (for the German Society for International Legal Co-operation, on the ECHR and its procedural rules), 2001 and 2002 in the framework of the EU-China Legal Exchange Programme, 2002 in Hungary (on the ECJ).

> complacency, for now a new challenge had arisen which he invited his audience to confront. This was 'the rise of an increasingly activist, left-wing and even elitist philosophy of law that is flourishing not in the United States but in foreign courts and in various international courts and bodies'.
>
> Chertoff gave the example of 'passenger name record data'. In order to enhance its capacity to identify people entering the United States who have connections with terrorists, the Administration sought access to information provided to airline companies and travel agencies by passengers when they purchase air tickets (address, telephone number, credit card details, *etc*). In so far as the information would come from Europe, this had led to difficulties because certain members of the European Parliament had objected on privacy grounds. Chertoff reported that, in fact, these difficulties had been resolved satisfactorily. But he explained that the incident focused his attention on the extent to which 'what happens in the world of international law and transnational law increasingly has an impact on my ability to do my job and the ability of the people who work in my department to do their jobs'."[24]

By identifying the transnational judicial discourse on fundamental rights as an offspring of a "left wing philosophy of law", Chertoff reveals his ideological motives behind the rejection of any kind of "foreign" influence. This attitude is echoed in many contributions supporting a U.S.-centred legal discourse: transnational constitutionalism is identified with judicial activism, and this, in turn, is identified with a kind of left-wing rights activism.[25]

The U.S. domestic disputes about "the laws of other states", and whether these can be taken into account by the Supreme Court, or by the courts in general, end up in a methodological parochialism. There are convincing reasons for the assumption that international law and the legal practices of other states can represent a reasonable standard of societal development.[26] If one is watching the world from "the shining city upon the hill" (Ronald Reagan/John Winthrop), however, it may be fruitless or even counter-productive to look closely into the valleys and gorges of global legal diversity, in search of common denominators or inspirations. Many, if not most, countries do not have such an elevated position; they believe in, and are bound by, transnational and supranational standards, and they sometimes even act accordingly. It is, therefore, safe to say that the sharp dispute about "the law of other states" says a lot about rifts in U.S.

24 M. Chertoff, Remarks at the Federalist Society's Annual Lawyers Convention, 17 November 2006. The complete text of his speech can be found at www.dhs.gov/xnews/speeches/sp_1163798467437.shtm. S. Marks, note 20 *supra*, extensively reports about, and comments upon, Chertoff's speech.

25 Steven Calabresi is one of the most radical representative of this fraction, see S. Calabresi, "'A Shining City on a Hill': American Exceptionalism and the Supreme Court's Practice of Relying on Foreign Law", (2006) 86 *Boston University Law Review*, pp. 1335–1416. For Calabresi, a reference to non-US-law is un-American and unpatriotic.

26 Harold Koh has convincingly argued that the legal system of the U.S. has always been oriented towards a kind of "standards of civilisation", and that it has a strong universalist tradition: H. Koh, "International Law as Part of Our Law", (2004) 98 *American Journal Of International Law*, p. 43.

jurisprudence and academia, but not much about methodological issues of comparative constitutional borrowing.

The ideological rift between the Scalia faction and the Breyer faction within the Supreme Court is situated along the lines of originalism and constitutional dynamism.[27] In theoretical terms, it is a conflict about the methods of constitutional interpretation: the "originalist" position is grounded in a conscious defence of a U.S. *Sonderweg*, and its background philosophy reveals an almost religious belief in an American exceptionalism.[28] No other jurisdiction seems to lay such an emphasis on the possibility of only one "correct", sacred method of constitutional interpretation as the originalists in the U.S. do. To the contrary, methodological interpretative pluralism is the norm in many jurisdictions all over the world; for example, the German Federal Constitutional Court simply lacks factions which believe that certain interpretative techniques are illegitimate from the outset. The South African Constitution even requires that the South African courts, "when interpreting the Bill of Rights...may consider foreign law" (Article 36 of the 1994 Constitution of the South African Republic). This simply codifies what has become a global judicial practice: mutual observation and Comparative Constitutional Borrowing (CCB).

The ideologically ossified U.S. discourse conceals another important facet of the emerging transnational legal discourse: it has developed – most notably after the end of the cold war – for precisely the opposite reason than simply to establish a single and uniform world order. Apart from obvious functional grounds of market effectiveness and stability, there is at least one decisive aspect of *democracy* that supports and potentially legitimates a co-operative creation of supra- and trans-national law: it has the potential to "compensate the shortcomings of constitutional nation-states" (Ch. Joerges)[29] by forcing them to take the interests of the "others" into account.[30] This still seems alien to democratic nationalists like Chertoff. His speech shows both a deep concern about being able "to do his job" when facing obstacles arising from "international law and transnational law", but, at the same time, also shows a profound neglect towards the interests of others and the potentially harmful external effects of

27 A public dispute between the Supreme Court Justices Antonin Scalia and Breyer at the Washington College of Law at American University on 13 January 2005 laid these positions bare. A full transcript of the discussion can be found at: www.wcl.american.edu/secle/founders/2005/050113.cfm. – "Originalists" hold that the U.S. constitution and its amendments should be interpreted along the lines of the "original" will or intention of the Founding Fathers, while the non-originalists (which seem to form the Court's majority at present) support a constitutional interpretation with regard to developing standards of the international community. For the latter, see the judgments in the following cases: *Atkins* v *Virginia*, 536 U.S. 304 (2002), *Roper* v *Simmons*, 543 U.S. 551 (2005), and *Lawrence* v *Texas*, 539 U.S. 558 (2003).

28 S. Calabresi (note 25 *supra*).

29 Ch. Joerges, "European Law as Conflicts of Law", in: Ch. Joerges and J. Neyer, Deliberative supranationalism revisited, 20/2006 *EUI Working Papers, Law*, 21.

30 For an extension of the concept of "otherness" in the context of the EU, see the contribution of A. Cebada Romero (Chapter 4 in this volume).

actions of the US government upon others. Chertoff finds it irritating that "some members of the European Parliament" should have a say in matters which he sees as purely domestic. These irritations, however, are a positive effect of supra- and trans-national constitutionalism, and not a flaw.

Some proponents of American parochialism do not even see the obvious irony in their argumentation. McGinnes and Somin, for example, hail the democratic quality of "the superpower law of the US" and qualify international law as a kind of second-class law ("raw international law") because of its democratic deficit. They overlook that domestic US law - due to its external effects, as in the case of passenger data transferred to US authorities mentioned by Chertoff - is well-able to affect the *democratic processes* in all other countries outside the U.S.: these persons might worry what their data protection laws and rights are worth if one country can dictate all the conditions of the data transfer. According to McGinnes and Somin, however, the foreigners affected by US domestic law should not worry:

> Because of its structural position in the international system, the United States is likely to generate public goods, including good legal norms, for the rest of the world.[31]

We hope so, but this is not the idea behind the concept of democratic self-government.

However, the US Supreme Court has not followed the suggestions of the "originalists". Instead of turning to judicial nationalism, it has perpetuated the internationalist tradition of US law and jurisprudence.[32] This does not solve the potential problems of a global constitutional juristocracy, but it does re-inforce the insight that there is no way back to legal isolationism. As a consequence, we will have to analyse the structural change caused by the emergence of supra- and trans-national constitutionalism. For a start, we can state the fact that Comparative Constitutional Borrowing is based upon, and embedded in, the judicial culture of argumentation and justification. It is seen here as a practice, an existing *discursive reality*, and one that makes sense in the given context of constitutional adjudication. Therefore, the central issue is not whether or why constitutional courts should use CCB, but how they do it, and in which environment.

3. The New Senator Class[33] in Action: Venice Commissions, Constitutional Court Conferences, and Global Constitutionalism Seminars

In order to justify the claim that CCB is a discursive reality, one might turn to judicial decisions and count the number of cross-references, conceptual borrowings, or mutual

31 J.O. McGinnis and I. Somin, "Should International Law Be Part of Our Law?", (2007) 59 *Stanford Law Review*, pp. 1175–1247, at 1176.

32 For a detailed account of this tradition, see H. Koh, note 26 *supra*.

33 The "Senator Class" is *Lufthansa's* highest frequent-flyer status.

citations. This statistical approach, however, will most probably lead only to disappointing results. It is rather rare that domestic constitutional courts, or supra- and trans-national courts, expressly refer to non-domestic legal material or decisions, even if these incidents appear to be on the rise.[34] Constitutional courts are, after all, not an international law or a transnational constitutionalism seminar. Non-domestic legal material finds its way into court decisions in ways other than by direct quotations: preparatory opinions of the judges and legal advisors often contain such arguments, and the parties' lawyers argue more and more frequently with non-domestic material, thus forcing the judges to react to it.

A second, and better, way of measuring the extent of supra-and trans-national constitutionalist discourses than counting quotations might be to analyse which and how constitutional ideas migrate from one jurisdiction to another, or to supra- and trans-national constitutional arenas. This approach can certainly verify that constitutional arguments and principles do wander; they are taken up by other jurisdictions, and they are re-moulded into a fitting element or principle for purposes of domestic adjudication.[35] A lot may be "lost in translation", but there are certainly gains, too. What this approach cannot deliver, however, is an idea about how these arguments and principles make their way across jurisdictions – is there a master plan, or does it solely depend upon the language skills of the respective judges, or upon the degree to which decisions are translated into a widespread language, that concepts migrate? In other words, it may just be pure chance that some ideas migrate and others do not.

How, then, can CCB be measured, if not by a quantitative analyses or a scholarly reconstruction? I suggest that we take the incidents of cross-references between jurisdictions, and incidents of the migration of constitutional ideas, solely as indicators of an ongoing practice, but not as the practice itself. Instead, we should look behind the curtains and turn to the *discursive worlds* that link institutional actors (and not only analyse their products, the judgments). A stock-taking of constitutionalist activities beyond the domestic sphere reveals enormous activities in a variety of fields. Three major interfaces can be distinguished: the Council of Europe (CoE) as a politico-legal actor which promotes constitutionalism in Europe and beyond; various networks of

34 Two more recent examples from the German context are: (1) the *Muslim butcher* case, in which the *Bundesverfassungsgericht* (Federal Constitutional Court, FCC) approvingly cites the Austrian (!) Constitutional Court in order to re-inforce its argumentations: www.bverfg.de/entscheidungen/rs20020115_1bvr178399en.html, paragraph 37, and (2) the Treaty of Lisbon case, in which the FCC expressly refers to the ECJ decision in the *Kadi* case, albeit only in order to establish its own right to control whether an EU legal act is *ultra vires*: www.bverfg.de/entscheidungen/es20090630_2bve000208en.html, paragraph 340.

35 One prominent example is the principle of proportionality which has become a key element of EC/EU constitutional law (a "general principle of EC law", in the wording of the ECJ): it is a modified version of the principle of proportionality which was created by the German FCC in its early jurisprudence and which has become a fundamental pillar of the whole legal system ever since. In turn, the origins of the "German" principle may be traced back to the "scrutiny"-jurisprudence and the various tests applied in this context by the US Supreme Court.

constitutional courts, connecting the judges and re-inforcing transnational dialogues; and academic support of these activities.

3.1. The Council of Europe and its Venice Commission

The Council of Europe (CoE), based in Strasbourg (France), now covers virtually the entire European continent, with its 47 member countries. It was founded on 5 May 1949 by 10 countries and is the political body of the 1950 European Convention on Human Rights (ECHR). Its official objectives are:

- to protect human rights, pluralist democracy and the rule of law;
- to promote awareness and encourage the development of Europe's cultural identity and diversity;
- to find common solutions to the challenges facing European society;
- to consolidate democratic stability in Europe by backing political, legislative and constitutional reform.[36]

The CoE is quite an ambitious institution, with activities in fields such as human rights and legal affairs, democracy and political affairs, international law and terrorism, social cohesion, education, culture and heritage, youth and sport.[37] Currently, it holds special campaigns in the following fields: "Speak-out against discrimination", "Europe against the death penalty", "Building a Europe for and with children", "Stop domestic violence", and "Dosta! Fight prejudice towards Roma".

The Venice Commission was set up in 1990 by the CoE. Its original task was to accompany the transition of Eastern European countries from socialist to liberal-democratic societies. This included the enactment of new constitutions, and the new establishment of constitutional courts (or comprehensive institutional reforms of existing constitutional courts). After the transition phase of the 1990s, the Commission was renamed "The European Commission for Democracy Through Law". It serves now as the Council of Europe's advisory body on constitutional matters, and it calls itself "an internationally recognised independent legal think-tank".[38] Its reach is larger than the CoE itself: All 47 Council of Europe member states are members of the Venice Commission; in addition, Kyrgyzstan joined the commission in 2004, Chile in 2005, the Republic of Korea in 2006, Morocco and Algeria in 2007, Israel and Tunisia in 2008, and Peru and Brazil in 2009. The Commission thus has 56 full members in all. Belarus is associate member, while Argentina, Canada, the Holy See, Japan, Kazakhstan, Mexico, the United States and Uruguay are observers. South Africa and Palestinian National Authority have a special co-operation status similar to that of the observers.

36 The current Council of Europe's political mandate was defined by the third Summit of Heads of State and Government, held in Warsaw in May 2005.

37 The website of the organisation, www.coe.int, contains detailed information about its activities.

38 Www.venice.coe.int/site/main/Presentation_E.asp.

The European Commission and OSCE/ODIHR participate in the plenary sessions of the Commission.

It works in four key areas: constitutional assistance, elections and referendums, co-operation with constitutional courts, and transnational studies, reports and seminars. The Commission is composed of "independent experts who have achieved eminence through their experience in democratic institutions or by their contribution to the enhancement of law and political science" (Article 2 of the revised Statute). The members are senior academics, particularly in the fields of constitutional or international law, supreme or constitutional court judges, or members of national parliaments. Acting on the Commission in their individual capacity, the members are appointed for four years by the participating countries.

The Venice Commission is buzzing with activities that revolve around constitutionalism. In 2002, it established the "Joint Council on Constitutional Justice". On the basis of Article 3 of the revised Statute of the Commission, this body now comprises the liaisons officers from constitutional courts and equivalent bodies. The institution of a presidency of the Joint Council, representing the constitutional courts and the Sub-commission on Constitutional Justice respectively, further underlines that the participating constitutional courts play a major role in this co-operation.

It is needless to say that the meetings under the wings of the Commission provide for a dissemination of constitutionalism in every respect.[39] The topics of its meetings and seminars range from single-country topics to the analysis of general constitutional principles and their application.[40]

3.2. *Networking*

The CoE organises a considerable part of networking activities in the field of constitutionalism, but this is not the only forum of such a kind. The courts themselves have organised regular meetings in the framework of the "Conference of European

39 The following selection of events represents the typical routine work of the Commission; they are taken from its website agenda:
- 18/06/2009 8th meeting of the Joint Council on Constitutional Justice (Tallinn);
- 10/11/2008 Seminar on the occasion of the 5th Plenary of the UACCC Scientific Symposium on "Fair Trial" (Saana);
- 30/10/2008 Colloquy on Constitutional Interpretation (Algiers);
- 25/10/2008 Seminar on "Models of Constitutional Jurisdiction" (Ramallah);
- 03/10/2008 XIII Yerevan International Conference on the Fundamental Constitutional Values and Public Practice (Yerevan);
- 01/09/2008 International Symposium on the "Separation of Powers and Adjudication in the 21st Century" and "Preparatory Meeting for the World Conference on Constitutional Justice" (Seoul).

40 For example, on 30 May 2007, it hosted the following event: "6e réunion du Conseil mixte sur la justice constitutionnelle – Mini-conférence sur 'Le principe de proportionnalité'".

Constitutional Courts" which was set up in 1972.[41] As of 2008, it had 39 members. The conference holds meetings about every three years; for example, the last (XIII and XIV) meetings took place in Nicosia/Cyprus in 2006, and in Vilnius/Lithuania in 2008.

Apart from these regular general meetings, all constitutional courts routinely visit each other, a practice which generates additional opportunities for exchanges about judicial review and constitutional adjudication.[42] This dense carpet of mutual visits also includes the major supra- and trans-national judicial actors in Europe, namely, the European Court of Human Rights and the European Court of Justice. What these numerous meetings and visits represent is not a "constitutionalism conspiracy", but a *practice of iteration* and dialogical development of constitutionalism. The relationships between national, supranational and transnational courts in Europe are not free from tensions; on the contrary, conflicts between the ECJ, on the one hand, and a number of European constitutional courts, on the other, are legendary.[43] The regular meetings and mutual visits of the constitutional courts, the ECJ, and the ECtHR may, therefore, also serve as arenas in which conflicts about judgments and disagreements about the interpretation of fundamental rights can be played out in the open (although not in public, as the meetings are not accessible to the general public, or to the press).

Other arenas for such debates are law reviews and legal journals. Constitutional court judges and judges of the ECJ and the ECtHR, and especially the Presidents of these institutions, regularly publish articles on the jurisprudence of their respective institutions. Present and former court presidents such as Jutta Limbach (German FCC), Luzius Wildhaber (ECtHR), and Vassilios Skouris (ECJ), to name a few, have written numerous interventions in the on-going consensual and conflictual discourse about the European constitutional order. These articles touch upon issues such as the migration of constitutional ideas, the function of the ECtHR and the ECJ, and the rising complexity of European fundamental rights adjudication. In addition, constitutional court justices explain their judgments in special fields, such as free speech, or use the forum of law journals to calm the waves after heated debates have erupted about certain judgments.[44]

41 Additional information can be found at: www.confcoconsteu.org/, a website which was established by the organizers of the XII meeting in 2002, and at www.lrkt.lt/conference3.html, established by the organizers of the XIV meeting.

42 According to the press releases website of the German FCC, for example, in July 2009 a delegation of the FCC visited the constitutional courts of Slovakia and the Czech Republic, in June 2009 a delegation of the Hungarian constitutional court visited the FCC in Karlsruhe, in May 2009 a delegation of the FCC visited the Austrian constitutional court, and so on: www.bverfg.de/presse.html.

43 The *Maastricht* decision of the German FCC has encouraged a number of other constitutional courts (of Italy and Spain, for example) to send out signals to the ECJ that they reserve themselves the right to declare EC/EU law unconstitutional. It is predictable that the 2009 decision on the *Treaty of Lisbon* (decision of 30 June 2009, Case no 2 BvE 2/08 and others) will have a similar effect as it contains the FCC's warning that it will strictly scrutinise the limits of the EU's competences, see www.bverfg.de/entscheidungen/es20090630_2bve000208en.html, para. 339–340.

44 W. Hoffmann-Riem, "Die Caroline II-Entscheidung des BVerfG- Ein Zwischenschritt bei der Konkretisierung des Kooperationsverhältnisses zwischen den verschiedenen betroffenen Gerichten",

3.3. *Academic Support*

A third, and closely connected, arena is legal academia. Legal research on supra- and trans-national constitutionalism has mushroomed in the last decades. Comparative law, once almost exclusively a domain of private law, has embraced constitutionalism, and more and more textbooks on comparative constitutional law have been published in recent years.[45] European and U.S. law departments have created centres and institutes which are dedicated to the study of supra- and trans-national constitutionalism and its institutional embodiments, the courts.[46] Their conferences and workshops provide for a proliferation and dissemination of the constitutionalism discourse. For example, The Hague Institute for the Internationalisation of Law (HiiL)[47] initialised a conference in 2008 with the title "Law of the Future – The Changing Role of Highest Courts in an Internationalising World", in which the patterns and processes of global constitutionalism were analysed from many different angles.

It is clear that these activities are based upon a consensus about the usefulness and meaningfulness of constitutional dialogues, even if fundamental differences in the conceptualisation and in theoretical approaches remain. Moreover, these parallel activities result in the establishment of a distinct knowledge network, a *new discursive world* in which the actors confirm and re-confirm their mutual understanding and interpretation of the "reality", of legal texts, and of legal principles alike.

These trends are echoed by observations from an international law perspective: while the influence of the International Court of Justice seems to vanish in the face of an ever-growing proliferation of courts and court-like institutions within self-contained regimes such as the WTO or the UNCLOS,[48] the internal balances within international law are changing, too. Human rights law, which used to be just one of many sub-categories of international law, has been converted in recent decades into a different legal material, an ever denser web of texts and institutions; in short, it has moved from contractual consent to a constitution of a sort. Some scholars are already working on the establishment of a

(2009) 62 *Neue Juristische Wochenschrift*, pp. 20–26. The title hints at the dispute between the German FCC and the ECtHR in the *von Hannover* case (Caroline von Monaco).

45 One example is Norman Dorsen, Michel Rosenfeld, Andras Sájo and Susanne Baer, *Comparative Constitutionalism*, (St. Paul: West Publishing, 2003).

46 A non-representative enumeration includes: the European University Institute in Florence (www.eui.eu) as a unique research institution; the Centre for International Courts and Tribunals at the University College London; the Global Law School at New York University; the Yale Global Constitutionalism Seminar, and many others.

47 Www.hiil.org/.

48 For a definition of "self-contained regimes" and a discussion about the phenomenon of fragmentation in international law, see "Fragmentation of International Law: Difficulties Arising From the Diversification and Expansion of International Law", Report of the Study Group of the International Law Commission, A/CN.4/L.702, 18 July 2006.

"World Court for Human Rights".[49] This is quite an ambitious project, given the fact that domestic and international human rights courts (constitutional courts, the ECtHR, the Inter-American Court of Human Rights) all demand the exhaustion of domestic remedies before access will be granted. If the World Court for Human Rights applies this principle, claimants will have to have a robust health and a persistent character in order to survive the procedures. As human rights cases have often already toured for ten to fifteen years through the national courts before they arrive at international tribunals such as the ECtHR, and because the proceedings before these institutions tend to last another three to five years, pushing a case to the World Court will become a life-long task. Legal history tells us that such a kind of mega-institution will be overburdened, and most probably become insignificant or ineffective over time.[50] This pessimistic outlook notwithstanding, the mere fact that such a court is on the agenda shows the eminent influence of the constitutionalism discourse.

4. European Constitutionalism: From Borrowing and Lending to Hierarchisation?

Even if a World Court for Human Rights is still far away, regional entities have already moved into the direction of supra- and trans-national constitutional adjudication. The most advanced system is based in Europe: European Constitutionalism, which was initialised by the U.S. after the Second World War, and taken up by the Council of Europe, is nowadays already two steps ahead of the U.S. and its nervous discussion about transnational references in judgments: The European Union has established a superior legal order *vis-à-vis* its Member States, and the European Court of Human Rights has evolved into a very busy and active decision-making machinery in the field of human rights interpretation. Both developments touch upon the nerve of domestic constitutional orders: They call the role and position of constitutional courts as the "guardians" of the

49 Research on the project of a World Court for Human Rights is financed by the "Swiss Initiative to Commemorate the 60th Anniversary of the Universal Declaration of Human Rights", see www.udhr60.ch/research.html. Two research projects, one led by M. Scheinin (see www.udhr60.ch/report/hrCourt_scheinin.pdf) and the other led by M. Nowak and J. Kozma (see www.udhr60.ch/report/hrCourt-Nowak0609.pdf) are already working on the topic.

50 A fitting example is the *Reichskammergericht*, the Imperial Chamber Court in Wetzlar. The Holy Roman Empire of the German Nation had established this institution in order to settle legal disputes within the Empire on a steadier basis. Its jurisdiction changed through the centuries, but most of the times comprised at least Germany, Belgium, Austria, Hungary, Slovenia, and parts of France and Italy. Access was granted also to individuals (subordinates, "*Unterthanen*"), and not only to members of the aristocratic élite. The *Reichskammergerichtsordnung*, the procedural order of the Court, even opened the appeals procedure for "*arme partheien*", poor parties, who were granted legal aid in case they could not afford a lawyer. During the 300 years of its existence (from 1495 until 1806), about 80,000 appeals reached the *Reichskammergericht*. It was, however, also notorious for its sluggishness: the proceedings could last decades, and some of them lasted longer than a century. For its role in the development of a rule of law/*Rechtsstaat* concept, see Bernhard Diestelkamp, *Reichskammergericht und Rechtsstaatsgedanke. Die Kameraljudikatur gegen die Kabinettsjustiz*, (Heidelberg: C.F. Müller, 1994).

respective national constitutional order radically into question, and they challenge the interpretative monopoly of the courts.

Ever since the 1993 *Maastricht* judgment of the German Federal Constitutional Court (FCC), a nervous dialogue has been initiated across Europe, about constitutionalism and democracy, about the synchronicity of constitutional ideas, and about the relationship between the EU Member States' constitutions and the EU "constitutional" structure. The originally bipolar structure of this judicial dialogue – if we reduce it to, for example, the relationship between the German FCC, the French *Conseil Constitutionnel*, the Italian *Corte Constituzionale*, and the ECJ, respectively – has turned into a multipolar structure in recent years, with the ECJ, and most recently the ECtHR, becoming increasingly important players in the field of constitutional law. In this multipolar context, explicit or implicit comparative constitutional borrowing is an inevitable consequence.

However, as lawyers and judges across Europe learn more and more to use and apply the tools of referring to comparative constitutional arguments, new questions will arise: will the traditional constitutional structures that have grown in the European nation states fall victim to the ECJ and the ECtHR jurisprudence? And from a perspective that is informed less by constitutional nationalism but more by democratic constitutionalism, one might ask: if there is such a thing as the "Common Core of European Constitutional Law in the Making", does this leave any room for a thorough discussion of contested constitutional concepts such as the welfare state, public order, or "hard" cases in fundamental rights law? And finally, which methodology – beyond cherry-picking – is appropriate for the complex task of containing tendencies of "judicial imperialism"?

Many judicial reactions to the ever-growing complexity of European constitutionalism are characterised by *tactics of avoidance*: instead of creating and staging open conflicts, constitutional courts tend to fire warning shots at the ECtHR and the ECJ but stop short of an open rift. Judges of national courts as well as ECJ judges insist upon a co-operative relationship between the ECJ and national constitutional courts. These friendly gestures, however, cannot hide a growing uneasiness about a perceived erratic course of the ECJ[51] and the undecided function of the ECtHR as a supreme or constitutional court, an international instrument, or both.[52]

51 See, for example, the critique of Ch. Schmid (Chapter 15 in this volume).

52 For a detailed analysis, see A. Cebada Romero and R. Nickel, "El Tribunal Europeo de Derechos Humanos en una Europa Asimétrica: ¿Hacia el Pluralismo Constitutional?", in: Pablo Antonio Fernández Sanchez (ed.), *La obra jurídica del Consejo de Europa (en commemoración del 60 aniversario del Consejo de Europa)*, Sevilla: Ediciones Gandulfo, 2010, p. 791–820.

Both the ECJ and the ECtHR have been heavily criticised in recent times for their "intrusive"[53] and "too detailed"[54] judgments. For example, the decision of the ECJ in the *Mangold* case and the decision of the ECtHR in the *von Hannover* case have been greeted, almost unanimously, with severe criticism, and have caused even alarmist and angry comments in Germany.[55] The *Taxquet* decision of the ECtHR on jury trials not only stirred emotions in Belgium, from where the case originated, but also in Norway, where the criminal court system shows similar features and where the fear is rising that the country will have to adopt a completely new system of criminal procedure prescribed by the ECtHR.[56]

European constitutionalism is messy. The function of its judicial actors is all but clear: Is the ECJ the Supreme Court *and* the constitutional court of the EU? Is the ECtHR the constitutional court of the EU *and* of its Member States? Does an EU Member State like Germany or Spain now have *three* constitutional courts (i.e., courts that define the contents and range of fundamental rights) instead of one? Are the hierarchies established in one legal order (for example, the EU) binding upon other legal orders (for example, those of Germany or Spain), and, if so, to what extent? The latter question will most certainly be the subject of lively discussions in the years to come.[57] "Conflict born of diversity will continue to characterise the process of European integration",[58] and,

53 Roman Herzog, the former German President, and former President of the Federal Constitutional Court as well as President of the Convention which drew up the EU Charter of Fundamental Rights, demanded "Stop the ECJ" in an article written for the *Frankfurter Allgemeine Zeitung*. Herzog found "adventurous legal constructs" in the judgments of the ECJ, and asked the FCC to take up again its watchdog function against "intrusions" of the ECJ: "Stoppt den EuGH", *FAZ*, 08 September 2008. A counter-critique by Lenz lists all cases mentioned by Herzog and claims that Herzog does not accurately restate the facts and the reasoning of the ECJ: C.O. Lenz, "Anmerkungen zu den Fällen aus dem Aufsatz von Prof. Herzog 'Stoppt den Europäischen Gerichtshof' in der FAZ vom 8.9.2008", Walter Hallstein Institut, *WHI – Paper* 1/09, www.whi-berlin.de/documents/whi-paper0109.pdf.

54 Lord Hoffmann, one of the most prominent UK law lords, has publicly criticised the ECHR and its jurisprudence as "inconsistent", that the court has "assumed power to legislate", and that its decisions are too intrusive: "It has been unable to resist the temptation to aggrandise its jurisdiction and to impose uniform rules on Member States. It considers itself the equivalent of the Supreme Court of the United States, laying down a federal law of Europe". Lord Hoffmann, "The Universality of Human Rights", Judicial Studies Board Annual Lecture, London, 19 March 2009, available at: www.jsboard.co.uk/downloads/Hoffmann_2009_JSB_Annual_Lecture_Universality_of_Human_Rights.doc, p. 14 and 21. See, also, the (critical) comment by Afua Hirsch: "Judges: can't live with 'em...", *The Guardian*, 06 April 2009, available at: www.guardian.co.uk/commentisfree/libertycentral/2009/apr/06/law-eu.

55 See Herzog (note 53 *supra*). For an overview, see J. Wieland, "Der EuGH im Spannungsverhältnis zwischen Rechtsanwendung und Rechtsgestaltung", in: (2009) 62 *Neue Juristische Wochenschrift*, pp. 1841–1845.

56 I.L. Backer, "Definition and Development of Human Rights in the International Context and Popular Sovereignty – A Comment", presented at the UNIDEM Seminar Frankfurt am Main, 15–16 May 2009, p. 8, on file with author.

57 The German FCC judgment on the *Treaty of Lisbon* (note 43 *supra*) has laid the groundwork for a renewed discussion about the *constitutional* limits of European integration, and it is quite predictable that other constitutional courts will follow suit.

58 Ch. Joerges, in this volume, Chapter 18, sub Part IV.1.

one may add, also the development of supra- and trans-national constitutionalism. What remains, however, is the fact that all of these courts are involved in the discoursive definition and re-definition of fundamental rights as "higher law".

5. Casework: The Practice of European Constitutionalism

Verba docent, exempla trahunt: The practice of European Constitutionalism is most visible in cases in which two legal orders contain the same or similar legal guarantees, and in cases in which it is unclear whether a fundamental right expressly granted in one order is also part of the second order. In the following, I will present and discuss two representative cases in which such a *doublement* played a decisive role.

5.1. The Omega Case (European Court of Justice)

Does the EU legal order contain an individual right to human dignity, or a principle of human dignity? This was one of the leading questions in the *Omega* case.[59] The Omega Company wanted to open an amusement centre in which customers were invited to play "Gotcha", an indoor game in which the participants shoot each other with weapons filled with ink bullets. The goal of the game is to hit the other players, and to bring them down. The city of Bonn in Germany issued an order prohibiting the game, arguing that the game threatened to violate the *ordre publique* (*Öffentliche Ordnung*) of the Federal Republic because it simulates acts of homicide, and that the prohibition order was necessary for the protection of human dignity, which is enshrined in Article 1 ch. 1 of the *Grundgesetz* (basic law). The case involved companies from other EU Member States, and was finally referred to the European Court of Justice. According to *ex*-Article 6.2 of the Treaty on European Union (now Article 6.3 TEU), the Union:

> [S]hall respect fundamental rights, as guaranteed by the European Convention for the Protection of Human Rights and Fundamental Freedoms signed in Rome on 4 November 1950 and as they result from the constitutional traditions common to the Member States, as general principles of Community law.

Article 6.2 TEU, therefore, does *not* contain a collection of constitutional rights; it refers to the European Convention and the "constitutional traditions common to the Member States", without any further explanation on how to find and extrapolate these common constitutional traditions. The ECJ held that the EU legal order does contain "respect for human dignity as a general principle of law". The following are the key paragraphs of this decision:

> 32. In this case, the competent authorities took the view that the activity concerned by the prohibition order was a threat to public policy by reason of the fact that, in accordance with the conception prevailing in public opinion, the commercial exploitation of games involving

59 ECJ, Case C-36/02, judgment of 14 October 2004.

the simulated killing of human beings infringed a fundamental value enshrined in the national constitution, namely human dignity. According to the Bundesverwaltungsgericht, the national courts which heard the case shared and confirmed the conception of the requirements for protecting human dignity on which the contested order is based, that conception therefore having to be regarded as in accordance with the stipulations of the German Basic Law.

33. It should be recalled in that context that, according to settled case-law, fundamental rights form an integral part of the general principles of law the observance of which the Court ensures, and that, for that purpose, the Court draws inspiration from the constitutional traditions common to the Member States and from the guidelines supplied by international treaties for the protection of human rights on which the Member States have collaborated or to which they are signatories. The European Convention on Human Rights and Fundamental Freedoms has special significance in that respect [...].

34. As the Advocate General argues in paragraphs 82 to 91 of her Opinion, the Community legal order undeniably strives to ensure respect for human dignity as a general principle of law. There can therefore be no doubt that the objective of protecting human dignity is compatible with Community law, it being immaterial in that respect that, in Germany, the principle of respect for human dignity has a particular status as an independent fundamental right.

35. Since both the Community and its Member States are required to respect fundamental rights, the protection of those rights is a legitimate interest which, in principle, justifies a restriction of the obligations imposed by Community law, even under a fundamental freedom guaranteed by the Treaty such as the freedom to provide services (see, in relation to the free movement of goods, Schmidberger, paragraph 74).

36. However, measures which restrict the freedom to provide services may be justified on public policy grounds only if they are necessary for the protection of the interests which they are intended to guarantee and only in so far as those objectives cannot be attained by less restrictive measures (see, in relation to the free movement of capital, Église de Scientologie, paragraph 18).

37. It is not indispensable in that respect for the restrictive measure issued by the authorities of a Member State to correspond to a conception shared by all Member States as regards the precise way in which the fundamental right or legitimate interest in question is to be protected. Although, in paragraph 60 of Schindler, the Court referred to moral, religious or cultural considerations which lead all Member States to make the organisation of lotteries and other games with money subject to restrictions, it was not its intention, by mentioning that common conception, to formulate a general criterion for assessing the proportionality of any national measure which restricts the exercise of an economic activity.

> 38. On the contrary, as is apparent from well-established case-law subsequent to Schindler, the need for, and proportionality of, the provisions adopted are not excluded merely because one Member State has chosen a system of protection different from that adopted by another State [...].

For these reasons, the Court confirmed the compatibility of the decisions of the German courts and the prohibition order of the City of Bonn with Community law. On the surface, this judgment seems to represents a wise decision for constitutional pluralism: According to the ECJ, there is no need for EU-wide common standards of judicial review regarding measures that are justified by reference to the protection of fundamental rights, such as human dignity. This allows for different standards of protection in the Member States; local knowledge and "odd details" of local constitutionalism are not disregarded, and forceful legal integration by means of a constitutionalism by stealth is avoided. On a second look, however, the decision adds another piece to the puzzle of European Constitutionalism. It states that the concept of human dignity – and its protection – represents a principle of European law in the sense of Article 6.2 TEU. It arrives at this conclusion without any research into the constitutional traditions common to the Member States – and such an inquiry, had it been made, would have revealed that there is no such "common" tradition. Not all EU Member State constitutions contain a legal concept of human dignity which gurarantees it *as an individual right*, and to some – such as the UK – such a concept is completely alien to the legal system. Additionally, only few Member States would interpret the protection of human dignity in a way that it could also be used *against* its bearers (in the *Omega* case, the players of Gotcha). In the end, the ECJ created a "new" common constitutional concept in the name of constitutional pluralism.

5.2. The Case Von Hannover v Germany (European Court of Human Rights)

Another example for a creeping constitutionalisation of legal orders can be found in the *Von Hannover* v *Germany* decision of the European Court of Human Rights (ECtHR).[60] This decision re-defined – and strained – the relationship between the German constitutional court and the ECtHR.

The European Convention on Human Rights had, for a long time, only been an additional instrument of human rights protection in Germany (as in most of its European Member States). Due to the comprehensive guarantees of basic rights in the *Grundgesetz* from 1949 and the active role of the FCC in the implementation of these rights in the German legal order, the 1950 Convention had a very limited significance in Germany. Only since the intensifying of the European integration in the 1990s and the introduction of a "new" ECtHR through Protocol 11 to the Convention has it gained increasing importance in the national context. Three particular reasons can be identified for this development: access to the ECtHR is much easier now than it was before 1998 when admissibility applications were first considered by the European Commission on

60 Case of *Von Hannover* v *Germany*, application no. 59320/00, judgment of 24 June 2004.

Human Rights; a public relations offensive after 1998 increased awareness about the ECtHR within the populations of the Member States; and finally, the number of contracting states of the Council of Europe has risen dramatically, so that nowadays 47 countries have signed the Convention, and the ECtHR's 47 judges have to deal with tens of thousands of applications. According to recent statistical data, the backlog of cases is impressive: on 1 January 2010, almost 120,000 applications were pending before a decision body.[61] Due to the large number of judgments delivered, the Court even had to establish an internal clearing-house in order to keep track of its own jurisprudence.

The *Von Hannover* judgment is remarkable because it reviews[62] a "hard case" in the jurisprudence of the German FCC – and it rejects the FCC's wider concept of freedom of the press in favour of the right to privacy of VIPs. The case dealt with the publication of secretly shot photos, all of them showing Caroline von Hannover, Princess of Monaco, in a variety of situations. Both courts had to balance the rights involved. The German FCC declined to differentiate between "useful" and "useless" information delivered by the press, and it also rejected the idea that pure entertainment in the tabloid press is not part of the general public and is not, therefore, protected by the freedom of the press.[63] In contrast to this, the ECtHR demands that photos and/or articles in the press need to contribute to a debate of general interest in order to survive the breach-of-privacy test:

> 63. The Court considers that a fundamental distinction needs to be made between reporting facts – even controversial ones – capable of contributing to a debate in a democratic society relating to politicians in the exercise of their functions, for example, and reporting details of the private life of an individual who, moreover, as in this case, does not exercise official functions. While in the former case the press exercises its vital role of 'watchdog' in a democracy by contributing to 'impart[ing] information and ideas on matters of public interest' [...], it does not do so in the latter case.

Following a stricter concept of the freedom of the press, as it is established, for example, in France, the ECtHR held that no watchdog function had been exercised in the case before it,[64] and it declared that there had been a violation of Article 8 of the Convention.

61 For more detailed information, see the report "50 years of activity", available on the Court's website: www.echr.coe.int.

62 Technically, however, the ECtHR cannot "review" national law or national decision – it can only state a violation of convention rights and grant a just compensation, see Articles 41 and 46 of the Convention.

63 See paragraphs 97–98 of the first decision in this matter which laid the constitutional ground for later decisions: FCC, judgment of 15 December 1999, Case no. 1 BvR 653/96, available in German at: www.bverfg.de/entscheidungen/rs19991215_1bvr065396.html. The second decision was subject of the ECHR decision: FCC, judgment of 26 April 2001, case no. 1 BvR 758/97 *et al.* An English translation can be found at: www.bverfg.de/entscheidungen/rk20010426_1bvr075897en.html.

64 "The Court considers that the publication of the photos and articles in question, the sole purpose of which was to satisfy the curiosity of a particular readership regarding the details of the applicant's private life, cannot be deemed to contribute to any debate of general interest to society despite the applicant being known to the public [...]", paragraph 65 of the judgment.

With this decision, it materially re-defined the content of the right to freedom of the press for all 47 member states of the convention.

The decision is an example of conflicting conceptual overlap, of a *dedoublement*: both the German constitution and the Convention contain a right to privacy and a guarantee of the freedom of the press. The obvious question in such a context – Who is the final arbiter? – can be answered easily: formally, the ECtHR can only state a violation of convention rights and grant a just compensation, see Articles 41 and 46 of the Convention, but it cannot overturn a domestic court decision. The legal situation, however, is far more complex than this. According to the jurisprudence of the FCC, courts are generally obliged to take the jurisprudence of the ECtHR into account (whereby the term "generally" needed closer definition), and if a court disregards the reasoning of the ECtHR, the claimant can successfully lodge a constitutional complaint: the neglect of ECtHR decisions potentially constitutes, in itself, a violation of the *Rechtsstaat*/rule of law principle.[65] In the *Von Hannover* case, later decisions both of the *Bundesgerichtshof* (Federal Court of Justice) and the FCC integrated the ECtHR position into their judgments, although not without adding certain nuances to their interpretation of the right to freedom of the press.

The *Von Hannover* decisions, whose twists and turns cannot be fully explored here, confirm the thesis of an on-going constitutional discourse about the contents and limits of fundamental rights. Domestic courts, and constitutional courts, increasingly apply the art of distinction, well-known to common law countries, in order to avoid head-on collisions with the ECtHR. This *tactic of avoidance* represents a soft answer to the potential ambitions of the ECtHR to become *the* constitutional court of Europe.

6. Constitutional Conflicts Law

What is left of the fear of a transnational constitutional juristocracy? Courts, it seems, are inevitably the central actors in the new transnational global society, and they inevitably foster a constitutionalisation of its legal order(s). The results are multiple legal regimes – and multiple regime-collisions of a growing complexity – with courts as gateways and interfaces. The European Union and the European Convention on Human Rights are but two of many such regimes that have left the traditional forms and

65 This jurisprudence was expressly confirmed in the infamous *Görgülü* case, available in English at: www.bverfg.de/entscheidungen/rs20041014_2bvr148104en.html (judgment of 14 October 2004, case no. 2 BvR 1481/04). Mr Görgülü had successfully lodged a complaint according to Article 34 of the European Convention. The lower court ignored the decision of the ECtHR in favour of Mr Görgülü, and the FCC delivered its judgment of 14 October 2004. In the following time, the lower court again ignored the ECHR jurisprudence, which led to another – successful – constitutional complaint: www.bverfg.de/entscheidungen/rk20050405_1bvr166404.html. The lower court still ignored the judgments of the ECtHR and the FCC. In its decision on the third – successful – constitutional complaint of Mr Görgülü the FCC plainly accused the lower court of arbitrariness. Criminal proceedings against the judges of the lower court are pending.

procedures of traditional international law far behind. The WTO panels and its Appellate Body, the International Criminal Court, the dispute settlement system of NAFTA, the new MERCOSUR court, the International Court on the Laws of the Sea – all these judicative bodies constantly deliver decisions on conflicting legal orders, and this list of institutions can easily be prolonged.

These institutions open up a common legal space, and – at least in Europe – they also open up a common constitutional space. This space, however, is characterised by diverse and overlapping constitutional regimes with diverse legal traditions and legal-political preferences. This diversity even appears within a single framework such as the European Convention of Human Rights. In addition, and for lack of clearly-defined hierarchies, even the instances of Comparative Constitutional Borrowing, and the constant iterations of constitutionalism as such, are too thin to produce a uniform, material "constitution", a single common core of European constitutionalism. Details matter, and they resist uniformity.

Constitutionalism nonetheless provides a meaningful frame of reference. The democratic deficit of trans- and supranational constitutionalism, however, is obvious: in the national arena, constitutional courts are exposed to protest and criticism by the press and the general public at large. The courts are *embedded* in a conflictual, legal-political discourse about the contents and the limits of fundamental rights. No such "thick" public exists on the global level, and not even on the European level can we find a comparable aggregation of public oversight and political control. Thus, as long as there are no easy solutions for the democracy problem at hand, constitutionalism itself has to be created and formed in a way that is conscious of these deficits.

Constitutional authoritarianism is clearly not the answer to the problem of judicial disembeddedness, nor is it legal pluralism. While concepts of legal pluralism[66] have aptly described and embraced the existence of such a variety of legal orders, their cognitive and explanatory force is rather limited as they cannot explain how conflicts between different legal orders can be properly defined, contextualised, and finally solved (or avoided). A "constitutional conflicts law" needs a more structured and procedural approach towards the problem of unity (of the fundamental ideas of a legal order) and diversity (of their concrete definition and application).

The varieties of European constitutionalism in the European constitutional laboratory may provide some answers. The ECHR, for example, is constantly in a situation in which it needs to define the "European Public Order" embodied in the European Convention on Human Rights, while, at the same time, it has to pay its tribute to the national constitutional orders of the Member States. This constellation is tempting for a court with a tendency for judicial activism, and the court has, more than once in recent times,

66 For an overview, see N. Walker, "The Idea of Constitutional Pluralism", in: (2002) 65 *Modern Law Review*, pp. 317–359.

been accused of overstepping its territory. In its *Bosphorus*[67] decision, however, the ECtHR went down a different path: it had to define its role *vis-à-vis* the EC/EU legal order, and it came up with a distinctive and creative solution. It stated that the EC/EU legal order provides for a sufficient degree of legal protection, and that a complainant has to show that, in his or her case, this general level of protection has not been met. This hurdle, although not as steep as the *Solange II* admissibility hurdle set up by the German FCC in relation to constitutional oversight over EC/EU law,[68] represents another possible path for a settlement of conflicting constitutional orders: mutual recognition as the rule, stricter scrutiny as the exception.

Such a mechanism, if further developed and cautiously applied, would combine respect for the legal traditions which have grown over long periods of time, and for local preferences and "odd details" with a necessary sense of the promises of constitutionalism. It may serve as one element of a future constitutional conflicts law.

67 ECtHR, *Bosphorus Hava Yolları* v. *Ireland*, Application no. 45036/98, judgment of 30 June 2005, www.echr.coe.int/echr/en/hudoc.

68 See BVerfGE 73, 339 (1986), *Solange II*: Constitutional complaints that are based upon a claim for the unconstitutionality of EC/EU law are inadmissible unless the complainant shows in a detailed analysis that the *general* level of human rights protection within the EU has sunk below the *general* level of protection guaranteed by the German constitution. This Herculean task that has not been met in the last 23 years since the judgment was handed down in 1986. – The latest judgment in EU matters, the *Treaty of Lisbon* decision (note 43 *supra*) expressly allows for complaints directed at EU legal acts which are *ultra vires*, but it has again confirmed the *Solange II* rationale with regard to constitutional rights protection.

Florian Rödl

CHAPTER 13. REGIME-COLLISIONS, PROCEDURALISED CONFLICT OF LAWS AND THE UNITY OF THE LAW: ON THE FORM OF CONSTITUTIONALISM BEYOND THE STATE

1. The "Conflict of Laws" Approach in Constitutionalism Beyond the State

"Constitutionalism" has become one of the leading catchwords in legal theory. This is particularly true for reflections on processes of condensed juridification beyond the state.[1] It seems common ground now that the concept of constitution is not necessarily bound to the concept of state.[2] In other words, entities which are not states, but are condensed contractual regimes, are said to be able to have constitutions or may be constitutionalised. These entities are usually located at supra-state level and comprise a plurality of states, such as the United Nations, the European Union, or the World Trade Organisation.[3] For many observers, this dissolution of the constitution from the state does not change much in the understanding of the concept of a constitution. Though not openly acknowledged, the underlying idea is that a constitution beyond the state is something quite similar to a state constitution; the only difference being the very fact that the entity with which the concept is linked is not a state. In particular, a constitution

1 See, for example, the two collections by M. Loughlin and N. Walker (eds), *The Paradox of Constitutionalism: Constituent Power and Constitutional Form*, (Oxford: Oxford University Press, 2007); Ch. Joerges and E.-U. Petersmann (eds), *Constitutionalism, Multilevel Trade Governance and Social Regulation*, (Oxford: Hart Publishing, 2006).

2 See the paradigmatic titles of publications by A. von Bogdandy and J. Bast, *Principles of European Constitutional Law*, (Oxford: Hart Publishing, 2007); Nicolaos Tsagourias, *Transnational Constitutionalism: European and international models*, (Cambridge: Cambridge University Press, 2007); H. Eberhard *et al.*, *Reflexionen zum Internationalen Verfassungsrecht*, (Vienna: WUV-Univ.-Verlag, 2005).

3 B. Fassbender, "The United Nations Charter as the Constitution of the International Community", in: (1998) 36 *Columbia Journal of Transnational Law*, pp. 529–620; J.H.H. Weiler and M. Wind (eds), *European Constitutionalism Beyond the State*, (Cambridge: Cambridge University Press, 2003); E.-U, Petersmann, "Constitutionalism and WTO Law", in: D.L.M. Kennedy and J.D. Southwick (eds), *The Political Economy of International Trade Law*, (Cambridge: Cambridge University Press, 2002), pp. 32–67.

beyond the state also establishes a vertical hierarchy of legal norms, which subordinates the law of the state under the newly established supra-national constitutional law.

Against this backdrop, the main focus in research is on how this vertical hierarchy is to be enforced. Only in rare cases, the focus is on how the basic principles enshrined in a modern state's constitution, i.e., rule of law, democracy, solidarity can be transformed or preserved under the new circumstances.[4] In contrast to this kind of – certainly widely differentiated – mainstream theory on constitutionalism beyond the state, there exists a different approach. It is the "conflict of laws" approach. This approach holds that to understand constitutionalism beyond the state in firm analogy to state constitutions is misleading. Instead, constitutionalisation beyond the state is a process of generating legal norms which are best understood against the backdrop of the legal discipline of conflict of laws. The proper discipline of conflict of laws tackles the problem of collisions of national legal orders, in which each strives for the application of its own particular norms to a given transnational legal relation. Hence, conflict of laws is a discipline which could not, and, indeed, did not start right away with an idea of vertical hierarchy. On the contrary, the problem of conflict of laws is, from its outset, a collision of legal norms of, by definition, the *same* status and dignity. Corresponding to this, the main focus of the conflict of laws approach to constitutionalism beyond the state is concerned not with the establishing, justifying and enforcing vertical hierarchies, but with horizontal, diagonal and heterarchical relations between different national, supranational and functional legal orders.

Gunter Teubner and Andreas Fischer-Lescano, on the one hand, and Christian Joerges, on the other, are important representatives of the conflict of laws approach. To present the two approaches by their labels, Teubner and Fischer-Lescano call for a "law of regime collisions",[5] while Joerges postulates a "proceduralised law of conflict of laws".[6]

4 Ph. Allot, *Towards the International Rule of Law*, (London: Cameron May, 2007); R. Bellamy, *Constitutionalism and Democracy*, (Aldershot *et al.*: Ashgate, 2006); J. Habermas, "The Post-national Constellation and the Future of Democracy", in: *ibid.*, *The Post-national Constellation*, (Cambridge MA: MIT Press, 2001); E.O. Eriksen, Ch. Joerges and F. Rödl (eds), *Law, Democracy and Solidarity in a Post-national Union*, (London – New York: Routledge, 2008).

5 A. Fischer-Lescano and G. Teubner, *Regime-Kollisionen. Zur Fragmentierung des globalen Rechts*, (Frankfurt aM: Suhrkamp Verlag, 2006); *ibid.*, "Regime-Collisions: The Vain Search for Legal Unity in the Fragmentation of Global Law", (2004) 25 *Michigan Journal of International Law*,pp. 999–1045.

6 See, in particular, Ch. Joerges, "The Challenges of Europeanization in the Realm of Private Law: A Plea for a New Legal Discipline", in: (2005) 24 *Duke Journal of Comparative and International Law*, pp. 149–196; *ibid.*, "Constitutionalism in Postnational Constellations: Contrasting Social Regulation in the EU and in the WTO", in: Ch. Joerges and E.-U. Petersmann (eds), *Constitutionalism, Multilevel Trade Governance and Social Regulation*, (Oxford: Hart Publishing, 2006), pp. 491–527; *ibid.*, "Rethinking European Law's Supremacy: A Plea for a Supranational Conflict of Laws", in: B. Kohler-Koch and B. Rittberger (eds), *Debating the Democratic Legitimacy of the European Union*, (Lanham MD: Rowman and Littlefield, 2007), pp. 311–327.

This chapter will attempt to examine the two positions on a fundamental issue, namely, the issue of the unity of the law. For a long time, the problem of the unity of the law has functioned as a dividing line in the theory of conflict of laws.[7] The hegemonic position in scholarship has moved from affirmation (*universalism*) to the rejection (*particularism*) of this very idea of the unity of the law. But there are doubts that the latter can continue to prevail in the era of globalisation which is accompanied by an increase and a consolidation of transnational law-mediated economic and social interaction.[8] Hence, it seems worthwhile to examine more closely whether the new conflict of laws-approaches of Teubner and Fischer-Lescano, and of Joerges draw from the *universalist* or from the *particularist* heritage of conflict of laws-theory.

2. Universalism versus Particularism in Private International Law Theory

Questions of form are always fundamental questions.[9] The question of whether a conception of conflict of laws represents a *universalist* or a *particularist* approach refers to the *form* of (a conception of) conflict of laws. According to the *universalist* approach, conflict of laws is to be understood as a universal and uniform law which is common to all legal orders which are co-ordinated under the conflict rules provided. The *particularist* approach, in contrast, conceives conflict of law-rules as an intrinsic part of one of the concurring legal orders; there are as many sets of conflict rules as there are legal orders. It is only accidentally that these sets of conflict rules have the same content; they are, hence, essentially different. According to the *particularist* approach, each legal order provides comprehensive co-ordination for all legal orders, but in a different way.

While the *universalist* form was the guiding idea in classical thinking about conflicts of laws in the Nineteenth century, it is supported only by very few today. The form of conflict of laws which prevails both in theory and doctrine today (and which operates tellingly more and more as "private international law") is, in turn, strongly *particularist*.

2.1. Classical and Modern Universalism

Classical universalism in conflict of laws is strongly linked with the name and writing of Friedrich Carl von Savigny.[10] It was Savigny who propagated forcefully that conflict rules, which determine the national legal rules to apply to a transnational private legal

7 A. Mills, "The Private History of International Law", in: (2006) 55 *International and Comparative Law Quarterly*, pp. 1–50.

8 On this, see F. Rödl, Weltbürgerliches Kollisionsrecht. Über die Form des Kollisionsrechts und seine Gestalt im Recht der Europäischen Union, Ph.D-thesis, Florence, 2008; G. Scherer, Das Internationale Privatrecht als globales System, Ph.D-thesis, Berlin, 2005, available at: http://edoc.hu-berlin.de/dissertationen/scherer-gabriele-2005-10-24/PDF/Scherer.pdf.

9 E. Weinrib, *The Idea of Private Law* (Cambridge MA – London: Harvard University Press, 1995), p. 25 *et seq.*

10 F.C. v. Savigny, *System des heutigen römischen Rechts*, Vol. 8 (1849), (reprint: Aalen: Scientia, 1981).

relationship, had to be the same for, and common to, all nations. He formulated a guiding principle, which sounded like a version of Kant's categorical imperative, for the searching of appropriate conflict rules for transnational legal relationships:

> we have here always to ask ourselves whether such a rule is likely to be suited for incorporation into this law [on conflicts of local laws, F.R.] which is common to all nations."[11]

Savigny's claim for the unity of the law of conflict of laws was conceptually connected with a second universalism. This was the idea of the universality of private legal status and relationship. Savigny thought that the canon of private legal status and relationships, i.e., capacity and corporation, contractual and non-contractual obligations, property, family, succession, was not only empirically the same in all legal orders, but also, more importantly, that the national rules constituting these private legal status and relationships might differ in content but did not change their common essence. The respective essence of a private legal status or relationships remained the same, notwithstanding the particular legal and social circumstances in which they were embedded, and notwithstanding which particular state was involved in the transnational case.[12] Upon the basis of this claim of a ubiquitous essence of private legal status and relationships, Savigny could conclude that the conflict rule to determine the law applicable to a transnational legal relationship, which is to be common to *all* nations, was to be found by way of close scrutiny of this very essence of the legal relationship. This led him to the famous methodological metaphor, cited to this day, that, in order to find the proper national legal order to be applied to a transnational private legal relationship, one had to look for the spatial "seat of a private legal relationship" (*Sitz des Rechtsverhältnisses*).[13] In other words, each private legal status or relationship has a spatial "seat" in the world, which connects the legal relationship with a national legal order; for example, the "seat" of legal capacity is the person's domicile, which leads to the application of the legal order of the nation in which the domicile is located, or, to give another example, the "seat" of a contract is its place of performance leading to that nation's legal order where the place of performance is located. The seat of status or relationship must not be determined by reflecting on societal circumstances, but by inspection of the pure status or relationship as it is given in its essence. Hence, Savigny's classical universalism resulted in a small number of conflict rules which connected each private legal relation with the legal order of a certain state, and with the selfsame action established a universal order of jurisdiction to prescribe in private law.

The second of Savigny's universalist ideas, the idea of a universality of private legal relationships stripping them of their legal and societal embeddedness, lost its persuasive power in the Twentieth century. It was considered to represent an apolitical understanding of private law. Critical scholars put forward that private law was not an

11 F.C. v. Savigny, *op. cit.*, 114.
12 F. Rödl, *op. cit.*, 72 *et seq.*
13 F. C. v. Savigny, *op. cit.*, 28.

area distinct from public law, and, in particular, that it was equally saturated with public policy aspects, a fact which would not allow determining the jurisdiction of states in private law according to an alleged essence of the private legal relationship. Instead, it was the often differing "governmental interest" of states which should determine the reach of domestic law in the transnational sphere.[14]

However, this second of Savigny's universalist ideas, which refers to the idea of the universality of private law relations, was often not properly distinguished from the first, the universalist idea of a unity of the law of conflict of laws. Thus, many saw the latter idea also hit by their criticism of Savigny's a-political understanding of private law. But the two are actually independent. Thus, accepting that the content of private law rules which determine rights and duties in private legal relations depends from their social and legal embeddedness does not exclude the ideal of unity in conflict of laws. What it does exclude is only that the law of conflict of laws takes the form which was propagated by Savigny, namely, a small number of multilateral rules. This position, although only rarely defended, can be called the modern universalism of conflict of laws.[15]

Certainly, for both the classical and the modern versions of universalism, there is the problem of how this universal legal order for conflict of laws which preserves law's unity can be conceptualised, given that there is no higher legal source from which the conflict rules could emanate. But this problem can be solved: One has to understand all institutions, and in particular courts, which articulate conflict rules as participating in a common enterprise to articulate a common law of conflict of laws.

Though the classical and the modern universalism are based upon different understandings of private legal relations and private law, the driving force behind the two universalisms is the same: it is the idea that law must be conceptualised as being submitted to the idea of its unity. This means that conflicts of legal orders, each concurrently striving for application on a given case, have to be subject to a legal solution of the conflict derived from a higher ranking order. Otherwise, there would be no valid law at all but only competing mental representations of law. And the prevalence of one representation over the other will depend on coincidental circumstances (i.e., the place of the court where the suit was first filed or where the first judgement was issued, the location of distrainable assets, *etc.*). In other words, whether one can have the idea of law at all, depends on the commitment to the idea of unity of (conflicts) law.[16]

14 B. Currie, *Selected Essays on the Conflict of Laws*, (Durham NC: Duke University Press, 1963); Ch. Joerges, *Zum Funktionswandel des Kollisionsrechts*, (Berlin: Walter de Gruyter – Tübingen: Mohr, 1971).

15 F. Rödl, *op. cit.*, 80, 121 *et seq.*

16 F. Rödl, *op. cit.*, 22 *et seq.*

2.2. *The Political Particularism Prevailing Today*

The doctrine of today's discipline of Private International Law stands in sharp contrast to universalism.[17] Its essential trait, also according to its self-understanding, is its deliberative particularism.[18] This means that the law on conflict of laws is not part of a superior and unique legal order. On the contrary, the law of conflict of laws is understood as a part of the same legal orders which are competing for application on a given case; thus, each legal order comprises particular conflict rules which can be, and often are, different from the conflict rules of the concurring legal orders. In other words, foreign legal orders and foreign private laws are not neglected, but their spatial reach is determined according to the prerogatives of the domestic legal order. One player in the jurisdictional conflict is, at the same time, the arbitrator of the selfsame conflict. In this way, Private International Law also subscribes to the context-dependence of private law rules, but it sacrifices, with the same action (as did most of the critics of Savigny), the idea of universalism in conflict of laws.[19]

It is important to note the specific reason for the essentially anti-universal attitude of today's Private International Law. It is not that the doctrine thinks that a universal conflict of laws is unlikely or impossible to achieve. The reason is, instead, the partisan attitude of the discipline – although a common discipline in all legal orders – towards the domestic legal order. The grounding of this attitude is in core the understanding of sovereignty which underlies this legal order. The idea of sovereignty, which is not only the source for private law rules, but is also the source for private international law rules, excludes that it functions as a neutral arbitrator acting from a viewpoint superior to the concurring private laws. The state origin of private international law prevents it from performing a supra-state function. The idea of the sovereignty of states trumps the idea of the unity of the law.[20]

3. The Form of Conflict of Laws in Constitutionalism beyond the State

3.1. *Fischer-Lescano's and Teubner's Law of Regime-Collisions*

Fischer-Lescano's and Teubner's approach starts with the assumption that, today, the sphere of international and transnational law is characterised by a pluralism of legal regimes, which have emerged as a supplement of the transnationalisation of functionally

17 The main reference for the following is K. Schurig, *Kollisionsnorm und Sachrecht. Standort und Methode des Internationalen Privatrechts*, (Berlin: Duncker and Humblot, 1981).

18 See, for example, K. Schurig, *op. cit.*, 295.

19 F. Rödl, *op. cit.*, 91 *et seq.*

20 Schurig denotes the predominant doctrine of private international law not a sovereigntist but an autonomist position (compare G. Kegel and K. Schurig, *Internationales Privatrecht*, ((Munich: C.H. Beck, 2004)), p. 186). This choice in wording is related to a tacit claim that private international law should actually not be formed by the states' legislator but by the states' courts, listening carefully to legal scholarship.

differentiated social systems.[21] Fischer-Lescano and Teubner observe that each of these regimes claims legal and constitutional autonomy *vis-à-vis* other regimes and *vis-à-vis* state law. In many cases, the regimes' claim for constitutional autonomy is directly manifested with the institutionalisation of a highest court, which is to adjudicate the legal disputes which arise from the regime's own law with final authority.[22] Presumably, it is this very claim of constitutional autonomy which justifies, according to Fischer-Lescano and Teubner, the drawing of an analogy from the pluralism of functional legal regimes at international or at transnational level to the pluralism of national private laws which is the subject of traditional conflict of laws. A further exploration of this analogy leads Fischer-Lescano and Teubner to their main thesis: the interaction or mediation between functional legal regimes should be submitted to a new paradigm delivered by conflict of laws.[23]

As stated in the introduction, the following treatise focuses on the question of the form of the conflict of laws-paradigms which are put forward for understanding constitutionalism beyond the state. Hence, the question for the law of regime-collisions envisioned by Fischer-Lescano and Teubner is precisely whether it is to be conceptualised as universal law or as particularistic law.

3.1.1. Epistemically Grounded Particularism

It is evident from Fischer-Lescano's and Teubner's account that they perceive themselves as critical towards any kind of universalism in law and even of intellectual attempts to reconstruct universalism in law.[24] For this reason, one is inclined to attribute a particularist approach to Fischer-Lescano's and Teubner's law of regime-collisions, which is the very same stance adopted by traditional private international law.

It has been explained above that, for the doctrine of private international law, the reason to subscribe to particularism and to battle against theoretical attempts for universalism was the doctrine's strong commitment to the concept of state sovereignty. The idea of state sovereignty, encompassing the authority to determine the law to be applied in transnational cases adjudicated by domestic courts, conflicted with the universalist idea of a conflicts law which was conceptualised as a neutral arbitrator between the competing claims of different states to apply their private laws in such cases. At this point, it seems worthwhile to question whether the analogy of states and functional regimes insinuated by Fischer-Lescano and Teubner can be driven further, i.e., with regard to the adequate reason to be given against universalism and in favour of particularism. If their idea was, indeed, to exploit the said analogy even further, then the reasoning could go as follows: functional legal regimes – or maybe their underlying

21 A. Fischer-Lescano and G. Teubner, *Regime-Kollisionen*, *op. cit.*, 23 *et seq.*, 25 *et seq.*

22 Ibid., 41 et seq.

23 Ibid., 57 et seq.

24 *Ibid.*, 10 *et seq.*, 24, 57, 170.

functional rationality[25] – not only claim their legal and constitutional autonomy, but these claims are also normatively valid. Similar to the sovereignty-claim of the nation state, the autonomy-claim of the functional regime would encompass the right and the authority to determine the law to be applied to the cases adjudicated by the regime's courts, contrary to the idea to subject the regimes to a kind of superseding and neutral conflict of laws-rules. In short, as is the case for the state sovereignty, the autonomy of regimes trumps the unity of law.

There are indications that this is, indeed, the argument which Fischer-Lescano and Teubner wish to advocate. More than once, the authors put forward that no functional rationality underlying the functional differentiation of international and transnational regimes should supersede or absorb other functional rationalities.[26] This imperative of mutual respect between functional rationalities and their related legal regimes certainly sounds fine and looks attractive at first sight. But the foundation for this general claim has barely been explored by Fischer-Lescano and Teubner. It is, however, difficult to see why this kind of suggestion does not commit them to the further idea that any functional rationality with its related legal regime is maintaining a kind of natural right to persist – maintaining as much autonomy as possible. Yet, such a strong essentialist claim for functional rationalities and related legal regimes could hardly be defended at all. In order not to stop the discussion at this point, it is, therefore, assumed that both the existence and the persistence of functionally differentiated international legal regimes have neither normative standing nor implication in the thinking of Fischer-Lescano and Teubner. They might take this differentiation simply as a given; a given one has to cope with.[27]

But if this is true, then our original question remains unresolved: What is the foundation for Fischer-Lescano's and Teubner's determined anti-universalism which is to characterise their idea of a law to mediate the legal collisions of functional legal regimes? Maybe, the reason is rather of epistemic provenance. A short version of such a probably long story could go as follows: there is no superseding legal order available which could provide a universal law for regime-collisions. Hence, only the parties of the collisions themselves – national legal orders in the case of collisions the private laws of nation states, functional regimes in the case of regime collisions – are able and competent to produce the solutions in, and with effect for, their respective jurisdiction. In this situation, it is impossible for these solutions, which are developed by each functional regime on its own account, to be understood as instances of a neutral and universal law of conflict of laws. The reason is epistemic in nature: a functional regime, even if it was normatively willing, is epistemically not able to articulate a neutral solution for two or even more concurring rationalities, one of which is represented by the adjudicating

25 *Ibid.*, 25 *et seq.*, 50.

26 *Ibid.*, 57 *et seq.*, 89, 130, 170 *et seq.*

27 N. Luhmann, *Die Wirtschaft der Gesellschaft*, (Frankfurt aM: Suhrkamp Verlag, 1994), p. 344: "Man kehrt nicht ins Paradies zurück."

regime itself.[28] Hence, the law of regime-collisions must be conceived as being particularistic, not due to the dignity of the regimes' autonomies, but due to their epistemic capabilities.

This epistemic claim is as equally strong as the normative claim considered above was. It can only be assumed that it roots in basic beliefs developed in systems theory. Leaving aside whether these beliefs can, indeed, be grounded, what is to be inferred from them is that, in contrast to the doctrine in private international law, the reason for particularism in the case of regime-collisions would not give normative support for the kind of partiality which is linked to the essential particularism in the case of private international law. But with this move the whole conceptual picture changes: State sovereignty denied any *normative* obligation to strive for the law's unity in conflict of private laws. The functional differentiation underlying legal regimes, in turn, does not deny a normative obligation to strive for law's unity, but takes it epistemically impossible for the unity of law ever to be achieved. This picture opens a conceptual option which is neither explicitly discussed nor rejected by Fischer-Lescano and Teubner, namely, that, for the law of regime collisions, the idea guiding each regime's adjudication of regime-collisions might, indeed, be an idea of a universal law, but that, for reasons of epistemic constraints, a universal law idea will never be achieved in reality; for this tragic reason, the law of regime-collisions will always remain particular. As a result, Fischer-Lescano and Teubner might like to argue that it is better and more sincere to admit this – in their view – undeniable epistemic fact.

3.1.2. The Reason to Submit Regimes to Conflict Rules

At this point, a new problem arises. If it is not normatively wrong, but epistemically impossible, for the functional regime to contribute to the articulation of a neutral and unitary law of regime-collisions – as is advocated by universalism in conflict of private laws – why is it then a regime's obligation to reflect on "foreign", i.e., on the law of other functional regimes at all? For a legal regime, as well as for a national legal order, the collision with the legal order of another regime or another state does not come naturally, nor does it occur by accident. It depends on the perception of these foreign legal orders as being similar to "the own" legal order. Only this condition of (mutual) acknowledgment between states or legal regimes leads to a collision of private laws or of regimes which can then, indeed, be represented not only from the exterior perspective of an observer but from the interior perspective of the state or regime.

What, then, are the reasons for a functional regime to acknowledge other legal regimes as equals, so that the law of a foreign regime may, indeed, collide with the regime's own law? Again, this problem is not systematically elaborated by Fischer-Lescano and Teubner, so that one has to try to trace their argument carefully from their rich general account. Again, it might help to resort again to the claims of the doctrine of private

[28] A. Fischer-Lescano and G. Teubner, *op. cit.*, 61, 81, 86, 164.

international law. The reason to submit the states' private law rules to the conflict rules generated by private international law, which is prominently given by the doctrine for the case of conflicting private laws, is that it is, on the one hand, advantageous for the nation state to acknowledge foreign private law as law.[29] But it must be assumed that Fischer-Lescano and Teubner would not resort to such an analogous claim. It is hardly convincing that functional regimes might draw similar advantages from the acknowledgement of their fellow regimes as nation states do with regard to their fellow states. On the other hand, the doctrine of private international law submits that to acknowledge other states' private law as the respective states' own private law is a requirement of public international law. This argument does not seem to be reflected in the approach of Fischer-Lescano and Teubner, as they would deny the existence of any superseding, hierarchically highest public international law.[30]

But there might be an alternative account which supports Fischer-Lescano's and Teubner's idea of a law for regime-collisions which pre-supposes the (mutual) acknowledgement of legal regimes. It is quite evident that Fischer-Lescano and Teubner do not really feel the need to explain why regimes have to acknowledge their fellows as equals and therefore to submit their own norms to regime-collision rules at all. Instead, they suggest several times that all one can strive for today is a law for regime-collisions.[31] But this proposition represents a valid reason for a law of regime-collisions only if one tacitly adds a further premise, namely, that the law's unity remains the guiding ideal. If the unity of law was not the guiding ideal, the "all one can strive for" given as the reason for the obligation for regimes to submit to a law of regime-collision would lose its grounding function. As a result, it turns out that Fischer-Lescano and Teubner do still, albeit tacitly, subscribe to the normative ideal of the unity of law, but they take this ideal to be unattainable given the functional differentiation of modern society.

3.1.3. Really an Anti-Universalism?

To repeat the form of the law of regime-collisions elaborated by Fischer-Lescano and Teubner as it was reconstructed in the two preceding paragraphs: the guiding ideal is the unity of law, but due to the functional differentiation of the modern world, the ideal of unity can only be approached (but never reached) by a law of regime-collisions; and, due to epistemic constraints of legal regimes, such a law of regime-collisions must be conceived as a particularistic law. Both suggestions support, independently of each other, the conclusion that the idea of a law of regime-collision stands in strong opposition to the idea of the unity of law, and, in this sense, also to universalism in conflict of laws.

It is clear that one cannot start an argument with the unity of law and end with its denial, and Fischer-Lescano and Teubner should feel uncomfortable with this conceptual situation. But the puzzle can be resolved, as the self-understanding of Fischer-Lescano and Teubner as anti-universalists rests on two conceptual

29 K. Schurig, *op. cit.*, 52.
30 A. Fischer-Lescano and G. Teubner, *op. cit.*, 48.
31 *Ibid.*, 57, 170.

misunderstandings of their main suggestions, which have just been repeated. The first misunderstanding is that Fischer-Lescano and Teubner reject the idea that the unity of law could result from a legal order rooted in a higher ranking source of law. But the – as such, convincing – rejection of this idea does not exclude the conceptual option to understand conflicts rules as an instrument pertaining the unity of law. The alternative understanding is just what universalism has argued in the case of conflict of private laws: the unity of law is still possible if all the institutions involved understand themselves to be participating in the articulation of a universal law for conflicts. Applied to the case of regime-collisions, the same thought would say that it is up to the regimes themselves to develop jointly such a legal system in order to resolve the jurisdictional conflicts between them. This common enterprise could not be secured by a superior law administered by a highest court, but only by way of submitting themselves to this enterprise. In conclusion, the opposition to an idea of conflict-rules derived from a higher source and administered by the highest court leaves the idea of the unity of law untouched.

Fischer-Lescano's and Teubner's second misunderstanding is that their doubts about the poor epistemic capacity of functional differentiated regimes would also support the suggestion that the idea of the unity of law had to be abandoned. Though each regime has to elaborate a law of regime-collision which resolves the jurisdictional conflicts between it and other functional legal regimes, the product will never be a shared and common law of regime-collisions as this is impossible for epistemic reasons.

At this point, it is useful to have a look to a parallel in philosophical epistemology: There are sceptical voices which claim that human beings actually do not share a common language, but that each and every human being has his or her own.[32] This is so although the participants of linguistic communication usually believe that the opposite is true. There are quite powerful arguments against this idea of "private language".[33] But in the given context, a rather different aspect is important: People behave in the same way, no matter whether the idea of a private language is true or false. They communicate as if they were sharing a common language and a common world, no matter whether this pre-supposition is factual or counter-factual.[34]

This pragmatic perspective might be a vantage point to reconsider Fischer-Lescano's and Teubner's *caveat* against the idea of unity: even if their epistemic claim were true, no practical difference would result from it. The courts of legal regimes would adjudicate on their jurisdictional conflicts as if they were articulating a common law in and for a

32 S. Kripke, *Wittgenstein on Rules and Private Language*, (Cambridge MA: Harvard University Press, 1982).

33 J. McDowell, *Wittgenstein on Following a Rule, in: Mind, Value and Reality*, (Cambridge MA/London: Harvard University Press, 1998), pp. 221–262.

34 It is telling that Fischer-Lescano's and Teubner's epistemic worry gets apparently lost when they describe the desirable interaction of courts: see A. Fischer-Lescano and G. Teubner, *op. cit.*, 71, 121 *et seq.*

common world. The suggestion that the aim of this practice is actually an illusion is a theoretical meta-comment by Fischer-Lescano and Teubner in the sense that it is not meant to change this practice. This was different in the case of private international law: there, emphasis was put on the state's sovereignty and thus the state was deliberately empowered to *partisan* decisions on the conflict of private legal orders. Such a partiality would go directly against Fischer-Lescano's and Teubner's intentions. Their particularism has no normative backup and thus provides no support for partiality. But if the theoretical meta-comment of epistemically grounded particularism does not change the adjudicative practice and does not even aim at changing it, then it becomes unclear what the very significance and role of the meta-comment is in the whole debate. The practical significance of an imperative directed to functional legal regimes to "adjudicate working thereby on a shared and unitary law of regime-collisions" is equal to an imperative to "adjudicate *as if* you were working on a share and unitary law of regime-collisions". One might, for reasons of simplicity, prefer the first version.

3.2. Joerges' Proceduralised Law of Conflict of Laws

Joerges does not start his project with similar strong beliefs about the (functional differentiation of the) world as Fischer-Lescano and Teubner do. Nor does he share their deep epistemic worries. His version of the conflict of laws-paradigm starts from a different point which will be explained below. However, preliminarily, it should be stressed that what follows does not treat Joerges' conflict of laws-paradigm in its entirety. It might be known that Joerges latest version,[35] which has been articulated for the European Union, distinguishes three dimensions of conflict constellations. The first dimension refers to conflicts between European norms, namely, the market freedoms and European competition law, and national norms which aim at a social embedding of the market. The second dimension refers to conflicts of regulatory rules, and of risk regulation in particular. The third dimension refers to conflicts between private or hybrid governance arrangements, as in the case of standardisation, with public law. The following account concentrates on the second dimension, which represents the essential form of Joerges' paradigm, and is the one which comes closest to his general understanding of the conflict of laws-problem. The other two dimensions are deducted from this general form, reflecting particular circumstances. The first dimension reflects particular conditions of European integration; the third dimension reflects the normative asymmetry between private and public norms.

3.2.1. The Reason to Submit Legal Orders to Conflict Rules

The rationale underlying Joerges' plea for conflict of laws is neither legal-theoretical, as in the case of classical or modern universalism in conflict of private laws, nor a tacit

[35] See Ch. Joerges and F. Rödl, "Reconstituting Democracy in Europe's postnational constellation by dint of conflict of laws", in E.O. Eriksen and J.E. Fossum (eds.), *RECON-Theory in Practice*, ARENA Report 2/09, Oslo: ARENA, 2009, pp. 307–334.

commitment to an ideal of universalism, which is lost in reality, as in the case of Fischer-Lescano and Teubner. Joerges' argument is different. He argues that nation states engaged in a world economy and a world society produce external effects which may burden their neighbouring states and their populations, but that these neighbours and their concerns are not represented in the democratic procedures of the nation states.[36] Hence, the fundamental democratic principle that those affected by legal norms must have an equal say in their genesis is constantly violated in the post-national constellation. Due to this situation, nation states have to take foreign interests and concerns into account, and the only mode with which to do this is by submitting their own law to conflict rules in order to mediate the conflict with laws of foreign states. Thus, Joerges' call for a law for conflict of laws is not based upon the concept of law and its unity, but on the concept of democracy, instead.

Certainly, one could think of an alternative: the unification of all peoples in a supranational, and, finally, in a world state which would then determine the law upon the basis of equal participatory rights of a world constituency. Joerges does not subscribe to this alternative, and his reasons are more pragmatic than conceptual. He has no conceptual objection against the idea of state-building at European or at world level. The only problem with these ideas is that they are unlikely to become a reality. And until then, one has to cope with the democracy-deficit of the nation state, anyway. This is why Joerges turns the omnipresent quest for the democratic legitimacy of the law of the multi-level system into a claim for a new law of conflict of laws.[37]

3.2.2. A Plea against Judicial Dominance

Joerges is not particularly concerned with the unity of law and legal universalism. The main concern which he stresses is that the generation of conflicts law is essentially not a case for the judiciary. A corresponding suggestion had once been submitted by Brainerd Currie even for conflict of laws for intra-federal conflicts in the Unites States.[38] The argument was that conflict of jurisdictions could not be understood as an adjudicative question, i.e., a question of law application. With the establishing of his proceduralised conflict of laws-paradigm for multi-level governance regimes, Joerges has adopted and generalised Currie's position.

What Joerges wants, at least for many areas such as regulatory and distributive policies, is to see the making of the law of conflict of laws proceduralised. This means, in his understanding, that the making of the law of conflict of laws must be politicised and democratised. The reasons are twofold. First – as has just been explained – he shares the

36 Ch. Joerges, Re-conceptualizing the Supremacy of European Law, op. cit., 317.

37 Ch. Joerges, Challenges of Europeanisation in the Realm of Private Law, op. cit., 189.

38 B. Currie, "The Constitution and Choice of Law. Governmental Interests and the Judicial Function", in: *ibid.* Selected Essays on the Conflict of Laws, (Durham NC: Duke University Press, 1963), pp. 188–282, at272, often cited by Joerges, for example, in *Re-conceptualizing the Supremacy of European Law, op. cit.*, 314.

view that the spatial reach of national jurisdiction is, if there is no superior law, in most cases, not a legal question, or, more precisely, not a question for legal adjudication. It must be political actors who are posited in a position of democratic accountability who have to generate the necessary conflict rules.[39] Second, to defer the making of conflict rules to the political process would lift the barriers which are enshrined into a pure judicial logic.[40] According to judicial logic, the solution of a conflicts case is usually restricted to the prevalence of either one or the other legal regime in a given case, or as a balancing of interests. Political proceduralisation, in contrast, would allow innovative solutions such as special substantive norms or default rules with exit options.

As a result, Joerges calls for a "conflict of laws" approach to the phenomenon of constitutionalisation, but he is opposed to the idea that the necessary "conflict of law" rules should be coined exclusively, or even dominantly, by a community of courts.[41]

3.2.3. Underlying Teleological Universalism

Now, we should ask ourselves, *how* is Joerges' position to be classified with a view to the dichotomy of *universalism* versus *particularism*? The answer, which will be tested here, is that Joerges' thinking represents a *teleological universalism*.

Joerges calls for an application of the conflict of laws-paradigm to multi-level governance regimes, such as the European Union or the World Trade Organisation. The question of whether this conflicts law has to be conceived of in terms of universalism or in terms of particularism has not been explicitly developed by him yet. However, it cannot be put into question the fact that the conflict rules are not to be autonomously developed by the nation states themselves, as is suggested and defended by private international law. The conflict rules are to be developed in institutionalised political procedures in which representatives of the legal orders involved are present (or – even if only in rare and specific cases – also by supranational courts as the European Court of Justice[42]). In contrast to modern universalism in conflict of private laws, Joerges does not resort to an idea of a universal law of conflict of laws as a result of a common enterprise of autonomous courts which again cannot be secured by legal means. Instead, he works with the much straighter idea of supranational political (and only in rare cases, judicial) institutions. From this straight conception of a supranational institutionalisation of the making of conflict rules, one cannot but infer that he focuses on conflict of laws rules which are common to all the jurisdictions involved into their making. Because these conflict-rules must only be conceived as common to all the jurisdictions involved and

39 Joerges, for example, in Re-conceptualizing the Supremacy of European Law, op. cit., 321 et seq.

40 Ibid.

41 See his rejection of the approach of A. Lowenfeld, the most important representatives of modern universalism in conflict of laws, in: Ch. Joerges, "Freier Handel mit riskanten Produkten? Die Erosion nationalstaatlichen und die Emergenz transnationalen Regierens", in: St. Leibfried and M. Zürn (eds), *Vom Wandel des Staates zur Staatlichkeit im Wandel*, (Frankfurt aM: Suhrkamp Verlag, 2006).

42 Ch. Joerges, Re-conceptualizing the Supremacy of European Law, op. cit., 320 et seq.

not as the same for all kinds of conflict constellations, Joerges appears as a clear-cut modern universalist.[43]

However, there are reasons why this position, which has just been developed, is not easy to spot in Joerges' work, and why even Joerges himself might not be satisfied with this account. The reason for this reluctance is connected to the answer which Joerges gives to a different problem: What happens if, in a given supranational context, there are no adequate *fora* established in which the relevant conflict of law rules can be developed in normatively valuable procedures. Joerges' answer is that, until such *fora* have been generated, the courts are not supposed to develop conflict rules on their own by presenting them as a result of adjudication. This would contradict Joerges' more fundamental claim against the a-political judicialisation of conflict of laws. According to Joerges, the courts are, in this situation, only called to exercise "comity".[44] But "comity", in turn, is an important and influential concept in the history of private international law. It stands for the idea of benevolent acceptance of foreign law by domestic jurisdiction, and it is traditionally understood as the *Gegenbegriff* to the idea of a superior (legal) obligation to find a neutral solution for a given conflict of legal norms. Thus, in this context, Joerges appears as a clear-cut adherent of particularism, albeit of a friendly version.

But this incidental turn to "comity" is literally a kind of "last resort". It is suggested here that it should be read as an instance of a passing retardation of a historic-teleological development. "Comity" is to be exercised only until the adequate *fora* for a proceduralised generation of conflict rules are established. But due to the normative obligation to cope with the external effects of national democracies, there is also an obligation to develop more and more of these *fora* and procedures. This normatively-driven process will and, indeed, should one day lead to a universal, though differentiated, legal order for conflict of laws. But today we find ourselves far from this situation, and thus we have to accept the resulting normative shortcomings. This is what might be called Joerges' teleological universalism.

4. Conclusion

Both adherents of a conflict of laws paradigm in constitutionalism beyond the state which have been investigated in this paper, Fischer-Lescano and Teubner, on the one hand, and Joerges, on the other, do not subscribe to the partisan particularism in the form that it is still defended by the doctrine of private international law. On the contrary, it could be demonstrated that both are adherents of the idea of the unity of law, and,

43 Joerges had advocated very early "vertical differentiations" in conflict rules depending from the parties involved: Ch. Joerges, *Zum Funktionswandel des Kollisionsrechts*, *op. cit.*, 157 *et seq.*

44 Most extensively elaborated in: Ch. Joerges, "Constitutionalism in Postnational Constellations: Contrasting Social Regulation in the EU and in the WTO", *op. cit.*

with this, also of universalism, in the one case in a tacit, in the other case in a teleological, form.

The chapter should end with an indication of why the idea of the unity of law deserves our particular interest, and why, therefore, all, and even mere tacit and mere teleological, attempts to retain the idea of the unity of law deserves our praise: Only by upholding the idea of the unity of law can any generation of legal norms be conceptualised as a democratic enterprise which includes all human beings as free and equal.

Miguel Poiares
Maduro

CHAPTER 14. THE CHAMELEON STATE
EU LAW AND THE BLURRING OF THE PRIVATE/PUBLIC DISTINCTION IN THE MARKET

The re-thinking of the traditional role of the state in the market has been accompanied by a variety of new forms of the exercise of public power and an increased blurring of the private/public distinction in the market.[1] It is now common, for example, for the state to intervene in the market not through the traditional mechanisms of regulation or public ownership, but in a private legal form, as another market participant. In some instances, it is the state that grants private operators the shield of a public legal form. There are also instances in which the state imposes on private entities the pursuit of actions that it itself may not be legally authorised to undertake. In all these cases, it becomes increasingly difficult to distinguish between private and public participations in the market and between the pursuit of traditional public goals and the pursuit of private interests the protection of which the state deems to be in the public interest. This difficulty does not simply represent a conceptual challenge for the law, it also blurs the traditional distinction between the market and the state as alternative modes of decision-making subject to different mechanisms of accountability.

In the realm of the EU, this phenomenon presents additional challenges, as the increased difficulty of distinguishing between forms of private and public action threatens to undermine the conceptual borders according to which the scope of some EU rules has been conceived. Furthermore, there is a risk that Member States may use this conceptual flexibility in such a way as to create forms of evasion from the application of the EU rules which they wish to reject. In some areas, such as free movement or state aid, for example, the state may feel tempted to assume a "private form" in order to evade the application of these rules, since, in principle, they are not applicable to private actors. In other areas, in contrast, regarding certain community rules which are only applicable to private activity, the state may give a "public form" to private behaviour in order to exempt itself from these rules.

1 This chapter is an updated and annotated version of the Keynote Address at the March 2006 European Law Conference at King's College, University of London. Naturally, the views expressed in this article are so in a purely personal capacity.

My analysis of a body of recent case law of the European Court of Justice will focus on three different areas in which this challenge emerges. I will try to identify how the Court has dealt with it in these different areas, and, finally, try to determine if there is (and, indeed, whether there can be) a coherent approach to this issue in its different manifestations. I would argue that such a coherent approach is emerging, and that it is founded upon a general requirement of consistency and coherence in state intervention in the market, and thus that this requirement aims to guarantee proper accountability of both the market and the state processes of decision-making.

My analysis will focus on cases spanning from 2003 to 2006. However, in some instances, these cases confirm or develop earlier decisions of the Court to which I will refer. Additionally, there are several cases which are currently pending at the Court which are of relevance to the overall theme of this talk. This only serves to demonstrate what, I believe, will be the growing importance in the Court's jurisprudence of cases concerning new forms of state intervention and/or participation in the market.

I have selected three areas of recent case law to address in the context of the overall topic of this article: (1) the concept of an undertaking; (2) the application of competition rules to the state (i.e., the co-ordinated application of Articles 10 and 81 EC); and (3) the so-called "golden share" cases. Other areas could have been included, including different aspects of the concept of state aid: its granting through private resources, and the criteria of private creditor and private investor.

1. The Concept of an Undertaking

Articles 81 to 86 of the EC Treaty are only applicable to undertakings. They are, in principle, not aimed at controlling state regulation of the market, which is susceptible to restricting free competition, but are, instead, addressed at the anti-competitive behaviour of undertakings (including, however, public undertakings and undertakings to which the state has granted special or exclusive rights). The concept of undertaking is, therefore, essential to the definition of the scope of application of these competition rules. It is well established that an entity engaged in an economic activity constitutes an undertaking for the purposes of EU competition rules. In the light of this, the *prima facie* application of competition rules to the state or state entities is based upon one fundamental criterion: whether a certain activity of the state or a public body is considered to be "economic activity".

The Court has had the opportunity to clarify the concept of economic activity, as applied to the state, in a series of judgments, one of the latest being its decision in *AOK*.[2] In this case, the Court had to assess the lawfulness of the practice of German "sickness

2 Joined cases C-264/01, C-306/01, C-354/01 and C-355/01, *AOK Bundesverband et al.*, [2004] ECR I-2493; see B.J. Drijber, (2005)42 *CML Rev*, pp. 523–533.

funds" which set the maximum re-imbursement sums for medical drugs, a practice that was challenged by pharmaceutical companies.

In order to determine whether the conduct of the German federal associations of sickness funds ("fund associations") violated competition rules, the Court first had to establish whether these associations could be considered as undertakings for the purposes of Articles 81 to 86. The fund associations, supported by the observations of the Commission, argued that their activities were not economic activities since they exclusively pursued a social function, had no profitable goal, and were organised under a principle of solidarity. In turn, the pharmaceutical companies argued that, since the sickness funds were in competition with each other with regard to the amount of the contributions to be paid by the insured people, the services provided, and both the management and the organisation of their services, their activity was an economic activity, and that, consequently, they ought to be considered as undertakings, subject to the application of competition rules.

The judgment of the Court began by recalling, in paragraph 46, that "[t]he concept of an undertaking in competition law covers any entity engaged in economic activity, regardless of the legal status of the entity or the way in which it is financed".[3]

The Court then analysed the nature of the activity in question. It recalled that, in the social security domain, it has developed a series of criteria which permit the exclusion of certain activities from the concept of economic activity. This is notably the case for entities that pursue an exclusively social goal, and whose activities are founded on a principle of solidarity, are devoid of a profit purpose, and where the contributions paid do not correspond to the services provided.[4] However, the Court also recognised that even entities that *partly* fulfil those criteria may still be considered as undertakings.[5] In other words, if the activity in question takes place in competition with other economic operators and/or if, even when pursuing goals of solidarity, it is, in effect, dominated by a principle of capitalisation, it must be qualified as an economic activity.

In the case in hand, the sickness funds exercised an activity with an exclusive social function, devoid of any profit purpose and were founded on the principle of solidarity. Moreover, the competition which was possible among them was restricted to a very limited set of circumstances and was also subject to a principle of solidarity (through the existence of a mechanism for re-distribution among the different sickness funds). The court concluded that this limited competition was not sufficient to attribute to their activity the nature of economic activity:

> The sickness funds are therefore not in competition with one another or with private institutions as regards grant of the obligatory statutory benefits in respect of treatment or medicinal products which constitutes their main function.[6]

3 *AOK*, cited above, paragraph 46.
4 *Ibid.*, paragraph 47.
5 *Ibid.*, paragraphs 49 and 50.
6 *Ibid.*, paragraph 54.

Furthermore, the fact that the Court has consistently maintained that the nature of an economic activity must be established *per se*, and not in the light of the overall activity of the entity in question (in other words, a certain entity can perform both economic *and* non-economic activities for the purposes of the application of competition rules), did not affect the outcome of this case, since the Court considered that, by simply determining the precise maximum amounts to be re-imbursed for medical drugs as imposed by the law:

> [T]he associations of sickness funds did not pursue a self-interest that could be distinguished from the purely social goals of the sickness funds.[7]

Thus, the judgment in *AOK* further clarifies the notion of economic activity and can help us shed light upon the underlying normative criterion that determines when state activity ought to be considered as an economic activity subject to competition rules.

Looking back, the starting point for the Court's inquiry into the notion of economic activity was the *Höfner and Elser* judgment. Here, the Court held that a public monopoly on employment procurement could be qualified as pursuing an economic activity since "employment procurement has not always been, and is not necessarily, carried out by public entities".[8] In itself, this might lead us to think that any activity susceptible to being performed by a private entity (or a profit-making entity in the more restrictive sense mentioned in the Opinion of Advocate General Jacobs[9]) would have to be included in the concept of an economic activity. This, however, would be too broad since, potentially, any activity (including defence) is susceptible to being carried out by private entities. It is for this reason, I would argue, that the Court has, in subsequent decisions, introduced some limits and refined this broad definition. The *Höfner and Elser* criterion is still frequently cited, but it has, in fact, been refined by a more detailed and complex set of criteria, as in the *AOK* case.

In fact, the broad reference in *Höfner and Elser* to activities susceptible to being carried out by private entities has to be contextualised by the circumstance which, in that case, the state *de facto* accepted the competition of some private operators with the public monopoly. What was relevant was that such activity took place in a market context as demonstrated by competition with private operators. When the court referred to activities which can be pursued by private entities, it therefore referred to activities which are carried out *under* market conditions. This effectively is in accordance with the criteria developed by the Court in all its subsequent decisions, and highlighted in the recent *AOK* judgment. It is in this light, too, that one should also read the reference in former Advocate General Jacobs' Opinions as to whether these activities could, at

7 *Ibid.*, paragraphs 62 and 63.

8 Case C-41/90 *Höfner and Elser* [1991] ECR I-1979, paragraph 22; see P.J. Slot, (1991) 28 *CML Rev*, pp. 964–988.

9 A.G. Jacobs' Opinion in case *AOK*, cited, delivered the 22 May 2003.

least in principle, be carried out by a private undertaking in order to make a profit.[10] The comparison with potential private operators is not relevant in all cases in which the latter could perform a certain activity, but only where they either *already* actually exercise that activity in competition with the state, or could do so under conditions similar to how it is exercised by the state. It is in this instance that the comparison criterion helps us to determine whether the state activity takes place in a market or under market conditions.

What is relevant is to ascertain whether the state excludes a certain activity from the market (in which case, it would be a non-economic activity), or whether the state, either in competition or under a monopolistic regime, pursues that activity as a market activity (in which case, it must be considered as being an economic activity). This inquiry can be carried out by using two concurrent criteria already highlighted in the *AOK* case.

First, if the activity is pursued in the same market by competing private and public bodies, the public bodies must also be subject to competition rules in order to avoid situations in which, while competing with private entities, the public bodies simultaneously claim immunity from competition law. The existence of private operators is, in itself, sufficient evidence that a market exists with regard to an activity which requires the application of competition rules. This was the purpose of the inquiry undertaken by the Court in *AOK* on the nature of the competition with regard to the activity undertaken by the sickness funds. A more recent case, *Cassa di Risparmio*,[11] dealt with the concept of an undertaking in the context of state aid, and concerned whether banking foundations could be considered as being undertakings for the purposes of receiving state aid. Here, the Court made an even clearer reference to this test by determining that there was no economic activity if the activity had an exclusive social character and was not exercised in a market in competition with other operators.

Second, even where the state has created a statutory monopoly for pursuing a certain activity, it is possible for its own activity to be carried out under market conditions; in this case, it still ought to be subject to competition rules. This is the focus of the inquiry undertaken in many of the Court's decisions (including *AOK*) on whether the activity in question is carried out with an exclusive social function and under a principle of solidarity, or whether it is carried out under a principle of capitalisation. To determine which of these principles dominates the activity in question, the Court has developed a set of balancing criteria which depend on the area in question, and include the services provided, how contributions are determined, its mandatory nature, the forms of solidarity embodied in the scheme, *etc.*[12]

10 See paragraph 27 of the Opinion in the *AOK* case and case C-222/04, *Cassa di Risparmio*, [2006] ECR I-289, Opinion of the Advocate General Jacobs, paragraph 78.

11 Case C-222/04, *Cassa di Risparmio di Firenze*, [2006] ECR I-289.

12 *AOK*, cited above.

To sum up, one could say that what determines whether a certain public activity amounts to an economic activity depends upon whether such an activity constitutes state participation in a market (as distinct from state intervention in the market). Modifying and refining the initial *Höfner and Elser* definition, economic activity exists when the activity in question is carried out by the state in the same way that a private operator in the market would pursue it (under a principle of capitalisation), or in competition with private operators. It must be recalled that this test serves only to determine whether the activity in question falls within the scope of the application of competition rules. It is still possible for the state to combine market and non-market conditions in a certain sector of activity, including imposing restrictions upon competition. However, in this case the activities in question would have to be assessed under the conditions put forth in Article 86(2). These will be undertakings entrusted with the operation of services of general economic interest whose pursuit of the tasks attributed to them has to be balanced with the goals of the competition rules under the criteria put in Article 86(2).

It is important to note that the case law is based on determining the true nature of the state action and imposes a requirement of consistency upon the state. If the state decides to undertake a certain activity under market conditions or to delegate it in part to the market, it must be subject to competition rules. Instead, if the Member State fully maintains a certain activity outside the market, precluding any competition and carrying it out under the principle of solidarity and not capitalisation, the activity is not subject to EU competition rules.

It is clear that by limiting the application of Articles 81 to 86 to undertakings, the EC Treaty did not intend to subject all Member State activities to competition rules. However, Article 86 also makes it clear that certain forms of Member State activity are covered by those rules. The need for consistency or coherence means that, if a state conducts itself as an economic operator, Articles 81 to 86 have to apply. The same principles guide the application of competition rules to the Member State whenever it ratifies, implements or re-inforces decisions taken by undertakings, as we will see next.

2. Article 10 and Competition Rules Granting Public form to Private Behaviour

Another form of blurring the distinction between private and public actions may also require the application of competition rules to the state. In this case, the predominant fear is that state measures which are not subject to these competition rules may, in effect, simply replace the anti-competitive behaviour of certain undertakings. It is not *public authority* that assumes a private form but, rather, *private interests* which may be disguised under the cover of state authority.

In principle, Articles 81 and 82 are only applicable to undertakings. However, it is also well known that the Court has interpreted these provisions together with the principle of loyal co-operation of Article 10 EC to establish that "while it is true that Article 86 [now Article 82 EC] is directed at undertakings, nonetheless it is also true that the Treaty imposes a duty on Member States not to adopt or maintain in force any measure which could deprive that provision of its effectiveness".[13]

Some have argued that this general statement of the Court ought to constitute the basis for an extensive application of competition rules, leading to its application to state rules whenever the latter could be said to threaten the objectives of the former. On the other hand, some favour a more literal reading of the Treaty provisions and argue that state legislation ought to be excluded from the scope of the application of competition rules independent of its impact on the values protected by the EC competition rules. While the first thesis emphasises the values of free competition embodied in EC economic law, the second thesis is based upon the assumption that EC rules ought not to interfere with the economic model of the state, and this is reflected in the Treaty-exclusive application of competition rules to undertakings.

Since the broader statement of the *GB-Inno* decision, the Court has taken a more careful but, in my view, substantially well-founded path in controlling State measures under these provisions. As we shall see below, the underlying normative approach is similar to that which guides the Court's case law on the concepts of economic activity and undertakings. According to a well-known line of cases, Articles 81 and 82 are only infringed by state measures in two cases: where a Member State requires or favours the adoption of agreements, decisions or concerted practices which are contrary to Article 81 EC or re-inforces their effects,[14] or where the state divests its own rules of the character of legislation by delegating to private economic operators the responsibility for taking decisions which affect the economic sphere.[15] In the first case, the agreement between private undertakings is external to the state, although it is required, favoured or has its effects re-inforced by the latter. In the second case, the state delegates its decision-making authority to the private entities.

In two well-known and relatively recent Opinions, Advocates General Jacobs and Léger have expressed their concern about the limits inherent to this approach, which they perceive as being too dependent on establishing the previously anti-competitive behaviour of the private parties themselves.[16] As a consequence, they have proposed somewhat revised criteria to determine the application of Articles 81 and 82 to measures taken by Member States. For these AGs, the measure in question does not constitute an infringement of Articles 10 EC and 81 EC, if (1) its adoption is justified by the pursuit of

13 Case 13/77, *GB-Inno-BM*, [1977] ECR I-2115, paragraph 31.

14 Case C-198/01, *CIF*, [2003] ECR I-8055, paragraph 46; see P. Nebbia, 41 *CML Rev* 2004, pp. 839–849.

15 Case 136/86, *Aubert*, [1987] ECR 4789, paragraph 23; case C-35/96 *Commission* v *Italy*, [1998] ECR I-3851; case C-35/99, *Arduino*, [2002] ECR I-1529, paragraph 35, and Order of 17 February 2005 in case C-250/03 *Mauri* [2005] ECR I-1267, paragraph 30.

16 Opinion of Advocate General Jacobs, Joined cases C-180/98 to C-184/98, *Pavlov*, [2000] ECR I-6451, paragraphs 160–163.

a legitimate public interest, and/or (2) if the Member States actively supervise the involvement of private operators in the decision-making process. However, in *Arduino*,[17] the Court apparently remained faithful to its traditional approach. The case concerned Italian legislation which fixed maximum and minimum honorariums for lawyers. While the final decision belonged to the Italian Minister, the Italian Bar association played an important role in the setting of the fees, subject to final governmental approval.

I believe, however, that the Court's traditional approach, if properly developed and understood, contains, in itself, sufficient elements to respond to the concerns of Advocates General Jacobs and Léger and may not be as restrictive as has been suggested. The risk with their proposal lies in the fact that the conditions imposed on the state were cumulative, which meant that any measure liable to affect competition would always have to be assessed in terms of the pursuit of a legitimate public interest. This might be too broad, and might risk overloading the Court by attributing to Articles 81 and 82 a role in reviewing most of the Member States' economic legislation. Instead, the second criterion suggested by Advocates General Jacobs and Léger can, and, in my view, ought to, be understood as being compatible with the criteria developed in the case law of the Court in this area.

These criteria appear to be dominated by the need to assess the true nature of state intervention in the market. The inquiry is whether the state's legislative process is dominated by a concern to protect the public interest, or, conversely, whether the degree to which private interests are being taken into account is likely to alter the overriding objective of the state measure, which is, therefore, to protect these interests. In my view, this requires a substantive interpretation of the test of delegation to private actors, which would be in accordance with Jacobs and Léger's requirement of effective Member State supervision. This interpretation guarantees that the application of competition rules is excluded only where it is due to a real submission to the public interest, and not where it is the product of capture of the political process by private actors. This requires a substantive assessment of the degree of involvement of the private entities in the legislative process, in order to guarantee that their participation at the stage at which a rule is proposed, or their presence within a body responsible for the drafting of the rule, does not have a determining influence on the content of the rule, and outweighs the taking of other interests into consideration. The purpose is to prevent the control of the public decision-making process by the private entities whose competition is at stake, leading to a legislative provision whose sole or predominant purpose might be the protection of certain private entities from the elements of competition, to the detriment of the public interest. I understand that such a procedural test might impose a certain burden on national courts, which would have to be entrusted with the factual analysis of such an effective state supervision. I believe, however, that this is both a more feasible

17 *Arduino* cited above; see A.J. Vossestein, (2002) 39 *CML Rev*, pp. 841–863.

and more normatively defensible solution than a solution based upon the anti-competitive effects of state measures.

I also believe that the Court's judgment in *Arduino* fits this approach. There, the Court stressed that it considered there to be real supervision by the state, and maintained that "it does not appear that the Italian State has waived its power to make decisions of last resort or to review implementations of the tariff".[18] The Court's disagreement with the Advocate General was more at the level of this fact-based assessment, rather than on a more profound normative level.

That the Court did not intend to restrict the application of competition rules further to the state was made clear in a subsequent case which appeared to maintain a broad interpretation of the application of competition rules and re-inforced its traditional arguments by making reference to the fact that:

> [S]ince the Treaty of Maastricht entered into force, the EC Treaty has expressly provided that in the context of their economic policy the activities of the Member States must observe the principle of an open market economy with free competition (see Articles 3a(1) and 102a of the EC Treaty, now Article 4(1) EC and Article 98 EC).[19]

In contrast to the case law reviewed in the previous section, the concern in these cases is not with the fact that a state may take a private form, and, in so doing, evade the application of certain EC rules; instead, the danger is that private interests may effectively control Member State decision-making to such an extent that the latter may simply serve as an instrument to protect the anti-competitive behaviour of the former. Again, a requirement of consistency is imposed upon Member State action. To evade the application of competition rules, its measures must correspond to an effective state intervention in the market, formulated in the light of the public interest in a decision-making process which is not controlled by the private entities that are supposed to be in competition in that market.

3. Golden Shares

The final area of case law that I wish to look at deals with the well-known "golden shares" cases. These are shares in privatised companies which the state has retained, and which grant it special rights in the context of a variety of important decisions concerning these companies and their business activities. In a series of infringement actions brought against several Member States by the European Commission, these measures were challenged on the grounds that they violated the free movement of capital and the rights of establishment. The cases in which the Court initially developed its approach date

18 *Arduino*, cited above, paragraph 40.

19 Case C-198/01, *C.I.F.*, [2003] I-8055, paragraph 47.

from the end of 2002.[20] But this approach was even more fully articulated in a judgment from 2003,[21] and recently confirmed in a judgment of 2 June 2005.[22] Mostly, I believe that this line of cases can help us provide a broader context to the two other areas of case law, which are both in the domain of competition law.

As in other areas of Community law, the Court is called in to define the limits that the EU legal order imposes upon the forms of Member State intervention in the market which, instead of constituting classic exercises of state intervention in the market (either by regulating the market or by public ownership of certain economic activities) make use of private instruments or market mechanisms while attempting to retain some form of public control over the latter. The question arises, in these instances, with regard to the limits and the control imposed on the forms of Member State action once the state has chosen the pursuit a certain function through traditional market mechanisms.

Advocate General Damaso Ruiz-Jarabo Colomer has argued that, since the state could, in principle, retain full control over certain companies though public ownership (which is, notably, protected by Article 295), it should also be possible for the state to retain a more limited form of control by retaining certain special rights in privatised companies.[23] Stated in even broader terms:

> It is almost unthinkable that the Treaty should be intended to allow the Member States to retain the full shareholding in any undertaking, with the maximum restriction on the freedoms of establishment and movement of capital which that implies, and, at the same time, to stand in the way of a liberalised system subject to limited administrative conditions which are non-discriminatory and, therefore, more in keeping with the aim of integration. To put it another way: if withdrawing financial activities from the private sector, by allocating them to publicly owned bodies (nationalisation or socialisation, pure and simple), creates a special system of ownership, as opposed to the ordinary system of ownership, there is no reason why a system of private ownership subject to special powers should not be viewed in the same way or should be treated less favourably.[24]

The Court did not follow this reasoning and took the view that Member States could not "plead their own systems of property, referred to in Article 222 of the Treaty, by way of justification for obstacles, resulting from privileges attaching to their position as shareholder in a privatised undertaking, to the exercise of the freedoms provided for by the Treaty".[25]

20 Case C-367/98, *Commission* v *Portugal*, [2002] ECR I-4731; case C-483/99, *Commission* v *France*, [2002] ECR I-4781; case C-503/99, *Commission* v *Belgium*, [2002] ECR I-4809; case C-98/01, *Commission* v *United Kingdom*, [2003] ECR I-4641; see H.Fleischer, (2003) 40 *CML Rev.*, pp. 493–501.

21 Case C-463/00, *Commission* v *Spain*, [2003] ECR I-4581.

22 Case C-174/04, *Commssion* v *Italy*, [2005] ECR I-4933.

23 *Commission* v *Spain*, cited above, and *Commission* v *United Kingdom*, cited above.

24 Commission v Portugal, France and Belgium, cited above, paragraph 66.

25 *Commission* v *Spain*, cited above, paragraph 67.

In my view, this position of the Court is in line with its case law in the two previous areas that I have reviewed, notably that related to the definition of the economic activity in which the state acts as a market participant. There is an obligation of coherence that is imposed upon the Member State once it decides to open a certain sector to the market.

This requirement is particularly important in the case of the privatisation of former state companies. In effect, while the Member State is entitled to maintain public ownership of certain companies by the Treaty, it is not entitled to be selective in the access that it grants to certain economic sectors once these are open to the market. If the state were entitled to maintain special forms of market control over privatised companies, it could easily frustrate the application of free movement rules by granting only selective and potentially discriminatory access to substantial parts of the national market. It is for this reason that once a Member State decides to privatise a certain company, the protection of the free movement of capital demands that the economic autonomy of this company be protected, except in cases where it is necessary to safeguard certain fundamental public interests recognised by Community law. The intervention of the state can no longer be determined by the purpose of securing economic control over the company in a manner which is contrary to the normal operation of the market. It can only be linked to pursuing a possible general economic interest which is associated with the company in question.

The Court has recognised that "certain concerns may justify retention by Member States of a degree of influence within undertakings that were initially public and subsequently privatised".[26] However, from the case law of the Court, it is clear that such influence must not be aimed at retaining economic or market control over the company, and must be limited to the objective of guaranteeing the fulfilment of certain public interest obligations. Once the state has taken the decision that it is in the public interest to privatise a certain company or sector of activity, it cannot attempt to retain economic control over the company by restricting, in effect, market access to that company. While the state may choose to maintain a certain company under public ownership, once it decides to privatise it, it must not set in place rules which can restrict access to that company by certain market operators, to the advantage of others or to the advantage of the state itself. Restrictions are therefore only acceptable if they are necessary for the pursuit of certain public interests attributed to these companies and are not put in place to guarantee the maintenance of a state economic control over these companies. It is for this reason that the Court has stressed the "principle of respect for the decision-making autonomy of the undertaking concerned".[27] As a consequence, if, on the one hand, the Court accepts that derogations to the fundamental principle of the free movement of capital may be accepted "if there is a genuine and sufficiently serious threat to a fundamental interest of society",[28] on the other hand, these derogations are limited to

26 *Commission* v *Belgium*, cited above, paragraph 43.

27 *Ibid.*, paragraph 49.

28 *Ibid.*, paragraph 47.

what is necessary to guarantee that "the performance, under economically acceptable conditions, of the tasks of general economic interest which it has entrusted to an undertaking" are not put in jeopardy.[29] It is also for these reasons that the state must identify the specific public interests that are worthy of protection, and that the rules which grant special rights to the state should be based upon objective and precise criteria that do not go beyond that which is necessary for pursuing that public interest and guaranteeing the possibility of effective review by the courts.

As in other areas, one can identify a requirement of consistency or coherence that is imposed on Member States. Once a decision has been taken to subject a certain area to the market, the state can no longer use its authority to exclude the application of certain EC rules that govern the internal market in that domain. If exceptions are authorised, this must be done under a limited set of circumstances and under the supervision of Community law and the courts (as is the case in the area of competition law with Article 86(2)).

4. Conclusion

The areas reviewed here are only examples of the increasing challenges that are arising for the application of EU rules to the new forms of state participation or intervention in the market, and the difficulty to distinguish between private and public legal forms of action. Clearly, this analysis could be extended to other areas. In the area of state aid, for example, it is foreseeable that this issue will gain importance as new legal forms are adopted by both the state and by private operators, or as the state comes up with new instruments for intervention which will make it more difficult to determine what constitutes state aid and what does not.[30]

However, the Court appears to be answering these challenges by developing a case law that is both flexible and built upon solid normative foundations. The criterion underlying these different areas of case law appears to be that a requirement of coherence or consistency is imposed on the state in its relationship with the market. This criterion can be said to make sense not only as a necessary tool for allowing the scope of EU rules to adapt to the changing faces of the state but also, in broader terms, for guaranteeing the different mechanisms of accountability inherent in the market and the state.

The power the state exercises in the political sphere is subject to democratic control. The market, in contrast, provides a different form of accountability which is dominated by competition, which is, itself, protected by competition rules. When the exercise of state power takes a public form and occurs outside the market, it is subject to the classical mechanisms of political and democratic accountability. Such public exercises of power are also assumed to take place under a decision-making logic which differs from that of

29 *Commission* v *Spain*, cited above, paragraph 82.
30 See the recent case *Cassa di Risparmio di Firenze*, cited above.

the actors in a market (though both can, at times, pursue the same goals). Instead, the use of a private legal form and the substitution of state intervention in the market by state participation in that market often entail the exclusion of these forms of state activity from the traditional mechanisms of political accountability. It is, therefore, essential, both in terms of proper accountability of the state and of control of any form of power, for such activity to be subjected to the mechanisms of accountability and the control of power inherent to the market. Finally, a consistency requirement is also important for the purposes of guaranteeing the transparency necessary for the functioning of the mechanisms of political accountability existent in the state's political process. This requires the state to make the logic of its decision-making correspond to what it itself proclaims.

This requirement of coherence also operates at the level of the market in two ways. Firstly, by guaranteeing that, when the state acquires a private form and is no longer subject to the classic mechanisms of public accountability, it becomes subject to the alternative mechanism of accountability inherent in the market (mainly competition). Secondly, by guaranteeing that the state is not allowed to intervene to protect certain private operators from the mechanisms of accountability inherent in market competition.

PART III

SOCIAL RIGHTS AND SOCIAL JUSTICE – CAN "THE SOCIAL" SURVIVE EUROPEAN INTEGRATION?

Christoph U. Schmid

CHAPTER 15. FROM *EFFET UTILE* TO *EFFET NEOLIBÉRAL* A CRITIQUE OF THE NEW METHODOLOGICAL EXPANSIONISM OF THE EUROPEAN COURT OF JUSTICE

1. Introduction

European integration is in crisis. The crisis affects not only political integration, as illustrated by the failure of the Constitutional Treaty and the Treaty of Lisbon, but, less visibly, although not less importantly, also integration through law – in particular, legal adjudication as a common enterprise of European and national courts, newly labelled "judicial governance".[1] The critical state of judicial governance may, perhaps, best be shown in two core and socially "exposed" fields of the European economic constitution: consumer and labour law. With regard to the former, the European Court of Justice (ECJ) may increasingly be criticised for interpreting it as a law of economic integration only, without caring about consumer protection. For example, in a number of cases, including *Gonzalez Sanchez and Skov*,[2] by elevating the outdated and patchy 1985 Product Liability Directive to a maximum harmonisation standard precluding stronger consumer protection under national law, the Court has unexpectedly deprived consumers affected by defective foodstuffs and medicines of important remedies available under national law.[3] In labour law, one may currently observe an even more serious clash of the market freedoms, collective agreements and collective action rights. In the recent *Laval*[4] and *Viking*[5] cases, the ECJ allowed undertakings incorporated in Eastern European countries to undercut wages stipulated by collective agreements in Western European countries, and severely restricted the trade unions' rights to strike actions against such forms of "social dumping". In the *Rüffert*[6] case on public

1 See, in general, S. Frerichs, *Judicial Governance in der Europäischen Rechtsgemeinschaft*, (Baden-Baden: Nomos, 2008).

2 Case C-402/03.

3 See Cases C-183/99 *González Sánchez* [2002] ECR I-3901; C-52/00 *Commission* v *France* [2002] ECR I-3827 and C-154/00 *Commission* v *Greece* [2002] ECR I-3879.

4 Case C-341/05 nyr.

5 Case C-438/05 nyr.

6 Case C-346/06 nyr.

procurement, the Court even went as far as to forbid the respecting, until that time mandatory under regional German law for tenders, of minimum wages stipulated by collective agreements. Yet, if labour competition were to intensify at the expense of Western European workers who cannot survive in their home countries with lower Eastern European wages, the fear of the "Polish plumber", who became so prominent in the French "no" to the Constitutional Treaty, may eventually materialise. Never in the history of European integration has it, to date, happened that workers and trade unions are apparently beginning to distrust the EU on a large scale,[7] and that eminent academics voice crude warnings, such as "stop the ECJ".[8]

These problems are predominantly political in nature. Indeed, they reflect unavoidable tensions between legitimate objectives of the integration process, such as the free market *versus* consumer and worker protection, Eastern European aspirations to access the Western European labour markets *versus* Western European defence action of the social state. However, the conviction driving this chapter is that these tensions do not just have political, economic and social origins. Instead, just as with any other exercise of public power, judicial governance has a twofold dimension: input and output, i.e., procedure and substance. Though little reflected in European practice, a great deal of the legitimacy of judicial decisions depends on the input dimension, i.e., an unbiased, inclusive, deliberate, quick and effective procedure, and a sound legal reasoning and methodology in court decisions.

Yet, the ECJ's legal reasoning and methodology is often viewed as defective. To start with, the ECJ's style of legal reasoning, inspired by the French tradition, is too succinct and leaves too little room for arguments and persuasion, which would be a pre-requisite for the acceptance of the decision by the losing party and by the Member State whose national legal order might be affected by the judgement. Beyond that, the Court's reasoning is usually very formalistic and, contrary to the legislative procedure, does not normally extend to assessing the impact of a decision in the social and economic reality of national systems. An even more important criticism attaches to the ECJ's substantive orientation. Indeed, the Court is often reproached to perform the function of an "EU house court", with the maximisation of *effet utile* being its chief interpretative criterion. This translates into an expansionist approach which constantly extends the reach and effectiveness of European law.

This chapter will theoretically reconstruct and refine, illustrate examples of, and propose an alternative to, the Court's methodological expansionism. In a first part, I will expound the thesis that the judicial expansionism of the past decades was, notwithstanding its methodologically revolutionary character, generally acceptable in

7 Compare, for example, European Trade Union Confederation, Resolution: ETUC response to ECJ Judgments *Viking* and *Laval*, available at: www.etuc.org.

8 R. Herzog and L. Gerken, Stoppt den Europäischen Gerichtshof, Frankfurter Allgemeine Zeitung of 8 Sept. 2008, also available at: www.cep.eu; F. Scharpf, Mitbestimmung 7–8/2008, 18 *et seq.* (interview).

substance, as it was oriented at approximating, in breadth, depth and effectiveness, the EC/EU to a quasi-federal constitutional system and did not, generally, go beyond other existing federal systems. This thesis will be illustrated by pointing to important judge-made innovations in the structural and substantive constitution (Section 2). In the last years, though, the thesis continues, the Court increasingly practises a new kind of judicial expansionism which is no longer compatible with, but goes beyond, the federal constitutional paradigm. Instead, the new approach is characterised by methodological weaknesses and biases which translate into a serious imbalance in the European economic constitution – *effet utile* is being turned into an *effet néoliberal*. This trend will be shown by reconstructing two major instances of methodological defects in labour law: the Court's basic freedoms-bias in dealing with conflicting fundamental rights in primary law, and its excessive application of the pre-emption doctrine in secondary law. It is submitted that this constitutional imbalance puts at risk not only the methodological integrity of European judicial governance, but also the social and political legitimacy of the European system *tout court* (Section 3). What is required from the Court, I conclude, by drawing on Christian Joerges, is nothing less but an abandonment of judicial expansionism and a reorientation towards an alternative methodological meta-principle. This may be labelled reflexive balancing and aims at a methodologically impartial and politically sensitive co-ordination of European and national law (Section 4).

2. Judicial Expansionism in the Elaboration of the European Economic Constitution

Famously, important parts of the EU's structural (dealing with the legal relationship of the EU and its Member States) and substantive constitution were not contained in the Treaty of Rome, but were developed by the ECJ in decade long jurisprudence. In the latter, the core provisions on the free movement of goods, services, labour, companies and capital were developed from commands directed to Member States modelled on GATT 1947 first into subjective rights which excluded discrimination, then into prohibitions of limitations and positive action commands, and, finally, were extended even horizontally, i.e., among private parties.[9] Even though this line of judicial law making is truly revolutionary, and would certainly not have been foreseen by the founding fathers of the EEC in 1958, it has developed the free trade provisions into a common and widespread instrument – namely, fundamental economic rights which are also contained in national constitutions. Such rights enjoy, by definition, direct effect and protect their holders not only against discrimination, but also other unjustified, in particular, disproportional, limitations; and even their horizontal applicability among

[9] See, instead, of many, J.H.H. Weiler, "The Constitution of the Common Marketplace", in: P. Craig and G. de Búrca (eds), *The Evolution of EU Law*, (Oxford, Oxford University Press, 1999), p. 349.

citizens and enterprises represents a widespread development in many, if not most, European states.[10]

With regard to the structural constitution, this may again be regarded as ultimately relatively similar to federal systems. It is true that, starting from the public international law origin of the Community, the Court-made doctrines of direct effect, supremacy and state liability, were indeed revolutionary; the same is true for its often overlooked procedural counterpart, the transformation of the preliminary reference procedure (Article 234 EC), which was originally only meant to ensure uniform interpretation of EC law, into a mechanism of constitutional review of national law. Yet, the ensuing result, namely, that there exists a "higher law of the land" which is directly applicable and trumps over lower (regional) law is no anomaly, but rather the regular state of affairs in federal systems; the remarkable point is only that the founding fathers of the EC did not, apparently, envisage such a system. Even the direct effect of directives does not constitute a major exception. It may be true that the concept of directives, which according to Article 249 EC constitute implementation commands directed to the Member States only, is a special European feature. Yet, the Court's doctrine of direct effect is built on the universally recognised principles of *venire contra factum proprium* in the Roman law tradition, and *resp. estoppel* in the Common Law – whereby nobody is to be allowed to gain advantages by disrespecting the law.

Finally, the state liability doctrine which the ECJ deduced from nothing more than "the system of the Treaty"[11] in *Francovich* and the follow-up decisions does have European structural specificities. Indeed, due to the limited number of cases referred, the ECJ was not yet able to elaborate it into a comprehensive framework. Instead, among the elements for a liability claim, only the violation of a right guaranteed in EU law has been defined exhaustively at European level, whereas the causality and scope of the recoverable damage still need to be defined by national law, which is resorted to gap-filling. Thus, taken together, state liability law in Europe constitutes a complex, and probably typically European, mixture of European and national law. However, beyond these structural specificities, the existence, as such, of a state liability doctrine covering "legislative injustice" is a typical feature of all European states.

All in all, it may be concluded that major features of both the structural and the substantive constitution have been developed by courageous and, partly, even revolutionary moves of the Court, which went massively beyond the original design of the Treaty of Rome and converted the EU into a quasi-federal system. Yet, when compared to other federal systems, and apart from the fact that no other system has been created through judicial law-making to a similar extent, the structural and substantive constitution of the EU have only limited peculiarities. As the federal

10 See A. Colombi Ciacchi, G. Brüggemeier and G. Comandé, *Fundamental Rights and Private Law in the European Union*, vol. 2, (Cambridge: Cambridge University Press, 2008).

11 Case C-6/90 and C 9/90, *Francovich*, ECR 1991, 5537. See, for example, in English, R. Caranta, "Judicial Protection against Member States: A New Jus Commune takes Shape", (1995) 32 *CMLR*, p. 703.

transformation of the EU has been tacitly approved by the Member States over the years, this kind of old judicial expansionism may eventually claim legitimacy.

3. Recent Judicial Expansionism Translating into Neoliberal Results

In recent years, European integration has entered a new phase in various respects. With regard to form, the successful model of – politically less visible – incremental integration has partly been replaced by an integration of "*grands projets*", which have, up until now, been far less successful: the Nice Fundamental Rights Charter, the White Paper on Governance, which claimed a new form for the exercise of political power by the EU, the Constitutional Treaty and, what may be viewed as its societal counterpart, the project of a European Civil Code. With regard to substance, economic integration seems to have reached a new phase in which the persistence of different national varieties of capitalism is no longer accepted.[12] Instead, radical liberalisation efforts systematically challenge the institutions of continental style organised capitalism, in which a certain equilibrium between economic efficiency and social state objectives was established. This trend is illustrated by the struggles over the Takeover and the Services Directives, which have also negatively affected the ratification debate of the constitutional treaty.

This shift in economic integration is also supported by a novel kind of judicial expansionism practised by the ECJ. This is characterised not so much by new and more fanciful methodological inventions, but by the legal political results of law-making in politically sensitive fields. Indeed, the special feature of this new judicial expansionism seems to be that it goes beyond the federalisation paradigm and thus translates into a serious imbalance in the European economic constitution, with *effet utile* being turned into an *effet néoliberal*.

This trend is, perhaps, most visible in the instrumentalisation, by the ECJ, of parties' strategies to circumvent national regulation in order to favour integration, often with a de-regulatory flavour. Such a connotation may be associated with the famous *Centros* and *Inspire Art* cases in which the ECJ accepted the use of foreign letterbox companies, the English private limited company in particular, explicitly to circumvent national corporate law requirements *inter alia* on minimum capitalisation. Indeed, the ECJ decided that it is legitimate for a company to be governed no longer by the law of the place of its doing business (the so-called real-seat-theory), but by the law of the place of its incorporation (the incorporation theory) even if the actual place of activity is then transferred into another country. Whilst the ensuing liberalisation of company law may still be viewed as acceptable on account of its rationalising effects, it might become

12 This thesis is advocated by M. Höpner and Armin Schäfer, "A New Phase of European Integration", MPIFG Discussion Paper 07/4.

critical if extended to socially sensitive parts of national company law, such as the German co-determination system.[13]

Beyond *Centros* and its progeny, it is submitted that more dangerous effects of the ECJ's new judicial expansionism might materialise in consumer and labour law: namely, the Court's articulation of fundamental rights and market freedoms in primary law, which, in certain cases, amounts to a pro-market freedoms-bias (1), and its excessive application of the pre-emption doctrine in secondary law (2).

3.1. The Court's Articulation of Fundamental Rights and Market Freedoms

In the Court's articulation of fundamental rights and market freedoms, there have been important new developments in recent years. To start with, the 1999 Nice Charter has consolidated and extended the reach and intensity of the protection of fundamental rights in Europe. Though not yet formally integrated into EU law due to the failure of the Constitutional and the Treaty of Lisbon, both of which had contained the Charter, European institutions including the ECJ and the European Commission have often referred to the Charter and elevated its provisions to directly binding general legal principles.

Whereas the fundamental rights contained in the Charter may only be invoked against EC/EU measures, and not against national measures others than implementation und execution measures of EU law (Article 51 Charter), the ECJ has apparently disrespected this limitation in the *Karner*[14] case. In this case, a trader had challenged the prohibition, contained in Austrian unfair competition law, of advertising that the re-sold goods originated from an insolvent estate. After excluding a violation of the free movement of goods by assigning the case to the *Keck* exception of non-discriminatory selling arrangements, the Court also scrutinised the compatibility of this result with the freedom of commercial speech as laid down in Article 10 ECHR. It answered this question in the affirmative as the national provision clearly fell within the margin of discretion granted to national law. In reality, the Court would not even have been allowed to examine the compatibility of a purely national provision with the ECHR as part of EU law. The opaque justification brought forward by the Court according to which the national measure fell the within scope of application of EU law is absolutely not convincing as the application of the basic freedoms had been excluded before and no other affected provision of EU law had been mentioned. Perhaps, extending

[13] Beyond the economic constitution, the jurisprudence on the mutual recognition of driving licences based upon Directive 91/439/EC may, incidentally, be assessed in a similar light (see Cases C-239/06 and C-343/06, *Wiedemann and Funk*). In these decisions, the Court held that a Member State must recognise a driving licence obtained in a foreign state even when the licence had been withdrawn in the home state, for example, for drunk-driving and the exclusionary period for the re-issuance of the licence had not yet elapsed. The only requirement is that the interested person must actually have a registered domicile in the foreign state – a connecting factor which can easily be manipulated.

[14] Case C-71/02, ECR 2005, I-00.

fundamental rights even beyond the scope assigned to them by the Charter might be an invitation to the Member States which opted out to join the Charter, so as to enable them to insist on the limits to judicial review laid down therein.

Another strange combination of fundamental rights and the basic freedoms appeared in the *Carpenter* case: the spouse of a British citizen, who was a national of the Philippines, applied for a permit to stay in the UK, but her application was rejected and a deportation order was issued. The Court held this decision to violate Mr. Carpenter's (!) freedom of services, which was strangely extended so as to cover the protection of family life under Article 8 ECHR as well. According to the Court, the latter's ability to provide services to clients in other EU states would have been impaired if his spouse had been deported, due to the fact that she was responsible for the children when the husband was away on business. With all sympathy for this decision and for the Carpenters' family life, treating the wife as the husband's accessory in exercising his freedom of services is methodologically simply undefendable. Beyond that, it remains completely unclear when a fundamental freedom may be used to extend the scope of application of a basic freedom right. A more happy articulation of fundamental rights and basic freedoms took place in the *Schmidberger* and *Omega* cases. In the former, the Austrian government had granted permission for the Brenner motorway to be closed in order to allow a demonstration against the levels of pollution in the Alps caused by the heavy traffic. Schmidberger was a German company that transported goods on lorries, which argued that the closure of the Brenner Pass interfered with the free movement of goods. The latter was argued to apply also among private parties, in the sense that Member States had an obligation to counteract its violation by one party. In its decision, the ECJ recognised that the closure of the Brenner Pass restricted the free movement of goods, and then considered whether the restriction of the free movement of goods could be justified due to the concerns of the Austrian Government to protect the freedom of expression and freedom of assembly as laid down in Articles 10 and 11 of the ECHR. Emphasising the huge margin of discretion that the Member State authorities enjoyed in this "balancing of interests" exercise, it concluded that the Austrian measures were lawful. Importantly, the ECJ did not subject fundamental rights to a more or less strict and one-sided proportionality scrutiny, as it normally does in cases of limitations to the market freedoms. Instead, extending this text bilaterally, as it were, the Court also argued that restrictions of human rights by market freedoms need to be justified:

> Consequently, the exercise of those [fundamental] rights may be restricted, provided that the restrictions in fact correspond to objectives of general interest and do not, taking account of the aim of the restrictions, constitute disproportionate and unacceptable interference, impairing the very substance of the rights guaranteed.

Remarkably, the latter restriction integrates the German concept of a minimum content of a fundamental right (*Wesensgehalt*) into EU law. An analogous approach was taken by the Court in the *Omega* decision. Omega was a German company operating a laser installation known as a "laser-drome". The police authority of the city of Bonn issued an order prohibiting the operation of games involving firing at human targets. The argument was that these games constituted a violation of human dignity as guaranteed in Article 1 (1) of the German Constitution. Even though the appeal initiated by Omega against this order was dismissed by the *Bundesverwaltungsgericht* (Federal Administrative Court), the latter was, however, uncertain as to whether the prohibition was compatible with the freedom to provide services and the free movement of goods as guaranteed in the EC Treaty. The ECJ referred to its judgment in *Schmidberger*, and confirmed that the protection of fundamental rights justifies, in principle, a restriction upon market freedoms. The ECJ shared the opinion of the Advocate General that "the Community legal order undeniably strives to ensure respect for human dignity as a general principle of law". Thus, just as in *Schmidberger*, the ECJ accepted the government's reasons, and allowed that measures which seek to ensure respect for human rights may be justified.

Unfortunately, the high methodological standard practised in these two cases was not perpetuated in subsequent jurisprudence in the *Viking*, *Laval* and *Rüffert* cases on the conflict of the freedom of services with trade unions' right to collective action.

3.1.1. Freedom of Services Versus Trade Unions' Right to Collective action: the Viking, Laval and Rüffert Cases

Facts

In *Viking*, a Finnish firm owned a ferry, the Rosella, which plied its trade between Helsinki and Tallinn. The Rosella sailed under the Finnish flag and had a predominantly Finnish crew. Viking wanted to re-register the ferry in Estonia. The International Transport Workers' Federation (ITF) has a long-standing and well-known campaign against the use of flags of convenience: in other words, the use of the flag of one country (typically with lower labour standards) by a beneficial owner situated in another country. The ITF and its affiliate, the Finnish Seamen's Union (FSU), planned to take industrial action against Viking with a view to preventing the firm from re-flagging the Rosella. Viking applied to the High Court in London for an injunction to stop the trade unions' boycott, on the grounds that it infringed Article 43 EC, the right to freedom of establishment. The English courts' jurisdiction over the case was found to be established pursuant to the Brussels Regulation. At first instance, the English court held that the unions were in breach of Article 43. It did not consider it necessary to refer to the ECJ, and granted an injunction to restrain the unions' industrial action. The unions appealed. The Court of Appeal was much less certain that Article 43 was applicable to the unions, noting that the case raised complex issues about the article's role in cases between private parties which had not previously been addressed by the ECJ. Moreover, even if the unions were to be held to be in breach of Article 43, there were serious questions with regard to whether the unions' actions amounted to direct or indirect discrimination, and, if so, whether or not these actions could be justified. The Court of Appeal decided that these issues should be referred to the ECJ. After detailed consideration, the Court refused to grant Viking an interim injunction against the unions pending the hearing of the case by the ECJ.

In *Laval*, a Latvian building firm was awarded a government contract to renovate school premises in Vaxholm, Sweden. The firm posted some Latvian workers to Sweden to work on the building site. The local branch of the Swedish builders' union (*Svenska Byggnadsarbetareförbundet*) opened negotiations with Laval's Swedish subsidiary with the aim of extending the relevant sectoral collective agreement to the posted workers and negotiating wages for them. The negotiations failed and the union (supported by the electricians' union) began a blockade of Laval's building sites. This effectively put a stop to all work on Laval's sites and eventually resulted in Laval's Swedish subsidiary going into liquidation. Laval brought an action in the Swedish courts. The firm sought a declaration that the collective action was unlawful, an injunction to stop the action, and compensation from the unions for the losses that it had suffered. The Swedish labour law court (*Arbetsdomstolen)* referred questions to the ECJ on the interpretation of the Posted Workers Directive 96/71/EC, and Article 49 EC, on freedom to provide services.

In *Rüffert*, a German company won a tender with the *Land Niedersachsen* which involved construction work in a prison located at Göttingen. The public procurement law of that *Land* states that:

> [T]he contracts for building services shall be awarded only to undertakings which, when lodging a tender, undertake in writing to pay their employees, when performing those services, at least the remuneration prescribed by the collective agreement in the place where those services are performed (...)

The German company sub-contracted the work to a Polish company and it turned out that the Polish workers actually earned less than half of their German colleagues on the site. Therefore, the *Land Niedersachsen* annulled the contract and imposed financial penalties on the company.

Again, the ECJ produced a judgment along the lines of the Posting of Workers Directive. In its view, the situation in *Niedersachsen* did not fulfil the criteria to fix pay as set out in the Directive as the law does not itself fix any minimum rate of pay and the collective agreement in question had not been declared universally applicable. Again, the Court argued that the Posting of Workers Directive outlines the maximum level of protection for posted workers, and that, in a collective agreement, as in this case, a higher level of protection cannot be laid down.

The Decisions of the Court

In *Viking*, the Court pointed out, in a first step, that Article 43 EC could be applied horizontally, i.e., also with regard to collective agreements regulating gainful employment and the provision of services, and that collective measures such as strikes which aim at the conclusion of such an agreement were inextricably linked with the latter and were, therefore, covered as well. This horizontal extension of Article 43 was motivated by the fact that, given that working conditions are regulated in some states by legal regulation and in others by collective agreement, another result would create inequality. In a more fundamental respect, the Court held that collective measures protected by the freedom of association are not exempt from the freedom of establishment by virtue of Article 137 V EC, which excludes European harmonisation measures in this field. Instead, according to the Court, in the areas which fall outside the scope of the Community's competence, the Member States are, in principle, free to enact regulation, but it must, nevertheless, comply with Community law. This apparently innocent sentence means nothing less than that the scope of application of the market freedoms is basically unlimited. Moreover, the Court argued that the protection of fundamental rights including social rights is within the scope of application of Community law, which aims not only at economic, but also at social, integration.

In a second step, the Court examined whether – as the right to register a ship in another country is protected by the freedom of establishment, and collective measures had effectively limited that right – the collective action rights of trade unions constituted a lawful limitation of that freedom. This assessment was delegated by the ECJ to the national courts, who have to respect, however, a set of provisos laid down by the ECJ, which render it somewhat unlikely that collective measures would pass the test. In particular, on account of the proportionality principle, collective action would be allowed only to the extent that it was actually necessary for the protection of workers, and this would not be the case if their jobs were not in danger. Generally, no justification would be available if the ship-owner's freedom to register a vessel in another Member States was completely impaired. In such an event, the protection of workers would not be available as a defence. Indeed, as ITF's policy of combating the use of flags of convenience also applied to the re-registering of vessels in states with a higher level of workers' protection, it was not a suitable measure to promote this aim in the first place.

The *Laval* decision crucially revolves around the compatibility of the collective measures undertaken by the Swedish trade union with the Posted Workers Directive, which will be dealt in more detail with below. Without analytically clarifying the relationship between the directive and Article 49, the Court continued to reason that the compatibility of the trade unions' action with the latter provision would also need to be examined. After repeating that such action, based upon the unions' fundamental rights, was not outside the scope of application of Article 49 and that that provision applied horizontally, the Court also confirmed that Article 49 had been limited by the unions' strike and blocking actions. Then, the ECJ turned to the key issue of the justifications of this restriction through over-riding reason of public interest. As a matter of principle, the Court continued, a collective measure which aims at protecting workers against social dumping is an appropriate public interest, as the activities of the EC/EU as defined in Article 2 EC, and confirmed in several European and international conventions and other legal instruments, include not only an internal market, but also a social policy. Whereas a blockade is still covered by the objective of protecting workers, the Court concluded, the specific obligations in question which the trade unions tried to impose on the undertaking were no longer covered. This followed from the fact that several obligations went beyond the minimum standard of working conditions laid down in the directive. With regard to negotiations on minimum wages, these would, in principle, be allowed by the directive, but were not, in a national context:

> [C]haracterised by a lack of provisions, of any kind, which are sufficiently precise and accessible that they do not render it impossible or excessively difficult in practice for such an undertaking to determine the obligations with which it is required to comply as regards minimum pay.

Finally, the Court found that the Swedish law on worker co-determination which stipulated that foreign collective agreements could not be invoked in Sweden were discriminatory and therefore in violation of Article 49.

The *Rüffert* case also dealt with the Posted Workers Directive (see below) and Article 49 EC. Regarding the latter provision, the ECJ did not admit any justification based upon the rationale of protecting workers, as the regional legislation only applies to the public, and not to the private, sector. The ECJ also rejected other defence arguments: the financial sustainability of social security systems – which had prompted the Federal Constitutional Court to admit compliance with collective agreements (*Tariftreue*) – or ensuring the freedom of collective bargaining and the freedom of association.

Methodological critique

The conflict at issue between the European freedom of services and the national fundamental right of trade unions to take collective action may be labelled a diagonal conflict in which, logically, the supremacy of European law must not be applied formalistically for the very reason that different subject matters are touched upon. Instead, a more complex solution is wanted with a set of conditions that need to be respected.

First, it is still acceptable that the Court does not exempt collective agreements and action by trade unions from the applicability of the basic freedoms altogether, as it had decided in *Albany* with regard to the relationship of antitrust law and collective agreements. Indeed, such a solution would have allowed for an unlimited restriction of the freedom of services and would have excluded any balancing and compatibilisation of the two colliding fields. It is true that this jurisprudence constitutes a remarkable extension of the horizontality doctrine, which has, up until now, only been applied to collective actors, such as sports associations[15] or employers[16] with factual regulation power over others; in contrast, trade unions may only militate in favour of the conclusion of collective-agreements, and, hence, they do not possess unilateral regulatory power. But when the legal order, in order to enable societal self-regulation in the public interest ("private governance"), assigns a high degree of regulatory power and

15 Case 36/74, Walrave and Koch, ECR 1974, 1405; C-415/93, Union Royale Belge des Sociétés de Football Association ASLB/ Jean-Marc Bosman, ECR 1995, I-4921.

16 Case C-281/98, Angonese, ECR 2000, I-4139.

collective rights to the industrial parties together, they should, when exercising these powers, be bound to consider fundamental rules of general interest – such as the European market freedoms, which articulate the European interest in the free circulation of goods, *etc.* However, the constitutionally protected status of trade union rights urges a limitation of the reach and intensity of the market freedoms' influence on collective agreements, so as to enable a smooth co-ordination of both constitutional principles.

Not exempting collective agreements from the application of the basic freedoms is not, moreover, logically incompatible with Article 137 V EC, as this provision only excludes a harmonisation competence in this field. Yet, the impossibility of re-regulating a situation in which de-regulation has taken place through the application of the basic freedoms should induce the Court to grant a significant margin of discretion to national law – as it otherwise faces the danger of a "terrorist approach", in the sense of putting a "de-regulatory" bomb, although it is unable to do the "re-regulatory" reconstruction work afterwards.

Unfortunately, the Court has not opted for such desirable judicial self-restraint. Instead, its way of articulating the basic freedoms with industrial relations is not methodologically neutral, but confers significant advantages on the former. To start with, the basic freedoms are chosen as reference provisions against which industrial action needs to justify itself under the narrow limitations of the proportionality principle. This is, of course, the Court's ordinary way of scrutinising the compatibility of any national legislation with the basic freedoms. However, this approach is inadequate in the case of *fundamental* rights – which, in all Member States' legal systems and also in European law (to name just the Charter), enjoy the same rank and dignity as the basic freedoms. Why should industrial action rights – which have been established in the Member State only after century-long painful struggles and which are indispensable components of the welfare state upon which the social peace is built – need to justify themselves before the basic freedoms – why not, provocatively speaking, just the other way round? Who has ever decided on the supremacy of the basic freedoms in Europe over any other constitutional rights? As already mentioned, the Court had adopted an adequate "bilateral" perspective on the articulation of fundamental rights and market freedoms in *Schmidberger* and *Omega*, but it is neither clear nor coherent why it has not done so in the cases under review. As a result, the Court should not choose one right as a reference provision, but should evenly balance both, so as to maximise the practical effectiveness of both – a procedure named "practical concordance" in German methodology. Such a balancing exercise would also include adapting the justifications available for the restrictions of market freedoms to the specific situation of private parties in horizontal constellations such as the present one – a problem which had already been addressed in the context of the *Bosman* decision.

Contrary to what some might think, the defective methodological approach by the Court is not a minor issue, but generates important consequences. Indeed, the Court only briefly sketches industrial action rights as part of the general interest, and, therefore, as in principle admissible limitations to the basic freedoms, before it turns to focusing in much greater detail on the proportionality conditions that those rights need to satisfy. Thus, neither their autonomous scope of protection, nor their indispensable hard core are de-limited and reflected in any way. Moreover, industrial action rights are implicitly downgraded by the Court by presenting them as part of the general interest only. In their historically prior and still most important function, fundamental rights are subjective defence rights of citizens and enterprises against the state; they are, in other words, *exceptions* to the general interest, not incorporations thereof.

Beyond this, collective action rights are also treated inadequately in the framework of the proportionality principle: the Court protects them only to the extent they are necessary to ensure the protection of workers, which is treated as the paramount objective. Consequently, in the Court's view, collective action rights are not suitable to restrict the market freedoms when invoked in order to counteract the transfer of an undertaking to a country with a higher standard of labour protection. The same is true when security of employment is not at stake – as it had been argued in *Viking* when the company offered to carry out the re-flagging without dismissing crew members. As a result, when collective action rights are tied to the protection of workers, they are ultimately reduced to safeguarding existing jobs alone.

However, in the European constitutional tradition, collective actions have a completely different dimension: they are generally protected in their own right, not as the accessories of other rights. Collective agreements and action rights represent a sphere of societal self-organisation which goes beyond the protection of workers, but is directly relevant to the legitimacy of modern "multi arena-governance" (Héritier), composed of a wide array of private and public elements. As a result, the Court should have analysed whether the self-organising capacity of Swedish trade unions as part of the Swedish civil society would have been affected in its hard core if it forced Sweden to accept foreign collective agreements and social dumping upon the basis of the market freedoms. These implications of collective action rights should also have been reflected in a less restrictive application of the horizontality doctrine. Whereas this doctrine may, perhaps, be extended legitimately to important collective agreements and action rights substituting themselves effectively for state regulation on working conditions, the trade unions should, at any rate, be accorded a larger margin of discretion in exercising their collective rights. Ultimately, all these considerations should have conducted the Court to the fundamental question of whether it was entitled to interfere with, and gravely damage, the Swedish social model in which the self-regulation of workers, tenants and consumers, which plays a far larger role than elsewhere in Europe, and has enabled social peace and prosperity for at least the last century.

3.2. The Excessive Application of the Pre-emption Doctrine in Secondary Law

Another methodological weakness which has translated itself into a serious neo-liberal imbalance in the European economic constitution is provided by the Court's excessive application of the pre-emption doctrine in secondary law. As a correlate of the supremacy doctrine, pre-emption means that national provisions which concur with European provisions are displaced because European legislation has already dealt exhaustively with the subject matter in question or laid down the conditions for the applicability of national law exhaustively. Thus, contrary to the supremacy doctrine, it is irrelevant whether a national provision is in conflict or not with European provisions if the national norm only falls in a pre-empted area, which may also be a small area. Clearly, the pre-emption doctrine has a huge interventionist potential, as it may declare inapplicable a whole field of national law on account of a perceived contradiction with European law. In a constitutional macro-perspective, pre-emption indicates a shift of legislative competence in a given field from a concurring to an exclusive European competence.

Pre-emption is, in some cases, prescribed by conflicts of law rules contained in European legal instruments. Normally, however, the assessment of whether a certain area, or sub-field, is regulated exhaustively by the European legislator belongs to the ECJ, which has, as always, a huge degree of discretion in the application of this doctrine. The following example of the interpretation of the Posted Workers Directive in the *Laval* and *Rüffert* cases will show that, unfortunately, the Court applies this doctrine too restrictively, which curtails national law too much and overstretches the regulatory capacity of European law.

3.2.1. The Posted Workers Directive

The Posted Workers Directive of 1996, which regulates the working conditions of workers posted to another Member State, was enacted for several motives. First, in the leading case *Rush Portuguesa* of 1990[17], the ECJ had indicated, albeit only in an *obiter dictum*, that Member States were entitled to apply their entire legislation in the field of social and labour law including collective agreements to posted workers. Clearly, this legal position strengthens national industrial systems, including the position of trade unions, but weakens the chances of foreign companies to access domestic markets, and thus the effectiveness of the freedom of services. To counteract this trend, the Commission was in search of a compromise which would limit this freedom less.[18] The Member States, at that time only Western European States (!), not only wanted to regulate the legal position of posted workers, but also wanted to protect their labour markets against low wage competition ("social dumping") from other Member States. In this context, Germany and other Member States also wanted to safeguard their own pre-existing special legislation on posted workers, which might have come under pressure had the ECJ ordered the unaltered application, on anti-discrimination grounds, of ordinary national legislation in the field of social and labour law to posted workers as well.

17 Case C-113/82, ECR 1990, 1965.

18 M. Corti, "Le decisioni ITF e Laval della Corte di Giustizia", (2008) 27 *Rivista Italiana di Diritto del Lavoro*, p. 254 *et seq.*

The principal aims of the Posted Workers Directive are indicated in its 5th Recital: promoting transnational services through fair competition and the protection of workers, leaving Member State law on collective action unaffected (Rec. 22). Though not explicitly mentioned, the objective of counteracting social dumping may also be read into the term "fair competition". Technically, the directive did not envisage the harmonisation of substantive law, but limited itself to a private international law solution. According to its Article 3, host Member States are required to ensure the application to posted workers of a set of important working conditions, including maximum work periods, minimum paid annual holidays and minimum rates of pay, as stipulated in their own law and/or collective agreements or arbitration awards declared universally applicable; if neither of the two instruments exist in a Member State, the latter is also allowed to base itself upon collective agreements or awards generally applicable to all similar undertakings in the geographical area and in the profession or industry concerned and/or collective agreements concluded by the most representative employers' and labour organisations at national level and applied throughout the country, provided that equal treatment of domestic and posted foreign workers is ensured (Article 3 para. 8). According to Article 3 para. 7, though, these provisions "[s]hall not prevent application of terms and conditions of employment which are more favourable to workers".

The meaning of this provision is not entirely clear, and it might even seem that these ambiguous terms were chosen on purpose, as a kind of liberalist trap. It is true that the wording of the provision covers any more favourable employment conditions, irrespective of who has enacted them. However, it is also clear that this interpretation would admit any national rules, even rules which, under the pretext of granting high protection to posted workers, *de facto* shield the national labour market from posted workers by making their use prohibitively expensive. As a result, it has been submitted in the literature that the directive's objective of co-ordinating the laws of the Member States in order to ensure effective minimum protection (Recital 13) required a limitation of this provision to more favourable rules of the enterprise's state of origin.[19]

As mentioned, under the Swedish social model, industrial relations play a central role, and the regulation of working conditions is largely left to the industrial partners. This model does not fit well with the system of the directive. Conditions on working time and all the other types of conditions mentioned in the directive, with the exception of minimum wage conditions, are contained in the Swedish implementation statute, but collective agreements often lay down more favourable conditions for workers. Wage conditions are left entirely to collective negotiation, but minimum wages, in the technical sense, do not exist; instead, staggered wages reflecting the different categories of workers are usually negotiated for single building projects. Moreover, the collective agreement the Swedish trade unions wanted to force on Laval contained further provisions (*inter alia* rules on protection against dismissal, on contributions to

19 Corti (*loc. cit.*), p. 259 *et seq.*

insurance schemes and on compensations for union activities) which are not contemplated in the directive at all.

3.2.2. The Interpretation of the Posted Workers Directive in *Laval* and *Rüffert*

In *Laval*, the ECJ ruled that all three types of clauses and conditions contained in the collective agreement were incompatible with the directive. Significantly, and though this term is actually never used, the Court based this assessment upon a formalistic pre-emption reasoning.

With regard to the provisions on wages, the Court held that, as the negotiation of wages had been left to the trade unions, they had not been stipulated in one of the ways allowed by the directive, i.e. by national law, or by the collective agreements or the arbitration awards declared universally applicable, or by representative collective agreements chosen by Member State authorities as the relevant basis for minimum working conditions. Therefore, no lawful designation of minimum provisions by state authorities could be recognised.

With regard to the second group of working conditions contemplated by Article 3 a-g and implemented by Swedish legislation, the Court stressed that it was not lawful that working conditions contained in collective agreements could go beyond the minimum standard fixed by law. Instead, the directive needed to be interpreted not only as a minimum standard, but also a maximum standard, under which only the rules of the enterprise's state of origin could be invoked as more favourable rules in the sense of Article 3 (7). Otherwise, the Court argued, the directive would be deprived of its *effet utile* – apparently that of enabling only a limited restriction of the freedom of services through a set of basic minimum working conditions.

With regard to the third group of working conditions, i.e., conditions not contemplated by Article 3 a-g, but contained in the relevant collective agreements (such as conditions on contributions to pension and accident relief schemes), these are not at all justifiable unless they are necessary to uphold public order as defined in Article 3 (10), which was not the case here.

In *Rüffert*, the Court applied basically the same schematic pre-emption reasoning as in *Laval*. The requirement, contained in the law for public tenders of the *Land Niedersachsen*, of a declaration by the undertaking that the collective agreements of the relevant sector would be complied with was not covered by Article 3 (1) 1st indent of the directive, as it clearly did not lay down any minimum wages itself; the collective agreement in the construction sector at issue was not covered by Article 3 (1) 2nd indent and (8) of the directive as it had not been declared universally applicable; nor could it be qualified as a representative collective agreement in the sense of Article 3 (8) as it had not been qualified as such by a public authority; moreover, it did not constitute an agreement "generally applicable to all similar undertakings in the geographical area and in the profession or industry concerned" as foreseen in Article 3(8) as it was not applicable to private construction works.

3.2.3. Methodological Critique

The formalistic application of the directive triggers a host of methodological criticisms. At a technical level, it is questionable how the Court could, as it did, simply scrutinise the compatibility of national legislation and collective agreements with the directive. Indeed, no mention is made of the direct effect doctrine or *interprétation conforme*, and the lack, well established in earlier jurisprudence since *Marshall*, of the horizontal direct effect of a directive. Assuming that the Court did not want to discard all its previous jurisprudence on this matter, the only methodologically possible way to explain the Court's reasoning would be to read the whole content of the directive implicitly into the scope of application of Article 49 EC. Indeed, whereas the Court kept the scrutiny of Article 49 EC and the directive separate in the motivation of the decisions, it quoted both sources together in their operative summary. However, this approach is highly problematical, as reading all the detailed provisions of a directive into primary law would level out the difference between primary and secondary law and unduly assign the directive more weight on account of the hierarchy of norms.

The main substantive criticism attaches to the excessive pre-emptive effect accorded to the directive by the Court, notably through its restrictive interpretation of Article 3 (7). Generally, this interpretation presses the multiplicity of regulation, extending to posted workers, on working conditions in all Members States and of both public and private origin, into the straitjacket of a few legal provisions, which, most probably, were not intended by their drafters as an exhaustive regulation of the whole field. Indeed, as shown by its clash with the Swedish system of industrial relations, the Posted Workers Directive is manifestly incapable of doing justice to the host of social models that exist in Europe.

This predominantly legal policy-based criticism may be specified analytically in various respects. First, the Court's limitation of Article 3 para. 7 to more favourable norms on the working conditions of the country of origin is far from being persuasive. When the ECJ tries to base this interpretation upon the *effet utile* of the directive, it should be noted that it deprives Article 3 para. 7 of any meaningful *effet utile* in the first place. Indeed, under the Article 8 para. 2 of the Rome I – regulation, labour contracts are governed, in the absence of a valid choice of law, by the law of the country in which the worker usually works. This rule also applies in the case of a transitory posting to another country. As a result, the law of the country of origin is already applicable according to ordinary conflict of laws rules. The mandatory norms of the Posted Workers Directive allow for an exception to these rules only when the labour regulation in the country of origin does not comply with the minimal working conditions of the country of destination, as contemplated in Article 3 a–g of the directive. In the event that the law of the country of origin is more favourable for the worker than the law of the country of destination, the former applies anyway. Therefore, if limited, as the Court did, to the law of the country of origin, Article 3 para. 7 of the directive is deprived of any meaningful scope of application.

Second, it is questionable that the Court extends the directive's pre-emptive effect to any private collective agreement governing working conditions. Indeed, the directive only refers to the regulation of working conditions in legal or administrative provisions, collective agreements declared universally applicable, or representative agreements selected by public authorities; its extension *beyond* these categories not only constitutes a massive limitation on private autonomy, but also prevents Member States from regulating such agreements constructively in any other way. The excessive horizontal pre-emptive effect accorded to the directive by the Court is rendered worse by the fact that, pursuant to Article 3(10), the directive restrictions are only justifiable on grounds of public order (which is much more restrictive than the justifications applicable to the market freedoms under the *Cassis* doctrine), and that the Court even denies these exceptions to be invoked by trade unions.[20] Third, whereas the clash of fundamental rights of collective action and market freedoms has been dealt with in the scrutiny of Article 49 EC, the former have not been resorted to in the interpretation of the directive – notwithstanding the general duty of interpreting secondary law instruments in the light of higher-ranking sources, such as fundamental rights, in particular. One constructive way to pay heed to trade unions' fundamental right to collective action would be to restrict the escape clause for more favourable working conditions in the sense of Article 3(7) of the directive to the terms laid down in collective agreements; such terms could then still be subject to a basic review under Article 49 EC. However, even within the Court's pre-emption approach, there would have been interpretative leeway for an approach deferring to the autonomy of Member States and the trade unions: As AG Mengozzi has plausibly shown in *Laval*, the Swedish system, which implicitly delegates the determination of working conditions, including minimum wages, to the industrial parties, could have been assessed as a functional equivalent to working conditions laid down by law or by representative collective agreements in the sense of Article 3(8) of the directive.

3.3. *Evaluation*

Taken together, these methodological defects and biases in the articulation of fundamental rights and market freedoms and the application of the pre-emption doctrine confer decisive advantages to European market values over social values protected at national level. This novel kind of judicial expansionism goes beyond the state of affairs in federal constitutional systems as administered by national constitutional courts. In these systems, one may not find a balancing of economic and social values, in which the former enjoy massive methodological advantages which translate into a neo-liberalisation of the whole system. Also, whilst different versions of pre-emption doctrines exist in all federal systems, we are not aware of any similarly aggressive recent

20 ECJ, *Rüffert*, at no. 84.

application of this doctrine, which puts the social institutions to which we owe peace and prosperity under pressure, and which prevents state authorities from fulfilling their regulatory responsibility in entire areas of law. As opposed to the old judicial expansionism which successfully approximated the EU to a federal constitutional system, this new from of judicial expansionism cannot claim legitimacy, but, instead, puts at the risk the very legitimacy of the European system. Against this background, it might actually be that this form of judicial expansionism can only be stopped politically, for example, through the establishment of a competing judicial body to safeguard national legislative autonomy and competences, as recently proposed again by Roman Herzog. Nevertheless, we do still nurture the, perhaps, naïve hope that European judicial governance may be reformed from within, i.e., by the legal system itself. To this end, we claim that the ECJ needs to accept a widely different constitutional role for itself in the European multi-level system, similar to Christian Joerges' vision of European law as a conflict of laws instrument in the US tradition, capable of balancing both national and European interests.

4. A Plea for a New Constitutional Role of the EC in the European Multi-level System

In order to exercise a more legitimate adjudication, the ECJ would need to abandon its role of motor of the integration, and evolve into a true constitutional court aiming at a methodologically impartial and politically sensitive co-ordination of European and national law. This mandate may be further specified by multi-level governance theory, which focuses on the effectiveness and legitimacy of governance. According to this theory, the legitimacy of judicial governance is highest when it draws on the European constitutional provision in order to compensate "nation state failures". These include discrimination of all kind, the shifting of the externalities of domestic policies to neighbour states, violations of universal constitutional norms, such as freedom and equality rights, and also obvious irrationalities and inefficiencies of national governance, which harms both national and European citizens. Conversely, democratically rooted legitimate national institutions, social state institutions, in particular, which the EU is not realistically able to establish at European level, should not be affected by European intervention. In procedural terms, legitimate judicial governance should, as far as possible, refrain from hierarchically commanding and controlling national legal systems, but should, instead, focus on their stabilisation and compatibilisation with European basic values – based upon the insight that procedural framework-setting is more legitimate than the substantive balancing of competing values, which are often essential elements of the national identity. This kind of governance should aim at integrating all affected interests, including those of citizens and enterprises from other Member States not directly involved in the proceedings at issue. To this end, the ECJ would need to enter into a more constructive dialogue with national courts, in which the different legal traditions and their rooting in the different social, economic and political models should be considered, just as the different factual consequences of decisions in the various Member States should be. As a basic rule, the degree of European intervention should depend on the extent to which nation state failures exist.

Applying these guidelines to the articulation of fundamental rights of collective action, national social models and European market freedoms, we may subscribe to the answer given by Christian Joerges and Florian Rödl:

> National welfare state traditions do not, by definition, constitute a form of national state failure. Instead, the curtailing of legal guarantees of the social state through supranational law does not represent an acceptable intervention into national democracies but amounts to the demise of modern democratic self-determination.[21]

Following these guidelines, the cases *Viking*, *Laval* and *Rüffert* would have needed to be decided differently.

21 Ch. Joerges and F. Rödl, Von der Entformalisierung europäischer Politik und dem Formalismus europäischer Rechtsprechung im Umgang mit dem "sozialen Defizit" des Integrationsprojekts, ZERP DP 2/2008.

Nina Boeger

CHAPTER 16. PUBLIC SERVICE, AUTONOMY AND COMMUNITY LAW

1. Introduction

Can Community law resolve the conflict between the Member States' individual concern to control their public services, and their common concern to integrate Europe's service markets and keep them competitive? The question is, of course, far from new and follows familiar processes. The breadth of this subject-matter is considerable, including Europe's liberalised or partially liberalised network industries (electronic communications, utilities, postal services), but also non-harmonised services, such as waste and water management, health and social services.[1] All these are referred to as "public services" below.

All of Europe's networked industries have been affected by de-regulation as a consequence of negative integration – the application of EC competition law – and regulatory competition, leading to liberalisation and privatisation, and, eventually, to re-regulation by way of European-wide standards. The Commission continues its liberalisation course with some determination, and plans to introduce the value of competition into further public service sectors; thereby increasing Europe's influence over public services as they become subject to the full body of EU economic law.[2] The Court, on the other hand, continues to develop EU economic law in a way that suggests its interference in welfare states, including its core sectors of education, and social and health services, has not even come close to reaching its limits.[3]

In the context of negative integration or re-regulation, one theme dominating both EC competition law and the secondary legislation in this field is the level of autonomy afforded to Member States to define certain services as "services of general interest" and to protect them from the market so as to give effect to social goals. Whilst these social

1 See European Commission, Communication on 'Services of general interest, including social services of general interest: a new European commitment', COM (2007) 725 final, 20 November 2007.

2 Ibid.

3 G. Davies, "The Process and Side-Effects of Harmonisation of European Welfare States", Jean Monnet Working Paper 02/06, NYU School of Law, 2006.

goals will regularly be distributional (i.e., to achieve the distribution of certain goods in a way that the market cannot achieve), they may occasionally be further reaching, as they may include the protection of a "public service ethos" or other values.

In the networked industries, Member States have ceded a degree of freedom in the interest of liberalisation and the harmonisation of standards; but whilst they have withdrawn a great deal of their direct involvement in these sectors, they have retained both the control and the responsibility of defining and imposing "public service obligations" on market operators, in order to guarantee a broad minimum service to all citizens. The objective of these legislative "packages" is to reconcile the concern of the Member States to control their welfare states, with the Commission's concern with regard to the Internal Market. And one dominant view amongst academics especially in the UK (where liberalisation and privatisation has so far outpaced the rest of the Community) has been to analyse these as attempts to reconcile citizenship and social rights with the Internal Market.[4] Whilst the legislation generally concentrates on upholding competition by avoiding cartels, these public service obligations are seen as an effective way of ensuring that considerations of equity and access to all are not overridden by the concern for profit and shareholder value which drive market providers.

But are public service obligations the solution to many of the deep value-conflicts that underlie the debate on Europe's role in relation to public services? Do they capture all the existing values and benefits that we find underlying solidarity models of public service, and the enfranchising function of certain public services? Can we trust regulators to exert their influence on social issues, dressing them up as a public service obligation, in this way?

This chapter discusses these questions. It suggests that a sensible design for Community public service law will have to start from first principles: the concern for individual autonomy, the capacity of European citizens to shape their own lives. Autonomy can be, and has been, in much of the classical writings on political liberalism,[5] seen in either a

4 Malcolm Ross, for example, attests a "re-orientation of both values and governance" at Community level (M. Ross, "Promoting Solidarity: From Public Services to a European Model of Competition?" (2007) 44 *C.M.L.Rev.*, p. 1057, at 1057). Tony Prosser observes a "degree of synthesis of substantive principles" between the value of competition and public service values in Community law (T. Prosser, *The Limits of Competition Law: Markets and Public Services*, (Oxford: Oxford University Press, 2005), p. 239). Mark Freedland has spoken of an "ironic reversal of the role of the Community as the guardian of liberal free trade" into "the residual guardian of [national] welfarist ideals, in however diluted a practical form", (Mark Freedland, "Law, Public Services, and Citizenship – New Domains, New Regimes?", in: M. Freedland and S. Sciarra, *Public Services and Citizenship in European Law: public and labour law perspectives*, (Oxford: Oxford University Press, 1998), p. 28).

5 See, for example, F.A. von Hayek, *The Political Order of a Free People*, (London: Routledge, 1979) and J. Maynard Keynes, *The End of Laissez-Faire*, (London, Hogarth Press, 1926). These are explored in R. Bellamy, *Liberalism and Modern Society: An Historical Argument*, (Cambridge MA; Polity Press, 1992). See, also, C. Sunstein, *Free Markets and Social Justice*, (New York: Oxford University Press, 1997).

more formal or a more material way, but only from the perspective of the private individual, and not from their capacity to interact with other individuals as a political community in order to shape their collective destiny and, more particularly for the purpose of this chapter, the social obligations that they owe to one another in recognition of their mutual solidarity.

The chapter begins by setting out the various interpretations of individual autonomy (and their formal and material aspects), but argues that autonomy really depends on whether citizens retain control over which interpretation dominates, in any one context, in their legal system. It also shows how these issues are relevant to the debate on public services. It also explains how Community law has affected our individual and collective autonomy, yet has also internalised it within the original "compact" between the Community and the Member States, which leaves control over welfare with the latter.

The discussion then turns to the historical realities of public service organisation in the Member States and discusses the Community's influence, especially in the network-based industries. The aim is to illustrate how the "compact" really works in practice, and how it respects the autonomy principle. This is followed by a more critical assessment of these effects, in which it is suggested that, while the Community legislation manages to respect some distributional choices, it is somewhat less effective in paying the same respect to collective choices involving values.

2. Public Service, Law and Autonomy

At the heart of the debate about public service liberalisation in Europe lies the fact that the market, for all its effectiveness in producing efficiency and wealth, functions upon the basis of a formal conception of our individual autonomy.[6] It is this lack of concern for genuine equality of opportunity in a world in which not all citizens come to the market as equals, which creates, in the words of Tony Prosser, "at minimum a tension between the application of competition law to key public services, such as the public utilities, and the principles underlying the distinctive nature of these services".[7]

Self-determination, or autonomy, is about the opportunity to pursue one's own good in one's own way, the problem being that, even if all individuals are regarded by the state as being *formally* equal, material inequalities can just as effectively constrain their opportunity to pursue their own good in their own way. The beauty of freedom is lost on those who have insufficient means to support their daily needs, and, although they are free in law, they cannot live their lives as they would wish. The core function of the national welfare state is to achieve real equality of ability by securing the *material* conditions for the actual exercise of individual autonomy, in order to secure for *all* individuals a genuine opportunity to use the instruments which the state makes

6 See, also, N. Boeger, "Solidarity and EC Competition Law", (2007) 32 *E.L.Rev.*, p. 319.

7 T. Prosser, *supra* note 4, p. 17.

available to them to structure their relations with each other.[8] Whilst this most obviously involves direct transfers (social benefits), it also involves the guarantee of essential services to all citizens irrespective of wealth or privilege, including health and care services, social services (for example, social housing), local infrastructure (for example, waste disposal services), utilities, transport, post, TV, telephone and, most recently, internet, *etc.* The universal access to these services, both socially and geographically, produces material equality between citizens by equalising the chances to live an independent life as a pre-condition for them to participate in market activity, and to better their own lot in this way.

But as the state sets itself up as public provider, and for this purpose juridifies ever more spheres of activity ("service") that would otherwise be left to individuals to structure according to their own choices and desires (using either the market or non-economic forms of exchange ("caring and sharing")), it will increasingly come to control the lives of its citizens by imposing on their relationships the state's own idea of what will further their autonomy best. In this way, its social programmes threaten the very autonomy which they aim to protect. Social programming on the one hand, and private autonomy on the other are, in Habermas' words, locked into a "zero-sum game". In his words:

> [W]hat is awarded to the State in capacities for social regulation seemingly must be taken, in the form of private autonomy [from the individual] … From this point of view, the State and private actors are involved in a zero-sum game – what the one gains in competence the other loses.[9]

The inter-action between state and individual in this way will reduce the latter's autonomy, and is likely to produce other negative consequences such as regulatory capture, bureaucratisation, stagnation, high prices and a low quality of public services.

One way of avoiding this dilemma is, of course, to adhere to a rather more formalistic conception of individual autonomy by leaving the provision of public services to the spontaneous ordering of the market and relying upon its economic incentives to increase efficiency and consumer welfare. However, choosing this option, it has to be accepted that reliance on the market to provide "public" services can lead to conflicts between the motives of the market – concern for profit and shareholder value – and concern for the material equality that motivates the welfare state. The market presumes that we come to it as equals (formal equality), and it has little concern for material equality unless it is made to do so: in simple terms, an obligation to secure universal access, affordability or quality of public services may well secure social cohesion and social solidarity, but it is just as likely to undermine profitability. A minimum of social

8 Consider the concepts of "freedom from" and "freedom to", in: I. Berlin, "Two Concepts of Liberty", in: *Four Essays on Liberty*, (Oxford: Oxford University Press, 1969), p. 118; see, also, J. Habermas, *Between Facts and Norms*, (Cambridge MA: Polity Press, 1996).

9 J. Habermas, "Paradigms of Law" (1996) 17 *Cardozo Law Review*, p. 771, at 775.

law or regulation or, indeed, political intervention (public ownership) to enforce these social concerns does, as a matter of historical reality, exist in every modern welfare state. No state, in reality, divests itself entirely of the responsibility to provide these services, even if some states prefer a competitive model whenever possible, simply tweaking market incentives in order to introduce a minimum of social protection. As a consequence of this responsibility, every state relies on law as a medium to secure the conditions for its citizens' autonomy, and how "formal" or "material" that law should be is subject to political debate. Formal law, on the one hand, provides the instrument for individuals to order their relationships with one another so as to maximise their individual gain, but has no regard for the material inequalities that affect their real opportunity to do so. Material law, on the other hand, is sensitive to these material inequalities and is about the real equality of legal ability for individuals. Within the legal corpus of any modern state, there will be both formal and material law, and some law that is more material than formal, and some that is more formal than material. The point is that it is for the political community, working through the institutions of the state and engaging in continuous political deliberation, to determine the mix that will best secure its citizens' autonomy.

This last point is most important in so far as it highlights a degree of futility in the debate between the "socialist" and the "liberal" ideals of political ordering, which seems to lock the political community into a continuous oscillation between these two positions.[10] Instead, it leads us to focus on a third perspective, turning to the observation that the balance between formal and material law *must* be determined by those who will be the subjects of the mix. We are only truly autonomous if we are truly self-governing, and this encompasses not only our *private* autonomy, as addressees of the law, and its mix of formal and material norms, but also our *public* autonomy, as co-authors of that mix. To focus exclusively on optimising the private autonomy of individuals, by determining the appropriate balance between formal and material equality for itself, views us simply as the addressees of the law and fails to make any connection with our public autonomy. In order to self-govern themselves truly as a political community, citizens require a set of rules ("constitution") which ensures their entitlement to participate in the process of law-making (norm-setting). This is what Habermas calls the "procedural" paradigm of law that aims to realise the autonomy of citizens fully by taking into account the fact that this has a *public*, as well as a *private*, dimension. It is by giving effect to the procedural paradigm of law, which ensures collective self-determination (public autonomy), that we can avoid the dilemma of the welfare state, whereby the state's social programmes can threaten the very autonomy that they aim to protect. As long as these programmes are adequately connected to processes of democratic participation within the state, which tie them to the choices that individuals make as the citizens of a political community, they will truly reflect the collective political autonomy of the citizens as a democratic society.

10 See D. Chalmers, "The Reconstitution of European Public Spheres", (2003) 9 *ELJ*, p. 142.

3. Community Law and the Community "Compact"

The Community's nature as a supranational and principally economic union of Member States, on the other hand, characterises its relationship with both the individual and the collective self-determination of European citizens. In the absence of a European *demos* conferring "thick" democratic legitimacy on the European institutions,[11] its role continues to be characterised by an absence of any authority to develop, at Community level, the far-reaching social programming upon which our welfare states depend. The idea that autonomy can be fully realised only when both its public and private elements are secured, highlights that the Community suffers, as Fritz Scharpf has most famously diagnosed, from an "asymmetry" or "social deficit" characterising its constitutional make-up.[12] Following this idea, the principle of autonomy imposes a negative obligation on the Community not to tread where the nation state, albeit imperfect in its own ways,[13] operates as the *locus* of democratic legitimacy. It must fulfil its integrating role whilst paying respect to the fact that, as far as the development of social programmes goes, our control over the law-making process (i.e., their legitimacy) remains best secured at domestic level. This obligation is inherent in the original compact between the Member States and the Community, whereby the Member States retain sovereignty over their welfare states and the Community is assigned competencies to further the Internal Market, whose rules the Member States accept as a basis for resolving conflicts that touch upon their common concerns, particularly the desire to integrate their national markets. By insisting on such a compact, Community law protects our collective self-determination in a very real sense, by giving effect to the choices which we take as a national political community (*demos*) where we determine how we wish to order our society. "Unity in diversity" is the term Christian Joerges has chosen to describe this constellation of Europe, referring to its capacity to enforce a degree of mutual obligation between European citizens, and the Member States, towards one another, whilst striving to maintain and uphold the level of "thick" collective solidarity within the nation state and, more particularly, the national welfare state.[14]

The Community has far from addressed its social asymmetry. The Court's constitutional interpretation of the Community's economic law can formalise national laws, imposing the law of the market on materialised national laws. To avoid the "formalising", de-regulatory, effects of negative integration, the Member States are given the

11 The "no *demos*" problem set out by Joseph Weiler; the *demos* being marked by an "organic-cultural identification and sense of belongingness", see J.H.H. Weiler, "Does Europe need a constitution? *Demos*, *telos* and the German Maastricht Decision", (1995) 1 *ELJ*, p. 219, at 256.

12 F.W. Scharpf, "The European Social Model: Coping with the Challenges of Diversity", (2002) 40 *JCMS*, p. 645.

13 See, for example, D. Marquand, *Decline of the Public*, (Cambridge MA: Polity, 2004).

14 See, for example, Ch. Joerges, *Democracy and European Integration: A Legacy of Tensions, a Re-Conceptualisation and Recent True Conflicts?*, European University Institute, Florence, working paper LAW No. 2007/25 and *Rethinking European Law's Supremacy*, European University Institute, Florence, working paper LAW No. 2005/12.

opportunity, but also carry the burden, of justifying their social programmes before the Court. European legislation increasingly re-introduces harmonised standards (such as universal service requirements) at European level, also with a view to prevent and react to the formalisation (de-regulation) of national law. These processes have extensively affected the networked industries, where the application of EC competition law has led to the abolition of public monopolies. The application of derogations, most notably Article 86(2) EC, has softened the process but has not stemmed the tide, and extensive sector-specific Community legislation has been enacted to secure the objectives of both liberalisation and certain social standards (see further below).

What the Community has yet failed to address is the paradox between its continuing lack of legitimacy – for want of a European *demos* – to take on the broad social programming that takes place at nation state level, and, on the other hand, its growing role as legislator re-instating social standards at European level to stem the consequences of de-regulation following negative integration.[15] Problematic as they are in their practical implementation, it is precisely because of this paradox that the principles of the original compact continue to characterise the Community's constitutional make-up.

This, finally, takes us back to the debate over public services in Europe. In this and the previous section, I have sought to illustrate that, at the heart of this debate lies the genuine concern of every political community, working through the instruments of the state, to pursue its own good in its own way, and to be in control of its own fate. By creating the appropriate institutional design for public services ("public service regime") in their own national territory, each Member State in effect strives to maximise not only the private autonomy of its citizens, by ensuring that there be an appropriate mix between material and formal laws, but also their collective public autonomy, by securing the appropriate means of public accountability, so as to uphold the citizens' collective control over their own destiny. As these public services are subjected to the pressure of formalisation (de-regulation) in the Community's constitutional constellation, the Community faces the paradox of a gradual role reversal between the Community and the Member States, where increasingly, Community legislation addresses material standards, but without any "thick" legitimation to develop and enforce social programmes. The Community's compact, whereby the Member States retain control over these programmes, plays a vital role in securing the citizens' collective public autonomy in the Community's constitutional constellation.

The next section turns to the concrete reality of public service regimes in Europe. The argument advanced is, broadly speaking, that there has been a degree of convergence amongst public service regimes, especially in the networked sectors, following their liberalisation upon the basis of Community law. Whilst in some Member States, the

15 M. Poiares Maduro, "Europe's Social Self: The Sickness unto Death", in: J. Shaw (ed), *Social Law and Policy in an Evolving European Union*, (Oxford: Hart Publishing, 2000).

introduction of competitive markets unsettled long-standing legal values, or even constitutional protection of public service values, in others, such as the UK, it meant that public service values would now be expressed through law, where they had not enjoyed legal protection before.

4. Continental and Anglo-Saxon Public Service Traditions

There exists, across the EU, a diversity of public service regimes and traditions (tradition here referring to the regime as seen in its historical context). Accounting for their variety would, however, go way beyond the scope of this chapter. In the following description, I shall therefore draw heavily on the existing materials, especially on Tony Prosser's[16] recent study of what he loosely terms the "Continental" and "Anglo-Saxon" public service traditions (the former mainly based upon French and Italian experiences, the latter based upon those in the UK).

Prosser's research makes apparent some historical differences between the two traditions. Broadly speaking, the Continental tradition is marked by a *system* of public service, whereby public service values are protected in the corpus of administrative law, and, in the case of France, through strong constitutional principles that firmly embed a public responsibility to ensure public service provision. In the UK tradition, on the other hand, public services have developed rather more pragmatically as a *conglomeration* of various essential facilities, the provision of which is, in the main, protected by political means and political discretion. Both traditions originate, broadly speaking, from the end of the Nineteenth century when public service emerged for the first time as a reference principally to basic utilities that were provided as part of municipal infrastructure, as a response to the industrialisation of society and the change in its basic needs that this signified for the population at the time. But while their historical origins broadly coincide, real differences exist at the level of principle, that also reflect on their organisation. In the UK, utilities were regarded as a matter for public organisation, but mainly for pragmatic reasons. The point was to organise them most effectively in order to allow individuals to pursue their lives freely and participate in the industrial age. This meant, amongst other things, that throughout much of the Twentieth century, the UK's public service regimes was organised mainly by political means, notably through the nationalisation of utilities. Public service values and "the public interest" would be protected as a matter of political discretion, either of the relevant minister or the bodies designated for that purpose, which Prosser, however, describes as "remarkably ineffective".[17]

In the Continental jurisdictions, on the other hand, it soon emerged that public responsibility to provide essential facilities to all citizens was regarded as a matter of

16 T. Prosser, note 4 *supra*.
17 *Ibid.*, p. 42.

principle and theorised accordingly.[18] Thus, the notion of public service became important not only as a matter of practical organisation, but also as a real way for the community to identify its solidarity obligations towards one another. This is reflected in a high level of theorisation of public service, especially with regard to utilities.

In France, these theoretical underpinnings derive from the writings of Leon Duguit and his work, which follows the ideas of the social theorist Emile Durkheim. Duguit considered the value of *fraternité* to be at the heart of the society of the French republic, and, accordingly, reasoned that social solidarity and the co-operation of social groups through public service formed an essential part of that society.[19] He drew heavily on Durkheim in formulating social interdependence and social morality as quintessential to man in society, and eventually in established his claim that there lay a moral and legal obligation on the state to ensure the provision of certain basic services to all citizens.[20] These obligations eventually led to the constitutional protection and enshrinement of "public service" as a French constitutional principle which continues to date.

Very similar ideas are embedded in German public law (we may add the German model as a further example of a Continental public service regime). Whilst lacking the status of a constitutional dogma,[21] the German doctrine on public service (*Daseinsvorsorge*) is equally strong in imposing on the state a responsibility as public provider.[22] Its theoretical roots, formulated by the jurist Ernst Forsthoff, who drew on the earlier writings of the philosopher Karl Jaspers and the public lawyer Otto Mayer, identify state authority, rather than solidarity, as the driving force of public services; asserting that only a "strong state" relying on public administration was capable of effectively managing the provision of essential public services.[23] Naturally, this meant an emphasis on hierarchy, with a strong system administrative law which lent itself to this task. Even though the German doctrine has shed much of its original emphasis on state authority, the use of administrative law to organise the provision of public services systematically

18 *Ibid.*, p. 94.

19 L. Duguit, *Law in the Modern State*, (1970, translation F. and H. Laski, first published in English 1919); or, in original French, his *Les transformations des droit public*, (1913).

20 E. Durkheim, *The Division of Labour in Society* (1984, translation W.D. Halls); see, also, T. Prosser, 'Regulation and Social Solidarity', (2006) 33 *J.L.S.*, p. 364, at 379–381.

21 Although, see S. Broß, "Daseinvorsorge – Wettbewerb – Gemeinschaftsrecht", (2003) 18 *Juristenzeitung*, p. 874, who argues to the effect that the principle is protected in the German constitution (*Grundgesetz*) as interpreted by the German constitutional court.

22 See D. Scheidemann, Der Begriff der Daseinsvorsorge: Ursprung, Funktion und Wandlungen der Konzeption Ernst Forsthoffs, (Göttingen/Zurich: Muster-Schmidt, 1991); C. Schütte, Progressive Verwaltungswissenschaft auf konservativer Grundlage – Zur Verwaltungslehre Ernst Forsthoffs, (Berlin: Duncker & Humblot, 2006); E.-J. Mestmäcker, "Daseinsvorsorge und Universaldienst im europäischen Kontext", in: F. Ruland, B. Baron von Maydell and H.-J. Papier (eds), Verfassung, Theorie und Praxis des Sozialstaats, (Heidelberg: C.F. Müller, 1998), p. 635.

23 E. Forsthoff, *Die Verwaltung als Leistungsträger* (Stuttgart/Berlin: Kohlhammer, 1938); and his *Lehrbuch des Verwaltungsrechts*, 1st volume (10th ed., Munich: C.H. Beck, 1973).

as a matter of public law, even where they rely on co-operation between public and private sectors, continues to date,[24] as does the perception of a public responsibility to ensure their provision.

One can trace these historical differences between the Continental tradition and the Anglo-Saxon tradition to date. Today's Anglo-Saxon regime, still dominated by its history of political liberalism, lends itself to economic ordering.[25] Continuing to take a pragmatic attitude to the development of public service values, the British legislator tends to rely heavily on ordinary competition law to regulate public services (ensuring efficiency and consumer choice), but has not, as yet, subjected the protection of public service values to any systematic codification at any level. Britain has reached a level of liberalisation which, the UK Office of Fair Trading reports, extends further than that which is currently enforced at Community level.[26] This situation has left the UK, which is not normally keen to take on European harmonisation initiatives, in a sort of model role in the continuing liberalisation process, with considerable influence as part of the mutual sharing of best practice, and, more concretely, the drafting of legislation.[27]

For the Continental regimes, on the other hand, liberalisation has only arrived relatively recently, and, as a rule, as a consequence of Community law. It has sparked real conflicts between economic principles and economic law on the one hand, and constitutional and administrative law and principles on the other. In these jurisdictions, a body of public service law based upon the idea that the state has a duty to ensure the equal treatment of citizens irrespective of its economic resources, which traditionally, has taken priority over competition law in cases of conflict, still exists.[28] Whilst this does not mean that the Continental regimes are irreconcilable with liberalisation, it means that, in these regimes, there continues to be a strong emphasis, in both public debate and legal design, on the distinction between the *organisation* of public service which may well be market-based, and the *substantive* responsibility for that organisation which remains firmly with the state.[29]

24 M. Bullinger, "Französischer service public und deutsche Daseinsvorsorge", (2003) 18 *Juristenzeitung*, p. 597.

25 T. Prosser and M. Moran, "Privatization and Regulatory Change: the Case of Great Britain" in: *idem* (eds), *Privatization and Regulatory Change in Europe*, (Buckingham: Open University Press, 1994), Chapter 3.

26 The UK Office of Fair Trading, for example, considers that "due to the extent of de-regulation and liberalisation of the economy that has occurred in the United Kingdom, it is unlikely that there will be a significant number of cases in which previous European Commission decisions [on the exception for 'services of general economic interest' from competition law] will be directly relevant when considering whether the exclusion applies in the United Kingdom". Office of Fair Trading, *Services of General Interest Exclusion*, competition law guideline published 2004, point 1.12. See, also, Prosser and Moran, *supra* note 25.

27 E. Szyszczak, The Regulation of the State in Competitive Markets in the EU, (Oxford: Hart Publishing, 2007), p. 141.

28 Prosser, note 4 *supra*, p. 2.

29 *Ibid.*, pp. 106–107 and p. 239.

5. Liberalisation and the Community Legislation

Today, these regimes and traditions do have to be seen in the light of the gradual, piecemeal, liberalisation and re-regulation of the network-based industries. These developments were initially motivated by the application of ordinary EC competition law in those sectors, whereby existing inefficiencies in national public service regimes began to be exposed.[30] In addition, the UK's advanced liberalisation programmes served by way of example, and the Commission could conveniently pick up on the UK's experience. This chapter is not the place to recount the liberalisation process of the various sectors in detail and there certainly is a great selection of material providing such accounts.[31] Instead, I shall outline three characteristics of the Community legislation in this field.

The first characteristic of this legislation is that it generally views full liberalisation as an ideal which, even if not fully realisable, should be realised as far as possible.[32] This is linked closely to a second idea, namely, that, as the Commission states, "the objectives of developing high-quality, accessible and affordable services of general economic interest and of an open and competitive internal market are compatible and should be mutually supportive".[33] The key feature of the legislation is, therefore, "controlled liberalisation", defined as "gradual opening-up of the market accompanied by measures to protect the general interest, in particular through the concept of universal service to guarantee access for everyone ... ensuring adequate standards for cross-border services that cannot be adequately regulated only at national level".[34] In reality, this has taken a number of legislative packages in each sector (following periodic review and renewal), and, in some sectors, it has been more effective or speedier than in others.

The second characteristic of the legislation is the central role of public service obligations as the measures to protect the general interest of the service in question, which the Commission stresses continually. Member States may impose these obligations on market operators in order, broadly, to achieve distributive outcomes that the market alone could not achieve (often but not always referred to as "market failures"). The legislation also generally provides how they may finance these social goals; they will regularly be given a choice. The most important public service obligation has been the universal service obligation. A brief look at the telecommunications sector illustrates its

30 For a recent summary, see Szyszczak, note 27 *supra*, Chapters 2–4.

31 See, for example, Szyszczak, note 27 *supra*, Chapter 5; Prosser, *supra* note 4, Chapter 8; P. Slot and A. Skudder, "Common Features of Community Law Regulation in the Network-Bound Sectors", (2001) 38 *C.M.L.Rev.*, p. 87; C. Henry and A. Jenemaitre (eds), *Regulation of Networked Utilities: the European Experience*, (Oxford: Oxford University Press, 2001).

32 See, for instance, the third Postal Directive (2008/06/EC amending Directive 97/67/EC) which effects full liberalisation of the postal sector by 2010 and, in some Member States, 2012. The Directive abolishes the remaining reserved areas, but does include a universal service obligation.

33 Commission, Communication on Services of General Interest, note 1 *supra*, at point 2.2.

34 Commission, *Green Paper on Services of General Interest*, COM (2003) 270 final, at point 5.

central significance. The most developed liberalised regime in the Community to date, the telecommunications sector, has broadly been considered a success story in terms of protecting social goals within the context of liberalisation.[35] The liberalisation of telecoms also produced a first time legal definition of universal service as "a minimum set of services of specified quality which is available to all users independent of their geographical location and, in the light of specific national conditions, at an affordable price".[36] Sauter vividly describes that the introduction of such a legal obligation meant a real benefit for telephone-users, as waiting times for telephone connections were reduced dramatically.[37]

Apart from real improvement in terms of accessibility, a second advantage of the universal service concept is that it can introduce transparency. Prosser, for example, considers that "the closer specification of universal service and of the means of its financing has flushed out the costs of providing a universal service much more clearly and, at least in the UK, this has proved to be considerably less than suppliers had claimed".[38]

The third characteristic of the sector-specific legislation is that it has led to the establishment of a number of independent national regulatory authorities in Member States, implementing and monitoring the sector-specific legislative framework.[39] Their role is generally to work closely with national governments on the one hand, and to report to the Commission on the other. However, not all sector-specific legislation defines the role of regulatory agencies in as much detail as, for example, the initial legislation on telecommunications did. In the postal sector, for example, the reform of the postal regulators, ensuring their independence, impartiality and transparency issues, is an important regulatory issue. In some Member States, for example the UK, some of these regulatory agencies have competition law competences (for example, Ofcom). A number of questions still surround the role of regulatory agencies, including whether they are too much or too little interventionist, whether they are sufficiently accountable, produce transparent regulation, and whether they are too much or too little politically independent.[40]

35 T. Prosser, note 4 *supra*, at p. 186.

36 See, for example, Directive 97/33/EC on Interconnection in Telecommunications with regard to ensuring Universal Service and Interoperability through Application of the Principles of Open Network Provision [1997] O.J. L101/24 ('Interconnection Directive'), Article 2(1)(g).

37 W. Sauter, "Universal Service Obligations and the Emergence of Citizens' Rights in European Telecommunications Liberalization", in: M. Freedland and S. Sciarra, *Public Services and Citizenship in European Law: public and labour law perspectives*, (Oxford: Oxford University Press, 1998), p. 123.

38 T. Prosser, note 4 *supra*, p. 187.

39 N. Petit, "The Proliferation of National Regulatory Authorities Alongside Competition Authorities: A Source of Jurisdictional Confusion", in: D. Geradin, R. Munoz and N. Petit (eds), *Regulation through Agencies – A New Paradigm of European Governance*, (Cheltenham: Edward Elgar, 2005).

40 See: www.lse.ac.uk/resources/riskAndRegulationMagazine/magazine/summer2005/independentRegulatoryAgenciesInEurope.htm, accessed on 20 January 2008.

Bearing these concerns in mind, one of the most crucial features of the Community's sector-specific legislation is, therefore, that, whilst it delegates to the regulators the implementation of the liberalisation packages, it still leaves political responsibility with the public authorities of the Member States, who will, of course, be restricted by the terms of the legislation. Such responsibility includes, in particular, the responsibility to define universal service obligations, and even though, in practice, governments are likely to undertake this task in co-ordination with the regulator, it is here that we find the clearest expression to date of a continuing public responsibility to provide these services as essential facilities. It is here that the Community's compact takes effect; leaving to the national level, as the democratic *locus* in the Community, the decision of how it wishes to formulated these social obligations, within the bounds of the legislation.

6. What Public Service Obligations Do and Do Not Do

Considering these features, one would conclude that this legislation makes a real attempt at protecting our (national) autonomy by leaving the responsibility to define and impose public service obligations on market operators with the political institutions of the Member States.[41] In particular, it leaves the Member States with a margin of appreciation as to how far they take these obligations, within the bounds prescribed by the legislation. However, I shall use the remainder of this section to make a number of remarks which suggest that we have to take our autonomy more seriously than this.

In this context, the starting point has to be at the very heart of the Community's primary law. Article 86(2) EC provides the central substantive norm in this respect. It provides that the EC Treaty's rules, and especially EC competition law, apply to undertakings entrusted with services of general economic interest in so far as those rules do not obstruct, in law or in fact, the performance of those services. This provision is relevant well beyond the Treaty's primary law. Much of the liberalisation packages present the goal of "controlled liberalisation", to which they pay so much attention, in the context of the balance between competition and public service enshrined in Article 86(2) EC. It therefore sets out a central framework that runs not only through EC competition law as interpreted by the Court of Justice and the Court of First Instance, but also through the relevant secondary legislation, the Commission's competition decisions and finally the Commission's communications on public services.

The orthodox view, represented by the Commission and some academic commentators, is that this provision sets out a narrow derogation from the Treaty rules in favour of public services, subject however to a strict proportionality test,[42] requiring (a) a causal

41 See the commentary cited *supra* note 4; see, also, Sauter, note 39 *supra*.

42 See Commission, Communication on Services of general interest in Europe, COM (2000) p. 580; Commission, Report to the Laeken European Council on Services of General Interest COM (2001) p. 598; van der Woude, "Article 90: Competing for Competence", ELR: Competition Law Checklist

link between the measure in question and the objective of general interest, (b) that the restrictions caused by the measure are balanced by the benefits of the general interest, and (c) that the objective of general interest cannot be achieved through other less restrictive means.[43]

The Court, and some more recent academic commentary, on the other hand, both interpret Article 86(2) EC as setting out a softer test, which allows the Member States a greater margin of discretion than a strict proportionality set. In particular, this softer test will *not* go as far as asking whether the anti-competitive measure in question was the least restrictive measure to attain the general interest in question; instead, the test is whether it was objectively necessary (and suited) to attain a legitimate goal.[44] In a frequently cited passage, Ross constructs the jurisprudence as a methodological shift "from economic measurement to value judgement", whereby the Court now concentrates "on the justifications for protecting the service", rather than the economic viability of the service provider.[45]

The legislation, on the other hand, very much reflects the interpretation of Article 86(2) EC favoured by the Commission; read in this way, the provision relays a positive incentive to draft public service obligations, and provisions relating to their financing, so as to create the least interference with the market whilst protecting their social goals. It also means that, in practice, the goal of competition is being prioritised in the legislation, while public service obligations, and especially universal services, tend to be formulated as a minimum service.[46] The underlying rationale is that public service obligations, and the regulation of their financing, are seen as regulatory impositions on the market, which should be restricted to correcting market failures in a way that does not impose unnecessary costs on the regulated firms.[47]

1991 (1992) 60, at 62; Buendía Sierra, "Article 86: Exclusive Rights and other Anti-Competitive State Measures", in: J. Faull and A. Nikpay (eds), *The EC Law of Competition*, (Oxford: Oxford University Press, 1999), p. 273; E.-J. Mestmäcker, "Daseinsvorsorge un Universaldienst im europäischen Kontext", in: F. Ruland, B. Baron von Maydell, and H.-J. Papier (eds), *Verfassung, Theorie und Praxis des Sozialstaats*, (Heidelberg: C.F. Müller, 1998).

43 Buendía Sierra, note 43 *supra*, p. 315.

44 J. Baquero Cruz, "Beyond Competition: Services of General Interest and European Community Law", in: G. de Búrca (ed), *EU Law and the Welfare State In Search of Solidarity*, (Oxford: Oxford University Press, 2005), p. 196. Similarly, N. Boeger, "Solidarity and EC Competition Law", (2007) 32 *E.L.Rev.*, p. 319: the Court allows Member States a wider margin of appreciation, giving effect to the Community's compact, and regards solidarity as a "political trump" that the Member States may invoke against Community competition law.

45 M. Ross, "Article 16 E.C. and services of general interest: from derogation to obligation?", (2000) 25 *E.L.Rev.*, p. 22, at 24; taken up again in: M. Ross, note 6 *supra*; see, also, L. Soriano, "How proportionate should Anti-Competitive State Intervention be?', (2003) 28 *E.L.Rev.*, p. 112; and, finally, T. Prosser, note 4 *supra*, p. 15 ("the approach of the European courts has changed, from treating public services (or 'services of general interest') as unwelcome impediments to completing the single internal market to seeing them instead as independently valuable expressions of citizenship rights.").

46 Baquero Cruz, note 44 *supra*, p. 211.

47 Szyszczak, note 27 *supra*, p. 143.

This balance does affect the actual drafting of public service obligations. The Commission's proposal for the Third Postal Directive, for example, expresses the definition of the universal service in most precise terms – all citizens must have their mail collected and delivered at least once a day, five days a week – but also in a way that very much suggests this would be a minimum level of social protection compatible with the primary goal, to introduce and maintain an open and competitive market.[48] Arguing in similar vain, Baquero Cruz finds that, throughout the legislation, out of all the funding options (including direct state subsidies, cross-subsidisation or the creation of a compensation fund through the introduction of fees on new service providers or users), the creation of a public service fund is regularly the preferred option from the Community's point of view as it is the least distorting of competition.[49]

Not only does the priority, which the legislation gives to the value of competition, affect the actual drafting of those public service obligations that *are* being included in the legislation, it also means that some public service values may simply not find recognition as a public service obligation in the legislation and, eventually, fall by the wayside. Again referring to the postal sector, one example would be what the French *Conseil d'Etat* has referred to as the *dimension humaine majeure* – the enfranchising function – of French postmen. The *Conseil* explains:

> [...] rien ne emplace le passage régulier, jour après jour, dans chaque localité et auprès de chaque usager, d'un agent bien identifie et appurtenant a un service bien implante sure tout le territoires. Cette sole présence est plus porteur en elle-même de service public et de la solidaire que celui-ci exprime, que les prestations proprement dites confies au prépose [...][50]

In other words, the *Conseil* ascribes to postmen and postwomen not only a transport function, but also an import role in respect of community cohesion: the "human face" of the postmen and postwomen reflects the integration of the individual into a collective, into the state as the political community of all citizens. In its statement, the *Conseil* thus describes the essence of Duguit's understanding of public service as comprising an inclusive element, whereby it makes visible the "human" face of the state as a collective or political community, marked by a sense of mutual obligation and social solidarity which is part of human nature.[51]

One may put the *Conseil*'s emphasis of these "human" functions down as one of those fiercely national points of view, which, some would say, fails to catch the mood of times. The postal sector is today characterised by the influence of new technology, the growth in internet purchasing and the use of e-mail, leading to an increased volume of parcel

48 See, further, note 34 *supra*.

49 Baquero Cruz, note 44 *supra*, p. 205.

50 Rapport public 2002, Etudes et documents No. 53, Doc. Franc., pp. 215 *et seq*., in particular, p. 354.

51 See note 19 *supra*.

post and reduction of the letter market.[52] Business customers dominate the market, demanding efficiency, greater capacity and lower costs. It is certainly correct that there are today all the incentives for citizens and for businesses in particular to require an efficient postal service. But to conclude that, for this reason, citizens will not want to preserve these ancillary human functions of postal services would be premature. Instead, the challenge lies in translating these functions into the liberalisation process, especially if we are to take the Commission's remarks above, where it insists that liberalisation need not mean a sacrifice of "services of general interest", at face value.[53] Martin Bullinger, for example, suggests an "open service architecture" as a first step, whereby national postal incumbents are required to further open their local distribution networks to new entrants.[54]

Whether one has strong feelings for (French) postal workers or not, the example illustrates a more fundamental issue, namely, that there are some choices citizens will decide to take as a community, operating through the institutions of the state or local government, that it may simply not be possible to transpose, by way of recognition as public service, obligations within the paradigm of "market failure" regulation. The regulatory literature is full of accounts of this type of regulation as one amongst several regulatory techniques.[55] The advantage of this regulatory pluralism is that, in each context (bioethics, healthcare, environment, *etc.*), the technique can be matched so as to give best effect to the substantive policy choices.[56] The Community's liberalisation process, by entrenching the economics-based market failure approach to regulation, tends to neglect the existence of a plurality of regulatory approaches, thereby creating a problem in situations in which the Community legislation should, in reality, give effect to political choices concerning rather elusive social or moral values, rather than quantifiable distributional choices. These values may prove "unquantifiable" in the monetary terms of a cost-benefit analysis (i.e., assessment of whether the "benefit" of regulating the market outweighs the "cost" for market operators) and therefore impossible to identify as a "market failure"; or, as is more likely, if attempts are being made, there is a danger that some of its protection will be lost. One can think of a number of values in this context. David Marquand's work provides a fruitful ground for examples.[57]

52 Szyszczak, note 27 *supra*, p. 151.

53 Commission, *Communication on Services of General Interest*, note 1 *supra*, at point 2.2; cited in the text to note 34 *supra*.

54 M. Bullinger, note 24 *supra*, p. 604.

55 See, for example, T. Prosser, "Regulation and Social Solidarity", note 21 *supra*; J. Black, "Critical Reflections on Regulation", LSE Centre for the Analysis of Risk and Regulation, Discussion paper 4 (2002); B. Morgan, *Social Citizenship in the Shadow of Competition: The Bureaucratic Politics of Regulatory Justification*, (Aldershot: Ashgate Publishing 2003); B. Morgan and K. Yeung, *Introduction to Law and Regulation*, (Cambridge: Cambridge University Press, 2007).

56 C. Scott, "Services of General Interest in the European Union: Matching Values to Techniques", (2000) 6 *ELJ*, p. 310.

57 Marquand, note 13 *supra*.

One of the areas in which this may well be the case is the protection of a "public domain", and especially of the "public ethos" characteristic of this domain. Marquand defines the public domain by reference to its:

> [D]istinctive culture and decision rules. In it citizenship rights trump both market power and the bonds of clan and kinship. Professional pride in a job well done or a sense of civic duty or a mixture of both replaces the hope of gain the fear of loss (and, for that matter, loyalty to family, friends or dependants) as the spur to action.[58]

Ralph Dahrendorf specifies:

> In the public domain people act neither of the kindness of their hearts, nor in response to incentives, monetary or otherwise, but because they have a sense of serving the community.[59]

These statements make it clear that the public domain and the public ethos are both formulations of a set of rules which sets out ideals of human interactions, in the same way as, for example, the economic rules of the market are. However, they are based upon fundamentally different value judgements, and, in essence, a fundamentally different view of human nature. There are obvious parallels with Duguit's conception of social solidarity and public service, and also with Forsthoff's work, referred to above. The public responsibility to provide public services, which their work emphasises, and the sense of duty to a community (the "ethos" of public service), are essentially two sides of the same coin. A third and related value in this respect is public trust. Again, trust can be more concretely understood here by reference to rule-bound behaviour, rather than in the sense of an implicit trust or "understanding" (referring to cronyism or clanship), for example, amongst close-knit village communities, which would be impossible to transpose into a more open community. Marquand puts it thus:

> Citizens trust each other because, and to the extent that, they are citizens: because, and to the extent that, they know that public institutions are governed by an ethic of equity and service.[60]

Does the Community legislation allow Member States to regulate the market in order to protect any of these values? Would it be permissible, for example, for a Member State to ring-fence market segments in order to secure public trust in public service operations? What if the Member State was prepared to impinge, for that purpose, on market principles *more than would be necessary* (and go beyond what is permissible in order to ensure the provision of a minimum service by way of public service obligation)? One could think of such measures being discussed, for example, following large public health

58 *Ibid.*, pp. 1–2.

59 R. Dahrendorf *et al.*, *Report on Wealth Creation and Social Cohesion in a Free Society*, (London: Commission on Wealth Creation and Social Cohesion, 1995), p. 39.

60 Marquand, note 13 *supra*, p. 34.

scares or corporate scandals. Public broadcasting is an example in which the Community does, indeed, recognise the cultural necessity to ensure civic trust in the quality of these public programmes, and allows for regulation to that effect.[61] In other liberalised sectors, however, the sector-specific Community legislation would regularly prevent the Member States from taking those steps. Incidentally, in those sectors where general competition law alone provides the legal framework, the Court of Justice may accommodate some of these choices. In *Ambulanz Glöckner*,[62] for example, the Court was faced with the question of whether a public authority could benefit from a derogation from EC competition law pursuant to Article 86(2) EC, in which it had reserved the provision of ambulance services to certain non-profit providers. The legal arrangement shielded these services from the for-profit incentives of commercial providers and was set up to ensure, amongst other things, a quality of service that people could trust. This, in itself, can be seen as a value for the local community, which the authorities may see worthy of protection. The Court, applying the softer "necessity" test under Article 86(2) EC, rather than a strict "least restrictive measure" requirement, thus accepting that the public authorities had a margin of appreciation, concluded that Article 86(2) EC could apply if all the conditions of that provision were fulfilled. Almost certainly, a strict proportionality review would have meant the measure in question would have been declared disproportionate.[63]

The legislation is certainly not unconcerned with the positive effects of public trust and public ethos, and one central aim of the Commission's strategy so far has been ensure those same effects through on-going control, monitoring and evaluation of the quality of the services ("consumer satisfaction"), transparency and quality of decision-making processes.[64] However, this process, whilst it may take an interest in similar effects, shows little interest in public trust and public ethos as self-standing values. Instead, it relies on economics-based assessments, and sees these as ways to identify asymmetries in the market, and then to improve efficiency and delivery further.[65] Marquand and Dahrendorf however introduce an entirely different perspective altogether, rooted in social rather than economic theory. It takes a real interest in public trust and ethos as political values, and sees them as ends in themselves, making for a civilised community and improving our collective identity. Regulation is being imposed *for this reason*; indeed, it is not being "imposed" at all, as this would imply an "imposition" from the perspective of the market. Instead, the regulation grows organically out of the political choice of the community to order itself in this way, prioritising these social values over economic values. It reflects, in a very real sense, our collective self-determination as a society. Whether we revert to regulation in this way will, of course, depend on our understanding

61 Prosser, note 4 *supra*, Chapter 10.

62 Case C-475/99 *Ambulanz Glöckner* v *Landkreis Südwestpfalz* [2001] E.C.R. I-8089.

63 Boeger, note 7 *supra*.

64 Commission, Communication on Services of General Interest, note 1 *supra*, at point 4.3. See, also, Commission, White Paper on Services of General Interest, COM (2004), p. 374.

65 Clear in: Commission, Communication from the Commission: A Methodological Note for the Horizontal Evaluation of Services of General Economic Interest, COM (2002) final, p. 331.

of ourselves as individuals and as a collective, and may well mandate an understanding of our autonomy which is much more radically materialised than that revealed in the Community legislation described above (in particular, its market failure approach to regulation). Such an understanding is, perhaps, best expressed in T.H. Marshall's famous definition of social citizenship, which, in his words, ensures:

> [A] general enrichment of the concrete substance of civilised life ... an equalisation between the more and the less fortunate at all levels.[66]

7. Conclusion

In this chapter, I have suggested that, in considering Europe's role in the field of public services, we have to start from basic principles. These principles are enshrined in the Community's compact whereby Member States retain the political control over their welfare states whilst the Community enforces their common economic interests. At the heart of such compact lies a concern for our individual autonomy – the capacity of European citizens to shape their own lives. This capacity may be defined in a more formal or a more material sense, and, in reality, there will, in any political community, exist a mixture between the two interpretations; there will, in any one legal system, exist a body of materialised and formal law. It is for the political community, working through the institutions of the state, to determine the appropriate mixture between the two and to this effect, it will rely on the existing rules (the constitution) which ensure that the addressees of the law retain control over law-makers. Such political control is best secured at national level where, for all their practical flaws, democratic structures remain constitutionally embedded. In the absence of equivalent democratic structures at Community level, the role of the Community is, in principle, confined to furthering the Member States' common economic concerns (even if it involves the setting of European standards which – and here lies the paradox – address common social concerns) whilst protecting our political autonomy negatively, by respecting the political freedom of the Member States.

This, I suggested, is the yardstick against which we should measure Europe's role in the field of public services. In practice, the Community legislation in the network-based sectors goes some way to giving effect to the Community's compact. It reconciles the Member States' quest for political autonomy on the one hand, and their common concern for economic integration and competition on the other, for example, by leaving the political responsibility for defining and imposing public service obligations, within the bounds of the legislation, to the Member States. Responsibility, in this sense, carries both an imperative and a freedom. Whilst, on the one hand, it means that Member States cannot divest themselves of the responsibility to make sure that these services are provided on an equitable basis (set out in the public service obligation), it means, on the

66 T.H. Marshall, *Citizenship and Social Class and Other Essays*, (Cambridge: Cambridge University Press, 1950), p. 56.

other, that they are, by and large, relatively free in how they implement these obligations, within the bounds of the Community legislation.

I finally drew attention to a number of ways in which the legislation, in its current form, appears to pay insufficient attention to the Community's compact. First, it adopts an interpretation of Community law that gives relative priority to market integration and competition over public service, based upon a narrow interpretation of Article 86(2) EC (a strict proportionality test) which is not mandated by the EC Treaty or, indeed, the Court's jurisprudence. Following such an interpretation, the legislation, secondly, prioritises a regulatory approach based upon an economic rationale of market failure. As a result of the dominance of market failure regulation, some public service values may well find expression in the political process in the Member States, but may not translate into public service obligations and accordingly, find no means of protection in the Community's legislative framework. Thus, in its current form, the legislation shows a propensity to entrench the values of a market society and to crowd out other values, such as the public service ethos, the public domain or public trust, thereby reducing the autonomy of our political communities in Europe to determine for themselves what importance they wish to attach to these collective values in their political organisation, in the field of public services.

Wolf Sauter

CHAPTER 17. SERVICES OF GENERAL ECONOMIC INTEREST (SGEI) AND UNIVERSAL SERVICE OBLIGATIONS (USO) AS AN EU LAW FRAMEWORK FOR CURATIVE HEALTH CARE

1. Introduction

This chapter aims to discuss the following research question: What is the scope for using the legal concept of services of general economic interest to guarantee the provision of universal service in curative health care (or multi-product hospital care)?

1.1. Article 86(2) as an Exception to the Treaty Rules for Undertakings

The starting point is that Article 86(2) EC provides an exception to (or: exemption from) the Treaty rules in relation to undertakings that have been entrusted with carrying out services of general economic interest. This exception covers both the Member States' authorities which entrust carrying out services of general economic interest to one or more undertakings, and the undertakings concerned. It means that they are exempt from the relevant rules, i.e., these do not apply to them to the extent necessary to carry out their tasks. This mainly, but not exclusively, regards the application of the competition rules (i.e., *vis-à-vis* the Member States, the market freedoms can also be relevant[1]).

The exception of Article 86(2) EC is especially important, because, otherwise, European law can be characterised as essentially a binary system, classifying entities either as undertakings (i.e., carrying out economic activities bearing economic risk), or not, with important consequences in terms of the legal obligations that follow:

- as soon as services are provided by undertakings, the competition rules instantly apply in full force;

1 Such as with regard to the free movement of goods and services, and the freedom of establishment. Articles 31 (commercial monopolies) 81 and 82 (prohibitions on cartels and dominance abuse) EC can also be relevant *vis-à-vis* Member States. See J.L. Buendia Sierra, "Chapter 6: Article 86", in: J Faull and A Nikpay (eds), *The EU law on competition*, (2nd edition) (Oxford: Oxford University Press, 2007).

- if, on the other hand, the entities concerned are not undertakings, but are "solidarity"-based, they are excluded from the competition rules altogether.

This may occur while the actual services concerned are very similar or even identical, and has been the basis for much dissatisfaction with the EU legal framework. It leads to the central paradox that vertically integrated services provided by public authorities tend to be ignored by the Treaty, whereas introducing even a modicum of competition among undertakings providing the same services can lead to the Treaty articles being applied to the point where legitimate public interests may be threatened.[2]

Evidently, this binary system complicates efforts to introduce competition gradually or partially, while doing so is frequently not only a political necessity, but also desirable from the perspective of system stability in a liberalisation context (for example, to offer an adjustment period or transition phase, or to experiment with greater and smaller degrees of market freedom).

Article 86(2) EC offers a way out of this binary system, because it allows proportionate restrictions on competition to be imposed to the benefit of undertakings charged with services of general economic interest. It allows a tailor-made solution for each service of general economic interest. In The Netherlands, multi-product hospitals markets are an important example of markets that are presently encumbered with state regulation, for which the introduction of greater degree of competition is contemplated. This is the reason why Article 86(2) EC is examined here as a possible EU legal framework for multi-product hospitals. Another area for which Article 86(2) EC may be relevant is long-term care.

1.2. The Research Question in Detail

In greater detail, the research question addressed in this chapter is as follows: Does the Community law concept of services of general economic interest form a possible and appropriate legal framework for those parts of multi-product hospital care in The Netherlands that are deemed:
- Of general public interest (for example, "universal service"); and
- Not suitable for competitive provision (i.e., subject to market failure)?

It should be noted that, so far, the debate on services of general economic interest is not clearly focused in economic terms, especially with regard to the use of the market failure

2 Thus Joined Cases C-159/91 and C-160/91 *Poucet and Pistre* [1993] ECR I-637; Case C-70/95 *Sodemare* [1997] ECR I-3395; and Case T-319/99 *FENIN* [2003] ECR II-357, the solidarity element prevailed. The opposite occurred in, for example, Case C-328/94 *FFSA* [1995] ECR I-6025 and Case C-67/96 *Albany* [1999] ECR I-5751; Joined Cases C-115/97, C-116/97, C-117/97 and C-219/97 *Brentjens* [1999] ECR I-6025; and Case C-219/97 *Drijvende Bokken* [1999] ECR I-6121.

concept. However, both the incidence of services of general economic interest and the proportionality of the solutions found could usefully be couched in economic terms.

Hence, an additional research question could be whether standard economic reasoning on market failure could be applied to determine the scope or services of general economic interest, and whether, in this case, the outcomes obtained might differ from those of the existing process. This question will only be addressed briefly, as a possible precursor to further inquiry.

1.3. Scope

The scope of the discussion in this chapter is the relevant EU law on competition, free movement, state aid and public procurement. National law is not examined in any detail at this stage, but may be taken up in future. Likewise, it may be decided to broaden this chapter horizontally, for example, by extending it to cover long-term care.

1.4. Structure

The structure of this chapter is as follows: after this introduction, first, the general scope of Article 86(2) will be discussed; second, the debate on services of general economic interest is described; third, various definition issues including that of universal service, will be addressed, as well as the link with market failure; fourth, the scope of the Article 86(2) EC derogation, notably including proportionality, is discussed; fifth, public service compensation and state aid are discussed; sixth, this framework will be applied to the multi-product hospital sector, and finally, some conclusions are drawn.

2. The Legal Basis and Basic Purpose of Article 86(2)

2.1. Legal Basis

Services of general economic interest (SGEI) find their legal basis in Articles 16 and 86(2) of the EC Treaty itself, as well as in Article 36 of the Charter on Fundamental Rights. These provisions will be discussed briefly here.

2.1.1. Article 86 EC

Article 86 of the EC Treaty – as originally introduced in the 1957 Treaty of Rome at the outset of the European Economic Community – provides a special regime for public monopolies, and for undertakings granted "special and exclusive rights" by the Member States, in respect to "the rules contained in the Treaty".

Within the context of Article 86 EC, Article 86(2) of the EC Treaty provides a special rule for "*services of general economic interest*" (SGEI) which reads as follows:

> Undertakings entrusted with the operation of services of general economic interest or having the character of a revenue-producing monopoly shall be subject to the rules contained in this Treaty, in particular to the rules on competition, in so far as the application of such rules does not obstruct the performance, in law or in fact, of the particular tasks assigned to them. The development of trade must not be affected to such an extent as would be contrary to the interests of the Community.

The Article 86(2) EC exception is neither specified nor limited (in Article 86 EC or elsewhere) in the Treaty.

> While it is possible for the Commission to set out its own interpretation of Article 86(2) EC in greater detail by means of Commission Decisions or Directives based upon Article 86(3) EC, this possibility has rarely been used. An important reason for the Commission's reticence is that the European Parliament and Council object to the use of these instruments, which allow the Commission to "legislate" single-handedly. The Parliament and the Council see this as lacking in democratic legitimacy, which is perceived as undesirable given the general "democratic deficit" of the EU. The European Parliament, in particular, favours instruments adopted upon the basis of "co-decision", which give it a role equivalent to that of the Council. Thus, the call for a Framework Directive adopted upon the basis of co-decision also addresses a situation which is unsatisfactory for the European Parliament from an institutional point of view. The Commission tries to accommodate these concerns by consulting the European Parliament informally on horizontal draft measures based upon Article 86(3) EC.

2.1.2. Article 16 EC

Thirty years after Article 86 was introduced in the EEC Treaty, a new Article 16 EC on services of general economic interest was introduced by the Treaty of Amsterdam in 1997. This ambiguous text reads:

> Without prejudice to Articles 73, 86 and 87, and given the place occupied by services of general economic interest in the shared values of the Union as well as their role in promoting territorial and social cohesion, the Community and the Member States, each within their respective powers and within the scope of application of this Treaty, shall take care that such services operate on the basis of principles and conditions that enable them to fulfil their missions.

On the one hand, the core legal elements of the concept of services of general economic interest are confirmed ("without prejudice to"), while, on the other, they are connected to a diffuse set of objectives as if to balance these against the market freedoms. Moreover, a declaration attached to the Treaty of Amsterdam underlined the need to interpret this provision in the light of the existing case law on Article 86(2) EC.

The ambiguity of Article 16 EC may further increase due to the following addition, that was proposed by the European Convention in Article III-122 of the proposed Constitutional Treaty, which otherwise repeats Article 16 EC:

> European laws shall define these principles and set these conditions without prejudice to the competence of the Member States, in compliance with the Constitution, to provide, to commission and to fund such services.

It is not clear who will adopt these laws, the Commission, based upon Article 86(3) EC[3] – with the drawbacks from a democratic perspective mentioned above – or the European Parliament and the Council, based upon Article 95 EC, or a combination of both. Perhaps, this provision will eventually be used as (part of) the legal basis for a future Framework Directive on Services of General Economic Interest (i.e., if there is sufficient political support for this among the Member States and in the European Parliament).[4]

In addition, an interpretative protocol will be added to Article 16 Protocol on Services of General Interest in the upcoming review of the Treaty after the failure of the Constitutional Treaty:

> Article 1:
> The shared values of the Union in respect of services of general economic interest within the meaning of Article 16 EC Treaty include in particular:
> - the essential role and the wide discretion of national, regional and local authorities in providing, commissioning and organizing services of general economic interest as closely as possible to the needs of the users;
> - the diversity between various services of general economic interest and the differences in the needs and preferences of users that may result from different geographical, social or cultural situations;
> - a high level of quality, safety and affordability, equal treatment and the promotion of universal access and of user rights;
>
> Article 2:
> The provisions of the Treaties do not affect in any way the competence of Member States to provide, commission and organise noneconomic (*sic*) services of general interest.[5]

This protocol appears to add little of substance with regard to services of general economic interest themselves, other than highlighting, once again, the topicality of this issue and the deep concerns held by the Member States that something essential may

3 Article 86 EC is renumbered Article I-166 by the proposed Constitutional Treaty.

4 The European Trade Union Federation ETUC, and the Socialist People Party block in the European Parliament (PSE) are campaigning for a Framework Directive, collecting citizens' signatures for a petition in this direction.

5 Presidency Conclusions of the Brussels European Council of 21/22 June 2007.

slip from their control. However, it may be that, in the future, the values of "a high level of quality, safety and affordability, equal treatment and the promotion of universal access and of universal rights" will be fleshed out further as basic principles of services of general economic interest. The provision on "non-economic services of general interest", absurd as it may be (are the provisions on equal treatment of men and women in the workplace and the Working Times Directive no longer to apply to public librarians?) need not detain us here.

2.1.3. Article 36 Charter on Fundamental Rights

Meanwhile, the concept of services of general economic interest has likewise found its way into Article 36 of the Charter on Fundamental Rights, as follows:

> The Union recognises and respects access to services of general economic interest as provided for in national laws and practices, in accordance with the Treaty establishing the European Community, in order to promote the social and territorial cohesion of the Union.

Substantively, these provisions add little, if anything at all, to Article 86 EC or to the case law of the Court on this provision. Hence, the remainder of this chapter will not address Article 16 EC Treaty or Article 36 of the Charter on Fundamental Rights, but will be limited to Article 86 EC. First, we will examine its role and structure.

2.2. The Role and Structure of Article 86 EC

Article 86 EC provides a special regime not only for undertakings entrusted with providing services of general economic interest, which may be public monopolies, but also more generally for undertakings granted "special and exclusive rights" by the Member States, with respect to "the rules contained in the Treaty". It should be noted that this exception covers all Treaty rules, i.e., not only ("in particular") the free movement and the competition rules, but also the rules on, for example, state aid and public procurement.

Consequently, Article 86 EC is a key provision concerning the distinction between the public and the private spheres in EU law. It is structured as follows:

Article 86(1) EC formulates the general rule prohibiting the Member States from taking, concerning public undertakings or undertakings enjoying special and/or exclusive rights, any measures contrary to the rules contained in the Treaty. These treaty rules are further specified as the anti-discrimination provisions of Articles 28 and 49 (i.e., free movement), the competition rules, and the rules on state aid.

Article 86(2) provides a limited derogation from this general rule for services of a general economic interest and revenue-producing monopolies. This exception is limited to cases in which the rules of the Treaty, in particular, the free movement and competition rules, would obstruct such enterprises in the performance of their public interest tasks, and where the state measures involved do not encroach on the Community interest – i.e., repeating the familiar EU law requirements of necessity and proportionality.

Under Article 86(3) EC, the Commission is empowered to enforce the prohibition in Article 86(1) and the application of Article 86(2) EC by way of Directives and Decisions. As is the case for Article 86 EC itself, such Article 86(3) EC Directives are addressed to the Member States, not to undertakings directly (an undertaking charged with infringing Article 82 EC, for example, could, however, invoke the applicability of Article 86(2) EC in its defence).[6]

Article 86 EC is addressed to the Member States, not to undertakings directly. In summary, it prohibits the Member States from taking, in relation to the specific categories of undertakings mentioned above, any measures contrary to the Treaty, with a limited exception for services of general economic interest. The application of both the general rule and its exception are subject to Commission supervision. As such, Article 86 EC is also an elaboration of the principle of Community "good faith" set out in Article 10 EC (*effet utile*) that has led to extensive case law on market interventions by the Member States (but which will not be discussed here).

So far, there are few examples of horizontal measures based upon Article 86 EC. These are:
Rules on financial transparency of public undertakings (dating back to 1980);[7]
Rules on public service compensation (of 2005, twenty-five years later).[8]

Apart from this, there are only sectoral rules regarding services of general economic interest in various network sectors, which (apart from those relating to the telecommunications sector[9]) are not based upon Article 86. These will be discussed in

6 The provisions of Article 86 EC read as follows:" (1) In the case of public undertakings and undertakings to which Member States grant special or exclusive rights, Member States shall neither enact nor maintain in force any measure contrary to the rules contained in this Treaty, in particular to those rules provided for in Article 12 and Articles 81 to 89; (2) Undertakings entrusted with the operation of services of general economic interest or having the character of a revenue-producing monopoly shall be subject to the rules contained in this Treaty, in particular to the rules on competition, in so far as the application of such rules does not obstruct the performance, in law or in fact, of the particular tasks assigned to them. The development of trade must not be affected to such an extent as would be contrary to the interests of the Community; (3) The Commission shall ensure the application of the provisions of this Article and shall, where necessary, address appropriate directives or decisions to Member States."

7 Now codified in: Commission Directive 2006/111/EC of 16 November 2006 on the Transparency of Financial Relations between Member States and Public Undertakings as well as on Financial Transparency within certain Undertakings, *OJ 2006 L318/17.*

8 Community framework for State aid in the form of public service compensation, OJ 2005 C297/04; and Commission Decision of 28 November 2005 on the application of Article 86(2) of the EC Treaty to State aid in the form of public service compensation granted to certain undertakings entrusted with the operation of services of general economic interest, OJ 2005 L312/67.

9 Commission Directive 2002/77/EC of 16 September 2002 on competition in the markets for electronic communications networks and services OJ 2002 L249/21.

Section 4.3. below. However, as mentioned above, if Article III-122 of the Proposed Constitutional Treaty (ever) enters into force, it may eventually be used as an additional legal basis for a Framework Directive on Services of General Economic Interest.

In the proposed Constitutional Treaty, Article 86 EC is renumbered Article I-166, without changes apart from the fact that the Commission would henceforth be able to adopt *Regulations* instead of *Directives*. Because Regulations are directly binding and do not require implementing legislation at national level, this means the Commission's legislative powers with regard to services of general interest (and special and exclusive rights) would actually be strengthened. This is remarkable considering the long-standing objections held by the European Parliament and the Council against Commission legislation based upon Article 86(3) EC that were already mentioned above.[10]

3. The Debate on Services of General Economic Interest

3.1. Scope of the Debate

A number of landmark decisions by the Court of Justice in the telecommunications sector in the 1990s sparked a debate on Article 86 EC. In these cases, brought by a number of Member States against the Commission, the Court accepted that the Commission could abolish exclusive and special rights in this sector by means of Commission Directives.[11] Proponents of state intervention subsequently felt strengthened by further cases such as *Corbeau* (in which the Court found that exclusive rights and cross-subsidies between various activities could be acceptable in the context of ensuring the financial stability of a universal service system for postal services). They sought to broaden the scope for public interest exception in Article 86(2) EC respectively to limit the Commission's powers in order to be able to continue to intervene in "key" economic sectors without Community intervention based upon breaches of the Treaty.[12]

In this debate, parties fearing liberalisation and privatisation based upon EU law campaigned to give the "*service public*" a sound basis in the Treaty itself. Often, France was the standard-bearer for such efforts. However, the Commission appears to have been successful in drowning its opposition in a decade-long consultation exercise generating a series of papers that might charitably be defined as "harmless".[13] Although the *service*

10 It remains contested whether or not Article 86(3) EC Directives should be considered legislation, rather than an authoritative interpretation of the Treaty by the Commission.

11 Case C-202/88 *Terminal Directive* [1991] ECR I-1223; Joined cases C-271/90, C-281/90 and C-289/90 *Services Directive* [1992] ECR I-5833.

12 Case C-320/91 *Procureur du Roi* v *Paul Corbeau (Corbeau)* [1993] ECR I-2533.

13 See the barrage of communications from the Commission: Services of general interest in Europe, OJ 1996 C281/3; Services of general interest in Europe, OJ 2001 C17/4; Report to the Laeken European Council – Services of general interest, COM(2001)598 final; Green Paper on Services of General

public concept was eventually written into the new Article 16 EC on services of general economic interest of the Treaty of Amsterdam cited above, this was done in a manner involving no substantive changes to Article 86 EC, and which was characterised in the French Senate as a mere "consolation prize".[14] Equally harmlessly, the *service public* concept has found its way into Article 36 of the Charter on Fundamental Rights (likewise cited above).[15]

As mentioned, the ambiguity of Article 16 was enhanced by the addition that was proposed by the European Convention in Article III-122 of the proposed Constitutional Treaty: "European laws shall define these principles and conditions". According to the White Paper on Services of General Interest, "this provision will provide an additional legal basis for Community action in the field of services of general economic interest, within the powers of the Union and within the scope of application of the Constitution".[16]

The White Paper also states, in the context of the question of whether a Framework Directive on Services of General (economic) Interest is needed, that this question will only be examined once the Proposed Constitutional Treaty enters into force. In the absence of such a Framework Directive, it should be noted that, apart from the Treaty provision on Article 86(2) EC itself, at present, no specific legal instruments beyond the Electronic Communications and Transparency Directives, and the Public Service Compensation framework (Notice and Decision) exist. In other words, the field is still very much open, and the debate has so far produced very little apart from underlining the importance of Article 86(2) EC.

One outcome of the debate has been that, in addition to services of general economic interest and services of general interest, the "social service of general interest" has been identified, in spite of the fact that "under Community law, social services do not constitute a legally distinct category of service within services of general interest".[17] Although there

Interest, COM (2003), 270 final; White Paper on Services of General Interest, COM(2004) 374 final; Implementing the Community Lisbon programme: Social services of general interest in the European Union, COM (2006), 177 final.

14 *Rapport d'information fait au nom de la delegation pout l'Union européenne sur les services d'intérêt general en Europe* (No. 82, 2000–2001 of November 2000, rapporteur Hubert Haenel), at 20, cited in J. Baquero Cruz, "Beyond Competition: Services of General Interest and European Community Law", in: G. de Búrca (ed), *supra* note 1, p. 177.

15 "The Union recognises and respects access to services of general economic interest as provided for in national laws and practices, in accordance with the Treaty establishing the European Community, in order to promote the social and territorial cohesion of the Union".

16 White Paper, *supra* note 13, p. 6.

17 COM (2006) 177, *Implementing the Community Lisbon programme: social services of general interest in the European Union*, at 4. The specific characteristics of such social services of general economic interest are listed as including one or more of the following: they operate on the basis of solidarity, in particular by the non-selection of risks or the absence, of equivalence between individual contributions and benefits; they are comprehensive and integrate the response to differing needs; they are not for profit; they include the participation of voluntary workers; they are strongly rooted in (local) cultural

are a large number of services that might qualify as a social service of general interest, the question of what they would then qualify for has been wisely left open. Because they were specifically excluded from the Services Directive,[18] which gave rise to the discussion on social services of general interest, health services are not covered by this concept (although long-term care is), and are, instead, subject to a separate Commission consultation process.[19] Social services of general interest will, therefore, not be discussed any further here.

In substance, then, there is no relevant change: the entire public debate on services of general economic interest can be seen as a holding exercise by the Commission, intended to diffuse political tension on this topic, without having had much of an impact on the scope or meaning of services of general economic interest. A benefit of this outcome is that the Treaty, and EU law, have not been saddled with a far-reaching *service public* clause that could cripple future liberalisation efforts, for example, in network sectors or the social sphere. The drawback of this limited outcome is that certain basic elements such as definitions, the purpose of services of general economic interest, and the nature of the proportionality test remain hazy.

Before examining the relevant concepts and definitions in further detail, the position on the services of general economic interest of the main actors involved is briefly restated.

3.2. Position on Services of General Economic Interest of the Main Actors

Broadly speaking, three (types of) institutional actors have developed sometimes contrasting positions on the subject of services of general economic interest.

3.2.1. Commission

The Commission has been engaged in a drawn out consultation process over the past ten years concerning services of general economic interest, initially concerning services of general economic interest as such, then on services of general interest in the context of the Lisbon programme, and finally on social services of general interest in the context of the proposed Constitutional Treaty. As mentioned above, this was essentially a containment exercise, i.e., a defensive approach designed to forestall any weakening of the Commission's position and/or of Article 86 EC more broadly. More recently, the role of the Commission has become more pro-active:

traditions; an asymmetric relationship between providers and beneficiaries exists that requires third party financing.

18 Directive 2006/123/EC of the European Parliament and of the Council of 12 December 2006 on Services in the Internal Market, OJ 2006, L376/36, Article 2f: "This Directive shall not apply to: (...) healthcare services whether or not they are provided via healthcare facilities and regardless of the ways in which they are organized and financed at national level or whether they are public or private."

19 Community action on health services, *supra* note 13.

- By including, in Article III-122 of the Draft Constitution, an additional legal basis for Community action in the area of services of general economic interest and, in Article III-166, the possibility of Commission Regulations, instead of Directives;
- By adopting a Community framework based upon a Commission Notice and a Commission Decision in the area of public service compensation and state aid, following innovative case law by the Court of Justice (*Altmark Trans*).[20]

It appears that the Commission would be interested in enacting or sponsoring a General Framework Directive on services of general economic interest, but is waiting for the adoption and entry into force of the (revised) proposed Constitutional Treaty before making its move.

3.2.2. Member States

The Member States, in most cases led by France,[21] have likewise approached services of general economic interest defensively, albeit from the opposite side: they have invoked the concept as a competition defence in individual cases, while trying to construct alternative concept such as *service public* that would provide, in their view, even better cover for state intervention in the market process. When discussing the proposed Constitutional Treaty, however, they failed to agree on curtailing the scope of Article 86(2) EC and settled for ambiguous wording that added nothing much that was relevant to the text.

Because the Commission appears to have been successful in its attempt to keep Article 86(2) EC afloat, now, maybe, is the time for the Member States to adopt a more pro-active approach and to develop more systematic ideas about services of general economic interest at national level. This concept, after all, might be useful to shield certain services from competition, in so far as they are justified (i.e., necessary) in order to carry out a legitimate public service task. It can, therefore, be a useful tool for a process of managed liberalisation, for example, to help contain escalating costs in the social sphere regarding sectors such as healthcare and/or pensions, which are no longer affordable as state-run systems.

3.2.3. The Court of Justice

The Court can be said to have constructed a system that allows the Member States the freedom to intervene on behalf of services of general economic interest, even to the point of creating or maintaining monopolies, albeit subject to a non-discrimination and proportionality test.

20 Case C-280/00 *Altmark Trans* [2003] ECR I-7747.

21 Although, the *service public* idea resurfaced as one of the "key" objectives of The Netherlands (the other Member State that had voted "no" in a referendum on the proposed Constitutional Treaty) in negotiating a revised (Constitutional) Treaty.

Its recent case-law on public service compensation greatly increases the significance of the Article 86(2) EC exception, while stressing the need for a formal act of entrustment in order to benefit from this privileged regime. In other words, it appears to set out some decisive markers on the requirements to be met while sweetening the package by offering a safe haven from the state aid regime. Arguably, this has changed the incentive structure for the Member States, although they may be slow to realise this, continuing (as, recently, in the Dutch position on changes needed to the proposed Constitutional Treaty that led to the protocol that will be annexed to Article 16 in the impending Treaty revision and was discussed in Section 2.1. above) to propose primitive carve-outs from the Treaty regime that lack any precedent, broader legal basis or economic rationale.

4. Definition Issues

4.1. Overlapping and Incomplete Definitions

It should not come as a surprise that, as the outcome of a consultation process that was, arguably, not even intended to produce clear results, the definitions and use of concepts in this area are muddy. For example, the White Paper on Services of General Interest states:

> Services of general interest are at the core of the political debate. Indeed, they touch on the central question of the role public authorities play in a market economy, in ensuring, on the one hand, the smooth functioning of the market and compliance with the rules of the game by all actors and, on the other hand, safeguarding the general interest, in particular, the satisfaction of citizens' essential needs and the preservation of public goods where the market fails.[22]

And:

> The debate on the Green Paper has strongly confirmed the importance of services of general interest as one of the pillars of the European model of society. (...) It has also confirmed the existence of a common concept of services of general interest in the Union. This concept reflects Community values and goals and is based on a set of common elements, including: universal service, continuity, quality of service, affordability, as well as user and consumer protection.[23]

It does not immediately inspire great confidence that services of general interest are here declared to constitute no less than a pillar of the European model, while this category ("services of general interest") is, as such, non-existent in EU law. However, this term was apparently devised to be able to discuss the implications of the fact that the Treaty's internal market and competition rules cover only economic activities. In the course of

22 Green Paper, *supra* note 13, p. 3.
23 White Paper, *supra* note 13, p. 4.

the debate on Article 86, at least four different partially overlapping concepts have played a role:

- services of general economic interest;
- universal service (obligations);
- services of general interest;
- social services of general interest.[24]

4.1.1. Focus on Services of General Economic Interest and Universal Service Obligations

Because there are no formal or generally accepted definitions of these concepts, their mutual demarcation is tricky. For example:

- There is no standard definition of services of general economic interest in the Treaty or in secondary legislation,[25] but it is an EU law concept that appears in the Treaty. Descriptions of services of general economic interest provided by the Commission overlap with those of universal service.
- There is no standard definition of universal service (obligations) and it does not appear in the Treaty, but universal service obligations have been specified in secondary sectoral legislation, notably for telecommunications (and postal services). Moreover, the concept is applied (but not under this name) in other network sectors, in particular, transport and energy.
- There are no standard definitions of services of general interest or of social services of general interest and it would not matter much if there were, as they are not EU law concepts, but were introduced to facilitate and defuse the debate on services of general economic interest. They are thought to overlap, at least in large part, with services of general economic interest.

Only services of general economic interest and universal service obligations are EU legal concepts. Moreover, health services (or at least curative care, notably hospital services) have, in any event, been excluded from the scope of (social) services of general interest. Therefore, the focus of this chapter will be on the former two, i.e., services of general economic interest and universal service.

4.2. The Lack of a Definition of Services of General Economic Interest

Another way of looking at the absence of a definition is that the definition of services of general economic interest itself was left open because the EC Treaty gives the Member States a wide freedom to define missions of general economic interest and to establish the organisational principles of the services intended to accomplish them. This interpretation is plausible also given that successive (proposed) amendments of the Treaty have not come up with a definition.

24 See the documents referenced at *supra* note 13.
25 White paper, *supra* note 13, p. 7.

Another reason why there is no list of services of general economic interest, or of services that are not, is that the concept of services of general economic interest is a dynamic one. Perceptions of what such services comprise, or what they do not, vary between time and place.[26] Thus, according to the Commission's Green Paper on services of general interest:

> The range of services that can be provided on a given market is subject to technological, economic and societal change and has evolved over time. (...) Given that the distinction is not static in time, (...) it would neither be feasible nor desirable to provide a definitive a priori list of all services of general interest that are to be considered non-economic.[27]

Because the concept of services of general economic interest is a fluid one, providing a list of such services is not very useful. Nevertheless, there are several descriptions of the key elements of services of general economic interest that are useful. For example, the Green Paper listed the following as common elements of a Community concept of services of general economic interest:

> [...] in particular: universal service, continuity, quality of service, affordability, as well as user and consumer protection.[28]

According to the White Paper, however, services of general economic interest mean the following:

> [...] in Community practice, there is broad agreement that the term refers to *services of an economic nature* which the Member States or the Community *subject to specific public service obligations* by virtue of a general interest criterion (emphasis added).[29]

Here, the link between services of general economic interest and specific public service obligations is worth noting. Territorial coverage obligations are also mentioned frequently. It should be noted that all of these factors are also mentioned in relation to universal service, which raises the question what the relationship between universal service and services of general economic interest is.[30] This will be discussed in greater detail below.

26 Clearly, it is possible to provide a list of sectors in which the Court or the Commission have accepted the existence of a service of general economic interest in past cases: river port operations; establishing and operating a public telecommunications network; water distribution; the operation of television services; electricity distribution; the operation of particular transport lines; employment recruitment; basic postal services; maintaining a postal service network in rural areas; regional policy; port services; waste management; ambulance services; and basic health insurance. However this does not mean that these services should be regarded as services of general economic interest in all Member States, at all times. See Buendia Sierra, note 1 *supra*, pp. 629–30.

27 Green Paper, note 13 *supra*, p. 14.

28 *Ibid.*, p. 15.

29 White Paper, note 13 *supra*, p. 7.

30 See Case C-266/96 *Corsica Ferries France* [1998] ECR I-3949, paras 44–7 which suggest universal service obligations are co-extensive with services of general economic interest.

The Member States' freedom to designate services of general economic interest is almost absolute up until the moment pre-emption occurs, i.e., the point where the relevant services are defined by Community legislation, based either upon Article 95 EC harmonisation measures or on Article 86(3) EC Commission Decisions or Directives, or both. Until that time, the Commission merely checks the definition of services of general economic interest for "manifest error". The Community element is introduced only at the level of the proportionality test of the measures concerned. Hence, pre-emption and proportionality are two important categories that will likewise be discussed further below.

First, however, the relevance of the requirement of an act of entrustment, respectively a comparable legal context, will be addressed as constitutive elements of a service of general economic interest.

4.2.1. Act of Entrustment

Whether open-ended or not, a service of general economic interest in principle requires an explicit act of entrustment: this can be seen as a constitutive act (i.e., creating the service of general economic interest where there was none previously).[31]

The Court has made this absolutely clear with regard to public service compensation, where, in order to be classified as not constituting state aid, the compensation in question has to be paid to an entity formally entrusted with services of general economic interest.[32] The act of entrustment should involve a clearly identified addressee as well as clearly defined obligations based upon objective and transparent parameters, established in advance, for the calculation of compensation. Compensation should not exceed cost, plus a reasonable rate of return, and in cases where a public tender procedure is not followed the compensation should be based upon that of a (hypothetical) efficient undertaking.[33] This requirement, again, underlines the importance of the provision of specific public service obligations by virtue of a general interest criterion (for which compensation is required) as the core of a service of general economic interest.

Evidently, solutions that are not market-based are likely to require public funding of some sort. Nevertheless, it is clear that an explicit measure of entrustment as a constitutive legal act is highly desirable in any event. This is so not just to build up a file for the defence (as has frequently been the focus of Member States so far), but also in order to have a sound basis for the proportionality test that the services of general economic interest must meet.

31 See Cases T-204 and 270/97 *EPAC* [2000] ECR II-2267, paras 125–8 and the references there.

32 Case C-280/00 *Altmark Trans*, note 20 *supra*; Community framework for State Aid, note 8 *supra*; and Commission Decision on Article 86(2) EC and State aid, note 8 *supra*.

33 Case C-280/00 *Altmark Trans,* note 20 *supra*, paras 89–93.

4.2.2. Existence Derived from Broader Legal Context

Nevertheless, the need for an act of entrustment – at least where there is no issue of public service compensation – is not absolute. The Commission has held that, in the absence of a legal act clearly entrusting a market party with services of general economic interest, it is also possible that the existence of a service of general economic interest can be derived from the broader legal context. It has, in fact, done so with regard to health insurance companies in state aid cases in relation to risk equalisation schemes.[34] This is based upon a generous reading of a single Court judgment to this effect:

> The Member States [...] cannot be precluded, when defining the services of general economic interest which they entrust to certain undertakings, from taking account of objectives pertaining to their national policy or from endeavouring to attain them *by means of obligations and constraints which they impose on such undertakings* (emphasis added).[35]

This does not, however, constitute "*carte blanche*" for the Member States, as the services of general economic interest concerned must somehow be separated from other economic activities.[36] Because, in addition, no public service compensation must be at issue (or it is subject to the state aid rules), and thus the relevance of this approach is likely to be limited in terms of the number of cases affected.

4.3. The Definition of Universal Service

The second important concept that requires further discussion is universal service. In the debate on services of general economic interest, universal service has been defined as follows:

> [...] to guarantee access for everyone, whatever the economic, social or geographic situation, to a service of a specified quality at an affordable price.[37]

34 Risk equalisation decisions concerning Ireland and The Netherlands. Aid measure N46/2003 Risk equalisation system – Ireland; Aid measures N 541/2004 and N 542/2004 Financial reserves and risk equalisation system – The Netherlands. In The Netherlands, as a matter of national law relating to services of general economic interest in the context of the cartel prohibition in Article 11, the prohibition of dominance abuse in Article 25 and the context of merger control, Article 41(3) of the Competition Act, in the absence of a formal legal act, it is possible, in highly exceptional circumstances to derive the existence of a service of general economic interest from "a conglomerate of rules, agreements and decisions". Kamerstukken II 1995/96, 24 707. nr 3, p 64.

35 Case 157/94 *Commission* v *The Netherlands* [1997] ECR I-5699, para 40.

36 State aid cases N541/2004 and N542/2004, at 27, with reference to Case C-179/90 *Porto di Genova* [1991] ECR I-5889.

37 Green Paper, *supra* note 13, p. 4.

Slightly different descriptions are:

> The concept of a universal service refers to a set of general interest requirements ensuring that certain services are made available at a specified quality to all consumers and users throughout the territory of a Member State, independently of geographical location, and in the light of specific national conditions, at an affordable price.[38]

And:

> In a liberalised market environment a universal services obligation guarantees that everybody has access to the service at an affordable price and that the service quality is maintained and, where necessary improved.[39]

Ubiquitous access and uniformity are, thus, important features of universal service. At the same time, however, continuity, quality of service, affordability, and user and consumer protection are mentioned alongside universal service as objectives of public policy in their own right.[40] Likewise, the common elements of services of general interest cited above include:

> [U]niversal service, continuity, quality of service, affordability, as well as user and consumer protection.[41]

Again, universal service is juxtaposed along public policy objectives that it might well be judged to include. The clearest definition is, perhaps, the following one:

> It establishes the *right* of everyone to access certain services considered as essential and imposes *obligations* on service providers to offer defined services according to specified conditions including complete territorial coverage and at an affordable price.[42]

This clarification of universal service as a universal right for consumers, on the one hand, and a set of obligations imposed on undertakings, on the other, should be highlighted as one of the key characteristics of universal service.

However, there is, again, a partial overlap (affordability) with values that are elsewhere presented as possible public policy objectives in their own right. Hence, it remains an open question as to whether universal service includes these other values or not –

38 *Ibid.*, at 16, with reference to Article 3(1) of Directive 2002/22/EC of the European Parliament and of the Council of 7 March 2002 on universal service and users' rights relating to electronic communications networks and services (Universal Service Directive), OJ L108/51.

39 Green Paper, *supra* note 13, p. 16.

40 *Ibid.*, pp. 16–19.

41 White Paper, *supra* note 13, p. 4.

42 *Ibid.*, p. 8 (emphasis added).

although it is difficult to envisage a meaningful universal service obligation that would, apart from accessibility and affordability, fail to provide a specific level of quality (as imposing full national coverage for free at zero quality would be pointless).

However, universal service and services of general economic interest do not fully coincide. The concept of services of general economic interest is broader, and may include other values, besides those set out in universal service obligations.

Therefore, it is proposed here to regard the various public policy objectives listed alongside universal service as a catalogue of related objectives that belong to the sphere of universal service and must be linked in a meaningful manner in order to achieve a worthwhile universal service guarantee in a particular case. The three core public policy values for healthcare in The Netherlands, quality, affordability and accessibility, would fit very well with such a concept of universal service albeit that in the context of imposing universal service obligations to be met by particular undertakings, they would need to be specified at a particular level, i.e. as a deliverable.

Universal service is further described as both a flexible and a dynamic concept, the basic principles of which are to be defined at Community level, which can subsequently be implemented by the Member States.[43] In a liberalisation setting based upon Community legal instruments (such as in telecommunications and postal services) this may well be appropriate, but it can scarcely be the model where Community legal instruments regulating liberalisation are absent – as is presently the case in healthcare. In summary, the existing reasoning on universal service obligations is incomplete and not always clear. On the bright side, this means that there is room for a national interpretation of these obligations, much like there is for services of general economic interest in general.

It should also be noted that, despite the conceptual haziness described above defining universal service obligations in telecommunications and postal services, and having *de facto* universal obligations in energy, has proven to be of the greatest importance in enabling the liberalisation of these services: once the main public policy concerns were tackled in this manner, the road to liberalising the remainder of the relevant service was opened. In The Netherlands, the situation concerning healthcare is similar, given that a broad national consensus on the need for liberalisation already exists in the absence of EU law or policy on this point. Here, too, basic public policy concerns must first be addressed in relation to services not deemed fit for liberalisation on public policy grounds as a pre-condition for further liberalisation of services for which competitive provision is feasible.

Because services of general economic interest and universal service obligations are the key relevant EU law categories their interrelationship will be examined further in the next paragraph.

43 Green Paper, *supra* note 13, p. 16.

5. Services of General Economic Interest, Universal Service Obligations and Market Failure

This brief section is dedicated to formulating some proposals on how to link the concepts of services of general economic interest, universal service and market failure. The starting point is the manner in which universal service has, so far, been defined at EU level in practice.

5.1. Examples of Universal Service Defined at EU Level

So far, there is only a handful of sectors – mainly concerning networked industries – where universal service has been defined at Community level.

5.1.1. Natural Gas

Article 3 of the Directive on Common Rules for the Internal Market in Natural Gas (Gas Directive) does not use the words "universal service", but it does deal with public service obligations and consumer protection.[44] It allows Member States to impose on gas operators in the general economic interest, public service obligations which may relate to security, including security of supply, regularity, quality and price of supplies, and environmental protection, including energy efficiency and climate protection. In addition, they may take appropriate measures to protect customers in remote areas, and may appoint a supplier of last resort. In addition, the Member States may claim exemption from certain provisions in the Gas Directive, to the extent that their application would obstruct the services of general economic interest concerned.

5.1.2. Electricity

Article 3 of Directive on common rules for the internal market in electricity (Electricity Directive) provides for an exception for services of general economic interest in much the same language.[45] In this case, however, it is explicitly provided that the Member States are to ensure a universal service[46] in relation to all household customers and, where appropriate, small- and medium-sized enterprises, including the possibility of appointing a supplier of last resort and of imposing an obligation to provide connection according to specified terms. Additional consumer protection measures and an exemption from certain provisions in the Electricity Directive, to the extent that their

44 Directive 2003/55/EC of the European Parliament and of the Council of 26 June 2003 concerning Common Rules for the Internal Market in Natural Gas, repealing Directive 98/30/EC, OJ 2003, L176/57.

45 Directive 2003/54/EC of the European Parliament and of the Council of 26 June 2003 concerning Common Rules for the Internal Market in Electricity, repealing Directive 96/92/EC, OJ 2003, L176/37.

46 "That is the right to be supplied with electricity of a specified quality within their territory at reasonable, easily and clearly comparable and transparent prices".

application would obstruct the services of general economic interest concerned, are also provided.

5.1.3. Postal Services

Chapter 2 of the Directive on Common Rules for the Internal Market in Postal Services (Postal Directive) is dedicated to extensive rules governing universal service in the postal service.[47] Defined as "the permanent provision of a postal service of specified quality at all points in the territory at affordable prices for all users", the universal service obligations concerned are specified in great detail in the Directive as minimum norms to be met. The expression "services of general economic interest" is not used as such, nor are such services addressed apart from universal service: i.e., no services of general economic interest other than universal service are covered. It should be noted that the proposed amendments of the Postal Directive, apart from spelling out universal service obligations in much greater detail, abolishes and prohibits exclusive and special rights in this sector.[48]

5.1.4. Electronic Communications

The entire Directive on Universal Service and Users' Rights relating to Electronic Communications (Universal Service Directive) is dedicated to universal service and users rights in this field.[49] Member States must ensure that services covered by the Universal Service Directive are "made available at the quality specified to all end-users in their territory, independently of geographical location and, in the light of specific national conditions, at an affordable price". This covers access at a fixed location, directory enquiry services and directories, public pay telephones and special measures for disabled users, and a minimum set of leased lines. Member States may designate one or more undertakings to guarantee the provision of universal service and detailed rules on the compensation for universal service tasks are provided. No services of general economic interest other than universal service are covered.

From these examples, it may be surmised that, at least where services of general economic interest have so far been defined at Community level:

- within the context of services of general economic interest, other types of public service obligations can, and do, exist alongside universal service obligations;

[47] Directive 97/67/EC of the European Parliament and of the Council of 15 December 1997 on Common Rules for the Development of the Internal Market of Community Postal Services and the Improvement of Quality of Service, OJ 1998, L15/14.

[48] Proposal for a Directive of the European Parliament and of the Council amending Directive 97/67/EC concerning the full accomplishment of the internal market of Community postal services, COM (2006) 594 final.

[49] Directive 2002/22/EC of the European Parliament and of the Council of 7 March 2002 on Universal Service and Users' Rights relating to Electronic Communications Networks and Services (Universal Service Directive), OJ 2002, L108/51.

- universal service obligations may be imposed either on all undertakings active in the market, or on a limited number of operators (provider of last resort);
- services of general economic interest and universal service obligations, in particular, have been highly useful tools in achieving a working consensus underpinning the liberalisation of the bulk of the network sectors concerned.

5.2. Services of General Economic Interest in Relation to Universal Service Obligations

The above section on definitions leaves a number of questions on the relationship between service of general economic interest and universal service (obligations) unanswered, which will be addressed here:
- What is the scope of a service of general economic interest in relation to the scope of universal service, or universal service obligations? Do they overlap or coincide?
- Can one exist without the other? Are they different in scope and content, and, if so, how?
- How are they applied or imposed, and by which legal means?

Given the absence of a definition and a legal framework for services of general economic interest (such as a Framework Directive may provide in future), at first sight, it remains unclear whether an entire sector (such as public transport, refuse collection or health services) could be designated as a service of general economic interest, or only those parts where restrictions on the application of the Treaty are held to be necessary in order for the tasks concerned to be performed (with possibly some related services – as ancillary restraints – necessary to make public service provision feasible or affordable).

Likewise, it is not quite clear what the role of universal service or universal service obligations should be in this context.

5.2.1. Proportionality

First of all, it is proposed, here, to deal with this issue from a perspective of proportionality. That is to say that, in principle, it would appear more in line with proportionality to limit the application of the services of general economic interest concept to those cases in which it is clear in advance that particular restrictions in relation to EU law obligations concerning free movement, competition, state aid and/or public procurement will be necessary (and, therefore, proportional) to enable the undertaking(s) charged with the service of general economic interest to provide those services, in the sense that these services could not otherwise be provided to the requisite standard. Where this is not the case, reserving particular services to specific undertakings would simply not be necessary – and would, therefore, fail the proportionality standard included in Article 86(2) EC.

Approaching this issue from the other end, for example, starting from sectors in which governmental intervention takes place in the public interest as a whole would mean embracing practically all current areas of public policy without any clarity in advance on the question of whether meaningful restrictions would be involved that actually require resorting to Article 86(2) EC. It is also unlikely that, in this case, a proper discussion would take place on the proportionality of the restrictions on competition that would be necessary (proportional) to ensure that they met the Article 86(2) EC standards. This is, therefore, not a workable alternative.

This issue is further complicated by the role of universal service obligations. Arguably, these should coincide with services of general economic interest, to the extent that they constitute the deliverables which form the objective of entrusting an undertaking with carrying out a service of general economic interest, and any restrictions necessary are necessary in order for the undertaking concerned to be able to carry out its universal service obligation based upon a stable economic footing. In other words, the service of general economic interest would then constitute the provision of universal service plus, conceivably, those non-universal service elements of the service necessary in order to enable its provision (ancillary restraints) or to make this provision affordable (funding regime).[50]

However, at least in theory, the concept of services of general economic interest can cover public service obligations that are not universal service obligations in that they *are* in the general interest but *not* linked to territorial coverage (security of supply – and continuity – are examples of this).

5.2.2. Public Service Compensation

Apart from the issue of proportionality, another anchor point is the act of entrustment required by the Court to keep public service compensation out of the realm of state aid, which will be discussed in greater detail in a separate section below (*Altmark Trans*).

The link between formal entrustment and an Article 86(2) EC exemption from the state aid regime for public service compensation suggests that the Court supports the coincidence or concurrence between services of general economic interest and universal service (obligations). Clearly, the most suitable time to undertake this formal entrustment process would be a liberalisation context when certain (parts of) services break out of the solidarity-based vertically integrated state provision, so the market freedoms and competition rules become relevant. Coincidence does not mean that a service of general economic interest must fully correspond with a universal service obligation: it *may* do so, but *may also* cover additional elements.

[50] It is sometimes held that other types of services of general interest than universal service are conceivable. In the absence of concrete examples this further distinction is not used here. See Buendia Sierra, *supra* note 1, pp. 642–3.

5.3. *Services of General Economic Interest and Market Failure*

When deciding on the scope of services of general economic interest and universal service obligations, the concept of market failure (and/or government failure) is a logical starting point: after all, it is only in these cases that the services concerned are not already provided to the requisite standard by the market (and/or by public authorities) that market parties must be entrusted with the provision of particular services in the public interest.[51] It is submitted here that only where markets, in the absence of governmental action, fail, will it be possible to meet the EU law standard of necessity (proportionality)[52] that is required to invoke successfully the EU law concepts of services of general economic interest and universal service.[53]

Evidently, a Member State does not have to intervene or take additional measures if the public interest objectives (such as accessibility, quality and affordability) are ensured by the functioning of the market mechanism alone. However, if a Member State finds the market alone does not ensure the provision of the relevant public goods – i.e. market failure occurs – EU law allows the Member State to designate (one or several) universal service providers and to compensate them. Intervention should be objective, transparent, non-discriminatory and proportionate. This will ensure both legitimacy (rule of law) and overall welfare (social dimension).

Remarkably enough, to date, the definition of services of general economic interest under Community law has not systematically or explicitly been connected with instances of "market failure".[54] At the same time, there is ample discussion of the proportionality of services of general economic interest: it, therefore, appears logical to introduce the concept of market failure and the consequences thereof as a guiding principle in formulating the scope of services of general economic interest.[55] If market forces, left to themselves, sufficed to provide the public good at stake, there would be little point in intervening.

51 Sometimes economic and non-economic objectives are distinguished. This is wrong because the alleged non-economic objectives can usually be couched in terms of public goods and attempts to improve their delivery.

52 Admittedly, the strictness of this test would still depend on whether or not pre-emption by means of secondary EU law had occurred. As will be discussed further below, it is proposed here that this test would be one of whether a measure is "manifestly disproportionate" in cases where there is no Community legislation occupying the field, and "least restrictive means" where Community rules apply.

53 The concept only becomes relevant in EU law terms when a Member State invokes Article 86(2) EC. In other words, as long as a Member State does not claim the exception it need not be able to demonstrate a market failure.

54 See, however, J.W. van de Gronden, "The internal market, the state and private initiative: A legal assessment of national mixed public-private arrangements in the light of European law", (2006) 33 *Legal Issues of European Integration*, p. 105.

55 An exception is the Green Paper, *supra* note 13, p. 3.

For example, in health care *insurance* markets, two types of market failure are commonly said to exist:

- Adverse selection: whereby insurers compete on the risk profile of their customers, seeking to attract lower-risk consumers, rather than on the provision of services;
- Information asymmetry: which means that providers of health care have much better information about the need and scope for treatment, and the quality of the services provided than consumers and insurers. At the same time, consumers have better information about their own behaviour than the insurers, who act as third-party payers. This leads to:
  - Producer moral hazard: the problem that producers provide too much production (more than is efficient and socially desirable) and/or too little (less than is efficient and socially desirable), of the wrong kind, at quality levels that are too low and price levels that are too high;
  - Consumer moral hazard: the problem that third-party payments (by insurers) may lead consumers to consume more health services than they would if they had to finance these services directly.

In The Netherlands, these market failures have been addressed by mandatory universal health insurance, a prohibition on risk selection and on premium-differentiation backed up by a risk-equalisation fund (risk pooling and risk-adjusted transfer payments), an obligation on insurers to contract for adequate levels of care, and efforts to improve stock-taking, availability and exchange of quality data. Government intervention, in other words, has served to ensure that the relevant public good – universal affordable healthcare insurance coverage – was attained. According to the Commission, the sum of the measures concerned corresponds to entrusting the health insurers with a service of general economic interest.[56]

Asymmetric information as well as problems of moral hazard, adverse selection and agency problems (when providers of health services oversell) are present in health care markets other than health insurance. Some of these problems can, in large part, be resolved by means of market-based solutions.

For example, consumers of healthcare are uncertain and have asymmetric information compared to the providers of health services. They are unaware of if and when they will fall ill (stochastic demand), which types of health care and how much of these they need, and where to buy them (idiosyncratic preferences, costly search and co-ordination) and whether a treatment will be or has been effective (experience and credence good). However, consumers do not usually shop directly for health care, but act through secondary markets or intermediaries, with insurers absorbing the risk of uncertain demand, primary care physicians aiding consumers in their search for health services, and hospitals co-ordinating the need for complex health services. Finally, the risk of

[56] At present subject to appeal in Case T-84/06 *Azivo* v *Commission*, action brought on 13 March 2006 on Aid measures N 541/2004 and N 542/2004.

over-consumption may, for instance, be remedied by imposing capitation fees that allow hospitals and physicians to share the risk of over-consumption.

In other cases, it may be necessary to intervene, for example, to guarantee access to emergency services within certain minimum time-limits or distance limits, according to public good standards which may be higher than what the market would provide on its own. Academic (teaching) hospitals, research, top-referential care and expensive pharmaceuticals are, at first sight, other possible candidates for such intervention.

It should be noted that a market failure could be addressed in terms of, for example, imposing a universal service obligation, which could then still be implemented consistently with market principles, i.e., by market parties playing by market rules. Compensation from general tax revenues does not create a barrier to entry (and is subject to parliamentary control as part of the budget procedures). Funding by market participants should ensure that participants only contribute to the financing of the universal service obligation and not of other activities which are not directly linked to the provision of the universal service obligation.

One pertinent example is provided by the risk equalisation funds in health insurance mentioned above. In the event that such a solution is not feasible, in some cases there may be a case for public provision or public service compensation (again, various forms could be envisaged that range from a universal service fund to funding from general taxation revenues). In summary, an economics-focused approach to services of general economic interest seems appropriate, even though this is, so far, not made explicit by existing documents on services of general economic interest. The reasoning used to argue the proportionality of the measure imposed would have to address this issue.

Finally, it is important to realise that numerous market-based remedies of market failure are imaginable. For example, failures in primary markets can be remedied by means of creating secondary markets, and/or introducing intermediaries, guarantees and standards, quality-certification, *etc.* This is the case because, frequently, market failure is not the result of "too much" competition, but more probably the result of a lack of possibilities to compete, and/or a lack of (tradable) property rights.

6. Scope of the Article 86(2) EC Exemption

A number of formal legal categories determine whether Article 86(2) EC is at issue. These concern, first, whether the entity is involved is an undertaking, second, whether it has been entrusted with a task of general economic interest, and third, whether the restrictions imposed are in line with the legitimate public task.

6.1. The Concepts of Undertaking and Solidarity

This sub-section deals with the question of which types of entities may claim an Article 86(2) EC exemption. In the first place, it should be noted that the word "economic" in services of general economic interest refers to the nature of the activity concerned, and not to the public interest which may be non-economic in nature, for example, the promotion of public health.[57] The notion of "economic" services in important, in that the exemption of Article 86(2) EC applies to undertakings: public authorities acting as such are not subjected to the competition rules.

6.1.1. Undertakings

The first question is, therefore, how to define the concept of "undertaking". The case law of the Court on the concept of undertaking is functional in nature. This means that the legal form under which an entity is classified under national law is irrelevant:

> [...] having recourse to Member States' domestic law in order to limit the scope of provisions of Community law undermines the unity and effectiveness of that law and cannot, therefore, be accepted. Consequently, the fact that a body has or has not, under national law, legal personality separate from that of the state is irrelevant in deciding whether it may be regarded as a public undertaking within the meaning of the Directive.[58]

Instead, the core issue is whether or not the entity concerned is engaged in an economic activity:

> In the context of competition law (...) the concept of an undertaking encompasses every entity engaged in an economic activity regardless of the legal status of the entity and the way in which it is financed.[59]

An economic activity in turn is defined as follows:

> [...] any activity consisting of supplying goods and services in a given market by an undertaking constitutes an economic activity, regardless of the legal status of the undertaking and the way in which it is financed.[60]

57 See Buendia Sierra, *supra* note 1, p. 644.

58 Case 118/85 *Transparency Directive* [1987] ECR 2599, para 11. See the Opinion of AG Cruz Vilaca in Case 30/87 *Bodson* [1988] ECR 2479, para 32. It is nevertheless used as a "sanity check" in clear cases. See Opinion of AG Jacobs, Case C-41/90 *Höfner* [1991] ECR I-1979, paras 22–3.

59 Case C-41/90 *Höfner*, supra n. 58, para 21. See Joined Cases C-159/91 and C-160/91 *Poucet and Pistre*, supra n. 2, para 17; Case C-244/94 *FFSA*, *supra* note 2, para 14; Case C-67/96 *Albany*, *supra* note 2, para 77; Joined Cases C-115/97, C-116/97, C-117/97 and C-219/97 *Brentjens*, *supra* note 2, para 77; and Case C-219/97 *Drijvende Bokken*, *supra* n. 2, para 67; Joined Cases C-180/98 to C-184/98 *Pavlov et al* v *Stichting Pensioenfonds Medische Specialisten (Pavlov)* [2000] ECR I-6451, para 74; Case C-218/00 *Cisal* [2002] ECR I-691, para 22; Joined Cases C- 264/01, C-306/01, C-354/01 and C-355/01 *AOK* [2004] ECR I-2493, para 46.

60 Joined Cases C-180/98 to C-184/98 *Pavlov* [2000] ECR I-6451.

Offering goods or services in a market, in particular doing so for payment, and assuming the financial risks involved, means engaging in an economic activity as an undertaking. Likewise, offering goods or services in competition, or offering goods and services that could be subject to competition, means engaging in an economic activity as an undertaking. Thus, in the 1991 *Höfner* Case, the Court held that:

> The fact that employment procurement activities are normally entrusted to public agencies cannot affect the economic nature of such activities. Employment procurement has not always been, and is not necessarily, carried out by public entities."[61]

Similarly, concerning ambulance services in its 2001 *Glöckner* Case, the Court held that:

> Such activities have not always been, and are not necessarily, carried on by such [private non-profit] organisations or by public authorities.[62]

It is, therefore, possible to base a finding that a particular entity is an undertaking upon the fact that the activities concerned could be performed in competition. Clearly, this is the case for most activities. Hence, it may be concluded that "very few bodies involved in the organisation of health care are not to be considered undertakings".[63]

6.1.2. Solidarity

Financial solidarity and exclusion from competitive provision, on the other hand, are required for classification as a scheme which has an exclusively social function which means that the entities concerned are not regarded as undertakings and are excluded from the application of the competition rules altogether (but not from the market freedoms and public procurement rules). That is to say, in this case, Article 86(2) EC does not come into play because the activities concerned fall completely outside the scope of competition. In this case, the following factors are generally weighed:[64]

- The objective pursued by a scheme;
- Its compulsory nature;
- The manner in which contributions (i.e., not based upon person-specific risks) and benefits are calculated and managed (i.e., based upon the redistribution of contributions or on capitalisation involving active fund management);

61 Case C-41/90 *Höfner, supra* note 58, paras 22 and 23. See Case C-55/96 *Job Centre Coop* [1997] ECR I-7119; Case C-258/98 *Giovanni Carra* et al [2000] ECR I-4217. In the Case C-82/01P *Aéroports de Paris* [2002] ECR I-9297, para 82, the Court confirmed "the fact that an activity may be exercised by a private undertaking amounts to further evidence that the activity in question may be described as a business activity".

62 Case C-475/99 *Glöckner* [2001] ECR I-8089, para 20.

63 See V. Hatzpoulos, "Health law and Policy: The Impact of the EU', in: G. de Búrca (ed), *supra* note 1, p. 148.

64 Joined Cases C-159/91 and C-160/91 *Poucet and Pistre, supra* note 2; Case C-355/00 *Freskot* [2003] ECR I-5263. See Hatzpoulos, *supra* note 63, p. 111.

- The overall degree of state control;
- Redistribution within the scheme by cross-subsidisation;
- The existence of competing schemes.

By examining, on the one hand, whether the entity concerned is active on a market, respectively, the activities concerned could be provided under competitive conditions, and, on the other, whether or not the elements of solidarity prevail, it can be ascertained whether a particular entity should be regarded as an undertaking to which the competition rules apply. If it is a public authority, the competition rules do not apply, and Article 86(2) EC is irrelevant. If it is an undertaking, and if it engages in providing services of general economic interest, Article 86(2) EC may be invoked as an exemption, provided the demands of proportionality are met.

6.1.3. Rule of Reason

Finally, it should be noted that it is possible that undertakings engage in activities that restrict competition, but are not caught by the competition rules because they pursue an overriding public interest objective in a proportional manner. So far, this exception (or rule of reason) has only been applied in the context of Article 81 EC (restrictive agreements), not Article 82 EC (dominance abuse), and remains highly contested.[65]

6.2. *EU Law Rules Affected by Article 86(2) EC*

As mentioned above Article 86(2) EC serves to balance the Community objectives of market integration with national public service objectives. At the outset, it should be noted that these two are not necessarily in conflict, because opening up services to competition frequently leads to lower prices and a greater range of choice for consumers, i.e., to net improvements in the services concerned.

Keeping this in mind, the next question is which type of EU rules may be subject of the Article 82(2) EC exemption. The relevant rules are these on:
- free movement (of goods, services and capital, freedom of establishment);
- competition;
- state aid;
- public procurement;
- commercial monopolies;
- concessions.

In principle, the rules on free movement and public procurement and concessions apply to public authorities, and the competition and state aid rules apply to undertakings.

65 Case C-67/96 *Albany, supra* note 2; Joined Cases C-115/97, C-116/97, C-117/97 and C-219/97 *Brentjens, supra* note 2; Case C-219/97 *Drijvende Bokken, supra* note 2; Case C-309/99 *Wouters* [2002] ECR I-1577; and Case C-519/04 P *Medina* [2006] ECR I-6991.

The Community objective of market integration and national public policy objectives are not necessarily in conflict: the opening of services to competition generally leads to lower prices and increased choice for consumers.[66] Sometimes, however, national policy objectives and Community policy objectives have to be co-ordinated. It is for this purpose that Article 86(2) exists:

> [...] which provides that services of general economic interest are not subject to the application of Treaty rules to the extent that this is necessary to allow them to fulfil their general interest mission.

And

> This means that under the EC Treaty and subject to the conditions set out in Article 86(2) the effective performance of a general interest task prevails, in case of tension, over the application of Treaty rules.[67]

The starting point, therefore, is that Article 86(2) EC provides an exception for services of general economic interest, to the Treaty rules. Second, however, this exception only applies to the extent that this is strictly necessary for performing the functions of services of the general economic interest concerned. This raises the issues of proportionality and pre-emption.

6.3. *Proportionality and Pre-emption*

In the first place, it is important to highlight that, because Article 86(2) EC is an exception, it is interpreted in a restrictive manner and must be invoked by the parties that seek to benefit from it: i.e., the Member State and/or the undertaking concerned, if challenged, must invoke the exemption and accordingly must meet the relevant burden of proof. This section is primarily concerned with the question of what this burden of proof is in the context of proportionality.

Under Community law, there are, in principle, two types of proportionality test, with a different degree of stringency. To determine whether national measures can qualify as entailing infringements of the Treaty rules that are "necessary" in order to ensure services of general economic interest, it is, therefore, important which type of proportionality test is applied, and when. The two types of proportionality test are:
- Manifestly disproportionate (the "mild" test). In this case, it will suffice if the measures imposed are *prima facie* suitable to achieving the task at hand;
- Least restrictive means (the "strict" test). In this case, of all imaginable measures, the one chosen must involve the least restrictions on market freedom.

66 See Buendia Sierra, *supra* note 1, p. 626.
67 White Paper, *supra* note 13, p. 7.

Key to this issue is the 1990 agriculture case *Fedesa*, in which the Court distinguished between the "manifestly disproportionate" and "least restrictive means" regimes, in a case regarding the legality of a number of Council Directives in the agricultural field, as follows:

> The Court has consistently held that the principle of proportionality is one of the general principles of Community law. By virtue of this principle, the lawfulness of the prohibition of an economic activity is subject to the condition that the prohibitory measures are appropriate and necessary in order to achieve the objectives legitimately pursued by the legislation in question; *when there is a choice between several appropriate measures recourse must be had to the least onerous*, and the disadvantages caused must not be disproportionate to the aims pursued.
>
> However, with regard to judicial review of compliance with those conditions it must be stated that in matters concerning the common agricultural policy the Community legislature has a discretionary power which corresponds to the political responsibilities given to it by Articles 40 and 43 of the Treaty. Consequently, the legality of a measure adopted in that sphere can be affected only if the measure is *manifestly inappropriate* having regard to the objective which the competent institution is seeking to pursue.[68]

It is submitted here that, with regard to the Member States, the same logic applies, but with a reverse outcome: where there is no Community norm that has occupied the field (pre-emption), the lighter "manifestly disproportionate" administrative law test prevails; where pre-emption has occurred, Member States may only intervene based upon "the least restrictive means".

This issue has been resolved in the *Corbeau* and *Almelo* Cases where the Court was willing to accept monopolies for services of general economic interest that were broader in scope than the universal service concerned.[69] Implicitly, therefore, such restrictions (ancillary restraints) were held not to be manifestly disproportionate, while they would, clearly, have failed a least restrictive means test, because other measures (such as funding of universal service obligations from general tax revenue) would clearly have been available. In such cases, the Member State has to be prepared to demonstrate that the broader scope is necessary to perform the universal service obligation, i.e., that the performance thereof is not merely hindered or made more difficult, but would otherwise be impossible.[70] This requires comparing the net cost of providing a universal service against the economic advantages inherent in the state measure at issue, as well as any

68 Case C-331/88 *Fedesa* [1990] ECR I-4023, paras 13–4 (emphasis added), with reference to Case 265/87 *Schraeder* [1989] ECR 2237, paras 21–2.

69 Case C-320/91 *Corbeau*, *supra* note 12, paras 15 *et seq*; Case C-393/92 *Almelo* [1994] ECR I-1521 paras 46 *et seq*. See Case C-475/99 *Glöckner*, *supra* note 62, which suggests the outer limit of such ancillary restraints is the ability to meet demand, i.e., to maintain efficient operations in the associated services (in this case, patient transport services in addition to emergency services).

70 Case T-260/94 *Air Inter* [1997] ECR II-997, paras 138–9.

other forms of compensation received (such as state aid).[71] Evidently, over time, circumstances may change.

The conclusion that pre-emption is relevant to the proportionality test may be drawn from the Electricity cases. When faced with the Article 226 EC Treaty, infringement cases concerning national electricity monopolies in The Netherlands, France and Italy, the Court has clearly opted for judicial restraint by stating the burden of proof on the Member States "*cannot be so extensive as to require the Member States [...] to [...] prove, positively, that no other conceivable measure, which by definition would be hypothetical, could enable those tasks to be performed* under the same conditions".[72]

The Court went on to show that the Commission had neglected to elaborate on the nature of the Community interest involved – even in terms of the effect on Community trade.[73] It clearly held that the Commission should have acted under Article 86(3) EC to back up its allegations:

> [...] it was incumbent on the Commission, in order to prove the alleged failure to fulfil obligations, to define, subject to review by the Court, the Community interest in relation to which the development of trade must be assessed. In that regard, it must be borne in mind that Article 90(3) [now Article 86(3)] of the Treaty expressly requires the Commission to ensure the application of that article and, where necessary, to address appropriate Directives or Decisions to Member States.[74]

Specifically, the Court held that the Commission should have demonstrated how "*in the absence of a common policy* in the area concerned, development of direct trade between producers and consumers, in parallel with the development of trade between major networks, would have been possible".[75] Hence, in the absence of Community measures, the Court will not consider itself bound to judge on the feasibility of alternative regulatory solutions, even if these may, theoretically, be more consistent with EU law.

71 Buendia Sierra, supra n 1, at 640–1.

72 Case C-157/94 *Dutch Electricity Monopoly* [1997] ECR I-5699, para 58; Case C-159/94 *French Electricity and Gas Monopoly* [1997] ECR I-5815, para 101; Case C-158/94 *Italian Electricity Monopoly* [1997] ECR I-5789, para 54 (emphasis added).

73 Case C-157/94 *Dutch Electricity Monopoly, supra* note 72, paras 66–73; Case C-159/94 *French Electricity and Gas Monopoly, supra* note 72, paras 109–16.

74 Case C-157/94 *Dutch Electricity Monopoly, supra* note 72, para 69; Case C-159/94 *French Electricity and Gas Monopoly, supra* note 72, para 113.

75 Case C-157/94 *Dutch Electricity Monopoly, supra* note 72, para 58; Case C-159/94 *French Electricity and Gas Monopoly*, supra n. 72, para 71 (emphasis added). See Joined Cases C-147/97 and C-148/97 *Deutsche Post* [2000] ECR I-3061. Here, in the absence of agreements on terminal dues between postal operators that would allow Deutsche Post to execute its public service task in a financially balanced manner, legislation allowing Deutsche Post to charge international mail at (higher) national rates did not cause it to infringe Article 86 EC.

As no Community framework is, to date, in place for health care – i.e., there is no pre-emption of national rules by Community rules – this means that the mild "not manifestly disproportionate" test should be applied. In fact, this is also the test applied by the European Commission in the Irish and Dutch risk equalisation scheme cases.[76]

In order to pass this test, the following must be shown:

> [...] in order that the derogation to the application of the rules of the Treaty set out in Article 90(2) [now Article 86(2)] thereof may take effect, it is not sufficient for the undertaking in question merely to have been entrusted by the public authorities with the operation of a service of general economic interest, but it must be shown in addition that the application of the rules of the Treaty obstructs the performance of the particular tasks assigned to the undertaking and that the interests of the Community are not affected [...].[77]

Thus, depending on the criterion used the proportionality test involves two or three steps:
- a causal link between the measure and the objective of general interest must be established;
- the restrictions caused by the measure are balanced by the benefits obtained in terms of the general interest (this is last step of the "not manifestly disproportionate" test); and
- finally, the objective cannot be achieved by less restrictive means (this is the last step of the "least restrictive means" test).

It is held here that – in the absence of pre-emption – the second step would suffice in the context of a "not manifestly disproportionate" test. Meanwhile, it should be noted that this approach to proportionality remains contested and merits further separate consideration in follow-up research across various EU law procedures in which the concept is applied.

6.4. *A Three Step Approach*

In order to minimise the issues of overlap and to provide a logical sequence in the steps that need to be taken in defining a service of general economic interest and its related universal service and other public service obligations, the following three-step approach is proposed:

76 Risk equalisation decisions concerning Ireland and The Netherlands. Aid measure N46/2003 Risk equalisation system – Ireland; Aid measures N 541/2004 and N 542/2004 Financial reserves and risk equalisation system – The Netherlands.

77 *Case C-179/90 Porto do Genova, supra* note 36, para 26, citing Case 311/84 *CBEM* v *Compagnie Luxembourgeoise* [1985] ECR 3261, para 17, and Case C-41/90 *Höfner, supra* note 58, para 24.

- First, the universal service and/or other public services should be defined: this means deciding which rights are deemed to exist (or to be necessary) with regard to a particular service to consumers.
- Second, an analysis is necessary of which of these consumers' rights, as a result of market failure, would not be adequately provided in a market setting – i.e., after market-based remedies against the market failure concerned are imposed – and might, therefore, require imposing universal service obligations or other public service obligations, and what the precise content of these obligations would be. This latter question can be determined based upon the following questions:
  - What would be the *proportionate remedy* to the market failure concerned that could benefit from an exemption? Is it necessary to impose obligations on all undertakings in the market or should one or more operators with specific obligations be designated? Again, when looking at remedies, solutions that allow competition to work (for example, the risk equalisation system) should be considered as a first choice.
  - Do the undertakings concerned need an *exemption from certain Treaty obligations* in order to perform their task to the required standard?
- The third question is that of the need for ancillary restraints. Should the undertakings concerned receive any *rights and/or obligations in excess of the scope of the universal service and/or other public service obligations* themselves?
  - The answer to this last question then defines the *scope* of the service of general economic interest.[78]
  - An *act of entrustment* and *an objective, transparent and proportional compensation mechanism* are required (subject to the *Altmark Trans* case law of the Court and the Commission framework on public service compensation).

6.4.1. Choice of Organisation

It is for the public authorities involved to decide whether they provide these services directly through their own administration, or whether they entrust the service to a third-party (private or public entity). Designating "in house" service providers as charged with services of general economic interest can lead to an infringement of the competition rules in the following three cases:
- where the public service requirements concerned are not (properly) specified;[79]
- where the provider charged is manifestly unable to meet demand;[80]
- where there is an alternative way of fulfilling the service of general economic interest requirements that would have a less detrimental effect in competition.[81]

78 The notion that a service of general economic interest might involve services broader than the universal service concerned in order to guarantee its economic viability can be traced back to Case C-320/91 *Corbeau, supra* note 12.

79 Case C-66/86 *Silver Line Reisebüro* [1989] ECR 803.

80 Case C-41/90 *Höfner supra* note 58.

81 Green Paper, *supra* note 13, at 24, citing the CFI in Case T-266/97 *Vlaamse Televisie Maatschappij* [1999] ECR II-2329.

Where a third-party is selected, the public procurement rules will generally apply, or, in the event that this is not the case, rules of transparency, equal treatment, mutual recognition and the protection of individual rights will apply (alongside the norms set out in Commission's Communication on Concessions under Community Law).

7. Compensation for Public Service Obligations

Relatively recently, a complete framework for public service compensation has been created, as the Court's decision in *Altmark Trans* was followed by a Commission Notice and Decision on this issue. The importance of this framework goes beyond compensation as such, because it addresses the issue of the legal basis and changes the incentive structure for Member States and undertakings alike. As a result, there are now clear benefits to a formal designation as a service of general economic interest. At the same time, a clear legal basis facilitates the carrying out of a proper proportionality test.

7.1. *Four-Part Test*

In its *Altmark Trans* Case of 2003, the Court, for the first time, set out a four-part test to determine whether or not, in the context of Article 86(2) EC, state aid might be involved:

- First, the recipient undertaking must actually have public service obligations to discharge, and the obligations must be clearly defined. […];
- Second, the parameters of the basis upon which the compensation is calculated must be established in advance in an objective and transparent manner, in order to avoid it conferring an economic advantage which may favour the recipient undertaking over competing undertakings […];
- Third, the compensation cannot exceed what is necessary to cover all or part of the costs incurred in the discharge of public service obligations, taking into account the relevant receipts and a reasonable profit for discharging those obligations. […];
- Fourth, where the undertaking which is to discharge public service obligations, in a specific case, is not chosen pursuant to a public procurement procedure which would allow for the selection of the tenderer capable of providing those services at the least cost to the community, the level of compensation needed must be determined upon the basis of an analysis of the costs which a typical undertaking, well run and adequately provided […] so as to be able to meet the necessary public service requirements, would have incurred in discharging those obligations […].[82]

[82] Case C-280/00 *Altmark Trans*, *supra* note 20, paras 89–93. See Joined Cases C-34/01 to C-38/01 *Enirisorse SnA v Ministero delle Finanze (Enirisorse)* [2003] ECR I-14243, para 31 *et seq*. The *Enirisorse* case finally clarified that collecting and allocating (part of) charges levied on other undertakings to the benefit of an undertaking charged with services of general economic interest may constitute state aid.

Compensation for public service missions that meets these criteria will not constitute state aid. If such compensation does not meet these criteria, it will be subject to the state aid rules. Note the fourth condition of *Altmark Trans* which provides for the situation "where the undertaking which is to discharge public service obligations, in a specific case is not chosen pursuant to a public procurement procedure", in which case the funding is based not upon actual costs but on the costs of a (hypothetical) effective undertaking.

7.2. The Commission Notice and Decision

Following the *Altmark Trans* judgment of the Court of Justice, the Commission has spelled out the conditions under which compensation for services of general economic interest is not considered state aid. However, it should be noted that a related question is whether charging particular undertakings with the provision of services of general economic interest is subject to the public procurement rules.

The Commission has built on *Altmark Trans* by adopting a Notice with a Community framework for state aid in the form of public service compensation (Commission Notice),[83] and a Commission Decision to deal with those cases in which the public service compensation concerned does not meet the *Altmark Trans* criteria and therefore constitutes state aid (Commission Decision).[84]

The Commission Notice re-states the fact that Member States have wide discretion in designating services of general economic interest, and that the Commission can only control for manifest errors in this designation. It encourages the Member States to consult widely, in particular among consumers, prior to defining public service obligations. An official act is required, which must specify the:

- precise nature and the duration of the public service obligations;
- undertakings and the territory concerned;
- nature of any exclusive or special rights assigned to the undertaking;
- parameters for calculating, controlling and reviewing the compensation;
- arrangements for avoiding and repaying any over-compensation.

Concerning compensation, the Notice emphasises that cross-subsidisation on activities not constituting services of general economic interest constitutes incompatible state aid. Compensation must be based upon costs plus a reasonable profit, including "all or some of the productivity gains during an agreed limited period". A reasonable rate of return means taking into account the risk or absence of risks incurred by the undertaking, in particular, in the presence of special and exclusive rights. Accounting separation is required where the undertaking concerned carries out other activities alongside the provision of services of general economic interest. Detailed rules pertaining to costs

83 Community Framework for State Aid, *supra* note 8.

84 Commission Decision on Article 86(2) EC and State Aid, *supra* note 8, preamble, para 16.

include a definition of the costs to be taken into account as covering all variable costs associated with the service of general economic interest and, where applicable, a proportion of fixed costs common to other activities.

The Commission Decision is dedicated to public service compensation that does not meet the criteria set out in *Altmark Trans* and/or in the Commission Notice, and, consequently, constitutes state aid that may be either admissible as such, or inadmissible (i.e., that is illegal and must be repaid). In order to avoid the need for notification, a *de minimis* rule is linked to quantified aid limits specified per sector, provided the service of general economic interest is imposed by an official act that meets the requirements set out in the Notice (and listed above). The Decision explicitly provides that hospital funding is exempt from the obligation of prior notification of services of general economic interest provided by hospitals under the state aid rules as long as it is proportionate to the actual costs of the services provided, irrespective of the amounts received, and provided that these services are qualified as services of general economic interest. Thus, Paragraph 16 of the pre-amble of the Commission Decision on SGEI compensation states:[85]

> [...] hospitals providing medical care, including, where applicable, emergency services and ancillary services directly related to the main activities, notably in the field of research [...] should benefit from the exemption from notification provided for in this Decision, even if the amount of compensation they receive exceeds the thresholds laid down in this Decision, *if the services performed are qualified as services of general economic interest by the Member States.* [emphasis added]

It appears that the possibility of benefitting from this provision in itself would put an exceptional premium on formally qualifying the relevant parts of hospital services as services of general economic interest.

8. Particular Reasons for Researching Services of General Economic Interest in Hospital Care

Health services were considered, in principle, to form part of the services of general economic interest in the White Paper,[86] and to form the topic of a paper on health services and social services. However, after health services were eventually dropped from the Services Directive,[87] they were not covered by the White Paper on Social

85 Commission Decision of 28 November 2005 on the application of Article 86(2) of the EC Treaty to State Aid in the form of public service compensation granted to certain undertakings entrusted with the operation of services of general economic interest, OJ 2005, L312/67, preamble, para 16.

86 White Paper, *supra* note 13, pp. 16–17.

87 Directive 2006/123/EC of the European Parliament and of the Council of 12 December 2006 on services in the internal market, OJ 2006, L376/36, Article 2f excludes health services. The Services Directive contains a special regime for services of general economic interest. According to its Article 1(3) The Directive does not require the Member States to abolish their monopolies, nor does it derogate from the freedom of the Member States to designate services of general economic interest, and the financing of services of general economic interest is outside the scope of the Services Directive.

Services of General Interest,[88] but by a separate communication (which, in turn, was focused on trans-national provision of health services and not on services of general economic interest).[89]

There are a several reasons for researching the possible usefulness of the concept of services of general economic interest in relation to healthcare in The Netherlands.

- First, it appears that the liberalisation of (important) parts of curative hospital care (but also planned future liberalisation of long-term care) gives rise to increasing problems in EU law terms. Oddly, full state provision is met with relative indifference in EU law, whereas even partial liberalisation gives rise to tension in relation to the competition, state aid and free movement rules, to name but a few. Arguably, qualification as (a) service(s) of general economic interest could be a safe haven for those parts of curative hospital care that have "universal service" characteristics, but are not suited for provision under competitive terms, and, therefore, require an alternative funding regime to the market mechanism.
- Second, simultaneously the European Commission, after a number of years of defensive back-pedalling on services of general economic interest, has latched onto recent case law (notably *Altmark Trans*)[90] to launch a more pro-active approach on the funding side of the SGEI issue ("public service compensation"). Notably, a legal act is required to benefit from the services of general economic interest exemption under the state aid regime, with important consequences for funding. For hospital services in particular, an even more relaxed EU regime is in place, provided that a formal act of entrustment with carrying out a service of general economic interest is involved.
- Third, at the same time, after being excluded both from the Services Directive and the recent Communication on Social Services of General Interest, hospital services are the subject of a special track based upon a separate consultation.[91] The Commission was scheduled to report on this before the summer of 2007. It should be noted that, although health services are not covered by the Services Directive, they remain subject to the Treaty provisions on free movement and competition.[92] Thus, the exception to these rules for services of general economic interest remains relevant.

Its Article 15(4) on the freedom of establishment provides that services of general economic interest are not subject to the procedural requirements set out in that Article in so far as their application obstructs the performance, in law or in fact, of the particular task assigned to them. Article 17(1) determines that services of general economic interest benefit from a derogation from the freedom to provide services.

88 White Paper, *supra* note 13, p. 3.

89 Community action on health services, *supra* note 19.

90 Case C-280/00 *Altmark Trans*, supra n. 20.

91 Community action on health services, *supra* note 19. Note, however, that there is no comparable exception for long-term care, which is consequently covered by the Services Directive. The consequences of this remain to be explored.

92 Providing Healthcare is an economic activity: Joined Cases C-180/98 to C-184/98 *Pavlov*, *supra* note 59. Third-party paying makes no difference to this: Case C-352/85 *Bond van Adverteerders* [2988] ECR 2085.

- Fourth, both the Commission and the Court have recognised the existence of services of general economic interest in respect of general health insurance,[93] respectively emergency ambulance services.[94] In combination with the finding that most health services are provided by undertakings, this means that, in principle, there should be appreciable scope for defining services of general economic interest in health care, respectively multi-product hospital services.[95]

Both health care and long-term care (of which the former is not covered by the Services Directive and social services of general interest, while the latter is covered by both) are subject to market failures that could provide reasons for the services of general economic interest instrument to be applied.

Focusing on multi-product hospital markets, the main areas in which market-based solutions are, at present, usually considered insufficient to remedy the market failures at hand are the following four:
- Emergency care (including emergency ambulance services);
- Top-referential care;
- Academic training and care;
- Very expensive and rare pharmaceuticals.

These areas are mentioned here only by way of example – it may well be that, where economies of scale in emergency care and top-referential care are significant, competition "for" the market is possible, instead. Likewise, if better product descriptions and better measures of output for academic training and care become available, market-based solutions may well work here, too.

Nevertheless, excluding (even by way of example) these areas from the market-oriented reform now planned in The Netherlands for multi-product hospitals (subject to a price-cap based upon yardstick competition) means that alternative funding systems and regulatory solutions have to be found. And if political pressures are taken into account, they are, at least presently, the prime candidates for a designation as services of general economic interest.

For long-term care, the main category, in which the scope for market-based solutions is extremely limited, concerns care for the multiply-handicapped for which funding cannot be based upon risk-equalisation schemes. It should be noted, however, that even where competition on insurance markets may, in this case, not be feasible, this should not mean that competition among providers could not work (even at the level, much neglected in today's practice, of using proper procurement mechanisms). The latter should, therefore, be examined as the solution of first resort.

93 Aid measures N 541/2004 and N 542/2004, at present subject to appeal in Case T-84/06 *Azivo* v *Commission*, action brought on 13 March 2006.

94 Case C-475/99 *Glöckner*, *supra* note 62.

95 Joined Cases C-180/98 to C-184/98 *Pavlov*, *supra* note 59.

Other examples that may be relevant candidates for services of general economic interest include, for example, immunisation programmes, where considerable externalities are at play.

9. Conclusion

In principle, the national public interest should usually be in line with the EU market freedoms and competition law, because the latter result in lower prices and greater choice for consumers. However, where market failure may lead to sub-optimal provision of public goods (such as the desired level of health care or of specific healthcare services, such as emergency services), there may be a case for public intervention in terms of imposing universal service obligations (provider of last resort) on one or more undertakings that are active in the market. Even in this case, competitive provision within certain limits may be feasible (for example, health insurance markets subject to universal coverage without risk selection) and should be explored even within the context of services of general economic interest – not least in order to meet the requisite proportionality standard.

It is for the purpose of balancing the public interest and market freedoms that Article 86(2) EC provides an exception to the Treaty rules for services of general economic interest. This exception only applies to the extent that this is strictly necessary for performing the functions of services of general economic interest concerned. It serves to reconcile the public interest identified as such at national level as the reason for introducing a service of general economic interest with respect for the Treaty rules by means of a proportionality test.

In the absence of a Community standard, the applicable proportionality test is whether the infringements of the Treaty rules were "manifestly disproportionate" or not. Where secondary Community law applies (i.e., pre-emption of national norms by Community norms) a stricter "least restrictive means" test may be applied. In a number of economic sectors (notably the network industries or utilities such as electronic communications, postal services and energy) the scope and content of services of general economic interest has been defined at Community level by means of Directives. This has served to identify clearly the scope of the exceptions involved and thereby the application of the general rule, i.e. the development of open markets with full competition.

Based upon the Community experience to date, a service of general economic interest normally consists of:

- universal service rights for consumers and related universal service obligations for one or more undertakings;
- and/or of other public service guarantees;
- and of ancillary services necessary to fulfil those universal service obligations and other public service guarantees;
- and of a compensation mechanism (financial remuneration).

To be recognised as such, in principle, services of general economic interest are set out in an act of entrustment, the contents of which have been specified in the Community Framework on Public Service Compensation based upon the *Altmark Trans* judgment of the European Court of Justice. Compensation is based upon costs plus a reasonable rate of return. Where public procurement procedures were not used to select the provider of the service of general economic interest, the standard used is that of an efficient firm. If these standards are met, the state aid rules do not apply.

If services of general economic interest fail to meet the criteria set out in *Altmark Trans*, but are designated *for healthcare* according to the standards set out for an act of entrustment, the related financial compensation does not require prior notification as state aid. If services of general economic interest are designated as such, this has an impact not only on EU law but, at least in The Netherlands, also in national law, given the use of a services of general economic interest standard across the board in the Dutch competition law: i.e., concerning the cartel prohibition, prohibition of dominance abuse and merger control.

The proportionality test (necessity) requires that the scope of services of general economic interest remains restricted to the necessary minimum. In the context of harmonisation, this text is based upon the least restrictive means, while, in the absence of harmonisation, the Member States retain greater freedom, and the relevant test is whether the measures concerned are manifestly disproportionate. This approach can help to resolve debate on the possibility of liberalising certain health services given that, for example, universal service to consumers can be guaranteed in this way, opening up the road to liberalisation.

Using the instrument of services of general economic interest requires taking clear decisions to define closely the public interest involved, because the scope of services of general economic interest is limited to what is necessary to attain the relevant public interest objectives. Market failure arguments will be key here. By defining services of general economic interest, the scope for liberalisation and market-based provision of the remaining services also becomes clearer. This exercise would, therefore, be particularly useful in markets in transition where, in a liberalisation context, the need for public interest exceptions is raised. Hence, services of general economic interest deserve to be analysed further as a tool to guarantee the public interest in the context not only of multi-product hospital care, but also in relation to long-term care.

In the context of a more thorough analysis *inter alia*, the following question should be addressed: Would the application of the services of general economic interest framework not only provide for the requisite exceptions to free movement, state aid, public procurement and competition rules – but also be compatible with adequate safeguards against distortions of competition in the competitive segments of the multi-product hospital market(s)? And, if so, how could this be guaranteed?

PART IV

CONCLUSIONS

Christian Joerges

CHAPTER 18. INTEGRATION THROUGH CONFLICTS LAW ON THE DEFENCE OF THE EUROPEAN PROJECT BY MEANS OF ALTERNATIVE CONCEPTUALISATION OF LEGAL CONSTITUTIONALISATION*

1. Introduction

The appellation "*hélas*" has twice been applied to Europe, latterly by Jürgen Habermas, in a collection of essays dating from 2008,[1] but also much earlier by Hans Magnus Enzensberger, whose characterisation of the European context is surely just as fitting now as it was at the time of the great take-off of European legal studies in the late 1970s.[2] Nonetheless, the current situation could not be more different. Contemporary Europe is suffering acute growing pains: it can no longer master its mass of competences; its Court, once the real hero of the integration project, is now much criticised – and that with unprecedented bitterness; its high constitutional ambitions have been rejected in popular referenda, and downgraded to a "Treaty on the Functioning of the European Union" – whose new modesty has not yet been fully appreciated, and which provoked meandering comments by the German constitutional court. In those early years, Europe's problems were very different: all that Europe suffered from then was an utter disregard. Within universities, European law was an optional subject with very little resonance. Public lawyers took some note of its institutional characteristics, national bureaucracies tackled the plethora of obstacles to free trade, competition law operated as a means of market integration, while European private law was non-existent The appearance, only a few years later, of a charismatic Commission President who would assert the Community character of 80% of the law touching upon the European

* Translated by Michelle Everson.

1 Jürgen Habermas, *Ach Europa*, (Frankfurt aM: Suhrkamp Verlag, 2008); *Europe: the Faltering Project* (London: Polity, 2009).

2 Enzensberger's cry of "Alas Europe" relates to a travel journal which he published only in 1987, but which was undertaken much earlier; useful references may be found about Hans Magnus Enzensberger's unwilling Eurocentrism in, *idem*, *Politische Brosamen*, (Frankfurt aM: Suhrkamp Verlag, 1982), p. 31 *et seq.*).

economy,[3] was, then, a far-off dream that disturbed no-one's slumbers.[4] Clearly, much has happened since, and, equally clearly, this "much" has not been the quite the right thing.

2. Structuring the Argument

The importance of the re-orientation of European law demanded by the title of this chapter will be exemplified mainly with regard to the, so-called, European social dimension. This topic was the object of grievous French-German quarrels during bargain over the Treaty of Rome, but was then widely neglected during the so-called golden age of "embedded liberalism". Only very occasionally was a warning articulated that a European project founded within economic and technocratic precepts would sooner or later face its own crisis of acceptance.[5]

At that time, such concerns were new. Today, they are far more common. This observation is designed to segue smoothly into the questions posed in the following sections. First, attention is paid to the question of why "social Europe" played such a subordinate role within the institutional design of the Community, and why it was possible to disregard it for so long (Section 3). Second, three modes of addressing "institutionalised" Europe's "social deficit" are presented, in order to facilitate a more nuanced and comprehensive description of the institutional *status quo* (Section 4.1) and, alongside, a starkly distinctive alternative (Section 4.2), as well as an attempted

3 Jacques Delors, "Europa im Umbruch: Vom Binnenmarkt zur Europäischen Union", in: EU Commission (ed), (1992) 9 *Europäische Gespräche*, p. 12.

4 Certainly, Delors' statement is anything but clear: see Thomas König and Lars Mäder, "Das Regieren jenseits des Nationalstaates und der Mythos einer 80-Prozent-Europäisierung in Deutschland", (2008) 49 *Politische Vierteljahresschrift*, pp. 438–463; Annette Töller, "Mythen und Methoden: Zur Messung der Europäisierung der Gesetzgebung des Deutschen Bundestages jenseits des 80-Prozent-Mythos", (2008) 391 *Zeitschrift für Parlamentsfragen*, pp. 3–17; Daniel Göler, "Europäisierung hat viele Gesichter. Anmerkungen zur Widerlegung des Mythos einer 80-Prozent-Europäisierung", (2009) 50 *Politische Vierteljahresschrift*, pp. 75–79.

5 A Bremen patriot may be entitled to mention that Bremen's mayor, Hans Koschnik, was among the very few to articulate such concerns in his opening speech, "Vom Europa der Kaufleute zum Europa der Bürger" (From an entrepreneurial Europe to a citizens' Europe), at the *Gustav-Radbruch Forum of the Arbeitsgemeinschaft Sozialdemokratischer Juristen*, Bremen, 6–7 April 1979, (pp. 9–18 of the documentation) – and, on that occasion, announced the founding of Bremen's "Centre for European Law and Politics" with its specific, at the time quite original, orientation (a memorandum of 1979, submitted by the present author, on the agenda of the centre warned: Over time, "the institutional structure of the EC" would reveal itself as lacking in the necessary capacity to overcome "growing political, economic and social problems", since "the guarantee given for economic freedoms [in the EEC Treaty] favoured a form of economic internationalisation", which would not only overburden the steering capacity of the nation states, but also that of the EC, and that would, at the same time, make implementation of national social programmes even harder. Given this problem, the vital issue was one of the identification of an integrationist research perspective, informed by the social sciences and by lessons drawn from the study of the political economy, within which the conditions could be discovered under which the institutionalisation of the EC might be made reconcilable with a social constitution (Christian Joerges, "Aufgaben und Organisationsstruktur eines Zentrums für Europäische Rechtspolitik", Manuscript, Bremen, 1979).

corrective review of treaty alterations made from Maastricht to Lisbon (Section 4.3). Titular aspirations are then elaborated in the fourth section (Section 5) and are then, finally, given exemplary expression in a summarising conclusion (Section 6).

3. The Social Deficit within the Integration Project

History can no longer be altered, but can only be told and re-interpreted. The Schuman plan of 1950, which is deemed to be the birth hour of the integration project,[6] prepared the way for a fundamental shift, for the overcoming of a warlike past of nationally-defined enemies and dictatorial regimes. In contrast to this heritage, the new Europe promoted "peace, prosperity and supranationalism".[7] The politicians of the founding generation, indelibly marked by their wartime experiences, were not concerned with the establishment of a *democratic* polity. They were, nonetheless, aware that their purely economically-oriented integration projection, limited to the creation of a common market, neglected the welfare state structures that were constitutive of the founding Member States. Infinitely more demanding options than those enshrined within the Treaty of Rome were discussed: Fritz Scharpf, in one of his most trenchant analyses, asks:

> [W]here would we now be if, in the 1956 negotiations leading to the Treaties of Rome and the creation of the European economic Community, French (socialist) Prime Minister, Guy Mollet, had had it his way?

Mollet had attempted to make harmonisation of social regulation and tax burdens a pre-condition for the integration of industrial markets – and had garnered support for his plans from the French economic sector.

> Would this attempt to harmonise social policies have succeeded, or would it have blocked the entire European integration project?[8]

This is a good question, but it is also one that, clearly, nobody can answer.

3.1. The De-Coupling of the Economic from the Social Constitution

In the same article, Scharpf characterises the history of what actually happened within Europe as being one of the "de-coupling" of economic integration from the social constitution (or from the various social constitutions of the Member States). The Member States retained their competence to regulate the social sphere; Europe, in contrast,

6 6 May 1950 (www.centre-robert-schuman.org/docs/declaration-robert-schuman-9-mai-1950.pdf.).

7 Thus, Joseph H.H. Weiler in one of his most impressive essays, "Fin-de-Siècle Europe", in: Renaud Dehousse (ed), *Europe After Maastricht: An Ever Closer Union?*, (Munich: Beck, 1994), pp. 203–216.

8 Fritz W. Scharpf, "The European Social Model: Coping with the Challenges of Diversity", (2002) 40 *Journal of Common Market Studies*, pp. 645–670, at 645–646.

became responsible for the opening up of national economies and their sublimation within a common market. "De-coupling" is not simply an analytical concept, it also has negative connotations, reminding us that social and economic constitutions are married together within welfare state democracies, thus also raising the question of the potential impact of a divorce between these two devoted partners – or, in other words, asking whether the economic integration of Europe might also lead to social disintegration within its Member States.

Indeed, contemporary academic commentary on Europe rarely, if ever, addressed such uncomfortable challenges in this stark form. Looking back, however, we can still discern how the then current conceptualisations of the governance of an integration project that was already underway, avoided any such difficulties. Instead, these questions were either re-formulated, strategically operationalised, or simply ignored.

Most strikingly, Hans Peter Ipsen, the Nestor of German European law, provided a conceptually rigorous reformulation of integration within his grandiose theory of "purposive associations".[9] This characterisation of Europe lay at the heart of Ipsen's attempts to reconcile the European Economic Constitution with the democratic constitutions of the Member States. The formulation similarly proved sufficiently progressive to encompass the increasing variety of competences that Europe had garnered for itself, alongside "the economic" sphere. Nonetheless, by virtue of his qualification of the tasks to be achieved at European level as "material technocratic competences", he likewise immunised the Community against demands for "political" democratic control. This approach drew predominantly upon the preparatory work of Ernst Forsthoff, for whom "the social" was, by virtue of its very nature, an administrative task, which was incompatible with the governing "rule of law" ideal that was found within the German Constitution.[10] We will return to this theme in the course of this chapter.[11]

Commentary on the new European integration constellation made strategic use of German "ordo-liberalism", doing so most intensely within so-called "second generation" conceptualisations. For a first generation, who played their part in the development of

9 Hans Peter Ipsen, "Der deutsche Jurist und das Europäische Gemeinschaftsrecht", *Verhandlungen des 43. Deutschen Juristentages*, (Munich: Beck, 1964) Volume 2, p. 14 *et seq.*; *idem*, *Europäisches Gemeinschaftsrecht*, (Tübingen: Mohr/Siebeck, 1972), p. 176.

10 Ernst Forsthoff, "Begriff und Wesen des sozialen Rechtstaates", (1954) 12 *Veröffentlichungen der Vereinigung der Deutschen Staatsrechtslehrer*, pp. 8–35. This legacy gets surprisingly little attention even in Marcel Kaufmann's thorough analysis of Ipsen's work (see his *Europäische Integration und Demokratieprinzip*, ((Baden-Baden: Nomos, 1997)), p. 157 *et seq.*, p. 212 *et seq.*) and in Peer Zumbanses more recent discussion of Fortshoff's work, see his *Ordnungsmuster im modernen Wohlfahrtsstaat*, (Baden-Baden: Nomos, 2008), p. 106 *et seq.*

11 See Section V below. On the relationship between the traditions, see Christian Joerges, "Europe a *Großraum*? Shifting Legal Conceptualisations of the Integration Project", in: Christian Joerges and Navraj S. Ghaleigh, *Darker Legacies of Law in Europe: The Shadow of National Socialism and Fascism over Europe and its Legal Traditions*, (Oxford: Hart Publishing, 2003), pp. 167–191.

the concept of "the social market economy" during the early years of the Republic,[12] and, above all, for Walter Eucken,[13] the ordering structures of the social and the economic spheres "were interdependent constitutions".[14] The negative consequences of de-coupling were only easily ignored for as long as Europe remained marginally important, so that it was still possible – notwithstanding the opening up of national markets – to take the continuing functioning of socially-oriented "embedded liberalism" for granted.[15] Once this situation changed, however, a second ordo-liberal generation, under the leadership of Ernst-Joachim Mestmäcker, took a change in direction that proved to be of paradigmatic importance.[16] The ordering-interdependence theorem was discarded, and Europe became, instead, the protector of an economic constitution dedicated to a "system of free competition", a constitution which had, as its mission, the alteration of national orders in order to ensure their conformity with the ordo-liberal system.

The most influential of all European lawyers, J.H.H. Weiler was able to confound our question with his elegant thesis that Europe led a form of double-existence, as a supranational legal community, on the one hand, and as an intergovernmental association, on the other.[17] In this manner, Weiler's reconstruction of the establishment of a supranational legal order by the ECJ was, likewise, also founded upon the *realpolitik* of political bargaining processes, so that he might assert the duty of politics to pay tribute to the social sphere.

3.2. *Europe as Agent of Reform*

In a startling twist of academic fate, Weiler only published the vital parts of his PhD dissertation, detailing his theory of the dual nature of the EC, in the 100th edition of the *Yale Law Journal* in 1991, there, contemporaneously – and still pre-Maastricht, but post the Single European Act (1987)[18] – to refute them in the light of the introduction of the

12 Philip Manow, "Modell Deutschland as an interdenominational compromise", Minda De Gunzburg Centre for European Studies, Working Paper 003/2001.

13 Walter Eucken, *Grundsätze der Wirtschaftspolitik*, (Tübingen: Mohr/Siebeck, 1951), in the paperback edition (Reinbek: Rowohlt, 1959), p. 124 *et seq.*

14 Milène Wegmann, *Früher Neoliberalismus und europäische Integration: Interdependenz der nationalen, supranationalen und internationalen Ordnung von Wirtschaft und Gesellschaft (1932–1965)*, (Baden-Baden: Nomos, 2002), especially p. 351 *et seq.*, for the importance of the political and social constitution for the project of economic integration (pp. 359–366).

15 See Fritz. W. Scharpf (note 8 *supra*) and more recently Stephan Leibfried and Herbert Obinger, "Nationle Sozialstaaten in der Europäischen Union, Zukünfte eines 'Sozialen Europas'", in: Martin Höpner and Armin Schäfer (eds), *Die politische Ökonomie der europäischen Integration*, (Frankfurt aM/New York: Campus, 2008), pp. 335–368.

16 References in Christian Joerges, "What is left of the European Economic Constitution? A melancholic eulogy", (2005) 30 *European Law Review*, pp. 461–489, at 469 *et seq.*

17 The core theses of his unpublished dissertation can be found in Joseph H.H. Weiler, "The Community system: the dual character of supranationalism", (1981) 1 *Yearbook of European Law*, pp. 257–306.

18 "The Transformation of Europe", (1990–91) 100 *Yale Law Journal*, pp. 2403–2485.

principle of majority-voting that foreclosed the important exit options of the Member States, which Weiler, the prophetic European law scholar who had trained in international law, did not wish to see foreclosed.[19] However, the pattern of European evolution was not only to destroy Weiler's theorem, but was also to undermine all established integration theories.

The prime suspect in this process was the programme "for the completion of the internal market", with which Jacques Delors, President of the Commission from 1985 onwards, was able to convince European politicians that Europe had to be, and could be freed, from its much-ridiculed "euro-sclerosis". Many of Delors' followers, but by no means Delors himself, had, as their primary aim, the radicalisation of the *finalité* of integration; that is, to paraphrase Karl Polanyi, the construction of an "disembedded market polity", or, to deploy the vocabulary of Michel Foucault, to bring an end to statal control over markets through the establishment of the mastery of markets over the states.[20]

Nonetheless, the results were not as expected. What had begun as an attempt to strengthen European competitiveness quickly descended – together with its corollary (deregulation) strategy – into a process whereby the EU was implicated within an increasing number of policy areas, and was thus required to develop an ever more complex regulatory machinery. The primary motivator here was the interest of the European legislator and the Commission in "social regulation" (consumer, labour and environmental protection), or new policy areas, the significance of which the ordo-liberal proponents of a "pure" economic constitution had fatally under-estimated. Of similar importance, but much less surprising, was the speed with which the integration process within the reach of the completion of the internal market was "deepened", and thus impacted upon an increasing number of policy areas. The significance of this development was not so much to be found in the intensity of its real-world impacts, but rather with regard to the symbolism of Europe's growing "social deficit", and the corollary introduction of new attempts to increase the European presence within the sphere of labour and social policy. With the Maastricht social protocol – "the agreement on social policy" – EU competences were broadened in the area of labour and employment policies, so that the once stark distinction between Europe's (apolitical) Economic Constitution and the political responsibility of the Member States for labour and social policy was now hopelessly blurred.

4. The De-coupling of Economic and Social Constitutions as a Challenge to Law

The long-term implications of the institutional concretisation of the European social deficit were, nonetheless, not yet visible. This was not simply by virtue of the fact that

19 Weiler, *ibid., at* 2453 *et seq.*, 2466 *et seq.*; see, also, *Fin-de-Siècle* (note 7).

20 Michel Foucault, *Naissance de la biopolitique.* Cours au Collège de France (Paris: Seuil/Gallimard, 2004), in particular, the lectures of 7 February 1979 (pp. 105–134) and of 14 February 1979 (pp. 135–164).

"embedded liberalism" still appeared to be remarkably stable, but was also a result of the degree to which the de-coupling of economic and social constitutions was reproduced within the dominant legal framework (Sections 5.1 and 5.2). In other words, it was very easy to relegate the problem to the status of one which might be solved solely within the semantics of intergovernmental bargaining and legal policy (Section 5.3).

4.1. The Internal Market as Agent of Inter-statal Redistribution

The European social deficit then took a very dramatic turn with the expansion of the Union. The issue was no longer simply one of the social deficit: in addition, the matter now included the intensification of socio-economic disequilibrium throughout the extended Union. This discrepancy was far greater than the development disequilibrium that had formed the subject matter to be overcome in earlier accession negotiations; transfer payments, however, – or a European Marshall plan, following the example of German re-unification – were not placed on the agenda.[21]

The ECJ has reacted to this new European constellation with three decisions, which have already become legendary.[22] In each of these cases, the Court has demanded the

21 The dozens of layers of enlargement support projects promoted by the EU and its Member States did not install fully-fledged social welfare regulations comparable to those of most of the old Member States; see, on the enlargement policies, the bitter remarks by M. Blecher, "Order or Noise – Order from Noise? Probleme der Entwickungszusammenarbeit (im Recht) und ihre Reform", (2007) 40 *Kritische Justiz*, p. 166 *et seq.* As he underlines, the distinction between economic supra-nationalism and national welfarism which was "decoupled" in the West was not only blurred in the East, where functional equivalents were simply non-existent. The accession states had, instead, to comply with the relatively meagre social policies of the *acquis*, without being in a position to establish any of the welfare models, which were (still) in place in the West. Large numbers of East European citizens were driven into economic migration with all its highly ambivalent social implications. On the other hand, the transformation of East European societies coincided with the increasing de-regulation strategies against the same social welfare structures in "old Europe" including the resort to "precarious" forms of labour and the weakening of classical unionist representation. These "developments", M. Blecher concludes, can be interpreted as the evolution of a new (and surely not democratically legitimated) factual "super-supremacy": the accomplishment of neo-liberal economic policies which have become the *new global governmentality* programme or *dispositive* (Foucault) subjecting all forms of present association to its rules. This new *modus operandi* has everywhere restructured economic, political, legal and social "constitutions", introducing a new form of governance in which entrepreneurial self-determination, self-care and self-responsibility of individual and social "bodies" have become core factors. Any reconstruction of the European integration project and of its "social deficit" must take this new (global) background and the concomitant re-politicisation of former "apolitical" contexts into account. See, also, M. Blecher, "Law in Movement", in: J. Dine, A. Fagan (eds), *Capitalism and Human Rights*, (Cheltenham: Edward Elgar, 2006), 80 *et seq.*; and *ibid.*, "Diritto in Movimento. Verso un Nuovo Diritto Comune", in: M. Blecher, G. Bronzini, J. Hendry, Ch. Joerges and R. Ciccarelli (eds), *Rivendicare il Comune. Governance e Nuovi Movimenti Sociali*, (Rome: EDS, 2009).

22 Case C-438/05, *International Transport Workers' Federation und Finnish Seamen's Union v Viking Line ABP and OÜ Viking Line Eesti*, judgment of 11.12.2007; Case C-341/05, *Laval und Partneri Ltd. v Svenska Byggnadsarbetareförbundet, Svenska Byggnadsarbetareförbundets avdelning 1, Byggettan und Svenska Elektrikerförbundet*, judgment of 18.12.2007; Case C-346/06, *Rechtsanwalt Dr. Dirk Rüffert v Land Niedersachsen*, judgment of 3.4.2008.

opening up of old European markets to service-providers from the new Member States, who, either on their own initiative, or in co-operation with western European investors, have busied themselves with the lowering of labour costs. The conflicts that have greeted such a legally-constructed utilisation of comparative cost advantages have, for the most part, been depicted in both academic and political commentaries not as inter-class conflicts, but as conflicts between rich and poor nations, less often as collisions between the workforce of saturated and low-cost labour markets (intra-class conflict). Justification for the law's wide-ranging toleration and promotion of such practices has similarly been greeted as a cheap form of reparation for the acceptance of the "*acquis communautaire*" by the accession countries.[23] Naturally, such descriptions cannot be found in this form within the reasoning of the ECJ. Here, the Court has, instead, based its argumentation upon the fundamental freedoms guaranteed by the treaties; freedoms that trump national labour-law provisions blocking market access, and even apply to oppositional strike measures that are legal within the Member States. The attempt to assert national labour law is curtly dismissed by the ECJ in its response to the arguments of the Danish Government in *Viking*:

> In that respect it is sufficient to point out that, even if, in the areas which fall outside the scope of the Community's competence, the Member States are still free, in principle, to lay down the conditions governing the existence and exercise of the rights in question, the fact remains that, when exercising that competence, the Member States must nevertheless comply with Community law [...] Consequently, the fact that Article 137 EC does not apply to the right to strike or to the right to impose lock-outs is not such as to exclude collective action such as that at issue in the main proceedings from the application of Article 43 EC.[24]

Among the authors who have underlined the dramatic implications of this reasoning is Loïc Azoulai, who has reconstructed it as a deep-seated alteration in the configuration of the integration project and its law.[25] The EC Treaty institutionalised European integration as a sectoral ("partial") project. In the meantime, however, we are now confronted with a new context of comprehensive ("total") integration, a form of integration that proceeded in rarely spectacular, but always seemingly logical, series of adjudicational steps taken by the ECJ to apply European law.[26] This observation is

23 See Michelle Everson, "European citizenship and the disillusion of the common man", in Section 2 of her contribution to this volume, (text accompanying note 59 *et seq.*), arguing starkly against those approaches.

24 *Viking* (paras 40 *et seq*). On the problems attending the regulation of competences in Article 137 EC, see Florian Rödl, "The Labour Constitution", in: Armin v. Bogdandy and Jürgen Bast (eds), *Principles of European Constitutional Law*, (Oxford: Hart Publishing, 2nd ed., 2010, pp. 623–658, at 636–37.

25 "The Court of Justice and the Social Market Economy" (2008) 45 *Common Market Law Review*, pp. 1335–1356.

26 "What the authors of the Treaty had in mind when drawing up the conditions for the construction of the common market was an economic integration, that is to say a "partial integration". In these conditions, the pre-eminence of the Treaty rules whose aim was to break open the national markets (free movement) was self-evident. The precedence of those rules was all the more accepted as their scope seemed to be limited to the economic and commercial sphere. It is no longer quite the same

correct characterization of the facticity the integration process.. It is also true, the law of integration entails the constituting of a "moving target", a legal situation that Ipsen, very early on in the history of integration, characterised as an "ever changing constitution" ("*Wandelverfassung*").[27] But change, we should assume, requires methodological rules and substantive justification; it must, surely, be constituted, so as to occur in a "constitution of change" and to ensure the validity of legal changes.[28] Here, however, Azoulai seems to restrict his analysis to a reconstruction of the Court's jurisprudence. He discusses the competence-based challenges to the ECJ's jurisprudence, as well as the problem of the restriction of the right to strike by means of comprehensive application of the economic freedoms – but then observes simply that the ECJ has risen above such challenges.[29] An ascription of such powers to the ECJ, however, would be extremely troublesome. It would raise the Court to the status of *pouvoir constituant* of the Union, affords it a power that allows it – autonomously and *en passant* – to rip national constitutional law up by its roots. Azoulai also makes it clear that this form of constitutionalising Europe is repugnant to him.[30] Yet, it is nonetheless true that his characterisation of the current jurisprudence of the ECJ is an adequate reconstruction of the Court's move towards an "integration through markets" project that radicalises Jacques Delors' internal market programme.[31]

4.2. *The De-Coupling of the Social from the Economic Constitution as a "Social" Integration Compromise*

Florian Rödl has defended a contrasting approach.[32] In common with Azoulai, he insists that the de-coupling of labour and economic constitutions within Europe has not resulted in the creation of a state of nature within which the law is as indifferent to the social

when one moves to a regime of "total integration", which is the present situation. Because the scope of application of Community law has constantly widened, there is virtually no area of economic and social life which escapes, in principle, the effect of the Treaty rules." (Azoulai, *ibid.*, 1346).

27 Hans Peter Ipsen, "Europäische Verfassung – Nationale Verfassung" (1987) *Europarecht*, pp. 195–213, at 201).

28 See Christian Joerges, "Europäische Konstitutionalisierung", in: Hauke Brunkhorst, Regina Kreide and Cristina Lafont (eds), *Habermas-Handbuch: Leben – Werk – Wirkung*, (Stuttgart: J.B. Metzler, 2009).

29 Azoulai (note 25), p. 1341 *et seq.*

30 "This extension produces a legitimacy problem, and also, in practice, a *problem of boundaries*", Azoulai (note 25), p. 1341 *et seq.*

31 Azoulai correctly draws attention to relevant passages (*ibidem*, p. 1347) found in the opinion of AG Maduro and within his earlier well-known dissertation *We the Court: The European Court of Justice and the European Economic Constitution* (Oxford: Hart Publishing, 1998), especially at p. 50 *et seq.*: "...workers throughout Europe must accept the recurring negative consequences that are inherent to the common market's creation of increasing prosperity..., (*Viking*, para. 58); a comment that is also to be relativised in the light of the postulating commentary that "society must commit itself to ... the provision of economic support to those workers who, as a consequence of market forces, come into difficulties".

32 Florian Rödl, "Constitutional integration of labour law constitutions", in: Erik O. Eriksen, Christian Joerges and Florian Rödl (eds), *Law, Democracy and Solidarity in a Post-national Union*, (London-New York: Routledge, 2008), 152–172; see, also, *idem*, "The Labour Constitution" (note 24).

conditions of European citizens as it was during the era of *laissez-faire* liberalism. In contrast to Azoulai, however, who establishes a duty of solidarity out of the *fait accompli* of the eastern enlargement and the continuous advance of the integration *telos* – a duty which requires the workers of old Europe, as well as their unions, to tolerate wage competition with cheaper eastern European labour – Rödl argues from an historical perspective. Even though the EC Treaty contains no comprehensive normative expression of a labour constitution along the lines of those found within the Member States, the Member States (together with the Community following the Treaty of Amsterdam) have committed themselves in Article 117 EC to "the improvement of living and working conditions in Europe" and have likewise made it clear that the improvements supplied by the "workings of the common market" are expected to be furnished in line with the "procedures" foreseen by the Treaty, and are further required to be reconcilable with "its legal and administrative provisions".[33]

Rödl's arguments are expounded in accordance with the thoughts of the socially-reforming protagonists of critical theory:[34] The normative promise of the liberal model is not fulfilled in that it disregards the theoretical pre-conditions upon which it rests. Instead, such pre-conditions are, far more, "political-normative yardsticks", against which the elaboration of the EU labour constitution must be judged. A real-world process of integration cannot simply call upon the *compromesso storico* of the EEC Treaty in order to justify an undermining adjudicative attack – and thus the further realisation of the integration project – upon formal legal reasoning or the interpretative canon of von Savigny. By contrast, Rödl demonstrates how jurisprudence on Article 117 EC has continuously evolved, and thus asserts that the vital question is that of the *clarification* of the conditions under which it applies.[35]

His methodological approach protects him from the potential equivocation – between facticity and validity – which is risked by Azoulai. Instead, Rödl must confront the possibility – most disturbing to the lawyer who concerns himself with positive law – that the existing labour constitution of the EU cannot be reconciled with its normative promise. Rödl makes explicit reference to this difficulty, at the same time detailing the reasons why it has arisen:[36] the divergences between the welfare traditions of old European states are fundamental in their character, an economic disequilibrium that grew even greater following eastern European enlargement, as well as the stagnation in the establishment of social Europe following ratification of the Treaty of Maastricht (1993), as the gulf between normative promise, and the necessary legislative competences to realise it, has grown ever wider.

33 "The Labour Constitution" (note 24), at 630 *et seq.*

34 The classic being, Jürgen Habermas, *Zum Strukturwandel der Öffentlichkeit*, (Neuwied: Luchterhand, 1957); for reconstruction of the argument and application to modern circumstances, see John P. McCormick, *Weber, Habermas, and Transformations of the European State: Constitutional, Social, and Supranational Democracy*, (Cambridge: Cambridge University Press, 2007).

35 "The Labour Constitution" (note 24), at 632–3.

36 *Ibid.*, at 637–39.

The consequences to be drawn appear obvious, but are cautiously formulated: rather than amuse itself with the creation of a unitary labour constitution, the EU must learn to live with its variety of traditions and conflicting interests. The EU must establish a "supreme body of conflicts law", which will facilitate its treatment of variety within this "social integration compromise".[37] Rödl asserts that, in addition to a necessary concretisation of the "visionary norms of Article 117 EC" that is founded within a conflict-of-laws logic, there is still much room for the realisation of the free movement of workers under Article 39 EC and for focused measures of legal harmonisation. He underlines the fact that such a supranational form of conflicts law need not be created from scratch, but may, likewise, find its anchor and normative orientation within the "constitutional association of states" (*Verfassungsverbund*),[38] a point to which we shall return below.[39]

4.3. The Project of the Constitutional Treaty

In stark contrast to Azoulai and Rödl, who, however divergently, have sought to identify the social dimension of the EU within applicable European law, European politics and conventional legal science have continued to place their seemingly unlimited faith in the project of an incremental realisation of the European social dimension. The most important steps upon which such a hope is built were addressed above.[40] Incremental efforts were intensified as the European Convention took up its work in February 2002 and declared that it viewed its given task as being one of establishing a European Constitution. By virtue of this interpretation of its mandate, the Convention was also required to commit itself to the corollary evolution of a social Europe within its draft constitution. The fundaments which characterise the Convention's draft have, by and large, been taken up unaltered within the Treaty on the Functioning of the EU (TFEU). These are: the duty to establish a "highly competitive social market economy",[41] the preservation of services of general economic interest as "shared values of the Union",[42]

37 *Ibid.*, at 627–633.

38 *Ibid.*

39 Section V.

40 See, above, Section II.2.

41 Article 3(3), TEU (consolidated version of 15 April 2008).

42 Article 14 (ex Article 16 TEC); these services are certainly an important dimension of "social Europe"; see Wolf Sauter and Nina Boeger in this volume and out of an enormously growing literature recently Ulla Neergard, "Services of General Interest: What Aims and Values Count?", in: Ulla Neergaard, Ruth Nielsen and Lynn Roseberry (eds), *Integrating Welfare Functions into EU Law – From Rome to Lisbon*, (Copenhagen: *DJØF* Publishing, 2009), pp. 191–224; Graça Maria Araujo Fonseca, "The process of Europeanization of services of general economic interest. Remarks on particular cross-sectoral substantial and organizational features", Ph.D Thesis, EUI Florence, 2009; these services are, however, by no means an equivalent to Hermann Heller's *Sozialstaatlichkeit*; see, comprehensively, Claudio Franzius, *Gewährleistung im Recht*, (Tübingen: Mohr/Siebeck, 2009), p. 32 *et seq.*, p. 151 *et seq.*, alongside with his "Hermann Heller: Einstehen für den Staat von Weimar", (Manuscript Berlin 2009).

the recognition of "social rights",[43] and the new co-ordination competences for labour (similarly, employment) and social policies.[44]

It is unsurprising that the political process was unable to identify new solutions for the problem of social Europe at such short notice. It is a bit more surprising that the current academic commentary seems so complacent. Stability within the debate may have much to do with the enormous expansion of European secondary law and the ever more intense impact of European primary law and jurisprudence. Parallel to this expansion, long-standing internal divisions within European law have now intensified to the degree that we are witness to sectoral fragmentation within the law, with the result that different groups of European lawyers are no longer in a position even to take note of each other's work, much less, to understand it. This is also true for so-called "generalists", who will now find it even harder to identify overarching evolutionary aspects within individual areas of law. The Europeanisation of once purely national legal science seems not to have helped much: certainly, the business of reading and writing across national borders has intensified; but the Anglo-Saxon lawyers, who have done so much to promote Europeanisation, still seem unable to find a way out of their own national maze of particularistic legal thinking.

Paradoxically enough, the insensitivity of Anglo-Saxon scholarship towards the constitutional dimension of Europe's social deficit has its parallels "overseas". The general indifference of German European lawyers to the social deficit, also derives, and ironically so, from the fact that, during the constitutional debates of the early Bonn Republic, the majority of German public lawyers distanced themselves, from the ordo-liberal thesis that the Constitution had established its ordered rule, and had thus asserted itself against the constitutive powers of a democratically-legitimated parliamentary democracy. Ordo-liberal theory and politics remained the domain of economic and private lawyers, and this schism has also been reproduced within European legal debates. Within universities, the new subject of European law was placed under the umbrella of public law; meanwhile, economic lawyers were able to assert their theoretical and practical positions within European competition law. Here, such lawyers fought unequivocally for the dominance of the theory of the European Economic Constitution and,[45] concomitantly, were comprehensively able to refuse to engage with efforts to supply Europe with democratic legitimation.[46] At the same time,

43 Fundamental Rights Charter of the European Union, Title IV, solidarity.

44 See, above all, Article 5(2) and (3) TFEU. The legal impact of this supposed constitutionalisation of processes of public co-ordination, in contrast to the provisions of Article 147(1) TFEU [ex Article 127 EEC] and Article 153(2)(a) TFEU [ex Article 137 EEC] that have been in force since the Treaty of Amsterdam, have yet to be clarified.

45 The leading light here is Ernst-Joachim Mestmäcker, whose most important contributions may be found in his collected volume, *Wirtschaft und Verfassung in der Europäischen Union: Beiträge zu Recht, Theorie und Politik der europäischen Integration*, (Baden-Baden: Nomos, 2003).

46 See, only, Peter Behrens, "Die Wirtschaftsverfassung der Europäischen Gemeinschaft", in: Gert Brüggemeier (ed), *Verfassungen für ein ziviles Europa*, (Baden-Baden: Nomos, 1994), pp. 73–90.

representatives of public law freed themselves from the technocratic influences of Ipsen and Forsthoff, in order to take part in discussions on the European democratic deficit – similarly, and, for the most part, if not exclusively,[47] failing to construct the question of the socially-constitutive power of Europe as a democratic problem. This constellation is reproduced within Anglo-Saxon constitutionalism. The socio-political implications of integration and the overcoming of the social deficit institutionalised within the European construction are treated as practical-political problems, and are never understood as a constitutive pre-condition for the democratisation of the Union. Instead, the relevant elements within the Convention's draft constitution and within the Treaty of Lisbon are greeted with pragmatic relief, as, at the very least, possessing potential for incremental advance.

5. The Conflicts Law Alternative

The problem of the welfare state is the practical-political *bête-noire* of the European project. What is left to us when we postulate that the ability to create an economic and social order is a constitutive pre-condition for democratic legitimacy, but simultaneously recognise that the EU harmonisation of the economic and labour constitutions of the Member States is impossible, so that Europe must reckon with lasting socio-economic divergence between its constituent Member States? The treatment of legal divergence is the domain of conflicts law. How can this discipline be expected to aid in the overcoming of the problem of the social deficit? Its "poverty of social values" is legendary.[48] The same is true of its methodological nationalism, a nationalism that is actively cultivated by its most prominent representatives.[49]

5.1. European Law as Supranational Conflicts Law

Rather than repeat the line of argument that re-interprets European law as a new form of supranational conflict of laws,[50] commentary is here restricted to a depiction of its core messages.

47 For a notable exception, see Ernst-Wolfgang Böckenförde, *Welchen Weg geht Europa?*, (Munich: Carl-Friedrich-von-Siemens-Stiftung, 1997), p. 23 *et seq.*

48 Konrad Zweigert, "Zur Armut des Internationalen Privatrechts an sozialen Werten", (1973) 37 *Rabels Zeitschrift für ausländisches und internationales Privatrecht*, pp. 435–452.

49 See, the incisive analysis in the habilitation of Klaus Schurig, *Kollisionsnorm und Sachrecht. Zu Struktur, Standort und Methode des internationalen Privatrechts*, (Berlin: Duncker & Humblot, 1981); see also by Florian Rödl, "Weltbürgerliches Kollisionsrecht: Über die Form des Kollisionsrechts und seine Gestalt im Recht der Europäischen Union", Ph.D Thesis, EUI, Florence, 2008, p. 48 *et seq.*

50 For early versions, see Christian Joerges, "The Europeanisation of Private Law as a Rationalisation Process and as a Contest of Legal Disciplines -- an Analysis of the Directive on Unfair Terms in Consumer Contracts", (1995) 3 *European Review of Private Law*, pp. 175–192; "The Impact of European Integration on Private Law: Reductionist Perceptions, True Conflicts and a New Constitutionalist Perspective", (1997) 3 *European Law Journal*, pp. 378–406; "Deliberative Supranationalism" – A Defence", *European Integration online Papers (EIoP)*; 5 (2001) No. 8, available at: http://eiop.or.at/eiop/texte/2001-008a.htm.

Conflicts law as democratic commandment: A starting thesis, and one upon which the entire construction is built, argues that the schism between decision-makers and those who are impacted upon by decision-making is now growing ever greater. This schism is explained by Niklas Luhmann within his sociological risk theory: according to Luhmann, the problem arises because decision-making on risks is always characterised by the fact that the potential damage is not simply borne by individual decision-makers, and nor is it only suffered by the persons profiting from the decision.[51] The famously contrasting problem construction - one which is favoured here - is grounded within democratic theory. It is most clearly elaborated in an essay by Jürgen Habermas,[52] made public prior to the publication of his theory of the democratic constitutional state (*Between Facts and Norms*[53]), and later explained in greater detail:[54] increasingly, constitutional states are unable to guarantee the inclusion of all of those persons who are impacted upon by their policies and politics within their internal decision-making processes. The notion of self-legislation, however, which postulates that the addressees of a law are, at the same time, its authors, demands "the inclusion of the other".

The supranationality of European conflicts law: This normative argument in favour of a new understanding of existing EU law is significant in various respects. First, and primarily so, since it also furnishes a justification for the validity of the supranational jurisdiction - one which is notable only by its absence in the conventional juridical derivation of the principle of supremacy.[55] As a consequence of their manifold degree of interdependence, the Member States of the Union are no longer in a position to guarantee the democratic legitimacy of their policies. A European law that concerns itself with the amelioration of such external effects, i.e., which seeks to compensate for the failings of the national democracies, may induce its legitimacy from this compensatory function. With this, European law can, at last, free itself from the critique that has accompanied it since its birth; a critique that states that it is *not* legitimate. It can thus operate to strengthen democracy within a contractual understanding of statehood, without needing to establish itself as a democratic state.

The reconstruction potential: Clearly, such a democratic exoneration of European law is only possible to the exact degree that it may be reconstructed within this perspective, or that it may be furnished with a conflicts law orientation. This, however, is already, often

51 *Soziologie des Risikos* (Berlin: de Gruyter, 1991); colourfully and laconically summarised in, for example, *Das Recht der Gesellschaft*, (Frankfurt aM: Suhrkamp Verlag, 1995), pp. 141–143.

52 *Staatsbürgerschaft und nationale Identität*, (Zurich: Erkner, 1991).

53 *Faktizität und Geltung*, (Frankfurt aM: Suhrkamp Verlag, 1992), see Annex III, pp. 632–660.

54 *Die Einbeziehung des Anderen*, (Frankfurt aM: Suhrkamp Verlag, 2001), p. 86 *et seq.*

55 Unrivalled, the reconstruction of J.H.H.Weiler, "The Transformation of Europe" (1991/2:2413 *et seq.*); for a less praiseworthy forerunner of the supremacy doctrine, see Matthias Schmoeckel, *Die Großraumtheorie. Ein Beitrag zur Geschichte der Völkerrechtswissenschaft im Dritten Reich, insbesondere der Kriegszeit*, (Berlin: Duncker & Humblot, 1994), p. 226; Schmoeckel analyses, *inter alia*, Hans Peter Ipsen, "Reichsaußenverwaltung", in *Brüsseler Zeitung* (3.4.1943), reproduced in Hans Werner Neulen, *Europa und das 3. Reich, Einigungsbestrebungen im deutschen Machtbereich 1939–1945*, (Munich: Universitas, 1987), pp. 111–115.

enough, the case: European law has given legal force to principles and rules which serve the purpose of supranational "recognition" – the non-discrimination principle, the supranational definition and demarcation of legitimate regulatory concerns, the demands for justification for actions that are imposed upon national legal systems, and the proportionality principle – which supplies a legal yardstick against which respect for supranationally-guaranteed freedoms may be measured – and the demand that all public exercise of power pays due regard to fundamental rights. All these principles and rules may be understood as a concretisation of a supranational conflicts law, which guarantees that the actions of the Member States are reconcilable with their position within the Community.

Internal differentiation of conflicts law within the multi-level European system: The metaphor of the multi-level system asserts that European "rule" cannot be organised hierarchically.[56] This argument is reflected, not only within the apportionment of competences within the EU, but also by the fact that vast discrepancies exist in the operational resources available at each ruling level. Accordingly, we are able to distinguish between three forms of legal collision – vertical, "diagonal" and horizontal. Diagonal collisions are an important and unique feature of multi-level systems. They are a constant feature of life within the EU, since the competences required for problem-solving are, at times, to be found at the level of the EU itself, and, at other times, at the level of the Member States. This division of competences gives rise to two forms of potential conflict – on the one hand, between divergent EU and national political orientations, and, on the other, between divergent interest constellations in the Member States – so that very particular mediation arrangements must be identified. This need for mediation is true for all multi-level systems, but is particularly pressing in the case of the EU, where the existence of diagonal conflict has had, as its corollary, the evolution of a particularly intense degree of administrative co-operation, the institutionalisation of advice-giving instances, and the systematic construction of non-governmental co-operative relationships. This infrastructure may be understood as furnishing the integral components of a conflicts law, a law that may no longer restrict itself to the individual adjudication of situational cases of conflict, and which must, instead, constantly busy itself with the finding of general solutions to universal problems. At the same time, such conflicts law must be methodologically and organisationally open to evolution, which has seen the development of post-interventionist regulatory practices and legal forms within national law. Accordingly, we may identify three types of European conflicts law, which operate in three dimensions:[57] conflicts law of the "first

56 The reference is to Renate Mayntz, *The Architecture of Multi-level Governance of Economic Sectors*, MPIfG Discussion Paper (07/13), 22–24; *idem*, "Von der Steuerungstheorie zu Global Governance", in: Gunnar Folke Schuppert and Michael Zürn (eds), "Governance in einer sich wandelnden Welt", (2008) 41 *PVS Sonderheft*, pp. 43–60.

57 See, for more detail, Christian Joerges and Florian Rödl, "Zum Funktionswandel des Kollisionsrechts II: Die kollisionsrechtliche Form einer legitimen Verfassung der post-nationalen Konstellation", in: Gralf-Peter Calliess *et al.* (eds), *Soziologische Jurisprudenz: Festschrift für Gunther Teubner zum 65. Geburtstag*, (Berlin: de Gruyter, 2009, pp. 768–77); for similar terminological usage, though built upon

order" is flanked on the one side, by a conflicts law, which, most specifically in the realm of European comitology, has concerned itself with the elaboration of material (substantive) regulatory options, and, on the other side, by a conflicts law, which governs the supervision of para-legal law and self-regulatory organisation.

Conflicts law as the procedural constitutionalisation of Europe: It follows from the preceding sections that it would be factually and normatively mistaken to regard European law as a system of law dedicated to the incremental construction of a comprehensive legal edifice. Europe must, at last, take its own motto – found within the draft constitutional treaty ("unified in diversity"[58]) – to heart, and learn to accept the fact that its diversity will accompany it far into the future, so that conflict born of diversity will continue to characterise the process of European integration. It must further concede that this "process" should be overseen by a conflicts law, which, by virtue of its identification of the principles and rules that govern conflict, will generate the law of the European multi-level system. Europeanisation is not simply a process of change, it is also a learning process. Law cannot pre-determine the substance of such processes, but may yet secure its own normative character, by virtue of its self-dedication to the processes of law-making/legal-justification (*Recht-Fertigung*), which mirror and defend the justice and fairness within law.[59]

5.2. *Exemplary Application*

The current jurisprudence of the ECJ on collective labour law[60] provides us with a dramatic mirror to the virulence of interest conflicts and political differences within the Union. At the same time, each of the cases detailed below concerns the consequences of the European "social deficit", or the incomplete addressing of the social sphere within the institutionalisation of the integration project. Unfortunately, there is little room here for a detailed re-construction of these judgments. However, an effort is made to identify the major disjunction between the conceptual orientation of the ECJ and the approach promised by a European conflicts law. In turn, this juxtaposition facilitates the documentation of the main regulative principles offered by the conflicts law perspective.

a different conceptual base, Poul F. Kjaer, "Three-dimensional Conflict of Laws in Europe", *ZERP-DP* 2009/2.

58 Article I-8 Draft European constitutional treaty (ABl. C 310/1, 16/12/2004); a formulation now dispensed with within the Lisbon Treaty on the Functioning of theEU.

59 See Rudolf Wiehölter, "Recht-Fertigungen eines Gesellschafts-Rechts", in: Ch. Joerges and G. Teubner (eds), *Rechtsverfassungsrecht: Recht-Fertigung zwischen Privatrechtsdogmatik und Gesellschaftstheorie*, (Baden-Baden, Nomos, 2004), p. 13 *et seq.*); the English version ("Just-ifications of a Law of Society", in: Oren Perez and Gunther Teubner, (eds), *Paradoxes and Inconsistencies in the Law*, (Oxford: Hart Publishing, 2005), pp. 65–77, available at: www.jura.uni-frankfurt.de/ifawz1/teubner/RWTexte/justum.pdf; see, for a constructive application to EU law, Michelle Everson and Julia Eisner, *The Making of the EU Constitution: Judges and Lawyers Beyond Constitutive Power*, (Milton Park: Routledge-Cavendish, 2007), in particular, p. 41 *et seq.*

60 See note 22 *supra*.

5.2.1. *Viking* and the Relationship between Economic and Labour Law

The legal conflict found in the case of *Viking* was mentioned briefly above.[61] Finnish workers and unions mobilised against the re-flagging of a Finnish registered ferry, threatening strike action. They feared that Finnish sailors, remunerated under a Finnish collective bargaining agreement, would, in time, be replaced by cheaper contracted labour. According to Finnish law, both the collective bargaining agreement and the threatened strike in its defence were afforded legal protection. The employer, Reederei Viking, however, made recourse to European law, claiming that the Union's threatened strike action, together with the political activities (promotion of international solidarity strikes) of, *inter alia*, the International Transport Workers' Federation ("ITF"), were irreconcilable with Viking's freedom of establishment as guaranteed by Article 43 EC.

If the preceding arguments have convinced, it should be clear to the reader that the case entailed conflict between two incompatible legal regimes. European law guaranteed freedom of establishment (and provision of a service), but did not govern industrial disputes, referring, instead, to national law in this area (Article 137(5) EC). The arguments presented by *each* side in this case, revealed the uncomfortable fact that the realm of European law has now almost completely forgotten the primary elements of conflicts law. The defendants argued that:

> Freedom of association, industrial disputes regulation and lock-outs lay beyond the jurisdiction of Article 43 and its guarantee for freedom of establishment, since, according to Article 137(5) EC, the Community [...] had no competences.

This is, according to the defendants, the conflict was taking place *outside* the EU. By the contrasting token, however, the ECJ was very happy to accept the "hint" given by the plaintiff that, although Finland might enjoy the fundamental freedom to construct its own law on industrial disputes, "this competence must, at the same time, be exercised with due respect for Community law".[62] To the Court, then, it would appear that the de-coupling of labour and economic law leads to the subordination of the former. *Both* parties construct their thoughts in line with the category of a vertical collision. They make no effort to identify a conflict-ameliorating collision norm, and, instead, press for an *out-and-out* decision. For the defendants, the fact that Community law guarantees the rights of establishment of Union citizens is of no interest, since EU law has no jurisdiction over industrial disputes. For the plaintiffs – and, most particularly, the Commission in the character of the Commissioner for the Internal Market, Charlie McCreevy – the Community guarantee for establishment is concomitant with a finding that national labour law must be disapplied.

61 Section III.1.

62 *Viking* (note 21), para. 40.

The fatal superficiality of such conceptions becomes readily apparent, where, following the legendary insight of Ernst Rabel,[63] the case is reconstructed in line with the primary operation of conflicts law, namely, the operation called characterisation. This operation cannot supply us with ready-made answers, but it does make us aware of what is at stake in the present conflict. To cite Antoine Lyon-Caen:

> Dans les sociétés d'Europe de l'Ouest, le droit du travail s'est constitué par émancipation du droit du marché, dénommé moyennant les variations terminologiques qu'il importe de ne pas oublier: liberté du commerce ici, *freedom of trade* ailleurs... Ce n'est pas que des règles sur le travail n'existaient pas avant cette émancipation, mais elles relevaient d'avantage d'une police du travail, partie plus ou moins autonome d'une police du ou des marchés.[64]

What do we gain when we adopt this perspective? Most fundamentally, this construction reveals that the problem is one which has dramatic constitutional dimensions. Equally, however, this perspective makes it clear that the controversy must not be resolved by a decision that asserts the supremacy of the freedom of establishment. The jurisprudence of the ECJ is rich in alternative and better models. Amongst these, the much called-upon decision in *Albany* is striking,[65] since, in this case, the ECJ was happy to restrict itself and its own jurisdiction,[66] avoiding the temptation to label Dutch collective pension schemes as "cartels" under European Competition law, and seeking, instead, to establish a "national autonomy preserving, contemporaneously, community-oriented" mode of co-existence between these two legal forms.[67] Various suggestions have been made, detailing an appropriate conflicts-oriented solution, one which does not derive from the supremacy principle – AG Maduro argues in favour of compensation for workers impacted upon by re-flagging from – apparently national – funds, which do not, however, exist.[68] Florian Rödl concludes, following his analysis of the division of competences laid down in Article 137 EC, that Member State constitutions "must evolve

63 "Das Problem der Qualifikation", (1931) 5 *Rabels Zeitschrift für ausländisches und internationales Privatrecht*, pp. 241–288. Unfortunately, the importance of this insight is not common ground in European Legal Scholarship; see Armin von Bogdandy and Jürgen Bast, "The Federal Order of Competences", in *idem* (eds.), note 24, pp. 275–307, at 294.

64 Antoine Lyon-Caen, "Droit communautaire du marché v.s. Europe sociale", contribution to the conference "Die Auswirkungen der Rechtsprechung des Europäischen Gerichtshofes auf das Arbeitsrecht der Mitgliedstaaten", of 26th June (Berlin), organised by the Federal Ministry for Employment and Social Affairs; available at: www.bmas.de/coremedia/generator/27028/property=pdf/2008__07__16__symposium__eugh__lyon-caen.pdf; for a congenial interpretation of the French tradition, see Emmanuel Dockès, "L'Europe antisociale", (2009) 12 *Etudes*, pp. 11–17, and previously, Alain Supiot, "L'Europe gagnée par "l"économie communiste de marché"". Le Monde, 25 January 2008 and, *inter alia*, *Revue du Mauss permanente* (www.journaldumauss.net), and *Süddeutsche Zeitung*, 3 April 2008.

65 Case C-67/96 ECR [1999] I-5751.

66 See, however, Brian Bercusson, "The Trade Union Movement and the European Union: Judgment Day", (2007) 13 *European Law Journal*, pp. 279–308.

67 See, for incisive detail, Michelle Everson, "Adjudicating the Market", (2002) 8 *European Law Journal*, pp. 152–171.

68 See, the AG's opinion, para. 59, but also the critique of Azoulai (note 24), p. 1354.

norms, which open up a legal realm for inter-European transnational labour conflicts and for transnational collective bargaining agreements".[69] What might an ECJ, however, undertake to do in the lengthy interlude before national labour constitutions have been adjusted? Once again, we might identify illuminating models within existing jurisprudence which have promoted successful legal development without, however, foreclosing processes of political adjustment.[70] Certainly, this may have grown harder within the current political constellation, which requires the ECJ to identify both the peculiarities and the limits to its own constitutional mandate. Talk of "judicial self-restraint", however, no longer suffices. In a final analysis, the ECJ is not a central or final constitutional instance with the power to review the constitutional traditions of the Member States.

5.2.2. *Viking* and the Strike as a Social Right

Commentaries on the ECJ judgments emphasise that these cases also contain the first explicit recognition that the right to strike is also a "fundamental right", forming "a fundamental right which forms an integral part of the general principles of Community law the observance of which the Court ensures".[71] The positive tone of the sentence, nonetheless, deceives, masking the nature of the conflict that the ECJ was called upon to solve. The conflict derives from the incompatibility of national regulation on industrial disputes with the EU's economic freedoms, and cannot, therefore, simply be resolved by means of transposition of the conflictual relationship into a purely European legal realm, whereby it is then solved – *per natura* – by means of the declaration of the hierarchical precedence of the four freedoms. This transposition of the conflict to the European legal realm, however, is not a simple flight of legal fancy on the part of the ECJ, which, instead, achieved this result by asserting that the right to strike relates to the fundamental principles of the EU. Given that these principles were primarily established in order to review legislative action, their application here – against private actors – is, nonetheless, inappropriate.

5.2.3. *Laval* and the Limits to the Doctrine of Pre-emption

Laval, formally registered in Latvia, tendered for the work of renovating a school in the suburbs of Stockholm, winning the contract as a result of its cheaper labour costs. In May 2004, Laval sent a dozen workers to the building site. Laval engaged in negotiations on entry into the local Swedish collective-bargaining agreement, but these failed. As work finally began in November 2004, Swedish unions reacted with boycott measures of such intensity that Laval ceased its operations. Just as was the case in *Laval*, such

69 "Labour Constitution" (note 23), Section IV.3.

70 See, the analyses of Christian Joerges, "The Challenges of Europeanization in the Realm of Private Law: A Plea for a New Legal Discipline", (2005) 24 *Duke Journal of Comparative and International Law*, pp. 149–196; also available at: www.iue.it/PUB/law04-12.pdf.

71 Case C-438/05, para. 44.

measures were legal under Swedish law. The ECJ was able to refer to its *Laval* judgment, given only a week before. In addition, the opportunity arose to review the application of the Posted Workers Directive,[72] which is the sole focus of the following section.

The Directive, adopted in 1996, following tortuous negotiations, concerns the "importation" into high-wage economies of cheaper labour from low wage economies. The Directive identified a compromise solution for the conflicts of interest which arise in such situations: Article 3 (1) of the Directive prescribes the application of certain defined working conditions to such arrangements, and demands, in particular, that the legally-binding minimum wage legislation of the host nation be applied for posted workers (Article 3(1)(c)). In its function, this is a collision norm, which both protects posted workers and secures the interests of employees within high wage economies, ensuring that the potential for the undercutting of wage levels within the host state is restricted.[73]

In its transposition of the Directive, Sweden sought to remain true to its industrial system of collective-bargaining, relying upon Article 3(8) of the Directive, which Swedish regulators construed as being an indication that such arrangements would continue to be valid. And, indeed, the general principles of Community law would seem to suggest that such an expectation was well-founded. In principle, Member States retain a regulatory competence in relation to those matters that can be demonstrated to belong to the category deemed by the Community to be valid "matters of public concern". Naturally, secondary law limits such national competence – but only to the degree that the claim to pre-emption by Community law of the area of national competence is sustainable. By the same token, the preamble of the Directive explicitly states (Recital 22) that the Directive does not impact upon "the laws of the Member States concerning collective action to defend the interests of the trades and professions". At the same time, Article 3 (1) (c) of the Directive states that minimum rates of pay are "defined by the national law and/or practice of the Members States to whose territory the worker is posted". These provisions seem a bit opaque. The doctrine of pre-emption doctrine seems to provide orientation in the deciphering of their impact on national autonomy – and that impact becomes dramatic if one interprets this doctrine in line with a leading law book:

> The sovereignty of EU law requires not only that it takes precedence over national law, but also that EU law, alone, determines its legal effects. It is a matter for EU law to determine which fields it governs, and what legal effect it has in those areas. These questions are anchored in the doctrine of pre-emption.[74]

72 Directive 96/71/EC, OJ L18/1996, 1.

73 For reconstruction of the fundamentals of conflicts law, see Florian Rödl, "Weltbürgerliches Kollisionsrecht" (Ph.D thesis, EUI, Florence, 2008), p. 234 *et seq*.

74 Damian Chalmers, in: Damian Chalmers *et al.* (eds), *European Union Law*, (Cambridge: Cambridge University Press, 2006), p. 188.

This definition of the doctrine draws upon a wholly orthodox understanding of the supremacy principle. Nonetheless, it similarly encapsulates the idea that the pre-emption doctrine serves the conflicts law function of demarcating and co-ordinating Community tasks with national competences. This interpretation is supported by the – very few – recent analysis of the practical application of the doctrine by the ECJ,[75] and may also be justified at the terminological level.[76]

An argument is to be found within the judgment, according to which, the Swedish practice of safeguarding wage-levels by means of legal recognition of collective-bargaining agreements, is not reconcilable with the Community interest: Swedish rules seemingly suffer from:

> [A] lack of provisions, of any kind, which are sufficiently precise and accessible that they do not render it impossible or excessively difficult in practice for such an undertaking [foreign service provider] to determine the obligations with which it is required to comply as regards minimum pay.[77]

However, precisely this form of indeterminacy is inherent to all industrial relations systems relying upon collective-bargaining, so that, in effect, the ECJ is thus demanding, no more nor less, than a complete re-formulation of Swedish law, in order that it pay due respect to the calculating interests of foreign firms. With this, the starting thesis again rears its ugly head that European integration is now dissolving national labour constitutions in favour of a market-oriented economic constitution.

A recent study, which seeks to demonstrate just how Sweden might adapt to the demands of the ECJ, has supplied the intelligent and carefully elaborated suggestions that, although industrial conflict measures should continue to draw upon and be based within existing collective-bargaining agreements, official information should be supplied by Swedish authorities on prevailing working conditions within Sweden.[78] This suggestion may be understood to embody a process of mediation between the demands of Swedish workers and the interests of foreign service-providers. It, nonetheless, remains to be seen whether this suggestion will survive a review in line with the excessively high standards set by the ECJ.

75 Eugene D. Cross, "Pre-emption of Member State Law in the European Economic Community: A Framework of Analysis", (1992) 29 *Common Market Law Review*, pp. 447–472 (the author argues in favour of recognition of "all instances of actual or potential conflict between Member State law and Community law... The division of competences and the principle of subsidiarity serve as orientation aids", at 471).

76 Andreas Furrer, *Die Sperrwirkung des sekundären Gemeinschaftsrechts auf die nationalen Rechtsordnungen*, (Baden-Baden: Nomos, 1994).

77 *Laval* (note 21), para. 110.

78 Swedish Government Official Reports, *Action in response to the* Laval *judgment*, (Stockholm: Fritzes Customer Service, 2008).

5.2.4. *Rüffert* and the Determination of the Purpose of National Laws

In its *Rüffert* judgment, the ECJ further entrenched its position. *Rüffert* concerned the legality of a tender proffered by one of the German *Länder*, Lower Saxony, which contained a clause indicating that the public authorities were bound to respect existing collective-bargaining agreements, so that tendering firms would also be required to abide by the relevant collective-bargaining agreements. Equally, partners contracting with public authorities would be required to transfer the duty to respect collective-bargaining agreements to any of these sub-contractors. Mr Rüffert, in his capacity as liquidator of the assets of *Objekt und Bauregie GmbH & Co. KG*, refused to recognise this obligation, sub-contracting individual tasks to a Polish firm. He was, accordingly, sued for non-performance by Lower Saxony. During the course of civil legal proceedings, the defendant argued that the state's provisions contravened Article 49 EC and the Posted Workers Directive. The ECJ confirmed this opinion: rules applying in Lower Saxony were irreconcilable with Article 49 since they prevented foreign service-providers from benefiting from lower wage costs within their country of origin. Lower Saxony's rules on tendering contravened the provisions of the Posted Workers Directive since they did not encompass or establish a universal duty on the part of the public authorities to respect collective-bargaining agreements, but, instead, only did so with regard to public tendering processes.

This logic is simply depressing. At the legal level, it fails utterly to convince, since it determines the purpose of rules binding the state to collective-agreements, without any reference to, or regard for, the intensive political discussions from which such provisions derive; a process that has more generally – with regard to similar provisions maintained within the *Land* Berlin – been recognised by the German Constitutional Court to be in accordance with the provisions of the German Constitution.[79] The German Constitutional Court does not share the ECJ's complacent conclusion that "respect for collective-bargaining does not constitute an employment protection measure". Certainly, the Court recognises the potential that collective-bargaining agreements may encroach upon constitutionally secured fundamental freedoms (above all, the right to property, Article 12(I) Basic Law). However, it was, nonetheless, convinced by the arguments of the Berlin legislator justifying such an encroachment:

> The combating of unemployment, together with measures that secure the financial stability of the social security system, are particularly important goals, for the realisation of which the legislator must be given a relatively large degree of decisional discretion, and especially so under current, politically very difficult, labour market conditions. This common interest, which the duty to respect collective bargaining agreements, contained within Article 1, paragraph 1, sentence 2 *Berliner Vergabegesetz*, seeks to serve, possesses an overwhelming importance.[80]

[79] Judgment of the First Senate (11 July 2006), 1 BvL 4/00.
[80] Para. 103.

The ECJ may be of a different opinion. It needs, however, to explain *why* its interpretation of the purpose of legislation might claim precedence, above all, over the judgment of the German Constitutional Court. European precedence is anything but self-explanatory, since legislation on collective-bargaining agreements and the Posted Workers Directive concern two very different legal subjects.

5.3. *The ECJ as Pouvoir Constituant?*

During legal conflict on the Treaty of Maastricht, the German Constitutional Court claimed for itself a "co-operative relationship" with the ECJ in the matter of the protection of fundamental rights.[81] This expectation on the part of the Court is not referred to by the ECJ within its judgments on posted workers. The conflicts law perspective developed here, however, concerns the appropriate demarcation of the constitutional functions of each of these decisional instances. We argue that the legitimacy of European law predominantly derives from that fact that it compensates for the structural "democratic deficit" of the nation state model. And it is precisely this function, which the ECJ is called upon to stabilise. Notwithstanding the fact that the ECJ's activities will often overlap the competences of national constitutional courts, this function, is, at core, an *aliud*. The ECJ is not a super-constitutional-court equipped with the power – *en passant* – to reformulate the constitutional orders of the Member States within preliminary reference proceedings. It must, instead, accept a very specific task, and one which the Member States are ill-equipped to fulfil: it must evolve a supranational law, one which mediates between the different European traditions and interests, and which appropriately resolves conflicts of interest.

6. Conclusion

"This may be true in theory, but it is not so in practice", reads the famous saying of Immanuel Kant.[82] In the conclusion to his *Tractatus*, Kant considers the suggestion that Europe might be brought from a position of constantly endangered peace – a condition resting upon the so-called "balance of powers – to a condition of perpetual peace; a proposition which clearly requires 'laws'", "to which each state must subject itself". Is this a simple utopia, a purely theoretical imagining? Kant laconically observes: "nowhere does human nature appear less appealing than in the relationship of great powers of entire peoples to one another and the proposition that a universal state" should be constructed, however "benevolent" it may sound, is always "laughed at".[83] Kant, the theoretician, however, does not allow himself to be confused: "what is true in theory by virtue of the imperative of reason, is also true in practice", is his incisive view. But how

81 Judgment of 12.10.1993, *BVerfGE* 89, 155, (1994) *Common Market Law Reports*, p. 57.

82 I. Kant, "Über den Gemeinspruch: Das mag in der Theorie richtig sein, taugt aber nicht für die Praxis", (Vol 9 of W. Weischedel's Kant Edition, *Werkausgabe der Wissenschaftlichen Buchgesellschaft*, (Darmstadt: Wissenschaftliche Buchgesellschaft, 1971)), p. 125 *et seq.*

83 Kant, *ibid.*, 171 and 172.

might this correctly-recalled "reason" assert its practical importance within the preternatural European world of states? This is a tortuous task, which must be faced by Europeans as if "moral-practical reason will finally triumph, all failed attempts notwithstanding".[84]

Given Europe's current nature, such a degree of decisiveness may be difficult to find. There are good reasons for a fundamental debate on the social deficit within Europe's integration project. Nonetheless, judgments such as those discussed here do not appear out of the blue, and the reactions that they provoke indicate that the issues raised are of highly sensitive significance. We know that there is no one comprehensive solution to the problem of the compatibility of the integration project with the social state. Meaningful treatment of Europe's conflicts of interests will require constructive work in many areas – a "tortuous task", indeed, just as Kant said.

84 Kant, *ibid.*, 172.

IUS COMMUNE EUROPAEUM

A peer-reviewed book series in which the common foundations of the legal systems of the Member States of the European Community are the central focus.

The *Ius Commune Europaeum* series includes horizontal comparative legal studies as well as studies on the effect of treaties within the national legal systems. All the classic fields of law are covered. The books are published in various European languages under the auspices of METRO, the Institute for Transnational Legal Research at the Maastricht University.

Recently published:
Volume 78: *The European Private Company (SPE): A Critical Analysis of the EU Draft Statute*, D.F.M.M. ZAMAN, C.A. SCHWARZ, M.L. LENNARTS, H.-J. DE KLUIVER and A.F.M. DORRESTEIJN (eds.)
Volume 79: *Constitutions Compared. An Introduction to Comparative Constitutional Law*, 2nd edition, A.W. HERINGA and PH. KIIVER
Volume 80: *Rechtsbescherming en overheidsovereenkomsten. De preventieve en jurisdictionele rechtsbescherming bij de gunning van overheidsovereenkomsten in Nederland, Frankrijk en België en de mogelijke invloed van de rechtspraak van het Hof van Justitie*, K. WAUTERS
Volume 81: *Derden in het contractenrecht*, I. SAMOY (red.)
Volume 82: *The Right to Specific Performance. The Historical Development*, J. HALLEBEEK and H. DONDORP (eds.)
Volume 83: *Financial Supervision in a Comparative Perspective*, M. POTO
Volume 84: *Enforcement and Enforceability – Tradition and Reform*, C.H. VAN RHEE and A. UZELAC (eds.)
Volume 85: *Fact-Finding in Civil Litigation. A Comparative Perspective*, R. VERKERK
Volume 86: *The Making of Chinese Condominium Law. A Comparative Perspective with American and South African Condominium Laws*, L. CHEN
Volume 87: *Effective Criminal Defence in Europe*, E. CAPE, Z. NAMORADZE, R. SMITH and T. SPRONKEN